Remaking American Communities

Our Sustainable Future

SERIES EDITORS

Charles A. Francis
University of Nebraska–Lincoln

Cornelia Flora
Iowa State University

Paul A. Olson
University of Nebraska–Lincoln

Remaking American Communities

A REFERENCE GUIDE TO URBAN SPRAWL

Edited by
David C. Soule

Foreword by Neal Peirce

University of Nebraska Press
Lincoln and London

Manufactured in the United States of America
∞
First Nebraska paperback printing: 2007

Library of Congress Cataloging-in-Publication Data
Urban sprawl.
Remaking American communities: a reference guide to urban
sprawl / edited by David C. Soule; foreword by Neal Peirce.
p. cm. — (Our sustainable future)
Originally published: Urban sprawl: a comprehensive reference guide.
Westport, Conn.: Greenwood Press, c2006.
Includes bibliographical references and index.
ISBN 978-0-8032-6015-3 (pbk.: alk. paper)
1. Cities and towns—United States—Growth. 2. Regional planning
—United States. I. Soule, David C. II. Title.
HT384.U5U74 2007
307.760973—dc22
2007013771

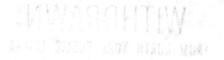

When I started this project, my dad was still alive and he and my mother had just entered their retirement village in Pennsylvania. While Dad will never get a chance to read this, I dedicate this volume to my mother, Jean Conder Soule, who has authored many books of her own, and gave me the heritage of putting words in print so that others may share them.

Contents

Contents

Foreword: Recent Emergence of Sprawl as an Issue in American Policy Debates

In the last half of the twentieth century, the physical—and social—fabric of the United States came unglued. This book is about the prime suspect—sprawl.

It's reasonable to argue that other, powerful forces worked to destroy the remarkable feelings of community cohesion that Americans felt at the end of World War II. Television, addictive from the days of its first flickering black-and-white images, lured people off their front porches and away from neighborhood chatter, causing them to retreat inside behind closed doors. Air-conditioning tamed a nation's perspiration rate but also sealed us off from each other, whether at home or in our automobiles.

Auto purchases soared, fueled by a surge of national prosperity; vehicle miles traveled and the ratio of vehicles to overall population climbed at an astounding rate. With federal policy driving hundreds of billions of dollars into highway construction and development of the Interstate Highway System, our collective love affair with the automobile prompted us to drive cars (1) for more and more varieties of trips and (2) constantly greater and greater distances.

Our zoning laws propelled us to embrace single-purpose developments—separate pods of residential subdivisions, commercial centers, and office buildings, all distanced from each other in a way that made auto use almost mandatory.

Mass commercialization and franchising, along with the incessant parking demands of the auto age, undercut Main Street retailing—department stores, small shops, and local restaurants alike. Strip malls and full-scale shopping centers, miles-long commercial alleys, and big box stores multiplied across the United States, indifferent to the older city and town centers whose commerce they were eviscerating.

And even this list is incomplete. Just a short list of other factors includes decades of federal housing policies pushing suburban over in-town housing, exclusionary housing as suburban towns resisted moderate or low-income residences, the flow of minorities into large urban centers, and higher crime rates in inner cities.

Assume some hostile power had set out, around the end of World War II, to design a set of trends and policies that would disperse us out across the countryside and deeply imperil the viability of American center cities and older towns; undercut our social relationships; divide us by income group and race; isolate any of us too young, old, or infirm to drive a personal automobile; magnify our dependence on foreign sources of oil; accelerate the consumption and depletion use of natural resources; and imperil our air and water. I doubt if they could have dreamed up a set of policies and trends so powerful.

The good news is that during the decade of the 1990s, even as we continued to sprawl wildly, a broad and growing range of Americans—scholars, analysts, civic activists, and others—began to cry, "Enough!"

Let us, they said, start to analyze and understand the forces dispersing American community and civilization. And let us begin to consider alternatives, from city and town revitalization to more balanced transportation systems, from a reconstruction of our damaged civic fabric to new forms of metropolitan governance capable of binding us together rather than continually tearing our society apart.

Why did this new awareness and interest emerge? One can select from a list of possible precipitating factors. In the midst of the 1990s, a decade of national economic expansion, traffic levels grew sharply, triggering major congestion. The consumption of treasured landscapes aroused increasing concern, and the powerful National Trust for Historic Preservation turned into a champion of town protection and less sprawl. The ISTEA and TEA-21 transportation bills mandated a voice for regions and for others than the roads-only state highway departments and included funding for a range of transportation enhancements, which, in sum, suggested that all the world does not need to lie under asphalt.

Simultaneously, interest in more sensitive physical forms increased among progressive developers, starting with the Urban Land Institute. A leadership role in new development directions was taken by a raft of foundations. And the country saw the emergence of such social equity analysts as Myron Orfield, David Rusk, and Manuel Pastor, rushing into the smart-growth debates, insisting that more intelligent development patterns can combat the alarming separation of classes, races, and incomes in the United States.

Still, when the history of America's turn of mind gets written, a major role will almost surely be accorded the New Urbanist architectural movement of the 1990s. With its stress on traditional town layouts, with its focus on the vital social connections that Americans instinctively miss in so much modern development, New Urbanism struck a responsive chord. It gave us an alternative vision to sprawl for the first time since World War II.

On the political side, Maryland Governor Parris Glendening gets credit for popularizing the "smart growth" term, starting with his 1997 legislation to conserve open spaces and support existing communities by giving counties a real choice. The Maryland bill gave localities a simple message: "Develop in a sprawling manner if you choose, but then don't come to the state for subsidies for roads and schools, water and sewer systems." The intended message was simply that the state's appropriate role is to preserve, not destroy community, and, most interestingly, that smart growth and fiscal prudence go hand in hand.

Simultaneously, Glendening moved to stop the all-too-familiar pattern of localities bulldozing older schools in favor of the big-enrollment, big-parking-lot schools recommended by the school building construction industry. Instead, his administration placed a priority on saving and refurbishing old schools instead. And with clear results: From 1991 to 1997, the percentage of Maryland's school construction funds supporting renovations and additions to existing schools—rather than new structures—soared from 34 percent to 82 percent.

In 2000–2001, as chairman of the National Governors Association, Glendening seriously and repeatedly engaged the country's chief state executives on growth issues. Indeed, it turned out he was hardly alone. Several governors were already espousing growth issues their own way—among them Independents Angus King of Maine and Jesse Ventura of Minnesota; Democrats Roy Barnes of Georgia, Ruth Ann Minner of Delaware, and Thomas Vilsack of Iowa; and Republicans Mike Leavitt of Utah and Christine Todd Whitman of New Jersey. In the following years, such officials as Democratic governors Jennifer Granholm of Michigan and Edward Rendell of Pennsylvania and Republicans Mitt Romney of Massachusetts and Mark Sanford of South Carolina took an active interest in the issue. Sanford, for example, was drawn to smart growth by the same issue of defending smaller, community-based schools that Glendening had championed in Maryland.

But no one suggests smart growth issues are or will be easy to advance in government, where they run up against the accumulated special interest camps of a half century and more of sprawl. Intense analysis of the phenomenon, from its history to laws to social and political dynamics, is critical. And we need to understand just how it interacts—in local politics, at the regional (I call it "citistate") level, and in state and federal policy.

In the long run, this is research on how to heal and remake an American community wounded by an unplanned development phenomenon gone amuck. In this book, David Soule and his colleagues take highly significant steps in that direction.

Neal Peirce

Preface

To address the complexity of this topic, the editor solicited some of the best thinkers in the country to contribute their current perspectives on the topic, including Neal Peirce, nationally syndicated columnist; Myron Orfield, architect of a new politics to address sprawl; Robert Yaro, currently the president of the Regional Plan Association and noted author and lecturer; David Rusk, former mayor of Albuquerque and author of the theory of "elastic cities"; and Curtis Johnson, president of the Citistates Group. The editor also secured significant commitments from emerging commentators, giving them a chance to fill out the important dimensions of the sprawl discussion.

Urban Sprawl: A Comprehensive Reference Guide divides the sprawl discussion into six major parts. Part I focuses on defining sprawl. While a succinct definition is elusive, the following simple one-sentence statement is offered to provide the essential elements:

> Sprawl is low density, auto-dependent land development taking place on the edges of urban centers, often "leapfrogging" away from current denser development nodes, to transform open, undeveloped land into single family residential subdivisions and campus style commercial office parks and diffuse retail uses.

What this definition misses are all the forces operating to make this development pattern happen. Sprawl is planned; it is a natural extension of public policies in place and refined over the last 50 years; it is the result of a legal framework; and it has social benefits and consequences that lead to a rich debate.

To flush out the definition, Part I places sprawl in an historical, legal, social, and planning framework. Editor David C. Soule wrote the first two chapters, which define sprawl and the management regimes that are established to regulate land uses that make sprawl what it is, and then place sprawl in an historical context. In

Chapter 3, Jay Wickersham provides an overview of the legal regimes of planning and zoning as a complement to the discussion of property and real estate laws. In Chapter 4, Ralph Willmer, a highly respected planning practitioner, discusses the current approach to land use, smart growth, and sprawl as seen "on the ground" in the community planning environment. In Chapter 5, Zenia Kotval and John Mullin of the University of Massachusetts provide an overview of the economics of sprawl. In Chapter 6, David Rusk confronts the problems of race and class, particularly in residential locations in metropolitan regions, and in Chapter 7, Meredith Cooper introduces the concept of social infrastructure. Drawing on the work of Robert Putnam and others, Cooper's chapter is the first major discussion of the social fabric of planning included in a "sprawl" volume. This emerging paradigm offers an important infusion of "people-based" planning principles to the traditional "place-based" planning model. Finally, because sprawl is now a political issue, at least in some states, Part I concludes with an overview of the politics of sprawl by David Soule (Chapter 8).

Part II outlines several important drivers of the sprawl dynamic. One of the more significant is the operation of the real estate market—the supply and demand for land, a fixed resource, for various uses, including residential, commercial, retail, and industrial (see David Soule's Chapter 9). However, transportation access (highways, transit, rail, air, etc.) is a critical component of the land development equation. In Chapter 10, Curtis Johnson provides an overview of this dynamic as it operates in one state, Minnesota, particularly in the Minneapolis/St. Paul region. Myron Orfield, another Twin Cities resident, has developed a sophisticated process for analyzing demographic and fiscal pressures in a region to determine strategic alignments among and between communities under stress for a "new politics." Orfield's study of the Atlanta region (Chapter 11) is included as an example of how such an analysis works. Orfield's Web site, included in Appendix I, has similar studies of over 20 other regions in the country.

Part III tackles the question "What's wrong with sprawl?" Because sprawl is often assumed to have a negative impact where it occurs, it is important to explore why. In Chapter 12, John Moynihan, planning director for the Roman Catholic Archdiocese of Boston, presents a compelling ethical argument on the impact of sprawl on the poor and people with limited choice in society. Once again, this argument is usually not included in discussions of sprawl. It is a critical component of why society needs to address this question in a straightforward, "no-holds-barred" discussion of race, class, and poverty. Sarah Gardner at the Center for Environmental Studies at Williams College presents the environmental argument (Chapter 13). Part III ends with David Soule's discussion of the cost of sprawl, a newly invigorated conversation among planners (Chapter 14).

Part IV gives an overview of the analytical disciplines that provide structure, theory, and measures for the various dimensions of sprawl. Chapter 15, by David Soule, provides an initial discussion of geography and demographics. In Chapter 16, Ron Thomas, current executive director of the Northeast Illinois Planning Commission in Chicago, provides a comprehensive discussion of the tools used by planners to engage citizens in a discussion of the future of their community and their region, mixing the creation of a "vision" for the future with a sophisticated set of tools that quantify impacts and assist in developing alternative scenarios that compare current trends and projections to more desirable outcomes.

Part V expands the exploration of sprawl with a series of cross-cutting issues. In Chapter 17, Ari Bruening, James Hlawek, and David Soule provide a discussion of the influence of property taxation on the dynamics of land use. In Chapter 18, Alex von Hoffman at the Joint Center for Housing Studies at Harvard University collaborated with David Soule to provide a framework for considering the immigration question in sprawl, another recent addition to this complex dialogue, recently introduced by the Center for Immigration Studies. Again, to our knowledge, this is one of the first treatments of this issue in a major reference work on sprawl.

Part VI explores a series of policy prescriptions introduced over the last few decades to deal with sprawl. In Chapter 19, Douglas Henton, John Melville, and John Parr offer a discussion of emerging efforts to consider a political geography that encompasses the economic geography in which sprawl operates. In Chapter 20, Terry Szold, professor at MIT's Department of Urban Studies and Planning and a professional planner, discusses some specific remedies planners are using to translate laws and regulations so that they provide a more satisfying development outcome. In Chapter 21, Robert Yaro discusses the historical and current context for major interventions to purchase and protect large tracts of land for posterity rather than letting them fall in the path of the development bulldozer. In Chapter 22, Angela Glover Blackwell and Radhika K. Fox provide an overview of smart growth strategies emerging to deal with the elusive consensus on how to act on the problem of sprawl in the United States in the twenty-first century.

Urban Sprawl includes a series of appendices to enhance its value as a reference. These appendices identify databases that are accessible to researchers, provide an annotated listing of Web sites that offer additional materials and local context, and list contact information for smart growth alliances around the country. We have also included in the appendices the Awahnee Principles for Resource-Efficient Communities, drafted in 1991 by a number of advocates for the New Urbanism paradigm, one of the primary responses to sprawl. A glossary offers brief, useful definitions of over 500 terms from planning, real estate, sociology, geography, economics, and political science that come up in the sprawl conversation. Each of these terms is presented in easily accessible language. Although a disclaimer is included to prevent the misappropriation of these definitions as legally defensible, the editor tried to remain accurate to the operational meaning of all the terms. The volume concludes with an exhaustive bibliography and a comprehensive index.

Acknowledgments

Any volume of this size and complexity requires many hands, minds, eyes, and hearts. Without the more than 20 contributors, this book would be limited to my own perspectives. All the contributors have participated in this adventure without compensation but with an earnest desire to expand our collective knowledge of the complex phenomenon of sprawl. I especially appreciate the contributions of Angela Blackwell Glover, Radhika K. Fox, Douglas Henton, Zenia Kotval, Curtis Johnson, John Mullin, Myron Orfield, John Parr, Neal Peirce, David Rusk, Alex von Hoffman, and Robert Yaro. Each of these people has an outstanding reputation in his or her own right and has numerous publications, and yet each willingly agreed to help me create this reference. I also want to thank colleagues and friends in the New England region who all have active careers and extensive commitments to civic and family life in this area. Jay Wickersham, Sarah Gardner, Terry Szold, John Moynihan, and Meredith Cooper have enriched this volume with local and national perspectives on this critical issue, which the environmental community has designated the number-one policy issue of the twenty-first century. I appreciate the patience of my editors at Greenwood Press, Michael Hermann and John Wagner, who maintained their patience with me through the many months of assembling, collating, and finalizing the articles. Thanks as well to my colleagues at the Center for Urban and Regional Policy at Northeastern University, especially Barry Bluestone, who referred me to Greenwood Press in the first place and provided critical support and encouragement along the way, and the staff and board of the Metropolitan Area Planning Council, who allowed me to take this on and provided valuable insights into the ground truthing of land use. There are hundreds of colleagues and friends in the planning profession who have taught me lessons along the way about the importance of citizen government and the intricacies of practicing planning until the early hours of the morning as they strove to make their communities safer and better places. I wish I could thank them all personally, but this volume will give them the satisfaction that they did teach me a few things.

Finally, my family, Rita, Rich and Michelle, Amy, Mike, Kayla, and Jacob deserve more praise than I can summon as they gave up evenings, weekends, and a few vacations together while I sat in front of the laptop, composing and editing.

Introduction

Today, there is a proliferation of interest and academic research on the topic of sprawl. As a research area, it offers interesting challenges as a legal question, a political consideration, and a social phenomenon.

As a legal question, sprawl "happens" in the context of a rich mixture of property and land use laws and regulations. Because many local governments pay for services, including K–12 education, using revenue derived from the property tax, land use is a fiscal question as much as it is an economic and environmental issue. Many current discussions of sprawl do not address this important component in enough detail to get to the root causes of sprawl-inducing behaviors. *Urban Sprawl: A Comprehensive Reference Guide* attempts to bridge that gap while still addressing the other components of the sprawl debate.

As a political issue, sprawl is getting increasing attention. Public interest groups now monitor ballot initiatives throughout the country that are linked to land-use policies. Several governors have succeeded in putting comprehensive regimes in place to target state investments to support "smart growth" and "sustainable development." The International City/County Management Association prepared a guidebook for municipal officials on principles for growing smart. The environmental community identifies sprawl as the number one challenge for the twenty-first century. This concern has led other groups, from developers and homebuilders to financial institutions and property rights organizations, to respond to this emerging agenda.

As a social problem, sprawl is a conversation about equity. As people migrate throughout a region or a state, not everyone has the same capacity for choice. Many commentators link sprawl and urban decay as two facets of the same set of social choices. The literature is replete with commentaries on race, class, and ethnic segregation, which are critical factors in the choice of residential and economic activity. Myron Orfield, a Minnesota legislator from the Minneapolis area and a contributor to this volume, has surveyed over 25 metropolitan areas in this country and documents the disproportionate share of burdens absorbed by older urban areas in metropolitan regions (Orfield, 2002).

This volume makes no pretense to being exhaustive on sprawl and its effects. It is intended to document the problem, identifying the social consequences and the preliminary policy constructs to frame future debates. However, there is an emerging political agenda on the subject, and this volume attempts to outline important parameters in defining the problem and innovations under discussion or in use to address it.

Based on 30 years of practice in regional and metropolitan planning, I believe that the country is both threatened and uniquely positioned to respond to these challenges. Because of our strong rebellious tendencies, our tenacious defense of the rights of the individual over the state, and our ingenuity, we are positioned to influence the course of events at the start of the twenty-first century.

New models of governance based on collaboration and cooperation that take precedence over command and control systems are being tested around the country. Further, if there is substantial market failure in the land-use economy, then surgical strikes are necessary to fix the legal framework. The location of transportation access points (interchanges, rail stations, etc.) and the expansion of urban infrastructure (water, sewer, and transportation) are critical factors in the movement of people in and through a region. Where and how these systems are extended and accessed have been and continue to be determinative in the distribution of growth and activity within regions experiencing the dynamic changes sprawl induces.

BIBLIOGRAPHY

Orfield, Myron. 2002. *American Metropolitics: The New Suburban Reality*. Washington, DC: Brookings Institution Press.

PART I

SPRAWL IN CONTEXT

1

Defining and Managing Sprawl

David C. Soule

DEFINING SPRAWL

According to the chronology in *Urban Sprawl* (Williams, 2000), William H. Whyte first used the term "urban sprawl" in an essay in 1958.[1] In 1967, Jean Gottmann, author of *Megalopolis* (1964), edited a volume with Robert Harper entitled *Metropolis on the Move: Geographers Look at Urban Sprawl*. It presented a summary of a conference held in 1964.

Defining sprawl is never an easy task. Sprawl is an elusive and often pejorative name for extensive, but low density, development in metropolitan regions outside the central city. To create a succinct working definition, we offer the following:

> Sprawl is low density, auto-dependent land development taking place on the edges of urban centers, often "leapfrogging" away from current denser development nodes, to transform open, undeveloped land, into single-family residential subdivisions and campus-style commercial office parks and diffuse retail uses.

A more precise working definition draws on several concepts. As people and jobs migrate out from the central city, pathways to sprawl follow transportation corridors. According to the *Planning Commissioners Journal*, sprawl is a problem "that affects urban, suburban, and rural communities. The results of sprawl range from loss of farmland to the decay of older urban centers."[2]

> In its path, sprawl consumes thousands of acres of forests and farmland, woodlands and wetlands. It requires government to spend millions extra to build new schools, streets, and water and sewer lines. In its wake, sprawl leaves boarded up houses, vacant storefronts, closed businesses, abandoned and often contaminated industrial sites, and traffic congestion stretching miles from urban centers.[3]

A survey of the literature in the field contains a rich mix of urban and metropolitan studies. However, in the last decade, there has been a proliferation of books and journal articles on the specific issue of sprawl. This is not by accident. As states have come to grips with rapid growth and change, they have passed legislation creating extensive planning regimes. An increase in ballot initiatives during the 1990s added to the saliency of this subject fostering interest on the part of foundations, publishers, and think tanks. Multiple titles in the comprehensive bibliography contain a direct reference to sprawl, smart growth, growth management, and sustainable development.

MANAGING SPRAWL

Nature of Land Use

Land use policies that allow sprawl to "happen" are built on a complex framework of laws and regulations. This chapter endeavors to enrich the discussion of sprawl by providing an overview of the legal regimes that affect, directly or indirectly, the use of land. It is essential that any management system designed to overcome the deleterious effects of sprawling development adequately address the complex legal environment in which these transformations take place. Local governments can and do influence the amount and rate of change in the uses of land within their borders. The "command and control structure" for managing land use, and therefore sprawl, is based in law and regulation. State laws enable the land-use management regimes, but usually private landowners and developers seek approval for their decisions from local planning and zoning boards (Diamond and Noonan, 1996).

Our foundational principles are a direct response to English feudal law (Platt, 1991) under which the king and his nobles owned all the land and leased it to tenants. We adopted the *allodial* paradigm instead that allows individuals to have clear title on property and real estate without paying tribute to the monarch or governmental in place. Someone always owns the land. If an individual (or corporation) does not own it, then it is in the public domain. Government has the right to dispose of its land holdings, which it does through a variety of mechanisms (Haar and Kayden, 1989). However, the nature of the American Revolution requires us to insert one additional premise that applies in a unique way. Property cannot be taken from individuals by the government without just compensation. This "takings" question is used from time to time by property owners who feel that local and state regulations overly restrict the rights of the owner.

Robert Burchell argues that the bias toward sprawl is embedded in the American psyche as part of the frontier mentality (Burchell et al., 1998, 14). Sprawl, in its broadest sense, has long been an American zeitgeist. Alexis de Tocqueville, touring the United States in the early 1800s, observed "no urban growth boundaries," but rather marveled at "America . . . where everything is in constant motion . . . and where no boundaries were set to the efforts of man." Today's sprawl is the frontier of long ago; it is akin to the postwar suburb—both of which have been extolled as defining American influences.

Burchell cites another more modern observer as follows:

Delafons describes the U.S. system of master planning, zoning, and subdivision control as heavily influenced by a "prairie psychology." He explains that U.S. development patterns are characterized by:

a) a supply of land which is viewed as virtually unlimited;
b) land that is open to all and property ownership rights that are encouraged and protected by the U.S. Constitution;
c) economic forces that are barely understood and should not be tampered with;
d) development professionals who prepare land for development and do not question whether the land should be developed (i.e., they make sure utilities are in place and feeder roads have been planned for); and
e) a basic distrust of elected and appointed officials, so that all procedures are codified and development that qualifies under these procedures does so "as of right," with minimal public review. (Delafons, 1962)

Sprawl is a broad description of suburban development as it has manifested itself on the American landscape. While sprawl is a particular descriptor of land-use transformation, it needs to be placed in a framework for analysis. Land is always transforming itself (meadows, forests, water channels, habitat, etc.). However, the human settlement pattern often radically, and usually permanently, changes undeveloped land to developed land.

Commercial development under the sprawl rubric is located on "strips" of highway. Some of it is standardized through national and regional franchises (7–11, McDonald's, etc.). Some of it is clustered in malls of various sizes and economic mix. All of it is principally accessible by automobile through curb cuts and parking lots. It feels cluttered and is often architecturally uninspired. Business development is located in office parks near major highways surrounded by seas of parking. Residential development is usually single-family detached housing on single lots in subdivisions or tracts. Usually, there are multiple automobiles garaged at each dwelling. Because of a legal framework, zoning land uses are substantially segregated from one another geographically making a personal vehicle a necessity.

Planners have made multiple arguments about the consequences of sprawl.

1. fiscal—the cost of sprawl—it's expensive! (*The Costs of Sprawl*, 1974; Burchell, 1998, 2002);
2. aesthetic—make your McDonald's look like our rural architecture (Arendt et al., 1994);
3. public health—don't poison the water;
4. traffic—Where did all these cars come from? (Downs, 1992);
5. elitist—this is my place, stay out (Downs, 1973).

From an aesthetic perspective, many consider sprawl to be ugly, demeaning the quality of life. It takes what makes a place special and unique and makes it "7–11-ville" (Palen, 1995). This has led to a "design" response from the architectural community.

While there are attempts like Galster's to measure sprawl in an objective way, it is clear that sprawl is basically normative. Many object to sprawl for various reasons.

First, it presumably uses land at an exhaustible rate that is unsustainable over time. Second, there is an equity issue. Not everyone benefits equally from the suburban phenomenon. Central cities, which typically act as acclimation centers for new immigrants and disadvantaged populations, become isolated. As scarce public and private dollars are invested, a disproportionate share of funds flows out of urban areas and into the countryside. Sprawl thus reinforces inequality (Downs, 1973).

Yet, with all these arguments against sprawl, there appear to be few places where concrete public policy opposes it. The question which needs to be asked is, "If sprawl is so bad, why do the majority of Americans choose this pattern of settlement?" Fischel (1985) and others argue that the market, and in fact the U.S. Constitution, limit the intrusion of regulatory regimes on the use of land. In a more recent offering, Fischel (2001) posits a "home-voter hypothesis" which pushes the argument even further, suggesting that the relationship between home owners and municipal corporations (i.e., cities and towns) leads to a structure of taxation, school policy, and land-use decisions which reinforce sprawl.

Around the country, different systems have been created to manage land use and its pernicious side effect—sprawl. Several states (such as Florida) have adopted aggressive command and control systems (Buchsbaum and Smith, 1993). Other states (Vermont, Oregon) vest power in regional systems wresting control of major land-use decisions away from local government. However, land use is managed at the local (municipal/county) level in most of the country.

Other Considerations

Beyond the land use/zoning discussion, sprawl "happens" based on interactions between a group of complex social, economic, and political forces. Many of these are discussed in considerable detail in this volume, but a few important factors need a brief introduction as to "why" they would appear in a discussion of sprawl.

Property Tax

Municipal tax policy is critical to understanding sprawl. From colonial days, taxes on the value of property have supported governmental expenditures. Land and improvements on the land are part of the theoretical and legal framework for this means of raising revenue.

Because of this linkage between property and municipal revenue, the literature about sprawl often refers to taxation as one of the stimuli for local decisions about land use. This is intensified in states that have a tax limitation in effect (e.g., Proposition 13 in California, Proposition 2½ in Massachusetts). In simple terms, these tax and expenditure limitation laws (TELs) restrict the amount that local governments can raise taxes. To avoid catastrophes in financing local expenditures, states have provided various forms of relief including voter approval for "overrides" or alternative taxation systems (e.g., local sales tax).

Property taxation leads to a critical challenge to any attempt to manage sprawl. Communities are forced to restrict and curtail expenditures. That was the intent of the interests that brought the tax caps forward in the first place. However, this financing mechanism provides an incentive to bring in any ratables to grow the pie. Interestingly, commercial and industrial growth offer a premium to communities as they need revenue because they consume less services than their taxes provide. Residential growth, on the other hand, is problematic to communities because the average single-family home consumes substantially more services, particularly if there are children in the school system, than the tax revenue from the home offsets. A recent study in the Boston region projects that a single-family residence in Bedford, Massachusetts, needs to be valued at $700,000 to generate enough revenue to pay for the services that the family, with two school-age children living in the house, will consume (*A Decade of Change*, 2001). According to one observer in California, "housing is the most undesired land use at the local level."[4] This "fiscalization of land use" is one more challenge to those intending to manage sprawl.

Social Dynamics

To correctly understand the dynamics of sprawl, several additional factors must be considered. A social framework is more normative and qualitative than other paradigms. It allows, and perhaps requires, an evaluation of winners and losers, equity adjustments, analysis of obstacles and impediments to equal access, and mechanisms to mitigate adverse impacts. It is impossible to discuss sprawl without including a presentation of the concept of social separation by race and class. Suburban development has often been about the flight of white populations from central cities and the economic separation of the affluent from the isolated concentrations of the poor in cities. This separation takes several forms.

Discrimination

Discrimination is an overt policy to benefit or exclude participation in an activity. There are activities that operate in the social and governmental structures with apparent similar effect. Most importantly, current census data show continuing economic and racial concentrations in metropolitan regions.

Economic Segregation

Economic segregation is intuitive. People with money have more choices than people without. In a metropolis, family wealth is made up of several factors—wages, assets, and business ownership (including stocks and bonds). As the family income increases and diversifies, wealth accumulations are invested in land, transportation, and additional business activity (Binford, 1985).

In the nineteenth and early twentieth centuries, wealthier families moved their residences away from the denser urban areas. Facilitated by expanding transportation improvements, social stratification began to manifest itself in geographic separation. Stilgoe and others point to the mythology of wide-open spaces as an economic goal (Stilgoe, 1988).

Social Class

Economic segregation only partially explains the dispersal of people in the region. Social class is particularly helpful in explaining why people who gain greater choice limit those choices to certain locations.

Several authors describe elaborate analyses in order to document social stratification by type of occupation (Carchedi, 1977). Lawyers rank higher than laborers. While the current effort of this researcher cannot justify such an analysis, the applicable theory is helpful for insights into the causes of sprawl.

For example, Boston culture is replete with nineteenth- and twentieth-century social stratification. Throughout this period the Brahmins (a social epithet designating the elite with "priestly" powers) have retained structures to influence and wield power (O'Connor, 1991).

Prestigious academic institutions maintain elaborate networks for collaboration, communication and interaction, which lead to economic, political, and social opportunity. In some ways, this benefits and adds clout to established older cities, as many executives work in the city and live in the suburbs (Palen, 1995). Myron Orfield's studies of the region identify communities which are under stress due to significant fiscal disparities.

Racial and Ethnic Segregation

American attitudes toward race are a significant component of the sprawl debate. Much of the discussion focuses on residential restrictions, many of which were written into manuals used by federal and state agencies in their guidance to mortgage lenders and real estate agents (Levine and Harmon, 1992).

As ethnic migration continued through the nineteenth and twentieth centuries, ethnic discrimination became a causal force in population movement as well. According to one planner, a community actually banned backyard truck gardens in the first part of the century to discourage Italian Americans from locating there.[5]

But the "complexion" of cities and regions is changing dramatically. Traditional racial minorities (black, native American) are being overwhelmed as a significant in-migration of Asian Pacific immigrants has begun to shift the relative percentages and the overall numbers. The Hispanic population represents an increasingly significant portion the nation's population.

One would expect that de jure discrimination, which is illegal, would be a thing of the past. Numerous laws and regulations at the municipal, state, and federal level have been enforced by aggressive public regimes over the past few decades. However, there are still continuing concentrations of racial and ethnic minorities in metropolitan regions.

Environmental Law

With the environmental community declaring "sprawl as the number one environmental issue for the 21st century," it is appropriate to briefly explore how environmental laws affect the issue. Broad statutory powers exist which protect water supplies, wastewater management, wetlands, and other environmental issues. These statutes provide to state and local governments a range of powers designed to overcome deficiencies in the land management systems. While these laws are primarily environmental measures, they also address Hardin's dilemma about governing the "commons" (Hardin, 1968). Planning and zoning regulate specific parcels of land and the impacts of the use of that parcel on abutting parcels. However, the existing planning laws inadequately account for the cumulative effects of development on the natural ecology of the land. As a consequence, environmentalists demanded a more aggressive management of the externalities of development.

Creative land-use planners at the local, regional, and state level can use the environmental regulations as an effective technique to manage sprawl. For example, open space acquisitions permanently remove land from the development pool. While this is the most effective deterrent to consumptive land-use practices, wetlands and watershed protection regulations substantially restrict the land uses in the critical environmental areas (see Chapter 13 in this volume). Even the concept of a sprawl impact statement is under discussion (Wickersham, 2001).

Wastewater management systems, particularly on-site septic systems, have an important impact on the health and safety of the community. They also have a direct impact on the density of development allowed on a parcel of land. Consequently, the development, extension, and upgrading of municipal wastewater management systems allow concentrated land-use activity, while on-site waste management induces the opposite effect. Many local officials worry that the current planning and zoning framework is inadequate to maintain rural densities in communities with on-site systems.

Finally, interbasin transfers (taking water out of one river basin for use and discharging it in another through wastewater treatment systems) are being monitored aggressively by water activists. If these laws were in effect earlier in the century, none of the large metropolitan water systems in the country could have been created. The state and federal governments have adopted watersheds as the basis for a number of programs and regulations. Tough enforcement of interbasin transfers will substantially restrict where communities can go to create new water supplies and new discharges. This will make water one of the fundamental components of a sprawl management agenda in the future.

Public Education Finance

The link to the property tax to local expenditures is emphasized in public education. State laws provide the basis for financing K–12 education through the local revenue sources—i.e., the property tax. Many states have faced challenges to this mechanism in the courts. Rich communities can offer better public education to their children than poorer districts.

With new funding came accountability. School districts are often now required to test students at various grade levels. In Massachusetts, passing the Massachusetts Comprehensive Assessment System test has now become mandatory for every graduating senior. A new acronym, MCAS, is on the lips of every high school student in the state. When results are posted every year, the test scores are front-page news. Every school is ranked and every local official wants to know how their students are doing and, if the results aren't good, why?

As the MCAS history has developed, the scores of good school districts become fodder for real estate brokers to bring people to town because "your kids will get a great education." One planner forecasts that MCAS scores are "all we need to predict which towns will grow."

FINAL THOUGHTS

In summary, sprawl is a widely discussed problem facing metropolitan areas throughout the country. Research tools are emerging which allow various aspects of the phenomenon to be described in a more analytical way. This is stimulating significant new discussion in the literature which is presented in the next chapter. Finally, while changes in land use have been happening over long periods of time, policies to manage and redirect these in a more equitable and efficient way are receiving significant attention.

NOTES

1. Williams, 2000, p. 43.
2. "Sprawl Resource Guide," *Planning Commissioners Journal*; see Web site at pcj@together.net.
3. Maryland Governor Parris N. Glendenning, *A New Smart Growth Culture for Maryland*, downloaded from pcj@together.net.
4. Soule, 2004.
5. Private conversation with practicing planner.

BIBLIOGRAPHY

Arendt, Randall, Robert Yaro, Elizabeth A. Brabee, Harry L. Dodson, and Christine Reid. 1994. *Rural by Design: Maintaining Small Town Character*. Chicago: American Planning Association.

Binford, Henry C. 1985. *The First Suburbs: Residential Communities on the Boston Periphery 1815–60*. Chicago: The University of Chicago Press.

Buchsbaum, Peter A., and Larry J. Smith, eds. 1993. *State and Regional Comprehensive Planning: Implementing New Methods for Growth Management*. Chicago: American Bar Association.

Burchell, Robert W. et al. 1998. *The Costs of Sprawl—Revisited*. Washington, DC: National Academy Press.

Burchell, Robert W. et al. 2002. *Costs of Sprawl—2000*. Washington, DC: National Academy Press.

Carchedi, Guglielmo. 1977. *On the Economic Identification of Social Classes*. London: Routledge and Kegan Paul.

The Costs of Sprawl: Detailed Cost Analysis. 1974. Washington, DC: Real Estate Research Corporation and U.S. Government Printing Office.

A Decade of Change: Growth Trends in the Greater Boston Area—1990 to 2000. 2001. Boston: Metropolitan Area Planning Council.

Delafons, John. 1962. *Land-Use Controls in the United State*s. Cambridge, MA: MIT Press.

Diamond, Henry L., and Patrick F. Noonan, eds. 1996. *Land Use in America*. Washington, DC: Island Press and Lincoln Institute of Land Policy.

Downs, Anthony. 1973. *Opening up the Suburbs: An Urban Strategy for America*. New Haven, CT: Yale University Press.

Downs, Anthony. 1992. *Stuck in Traffic: Coping with Peak-Hour Traffic Congestion*. Washington, DC: Brookings Institution.

Fischel, William A. 1985. *The Economics of Zoning Laws: A Property Rights Approach to American Land Use Controls*. Baltimore: The Johns Hopkins University Press.

Fischel, William A. 2001. *Home-Voter Hypothesis: How Home Values Influence Local Government Taxation, School Finance, and Land Use Policies*. Cambridge, MA: Harvard University Press.

Getting to Smart Growth: 100 Policies for Implementation. 2002. Washington, DC: Smart Growth Network and International City/County Management Association.

Gottmann, Jean. 1964. *Megalopolis: The Urbanized Northern Seaboard of the United States.* Cambridge, MA: MIT Press.

Gottmann, Jean, and Robert A. Harper, eds. 1967. *Metropolis on the Move: Geographers Look at Urban Sprawl.* New York: Wiley.

Haar, Charles M., and Jerold S. Kayden, eds. 1989. *Zoning and the American Dream: Promises Still to Keep.* Chicago: Planners Press of the American Planning Association.

Hardin, Garrett. 1968. "The Tragedy of the Commons." *Science* 162: 1243–48.

Levine, Hillel, and Lawrence Harmon. 1992. *The Death of an American Jewish Community: A Tragedy of Good Intentions.* New York: The Free Press.

O'Connor, Thomas H. 1991. *Bibles, Brahmins, and Bosses: A Short History of Boston.* 3rd ed. Boston: Trustees of the Boston Public Library.

Palen, John J. 1995. *The Suburbs.* New York: McGraw-Hill

Platt, Rutherford H. 1991. *Land Use Control: Geography, Law, and Public Policy.* Englewood Cliffs, NJ: Prentice Hall.

Soule, David. 2004. "Confronting Housing, Transportation and Regional Growth." *Landlines* 16(2), available at http://lincolninst.edu/pubs/pub-detail.asp?id=889.

Stilgoe, John R. 1988. *Borderland: Origins of the American Suburb, 1820–1939.* New Haven, CT: Yale University Press.

Tocqueville, Alexis de. 1945. *Democracy in America.* New York: Knopf.

Toward a Sustainable Tax Policy: Tax Strategies to Promote Sustainable Development in Metro Boston. 2001. Prepared by the Metropolitan Area Planning Council in Conjunction with the McCormack Institute. Boston: U.S. Environmental Protection Agency.

Wickersham, Jay. 2001. "Managing Growth without a Growth Management Statute: The Uses of MEPA." Boston, April 2.

Williams, Donald C. 2000. *Urban Sprawl: A Reference Handbook.* Santa Barbara, CA: ABC-CLIO.

2

Historical Framework: Cities and Their Regions, Suburbanization, and Federal Policies

David C. Soule

CITIES AND THEIR REGIONS

Lewis Mumford, the most significant historiographer of city development, sees a continuum in human settlement. In his book *The City in History* (Mumford, 1961), he theorizes that the hunter needs a broad-ranging geography to stay alive and a transitory dwelling place. The farmer is "place related" and needs a dwelling to oversee, guard, and protect his investment in the land. Cities become necessary for the complex social interactions of a civilized society. Trade and commerce need a place for transactions. Legal and judicial disagreements need arbitration. Religion and culture focus on population centers. Tribal behaviors and turf establish actual boundaries between centers and their collective periphery.

Mumford posits that great cities have existed for 5,000 years. Their interactions with the surrounding countryside (agriculture, trade routes, territorial protection, law, commerce, and religion) have intensified as human activity became more complex.

Throughout history, the "city" was the meeting place for commerce, government, and religious activity. The "countryside" supported the city through agricultural activities. Industrialization gradually changed the nature of cities, creating a need for large urban labor forces and expanding wealth for "country gentlemen" to purchase for rural estates (Mumford, 1961).

Stilgoe (1988) traces this "lifestyle" change in the late nineteenth and early twentieth centuries as a fundamental force in the development of "borderlands" around many cities in the United States and in Europe. Other observers, Warner in particular, see transportation infrastructure as a change agent. Streetcar spurs poked through the urban edge and into the surrounding territories. People with enough wealth to purchase real estate moved out of crowding cities. They settled in the wide-open country on their own plot of land. The transportation systems made it possible for larger and larger numbers of people to live in one location and to work in another (Warner, 1978).

The culture of the land bifurcated as well. In the discussion of cities, the psyche of America is schizophrenic. On the one hand cities are important centers of business, government, and culture. On the other, as the density of human settlement increased to accommodate the growing needs of industry, cities became places of disease, fire, pestilence, and crime. The city-planning movement began in response to both of these critical human concerns (So and Getzels, 1988).

During the late nineteenth and early twentieth century, the countryside was a frontier full of opportunity and adventure through which people fulfilled Horace Greely's exhortation to "go west." It was also a place where folks from the cities could find gold and new commercial ventures could grow in place of grasslands and timber. However, it was also a place of safety and flight away from congestion. Stilgoe points to this fundamental division in American society as the principle reason for the transition of rural land to more intense uses (Stilgoe, 1988).

Municipalities and counties, which existed from colonial time, were transformed into metropolitan regions with the "suburbs" as the twentieth century progressed. In some parts of the country, annexation allowed cities to absorb the developing areas, retaining a more economically integrated unit (Rusk, 1993). However, in most New England states, colonial towns provided a mechanism that allowed the emerging areas to isolate themselves politically, economically, and socially from their city neighbors. As land-use policies became more sophisticated through the early twentieth century, local planning and zoning became tools for municipalities to control land use change. Used to enhance the quality of life, these tools occasionally became mechanisms to bar outsiders and preserve economic, racial, and ethnic stratification (Downs, 1973). The first planning and zoning laws were passed in the 1920s. By the 1940s, many communities had some form of local land use regulation.

The country lifestyle was available to everyone who could scrape together the down payment on a car and a house. That is, of course, unless you were black, Hispanic, or one of a number of other groups from whom the rest of the population was fleeing. This overt discrimination led to fierce fights in federal and state courts to overturn local regulations that were discriminatory in their intent or effect.

Rutherford Platt, in his book, *Land Use Control* (1991), theorizes that between increasingly complex human settlement patterns require sophisticated legal frameworks to manage land use. He lays out the process of land development in Western and particularly Anglo-American culture, tracing its legal basis. Platt suggests that feudal societies held land in common throughout the Middle Ages. Gradually, land grants were subdivided into smaller farms, estates, and ultimately focused on centers of commerce and culture. This tradition was exported through the colonial period of the European hegemonies of the sixteenth and seventeenth centuries. The specific manifestations vary according to the country settling the frontier. In New England, the English tradition prevails. In Florida, California, and the southwest, the Spanish tradition is manifest.

As the United States moved through its colonial period, land grants from the king allowed for the claiming of lands in the new world and the subdivision of those lands for private owners. The historical pattern of community settlement in Massachusetts is just one example of this phenomenon. The Massachusetts Historical Commission documents that settlement patterns followed native American trade and hunting routes (Bradley, 1982). Boston and Salem were settled in 1630. Their proximity to the Atlantic Ocean and their protected harbors established them as commercial hubs.

By 1640, the countryside of eastern Massachusetts was dotted with land-grant communities. The process of subdividing raw land into villages and countryside was well on its way 130 years before the American Revolution.

SUBURBANIZATION

According to Robert Fishman (Fishman, 1987), Chaucer uses the word "suburb" in the *Canterbury Tales* to describe the limbo places around fourteenth-century cities. They were the spaces where the "riffraff" collected. These people scratched out an existence through a variety of legal and illegal means. These places were looked down on by the gentry of society as under (sub) the dominance of the city (urbia).

Two important studies discuss the suburbanization, using the Boston region as a template. Henry Binford suggests that suburban development began almost immediately. He theorizes that exurban agriculture and manufacturing led to improvements in physical infrastructure to promote trade and commerce (Binford, 1985).

Warner, mentioned earlier, pinpoints the development of transportation systems, particularly the rail and interurban transit, as the principal driving force for suburban development. Beginning in 1830 and continuing through the next 170-plus years, transportation accessibility to the commercial center drove the development system (Warner, 1978).

As cities became more congested, sanitary conditions deteriorated, and wooden residential structures were tinderboxes set ablaze at the slightest spark. Greenspaces were hard to find and families with means longed for a different lifestyle (Stilgoe, 1988).

Country estates predated the modern suburb by millennia. However, Stilgoe theorizes that nineteenth-century magazines promoted a bucolic existence with fresh air, vast natural areas, healthy living conditions, and wonderful childhood memories. As the United States expanded through the frontier, those who chose not to journey thousands of miles from home could buy tracts of land near the emerging web of rail lines. Papa could travel to the busy work of the commercial center, while Mama and the children stayed safely at home in the country.

FEDERAL POLICIES AND SPRAWL

The federal government has contributed to sprawl through various policies including constitutional protections for private property, expenditures on highway expansion, housing subsidies, and various economic and environmental policies. Each of these is discussed briefly below with references to other chapters in this volume that provide more detailed profiles of some of the policies.

Private Property

One of the fundamental tenets of the American constitution is the role of the government in the protection of the rights of private property owners. Our colonial heritage is built on the foundation of land grants from the western European hegemonies that sent explorers to the "new world." The "colonists" who came with their hopes and dreams of religious freedom and a new future also came with a legal system that facilitated the subdivision of land grants for residential and commercial settlement. However, the European land systems that were feudal in nature, vesting significant rights (and wealth) in the hands of a few, were significantly transformed in the 150-plus years from the Jamestown and Plymouth settlements to the Declaration of Independence. The treatise of John Locke that formed the basis for the Declaration of Independence suggests that the role of the government is to protect "life, liberty, and *property* [italics mine]." The concept of the "pursuit of happiness" that replaces Locke's trinity in 1776 is certainly colored by the flavor of property rights.

Whether it was the quartering of troops, the confiscation of land for public (i.e., royal) purposes, or the heavy taxation of enterprise, the revolution completed a transformation of American property law into several constitutional principles that substantially underpin the framework for all regulatory systems that are discussed in this volume and are in use today to manage sprawl (or any land use, for that matter). While the Constitution does not specifically mention private property within the seven articles, several of the amendments do.

Once property is in private hands, the Fifth Amendment states:

> No person shall be held to answer for a capital, or otherwise infamous crime, unless on a presentment or indictment of a Grand Jury, except in cases arising in the land or naval forces, or in the Militia, when in actual service in time of War or public danger; *nor shall any person* be subject for the same offense to be twice put in jeopardy of life or limb; nor shall be compelled in any criminal case to be a witness against himself, nor *be deprived of life, liberty, or property, without due process of law; nor shall private property be taken for public use without just compensation.* (emphasis added)

Further, the Fourteenth Amendment extends this protection to prohibit states from abridging this right. The "takings" question has been adjudicated from time to time. Property owners who feel that local and state regulations overly restrict the rights of the owner have secured a hearing at the Supreme Court to test the limits of governmental oversight of the use of private property. State laws provide the legal framework for further property and real estate law.

Early Influences

Robert Yaro (Chapter 2 in this volume) suggests that there were significant reactions to the rapid expansionism of the eighteenth and early nineteenth centuries as the vast urban centers of the country became congested, dank, and dark. Stimulated by transcendentalists like Emerson and Thoreau, a young urban landscape architect named Frederick Law Olmsted emerged to carve out natural oases in the hearts of cities. While Olmsted was providing access to park lands inside of dense urban centers, another naturalist, George Perkins Marsh, watching the westward expansion fomented by Horace Greeley's famous challenge to "Go west, young man, go west," came to the troubling conclusion that "man is everywhere a disturbing agent."

Walter Muir, founder of the Sierra Club, was traversing the West and Midwest cataloguing and documenting the natural treasures of the wilderness. Through his influence, the national park system was authorized by Congress in 1916.

The young police commissioner in New York at the time, Teddy Roosevelt, came under both influences and by 1900, when he ascended to the presidency, he transformed the role of the federal government intervening to protect the land. However, influenced by another naturalist, Gifford Pinchot, Roosevelt concluded that, rather than preserving land simply for its natural beauty and wildlife habitat, the wilderness should be available for human use as well. Pinchot advocated a "joint use" doctrine of federal lands management. Pinchot, named to lead the Forestry Division of the U.S. Department of Agriculture in 1898 and then first head of the U.S. Forest Service, allowed active timber harvesting on federally owned land. This would be quickly extended to mineral rights and other joint uses such as live-stock grazing. These subsidies of private-sector activity on government-owned land continue to be an active policy controversy in twenty-first century America. However, from a sprawl perspective large tracts of land were permanently withheld from development through this mechanism.

Transportation as a Growth-Shaping Mechanism

Samuel Bass Warner was not the first urbanologist to understand the linkage between transportation systems and urban expansion. However, he is probably the most well known and certainly created a populist recognition of the connection (Warner, 1978). The streetcars he writes about were operated by private companies and the lands they accessed were private tracts owned by the same companies as speculative development real estate. The relationship that Warner describes significantly influences federal policy, as we shall see, in the second half of the twentieth century.

Moreover, the systems that Olmsted developed to create urban parklands were carefully and strategically linked together through urban parkways that allowed city dwellers to access the publicly available open space in their new Model T. This relationship between land use, transportation, and open space created a profound influence on the layout of the federal subsidized highway network, long before the creation of the interstate highway system. As early as the 1920s, federal aid was available to states for certain categories of roads. A route numbering system was in place and, while Routes 1 and 66 are probably the most celebrated in fiction and song, thousands of miles of roads became eligible for federal subsidies.

These same subsidies, however, were not available to railroads and urban transit systems. These would remain in private hands well into the second half of the twentieth century until finally the franchises were relinquished back to the cities and states as owners went bankrupt. Federal support for these systems would take even longer to develop and continue to be more difficult to sustain without the subsidies contributed by the motor fuels tax to the highway trust fund.

The Great Depression and the New Deal

Inheriting the results of a laissez-faire economic policy, which had plunged the country into its most devastating crisis since the civil war, Franklin Delano Roosevelt, a relative of the earlier president of the same surname, borrowed from Teddy's interventionist legacy. Adopting the economic policies of John Maynard Keynes instead of Adam Smith, FDR dedicated a massive infusion of federal cash into building, expanding, and refurbishing the American landscape. Through the Works Progress Administration (WPA) and other domestic efforts, thousands of unemployed workers were given jobs building roads and bridges, creating buildings in national and state parks, and extending urban water and sewer systems into the countryside. The New Deal not only provided an economic safety net for individuals and families, it set the stage for 50 years of federal presence and investment in the domestic arenas that had previously been the responsibility of state and local governments or private enterprise. It would take another reformer—Ronald Reagan—to turn the tide in a different direction. One would argue that Nixon and Carter had set the stage and that the disillusionment with war, stagflation, and deceit in the White House had changed public opinion against Washington. However, Reagan's philosophy about a severely limited federal domestic agenda is the dominant paradigm as we enter the twenty-first century.

Postwar Period

It took the pent-up demands of the postwar period to make the modern suburb. Palen (1995) suggests a powerful linkage between federal subsidies already mentioned for highways and housing, which, combined with accessible automobile loans and easy credit, set changes in motion. The conversion of raw land continued at such a pace, the land defined as "urbanized" in one region of Massachusetts in the second half of the last century grew at a rate of 300 percent, with more land converted during these few decades than in all the years from Plymouth Rock to the atom bomb.[1]

Suburban development patterns were underway throughout the early part of the twentieth century, but the period after World War II is replete with many federal policy changes that accelerated the sprawling of America. Two of these activities are so significant that it is impossible to discuss this issue without mentioning them. First, returning veterans received cheap and easy credit to purchase homes. Real estate interests purchased large tracts of rural land at the edges of large urban centers and subdivided the property into house lots (So and Getzels, 1988). Through the deft maneuvering of federal mortgage guarantees and tax policies, single-family home ownership became the American dream.

Second, in 1956, the federal government created the Interstate and Defense Highway Act. Originally, the project provided for the evacuation of cities in the event of nuclear attack and the rapid movement of troops. The country was ripe for a larger role of government in the expansion of infrastructure. Eisenhower used national defense, successfully, as a broad justification for this expansion. This system quickly changed into our interstate highway network that had the opposite effect of feeding cities with necessary workers every day from surrounding suburbs. The gasoline tax allowed an unprecedented self-financing mechanism—the "highway trust fund." Automobile manufacturers, petroleum refiners, and road builders created one of the strongest forces in American politics.

Other federal programs empowered the suburbanization of the countryside. As early as the 1945 Federal Housing Act, emerging communities received federal support for water and sewer systems. As federal policy continued to evolve, the Housing Act of 1954 became the vehicle for the urban renewal program. In its early stages, cities used the program to remove blighted neighborhoods from the landscape. The residents moved into other neighborhoods (So and Getzels, 1988). According to some critics, blight just moved across town while upwardly mobile people moved out to the countryside (Chapin and Kaiser, 1979). The mortgage deduction on the federal income tax created an additional subsidy for home ownership, which, in turn, provided additional political support for suburban development.

Fair Housing

However, not all people benefited equally from this new federal largesse. Racial attitudes and prejudice are especially insidious in the dispersion and stratification of people, particularly residential location. Much has been made in the literature about "white flight." According to Douglas Massey, housing discrimination in most urban markets against blacks is just as likely in northern cities and even more likely than in the South where one would expect a legacy of days gone by.[2] Throughout the mid-twentieth century, the federal government allowed and even empowered restrictive covenants in subdivisions that were using federal mortgage subsidies (Downs, 1973).

This overt discrimination led to fierce fights in federal and state courts to overturn local regulations that were discriminatory in their intent or effect. As So documents, the *Mount Laurel* decision in New Jersey in 1975 was the first and most far-reaching of the courts' actions. In summary, the National Association for the Advancement of Colored People sued the town of Mount Laurel because it failed to account for regional housing needs in its local planning. The court required the community to redress this lack and to respond to the regional, as well as the, local housing market (So and Getzels, 1988).

Early Smart Growth Responses

As the nation emerged from the post-war period and the interstate highway system opened up the countryside to suburban development, one agency, the Federal Housing Administration, later to become the U.S. Department of Housing and Urban Development, undertook the first national effort to stimulate local and regional planning.

HUD 701

Section 701 of the Housing Act of 1954 authorized the Federal Housing Administrator to provide grants to localities to undertake comprehensive plans designed to coordinate housing, transportation, infrastructure placement and capacity, and early efforts at conservation of natural resources. Based on these plans, grants for water and sewer projects became available to states and localities.

Areawide Planning

HUD was also the first federal agency to recognize that large-scale water and sewer systems needed to be undertaken on a regional or areawide scale to be cost effective. Using the "carrot" approach, HUD authorized a greater federal matching grant to localities that could demonstrate that their efforts were based on a regional plan. However, in order to create these plans, HUD stimulated the creation of areawide planning agencies throughout the country to undertake regional plans.

Metropolitan Planning Organizations (MPOs)

In 1973, the federal reauthorization of the highway trust fund introduced the first "metropolitan" planning system with "teeth." While earlier versions of the federal highway acts had required a "coordinated, continuing, and comprehensive planning" program (known as the "3c process") for states as they prepared their highway layouts, particularly in urban areas, the 1973 act *required* states to create metropolitan planning organizations (MPOs) in urbanized areas around the country. They set aside a dedicated financing stream by requiring states to pass through ½ of 1 percent of the federal highway appropriations to these MPOs. More significantly, the law *linked* the metropolitan plans, created by these organizations to the annual transportation improvement program (TIP). The regional transportation plan and the TIP must identify all projects eligible to receive federal funds. The MPOs were not capable of programming projects that could enhance (or detract from) sound land-use policy. Later iterations of the act merged transit and highway planning and funding together into "surface transportation," allowing flexibility between modes, added a series of "enhancements" that allowed for the use of highway funds for pedestrian and bicycle uses, and required a close coordination between land use and transportation.

Environmental Influences

Highways were not the only urban infrastructure systems to receive federal subsidies. Throughout the nineteenth century, scientists had established the relationship between pathogens and disease. While some of the more devastating scourges (such as plagues) were carried by animals, particularly denizens of dense and dirty urban places such as rodents and insects, other pathogens were waterborne and linked to inadequate treatment of human wastes. Since a principal mode of urban transportation before steam and electricity was the horse, animal wastes also provided a rich festering stew as well. Therefore, the first major thrust for upgrading urban infrastructure was not environmental in the modern sense, but came, instead, from the public health community.

Environmental Protection Agency (EPA)

Throughout the years, the U.S. Environmental Protection Agency (EPA) has "dabbled" in similar efforts to link regional planning and infrastructure investments. Section 208 of the Clean Water Act attempted to manage "nonpoint" water pollution sources through an areawide planning system. However, without linking the plans to specific funding strategies, the effort was abandoned.

The strongest linkage is between the State Air Quality Implementation Plans (SIPs) and the MPO plans and Transportation Improvement Programs (TIP). The SIPs require a sign-off on the TIPs by the state and federal air quality review agencies. In places under sanction for severe air quality problems, this tool can mandate that all transportation improvements improve the air quality.

In recent years, EPA has begun to target and invest in "smart growth" initiatives throughout the country. During the Clinton administration, EPA provided grants and established an awards program for emerging efforts. While this effort is substantially reduced at the present time, various tools and programs are offered on their Web site for review and guidance.

Environmental Impact Statement (EIS)

The Environmental Impact Statement (EIS), required for all major federally supported projects, has provided an opportunity for experimentation in quantifying the impacts of infrastructure expansion, particularly highway construction, on the land adjacent to the improvements. By quantifying the "induced growth" potential on surrounding environments, the opportunity for alternative mitigation efforts can be identified. Probably the most significant attempt to date has been the EIS for the widening of Interstate 93 in southern New Hampshire. EPA required the NH Department of Transportation to plan for and offer mechanisms to the abutting communities for managing the development that would inhere to the expanded highway capacity.

Water

Sophisticated urban water systems preceded the more elaborate treatment of wastewater. Part of the Olmsted genius and legacy was to harness this public health motive into his urban parks strategy. Flood control levies were integrated into the parkways. Aqueducts bringing water from distant reservoirs were covered over and became trail networks. "Pure" water from the country arrived in the cities with little need for treatment, at least under the prevailing science.

However, not everyone had the luxury of drinking from mountain streams. Many urban centers, built as they were on the banks of rivers, were forced to withdraw drinking water from the same water systems that they used to discharge their untreated sewage. Further, storm and sanitary sewers were combined under urban streets according to the scientific wisdom of the day. This meant that during storm events, significant volumes of untreated human waste as well as runoff from streets would be discharged into the river systems. Further, large river systems served more than one urban area and downstream cities were intensely impacted by the behaviors of their upstream neighbors. No coordinated regulatory framework existed. Moreover, significant untreated industrial wastes entered these same river systems.

Federal investment in urban water and sewer systems began as a component of postwar federal housing initiatives. States and localities could receive federal grants for up to 80 percent of the capital cost of treatment facilities. These subsidies, however, have been vastly curtailed over the last 20 years, leaving states and cities without a financial partner in fixing these costly systems. EPA continues to regulate discharges and can apply significant sanctions to non-performing communities.

National Pollution Discharge Elimination System (NPDES)

Like smokestack and tailpipe emission controls for air quality management, much of the industrial pollution entered water bodies through some kind of "pipe." These pipes may be the wastewater systems that carried human waste and storm water runoff or they may be separate conduits. Occasionally, these could be observed from the waterside or the riverbanks. The effects of the industrial pollutants were pernicious and extremely toxic to fish, wildlife, and, eventually, up the food chain to humans. Modern water quality planners point to the day the Cuyahoga River caught fire in Cleveland as a seminal event in transforming American policy on industrial pollution in lakes, rivers, and harbors. With the adoption of the Clean Water Act in 1965, urban sanitary sewers were already receiving significant (75%) federal subsidies. However, more aggressive interventions were now required.

The National Pollution Discharge Elimination System (NPDES) created a mandate to states to regulate these discharges and return the nation's waterways to fishable, swimmable, or even drinkable condition. Once again the initial reaction from industrial was combative, but, gradually, technology and public opinion helped to accomplish this.

Because our industrial history, like that of many countries, was linked to water, and many urban centers developed around the rivers and harbors, cities were an early beneficiary of the NPDES clean-up. However, they also were required to bear an increasing cost as federal subsidies for renovating, improving, and expanding their sanitary and storm sewers dried up.

Nonpoint Source

A much more difficult water pollution problem to manage and regulate is the runoff from streets, parking lots, and other impermeable surfaces. The federal government has attempted on several occasions to require states and localities to tackle this issue, with limited success. Interestingly, from a sprawl perspective, suburban and rural development contribute heavily to this form of pollution as well through widespread application of pesticides, fertilizer, and removal of natural barriers to erosion and sedimentation such as trees.

Air

Breathing bad air became a national concern as smog-laden Los Angeles became a poster child for all that was bad about the nation's flirtation with the automobile. Although Los Angeles' unique geography created special conditions that intensified a variety of airborne pollutants and trapped inside a large coastal basin surrounded by mountains, every major metropolitan area suffered from the health effects of this problem. As the science developed, linkages between air pollution and transportation (mobile sources) and smokestack industry (stationary sources) were clearly established. This set off a fight between the industrial interests of the Northeast and the Midwest and the transportation industry serving the entire nation.

It would take the 1970 Clean Air Act, one of the initial products of the emerging modern-day environmental movement, to create standards for measuring the health effects of different pollutants (criteria pollutants) on people (primary) and on plants, animals (secondary), and even structures and buildings. From these standards, a sophisticated set of sanctions was developed to encourage and then enforce the curtailment of emissions. States were required to develop implementation plans (SIPs) to manage quantifiable reductions in air emissions for both smokestacks and tailpipes. Both have had an impact on sprawl.

Mobile Sources

The internal combustion engine, burning fossil fuels, is a major source of a variety of criteria pollutants, including the key precursors to smog. While the personal automobile is the primary source, motorcycles, trucks and buses generate their fair share. Airplanes, lawnmowers, and other small engines contribute significantly to the deterioration of air in urban environments. As travel increased dramatically during the second half of the twentieth century, the cumulative impact of this technology became visible, literally, and the health effects on the entire human population began to appear, with special impacts on vulnerable populations such as the elderly, the young, and people with respiratory impairment.

The primary regulation introduced to limit the damage was the tailpipe emission program. Over the last few decades of the twentieth century, auto manufacturers were required to improve the efficiency of their engines and their exhaust recovery systems (catalytic converters). As older cars were replaced by newer vehicles and tailpipe testing programs were introduced in many states, significant improvements were realized. Individuals accommodated themselves to these requirements and, like other inconveniences such as airport security, began to see "clean cars" as an important and necessary part of life.

A by-product of the success of the tailpipe emission program was that automobile usage increased significantly over the last half of the century, despite occasional energy constraints. Attempts to tighten restrictions on mobile sources were pushed back by auto manufacturers. By allowing trucks to meet a lower standard, and classifying sport utility vehicles (SUVs) as trucks, federal policies have created a mixed bag of results. Our air is cleaner, but we are still driving more, increasing our demand for energy and for ever-expanding highway infrastructure.

Stationary Sources

While stationary sources (smokestacks) are a contributor to the deterioration of air quality, significant sanctions and technological advances have also reduced their impact. From a sprawl perspective, these reductions have had a positive impact on urban settings. Once heavily impacted by industrial pollution, cities are now more likely to compete for "cleaner" industries. However, the bad news is that many of the heavier manufacturing industries, which used to supply jobs to a vast array of skilled and unskilled workers alike, are leaving urban areas for other reasons and, in many cases, leaving the country entirely. Some hard-nosed critics continue to blame strict environmental regulations as a culprit in this departure, but most acknowledge that the cost of labor is the significant driver.

Indirect Sources

Other efforts were not as successful. An early attempt to mange the more diffuse impacts of land use through an "indirect source" permit failed to gain widespread support. Efforts by states to quantify the cumulative impact of traffic congestion by shopping malls, large employers, and other traffic generators were challenged in court by the development community on the basis that "background" congestion from pre-existing uses contributed significantly to local conditions and previously permitted land uses were not required to mitigate their impacts. In many large metropolitan areas, highly congested cities were required to adopt parking freezes while their suburban neighbors (and competitors) were allowed, and in fact required, to create large parking areas to meet the demands created by automobile traffic accessing office parks and shopping districts.

Wetlands and Coastal Zones

Wetlands are not always "wet" but are more often defined as soil types and conditions that contribute to seasonal variations in water resources. When "wet," these areas provide important wildlife habitat. Federal intervention came late in the game. Most aggressive early efforts at protecting and reclaiming wetlands were state initiatives.

The Coastal Zone Management Act enacted in 1972 empowered states to create significant protection of marshes and other coastal areas. The federal Wetlands Reserve Program compensates land owners willing to keep wetland areas off the market or out of production. One controversial proposal of the Clinton era was to require "no net loss" of wetlands for major land developments.

Brownfields

Another significant success for sprawl managers is the introduction of "brownfield" regulations to make sure that urban industrial sites, which became contaminated through previous use, could be reclaimed for productive use by new owners without the liabilities for massive and expensive cleanup. Spurred on, once again, by massive publicity about contamination incidents such as Love Canal, Congress first created "Superfund" legislation that allowed the cleanup of contaminated sites while aggressively pursuing the guilty parties and bringing them in front of a judge.

However, many urban (and occasionally suburban and rural) sites suffered under this cloud over their economic viability while these battles raged on and sprawl favored open "green fields" to these contaminated "brown fields." A number of sophisticated states developed interventions strategies to overcome this intractable situation. By intervening to reclaim the sites, states allowed them to be renovated to a condition that was less than pristine, but safe and viable for economic activity. New owners could proceed to bring the site on-line without fear of being liable for future damages. Meanwhile, the perpetrators of the prior contamination could still be pursued as necessary.

The federal government, seeing the wisdom of this alternate strategy, began to revise its approach and now actively supports a "brownfields" approach to previous contamination. From a sprawl perspective, this frees up many urban sites to compete successfully with suburban locations for new industrial and commercial development.

Economic Subsidies

One of the federal policies, least analyzed in the normative critique of sprawl, is the significant investments made to stimulate economic development in distressed parts of the economy. The granddaddy of these efforts is the Tennessee Valley Authority. Forming it in 1933 as part of the New Deal strategy to bring the country back from the depths of economic crisis, Roosevelt created a publicly-owned power utility to bring electricity and other utilities into the rural hinterlands of the mid-Atlantic and Southern states. It was clearly designed to "stimulate economic development and employment.... TVA also was important for demonstrating that government land use planning could be used to benefit the broad public in a region" (Kraft, 2001, p. 84).

In 1965, Congress authorized the creation of the Economic Development Administration (EDA) as an agency under the U.S. Department of Commerce. EDA targeted a number of investments in public works infrastructure designed to stimulate job creation in distressed areas. While some of these were focused on urban areas, a significant number led to industrial and office parks in rural areas which filled their sites with industries plundered from urban areas and from other states. These policies, while now significantly readjusted to avoid these predatory practices, nevertheless, are part of the federal policy system that helped create the phenomenon we call sprawl.

NOTES

1. "Vision 2020" slide show for Southeastern Massachusetts.
2. Massey and Denton, 1993, pp. 90–102.

BIBLIOGRAPHY

Binford, Henry C. 1985. *The First Suburbs: Residential Communities on the Boston Periphery 1815–60*. Chicago: University of Chicago Press.

Bradley, James W. 1982. *Historic and Archaeological Resources of the Boston Area: A Framework for Preservation Decisions*. Boston: Secretary of State.

Chapin, F. Stuart, and Edward J. Kaiser. 1979. *Urban Land Use Planning*. 3rd ed. Urbana: University of Illinois Press.

Downs, Anthony. 1973. *Opening up the Suburbs: An Urban Strategy for America*. New Haven, CT: Yale University Press.

Fishman, Robert. 1987. *Bourgeois Utopias: The Rise and Fall of Suburbia*. New York: Basic Books.

Kraft, Michael E. 2001. *Environmental Policy and Politics*. 2nd ed. New York: Longman.

Massey, Douglass S., and Nancy A. Denton. 1993. *American Apartheid: Segregation and the Making of the Underclass*. Cambridge, MA: Harvard University Press.

Mumford, Lewis. 1961. *The City in History: Its Origins, Its Transformations, and Its Prospects*. New York: Harcourt, Brace and World.

Palen, John J. 1995. *The Suburbs*. New York: McGraw-Hill.

Platt, Rutherford H. 1991. *Land Use Control: Geography, Law, and Public Policy*. Englewood Cliffs, NJ: Prentice Hall.

Rusk, David. 1993. *Cities without Suburbs*. Washington, DC: The Woodrow Wilson Center Press.

Smith, Zachary A. 2004. *The Environmental Policy Paradox*. 4th ed. Upper Saddle River, NJ: Prentice Hall.

So, Frank S., and Judith Getzels, eds. 1988. *The Practice of Local Government Planning*. 2nd ed. Washington, DC: International City/County Management Association.

Stilgoe, John R. 1988. *Borderland: Origins of the American Suburb, 1820–1939*. New Haven, CT: Yale University Press.

Warner, Sam Bass, Jr. 1978. *Streetcar Suburbs: The Process of Growth in Boston (1870–1900)*. 2nd ed. Cambridge, MA: Harvard University Press.

3

Legal Framework:
The Laws of Sprawl and
the Laws of Smart Growth

Jay Wickersham

Our laws actively shape our communities and our landscapes. This chapter describes how conventional or "Euclidean" zoning (from the definitive court case testing the constitutionality of zoning—*Village of Euclid* [Ohio] *v. Ambler Realty Co.*) has helped to create the landscapes of sprawl: low-density, single-use, automobile-dependent development on the urban fringe, with limited affordability of housing.[1] This chapter also suggests a variety of legal reforms that can help reverse this trend to foster smart growth patterns of development: higher-density, mixed-use developments in locations that foster a range of transportation choices and greater housing affordability.

The first part of the chapter describes the history and structure of Euclidean zoning and its role in postwar suburbanization. The second part describes the persistent failings of Euclidean zoning: the lack of planning, regional fragmentation, and exclusionary effects. The third part describes a range of potential reforms to Euclidean zoning at the local level, including "traditional neighborhood development" codes, local growth management systems aimed at affecting the pace of development, and inclusionary zoning. The fourth and final section describes a range of "smart growth" laws instituted at the regional and statewide scale, including major project reviews under Vermont's Act 250, state oversight of local planning in Oregon (urban growth boundaries) and Florida (concurrency requirements), and targeting of state infrastructure investments in Maryland.

Any proposed smart-growth laws, whether at the local or the state level, must be tested against certain broad questions. Do the laws give incentives for appropriate growth, or do they just constrain disfavored types of growth? Do the laws balance the regional benefits of growth against its localized impacts? Are there procedures to ensure the fair and predictable implementation of policy goals? Do regulations focus on public infrastructure investments or on private developments? And finally, do regulations dictate smart-growth results? Or do they seek to remove constraints that inhibit consumer choice, trusting that there is sufficient market demand for the residential and commercial development models favored by smart-growth advocates?

EUCLIDEAN ZONING: THE DOMINANT MODEL OF LAND-USE REGULATION

This section sketches the history and internal structure of conventional or "Euclidean" zoning. It then describes how changed development patterns after World War II revealed shortcomings in the Euclidean model.

The History of Euclidean Zoning

The dominant model of land use regulation in the United States is local zoning. Shortly after World War I, the wide implementation of zoning by local government rapidly won almost universal acceptance. New York City passed the first citywide zoning ordinance in 1916. In 1924, the U.S. Department of Commerce, under the leadership of Commerce Secretary Herbert Hoover, promulgated a Standard Zoning Enabling Act (SZEA).[2] By 1926, when the Supreme Court upheld the constitutionality of zoning against a takings challenge in *Village of Euclid v. Ambler Realty Co.*,[3] over 400 municipalities, with a total population of over 27 million, had zoning ordinances in place.[4] By 1930, forty-seven of the forty-eight states had zoning enabling acts, and over 900 cities, with a total population of more than 46 million (approximately 67 percent of the urban population), had zoning in place.[5] Today, almost every state and major city, with the exception of Houston, Texas, employs zoning as its principal tool of land-use regulation.

The success of Euclidean zoning is something of a historical accident. Around 1910, pioneers of the city planning movement, like Chicago architect Daniel Burnham and landscape architect Frederick Law Olmsted, Jr., focused upon the eminent domain power, as it was being used by government agencies in continental Europe, as the primary legal tool to implement their policy goals.[6] Within the urban core, these planners sought to use eminent domain to create elegant boulevards, parks, and civic buildings, as Baron Haussman had done for Napoleon III in late nineteenth-century Paris.[7] At the urban fringe, they looked to the way that German cities controlled what we now call sprawl by buying and landbanking large areas of land, replanning them as relatively dense, compact housing estates, and then re-releasing the land back on the private market.[8] Zoning, by comparison, was originally seen as a less important item in the planner's legal toolbox. The purpose of zoning was to stabilize existing areas once they had been properly planned, to ensure that they did not change too rapidly over time.[9]

The early planners were unable to obtain the broad powers of condemnation that they sought, both because of political opposition in the legislatures and because of the judicial doctrine of "excess condemnation" and cramped definitions of the "public use" requirement.[10] Zoning, by contrast, won wide and rapid support. By 1926, the year of the Euclid decision, all but five states had passed zoning enabling acts, most of them based on the SZEA.[11] By default, zoning took on its present function as a template for the creation of new urban and suburban districts. Zoning's underlying presumptions were also more aligned with an ideological shift in the planning profession during the 1920s. A functionalist view of the city as a large and smoothly operating machine took hold, heavily influenced by Frederick Winslow Taylor's studies of industrial efficiency.[12] Euclidean zoning, with its strict separation of uses and its comprehensive and uniform dimensional standards, fit right in. The functionalist view of the city, requiring the strict separation of uses, persisted as a particularly powerful ideological motivation for urban renewal projects in the 1950s, as well as for suburban sprawl developments.

Today, that functionalist template retains an air of inevitability. Our zoning remains stuck in the "Sim City" model of urban development. As in the popular computer game, each zone is set aside solely for single-family or apartment or commercial or industrial use, with little possibility and no incentives for the mixing of uses. Euclidean zoning is accepted as a given and reinforced by real estate developers, bankers, lawyers, architects, and city planners. We have lost sight of the fact that it doesn't mirror what we know about vital cities and regions.

The Structure of Euclidean Zoning

The basic structure of Euclidean zoning has changed little since the 1920s.[13] Zoning codes divide a community into uniform districts, or zones. Uniform districts ensure that property owners will be treated fairly. Within each district, all property owners are subject to the same regulations, governing three principal factors: allowable uses, allowable bulk (size and shape) of buildings, and density of development. District regulations define the "as-of-right" zoning entitlement that the owner can presume, without having to undergo a project-specific permitting process. Thus, uniform districts give property owners assurances as to what they, and their neighbors, will be permitted to do, thereby encouraging social stability and financial investment.

Use Restrictions

Within each district the code will list the permitted uses, as well as certain uses that may be "conditional" upon issuance of a permit. Any use that is not specifically listed as permitted or conditional is forbidden in that zoning district.[14] Most zoning codes, starting in the 1920s, initially used a system of cumulative or pyramidal use districts. (The term pyramidal refers to the way one can describe the system in a pyramid-shaped diagram.) Under a cumulative system, the most restrictive use district is the Single-Family Residential, which is placed at the top of the pyramid because the only allowable use is the single-family house. As one steps down the pyramid, through multifamily residential, commercial, and then industrial districts, more permitted uses are added in each district. The most permissive zone of all under the cumulative system is Heavy Industrial, where anything goes.

More recently, zoning codes have incorporated exclusive-use districts.[15] Under the exclusive use system, commercial and industrial zones, like residential, are limited to that particular set of uses. The result is a greater "sorting out" and separation of uses, of the kind that we observe in recent suburban development, as opposed to the more fine-grained mixing of different uses that characterizes older urban areas (particularly those developed before the adoption of zoning in the 1920s).

Dimensional (Bulk) Restrictions

For each district, the zoning code will set out restrictions on the size and locations of buildings and other structures within each lot. Setbacks (also described as yard depths) define the distances that a building must be set back from the front, side, and rear lot lines. Codes also define maximum restrictions on building height, often expressed both in feet and number of stories. Combining these two sets of dimensional restrictions will yield the "maximum dimensional envelope": an imaginary three-dimensional volume of space within which a building may be located.[16]

Density Restrictions

Zoning codes also include density restrictions, aimed at regulating the maximum intensity of development within a district. For residential zones, density controls may restrict the minimum lot size or the maximum number of dwelling units per acre. In urban areas, density is often controlled through the maximum Floor Area Ratio (FAR). FAR is calculated by dividing the total square footage of all floors of the building by the total square footage of the lot.[17]

Most zoning codes contain minimum requirements for off-street parking, expressed as the number of required parking spaces per dwelling units for residential uses or as the number of required parking spaces per 1,000 square feet of commercial development. For commercial developments on suburban sites, off-street parking requirements, rather than setbacks, minimum lot sizes, or FAR, often control the density on a lot.[18]

Zoning Procedures

Because the SZEA was drafted before the emergence of federal and state administrative procedure acts, it contains very few procedural requirements at the municipal level. A local, legislatively appointed Board of Adjustment reviews rules on amendments, grievances, special permits, variances, and nonconforming uses, subject to judicial review.[19] Courts give limited deference to special permit and variance decisions, which are usually treated as "quasi-judicial," while giving greater leeway to amendments or rezonings, which are usually treated as "quasi-legislative."[20] Standing in zoning cases is narrowly restricted to include only property owners, abutters, and other immediately affected parties.[21]

Zoning and the Constitution

Government's authority to impose zoning restrictions arises from the police power: the power to regulate private property to protect the public health, safety, and welfare. The 1926 Euclid decision firmly established the legal power to restrict allowable land uses and the bulk and density of new development. More recent decisions have upheld the expansion of government regulation to such areas as visual appearance, historic preservation,[22] and the protection of open space.[23]

The principal limit on government's regulatory power is the Takings Clause of the Fifth Amendment: "nor shall private property be taken for public use without just compensation." Since the 1920s, courts have applied the Takings Clause to require government compensation when a regulation deprives the landowner of all economically beneficial use of his or her land, unless such use would be barred on other grounds (for example, that it would pose a nuisance to neighboring landowners).[24] Note, however, that a severe diminishment in the value of the land will usually not qualify as a taking; courts rarely find that a taking has occurred unless the regulation is so restrictive that no development whatsoever—not even a single house—can be built on the property. Moreover, in measuring the impact of the regulation, the court will look at the value of the property as a whole.[25] Thus, a regulation that renders one lot unbuildable in a multi-lot subdivision will likely not be viewed as a taking. Another controversial subject in takings law has been the increasing use of exactions in the regulatory process; see below for a further discussion of this topic.

The Role of Zoning in Postwar Suburbanization

The trend towards suburbanization began in the nineteenth century, long before zoning appeared. The most rapid expansion of suburbia, however, began in the latter half of the twentieth century.[26] After World War II, America evolved into a predominantly suburban nation. Federal policies spurred the development of interstate highway systems and promoted inexpensive mortgages for suburban homes. First came the rapid development of large suburban subdivisions, followed by retail shopping centers, industrial parks, and office complexes. The old pattern of development, consisting of a commercial downtown core and surrounding urban and suburban residential areas, no longer exists. American metropolitan regions now consist of multiple commercial nodes, often known as "edge cities," linked by a net of highways.[27] These commercial areas frequently exceed the old downtown in size and activity. Today most Americans commute not from a suburb to downtown, but from one suburb to another.

Euclidean zoning has played a major role in the development of recent, distinctive suburban growth patterns. In suburban communities, the predominant pattern of zoning widely separates residential, business, and industrial uses, rather than permitting the much more fine-grained mixing of uses that is typical of older cities. Suburban zoning has encouraged very low population densities; residential lot size requirements ranging from one to five acres are not uncommon. Zoning also has encouraged patterns of "ribbon" or "strip" development along major roads, by setting aside large areas for low-density commercial use.

Euclidean zoning's low densities and separation of uses have created a dependence on private automobiles as the sole form of transportation in the suburbs. Cost considerations prohibit the development of public transportation systems, such as buses and railroads. Since people no longer live, work, and shop in a single area, each activity requires an additional automobile trip.[28] The reliance on automobiles has resulted in traffic congestion, land clearing for roads and parking lots, and air pollution.

Low-density suburban development patterns can radically affect the environment. Although each individual house may seem innocuous, the widespread expansion of public services, such as sewers and septic systems, road building, and clearing and leveling of lots, can destroy existing ecosystems. Suburban development can also radically transform the visual quality of the landscape. Strip commercial development along major roads gives an impression of an unending landscape of gas stations, shopping centers, and fast food outlets; two or three new houses built in the middle of a field can destroy the visual image of a long established farming community.[29]

Finally, low-density, large-lot residential zoning exacerbates high housing prices by raising the cost of land and municipal services in relation to each housing unit. Disparities in housing prices between older cities and newer suburbs have reinforced patterns of community segregation by class and race.

PERSISTENT FAILINGS OF EUCLIDEAN ZONING

Modifications of Euclidean zoning to regulate major projects and protect critical resources have had mixed success. This section discusses three persistent problems. First, because municipalities often are not required to undertake land-use planning or to conform zoning and other regulations to the provisions of a plan, local governments find it difficult to predict and shape long-term development trends. Second, because metropolitan areas are fragmented politically into many small municipal governments, local regulations are ineffective in dealing with large-scale land-use problems. Third, both local land-use regulations and new state and federal regulations with effects on land development have often been used as exclusionary devices, allowing communities to keep out unwanted activities and people.

Planning in the Context of Euclidean Zoning

The SZEA provides that local zoning should be adopted "in accordance with a comprehensive plan."[30] In 1928, only four years after issuing the SZEA, the U.S. Commerce Department issued a Standard City Planning Enabling Act (SPEA).[31] But for a variety of reasons, in many states Euclidean zoning does not rest on a legal underpinning of comprehensive planning.

First, the SZEA was never amended with explicit reference to the SPEA or even with a definition of "comprehensive plan," leaving the meaning of the statute unclear. Second, the SPEA itself took a narrow view of planning: It created a local planning commission that was separate from the zoning commission and gave it only the duties of mapping current and future streets, reviewing all public works, adopting regulations for subdivisions, and making recommendations for future land use trends.[32] The SPEA did not give the planning commission any power over the zoning ordinance or require that zoning conform to the plan. Finally, states and municipalities were much slower to adopt planning than they were to adopt zoning.

As a result, when confronted with the SZEA's command that zoning conform to a comprehensive plan, most courts have read this requirement tautologically: The zoning regulation is itself "the plan."[33] This reading permitted municipalities to adopt zoning without undertaking planning; further, when municipalities did plan, it allowed zoning to diverge significantly from the plan without any legal consequences.[34] Even today, the majority of states do not require local planning as a basis for local zoning.[35]

Governmental Fragmentation and Home Rule

The power to regulate land use rests in the state, as part of its general police power.[36] Zoning enabling acts based on the SZEA delegate that power to municipalities, but the state can always review or even rescind its grant of powers.[37] While most states grant some measure of legal autonomy to municipalities through home rule (under a state constitution, statute, or judicial doctrine), few states hold zoning to be among a municipality's inherent home rule powers. Moreover, even in such "strong" home rule states, courts have upheld the power of the state legislature to supersede local zoning where statewide interests are at stake.[38]

Nonetheless, to conclude that municipal regulation of land use is at the mercy of the state is to confuse form with substance. In fact, until the passage of the first regional and statewide land-use statutes in the 1960s, states had exercised virtually no oversight of local zoning. Throughout the United States, local control over land use through zoning is one of the most powerful ways in which municipalities exercise de facto home rule powers.[39] The use of zoning to defend home rule is linked to the fragmented nature of local government. Throughout the nineteenth century, cities grew both in population and in geographic size, thereby annexing unincorporated areas outside their boundaries. During the twentieth century, however, suburbs have increasingly resisted annexation.[40] The result is often a balkanized political landscape, in which large metropolitan regions that show a unity in geographic, economic, and social terms are broken up politically into dozens or even hundreds of independent municipal governments.[41]

Local Inability to Deal with Major Projects

Both the scale and the location of major new development projects tend to frustrate attempts at local control. Not only do local governments often lack the expertise to address the spillover effects of such developments, but their own self-interest may lead them to ignore such problems; most of the benefits may accrue to one city or town (in the form of new jobs and taxes), while the harms (traffic congestion, flooding from filled wetlands, air and water pollution, economic and social dislocations) spill over onto adjoining communities. The development patterns of "edge cities" exacerbate this problem. Since these new commercial cores developed according to their relationship to the highway, not to an existing town center, they frequently overlap the boundaries of two or more municipalities.[42]

Local Inability to Protect Shared Environmental Resources

A resource that extends over a broad area, whether natural (forests, mountains, lakes and rivers, wetlands, coastal zones) or man-made (historic districts, farmlands), poses the "tragedy of the commons" problems of degradation of a shared resource.[43] Where many actors share the use of an indivisible common resource, each is rationally impelled to develop the resource beyond its carrying capacity. Each individual's short-term gain will exceed individual harms, while harms will be spread out among all the users. Voluntary cooperation cannot overcome the constant risk of a few holdouts, still seeking their own gain. Where such an affected resource overlaps the boundaries of municipal governments, only an effective regional or statewide agency can regulate the private land market in a way that protects the resource from harm.

Exclusionary Effects of Local Zoning

Municipalities often manipulate their zoning powers to exclude unwanted activities and groups of people. With zoning decisions made at the local level, small, homogeneous communities that do not necessarily reflect the more general population in terms of class and race have the opportunity to control entrance into their neighborhoods. In the words of Richard Babcock, "zoning has provided the device for protecting the homogeneous, single family suburb from the city."[44]

The use of zoning for exclusionary purposes can take on several forms. "Fiscal zoning" seeks to bar uses that produce low taxes and high demand for municipal services, such as dense multifamily housing with many school-age children, in favor of uses that will produce high taxes and low demands for services, such as office parks and shopping centers. Proponents of the NIMBY ("Not in My Back Yard") syndrome use zoning to bar LULUs (locally undesirable land uses): projects that are socially necessary but disliked by their neighbors, such as prisons or waste treatment facilities.[45] In exclusionary zoning, municipalities use large-lot requirements within zoning districts limited to single-family homes to block the creation of affordable housing. This type of exclusionary zoning is often motivated by racial or class bias.[46]

LOCAL MODIFICATIONS TO EUCLIDEAN ZONING

This section begins by describing alternative physical models of development that underlie some of the strongest critiques of Euclidean zoning. It then goes on to describe a range of potential reforms to Euclidean zoning at the local level, including planned units developments (PUDs), design-based standards such as "traditional neighborhood development" codes, local-growth management systems aimed at affecting the pace of development, and inclusionary zoning aimed at creating affordable housing.

Garden Cities, Urbanists, and New Urbanists

All land use regulations embody, implicitly or explicitly, some vision of the physical character of the community—how buildings, streets, and other man-made structures are organized in relation to each other and to the natural environment.[47] Euclidean zoning embodies two images that are pervasive in American history: first, land subdivided into an infinitely extensible grid that serves as a tool of speculation, sale, and development;[48] and second, each parcel of the grid ultimately transformed into a single-family house sitting on its own private patch of green.[49]

In response, planners, designers, and other writers have articulated three critiques of how Euclidean zoning has shaped the physical character of our communities: the garden city critique of Lewis Mumford and others; the urbanist critique of Jane Jacobs; and today's New Urbanist critique, which incorporates elements of both.

The Garden City Critique

As early as the 1920s, Lewis Mumford and the other members of the Regional Planning Association of America popularized the garden city ideal as an alternative to rapid suburban growth.[50] The "garden city" vision of compact, self-contained communities surrounded by greenbelts and offering residents a full range of urban housing types, jobs, and cultural and recreational opportunities, was first articulated by the English reformer Ebenezer Howard.[51] The garden city ideal inspired the creation of a series of communities in Great Britain, culminating in the publicly funded New Towns built in the 1950s and 1960s.[52] Examples of garden cities in the United States include the town of Radburn, New Jersey, and three greenbelt towns built under the auspices of the Federal Resettlement Administration during the New Deal.[53] The garden city ideal remains today a vital, if often unacknowledged, influence on regional planning and alternatives to sprawl.[54]

Jane Jacobs and the Urbanist Critique

Jane Jacobs's 1961 masterpiece, *The Death and Life of Great American Cities*, contains one of the strongest criticisms of Euclidean zoning ever written.[55] At the heart of *The Death and Life* is an appreciation of economic diversity: the richness of business ideas and opportunities that flourish in a city. Jacobs understood that "the same physical and economic conditions that generate diverse commerce are intimately related to the presence, or production, of other kinds of city variety"—variety in its cultural opportunities, its physical settings, and its residents and visitors.[56] In other words, the same forces that make a city a good place to do business also make it a good place to live.

Jacobs showed how a city's economic and social vitality and diversity can be strangled or supported by the layout of its streets, parks, and buildings. She identified and described four urban design principles that are preconditions for the creation and preservation of vibrant, diverse cities: (1) high densities of population and activities; (2) mixtures of primary uses; (3) small-scale, pedestrian-friendly blocks and streetscapes; and (4) the retention of old buildings mixed in with new. An unabashed champion of density, Jacobs criticized Mumford and the garden city movement for their continuing concerns with urban density. In her view, dense, mixed-use districts are more active and safer both day and night.[57] The sorting-out of functions into single-use districts stifles the cross-fertilization of ideas and experiences that is so important to a city's economic and social health. "Without a strong and inclusive central heart, a city tends to become a collection of interests separated from one another."[58] Jacobs understood that streets and sidewalks, as much as parks, are the true public spaces of a city.[59] Old buildings, mixed in with new, offer cheap space for new businesses and low-cost housing, and they provide landmarks that anchor a neighborhood in space and time.[60]

The principles that Jacobs identifies as the necessary conditions for a vital, diverse city are directly at variance with the underlying presumptions of Euclidean zoning. Where Jacobs favors density, Euclidean zoning restrains density in order to reduce congestion, crime, and other urban ills. Where Jacobs favors a mixture of primary uses, Euclidean zoning separates or quarantines uses so that they will not infect one another. And where Jacobs wants to create pedestrian-friendly streetscapes and preserve older buildings, Euclidean zoning fails to address those issues (subdivision regulations, which evolved parallel to Euclidean zoning, typically require roadway designs based solely on the needs of automobile traffic).[61]

The Smart Growth/New Urbanist Vision

Key elements of both the garden city ideal and Jane Jacobs's vision have been incorporated into the smart growth and New Urbanism movements. Although there is no universally accepted definition of smart growth, it is best understood as the antithesis of sprawl. Smart growth advocates argue for a land development model that is more compact, focused on downtowns, town centers, and other previously developed sites, and characterized by higher densities and a sharper break between developed areas and protected open spaces. Smart-growth models also display a greater mix of uses, with residential, commercial, and civic activities more tightly inter-spersed. Such higher densities and mixed uses are intended to foster a wider range of transportation choices, including public transit, ride-sharing, bicycling, and walking. Thus, smart growth couples Jacobs's localized vision of dense, vital communities with the garden city movement's regional ideal of compact settlements surrounded by greenbelts.

The concept of "smart growth" first emerged in the planning community during the 1980s. The most extensive exploration and description of smart-growth policies and model legislation is the Growing Smart Papers issued by the American Planning Association between 1995 and 2002. Smart-growth advocates often make common cause with the "New Urbanism" movement, a group of architects, planners, and de-velopers who advocate reclaiming preautomobile patterns of city and town-building.[62]

In the past decade, smart-growth concepts have been adopted by many environ-mentalists and affordable housing advocates. As a political movement, smart growth now exists as an alliance among these three groups. The breadth of these smart-growth alliances is a potential source of strength and influence. But at the same time, there are potential tensions among alliance members: many environmentalists see the primary goal of smart growth as checking sprawl in suburban and rural areas, while their allies may see its primary goal as encouraging growth in cities and town centers. Affordable housing advocates, meanwhile, are concerned that new regula-tions may limit the supply of housing and raise its costs. These differing and some-times conflicting perspectives must be reconciled in any proposed legal reforms aimed at advancing smart growth policies.

Regulation of Major Projects

Euclidean zoning presumes small-scale, lot-by-lot development; it was not de-signed to regulate such projects as large residential subdivisions, industrial parks, of-fice complexes, regional shopping malls, and major mixed-use urban projects. To address such large-scale development, many zoning ordinances have been amended to permit Planned Unit Developments (PUDS). A PUD is a variety of highly site-specific zoning which may be authorized either through the issuance of a special per-mit, or through the adoption of a zoning amendment.[63] The most common form of PUD is "cluster zoning," in which housing units are grouped more closely together, permitting the preservation of larger areas of undeveloped green space. PUDs can also be used to mix different housing types (single-family houses, townhouses, and apartments) and different types of uses (residential, office, and retail). In return for the wider mix of uses, greater densities, and more flexible dimensional restrictions, PUDs typically provide greater public benefits, both on-site (such as increased open space) and off-site (such as contributions to infrastructure improvements). The zon-ing code should set out minimum land areas for projects to qualify as PUDs; many codes also cap the allowable height and density standards for such projects.

Effects of Project-Specific Reviews

On a project-specific basis, such review processes can counteract some of the ef-fects of Euclidean zoning. The mechanism of a PUD offers landowners the chance to work with local officials and citizens to develop a more imaginative project design that meets both development and community goals, without being limited by the constraints of Euclidean zoning. Approval of a special permit or a PUD can allow a higher level of density and a broader mix of uses than zoning would otherwise allow as-of-right. Through project review processes, communities have adopted discretionary urban design standards that favor the retention of existing street and block patterns, the preservation of older structures, and the reservation of ground-floor streetfronts for shops, restaurants, and other active uses.[64]

But there has also been a cost. Because these reforms are project-specific, and not comprehensive, the counterproductive, as-of-right requirements of Euclidean zoning have been sidestepped, not removed. To tempt developers into the project review process, regulatory systems will offer a density or height bonus to offset the increased time and costs that are involved. Such incentives can cause all parties to undervalue small-scale, incremental renovation and infill projects that can be so important for the stability of an urban district or a community. Thus, favoring large private investments can cause the same kinds of cataclysmic change as the public urban renewal projects of the 1950s. The project review process may also involve such intense bargaining—particularly when there are no clear and predictable standards to govern the outcome—that it is very frustrating for developers and communities alike. Sometimes the result is to cause the public to distrust the entire regulatory system.[65]

The Problem of Exactions

Exactions are public benefits that a property owner must provide as a condition of a project-specific review procedure, to offset the potential impacts of the proposed development. There are two principal types of exactions: land and money. Sometimes the developer may be required to dedicate a portion of the site for a public use to serve the new development: a park; a right-of-way for a road, transit line, or bicycle path; or a site for a fire station or school. More commonly a developer is required to pay for improvements to public infrastructure, such as roads, water supplies, sewers, or storm drainage systems, that will accommodate the increased impacts of the project.[66] Ordinances may also require developers to contribute "impact fees" or "linkage" trust funds for indirectly related public purposes, such as citywide programs to improve transportation, create affordable housing, or provide job training.[67] In either case, such payments should be set aside in a dedicated trust fund, to ensure they are used for their intended purpose.

Exactions have become widely used by cities and towns over the past 20 years, but the practice remains controversial. Developers often claim that requiring exactions imposes unequal costs upon new projects, to provide public services that should be paid for by all taxpayers. Some citizens have argued that exactions may distort the development review process in the other direction, enabling the permitting of over-scaled projects.

Courts and legislatures have set some limits on the use of exactions. The U.S. Supreme Court has twice ruled on the constitutionality of land dedications under the taking clause of the Fifth Amendment. In *Nollan v. California Coastal Commission*,[68] the Court held that there must be a "nexus" or relationship between the impacts of a project and the site area that it is required to set aside for public use. In *Dolan v. City of Tigard*,[69] the Court held that even where a nexus exists, the local permitting agency must show evidence that the exaction is "roughly proportional" to the project impacts. Although the U.S. Supreme Court has never ruled on the constitutionality of financial exactions, many state courts and legislatures have imposed similar rules on both land dedications and financial exactions, to ensure fairness and predictability for property owners. Many cities and towns have developed schedules that set predictable formulas for exaction payments, tying the amount of the predicted cost of infrastructure improvements.

Zoning for Density, Mixed Uses, and Urban Design

Although standard Euclidean zoning (along with subdivision and roadway standards) appears to be value-neutral, it actually favors large, free-standing, single-use buildings, surrounded by parking.[70] Thus, Euclidean zoning makes it nearly impossible to create a new development with the physical qualities that make older downtowns, urban neighborhoods, and town centers so attractive. As an alternative to the project-specific reviews described above, there is now broad experimentation going on nationwide into design standards and as-of-right zoning entitlements that can help create dense, mixed-use development patterns with an attractive, pedestrian-friendly urban character. Such codes are often known as "traditional neighborhood development" (TND) codes.[71] There are four specific zoning techniques that can help achieve the planning goals for TND districts: mixed use zoning; minimum density requirements/Floor Area Ratios (FARs); maximum parking requirements; and design standards for buildings, streets, and public spaces.

The most far-reaching use of TND codes may be found in the model zoning codes being developed by members of the New Urbanist movement. TND zoning codes began as privately enforced subdivision regulations in places like Seaside, Florida, and Mashpee Commons on Cape Cod. Now they are being adopted in communities across the nation.[72] Oregon has recently issued a new model zoning code, jointly sponsored by the Departments of Land Conservation and Development and Transportation, which incorporates many of these TND elements and is applicable to all of its towns and small cities.[73] Recently, Pennsylvania and Wisconsin have amended their state zoning and planning enabling acts to expressly authorize TND codes.[74]

Mixed-Use Zoning

Creating a successful TND district requires the intermingling of shops, restaurants, workplaces, and residences. Shops and restaurants allow residents and workers to run errands or get a meal on the way to or from the station. A variety of activities keeps sidewalks and other public spaces livelier and safer throughout the day and evening. The mixture of uses promotes the use of public transit, where it is available.

To address these issues, zoning codes should encourage and not discourage mixed-use development. Mixed uses are often encouraged in current zoning codes through density bonuses, through a special permit process. For example, to encourage residential development in a TND district, projects containing at least 50 percent residential uses could be allowed greater height and FAR.

It is more effective, however, to allow mixed uses on an as-of-right basis. The impacts of different uses may be addressed through "split zones." Split zones define the maximum density of both commercial and residential uses on a lot and define the total FAR that exceeds both. Thus, a developer has flexibility to respond to market forces in deciding whether or how to combine different project elements. But the developer cannot take advantage of the maximum buildout without developing a mixed-use project. For example, within a TND district that is targeted for denser residential uses, the zoning code sets a maximum FAR for commercial uses of 1.0, a maximum FAR for residential uses of 1.5, and a maximum total FAR of 2.0.[75]

Minimum Density Requirements/Floor Area Ratios (FARs)

A critical mass of density is required to provide the ridership necessary for a successful TND district. By concentrating development, more opportunities arise to replace trips in drive-alone automobiles by car- and van-pooling, bicycling, and walking. Denser development, particularly when it mixes retail, office, and residential uses, also has an improved "internal trip capture" rate: trips that otherwise would make someone drive to several different destinations can all be accomplished on foot within the same area.

Minimum density zoning carries out the goals of a community plan for a TND district by establishing a threshold for development density. The minimum density requirement may be expressed as a minimum FAR for commercial development, and as a maximum lot size or minimum number of units per acre for residential development. For multiple lots, minimum density can be averaged over the entire development, allowing the mix of larger lots with smaller lots.[76]

Maximum Parking Standards

Conventional zoning typically sets minimum parking standards, designed to ensure that all cars attracted by a certain use can be accommodated with on-site parking. This has had the effect of lowering development densities, producing large tracts of impervious pavement, and increasing areawide traffic problems.

Within TND districts zoning codes, zoning codes should establish maximum, rather than minimum, limits on the number of parking spaces to be provided.[77] Limiting the number of available parking spaces discourages automobile trips and provides incentives for greater transit use. Reducing the amount of land dedicated to paved parking lots allows on-site development densities to be increased, while preserving open space and reducing flooding and water pollution. Developments that need not build as much parking may be able to provide greater support for affordable housing.

Design Standards

From a design viewpoint, TND codes start with the design of the street: the width of travel lanes and sidewalk, the presence of parked cars, and the way that buildings front upon that street. Within urban districts, all streets must have minimum sidewalk widths and provide on-street parking. Within private building lots, parking should be set back to the side or rear of a building, to preserve the pedestrian character of the street.[78] TND zoning may also require mandatory shopfronts along the sidewalks in designated retail frontage locations. It may also require that arcades, stoops, or porches provide a human-scaled transitional zone. Special standards are established for civic spaces: parks, greens, and plazas. Standards also allow or encourage special architectural treatments for civic buildings, from government buildings and schools, to religious, cultural, and transportation facilities.[79]

Local Growth Management Regulations

Local growth management regulations are intended to alter the pattern and pace of development.[80] More specifically, their use is aimed at shifting from prevalent postwar patterns of low-density, monofunctional suburban sprawl to more compact development patterns with higher densities, a greater mixture of uses, and a sharper transition from urbanized areas to surrounding greenbelts. Proponents of growth management argue that limiting suburban sprawl preserves existing open spaces, thus strengthening natural ecosystems, offering opportunities for recreation, and maintaining the economic viability of farming and other rural industries. Higher densities can make public transportation, bicycling, and walking a feasible alternative to automobiles, thus lessening air pollution, energy consumption, and traffic congestion. From an economic viewpoint, steering new development to settled areas where transportation and other public services are already available keeps taxes and other costs low, strengthening the competitive position of businesses. Finally, higher residential densities can reduce housing costs by lowering the costs of land relative to each unit, thereby making housing more available to low- and moderate-income residents.[81]

Certain growth-management regulations, including development moratoria and caps on the number of building permits issued, are squarely aimed at halting growth outright, at least in the short term. Other strategies, most notably concurrency requirements, growth boundaries, agricultural zoning, and transferable development rights (TDRs), focus on steering long-term growth into more beneficial development patterns.

Courts have generally upheld growth-management regulations against "exclusionary zoning" challenges, so long as the municipality can show that the regulation is supported by long-term planning and is motivated by the desire to manage, but not stop, growth.[82] Some growth-management regulations attempt to promote the creation of affordable housing: For example, a concurrency regulation may give added weight to housing affordability when determining project approval, or imposition of a growth boundary may require an increase in residential densities within the designated growth area in order to counterbalance decreases in densities outside the growth limits.

Concurrency and Growth Boundaries

"Concurrency" requirements endeavor to affect the sequencing of development within a community.[83] Under a typical concurrency ordinance, any development beyond a very low density threshold can only proceed if the developer can show that required public services, primarily transportation and utilities, are or will soon be available. This determination may be made by allocating points to various required services with some minimum number to be met, or by requiring some minimum "level of service" (LOS) for certain specified services. The section "State and Regional Land Use Regulations" describes the use of concurrency requirements as the cornerstone of Florida's statewide smart growth program.

Growth boundaries attempt to limit the physical expansion of a community. Since around 1970, municipalities have defined boundaries which distinguish between "growth" areas, where densities are higher and urban development is encouraged, and "slow growth" or "conservation" areas, where development is discouraged to preserve natural resources and rural industries. "State and Regional Land Use Regulations" describes in considerable detail the use of growth boundaries in Oregon's statewide planning consistency program.

Thus, both concurrency and growth boundary requirements permit a municipality to link private development to public choices about the efficient allocation of roads, utilities, schools, police, fire, open space, and other public services. When used solely at the local level, however, such regulations may actually be counterproductive; the result may be to shift development to neighboring communities that lack such controls, thereby resulting in more dispersed development patterns on a regional scale.[84]

Agricultural Protection Zoning

An agricultural protection zone is intended to preserve existing farmland or land that has potential for agricultural production, by requiring large minimum lot sizes and limiting or forbidding uses other than agriculture.[85] Agricultural zones have most commonly been successful, politically and legally, in areas where there is widespread recognition of the importance of agriculture to the local or regional economy and where farmland has not come under significant development pressures. The minimum parcel size in an agricultural zone has been defined in different areas at anywhere from 20 acres to hundreds of acres—usually reflecting local conditions of what is necessary for successful farming. The number of dwellings is often limited; new dwellings should be located on soils least suitable for agriculture, and clustered on small lots whose development will not interfere with the efficient farm use of the rest of the land. This maximizes the amount of contiguous land still available to farm, while allowing farmers some profit from the residential value of their land.

Courts in some states, such as Massachusetts, have not been supportive of large minimum zoning lots. It is important to differentiate agricultural zoning from simple large-lot zoning. Many communities use large-lot zoning, where each new house must be on a minimum of from two to 20 acres, as a way to limit population growth in a community, particularly for those of moderate income. While there may be particular situations where large lot zoning is appropriate, more often it maximizes land consumption and ensures sprawl. The cost of public services, from roads to sewer lines to school bus routes, increases with large-lot zoning. Wildlife habitat is fragmented into lots that are "too large to mow, too small to hay." For agricultural zoning to be effective, it must require minimum lot sizes that effectively discourage nonfarmers from buying land.

Transferable Development Rights (TDRs)

A TDR program reduces development pressures on resources that need protection, like farmlands or historic properties, and allows denser development in appropriate locations, all the while trying to ensure greater financial fairness so the process does not create winners and losers. TDR is a regulatory technique that allows transfer of some or all of the development rights from one property to another.[86] TDR is based on the legally supportable concept that the rights associated with property ownership are divisible and can be marketed. A TDR regulation delineates "sending areas," in which the allowable density of development is reduced, and "receiving areas," where increased density of development is permitted. Landowners in a sending area can sell their development rights to landowners in a receiving area, who are allowed to build greater density as a result of buying those rights. Once development rights have been transferred from a sending property, its as-of-right buildout is permanently reduced. TDR programs may be expressly enabled by state statute or be based on municipal authorities. In some of the most successful programs, like the one in the New Jersey Pinelands, a publicly funded bank has been created to make a market. The bank purchases development rights from willing sellers and holds them until a buyer is found.

Inclusionary Zoning

Many communities have provisions in their zoning bylaws requiring or promoting the construction of affordable housing, either as a requirement or by offering incentives.[87] The requirement to include affordable housing can be made part of special permit review. The zoning code would stipulate that a minimum percentage of the total number of units—10 to 20 percent are common levels—be made affordable in new housing developments above a certain size. Some bylaws permit the developer to create affordable housing off-site or to make a financial contribution of equivalent value into a mitigation fund. Such inclusionary requirements may also be applied to large commercial developments which create demand for more housing. A requirement to provide affordable housing can also be imposed as a condition on projects seeking more density, floor area, or height than normally allowed.

As an incentive, the zoning code can provide density bonuses for developments providing affordable housing, both in multifamily projects and single-family subdivisions. In the latter case, flexible standards for lot dimensions and layout are necessary to accommodate the additional density and help reduce development costs.

STATE AND REGIONAL LAND-USE REGULATIONS

The regulatory tools discussed in the previous section—local zoning for traditional neighborhood development and growth management controls—can help communities move away from prevailing patterns of low-density, monofunctional sprawl, toward higher-density, more compact development. Nonetheless, when implemented solely at the local level, such controls may have only limited effects upon development patterns within larger metropolitan areas.

A number of states have adopted statutes that reassert some measure of statewide or regional control over local land development policies.[88] These statutes employ a variety of forms of land use controls: (1) statewide or regional land use classification; (2) state or regional regulation of major development projects; (3) state or regional regulation of critical resources; (4) statewide or regional requirements that local land use plans and zoning be consistent with statewide or regional policy goals; and (5) targeting of state infrastructure investments to designated growth areas. Each of these forms of regulation is discussed in more detail below.

Statewide and Regional Land-Use Classification

Classification of allowable land uses at a statewide or regional level offers a dramatic, but infrequently used, alternative to local land use regulation through conventional zoning.

Hawaii

The state land use program adopted in Hawaii in 1961[89] has a unique character. In Hawaii, the state, and not its municipalities, exercises primary control over land-use districting. A nine-member state land-use commission has the power to classify all lands in the state into one of four land-use districts: urban, rural, agricultural, or conservation. Within the broad district classifications created under the statute, counties and municipalities retain power to impose more detailed zoning controls in urban, rural, and agricultural lands. Control over conservation districts remains in the hands of the state department of land and natural resources. The statute allows local authorities to issue special permits for certain "unusual and reasonable" uses in rural and agricultural districts. Special permits for areas greater than 15 acres are subject to state approval.

Regional Programs

A unique bistate regional land use agency was created by California and Nevada in 1968 for the Lake Tahoe region. The Tahoe Regional Planning Compact,[90] which was ratified by Congress in 1969 so as not to violate the constitutional ban on interstate agreements,[91] created a 14-member planning agency, representing the two states equally.[92] The agency has the power to adopt a regional plan and to regulate a wide range of development issues, including zoning, subdivisions, floodplain and watershed protection, and shoreline development.[93] Development projects in the region are subject to local permitting requirements, but a local permit may be reversed by the agency.[94]

In 1971, New York State enacted the Adirondack Park Agency Act[95] to protect the resources of the 6-million-acre Adirondack Park, a unique combination of public and private lands which is expressly protected in the New York constitution.[96] Under the act, a state-appointed agency creates a comprehensive development plan to guide planning and development on the privately held lands that make up 60 percent of the Adirondacks. The plan classifies land into six different categories, each with its own allowable uses and standards for development. The agency can approve a local regulatory program if it is supportive of the policies of the regional development plan. Upon approval, the local government regains the power to approve smaller ("class B") development projects. The agency directly reviews and approves all major ("class A") development projects, and it can reverse any local variance granted for a class B project.

Other examples of regional land classification, all in areas with highly sensitive environmental resources, include the unorganized townships of northern Maine[97] and the New Jersey Pinelands.[98]

State and Regional Regulation of Major Development Projects

To deal with the spillover effects of major development projects, a state may require approval by a regional or state agency for all development projects beyond a certain threshold. Such approvals are required in Vermont, Maine, Florida, Georgia, the Adirondacks region of New York (see above), and the Cape Cod and Martha's Vineyard regions of Massachusetts. On procedural grounds, one may distinguish between those statutes that require a state or regional permit that is separate from local permits, like Vermont's Act 250, and those statutes, like Florida's Developments of Regional Impact (DRI) program, in which a state or regional agency may review and challenge local permit decisions.

Environmental Impact Review Programs

The National Environmental Policy Act of 1969 (NEPA),[99] and the many state laws modeled on NEPA,[100] require review of the environmental impacts of major public (and in some cases private) development projects, prior to government permitting, funding, land transfers, or other agency actions. Although such review is advisory,[101] as opposed to a formal permit, the complexity and length of the NEPA process can impose a heavy burden on a project, whether it is a publicly funded development supported by a constituency eager for action or a privately funded project in which the developer must continue to pay interest charges and other costs of delay. Thus, state regulators and citizens opposed to projects can use the impact review process as an effective check on major projects, even without express approval power.[102]

The state-level environmental impact review program in Massachusetts, conducted under the Massachusetts Environmental Policy Act (MEPA),[103] shows how such programs can be used to advance smart growth development policies. MEPA review differs from federal review under NEPA, as well as from analogous programs in other states, in two critical respects. First, unlike other programs, the decision as to whether the review of a project's environmental impacts has been adequate is made by the Secretary of Environmental Affairs, and not by the lead agency (such as a transportation agency or local government). Second, mitigation measures agreed to during MEPA review are enforceable, through the adoption of legally binding Section 61 Findings. Other strengths of the program include "bright line" regulatory standards that determine whether or not a project exceeds review thresholds, short review timelines with "deemed approved" standards, and inclusive requirements for public notice and participation in the review process.

The 1998 revisions to the MEPA Regulations modified the project-review thresholds to implicitly favor smart growth policies. Reviews are now required solely on the basis of project impacts, such as wetlands alteration, traffic and sewage generation, and creation of impervious surfaces, and not on the basis of project size or cost. This has had the effect of easing the relative burden of review on urban and redevelopment projects, while heightening the scrutiny of projects located in suburban and rural "greenfield" sites. MEPA review is a particularly powerful tool for shaping state agency investments in infrastructure—roads, transit, water supplies, sewers, and public buildings—because they are subject to broad-scope jurisdiction, extending to all potential environmental impacts.[104] In addition, the MEPA Regulations require that EIRs discuss projects in the context of relevant local and regional planning.[105]

Regional Permit Decisions (Vermont's Act 250)

Vermont's State Land Use and Development Act of 1970 ("Act 250")[106] created a two-track system, under which a developer must obtain a project permit from one of the nine regional Environmental District Commissions (EDCs), separate from any local permits. The threshold of review is very low, affecting all public and private construction projects "involving" 10 or more acres, and all residential construction projects of 10 or more units (in either case including multiple tracts under common ownership located within a five-mile radius).[107]

Under Act 250, an EDC may deny a regional permit if it finds a proposed project to be "detrimental to the public health, safety or general welfare." The applicant for the permit bears the burden of proof that the project will not cause undue air pollution, water pollution, soil erosion, or strain on water supplies, and that it conforms with local and regional land use plans. Opponents, on the other hand, must show that a project would unreasonably burden roads and other public services or would have "an undue adverse effect" on natural, aesthetic, or historic sites. Once the development receives a regional permit, it must still receive all other necessary state agency and local approvals.

Major project provisions similar to those of the Vermont act are found in Maine[108] and Georgia[109] and in the regional land-use acts regulating the Adirondacks region of New York (see above) and the Martha's Vineyard[110] and Cape Cod[111] regions of Massachusetts.

State and Regional Review of Local Decisions (Florida's DRI Program)

The Florida Environmental Land and Water Management Act of 1972[112] provides for regional regulation of any "development of regional impact" (DRI). The statute defines a DRI as a project with "a substantial effect upon the health, safety, or welfare of citizens of more than one county."[113] The Florida act differs from the statutes described above in two significant respects: (1) by setting a higher threshold of review,[114] the statute affects only the largest projects; and (2) by allowing the state planning agency to step in only to appeal a local project approval, the Florida act avoids duplication of permits and hearings.

When a project is classified as a DRI, the developer files an application with the local government, and the municipality holds a public hearing. The regional planning agency (RPA) issues a report evaluating the regional impact of the proposed development, reviewing the project's effect on the natural resources, economy, public services, and housing availability in the region. The municipality may then approve, approve with conditions, or deny the project, based upon its consistency with the local comprehensive plan and regulations, the State Comprehensive Plan, and the RPA's recommendations. If the state planning agency ("SPA") then disagrees with the local permit decision, it may appeal the decision to the Florida Land and Water Adjudicatory Commission.

Under the comprehensive 1993 amendments to the Act, Florida provided for the gradual phasing out of its DRI review. A project is exempted from DRI review if it is located within a municipality whose land-use plan and regulations have been found consistent with statewide goals.[115] Smaller towns and rural communities, which often lack professional planning staff, retain the option to continue participating in DRI review. Even where a municipality has been certified for exemption from DRI review, however, local approvals are still subject to appeal by the SPA, either upon the grounds that the project is inconsistent with the local, regional, or state land-use plan, or because the adverse impacts to identified state or regional resources would not be adequately mitigated. In such communities, the review thresholds for DRIs are raised in areas identified in the local plan as urban central business districts or regional activity centers.[116]

State and Regional Regulation of Critical Resources

Several state statutes deal with the problem of protecting an environmental resource of regional or statewide importance that overlaps municipal boundaries. The most far-ranging of these is the critical resources provisions of the statewide act in Florida. (The reader is also referred to the discussion of the New York Adirondacks statute above.)

Florida provides for state regulation of environmental resources in Section Five of the Florida Environmental Land and Water Management Act of 1972, which grants the state the power to designate a wide range of resources, both natural (wetlands, forests, mountains, wildlife habitats) and man-made (historic sites, farmlands), as "areas of critical concern."[117] The state planning agency (SPA) must recommend the designation of an area of critical concern to the legislature, which then adopts the designation by statute.[118] An area may be designated when development activities would have a significant impact on natural or historical resources, or on an existing or proposed public facility. Part of the SPA's recommendation includes "specific principles to guide the development of the area." To date, the legislature has designated four areas, including the Big Cypress Swamp (323,000 acres) and the Florida Keys (150-mile-long island chain).

Once an area has been designated, the SPA may approve local land development regulations and the local comprehensive plan if the plan and regulations comply with the development principles for the area. If a local government fails to submit the required information, or if the local plans and regulations do not comply with the development principles, the SPA recommends regulations and a comprehensive plan to the Administration Commission, which can then adopt them as a binding rule. More recently, the state has chosen to exercise oversight through the adoption of informal "management plans," seeking to persuade local governments to take protective steps themselves, rather than intervening and usurping their powers through the designation process.[119]

Similar critical areas provisions appear in a number of other states and regions. In Maryland, for example, the State Economic Growth, Resource Protection and Planning Commission sets regulatory standards for all "sensitive areas," such as streams and floodplains, until a municipality adopts its own planning standards.[120] In

Massachusetts, the regional commissions in the Martha's Vineyard and Cape Cod regions have the power to designate critical areas, to set development standards for those areas, and to issue project approvals.[121]

The Planning Consistency Model: State Oversight of Local Plans and Regulations

The Oregon statute offers an alternative model for state control over land use. Adopted in 1973, it relies on state oversight of local planning and zoning, rather than on direct state or regional regulation of major projects or critical areas.[122] The Oregon program is also prominent for its use of mandatory urban growth boundaries (UGBs). During the 1980s and 1990s, nine additional states have adopted planning consistency statutes modeled to some extent on the Oregon statute: Florida,[123] Georgia,[124] Maine,[125] Maryland,[126] New Jersey,[127] Rhode Island,[128] Tennessee,[129] Vermont,[130] and Washington.[131] This section focuses on the Oregon program, and to a lesser extent on Florida's planning consistency statute, which relies on "concurrency" requirements.

The Oregon State Land Use Act was adopted in 1973, during the same period of environmental reforms that included the creation of the Vermont and Florida statutes discussed above. Oregon, like Vermont and Florida, exhibited several characteristics which influenced environmental reform in the state: a wealth of natural resources, a strong reliance on tourism and outdoor recreation, and rapid population growth and development.[132] In addition, the Oregon statute also received strong support from then-Governor Tom McCall and from both parties in the legislature.[133] In 1975, after his term in office ended, McCall furthered environmental reform by helping to found 1000 Friends of Oregon, a public advocacy group which has been instrumental in shaping the implementation of the statute and in forging a coalition of support from environmental, development, and housing advocates.[134] The Oregon statute has survived four repeal efforts.

Ensuring the Consistency of Local Plans and Regulations with Statewide Goals

The consistency provisions are the heart of this model. Under Euclidean zoning, local planning, where it takes place at all, is seen as a self-contained activity. In contrast, statutes following the Planning Consistency model require that local plans be consistent with statewide (and regional, where applicable) goals. Further, while Euclidean zoning does not require consistency between zoning and local planning, the Planning Consistency model statutes require that zoning and other local regulations be consistent with a local plan, where it exists.

The consistency framework represents an attempt to strike a political compromise that will meet statewide goals without impairing the administrative efficiency of the system. In political terms, consistency requirements avoid directly infringing on attributes of local home rule by allowing municipalities to continue to plan and zone, while still exerting state oversight of these activities. Allowing local authorities to maintain a degree of control adds to the legitimacy of the regulations and is therefore politically attractive. In terms of efficiency, there is also an administrative argument for a continued strong local role. The complexity of land-use issues suggests that effective regulation and enforcement should be grounded in a knowledge of specific local conditions.

There is virtual unanimity among the states about the state-level policy goals of a planning consistency program. One study defines the eight goals common to nearly all statutes as follows: (1) protecting natural resources; (2) improving or maintaining water quality; (3) preserving forests and farmlands; (4) preserving historic resources; (5) preserving or creating open space; (6) encouraging economic development; (7) developing a multimodal transportation system; and (8) preserving or creating affordable housing.[135]

The Oregon act provides for a seven-member Land Conservation and Development Commission ("LCDC") with the power to adopt statewide land-use planning goals.[136] Under the act, each city and county must prepare a comprehensive land-use plan that complies with state planning goals.[137] These municipalities must also implement regulations, including zoning, that comply with both the local plan and the state goals.[138] LCDC has the power to review and "acknowledge" (approve) both plans and regulations[139] or to order a municipality to bring its plan or regulations into compliance with the goals.[140]

To persuade municipalities to plan may require both sticks and carrots. In Oregon, local plans are compulsory;[141] in other states planning is voluntary but highly encouraged, through offers of financial and other incentives. Almost all the states offer financial, and in many cases technical, aid to municipalities in preparing their plans.[142] Oregon also offers legal fees or representation to towns when their plans or regulations are challenged in court.[143] Some states strengthen their commands by threatening a broad cutoff of forms of state aid other than planning funds.[144] Another powerful incentive is the ability to charge developers with exactions that defray the offsite costs of development; some states make a municipality's power to charge exactions contingent on its adoption of a state approved plan.[145]

Defining Consistency for Local Plans and Regulations

The Planning Consistency model requires two levels of consistency: (1) consistency between the local plan and state goals, and (2) consistency of local regulations, including zoning, with the approved local plan and state goals. In each case, consistency involves a two-pronged test. First, the lower-level document must be compatible with the higher level plan—i.e., there should be no outright conflict between the two; and second, the lower-level plan must further the goals of the statute authorizing the development of plans—i.e., where active policy initiatives are called for, they must be carried out.[146]

Ensuring consistency between the local plan and state goals can be problematic. Since a land use plan by its very nature is aspirational and states general principles, the local plan may simply voice the same general aspirations found in the state goals. As a check on local planning, the statutes set procedural standards for municipalities: hearings, comments, and other forms of public participation.[147] Most of the statutes also specify the contents of a plan and the issues that must be addressed through policies and implementation strategies—e.g., land use, transportation, housing, economic development, public facilities, rural or open areas, natural or sensitive areas, implementation, and so on.[148]

A more intrusive form of oversight occurs when the state imposes more substantive requirements on local planning—particularly requirements to employ growth-management strategies or to combat local exclusion. By requiring that a local plan define an urban growth boundary or outline specific steps to increase housing affordability, the SPA, and subsequently the courts, can more easily check the local plan's consistency with state goals, since those goals are in concrete form.[149]

The second requirement, for consistency of local regulations with the approved local plan and the state goals, can be tested more easily. For example, the SPA can examine whether the regulations adequately protect critical resources, such as wetlands or historic districts, that are identified in the plan; or it can check that the amount of land zoned for commercial, industrial, or multifamily use corresponds to the economic projections and the demographic needs. Further, not only regulations, but also specific local actions such as rezonings, variances, subdivision approvals, and building permits, can be tested for consistency with the state and local plans. The more precise the criteria in the plans, the easier it is for the SPA and the courts to assess the validity of local actions.

Procedural Requirements for Local Planning

Procedural standards are often surrogates for the first consistency requirement, between statewide goals and local plans. Procedural standards on local planning also reflect a view of planning as an inclusive, and frequently messy, political process. This attitude manifests itself in two ways: provisions for public participation in the planning process and requirements that local plans be adopted by the municipal legislative body as a local ordinance.

For a plan to retain its credibility, it must be kept current.[150] Thus, almost all of the statutes require that plans be reviewed and amended, if necessary, on a regular basis—at least every 5 to 10 years, varying by states.[151] Most municipalities, however, amend their plans much more frequently than is statutorily required.

Overly frequent local-plan amendments can also raise problems. Municipal legislators can easily undermine sound planning principles by "spot planning" or "spot zoning"—amending the plan or the zoning regulations solely to make a specific project possible.[152] To address this problem, Oregon subjects zoning amendments to greater judicial scrutiny, by terming amendments "quasi-judicial" rather than "quasi-legislative" acts.[153] In addition, Oregon's LCDC has the power to review all post-approval plan changes; the sheer volume of changes, however, threatens to overwhelm such checks.[154] To deal with this problem more directly, some states set limits on how often a municipality may amend its plan or its regulations and also subject the amendments themselves to state review to ensure that any changes comply with statewide policies.[155]

Dispute Resolution

Since the inception of zoning, local land-use regulation has relied upon judicial review of all decisions—a process that is frequently slow, hampered by judges' lack of land-use expertise, and is often highly deferential to local officials. To overcome these problems, Oregon has created a unified process that sends all land use appeals to a specialized state board.[156]

Oregon's Land Use Board of Appeals (LUBA), a three-member panel appointed by the governor, is a cornerstone of its growth management program. LUBA has exclusive jurisdiction to review "limited land use decisions" by municipalities, and "land use decisions" by municipalities or state agencies.[157] "Limited land use decisions" are limited to subdivision approvals and site-plan review of projects located within an urban growth boundary. "Land-use decisions" encompass all other actions, including local project approvals, adoption or amendment of local plans and regulations, and LCDC acknowledgement of local plans and regulations.[158] LUBA's efficiency has allayed fears that state regulation would impede the land development process, while its fairness and expertise have encouraged higher and more consistent standards of local action throughout the state.[159]

Substantive Requirements for Local Plans: Urban Growth Boundaries

Requirements on local planning consistency can increase the efficiency of local regulation by helping to break down the fragmentation that exists in many municipalities between planning, zoning, conservation, and historic preservation agencies. But simply requiring that a municipality create a plan will not necessarily lead to any change in development patterns, because the act of planning by itself is policy neutral. For a state to work a broad change in land development patterns in furtherance of its environmental, economic, and social policies, there must be a change in the very structure of Euclidean zoning. Here, as in other respects, Oregon has been the pioneer, by requiring that all municipalities define an "urban growth boundary" (UGB).

A growth boundary regulation distinguishes between "growth" areas, where densities are higher and development is encouraged, and "slow-growth" or "conservation" areas, where development is discouraged in order to preserve resources. In Oregon, soon after adoption of the statute, the state's LCDC adopted growth controls as one of its 19 statewide goals, which guide state approval or rejection of local plans. Under Goal 14, "Urbanization," each municipality must delineate a UGB in its plan, to "define and separate 'urban' and 'urbanizable' land from 'rural' land."[160] To carry out this goal, each city in Oregon must project its long-range land-use needs over the next 20 years, based on estimates of population size and composition, economic activities, and other factors.[161] The city must then define a UGB encircling a compact area of land large enough to accommodate those needs.[162]

To give meaning to the UGB, a city must pursue very different policies on either side of the boundary. Inside the UGB, the city must actively accommodate housing needs for residents at all income levels, as well as provide for economic development.[163] In 1987, the legislature amended the planning statute with economic development requirements, providing for the availability of adequate amounts of land for commercial and industrial uses.[164] Each city with a population greater than 2,500 must also create a public facility plan, to ensure that adequate transportation and utilities will be available for all development within the UGB.[165]

Outside the UGB, the focus of regulation is to preserve existing natural resources and rural industries, primarily farming and forestry.[166] All lands classified with agricultural soils must be zoned within an exclusive farm-use (EFU) district. Forest lands require similar protection. The effect of this zoning is to bar all nonrural uses on farmlands and forests, with only minor exceptions.[167] Preservation of the economic viability of rural industries ranks above the environmental and aesthetic value of rural lands; thus, the program aims to prevent even "hobby farms" and "forest dwellings" by setting large minimum lot sizes in such areas. Approximately 60 percent of all nonurban private land in Oregon is classified as EFU property, and another 30 percent as forests, leaving only 10 percent as "secondary" (formerly called "marginal") rural lands where some development, such as low-density residential development and hobby farming might be permitted.[168]

Critics of growth management typically charge that such programs will hurt housing and businesses, by limiting the land supply and raising land costs.[169] Broadly speaking, studies of the economic effects of the Oregon program have refuted these charges. Within the UGBs, the Oregon program has been generally successful at increasing the amount of land available for multifamily housing (see discussion below) and for commercial and industrial uses.[170] Moreover, almost all new development in these categories has been located within the UGBs.[171] While studies have not proven that businesses have incurred lower costs as a result, they do show that there has been no significant impact on payroll growth in Oregon companies due to higher land prices or a heavier regulatory burden.[172] Outside the UGBs, the program has been very successful at preserving farmlands and forests, though piecemeal development due to lax enforcement has been a problem in some rural areas. Oregon farms have fared better, in economic terms, than farms in neighboring Washington, and better than national averages.[173]

Another criticism of growth management is that when its use is restricted to local governments, it ignores or even contradicts the regional patterns of development in the modern metropolis. To combat this problem, the Oregon LCDC gave the metropolitan governing body in the Portland area the authority to define the UGB for the entire region, which encompasses three counties and more than 30 municipalities and is home to over half of the state's residents.[174]

Substantive Requirements for Local Plans: Concurrency Requirements

"Concurrency" requirements, which address the link between public investment in infrastructure, particularly roads and highways, and private land development, play a central role in the Florida growth-management program. Under the Florida statute, local plans must first include a capital improvement element, showing how the municipality will "correct existing [or future] deficiencies" in public services;[175] the plan must then define "levels of service" (LOS) for six different categories of public services, including transportation, utilities, and open space. To gain local approval, all major development projects must satisfy the LOS requirements.

In implementing the concurrency provisions, the Florida SPA has looked most strictly at the requirements for water and sewer services.[176] Ensuring that municipalities meet the standards for transportation has proved more difficult, both because transportation LOS are more difficult to measure accurately and because the state has failed to provide the additional funding that local governments need to improve road and transit services. Some observers predicted that the concurrency provisions would lead to development moratoria, but that has not happened, due in part to the recent slowdown in development and in part to the SPA's more flexible attitude toward the transportation LOS standards.

Concurrency requirements raise additional issues. Particularly where transportation is concerned, inflexible application of concurrency requirements may actually exacerbate patterns of development sprawl. New projects migrate toward the urban fringe where there is less traffic on roadways and fewer demands upon public services. In response, the SPA has developed a policy in reviewing local plans that favors compact development patterns and discourages urban sprawl. Urban sprawl has been defined as "the extension of urban-type development into rural, agricultural, or other undeveloped or sparsely developed lands in a haphazard development pattern in which land uses are not functionally related to each other. Common patterns of urban sprawl are the ribbon pattern, leapfrog pattern, and concentric circle pattern." A Florida court has upheld this policy of discouraging urban sprawl as within the SPA's authority under the statute.[177]

Addressing the Problem of Local Exclusion

A number of states have squarely addressed the problem of local exclusion at the state level—either within their smart-growth programs or separately. In general, there are two distinct models that have been used: a state veto of local exclusion, on a project-by-project basis, or incorporation of state needs (particularly for affordable housing) into local planning.

State Overrule of Local Decisions

A Massachusetts statute, the "Anti-Snob Zoning Act," allows review by the state housing appeals committee when a municipality disapproves certain low- or moderate-income housing project applications. These applications are submitted under §21 to the local board of appeals instead of the local zoning boards.[178] There are similar laws in Connecticut and Rhode Island.

More broadly, the Florida DRI statute requires the RPA to address whether a proposed project will have a favorable impact on the economy of the region[179] or whether it will favorably affect "the ability of people to find adequate housing reasonably accessible to their places of employment."[180] Very few projects, however, have been successful at using either of these provisions to overturn local project disapproval. The Washington planning consistency statute provides that local plans and regulations cannot veto "essential public facilities," so long as they have been identified previously by a state agency which has assessed statewide needs.[181] Essential facilities are defined broadly to include all projects "that are typically difficult to site"; examples given in the statute include airports, prisons, waste treatment facilities, and group housing.[182]

Planning for Regional Housing Needs

Independent of its smart growth statute, New Jersey created a separate program for affordable housing, growing out of the landmark *Mt. Laurel* cases.[183] The New Jersey Fair Housing Act of 1985[184] created a statewide council to determine the need for low- and moderate-income housing within each region of the state. Under the Act, each municipality must submit to the council a plan showing how it will provide for its fair share of regional housing needs.[185] Communities must take active steps to meet their fair-share targets, including rezoning, building subsidized projects, requiring developers to set aside a certain number of affordable units, or allowing developers to pay exaction fees into a housing trust fund.[186] Communities can also negotiate with neighboring cities and towns to transfer up to one-half of their obligations.[187]

Oregon has effectively incorporated the *Mt. Laurel* "fair share" principle into its state-level planning consistency program. Goal 10, Housing, declares it a goal of the statewide program "to provide for the housing needs of citizens of the state."[188] Statewide, municipalities must remove barriers to "needed housing," which is broadly defined to include multifamily, manufactured, and government-assisted housing.[189] Within the metropolitan Portland region, the SPA has adopted a rule that all municipalities must meet specified citywide targets: At least half of all housing must be multifamily, and overall residential densities must average between 6 and 10 units per acre.[190] These requirements have greatly increased the amount of land zoned for multifamily housing within UGBS.[191] Average housing prices in Oregon have remained lower than in neighboring states and the country as a whole over the past 15 years, although it appears that the growth-management program may have had little effect on prices either way, because changes in demand influenced the market more than changes in supply.[192]

Linking Land-Use Planning and State Investment in Infrastructure

Decisions to invest private capital in land development are heavily influenced by access to public infrastructure: highways, roads, transit lines, water supplies, and sewer lines. Therefore, state decisions on where infrastructure is located can influence land development patterns as strongly as local zoning does. Yet preemption doctrine almost invariably exempts the projects of state government from local zoning controls.[193] Thus, a state highway agency is free to route a new road through an area designated by the municipality for open space conservation, even if the predictable result of the road project will be to create nearly irresistible pressures for private development at odds with the local plan.

For this reason, several recent state-level smart-growth programs, notably in Maryland, focus upon influencing state infrastructure investments. In Maryland, the state planning law identifies priority funding areas.[194] The areas include the existing urbanized portions of greater Baltimore and Washington, DC, existing cities, and additional priority areas designated by county governments. The county-level designations are limited to commercial areas zoned industrial or principally used for employment, or that are served or planned to be served by sewers. For residential areas, county-level designations are limited to areas served by sewers and developed or zoned at two units per acre and expansion areas beyond current development served by sewers and developed or zoned at 3.5 units per acre. Counties must certify such locally designated areas to the state Department of Planning for review and comment. The state program has led to locating investments in roads, schools, colleges, and state office buildings within existing cities and town centers, where they would not serve as an incentive to sprawl.

Other states employing growth-management statutes have been less successful at integrating state investments into the framework of land development policy. In Oregon, for example, the LCDC has found it much more difficult to control other state agencies than to exercise control over municipalities.[195] Only three states, Maryland, Rhode Island, and Washington, require that specific projects undertaken by state agencies follow approved local plans and regulations.[196]

NEPA and similar state-level environmental impact review laws can play a powerful role in shaping infrastructure investments. In Oregon, the construction of new regional light rail lines serving the eastern and western suburbs of Portland has been paralleled by the creation of clustered new developments, including multifamily housing, retail stores, and offices, around many of the new stations. These land-use policies arose out of a NEPA review, which compared the traffic, air quality, and land-use impacts of transit and highway improvements to serve the same corridor, ultimately finding greater benefits in the transit alternative when it was associated with a smart growth pattern of land use.[197]

NOTES

1. I use the term here in a descriptive, and not a pejorative, sense. "Sprawl" as a term to describe development patterns at the urban fringe was first popularized by William Whyte. See William H. Whyte Jr., "Are Cities Un-American?" in The Editors of Fortune, *The Exploding Metropolis* 23 (1958).

2. U.S. Department of Commerce, *A Standard State Zoning Enabling Act Under Which Municipalities May Adopt Zoning Regulations* (recommended 1926) [hereinafter *SZEA*], reprinted in 5 Arden H. Rathkopf & Daren A. Rathkopf, *Rathkopf's The Law of Zoning and Planning*, app. A, Edward H. Ziegler Jr., ed., 4th ed. & Supp. 1993 [hereinafter Ziegler].

3. *Village of Euclid v. Ambler Realty Co.*, 272 U.S. 365 (1926). For a wide-ranging set of essays on Euclidean zoning, see *Zoning and the American Dream* (Charles M. Haar and Jerold S. Kayden, eds., 1989).

4. Mel Scott, *American City Planning Since 1890* (1969), at 168–69, 192–98, 238.

5. Charles M. Haar and Michael A. Wolf, *Land-Use Planning* (4th ed. 1989), 189.

6. Scott, at 47–109.

7. Frank Williams, *The Law of City Planning and Zoning* (1922), 65–67, 77–79 (discussing French condemnation statutes); Donald Olsen, *The City as a Work of Art* (1986), 35–57 (discussing Baron Haussman and Paris).

8. Williams, at 39–41, 83–87; Seymour Toll, *Zoned America* (1969), 128–40.

9. Williams, at 210–64; Toll, at 128–40.

10. Williams, at 128–48; see also *Cincinnati v. Vester*, 33 F.2d 242. 244–45 (6th Cir. 1929), *aff'd* 281 U.S. 439 (1930) (discussing excess condemnation).

11. *SZEA*, sect. 3.

12. Scott, at 120–27, 250–52.

13. Although there are broad patterns of similarity that characterize Euclidean zoning nationwide, each state has developed its own distinctive legal rules. The general statements here, which reference a standard legal treatise, Daniel Mandelker, *Land Use Law* (5th ed., 2003), must always be confirmed in the laws of the specific state.

14. See generally Mandelker, ch. 5.

15. On cumulative versus exclusive use districts, see Mandelker, § 5.43.

16. *Id.* § 5.71–74.

17. *Id.* § 5.75.

18. *Id.* § 5.77.

19. See *SZEA*, § 7.

20. On the quasi-judicial/quasi-legislative distinction, see generally 3 Ziegler, § 42.03(1); Mandelker, § 6.68.

21. See generally 3 Ziegler, § 43; Mandelker, § 8.02–07.

22. *Penn Central Transportation Co. v. New York City*, 438 U.S. 104 (1978).

23. *Agins v. City of Tiburon*, 447 U.S. 255 (1980).

24. *Lucas v. South Carolina Coastal Council*, 505 U.S. 1003 (1992).

25. *Penn Central*; *Palazzolo v. State of Rhode Island*, 533 U.S. 606 (2001); *Tahoe-Sierra Preservation Council, Inc. v. Tahoe Regional Planning Agency*, 535 U.S. 302 (2002).

26. See generally Robert Fishman, *Bourgeois Utopias: The Rise and Fall of Suburbia* (1987); Kenneth T. Jackson, *Crabgrass Frontier: The Suburbanization of the United States* (1985).

27. Joel Garreau, *Edge City: Life on the New Frontier* (1991). Garreau defines an edge city as containing at least 5 million square feet of commercial space and 600,000 square feet of retail space—that is, several large office parks and a regional shopping mall. *Id.* at 6–7. Garreau mapped over 200 edge cities nationwide, including 15 or more in the Los Angeles, New York, and Washington metropolitan regions. *Id.* at 425–38.

28. See Robert Cervero, "Land-Use Mixing and Suburban Mobility," 42 *Transportation Quarterly* (1988), 429.

29. See generally William H. Whyte, *The Last Landscape* (1968).

30. *SZEA*, § 3.

31. Scott, 242–48 (1969). The full text of the SPEA, including all explanatory notes, can be found in American Law Institute, *A Model Land Development Code*, app. B (Tentative Draft No. 1, 1968).

32. See SPEA, *supra*, §§ 6, 7.

33. Haar, "In Accordance with a Comprehensive Plan," 68 *Harvard Law Review* (1954), 1154.

34. Babcock, *The Zoning Game: Municipal Practices and Policies* (1966), 120–25.

35. Ziegler, § 12.03; Mandelker, § 3.14–15.

36. Euclid, 272 U.S. at 387–88.

37. *Id.* at 390 (holding that state could override local zoning where general public interest far outweighs local interests).

38. See *Board of Appeals of Hanover v. Housing Appeals Comm.*, 294 N.E.2d 393, 409–14 (Mass. 1973) (state may override local zoning to provide for critical housing needs); *Snohomish County v. Anderson*, 868 P.2d (Wash. 1994), 116 (ordinance that mandates local planning, as required under statute, is not subject to home rule right of referendum).

39. See Richard Briffault, "Our Localism: Part I—The Structure of Local Government Law," 90 *Columbia Law Review* (1990), 1.

40. As of 1980, the city of Boston accounted for about 20 percent of its metropolitan area population, and its land area is just 3 percent of the total metropolitan region. In Chicago, the comparable statistics were 42 percent of the population and 6 percent of the land area; in Los Angeles, 40 percent of the population and 11 percent of the land area. Rutherford Platt, *Land Use Control: Geography, Law, and Public Policy* (1991), 145.

41. One count in 1961 identified 1467 separate governmental entities within the New York City region. *Id.* at 162.

42. See Garreau (1991), at 46 (discussing New Jersey metropolitan area); *id.* at 185 (discussing Phoenix).

43. Garrett Hardin, "The Tragedy of the Commons," 162 *Science* (1968), 1243.

44. Babcock, at 3.

45. Michael Dear, "Understanding and Overcoming the NIMBY Syndrome," 58 *Journal of the American Planning Association* (1992), 288.

46. *Id*. Exclusion of high-density housing, largely motivated by racial and class fears, has been a driving force in the acceptance and use of zoning since its inception. See Toll, at 196–97 (1969); Kenneth Baar, "The National Movement to Halt the Spread of Multifamily Housing, 1890–1926," 58 *Journal of the American Planning Association* (1992), 39. Justice Sutherland in his *Euclid* opinion described the apartment house as a "parasite" that destroys the desirability of a residential neighborhood of detached homes. *Euclid*, 272 U.S. at 394.

47. See Michael Kwartler, "Legislating Aesthetics: The Role of Zoning in the Design of Cities," in *Zoning and the American Dream*, 187.

48. See Vincent Scully, *American Architecture and Urbanism* (new rev. ed. 1988).

49. See John Stilgoe, *Borderland: Origins of the American Suburb, 1820–1939* (1988), at 93–120.

50. Lewis Mumford, "The Ideal Form of the Modern City" and "The Regional Framework of Civilization," in *The Lewis Mumford Reader* (Donald L. Miller, ed., 1986), 162–75, 207–16.

51. Ebenezer Howard, *Garden Cities of Tomorrow* (1902).

52. Walter Creese, *The Search for Environment* (1966).

53. See Scott, at 259–60, 335–42; Clarence S. Stein, *Toward New Towns for America* (1957).

54. See, e.g., Jonathan Barnett, "Accidental Cities: The Deadly Grip of Outmoded Zoning," *Architectural Record*, February 1992, at 94, 98–101. On the ecological approach to regional planning, see generally Ian L. McHarg, *Design with Nature* (1969). For an adaptation of the garden city ideal to the multi-nodal reality of the modern metropolitan region, see Kevin Lynch, *A Theory of Good City Form* (1981), 293–317.

55. Jay Wickersham, "Jane Jacobs's Critique of Zoning: From *Euclid* to Portland and Beyond," 28 *Boston College Environmental Affairs Law Review* (2001), 547 [hereinafter Wickersham, "Jacobs"]; David Hill, "Jane Jacobs's Ideas on Big, Diverse Cities: A Review and Commentary," 54 *Journal of the American Planning Association* (1988), 302.

56. Jane Jacobs, *The Death and Life of Great American Cities* (1961), 150–51.

57. *Id*. at 154–56.

58. *Id*. at 165–74.

59. *Id*. at 29–88, 178–86, 363–68.

60. *Id*. at 187–90, 193–99, 384–88. Jacobs was influenced by Kevin Lynch's investigations into how city-dwellers perceive the physical organization of their communities. See Kevin Lynch, *The Image of the City* (1960).

61. Wickersham, "Jacobs."

62. See generally Michael Leccese and Kathleen McCormick, eds., *Charter of the New Urbanism* (2000); Andres Duany, Elizabeth Plater-Zyberk, and Jeff Speck, *Suburban Nation* (2000); Peter Calthorpe, *The Next American Metropolis* (1993).

63. See Mandelker, § 9.24–30.

64. On New York City's pioneering use of such innovations, see Norman Marcus, "Zoning from 1961 to 1991: Turning Back the Clock," in *Planning and Zoning New York City* (Todd W. Bressi, ed., 1993), 61–102. On special review procedures in urban zoning, see Clifford L. Weaver and Richard F. Babcock, *City Zoning* (1979) at 58–69, 119–31. For a comprehensive example of project-specific standards within a special review district, see Boston, Mass. Zoning Code, art. 38 Mid-Town Cultural District.

65. Weaver and Babcock, at 181–97.

66. R. Marlin Smith, "From Subdivision Improvement Requirements to Community Benefit Assessments and Linkage Payments: A Brief History of Land Development Exactions," 50 *Law and Contemporary Problems* (1987), 5, 7–16.

67. *Id*. at 16–28; Donald L. Connors and Michael E. High, "The Expanding Circle of Exactions: From Dedication to Linkage," 50 *Law and Contemporary Problems* (1987), 69.

68. 483 U.S. 825 (1987).

69. 512 U.S. 374 (1994).

70. Kwartler, "Legislating Aesthetics."

71. See Brian Ohm and Robert Sitkowski, "The Influence of New Urbanism on Local Ordinances: The Twilight of Zoning?" 35 *Urban Lawyer* (2003), 783.

72. *Id.* at 788–93.

73. See generally See also Oregon Transportation and Growth Management Program, *Model Development Code & User's Guide for Small Cities* (1999) [hereinafter *Oregon Small Cities*].

74. 53 PA. CONS. STAT. ANN. § 10701-A; WIS. STAT. ANN. § 66.1027(3). See Brian Ohm and Robert Sitkowski, "Enabling the New Urbanism," 34 *Urban Lawyer* (2002), 935.

75. See Toronto, Ontario, Zoning By-Law No. 4, § 8-85-8(3).

76. Minimum densities are widely used in communities around the country, including Durham, North Carolina; Austin, Texas; Sacramento, California; and Gresham and Portland, Oregon. See also *Oregon Small Cities*.

77. Maximum parking standards have been widely used in Oregon and other zoning. The Boston Transportation Department has set goals for reducing parking for projects located in city neighborhoods adjacent to transit stations, at ratios ranging from 0.75 to 1.25 spaces per residential unit, or per 1000 square feet for commercial projects.

78. See Duany Plater-Zyberk & Co., Transect-based Neighborhood Development Code (July 2000).

79. *Id.*

80. See Wickersham, "The Quiet Revolution Continues: The Emerging New Model for State Growth Management Statutes," 18 *Harvard Environmental Law Review* (1994), 489. Much of the literature, including my own earlier article, uses the term "growth management" instead of "smart growth." Growth management is a term that first found wide usage in the 1980s to describe local land-use regulations that limit or condition growth through such devices as phased or tiered development, growth boundaries, building permit caps, and moratoria. See Douglas R. Porter, *Managing Growth in America's Communities* (1997). Smart growth is a more inclusive term for programs that address regional, state, and federal roles, pay greater heed to environmental concerns, and focus on location and design of infrastructure as well as private development. See generally Robert Freilich, *From Sprawl to Smart Growth* (2000).

81. David R. Godschalk, "In Defense of Growth Management," 58 *Journal of the American Planning Association* (1992), 422.

82. *Golden v. Planning Bd. of Ramapo*, 285 N.E.2d 291, 296 (N.Y. 1972); *Construction Indus. Ass'n v. City of Petaluma*, 522 F.2d 897, 906, 908–09 (9th Cir. 1975), *cert. denied*, 424 U.S. 934 (1976).

83. See Thomas Pelham, "From the Ramapo Plan to Florida's Statewide Concurrency System," 35 *Urban Lawyer* (2003), 113.

84. Chinitz, "Growth Management: Good for the Town, Bad for the Nation?" 56 *Journal of the American Planning Association* (1990), 3.

85. See generally Mandelker, § 12.12.

86. *Id.*, § 12.16.

87. *Id.*, § 7.26–31.

88. For an early exposition of this movement, see F. P. Bosselman and D. L. Callies, *The Quiet Revolution in Land Use Control* (1971). For studies of the first wave of state and regional statutes adopted around 1970, with particular emphasis on the Florida and Vermont statutes, see John M. DeGrove, *Land, Growth and Politics* (1984); and Robert G. Healy and John S. Rosenberg, *Land Use and the States* (2nd ed. 1979). On the second wave of state and regional statutes in the 1980s, see *State and Regional Comprehensive Planning: Implementing New Methods for Growth Management* (Peter A. Buchsbaum and Larry J. Smith, eds., 1993); John M. DeGrove with Deborah A. Miness, *The New Frontier for Land Policy: Planning and Growth Management in the States* (1992); Dennis E. Gale, "Eight State-Sponsored Growth Management Programs: A Comparative Analysis," 58 *Journal of the American Planning Association* (1992),

425; and Wickersham, "The Quiet Revolution Continues." On the third wave of statutes in the 1990s, and an analysis of the political prospects for further reforms, see Patricia Salkin, "Smart Growth at Century's End," 31 *Urban Lawyer* (1999), 601.

89. Haw. Rev. Stat. §§ 205-1 to 205-18; see DeGrove, *Land* 10–48.

90. Cal. Government Code ~ 66801; Nev. Rev. Stat. 277.200.

91. Pub. L. 91–148,83 Stat. 360 (1969) (approval of bistate compact under U.S. Const. art. 1, § 10, cl. 3).

92. Tahoe Regional Planning Compact, art. 3(a)(I), (2).

93. See *California Tahoe Regional Planning Agency v. Jennings*, 594 F.2d 181 (9th Cir.), *cert. denied*, 444 U.S. 864 (1979) (upholding RPA regulation setting height limit, with local variances permitted).

94. See *Younger v. Tahoe Regional Planning Agency*, 516 F.2d 215 (9th Cir.), *cert. denied*, 423 U.S. 868 (1975); *Lakeside Community Hospital v. Tahoe Regional Planning Agency*, 411 F. Supp. 1150 (D. Nev. 1978) (RPA may deny permit application without prejudice, pending completion of air quality plan).

95. N.Y. Exec. L. art. 27, §§ 800–820.

96. See N.Y. Const. art. 14, § 1.

97. Me. Rev. Stat. tit. 12, §§ 683–685-C.

98. N.J. Stat. Ann. § 13:18A-1 49.

99. 42 U.S.C. §§ 4321–4370d.

100. Currently, 15 states have adopted "little NEPAs," and 10 more have adopted statutes with similar provisions governing at least some projects. 1 Ziegler, § 7B.

101. 42 U.S.C. § 4332(2)(C); see *Vermont Yankee Nuclear Power Corp. v. Natural Resources Defense Council, Inc.*, 435 U.S. 519, 558 (1978) (NEPA review is "essentially procedural").

102. Platt, at 305–07.

103. M.G.L. ch. 30, ss. 61–62H; 301 CMR 11.03. See Jay Wickersham, "EIR and Smart Growth," *Urban Land* (May 2003).

104. 301 CMR 11.01(2)(a).

105. 301 CMR 11.07(6)(g)(8).

106. Vt. Stat. Ann. tit. 10, §§ 6001–6108. See Healey and Rosenberg, at 133–35.

107. See *Committee to Save the Bishop's House, Inc. v. Medical Ctr. Hosp., Inc.*, 400 A.2d 1015 (Vt. 1979) (considering scope of affected developments under Act).

108. Me. Rev. Stat. tit. 38, §§ 481–489C.

109. Ga. Code Ann. § 50-8-7.1(b)(3).

110. Mass. Acts 831, as subsequently amended by 1979 Mass. Acts 319.

111. 1990 Mass. Acts 716.

112. Fla. Stat. ch. 380.

113. The DRI provisions survived a major court challenge in *Graham v. Estuary Properties, Inc.*, 399 So. 2d 1374 (Fla.), *cert. denied*, 454 U.S. 1083 (1981) (denying permit for project not a taking, but justified on grounds of pollution prevention and protection of environmentally sensitive areas).

114. DRIs include airports; recreational facilities with more than 10,000 seats; office projects over 300,000 square feet or 30 acres; ports and marinas for over 150 vessels; retail projects over 400,000 square feet or 40 acres; and hotels with over 350 rooms. Fla. Stat. ch. 380.0651(3).

115. Fla. Stat. ch. 380.06(27).

116. *Id.* ch. 380.06(2)(e).

117. *Id.* ch. 380.05.

118. In 1979, the Florida Supreme Court found the prior authorization of the state agency to designate a critical area through an administrative rule to be an unconstitutional delegation of legislative power to the executive. See *Askew v. Cross Key Waterways*, 372 So. 2d 913, 925 (Fla. 1978). The statute was then amended.

119. See DeGrove, *Land*, at 151–53.

120. Md. State Fin. & Proc. Code Ann. § 5–709. For other states, see Del. Code Ann. tit. 29, § 9212; Me. Rev. Stat. tit. 5, §§ 13076.13079; Minn. Stat. §§ 116G.Ol-.15; Nev. Rev. Stat. §§ 321.655, .770.

121. 1977 Mass. Acts 831, §§ 7–11 (Martha's Vineyard); 1990 Mass. Acts ch. 716, §§ 10, 11 (Cape Cod). See *Island Properties, Inc. v. Martha's Vineyard Comm'n*, 361 N.E.2d 385 (Mass. 1977) (critical area regulations are not affected by zoning "freeze" effected by statute authorizing local subdivision approvals).

122. Or. Rev. Stat. § 197. See generally DeGrove, *Land*, at 235–90; Gerrit J. Knapp and Arthur C. Nelson, *The Regulated Landscape: Lessons on State Land Use Planning from Oregon* (1992); Robert L. Liberty, "Oregon's Comprehensive Growth Management Program: An Implementation Review and Lessons for Other States," 22 *Environmental Law Reporter* (1992), 10,367.

123. Fla. Stat. chs. 163.3161–3243. See DeGrove, *Growth Management*, at 7–31; Thomas G. Pelham, "The Florida Experience: Creating a State, Regional, and Local Comprehensive Planning Process," in Buchsbaum and Smith, at 95–124.

124. Ga. Code Ann. §§ 36–70, 50–58.

125. Me. Rev. Stat. Ann. tit. 30-A, H 4311–4344.

126. Md. State Fin. & Proc. Code Ann. §§ 5-701 to 5-7 A-02.

127. N.J. Stat. Ann. H 52:18A-196 to -207. See DeGrove, *Growth Management*, at 33–50; Peter A. Buchsbaum, "The New Jersey Experience," in Buchsbaum and Smith, at 176–90.

128. R.I. Gen. Laws § 45-22.2.

129. Tenn. Pub. Ch. 1101.

130. Vt. Stat. Ann. tit. 24, §§ 4301–4387.

131. Wash. Rev. Code Ann. § 36.70A. See DeGrove, *Growth Management*, at 117–35; Larry J. Smith, "Planning for Growth, Washington Style," in Buchsbaum and Smith, at 138–55.

132. DeGrove, *Land*, at 235–37.

133. See generally DeGrove, *Land*, at 237–48 (voting did not split along partisan lines, but along geographic lines).

134. *Id*. at 278–79; Liberty, at 10,390.

135. Wickersham, "Quiet Revolution."

136. Or. Rev. Stat. §§ 197.030–.065, .225.

137. *Id*. § 197.175. The state supreme court found that municipalities are required by statute to conform local zoning decisions and ordinances with a local plan. See *Baker v. City of Milwaukie*, 533 P.2d 772 (Or. 1975) (citing Or. Rev. Stat. § 227.240(1) (repealed 1975)).

138. Or. Rev. Stat. § 197.175.

139. *Id*. § 197.251.

140. *Id*. § 197.320.

141. *Id*. § 197.175.

142. Wickersham, "Quiet Revolution."

143. Or. Rev. Stat. § 197.265.

144. Wickersham, "Quiet Revolution."

145. *Id*.

146. The only statute to fully define consistency at both stages is Florida's. See Fla. Stat. ch. 163.3177(10)(a) (defining consistency of local plan with state goals); Fla. Stat. ch. 163.3194(3)(a) (defining consistency of local regulations and development orders with local plan). In Oregon the doctrine developed judicially. See *Baker v. City of Milwaukie*, 533 P.2d 772,777–79 (Or. 1975) (requiring conformity between local zoning decisions and ordinances with the local plan).

147. Wickersham, "Quiet Revolution."

148. *Id*.

149. *Id*.

150. Charles M. Haar, "The Master Plan: An Impermanent Constitution," 20 *Law and Contemporary Problems* (1955), 353.

151. Or. Rev. Stat. § 197.633(2) (four to ten years).

152. See 1 Ziegler, § 12.12; 2 Ziegler, ch. 28.

153. See *Fasano v. Board of Comm'rs*, 507 P.2d 23 (Or. 1973). The Fasano principle has been codified in the municipal zoning act, Or. Rev. Stat. § 227.175(4).

154. Wickersham, "Quiet Revolution."

155. *Id.*

156. Or. Rev. Stat. § 197.810.

157. *Id.* § 197.825(1); see *Dunn v. City of Redmond*, 735 P.2d 609 (Or. 1987).

158. Or. Rev. Stat. § 197.015.

159. Wickersham, "Quiet Revolution."

160. Liberty, at 10,375–76.

161. *Id.* at 10,376.

162. *Id.* See also *1000 Friends of Oregon v. Land Conservation and Dev. Comm'n*, 642 P.2d 1158 (Or. 1982) (holding that UGB may not be based solely on the political boundary); *Willamette Univ. v. Land Conservation and Dev. Comm'n*, 608 P.2d 1178 (Or. Ct. App. 1980) (holding that UGB must be based solely on city's determination of future growth needs, and not on irrelevant political boundaries).

163. Goal 9 (Economic Development) is "to provide adequate opportunity . . . for a variety of economic activities."

164. Or. Rev. Stat. § 197.712(2)(c).

165. *Id.* § 197.712(2)(e). This requirement also furthers Goal 11 (Public Facilities and Services), which calls for the "timely, orderly, and efficient arrangement of public facilities and services . . ." and Goal 12 (Transportation), envisioning "a safe, convenient, and economic transportation system."

166. Thus, Goal 14 (Urbanization) complements Goal 3 (Agricultural Lands), "to preserve and maintain agricultural lands," and Goal 4 (Forest Lands), "to conserve forest lands by maintaining the forest land base."

167. Wickersham, "Quiet Revolution."

168. Wickersham, "Quiet Revolution."

169. See Knaap and Nelson, at 70, 171–72.

170. Between 1975 and 1982, the amount of vacant land zoned for industrial use within the 10 largest Oregon urban jurisdictions increased 79 percent. Liberty, at 10,380.

171. Several case studies during the late 1980s showed that between 80 percent and 96 percent of all new commercial industrial developments were located within UGBs. *Id.* at 10,378.

172. See Knaap and Nelson, at 174–78 (study of payroll growth in various Oregon industries).

173. *Id.* at 147.

174. *Id.* at 51; DeGrove, *Land*, at 245–47.

175. Fla. Stat. ch. 163.3177(3). See DeGrove, *Growth Management*, at 16–22; Pelham, at 95, 107–08.

176. See Pelham, at 114–16.

177. *Home Builders and Contractors Ass'n of Brevard v. Dept. of Community Affairs*, 585 So. 2d 965, 968 (Fla. Dist Ct. App. 1991) (holding that SPA may apply policy discouraging urban sprawl in adjudicatory decisions on individual plans).

178. Mass. Gen. L. ch. 40B, §§ 20–23; see generally *Board of Appeals of Hanover v. Housing Appeals Comm.*, 294 N.E.2d 393 (Mass. 1973) (upholding statute against constitutional challenges).

179. Fla. Stat. ch. 380.06(12)(a)(2).

180. *Id.* ch. 380.06(12)(a)(5).

181. Wash. Rev. Code Ann. § 36.70A.200(2).

182. Wash. Rev. Code Ann. § 36.70A.200(l).

183. The *Mt. Laurel* doctrine declares that, under the equal protection clause of the New Jersey constitution, a municipality may not employ zoning and other land use regulations to avoid providing its fair share of regional needs for low- and moderate-income housing. *Southern Burlington County NAACP v. Township of Mt. Laurel* ["Mt. Laurel I"], 336 A.2d 713 (N.J. 1975), *cert. denied*, 423 U.S. 808 (1975); *Southern Burlington County NAACP v. Township of Mt. Laurel* ["Mt. Laurel II"], 456 A.2d 390 (N.J. 1983).

184. N.J. Rev. Stat. §§ 52:27D-301 to -329. For the generally favorable response of the New Jersey Supreme Court to the Act, see *Hills Dev. Co. v. Township of Bernards* ["Mt. Laurel III"], 510 A.2d 621 (N.J. 1986), and *Holmdel Builders Ass'n v. Township of Holmdel* ["Mt. Laurel IV"], 583 A.2d 277 (N.J. 1990).

185. See N.J. Stat. Ann. § 52:27D-309.

186. See *id.* § 52:27D-311.

187. See *id.* § 52:27D-312(a).

188. Liberty, at 10,378.

189. Or. Rev. Stat. § 197.303 ("needed housing" defined); *id.* § 197.312 (limitations on local actions). See Knaap and Nelson, at 78–80.

190. See LCDC, Metropolitan Housing Rule.

191. Within the metropolitan Portland region, the amount of land available for multifamily housing more than tripled between 1977 and 1982, and the total number of buildable units increased from 129,000 to over 301,000. Liberty, at 10,379.

192. See Knaap and Nelson, at 84–87.

193. See, e.g., *Diversified Properties, Inc. v. Town of Hopkington Planning Bd.*, 480 A.2d 194, 195 (N.H. 1984). See generally 3 Ziegler, ch. 31.

194. See Md. Stat. Fin. & Proc. Code ss. 5-7B-l–10 (stringent restrictions on state investment in infrastructure outside of designated urbanized areas).

195. Liberty, at 10,375.

196. Md. State. Fin. & Proc. Code Ann. § 5–7 A-02(a) (allowing some exceptions for "extraordinary circumstances" when no "reasonably feasible alternative exists"); R.I. Gen. Laws § 45-22.2–10; Wash. Rev. Code Ann. § 36.70A.103. In both Florida and Vermont, a local plan is one of the factors to be taken into account in granting a permit to a major public or private development project.

197. 1000 Friends of Oregon, *Making the Connections: A Summary of the LUTRAQ Project* (pamphlet).

4

Planning Framework: A Planning Framework for Managing Sprawl

Ralph Willmer

While not a new description of the current state of land development, sprawl is receiving increasing attention in the planning community. We are hearing about sprawl all the time, and it seems that each month a new volume appears describing one aspect or another of this concept of urban sprawl. The word alone carries negative connotations. We may think of the nearby strip malls, the expanses of asphalt parking lots, or the large subdivision where a farm used to be. We live with congested roads, dense development, and contaminated drinking water sources. While people experience these quality-of-life concerns every day, the issue has never really risen to the level where legislators have taken notice. That, however, is beginning to change. Traffic congestion; loss of open space, forest, and agricultural land; impacts to natural resources; high capital costs to provide infrastructure to accommodate new growth; and a sense of loss of community character are all symptoms of sprawl. As land becomes scarce, development tends to move toward those marginal parcels that are more environmentally sensitive or have other impediments to development.

Growth management is a systematic approach to regulating growth that attempts to steer development to areas where growth is appropriate while protecting those areas where resource protection is an important concern. The goal is to maximize the benefits of growth and protect areas where new development should be minimized. Growth management is practiced primarily at the local level, although it is frequently directed by state legislation. This changes the rules of development since there will be an increase in municipal control.

A growing number of states have either enacted or are considering legislation designed to encourage the preparation of comprehensive land-use plans and the use of growth-management techniques that attempt to accommodate growth in a rational manner. These laws will impact the way in which the development process unfolds in the near future.

SPRAWL AND ITS IMPACTS

Sprawl can generally be defined as the spread of low-density, segregated-use, automobile-dependent development that tends to be located on previously undeveloped land away from urban centers. Statistics demonstrate that the rate of land lost to development is far more substantial than the rate of population increase. Thus, the commercial development along highway corridors, as well as the multitude of one- and two-acre residential lots all contribute to the consumption of previously undeveloped land that contributes to sprawl. Federal housing policies benefited single-family home construction over multifamily, further exacerbating the sprawling development patterns in our cities and towns.

Local land-use regulation contributed as well. Many zoning codes created residential zoning districts and commercial zones with large minimum lot sizes that discouraged compact development. Gradually, developers moved away from the inner core of urban centers and small village centers, spawning the growth of highway-dependent commercial development in the form of small strip malls, large box retailers, and massive shopping centers.

The impacts of sprawl are numerous.

- There are physical and environmental impacts such as traffic congestion and its resultant air pollution, water quality concerns, sewage disposal, loss of wetland resources, and stormwater runoff.
- Community character is altered by the loss of open space, the conversion of agricultural and forest land to other residential and nonresidential uses, and the increased density of development within the municipality.
- Finally, there are fiscal considerations, including the cost of community services provided to new development and the need to provide new and improved infrastructure, at great expense, to accommodate the new growth.

ENVIRONMENTAL PROTECTION

In planning and growth-management strategies, the connection between land use and the environment is a particularly strong one. In fact, the current interest in sprawl has been largely stimulated by an increasingly strong environmental critique of current land-development practices. Local land-use policy and regulations should not be established without first understanding the basic environmental framework and carrying capacity of the land within the jurisdiction. Based as they must be on protecting public health and safety, local regulations need a clear nexus with a legitimate public interest in environmental protection. This framework extends beyond the frequently mentioned issues of water quality and open-space preservation to the very nature of land use itself.

A sound planning process will include an inventory of natural resources and open spaces in order to best determine where it is appropriate to develop, how development should be regulated, how important or especially sensitive resources should be protected, and where development should be concentrated and precluded.

All too often, planners find that the zoning codes that govern land-use patterns are archaic and have not taken into account the impacts of development. Open spaces are frequently dissected into small, privately owned back yards as one single-family home after another is developed on large lots without regard for how this type of development pattern will impact upon the character of the community.

ECONOMIC POLICY

Even the business and home building community has recognized the impacts of sprawl on our economy. A 1996 report, entitled *Beyond Sprawl*, co-sponsored by the Bank of America, cites a variety of costs resulting from sprawl including a decreased tax base and municipal services, liability for abandoned contaminated properties, and increased commuting times for employees. The July 1998 issue of *Builder* magazine was devoted entirely to the issue of sprawl and how builders can respond to the concerns raised.

EMERGING POLITICAL CONSENSUS

The vast array of impacts arising from unchecked sprawl has generated increasing attention over the years. Many of these impacts affect the quality of life and the character of the community, sometimes in very profound ways. However, because the local residents of a municipality so readily notice these types of impacts, the interest in managing sprawl has become more apparent.

This was borne out in the recent elections. Citizens around the nation voted for measures designed to check unmanaged growth such as historic preservation, protection of farmland and open space, and urban growth boundaries. In recent years, voters also approved billions of dollars in funding for conservation, urban revitalization, and smart growth initiatives.[1]

A number of states, in recognition of these issues, have attempted to proactively manage growth through legislation that establishes a new series of planning approaches designed to ameliorate the impacts of growth. The common purpose has generally been to try and manage growth in a manner that does not limit or restrict new growth. Rather, the emphasis is to find a means to direct growth where it is appropriate while taking efforts to protect or preserve land where new development may be inappropriate.

SMART GROWTH

Smart growth is the antithesis to sprawl. The American Planning Association (APA), in its Policy Guide on Smart Growth, defines smart growth as follows:

Smart growth means using comprehensive planning to guide, design, develop, revitalize and build communities for all that:

- have a unique sense of community and place;
- preserve and enhance valuable natural and cultural resources;
- equitably distribute the costs and benefits of development;
- expand the range of transportation, employment, and housing choices in a fiscally responsible manner;

- value long-range, regional considerations of sustainability over short-term incremental geographically isolated actions; and
- promote public health and healthy communities.

Compact, transit accessible, pedestrian-oriented, mixed-use development patterns and land reuse epitomize the application of the principles of smart growth.[2]
Moreover, APA's policy suggests that

> In contrast to prevalent development practices, Smart Growth refocuses a larger share of regional growth within central cities, urbanized areas, inner suburbs, and areas that are already served by infrastructure. Smart Growth reduces the share of growth that occurs on newly urbanizing land, existing farmlands, and in environmentally sensitive areas. In areas with intense growth pressure, development in newly urbanizing areas should be planned and developed according to Smart Growth principles.[3]

CHARACTERISTICS OF SMART GROWTH

In its June 1998 issue of *Urban Land*, the Urban Land Institute summarized the characteristics of smart growth. These characteristics include:

- Development that is economically viable while preserving natural and open space resources.
- Streamlined and predictable permitting, especially for projects that promote economic development and environmental protection.
- Infrastructure is maintained and improvements are implemented to serve new residents and businesses where new development is appropriate.
- Municipalities, nonprofits, the private sector, and the citizenry work together toward mutual goals.
- Redevelopment is focused on infill parcels, brownfields, and the reuse of vacant buildings rather than greenfields, or undeveloped land.
- Compact development is encouraged in existing commercial areas and new town centers, as well as around transportation facilities.
- Safety of and accessibility for pedestrians ensured through planning and design reviews.
- Recognition of the economic vitality of traditional downtowns and urban neighborhoods.[4]

Numerous other organizations have added their voice to the debate regarding Smart Growth. APA, in its Policy Guide on Smart Growth, established a number of detailed core principles that apply to smart growth (see the appendix at the end of this chapter).
The National Association of Home Builders (NAHB) has also established a policy on smart growth:

- Planning for and accommodating anticipated growth in economic activity, population, and housing demand as well as ongoing changes in demographics and lifestyles while protecting the environment.

- Providing for a wide range of housing types to suit the needs, preferences, and income levels of a community's diverse population.
- Adopting a comprehensive land-use planning process at the local level that clearly identifies land uses, such as residential, commercial, recreational, and industrial as well as land to be set aside as meaningful open space.
- Adopting balanced and reliable means to finance and pay for the construction and expansion of roads, schools, water and sewer facilities, and other infrastructure required to serve a prosperous community.
- Using land more efficiently by allowing higher density development and innovative land use policies and encouraging mixed-use and pedestrian-friendly developments with access to open space and mass transit.
- Revitalizing older suburban and inner-city markets and encouraging infill development.
- Ensuring that planning is the exclusive province of local units of government.[5]

Similar in concept to smart growth is new urbanism or neotraditional development—in fact, sometimes the terms are used interchangeably. However, new urbanism and neotraditional development address design issues more directly, particularly in traditional neighborhood developments. There is a greater focus on creating development on a more human scale. New urbanist communities contain a diverse range of housing and jobs and are walkable.

The Congress for the New Urbanism (CNU), in its charter states:

We advocate the restructuring of public policy and development practices to support the following principles: neighborhoods should be diverse in use and population; communities should be designed for the pedestrian and transit as well as the car; cities and towns should be shaped by physically defined and universally accessible public spaces and community institutions; urban places should be framed by architecture and landscape design that celebrate local history, climate, ecology, and building practice.[6]

Upon close examination, these organizations have very similar views of smart growth, with one notable exception—NAHB's policy suggests that planning is solely a local governmental responsibility. While some of the other organizations do not speak directly to this issue, APA clearly believes that planning functions are properly addressed at all levels of government.

The underlying principle of smart growth is the preservation of land and natural resources. On both the local and regional levels, environmental resources, agricultural and forest lands, and open spaces can be protected through more compact building forms, infill and brownfield redevelopment, and some reduction in the requirement for wide streets and excessive parking. More compact development patterns also reduce the dependence on the automobile by shortening or eliminating trips, thereby creating less pollution and energy consumption.

One of the largest financial burdens faced by government at all levels is the capital cost of providing infrastructure to service the needs of new growth. These costs include those for land acquisition and construction. Additionally, there is the expense of operation, maintenance, and repair of that infrastructure. Compact development patterns can reduce this burden by limiting the need for new roads, water and sewer lines, emergency services, and schools. As an example, streets are commonly built too wide for the area they serve. Thus, in areas where density is low, the streets should be narrower because they tend to support less traffic that travels at slower speeds.

The mix of uses created by locating residential structures in close proximity to stores, offices, services, schools, and parks creates a land-use scenario that allows for increased pedestrian and bicycle access. Again, this can result in a reduced amount of automobile use by eliminating or shortening trips. Additional advantages include greater safety due to an increased number of people, greater convenience for residents, and a variety of housing types and levels of affordability.

Compact development requires safe and efficient transportation. In order to accommodate the increased pedestrian and bicycle usage, streets and sidewalks need to be properly designed. Thus, smart development patterns include reasonable walking distances between different land uses, support for mass transit, bicycle lanes and racks for locking bikes, placement of parking away from the front of buildings, limiting the use of curb-cuts, and orientation of the building doorways and windows toward the sidewalks where the street activity takes place. Traffic-calming techniques and street design that slows traffic, disperses congestion, or diverts heavier traffic away from pedestrians will augment safety.

Human-scale design relates to the design and orientation of the buildings in a manner that enhances the experience of pedestrians, bicycle riders, and motorists alike. When mixed-use, compact development patterns are permitted, design guidelines encourage orientation of buildings and porches toward the sidewalks and streets. The buildings should be similarly sized in terms of floor area and height, and landscaping should be required as a buffer and to improve parking areas and streetscapes.

OPPOSING POINTS OF VIEW

Not all planners agree that sprawl is bad or that smart growth is the antidote. Many professionals agree that the current land-use pattern, especially in suburban areas, is exactly what the American people want. Although federal road-building policies may have played a role in shaping suburban growth patterns, we need to recognize that the American culture is very automobile-centric and the American Dream has historically been to purchase your own home and drive your car wherever you need to go. Thus, the market has merely provided what the consumers crave—single-family homes on adequately sized lots (i.e., ½- to 1-acre lots). It is only later that many planners are beginning to understand the ramifications of such growth.

Advocates of affordable housing argue that many of the smart-growth principles (sometimes demonstrated in new communities built to smart growth or new urbanism specifications) will not and cannot achieve the goal of housing affordability. Concerns are frequently raised over neighborhood gentrification and the displacement of low-income residents. Since smart growth and new urbanism advocate housing choice to provide housing for a greater range of incomes, a properly developed plan can overcome this problem. A number of zoning techniques such as mixed-use allowing apartments in commercial districts and inclusionary housing are a couple of examples of how housing affordability can be enhanced.

Other advocates believe that many smart growth initiatives focus on single issues, such as open space preservation, transportation, or village centers. By definition, while they may advance certain goals of a community, they do not represent comprehensive smart solutions to broader problems. However, implementation of smart growth and new urbanist techniques will bring about comprehensive solutions to today's land use planning challenges.

Additional criticism focuses on density and its impacts, especially traffic. It is difficult to convince the public and local officials of the benefits of denser development in certain locations due to the perceptions that impacts are actually worse as a result. Traffic is inevitable in more densely developed areas, but that traffic is confined to a smaller area, travels at a slower rate of speed, and is at an overall reduced level because of the effort to develop alternatives to automobile travel.

Thus it is important to educate citizens and decision makers about the benefits of smart growth, new urbanism, and other planning techniques currently in vogue. Furthermore, it is important to address these planning issues the way it was taught in planning school—comprehensively. By applying smart growth principles to the variety of planning concerns faced by planners, these conflicts can be minimized by understanding the obstacles to smart growth and how to overcome them.

OBSTACLES TO SMART GROWTH

Development patterns today typically follow the "cookie-cutter" grid subdivision and highway strip patterns that have been popular with builders since the mid-1900s. A quick review of local land-use regulations in many municipalities across the country will yield a similar result. This type of development pattern is encouraged or even required under these codes. Development that incorporates the principles of smart growth is either prohibited outright or would require special permits that lengthen the permitting process, thereby creating disincentives for developers.

This is particularly true for larger-scale developments proposed as infill projects, mixed-use, new urbanist traditional neighborhood centers, or planned unit developments (PUDs), which cause neighborhood concerns regardless of whether the proposal adheres to smart-growth design. Many people fear the impacts of such large developments. They also have trepidations over "the unknown"—land-use and design criteria that may encourage denser development in certain areas, regardless of the smart-growth tools that may be employed in the design.

Obstacles to smart development can be found in old or the lack of master or comprehensive plans. This problem is often complicated by local regulations that are archaic. Examples include zoning ordinances, subdivision regulations, environmental and health regulations, building codes, and transportation regulations. Many municipalities have standards that do not account for or contemplate current land uses and patterns. For example, numerous codes do not allow mixed uses or multifamily housing, or have parking requirements that are based upon decades-old needs. This may be further exacerbated by state planning and zoning statutes that may prohibit, or may not specifically authorize, the use of modern land-use tools and techniques that implement smart-growth principles.

There are numerous design features to smart growth, new urbanism, and neotraditional development that frequently encounter impediments to implementation. This is due in part to a misunderstanding of the goals to be achieved through state-of-the-art planning techniques and the need for the public to see how these techniques would actually be employed in a development project. Examples of these features can include:

- reducing street width,[7]
- traffic-calming techniques,
- pedestrian and bicycle enhancements,
- allowing streets to connect to adjoining neighborhoods (in contrast to cul-de-sacs),
- use of on-street parking to meet minimum parking requirements,
- shared parking,
- planting of street trees and other landscaping improvements,
- use of alternative paving materials,
- zero lot-line development and reduced setbacks,
- mixed-uses, particularly apartments over stores or offices,
- smaller minimum lot sizes, and
- architectural and design standards to create or maintain existing community character.

BREAKING THE BARRIERS TO EFFICIENT USE OF LAND RESOURCES

Sprawl conditions are accelerated by development on vacant land or greenfields. Frequently, such parcels are valued open spaces, land managed as forest, or agricultural land that is often still under cultivation. Not only does this result in a loss of community character, but also it deprives the city or town the opportunity to permanently protect land that has environmental resource value.

The alternative is encouragement of more infill development and the redevelopment of remediated brownfield sites. The challenge to use of infill properties is that they may have constraints placed upon them due to the site's inability to meet existing zoning requirements, such as inadequate size or setbacks. Thus, unnecessary impediments are placed on infill development since many zoning codes are rigid with respect to these dimensional standards.

The smart-growth alternative is to relax the dimensional requirements by either reducing or even eliminating them under certain conditions. This allows buildings to be built close to one another by reducing side-yard requirements and to align directly with the sidewalk without having a front yard setback. On larger lots, overall project density can be maintained by clustering buildings closer together to create a more homogeneous neighborhood or village center, while creating the flexibility in site design to preserve open space and the natural features of the parcel. Allowing increases in building height can minimize horizontal growth patterns that consume more land. These techniques also help to minimize the amount of impervious land created, and subsequent runoff is reduced.

Typical street design standards also tend to encourage greater consumption of land because they often require street widths that exceed what is necessary to handle the volume of traffic. This is especially true for residential streets. Even if the land preserved by using narrower streets (which coincidentally can serve to slow traffic) is used for median strips, open-space buffers, or sidewalks, a more pleasant local character can be achieved.

Similarly, many municipal land-use codes require more parking than is necessary, thereby increasing the amount of land to be rendered impervious. There are many opportunities to account for on-street parking and encourage shared parking, particularly between uses that have peak usage periods at different times of day. Most parking regulations contain requirements for a minimum number of parking spaces for various uses. Setting standards for a maximum number of spaces as well will avoid the problem of vast underutilized parking areas and the related aesthetic and environmental problems. Moreover, parking design standards do not always require landscaping.

The major environmental consequence of wide streets, driveways, and excessive parking is the increased generation of stormwater that requires management. Pavement reduction or alternative surfaces (particularly for driveways) will minimize the volumes of stormwater to be collected and treated and therefore make more efficient use of infrastructure related fiscal resources.

BREAKING THE BARRIERS TO PROVIDE TRANSPORTATION OPTIONS

A twenty-first-century planning framework must include comprehensive transportation policies that reduce our use and dependence on the automobile as a primary mode of transportation by focusing on how transportation policy is integrated into land-use policy and how pedestrian-friendly communities can be enhanced. Sprawling land-use development patterns have historically been aided and abetted by federal, state, and local policies, albeit unwittingly. There are numerous reasons for this, but first and foremost, we can blame our never-ending reliance on the automobile. Access to highways made automobile travel desirable. Federal transportation policies and budgetary decisions strongly favored highways over transit. Single-family-home and commercial-strip development yields more dependence on the automobile, leading to more inefficiencies in transportation and the use of municipal fiscal resources.

One of the major tenets of smart growth is to provide a greater diversity of transportation options, particularly by improving pedestrian and bicycle accessibility. The goal is to reduce dependency on the automobile for short trips at a minimum. As previously described, the key to success in reducing automobile trips is to allow for a more compact development pattern that minimizes the distances people have to walk to reach their destinations.

Transit-oriented development (TOD), or a concentration of development around a transit stop, or node, can accomplish a great deal in reducing car trips. Compact development, particularly offices and other business uses near transit nodes, can encourage people to use mass transit as an alternative to the car. Belzer and Autler (2002) describe TOD as follows:

> More intensive mixed-use development alone can allow an increase in walking and bicycling within the neighborhood; when a transit connection is added to the mix then auto-free travel to other parts of the metropolitan area become

more feasible. Less automobile use means less consumption of fossil fuels, less air pollution, and lower spending on transportation. When the characteristics of a particular place are recognized as supportive of lower personal transportation costs, the monetary benefits can be captured by both individuals (in the form of greater mortgage borrowing power) and the community (in the form of lower development costs stemming from reduced need to build expensive parking). In short, transit-oriented development can be a central part of a development paradigm that is more environmentally sustainable and more socially just, and that contributes to both economic development and quality of life.

TOD has also encountered some difficulty in public acceptance for many of the same reasons described earlier. Despite the benefits to be derived from the intensification of development around transit stops, resistance to the increased density still must be overcome.

Design issues at the street level also need to be addressed as part of the smart growth and new urbanism strategy. For example, streets that are wider than necessary only serve to accommodate the use of the automobile while discouraging the construction of wider sidewalks or the establishment of bicycle lanes. Narrower streets, traffic-calming techniques, and parking will slow down traffic. Furthermore, streets that do not connect, such as long dead ends and cul-de-sacs, create additional barriers to pedestrian travel and can aggravate sprawl conditions.

Even a simple requirement that sidewalks be built represents a pedestrian access improvement in many municipal regulations. However, they will increase the amount of impervious surfaces created in new development projects, so it is important to be able to strike the balance between creating a pedestrian-friendly setting while minimizing potential environmental degradation. A balance can be obtained through stormwater management and mitigation, as well as the use of more permeable materials and environmentally friendly designs where appropriate.

THE NEED TO ENSURE PROPER IMPLEMENTATION

Implementation is the key to the success of any smart-growth program. Without the proper regulatory tools and a somewhat flexible development review process, smart growth would be unattainable. The flexibility in the program provides a means for applying design standards that address the specific conditions of the project site. Rigid standards inhibit the creativity necessary to promote these smart growth principles.

Local land-use codes inherently contain obstacles to successful implementation of smart-growth strategies. A variety of procedural details can hinder the regulatory flexibility that can be important in realizing the planning goals of smart development. The solution is to revise these codes to create more of a level playing field between conventional development proposals and those in which more creative development scenarios are proposed.

Examples of procedural provisions that inhibit implementation of smart growth include a burdensome permitting process that is unnecessarily time-consuming or imposes excessive conditions. When faced with more conventional proposals that do not have additional layers of regulatory review, developers naturally gravitate to those permit reviews that are quicker, more predictable, and therefore cheaper.

The lack of regulatory flexibility is further confounded by design review processes that are too discretionary or have vague standards. Most review boards do not have the planning expertise to adequately apply sophisticated standards to complex development projects. One approach that has been utilized in some jurisdictions is to establish two sets of review standards—one that is specific and prescriptive and another that provides some degree of flexibility to let the review board employ some discretion in the decision-making process. The developer would have the choice as to which approach should be taken.

Another key component to the implementation of smart growth is education. While planners may understand the benefits, it is important for local officials and the public to understand them as well. With greater understanding of smart-growth tools and techniques, public acceptance will increase, as will implementation of these measures. All stakeholder groups must be involved in the process of creating new ordinances and regulations, as well as the project review process.

SUSTAINABLE DEVELOPMENT

Perhaps one of the hardest terms in planning to define is sustainable development. It seems to be somewhat "in the eye of the beholder," although some basic environmental characteristics can be found consistently in the literature. In fact, Krizek and Power include an appendix in their report that contains almost two dozen different definitions and nine sets of principles to further clarify sustainable development.[8]

One of the more commonly cited international policy statements on the issue of sustainability is the report of the Bruntland Commission (formally known as the United Nations World Commission on Environment and Development) in 1987. The Commission defines sustainable development this way: "Development that meets the needs of the present without compromising the ability of future generations to meet their own needs."[9]

Furthermore, the Commission outlined the key principles of sustainability:

- Needs of the future must not be sacrificed to the demands of the present.
- Humanity's economic future is linked to the integrity of natural systems.
- The present world system is not sustainable because it is not meeting the needs of many, especially the poor.
- Protecting the environment is impossible unless we improve the economic prospects of the earth's poorest peoples.
- We must act to preserve as many options as possible for future generations since they have the right to determine their own needs for themselves.[10]

The concept behind sustainable development is the need to strike a balance between social equity, economic prosperity, and environmental integrity. Among the key characteristics of sustainability are:

- inter- and intra-generational equity;
- protecting and living within the natural carrying capacity of the natural environment;
- minimization of natural resource use; and
- satisfaction of basic human needs.[11]

As described by Porter, sustainable development can be practiced at several different levels—community, project, and individual building.[12] At the community level, it involves judiciously using the land so as to minimize adverse impacts on natural resources when developing open spaces and ensuring that these resources are protected and restored during the development process. As alternatives to building on greenfields, sustainable development principles encourage the use of existing structures and systems and creating the economic incentives necessary to implement that goal.

Another recommendation is to "expand the range of and increase access to economic and social opportunities by recognizing the increasing diversity of needs, stimulating interaction within the community, and connecting to existing communities and neighborhoods."[13]

Finally, on the community level, transportation options and access need to be expanded in concert with new development and other infrastructure needs. However, investment in new public facilities should be concentrated on those that promote compact development.

At the project level, one must work within the natural setting of the project site to ensure that the system is preserved and enhanced. For example, native vegetation should be maintained, systems should be in place to mange stormwater runoff, and the existing topography should be respected. Existing infrastructure should be used and the use of impermeable materials ought to be avoided where possible. Mixed-use projects are to be encouraged in order to create a special sense of place that establishes a sound economic and social environment for both housing and commercial enterprises. Even the conception and design of projects can contribute to sustainable development by incorporating many of the concepts addressed above prior to construction.

At the individual building level, building footprints can be minimized while preserving the natural features of the site. Conservative use of resources in building construction and operation, as well as waste reduction, will help to address sustainable development objectives. Developers could employ local labor and use locally purchased materials.

As an example of sustainable development at the individual building level, the concept of green buildings has become a recent trend in land-use development. Buildings waste an enormous amount of energy through inefficient design and improper siting. By applying the concepts of green development, substantial savings in energy consumption can be achieved. Green buildings tend to take advantage of locations near transit nodes and bicycle paths to reduce automobile traffic, are designed with energy efficiency as a goal (building orientation, energy-efficient appliances, heating, lighting and cooling, etc.), are made with recycled and environmentally friendly building materials, and conserve water resources.

From a local planning perspective, the goals of sustainable development can be achieved through a variety of local zoning and regulatory programs. Many of these provisions are similar to those included in the smart-growth tool box. The planning goals can include, but not be limited to, increasing density where appropriate and seeking ways of minimizing automobile traffic; encouraging alternative transportation modes; increasing housing choice, affordability, and availability; planning energy efficiency; redeveloping brownfields and infill properties rather than greenfields; preserving valued open spaces and creating networks that connect them; protecting drinking water supplies; striking a balance between job and housing location to minimize commuting time and distance; and generally understanding the carrying capacity of the land.

Additional nontraditional planning issues also arise such as wildlife habitat conservation, proper solid waste reduction and disposal practices, and energy conservation and the use of alternative energy sources.

GROWTH MANAGEMENT WILL ALTER THE DEVELOPMENT LANDSCAPE

The planning concepts described above arise as a result of the attention paid to sprawl and its environmental and quality of life impacts. Developers, in turn, must be cognizant as to how this changes the way in which future land use decisions are to be made.

One immediate outcome is that municipalities and counties will be embarking on the planning process, whether mandatory or not, in order to create baseline information about existing development trends and future build-out. This is important if the county, city, or town is to make important decisions in the future regarding, for example, infrastructure needs, open-space preservation, and water supply protection.

Developers must recognize that these planning efforts and the concerns about sprawl as they proceed with development plans. For example, development designs should incorporate best-management practices and other techniques that protect resources, provide for documented housing needs, minimize impacts to infrastructure, respect community character, and encourage transportation modes other than the automobile. Infill and redevelopment projects that preserve open space can provide the dual benefit of saving greenfields from development while using undeveloped or underutilized land.

Increasingly, development projects are going to be directed to areas where an adequate infrastructure already exists or where the municipality has planned and budgeted future expansion, such as within urban growth boundaries. Communities are also more sensitive to the issue of the cost of providing services to accommodate existing and new growth. For instance, many recent studies indicate that residential development does not pay for itself, primarily due to the high cost of public education. Many school districts closed, demolished, or reused underutilized school buildings during the 1970s and 1980s. In recent years, however, the baby boomers began having children and school enrollment started to increase, resulting in the need to expand existing schools or build new ones. The fiscal cost of sprawl is simply a burden that the public sector can no longer afford to carry.

Therefore, municipalities and counties may look for alternative means for obtaining funding to meet these capital costs. A number of states have enacted legislation allowing for the imposition of impact fees. Simply put, these fees are paid by developers to offset the cost for capital facilities resulting from new development. The standards for adopting a legally defensible impact fee system have been established in the case law from around the country.

Additionally, development will be steered away from land deemed valuable for preservation purposes. Projects proposed for other areas generally may not be allowed or will not have the benefit of infrastructure provided by the public sector. Thus, development outside village centers and urban growth areas may cost the developer substantially more money.

Municipalities may be more interested in supporting existing downtowns and town centers rather than highway commercial land uses that are automobile dependent. As a result, urban redevelopment projects that incorporate certain design concerns, pedestrian friendliness, and reuse of existing, underdeveloped, obsolete structures are likely to be favored over large projects on undeveloped land. Brownfield redevelopment will likely become more commonplace as state legislatures (and maybe the U.S. Congress) lift the financial and legal barriers to reuse of contaminated properties.

Local regulations can provide incentives for smart-growth development, as well as specific requirements that govern how development is to occur. These can include a variety of growth-management tools and techniques that address the location, timing, and standards for development. As planning efforts move forward, local regulations that implement the plans can be expected.

However, land-use controls are not the only answer. Decisions regarding the public expenditure for services and infrastructure improvements, the location of utilities, the management of public land and facilities, and the generation of revenue can affect how growth is managed.

CONCLUSION

Growth management in general and smart growth in particular has shifted the debate over growth and development. Instead of limiting discussion to whether growth should occur, consideration must be given to how and where growth should occur. The answer will differ with each jurisdiction, but a much more careful analysis must be undertaken to understand the ramifications of growth.

In the meantime legislation will evolve that encourages long-range planning incorporating the concepts of growth management and smart growth. Localities will become more cognizant of the physical and fiscal impacts of growth and will look for the means to manage it. Planning becomes more interdisciplinary as a result, and a more comprehensive vision for our future will be generated.

APPENDIX 4.1: APA CORE PRINCIPLES OF SMART GROWTH

A. **Recognition That All Levels of Government, and the Nonprofit and Private Sectors, Play an Important Role in Creating and Implementing Policies That Support Smart Growth.** Every level of government—federal, state, regional, county, and local—should identify policies and practices that are inconsistent with Smart Growth and develop new policies and practices that support Smart Growth. Local governments have long been the principal stewards of land and infrastructure resources through implementation of land-use policies. Smart Growth respects that tradition, yet recognizes the important roles that federal and state governments play as leaders and partners in advancing Smart Growth principles at the local level.

B. **State and Federal Policies and Programs That Support Urban Investment, Compact Development, and Land Conservation.** State and federal policies and programs have contributed to urban sprawl and need to be re-examined and replaced with policies and programs that support Smart Growth, including cost effective, incentive-based investment programs that target growth-related expenditures to locally-designated areas.

C. **Planning Processes and Regulations at Multiple Levels That Promote Diversity, Equity and Smart Growth Principles.** All planning processes, as well as the distribution of resources, must be equitable. A diversity of voices must be included in community planning and implementation.

D. **Increased Citizen Participation in All Aspects of the Planning Process and at Every Level of Government.** Appropriate citizen participation ensures that planning outcomes are equitable and based on collective decision-making. Planning processes must involve comprehensive strategies that engage meaningful citizen participation and find common ground for decision-making.

E. **A Balanced, Multi-Modal Transportation System That Plans for Increased Transportation Choice.** Land use and transportation planning must be integrated to accommodate the automobile and to provide increased transportation choices, such as mass transit, bicycles, and walking. Development must be pedestrian-friendly. All forms of transportation must be reliable, efficient and user-friendly, allowing full access by all segments of the population to housing, employment, education, and human and community services.

F. **A Regional View of Community.** Smart Growth recognizes the interdependence of neighborhoods and municipalities in a metropolitan region and promotes balanced, integrated regional development achieved through regional planning processes.

G. **One Size Doesn't Fit All—A Wide Variety of Approaches to Accomplish Smart Growth.** Customs, politics, laws, natural conditions, and other factors vary from state to state and from region to region. Each region must develop its own approach to problem solving and planning while involving the public, private and non-profit sectors. In some areas, this may require a significant change in perspective and culture, but such changes are necessary and beneficial in obtaining the results that Smart Growth aims to achieve.

H. **Efficient Use of Land and Infrastructure.** High-density development, infill development, redevelopment, and the adaptive re-use of existing buildings result in efficient utilization of land resources and more compact urban areas. Efficient use of public and private infrastructure starts with creating neighborhoods that maximize the use of existing infrastructure. In areas of new growth, roads, sewers, water lines, schools and other infrastructure should be planned as part of comprehensive growth and investment strategies. Regional cooperation is required for large infrastructure investments to avoid inefficiency and redundancy.

I. **Central City Vitality.** Every level of government should identify ways to reinvest in existing urban centers, to re-use former industrial sites, to adapt older buildings for new development, and to bring new development to older, low-income and disadvantaged neighborhoods.

J. Vital Small Towns and Rural Areas. APA recognizes that inefficient land use and low-density development is not confined to urban and suburban areas, but also occurs around villages and small towns. Many once thriving main streets are checkered with abandoned storefronts while a strip of new commercial activity springs up on the edge of town together with housing and public facilities. Programs and policies need to support investment to improve the economic health of small town downtowns and rural community centers. The high cost of providing basic infrastructure and services in rural communities demands efficient use of existing facilities and compact development. Housing choices in rural areas need to take into account changing needs resulting from shifting demographics, the cost of providing services and infrastructure, and the cost of services and infrastructure capacity, and must address upgrading of existing housing as an alternative or complement to new development. Smart Growth is critically important in rural and small town economic development initiatives because the limited availability of public funding means each dollar must accomplish more.

K. A Greater Mix of Uses and Housing Choices in Neighborhoods and Communities Focused Around Human-Scale, Mixed-Use Centers Accessible by Multiple Transportation Modes. Mixed-use developments include quality housing, varied by type and price, integrated with shopping, schools, community facilities and jobs. Human-scale design, compatible with the existing urban context, and quality construction contribute to successful compact, mixed-use development and also promote privacy, safety, visual coherency and compatibility among uses and users.

L. Conservation and Enhancement of Environmental and Cultural Resources. Biodiversity, green infrastructure, and green architecture are integral to Smart Growth. Smart Growth protects the natural processes that sustain life; preserves agricultural land, wildlife habitat, natural landmarks and cultural resources; integrates biodiversity, ecological systems and natural open space (green infrastructure) into the fabric of development; encourages innovative stormwater management; is less consumptive and more protective of natural resources; maintains or improves air quality, and enhances water quality and quantity for future generations. Energy conservation is a major benefit and result of Smart Growth, helping to create more sustainable development and allow people to meet current needs without compromising the needs of future generations. Green architecture incorporates environmental protection and reduced natural resource consumption into the design and construction of buildings, also enhancing the comfort and health of the occupants.

M. Creation or Preservation of a "Sense of Place." A "sense of place" results when design and development protect and incorporate the distinctive character of a community and the particular place in which it is located. Geography, natural features, climate, culture, historical resources, and ecology each contribute to the distinctive character of a region.

Source: American Planning Association Policy Guide on Smart Growth, adopted by the APA Board of Directors, April 2002.

NOTES

1. Moe, 1998.
2. American Planning Association Policy Guide on Smart Growth, adopted by the APA Board of Directors, April 2002.
3. Ibid.
4. Pawlukiewicz, 1998, pp. 46–47.
5. National Association of Home Builders, www.nahb.org.
6. Congress for the New Urbanism, www.cnu.org.
7. A frequent critic of changes in street design is the local fire department, which worries that emergency vehicles would have difficulty maneuvering in a more restricted location.
8. Krizek and Power, 1996.
9. Porter, 2000, p. 5.
10. Ibid.
11. Krizek and Power, 1996, p. 7.
12. Porter, 2000, pp. 22–23.
13. Ibid., p. 22.

BIBLIOGRAPHY

American Planning Association. 1996. "Modernizing State Planning Statutes." *Planning Advisory Service*. Chicago: Author.

American Planning Association. 2002. *Growing Smart Legislative Guidebook*. Chicago: Author.

Anderson, G., and H. Tregoning. 1998. "Smart Growth in Our Future?" In *Urban Land Institute on the Future Smart Growth—Economy, Community, Environment*. Washington, DC: Urban Land Institute.

Bank of America, California Resources Agency, and Greenbelt Alliance. 1996. *Beyond Sprawl: New Patterns of Growth to Fit the New California*. San Francisco: Authors.

Belzer, Dena, and Gerald Aulter. 2002. "Transit Oriented Development: Moving From Rhetoric to Reality." Washington, DC: The Brookings Institution Center on Urban and Metropolitan Policy and The Great American Station Foundation.

Builder Online. 1998. Washington, DC: Hanley-Wood, July.

Commonwealth Research Group and McGregor & Shea. 1995. "Cost of Community Services in Southern New England." Boston: Southern New England Forest Consortium.

Davidson, Michael, and Fay Dolnick. 2004. *A Planners Dictionary*. American Planning Association.

English, M., J. Peretz, and M. Manderschied. 1999. "Smart Growth for Tennessee Towns and Counties: A Process Guide (Draft)." Knoxville: University of Tennessee, Energy, Environment, and Resource Center.

Francis, J., and A. Leaby-Fucheck. 1998. "Smart Growth and Neighborhood Conservation." *Natural Resources & Environment* 13(1).

Kay, Jane Holtz. 1997. *Asphalt Nation—How the Automobile Took Over America and How We Can Take It Back*. New York: Crown Publishers.

Knack, Ruth Eckdish. 2000. "Contrarians." *Planning Magazine* (American Planning Association) 66(12).

Krizek, Kevin, and Joe Power. 1996. *A Planner's Guide to Sustainable Development*. Chicago: American Planning Association.

Liberty, R. 1998. "Planned Growth: The Oregon Model." *Natural Resources & Environment* 13(1).

Moe, R. 1998. "Fed Up with Sprawl." *New York Times*, November 11.

National Neighborhood Coalition. 2001. "Smart Growth for Neighborhoods: Affordable Housing and Regional Vision." Pamphlet.

Pawlukiewicz, M. 1998. "What Is Smart Growth?" *Urban Land* 57(6).

Porter, Douglas. 2000. *The Practice of Sustainable Development*. Washington, DC: Urban Land Institute.

Rocky Mountain Institute. www.rmi.org.

Slone, Daniel K. 2003. "Overcoming Impediments to Implementation of New Urbanism." *New Urbanism: Comprehensive Report & Best Practices Guide, New Urban News*.

Smart Growth Network. 2001. "Affordable Housing and Smart Growth—Making the Connection." Washington, DC: Author.

Ward, M., K. Brown, and D. Lieb. 1998. "National Incentives for Smart Growth Communities." *Natural Resources & Environment* 13(1).

5

Economic Framework: The Economics of Sprawl

Zenia Kotval and John Mullin

This chapter addresses the evolution of economic regions, explains economic theories that attempt to understand the development phenomenon, identifies critical determinants of growth and sprawl, and lists transferable lessons for future economic development and land-use planning. In essence, we attempt to identify and explain critical aspects of regional economic development and how it influences and is in turn influenced by sprawl.

Numerous indicators have developed to determine a region's performance. Microeconomic theory can be applied to regional geography to determine the current state of the region. Because economic data is time specific, a region's performance can be measured and compared at different periods. Total employment, firm composition, agglomeration indices or the more sophisticated "cluster" analysis (Porter, 1980), per capita income, and job stratification are all used to measure how well a region is doing. Because these are standard metrics, they can also be used to measure one region's performance against another. Regions can be compared with national and global economies as well. Recently, Porter's team has provided a Web site (www.data.ics.hbs.edu) that allows this type of analysis to be performed at a regional and state level with insights on how the region's 41 clusters of industries compare.

Part of the premise for seeing the regional nature of economies is that they represent a large enough geography to model the dynamics of a "local" economy. Unlike state and national economic analysis, regional economics allows researchers to look below the big picture summaries of economic performance allowing more focused insight into the critical dimensions of the economic development of metropolitan areas.

ECONOMIC REGIONS EVOLVE OVER TIME

Part of the phenomenon of sprawl is the way in which the regional economy intersects with the use of land. Of particular interest to this research is the relationship between cities and their suburbs in metropolitan areas. Regional economics is a specialized branch of economic theory (Bendavid-Val, 1991). Jane Jacobs's study *The Economy of Cities* emphasizes that cities and their regions are inextricably tied together (Jacobs, 1969). Neal Peirce and Curtis Johnson, both contributors to this volume, have resurrected the term "Citistates" to describe the twentieth-century American metropolis. The success or failure of these large regions is dependent on a number of strategic processes to enhance the relative competitive advantage against all others. Increasingly, this has taken on an international dimension as American regions are constantly compared with cities of the world (Peirce et al., 1993).

Economies of regions are first and foremost a product of history. Take the Tidewater Region of Virginia, for example, where it is clear that the first settlers in the seventeenth century foresaw the value of an agricultural economy and scattered communities. To this day, the legacy of this direction can be noted in county after county with their small villages, open lands, and inevitable county seat. By contrast, southern New England was laid out on a tight mosaic of clearly defined towns clustered along the waters' edge or along long-dated crossroads. Here there was a mixture of agriculture and, right from the start, the creation of small manufacturing enterprises. Indeed, the term "county" in New England is virtually meaningless. In fact, some states have greatly diminished the powers of counties to the point that in Connecticut and parts of Massachusetts they exist only as a historic description. In both cases, the style or type of settlement pattern was critical to the regional economies that evolved. In New England, for example, we can point to two key raw materials that were important in its evolution: forests and iron. The forests provided the basic material for domestic construction and shipbuilding. The cutting of this timber required skill and innovation, which over time was gained by the Puritans and other settlers. These skills were quickly transferred to shipbuilding. At the same time, shipbuilding required iron. This resource could be found throughout southern New England and became a focal point for public-private investment. In fact, the largest and most awe-inspiring example of a public private investment of the seventeenth century was the Hammandsworth Iron Works, located in what is now Stoughton, Massachusetts.

Through the combination of wood, iron, skilled workers, and a public-private partnership rose New England's first industrial cluster, shipbuilding. The demand for sail makers, carpenters, blacksmiths, rope makers, tanners, warehouse operators, and retailers also expanded. It is little wonder that, given the desire of New Englanders to both farm and make things, that they become "jacks of all trades" and "yankee tinkerers." In the eighteenth century, the presence of these resourceful and innovative workers, along with the availability of investment capital, gave rise to the creation of the American System of Manufacturing, which evolved in the Connecticut River Valley with Springfield as its center. Another cluster emerged, toolmaking, which continues even today. The combination of toolmaking, the skills required to make ships, and investment capital formed the basis for the rise of nineteenth-century textile and shoemaking clusters which were powerful economic forces in New England for almost a century. As with modern-day clusters, the owners of the enterprises were committed to constant improvement and innovation. It was these attributes, along with the region's educational resources, that stimulated inventors to develop their "high technology" industrial products in New England.

The point is simply this: One cannot simply create an industrial base or form an economic region instantaneously. They are built upon settlement patterns, work ethic, innovations and investments of previous periods. History counts!

ECONOMIC REGIONS ARE CONNECTED

The notion of connectedness is cultural, psychological, and infrastructural. Annalee Saxenian (1996), in her seminal book comparing the culture of Silicon Valley to Massachusetts's Route 128, identified the informal sharing of ideas as a positive factor in Silicon Valley and one that was missing in New England. This sharing was critical in bringing new products to market, in creating new inventions, and in being constantly innovative. From a New Englander's perspective, the culture has been far more inward looking. It is the laboratory experience that has tended to be far more important. It is the product for innovation's sake that is more apt to be a desired end. Further, while the region has a rich history of creating new clusters, it also has a record of allowing other regions to take its ideas and bringing them to market. Therefore, the fact that New England's economy keeps reinventing itself is not surprising.

In terms of infrastructure, the ability to provide the basic elements needed to make things (i.e., water, electricity, gas) represents a fundamental part of any economic development strategy. Nowhere can this be better noted than with the creation of the Tennessee Valley Authority and its impact upon the Tidewater Region. We can also note the importance of highways. The beltways around Boston (Route 128 and Interstate 495), the interstates that connect Raleigh, Durham, and Chapel Hill (the Research Triangle), and the new automobile corridor that connects the Saturn, Mercedes, and Toyota Plants in Tennessee are all examples of this phenomenon.

In a psychological sense, there is something to be said about being able to identify a region in the public's eye. If we say Detroit, Pittsburgh, or Fort Worth, our minds would typically think of automobiles, steel, or cattle. If we say San Jose, Boston, or Raleigh-Durham, our minds shift to the high-tech firms of Silicon Valley, Route 128, and the Research Triangle. In a wider sense, we identify the Frost Belt with declining manufacturing and the Sun Belt with emerging industries. In all of the above, there is a sense of identity and being part of a region.

ECONOMIC THEORIES AND THE FORMATION OF ECONOMIC REGIONS

Theories supporting different economic growth and development patterns abound. Most can be categorized as either place-based, sector-based, or incentive-based theories. The key place-based theories include Location Theory, Central Place Theory and Neoclassical Growth Theory. Sector-based theories include Economic Base Theory, Staple (Export-based) Theory and Product Cycle Theories. Incentive-based theories include Attraction Theory and theories that build on entrepreneurship. (See the United States Department of Commerce, Economic Development Administration website for a discussion of Economic Theories—www.eda.gov)

The economic theories most applicable to this chapter are place-based theories. Let's begin with *Location Theory*. Simply stated, the theory contends that industry will locate in areas that optimize movement between raw materials, processing, and delivery to the market. It assumes transportation networks are the key to moving goods across the spectrum. Although this theory still holds true for some heavy industrial sectors, in a day of knowledge economies, value-heavy, weight-light products, service-based industrial sectors, and changes in technology and communications, location theory holds less of a prominent position. What does this mean for economic growth? Economic regions (and industrial clusters) are less likely to be dependant on heavy transportation networks and more dependant on telecommunication and knowledge networks. They could thrive in places very distant from the traditional economic core.

Another common place-based theory is *Central Place Theory*. According to this theory, places are hierarchical in nature. Some places are central to industry and become powerful economic regions. These central places depend on smaller, well-connected regions to supply labor and materials in a timely and efficient manner. There is a function for both the central place and the feeders that enable the region to interact as an economic whole. This theory still holds true in the sense that large cities and traditional cores will house the home office locations and the functions that require constant face-to-face interactions. Satellite and processing functions are likely to take place in areas outside the major metropolis where land, labor, and the cost of living is cheaper.

Another place-based theory, the *Neoclassical Growth Theory*, says that economic regions will reach equilibrium if market forces are left alone (little or no government intervention). Capital mobility will move from a region where the cost of doing business is high to ones where it is low or more competitive. Thus economic capital moves to an area that needs an economic boost. Another theory, *Attraction Theory*, takes a different point of view. Attraction theory says that any region, through government intervention, can make itself attractive to industry by providing incentives and subsidies for growth. This theory makes the case for more intervention and the strong need to shape market forces.

There are other economic theories that explain how economic regions function (product cycle theories), what creates sustainable economic development (export-based theories), what industries create regional multiplier effects (economic-base theories), and what dynamics make industries more competitive (cluster theories). However, these don't necessarily attempt to justify the physical movement of economic activity in and between regions.

Having discussed the theoretical rationale for evolving economic regions, lets move to the practical determinants of growth and sprawl.

Determinants of Sprawl

In some basic sense, sprawl is growth outside of traditional metropolitan area. One of the major distinctions between growth in European countries and in the United States is that Europeans are less dependent on automobiles and invest far more on regional, national, and international transportation infrastructure than the United States. New growth or expansion in Europe tends to be polycentric. Growth occurs around smaller existing communities connected by efficient and adequate transportation networks (rail, air, and road) to larger metropolitan areas. Growth in the United States is primarily monocentric, that is, it sprawls out along road networks away from metropolitan areas. These developments lack traditional centers and balanced land uses. They often start out as residential tracts that attract commercial and economic development at a later date. Most planners and environmentalists are frustrated at the seemingly endless, unplanned growth. Growth, however, will continue. Americans love their automobiles, want to live in bigger houses, want to own their own land, and want to dictate their environment. The following section discusses some of the key determinants of growth (and sprawl).

People's Preferences

The ongoing sprawl in the United States can be traced to three fundamental factors: the desire of Americans to be connected in some way with nature, the desire of Americans to own automobiles, and the desire to own a single-family home. The earliest manifestation of this could be found in the expansion of streetcar and commuter line suburbs, whether it was into Westchester County, New York, Philadelphia's Mainline, or Boston's inner suburbs. Later, in the decade after World War II, came America's housing policies that stimulated the inexpensive purchase of single-family homes and the creation of the nation's interstate highway system. The most vivid examples of the results of this set of policies were the post–World War II track housing developments that detail the landscape. Even as planners and environmentalists lament the loss of farmland, the added costs of infrastructure, and the social and economic costs of this development pattern, people are still moving out of the inner cities and into the suburbs. Houses and housing lots are getting bigger, and there seems an insatiable demand for suburban tracks of land. The move back to center city is for a select few people in a select few cities. The average American family still lives the American dream of a single-family home on a quarter-acre lot away from the distressed areas of center city. As long as this preference is dominant, suburban growth (often in the nature of sprawl) is here to stay.

The Role of the Automobile

The economics of sprawl cannot be examined without considering the automobile. Along with the single-family home, the automobile will not go away. We can talk about mass transit, virtual offices, or cyberspace but the fact remains that we are still willing to suffer the Hollywood Freeway, Detroit's Eight Mile, or DC's Beltway for hours at a time. We will build mass-transit systems but, once again, how many of middle-class Americans use them? In many cities, the mass-transit systems work tremendously, with the net result of thousands of automobile trips being replaced. However, in other instances, mass-transit systems are simply the means of movement of the poor. Simply put: We, as planners, must accept that, at least in the near future, the privately owned automobile is the transportation mode of choice. In any meaningful way, there will be no change. Moreover, the numbers of vehicles per household, as we age, as we prosper, and as automobiles decline in relative cost will only increase. What is the meaning of this in terms of the economics of sprawl?

Economic Development Follows People

No sooner did people choose suburbs as their preferred place to live than retailers, realizing that the market for their goods was now distant from their center city locations, also moved to new locations closer to the suburbs and at the junction of new highways. The early work of Victor Gruen (Gruen and Smith, 1960) in his plan for a ring of malls around Fort Worth provided a prototype that is still in vogue today. Concurrent with the move of people and markets to suburbia was the realization by industrialists that their skilled workers had relocated and that there was a dramatic shift in how products were made and delivered.

Prior to the war, there was a tendency to manufacture products in a multistoried plant where employees could walk to work and where the products could be easily shipped by train. After the war, new industrial systems shifted to horizontal operations which required production to occur on one floor. Thus, the multistoried mill buildings became increasingly obsolete. Moreover, the creation of the interstate highway system meant that moving goods by truck became increasingly economical. Finally, government tax and economic policies provided a large financial advantage to industrialists who built new structures. In short, because the skilled workers had moved outward, industrial operations required expansive space, trucking was more efficient than rail, and we began to see the shift of industry following the residential and commercial sectors. The net result of this is the industrial or office park, set in campus-like settings with low densities.

THE LOCATION QUESTION

Scholars from Christaller to Florida to Porter have long identified certain characteristics that describe how and where industry locates. Christaller's Central Place Theory describes the hierarchy of places, Florida (2003) has created a concept called the creative class, and Porter (1998), arguably the most famed analyst, has clearly articulated the rise of clusters. In all three of these perspectives the concept of geography and "place" becomes important in providing a crucible for industry. And perhaps more importantly, this crucible has changed over time. What worked in the nineteenth or first half of the twentieth century most likely will not work today. And the rationale for placing industry today will not be the rationale tomorrow. However, we can identify certain critical factors that are influencing the place of industry across the country.

The most fundamental point is that there are major differences between urban, suburban, and rural locations. Our urban areas are far less inclined than in times past to serve as places of large-scale manufacturing operations or even massive office complexes. The increasing role of automation and the placing of assembly operations offshore have contributed to a steady change for such companies. Our suburban areas have been far more attractive due to the availability of space, the availability of pleasant, parklike industrial settings, and easy automobile access. Our rural areas, because of a lack of infrastructural facilities and inaccessibility, are least apt to be welcoming. However, in each type of community there are still means of limiting sprawl. For example in our urban areas, there are still pockets of manufacturing, built upon our nineteenth-century heritage that are surviving quite well. Indeed, in parts of Chicago, New York, Boston, and Portland, zoning districts designed to protect these areas have been created. These districts were approved even though their conversion to a combination of office, artist lofts, residences, and retail would most likely have resulted in a greater return on municipal investments. These companies, mainly small operations, can add to the character of the urban fabric. They also can help to prevent sprawl. It is clear however, large industrial operations will never return to these areas. In the suburbs, the low density provides an interesting site planning challenge. With appropriate upgrades in infrastructure, there is no reason that the densities cannot be expanded. Much as our malls have gone multistory, so could many of these industrial structures—particularly if they cater to multiuse or multitenants. In urban, suburban, as well as rural areas, there is one new infrastructural element that has become crucial: high-speed Internet connectedness. Fiber-optic connections provide a tremendous advantage to an area. For the first time, many businesses are geographically independent. They can carry on their activities without their clients having any knowledge of their whereabouts. One calls an (800) number for an insurance company—the call is answered in Ireland. One calls an (800) number for Singapore Airlines—the call is answered in India. This trend is only likely to increase over time. We don't know the full ramifications of this yet. We do know that more and more workers are spending an increased amount of time at home and that trips to the office are likely to be fewer. At the same time, it may well mean that companies can actually house more workers in their plants via "hot desks" and shared office cubicles. In the long term this will certainly have an impact on commuting patterns.

There is one more point that should be made concerning the influence of community type on economic development: the notion of security. Michael Porter has said that security in all of its forms, from protecting workers to making salespeople comfortable to the psychology of protection, is absolutely essential to attracting and maintaining good companies. If this sense of security is lacking, then it is unlikely that high quality companies will feel compelled to locate or stay therein. Security counts!

Chasing the Tax Base

For years and years, our Southern states, far more than any other region, have actively recruited firms from other areas. They have done so armed with economic incentives ranging from free land to free workforce training to tax abatements. In a national and an absolute sense, tax-base chasing makes little sense, for it becomes a zero-sum game. At a regional level, communities that succeed in attracting well-run companies that pay a living wage, that are good corporate neighbors, and pay their taxes will have a decided advantage. In short, those communities that have well-planned, well-integrated economic development plans have a higher quality of life than those that do not. The correlation is most pronounced between tax-base enhancement and good schools. As long as school costs are local (or county) in nature, we will continue to see tax-base chasing. Indeed, one of the single greatest determinates of a high quality of life is the accomplishments of local schools: Good local schools attract good families and good companies. And given the increasing cost associated with good schools, a strong industrial/commercial-orientated tax base is a necessity.

The Role of Labor Markets

The role of labor in our economy is changing dramatically and will have profound consequences on where and how we live. There are several factors at work: First, women have increasingly entered the workforce to the point of "full employment" (approximately 80 percent) of all women; the remainder will either be unemployed or drop out by choice to raise children or to serve as "home workers"). While there is still wage irregularity, the gap is slowly but steadily narrowing. Secondly, the American tradition of "job churning" shows no signs of abating. Labor experts have long noted that a high-school graduate today can expect to have between 1 and 12 jobs in his/her lifetime. This, coupled with the fact that 20 percent of Americans move each year, means that our workers will be highly mobile and will follow the jobs. Thirdly, Americans are working at an increasingly younger age and staying in the workforce for longer periods. Concerning the younger group, the increasing number of teenagers now working is changing the character of high-school life. Many large high schools have cut back on their extracurricular activities because of the lack of participants. Concerning the elderly, there are myriad factors, ranging from necessity (poor pensions, high medical costs) to boredom, that have contributed to this factor. Finally, the American worker must be educated. Our future economic base is reliant upon research and development, on knowledge-based industries, and on prototype manufacturing. An uneducated worker will not make a living wage in our future economy. First, in order to "make it" in America, the worker in the near future will require at least an associates degree level of education: It is at this level that well-paying (i.e., living-wage) jobs are found. Moreover, given the increasing sophistication of equipment and the need to be highly computer literate, it is the technical proficiency of the community-college graduate that is in demand. Beyond the educational attainment of the students, community colleges have had a remarkable success record in providing retraining for the unemployed or displaced worker, certificate programs for those in the workforce, and even individualized training in plants themselves. We know of no region where an economic recovery has occurred without the support and participation of a strong community college.

What does all of the above mean in terms of preventing or controlling sprawl? In a basic sense, it means that careful economic development at the regional level is critical: The problems are too big for townships but too personal for the state level. Also in a basic sense, it means that a successful regional economy will have to be diverse, accept change, and be responsive. It is clear as well, that education is crucial to insuring that the region is prepared to accept and embrace the sense of constant economic change that it will inherit. Established metropolitan areas and core cities that embody these characteristics will be in a better position to limit sprawl and sustain and attract development within its boundaries.

ON REGIONAL CYCLES

Many authors, including Markusen (1985), have hypothesized that business cycles for clusters of firms and the economic cycles of regions have similar attributes: There is a spark, they grow, they cluster, they mature, and they decline. Take for example, Eastern Massachusetts: the shedding of the textile industry, the shedding of the shoe industry, and the collapse of shipbuilding. These are three of the key nineteenth-century industries that helped to sustain the region well through World War II. We can also note the quick rise and partial collapse of the region's radio-stereo industry as firms such as General Radio, Scott, and KLH are but a shadow of themselves and, of course, the startling collapse of the region's computer industry as giant firms such as Data General, Digital, and Wang, among others, no longer exist. But, in each case, the region has reinvented itself. Consider that textiles were replaced by electronics, which were replaced by computers, which were replaced by software, biotechnology, and nanotechnology. Eastern Massachusetts has become the largest nanotechnology center in the nation in terms of jobs. We also know that, in the years ahead, we will also begin to shed this wave of industries. Given all of the above, the point is that regions cannot plan for one industry, regions cannot put all their bets in one product line but should seek constant improvement, and regions cannot hold onto the past but instead must stimulate and accept change. Above all, regions cannot be afraid to hurry history along: They must realize that they cannot hold on to a competitive advantage forever, but can use their state of the art infrastructure, their institutions, and the skills of their workforce to serve as a launching pad for the next wave.

The Socioeconomic Consequences

Planners and environmentalists have boldly spoken about the costs of sprawl. There is little doubt that growth outside of the built-up areas sustain infrastructure and utility costs. New roads, new water and sewer systems, and new utilities all carry a significant price tag. Too often this added cost is reflected in the price of homes and building sites. As such, they attract a group of persons who have the ability to pay this premium. The net result is that only the more affluent can afford to live in these communities. Furthermore, the fact that these new communities are not serviced by mass transit or linked infrastructure forces people to be more dependant on multiple cars per family. Again, the social cost of this type of development is that it will only attract people who can afford to own multiple vehicles. Too often, suburbs are facing a job-housing imbalance where large-lot suburban homes are priced too high for the average suburban worker. Workers need to drive longer distances to find affordable housing sites or commute from the cities. This increases both commuting distances and congestion.

Furthermore, when new industries and employment opportunities move into areas that are already built up and that have a localized economy, it brings with it an influx of people. This sudden influx can be disruptive. Lets assume for a moment that the commuters begin slowly but steadily to move into a blue-collar, low- to moderate-wage community. By so doing, they immediately cause property values to rise, place pressure on local companies to raise hourly wages in a highly competitive industrial group, and generally cause a shift in values. All of this can cause a disruption to the firms, businesses, workers, and community itself.

Today, one is also very much aware of the efforts to control growth through such smart-growth regulations as the purchase of development rights, open space acquisition, and growth-cap ordinances. Generally, such measures at the local level protect community character, provide open space, incorporate nature into the community, and enable the community to meet its needs in a steady, planned manner. However, at a regional level where there are growth pressures, the net impact may well be to increase sprawl: It simply causes the growth to move to the next community, further increasing commuting time and spreading out growth. The key point is this: Growth must be accommodated and will result in changes in land use somewhere. When it is blocked in one community it will move to the next community and continue to contribute to sprawl. Consider Cape Cod, Massachusetts, which because of tremendous planning has protected an extensive part of the region's historical character and natural habitat. One result of this is that housing prices have risen so dramatically that young families can no longer afford to live there, working-class families are increasingly nonexistent, and there is little racial diversity. The Cape has become a haven for the over-55 set. Indeed, because their values tend to reflect the needs of the elderly (highly understandable), there has been less and less support for local schools, causing those families that could afford to live on the Cape to consider living elsewhere. The notion of balanced development needs to be addressed.

CONCLUSION

And thus, today, we are a society that continues to push outward and outward, increasingly removing farmland and open space from our communities and changing our community character. We can note the following trends.

Government economic policies will continue to give advantages to companies that build new structures. At times these will be in the form of tax credits for hiring new workers, tax deduction advantages that speed up the depreciation process, grants for infrastructure improvements, or workforce enhancement agreements. These incentives will inevitably aid the suburbs rather than city centers. They will also contribute to a decline in industrial and office uses in core areas.

Incentives designed to stimulate brownfield revitalization are insufficient to attract high-end investors into core areas. We have found that there are several factors for this failure. First, the processes are time consuming and costly. Secondly, the means of getting to these sites is difficult. Thirdly, there is often resistance from residential neighbors to having a new facility in the immediate vicinity. Finally, no matter how clean these sites have become, there is still a sense of stigma about them.

It will be increasingly difficult to place industry in built-up areas. Indeed, in many parts of the East Coast there is already a shortage of prime industrial land. In fact, in all of Rhode Island, there are only two sites presently on the market that meet the standards of a first-class industrial park. Several factors are causing this to happen. In the absence of strict performance standards, industrial operations are frequently noisy, cause vibrations, use excessive lights, and create heavy truck traffic. If any of these "touch" the residential sectors of a community, then one can expect resistance. Above all, there is the fear of environmental damage occurring as a result of industrial processes. Echoes of Bhopal, Love Canal, Three-Mile Island, Erin Brockovich or *Civil Action* often thwart placing of industrial facilities. There is still a fear of industrial plants and, given that investment in homes is arguably the largest one will ever make, people have a right to echo their concerns.

Where industry is placed, it will be at an increasingly lower density than today. The idea of high-density industrial development is clearly a product of past times. Today, we are seeing industrial parks where building footprints are far less than 15 percent of the total land in the parcel in question. While this approach matches the desires of employees to work in quiet, pleasant surroundings that are well separated from surrounding uses, they are taking up a considerable amount of acreage, not to mention increased infrastructure and service costs.

When industry is separated from the town by open space and new infrastructure systems are required, the open space will become more intensely used. In other words, if sewer and waterlines are placed in farm, forest, or orchard lands, then the pressure to rezone these parcels to a higher use can be expected. Most often, it will raise the assessed value of the properties and cause the landowners to realize that selling the land would be more advantageous than continuing to try to farm or grow trees.

Finally, we must come to terms with the fact that growth will continue. How one deals with these development patterns will dictate the landscape. Personal preferences, unintended consequences of government policies, scale and nature of development control (including smart growth initiatives), and investment (or lack of) in infrastructure and utilities will all play a significant role in the way we live, work, and play in the future.

BIBLIOGRAPHY

Bendavid-Val, Avrom. 1991. *Regional and Local Economic Analysis for Practitioners*. 4th ed. New York: Praeger.

Benfield, F. Kaid, Matthew D. Raimi, and Donald D. T. Chen. 1999. *Once There Were Greenfields: How Urban Sprawl is Undermining America's Environment, Economy and Social Fabric*. New York: National Resources Defense Council with the Surface Transportation Policy Project.

DeVillars, John. 2002. Foreword. In Terry Szold and Armando Carbonell, eds., *Smart Growth: Form and Consequence*. Cambridge, MA: Lincoln Institute of Land Policy.

Economic Development Administration, U.S. Department of Commerce. 2003. "Defining Economic Development." Available at http://12.39.209.165/xp/EDAPublic/Research/EcoDev.xml#EDT.

Florida, Richard. 2003. *The Rise of the Creative Class: And How It's Transforming Work, Leisure, Community and Everyday Life*. New York: Basic Books.

Glaeser, Edward, and Matthew Kahn. 2003. *Sprawl and Urban Growth*. Cambridge, MA: Harvard Institute of Economic Research.

Gruen, Victor, and Larry Smith. 1960. *Shopping Town USA: The Planning of Shopping Centers*. New York: Van Nostrand Reinhold.

Jacobs, Jane. 1961. *The Death and Life of Great American Cities*. New York: Random House.

Kotval, Zenia, and John Mullin. 1993. "A Balanced Approach to Industrial Planning: The Greenfield Versus Brownfield Debate." *Economic Development Commentary* 17(2): 18–23.

Markusen, Ann R. 1985. *Profit Cycles, Oligopoly, and Regional Development*. Cambridge, MA: MIT Press.

Peirce, Neal R., Curtis W. Johnson, and John Stuart Hall. 1993. *Citistates: How Urban America Can Prosper in a Competetive World*. Washington, DC: Seven Locks Press.

Porter, Michael. 1998. *Competitive Advantage: Creating and Sustaining Superior Performance*. New York: Free Press.

Porter, Michael E. 1980. *Competitive Strategy: Techniques for Analyzing Industries and Competitors*. New York: Free Press.

Saxenian, Annalee. 1994. *Regional Advantage: Culture and Competition in Silicon Valley and Route 128*. Cambridge, MA: Harvard University Press.

6

Social Framework: Sprawl, Race, and Concentrated Poverty—Changing the "Rules of the Game"

David Rusk

Over the last dozen years, I have crunched several decades of census numbers for all of the 331 metropolitan areas and now the 462 urbanized areas of the United States. I have spoken and consulted in more than 100 metropolitan areas and have analyzed demographic, social, and economic trends down to the neighborhood level in almost 70 such regions.

Both analysis and experience convince me that two factors have largely shaped how our metropolitan areas have developed—sprawl and race. Sprawl and race interact with each other. They are linked most clearly through the concentration of poverty.

Concentrated poverty is urban America's core problem—both socially and geographically. Concentrated poverty creates push-pull factors. Push factors—high crime rates, failing schools, falling property values, and often higher tax rates—push middle-class families out of poverty-impacted neighborhoods in central cities and many older suburbs. Pull factors—safer neighborhoods, better schools, rising home values, often lower tax rates—pull such families to newer suburban areas.

It is not any "superior virtue" of suburban governments that is responsible for suburban pull factors. Pull factors simply reflect the fact that most suburbs are low-poverty areas. Both push and pull factors are largely opposite sides of the same coin—the concentration of poverty.

Concentrated poverty is also a highly racialized phenomenon. Nationally, almost twice as many residents of our metro areas are poor and white as are poor and black or poor and Hispanic. Yet poor whites rarely live in poor neighborhoods (where poverty rates exceed 20 percent). Only one-quarter of poor whites live in poverty-impacted neighborhoods; three-quarters live in working-class or middle-class neighborhoods scattered all over our metropolitan areas. By contrast, half of poor Hispanics and three-quarters of poor blacks live in poor neighborhoods in inner cities and inner suburbs.

What does this mean? For one thing, if you are poor and white, the odds are three out of four that at your neighborhood school your own children's classmates will be primarily middle-class children. If you are poor and black, the odds are three out of four that your own children will be surrounded by other poor school children. The socioeconomic backgrounds of a child's family and of a child's class-mates are the strongest influences shaping school outcomes. Housing policy is school policy. Let's examine sprawl, race, and concentrated poverty in turn.

THIN EDGES, THINNING CORE

Sprawl is like pornography—hard to define but you know it when you see it. Others have made many attempts to define sprawl, but to illustrate a very basic trend for urbanized areas, I have turned to one set of simple statistics—the ratio of the growth of urbanized population compared to growth of urbanized land.

In 1950, 69 million people lived in 157 urbanized areas that covered 12,747 square miles. By 2000, those same 157 urbanized areas contained 153 million residents in 52,090 square miles of developed land—about double the population (121 percent growth) occupying over four times as much land (a 309 percent growth rate). In other words, nationwide, during these 50 years, new development consumed land at 2½ times the rate of population growth. A region like Orlando urbanized land far more rapidly (1,720 percent growth) but absorbed a much greater rate of population growth (1,482 percent). Orlando's land-to-population growth ratio was 1.2 to 1. By contrast, in the Detroit area urbanized population grew 42 percent but urbanized land ex-panded 198 percent—almost five times the population growth (4.7 to 1).

Which region experienced more sprawl—Orlando or Detroit? By my standards, the Detroit area: The imbalance between population growth and land consumption was greater. High land-to-population growth ratios reflect not only low-density de-velopment on the urban fringe but also steady depopulation of the urban core. Dur-ing those five decades, the city of Detroit lost 49 percent of its peak population (from 1,849,568 in 1950 to 951,270 in 2000), yet the city's hollowed-out neighborhoods did not cease being "urbanized." Some population loss was the inevitable (and fairly be-nign) result of smaller household size. But most reflected middle-class flight from the city—pushed out by the social problems rising from growing concentrations of poverty.

Jim Crow by Race—Jim Crow by Income

From 1970 to 2000 residential segregation declined modestly in most metro areas. Using a common dissimilarity index (in which 100 = total apartheid), Table 6.1 mea-sures residential segregation of African Americans in 16 large northern metro areas and 17 large southern metro areas.[1]

Though racial segregation is declining, as Table 6.2 shows, economic segregation generally is increasing. Jim Crow by income is replacing Jim Crow by race.

Why are economic segregation indices so much lower (i.e., with scores in the 30s, 40s, and 50s) than racial segregation indices (i.e., with scores in the 50s, 60s, 70s, and 80s)? In part, the answer lies in the fact that American society has historically segre-gated more by race than by economic class.

Table 6.1. Change in Residential Segregation of African Americans in 33 Large Metro Areas from 1970 to 2000 (Dissimilarity Index: 100 = total racial apartheid)

Category	1970	2000
Northern Metro Areas (16)	84	74
Detroit	88	85
Milwaukee	91	82
Newark	81	80
Southern Metro Areas (17)	80	64
Atlanta	82	66
Charlotte	67	55
Oklahoma City	90	54
Average of 33 Metro Areas	82	69

Table 6.2. Change in Residential Segregation of Poor Persons in 33 Large Metro Areas from 1970 to 2000 (Dissimilarity Index: 100 = total economic apartheid)

Category	1970	2000[2]
Northern Metro Areas (16)	36	41
Detroit	39	45
Milwaukee	39	51
Newark	42	46
Southern Metro Areas (17)	37	36
Atlanta	40	36
Charlotte	38	30
Oklahoma City	36	34
Average of 33 Metro Areas	37	39

But a large factor is, as discussed above, that most poor whites do not live in poor neighborhoods. Table 6.3 summarizes the percentage of poor whites and poor blacks who live in census tracts with greater than 20 percent poverty rates. The percentages are substantially lower in southern metro areas because:

1. a proportion of southern poor blacks live in rural areas, whereas blacks are almost totally absent from northern rural areas and small towns,
2. during the 1970s and 1980s, southern regions, in general, experienced stronger economic growth than northern regions, and
3. the combined effect of faster racial desegregation and falling economic segregation in 7 of 17 southern regions (vs. only one of the 16 northern regions) reduced the growth of poverty-impacted census tracts.

Thus, race is the basis of concentrated poverty. In fact, race is the underlying factor that determines whether or not there are growing disparities between central cities

Table 6.3. Concentration of Poor Persons by Race in Poverty Census
Tracts in 27 Large Metro Areas in 1990[3]

Category	Poor Whites	Poor Blacks
Northern Metro Areas (12)	29%	82%
Detroit	30%	90%
Milwaukee	37%	91%
Newark	16%	64%
Southern Metro Areas (15)	21%	69%
Atlanta	10%	65%
Charlotte	10%	54%
Oklahoma City	34%	66%
Average of 27 Metro Areas	25%	75%

and their surrounding suburbs. In the face of ubiquitous low-density development, a city's ability to expand its municipal territory by annexation or consolidation directly affects its success or failure in maintaining market share. "Elastic" cities (like Charlotte and Oklahoma City) successfully defend their market share of regional growth through annexation. "Inelastic" cities (like Detroit, Milwaukee, and Newark) lose market share, with very adverse social, economic, and fiscal consequences. Inelastic cities cannot expand their boundaries through annexation to capture sprawling new subdivisions, strip shopping centers and regional malls, office complexes, and industrial parks.[4]

It is the issue of race that makes a city's market share so vital. The way different races are sorted into different neighborhoods and jurisdictions by the operation of segregated housing markets is the reason why significant economic and fiscal disparities emerge between inelastic central cities and their surrounding suburbs.

WHITE AMERICA VS. DIVERSE AMERICA

Since first publishing *Cities without Suburbs*, I have examined metro areas I had characterized as "White America" in greater detail. White America is composed of 57 metro areas that have no significant black or Hispanic populations—that is, less than 2 percent black residents and less than 5 percent Hispanic residents.

From the 2000 census Table 6.4 compares the average income of city residents as a percentage of the average income of suburban residents, a key measure of economic disparities, between metro areas with and without minority populations.

The first column breaks these 57 "minority-absent" metro areas into my standard elasticity categories, which are determined by the territorial expansion of their central cities. In "zero-elasticity" metro areas the 15 central cities (e.g., Scranton, Pennsylvania, and Binghamton, New York) did not expand their boundaries at all between 1950 and 1990. The 11 "low-elasticity" cities (e.g., Spokane, Washington, and Duluth, Minnesota) expanded their territory modestly (an average of 62%). Thirteen "medium-elasticity" cities (e.g., Green Bay, Wisconsin, and Cedar Rapids, Iowa) tripled their territory (206%). Twelve "high-elasticity" cities (e.g., Boise, Idaho, and Eugene, Oregon) and six "hyper-elasticity" cities (e.g., Rochester, Minnesota, and

Table 6.4. The Impact of Race on Metropolitan Disparities: Contrasting City-to-Suburb Income Percentages Between White America and Diverse America in 2000

Central City Elasticity Category	White America (57) Metro Areas	Diverse America (117) Metro Areas
Zero-Elastic	89%	68%
Low-Elastic	94%	78%
Medium-Elastic	97%	89%
High-Elastic	100%	97%
Hyper-Elastic	103%	99%

Redding, California) were very aggressive in municipal annexation, expanding 463 percent and 539 percent, respectively.

What is notable is that even very inelastic central cities in White America experienced little disparity between the average income of city residents and the average income of suburban residents. White America's zero- and low-elasticity cities averaged 89 percent and 94 percent of suburban income levels, respectively. Furthermore, in White America the most elastic cities had average incomes that were higher than their surrounding areas (103%).

The second column summarizes the results for 117 large metro areas with racially diverse populations, which I'll call "Diverse America." Though there were substantial variations among individual metro areas, the metro areas in Diverse America averaged 12–18 percent black and 7–18 percent Hispanic populations in different elasticity categories.

Highly segregated housing markets that concentrated most low- and moderate-income minorities in central city neighborhoods characterized the 24 zero-elasticity metro areas in Diverse America. Income levels in 24 zero-elasticity central cities averaged only 68 percent of suburban income levels. By expanding their city limits modestly (21%), Diverse America's 23 low-elasticity cities succeeded in capturing a modest, but positive market share of regional growth. Their city/suburban income percentage narrowed to 78 percent. As Diverse America's cities move progressively up the elasticity scale, increasing their market share, the income gap narrowed with their suburbs. The 24 hyper-elasticity cities expanded their city territories tenfold (944 percent), captured half of all metro population growth, and almost achieved income parity (i.e., 99%).

In every elasticity classification, the minority-absent cities of White America were closer to income parity with their suburbs than the minority-present cities of Diverse America. The gap ranged around 15–20 percentage points for relatively inelastic cities to half a dozen percentage points for more elastic cities. In effect, the ability of highly elastic cities in Diverse America to capture so much of their own suburban growth largely offsets the effects of their housing a moderately disproportionate share of their regions' poor, minority households.

RACE AND SPRAWL

How does a central city's racial composition affect the rate of the region's sprawl? Table 6.5 contrasts 18 urbanized areas in White America[5] with 19 urbanized areas in

Table 6.5. Land-to-Population Growth Ratios for 18 White America[6] vs. 19 Diverse America Urbanized Areas from 1960 to 1990

Urbanized Areas	Population Growth	Land Growth	Land-to-Population Growth Ratio
18 White America	69%	126%	1.8 to 1
19 Diverse America	44%	122%	3.0 to 1

Diverse America (in this case, the 15 most racially segregated metro areas that are virtually identical with the most "inelastic" metro areas).[7] Overall, White America consumed land at a rate only 1.8 times the rate of population growth compared to Diverse America's land consumption rate of 3.0 times the rate of population growth.

The racial composition and consequent concentration of poverty helped drive middle-class residents out of Diverse America's cities into new subdivisions in the ever-expanding urban fringe.

THE "SEGREGATION TAX"

Thus far, my discussion of social equity issues and urban sprawl has focused on poverty. However, the flip side of rapid outward expansion on the urban fringe is the slow abandonment of the urban core, and this exacts its price from black, middle-class homeowners as well—what I have called the "segregation tax."

To illustrate, for the first time the 1990 census provided information on both the value of the average home owned by members of different racial groups and the amount of the average homeowner's income by racial group. In 1990, for example, black homeowners in the six-county Baltimore metro area owned houses with a mean value of $69,600, while black homeowners' mean household income was $41,466.[8] In other words, for every dollar of household income, the average black homeowner received $1.68 worth of house.

White homeowners in Greater Baltimore (as might be expected) had a higher mean household income ($55,429) and a higher mean home value—a much higher-valued house ($133,000). For every dollar of household income, the average white homeowner received $2.40 worth of house.

In effect, for a dollar of income, the average black homeowner was getting only 70 percent (that is, $1.68 vs. $2.40) of the home value that the average white homeowner received. Or, inverting the mathematics, the average black homeowner was receiving 30 percent less home value per dollar of income than was the average white homeowner. Knowing that the Baltimore region was still highly segregated (a black/white dissimilarity index of 71 in 1990), I characterized the 30 percent disparity as a 30 percent "segregation tax."

In comparing what black and white homeowners get for each dollar of household income in America's 100 largest metropolitan areas in 1990, the value of the average African American homeowner's house was 18 percent less than the value of the average white homeowner's house.

That was the price exacted by the fact that the great majority of African American homeowners still lived in majority-black neighborhoods. Over three-fourths of homebuyers were white. With many whites ruling out buying homes in majority-black neighborhoods, competition for houses in black neighborhoods was automatically reduced, depressing home values. In effect, black homeowners were paying an 18 percent "segregation tax" on the value of their homes.

The level of "segregation taxes" on the value of African American homes covered a wide range. In the Riverside–San Bernardino, California, region, one of the more racially integrated metro areas in the United States, no "segregation tax" penalty was exacted. At the other extreme, in the Detroit region, the second most racially segregated metro area in the United States in 1990, the "segregation tax" was 43 percent.

In-depth, neighborhood-by-neighborhood analysis of metro Philadelphia (where the segregation tax was 39 percent) shows that a neighborhood's racial composition and poverty level explained almost 60 percent of the variation in the ratio of home value to homeowner income. A neighborhood's racial composition had roughly twice the impact of a neighborhood's relative poverty level.

In fact, comparing five of metro Philadelphia's wealthiest, majority-black neighborhoods with over 170 similarly wealthy, but majority-white, neighborhoods shows that homeowners in wealthy, majority-black neighborhoods still paid a 25 percent "segregation tax" in the form of reduced home values.

At the other end of the scale, comparing five of metro Philadelphia's lowest income, majority-white neighborhoods with almost 50 similarly low-income, but majority-black, neighborhoods shows that homeowners in poor white neighborhoods received a 58 percent bonus in home values over home values in poor black neighborhoods.

Unlike African Americans, the much lower levels of residential segregation experienced by Asians and Hispanics had no statistically significant impact on relative home values and home value-to-income gaps between whites and other minorities were small.

In short, there are two homeownership markets in America's metropolitan areas—one overwhelmingly white, the other overwhelmingly black. The higher the level of racial segregation, the higher the "segregation tax" that African American homeowners pay on the value of what is typically their biggest family asset—their home. As a result, the "wealth gap" between blacks and whites is greater than the "income gap"—a critical hurdle to moving the next generation of black households up the economic scale.

THE REGIONAL REFORM AGENDA

However we define "sprawl," the central issue really is what gets built where for whose benefit? It is clear that the current "rules of the game" are loaded against the interests of the poor, particularly the minority poor, and against the communities where they are concentrated.

Reversing these trends requires decisive actions to reform the regional "rules of the game." The key reforms are the following:

- To counteract growing fiscal disparities among local governments, institute regional tax base sharing.
- To combat accelerating urban sprawl and core community disinvestment, institute regional growth management.
- To reverse growing concentrated poverty and economic segregation, institute regional fair share low- and moderate-income housing.

Long-standing, successful models of each policy that can be adapted to most regions' circumstances exist.

Tax Base Sharing

Some 188 municipalities, 60 school districts, and 40 other special districts were required to participate in the Twin Cities Fiscal Disparities Plan by the Minnesota legislature in 1971. Under the mandatory tax base sharing system, 40 percent of the increase in business property valuation is pooled and redistributed by an equalization formula among the almost 300 participating governments. By 1998, the regional pool amounted to $410 million—about $165 per resident of the region per year. (By contrast, the Dayton, Ohio, area's ED/GE program, with its voluntarily negotiated tax base sharing program, amounted to about $1 per resident of the region per year.)

Growth Management

"You can't get Portland's growth management results without Oregon's law," I was once told. The Oregon legislature passed the path-breaking Land Conservation and Development Act in 1973. It required all 36 counties to develop comprehensive land-use plans meeting state standards and required Oregon's 240 municipalities to draw urban growth boundaries (UGBs) as part of the county plans. Since 1979, the Portland region's UGB has been in effect. It was devised by Portland Metro, the only directly elected regional government in the United States. The UGB has been very effective in controlling outward sprawl. From 1980–1990, Portland's urbanized population grew 14 percent, but urbanized land expanded only 11 percent; from 1990–2000, urbanized population ballooned 35 percent but urbanized land grew only 22 percent (including the Vancouver, Washington, portion, where a meaningful state growth management law was enacted only in 1991). By 2040, Portland Metro projects a 50 percent population growth (on the Oregon side only) but only 8 percent more urbanized land (within a slightly expanded UGB).

What is the impact of the UGB on social equity issues? Myron Orfield, president of the Metropolitan Area Research Corporation, reports that of the 25 largest metro areas, only in the Portland region have both the central city and its older, blue-collar suburbs gained regional market shares of tax base, jobs, and so on during the past decade. By preventing sprawling development on the urban fringe, Portland's UGB has turned market investment back into the core communities. Despite a rapid run-up in home prices during the mid-1990s' economic boom, fiscal disparities are shrinking, racial segregation is diminishing, and region's already low level of economic segregation may be diminishing as well.

Fair-Share Housing/Inclusionary Zoning (IZ)

The nation's model mixed-income housing program is Montgomery County, Maryland's, Moderately Priced Dwelling Unit (MPDU) ordinance. Adopted by the county council as the nation's earliest inclusionary zoning laws in 1973, the MPDU law requires that at least 12.5 to 15 percent of any new housing development of 35 or more units must be affordable to households in the lowest third of the county's income scale. Furthermore, the Housing Opportunities Commission (HOC), the county's public housing authority, is given right of first purchase for one-third of the "MP-DUs," or, in effect, 5 percent of every new subdivision.

Complying with the changed "rules of the game," since 1975 private, for-profit homebuilders have produced over 11,000 MPDUs integrated (generally seamlessly) into middle-class subdivisions. HOC has purchased over 1,700 MPDUs and rents more than 1,500 scattered in 220 different low-poverty neighborhoods. The result is that Montgomery County is one of the country's most racially and economically integrated communities.

Following Montgomery County's lead, at least 132 cities, towns, and counties have enacted inclusionary zoning (IZ) ordinances. About 13 million people (about 5 percent of the United States's population) now live in communities where local government mandates mixed-income housing.

IZ jurisdictions range in population size from giant Fairfax County, Virginia, (945,717) to the tiny town of Isleton, California, (818). Some 107 counties and municipalities in California (about one-fifth of all local governments in that state) have enacted IZ laws, but there are other clusters of IZ communities in the Washington, DC, and Boston regions (also high-cost housing markets). In September 2003, Highland Park, a Chicago suburb, passed the first IZ law in the Midwest; Madison, Wisconsin, adopted the region's second IZ law in January 2004.

Municipal governments have adopted IZ laws in at least 32 counties. The 32 pioneers averaged only 17 percent of their counties' population at the time they adopted their area's first IZ law. However, additional neighbors have followed suit, and a dozen county governments have enacted IZ laws for unincorporated land, so that IZ requirements now cover an average 54 percent of the 32 counties' populations.

For example, Pleasanton was less than 5 percent of the population in California's Alameda County when it adopted its IZ ordinance in 1978. However, similar laws enacted by San Leandro (1980), Berkeley (1986), Livermore (1986), Emeryville (1990), Dublin (1996), Union City (2001), Fremont (2002), and Alameda County itself (2000) have raised IZ coverage to 55 percent of that East Bay county's population.

Each community tailors its ordinance to its own housing needs and building industry scale. The key issues are minimum project scale ("trigger point"), percentage of inclusionary units required ("set-aside"), maximum income for eligible households, size of density bonus, and length of control period for resale prices or rents.

Inclusionary requirements are triggered by housing developments as low as a minimum of five units and as large as a minimum of 50 units. The most common threshold at which IZ is required is 10 or more units.

Set-aside percentages for affordable housing range from as low as 5 percent to as high as 35 percent. Almost three-quarters of the communities require setting aside between 10 and 15 percent of the total units in eligible developments as affordable housing.

Maximum eligible income ceilings range from 30 percent AMI (area median income) to 120 percent AMI. (The Federal Department of Housing and Urban Development provides annual AMI calculations for all metro areas.) Many communities apportion units among different income levels (for example, one-fourth of the units for less than 50 percent AMI, half of the units for less than 80 percent AMI, and one-fourth of the units for less than 120 percent AMI).

About 40 percent of all jurisdictions target all or a portion of the inclusionary housing for households under 80 percent AMI. Many of these allocate an additional proportion for households from 81–120 percent AMI. (All these communities are in Northern and Southern California and the Boston area, with their sky-high housing costs.)

One-fifth of all jurisdictions target all or a portion of the units for very low income households (50 percent AMI). Reaching even lower on the income scale typically requires funneling public housing subsidies into the program through actions such as having the public housing authority purchase affordable units outright or using housing vouchers in rental properties.

Density bonuses are utilized by 95 percent of all IZ laws as primary cost-offsets for homebuilders, though other methods are also common. In California, 44 percent of IZ laws offer fast-track processing, 42 percent waive certain fees, 42 percent allow reduction of certain standards (like parking requirements), and 38 percent provide cash subsidies.

Resale price and rent control periods generally are quite long in order to maintain a stable, long-term inventory of affordable housing. Only 14 programs have control periods of only 10 or 15 years. Twenty communities require a minimum 20-year control period; 47 require a 30-year control period; 7 require 40 to 45 years; 20 require 50 to 55 years; 5 specify 59 to 60 years; 4 specify 99 years; and 23 require IZ housing to be permanently affordable.

Metropolitan-wide coverage of IZ laws would be optimum, but exists nowhere. The good news is that inclusionary zoning is a policy that can be enacted and implemented jurisdiction by jurisdiction.

What would have been the impact if, over the past 25 years, regionwide inclusionary zoning policies had been in effect for the nation's 100 largest metropolitan areas?

- At least 2,250,000 more affordable housing units would have been produced. These generally would not have been in stand-alone projects, stigmatized as "subsidized housing," but would have been integrated as architecturally compatible houses, townhouses, and apartment units into new, overwhelmingly middle-class developments.
- By allocating two-thirds of the affordable units for purchase or rent by low-income households ("workforce housing"), at least one-third of the nation's shortfall in affordable housing could have been met by inclusionary zoning policies.
- By allocating one-third of the affordable units for purchase or rent by local public housing authorities ("welfare-to-workforce housing"), the trend towards greater residential segregation of very low-income households would have been prevented, even reversed. In fact, potentially, the level of economic segregation in 2000 could have been lowered below 1970 levels in most metropolitan areas.

Inclusionary zoning can be both smart business and Smart Growth. Effective laws assure that complying with inclusionary zoning mandates will also be profitable through providing density bonuses, waiving fees, or providing low-cost, public financing, or direct tax subsidies. Promoting more compact development and eliminating the "push-out" factor of high-poverty neighborhoods reduce pressures to urbanize farmland and natural areas on the urban fringe. Inclusionary zoning can help meet critical housing needs, reduce the concentration of poverty and slow urban sprawl.

Of greatest importance, however, inclusionary zoning can reverse the growth of economic segregation in the nation's public schools.[9] In 2003, I completed two major studies of the housing/schools linkage in metro Baltimore (with the eighth most economically segregated schools in the United States) and metro Denver (with the 13th most economically segregated schools).[10]

Metro Baltimore has only seven countywide school districts. While actions by school boards within each district to balance school enrollments socioeconomically would have hypothetically reduced economic school segregation by 15 percent from 61.7 to 53.5, modeling a regionwide, 20-year, mixed-income housing policy would have further reduced economic school segregation to 25.8—a 60 percent reduction!

For the Denver region, hypothesizing that the region's 17 school boards would carry out school assignment policies that would equalize low-income pupil enrollment among all elementary schools within each of the school districts, I calculated that the economic school segregation index would be reduced to 46.6—about a 20 percent reduction in economic segregation. However, reinforcing what school boards have the authority to do with an inclusionary zoning policy that city and county governments have the authority to enact would reduce the school economic segregation index to 13.9—a three-quarters reduction in economic school segregation! That would make metro Denver's schools the third most economically integrated in the nation. By achieving just half that level (27.8), which is readily within the range of realistic implementation, greater Denver would have the second most economically integrated schools of any major metro area.

HOUSING POLICY IS SCHOOL POLICY

"Social Engineering"

The dismissive phrase "social engineering" may doubtlessly occur to some after reading this discussion of inclusionary zoning. "America is not very good at social engineering," I have been told.

On the contrary, American society has been very effective at "social engineering." What was slavery? What was Jim Crow (southern-style and northern-style)? What was the purpose of racially restrictive deed covenants? Or of FHA- and VA-sponsored mortgage market "redlining"? Or (to be more contemporary) of large-minimum-lot residential zoning or of outright bans on apartment construction (both recently found unconstitutional violations of civil rights laws by a Federal District Court in Dallas)?

In my experience, when the existing rules of the game produce results that powerful beneficiaries like, they are blessed as the workings of a "free market." When reforms in the rules of the game are proposed that would produce results they disagree with, they are condemned as "social engineering."

Changing the Rules of the Game

In regions with multiple local, independent governments, the "have-nots" typically have no leverage to get the "haves" to institute voluntarily any such policies. Regional collaboration must be mandated by a higher level of government. Though the federal government powerfully shapes the housing market, local governments' broad land-use planning, zoning, and tax policies are controlled by state governments. Regional reformers must target state legislatures and governors.

After three decades only a dozen states have adopted statewide growth-management laws. In most states environmental organizations, farmland preservation groups, and similar groups have been unable to muster sufficient political strength to change the current rules of the game.

However, the past decade has seen the emergence of new recruits to the cause of tax base sharing, growth management, and inclusionary zoning:

- business groups like Chicago Metropolis 2020, the Silicon Valley Manufacturers Group, Greater Baltimore Committee, and Better York;
- alliances of declining suburbs like the First Suburbs Consortium in Ohio;
- big city mayors like Rochester's William Johnson and Grand Rapids' John Logie[11] (mayors are often ambivalent, seeing regionalism as potential infringement of their authority or dilution of their political power base); and
- faith-based coalitions, such as Northwest Indiana's Interfaith Federation, Baltimore's BRIDGE, and the New Jersey Regional Coalition.

Environmentalists focus on man's impact on nature. Civil rights groups target injustices to our fellow man. What I have learned in the scores of communities that I have worked with over the past eight years is that the civil rights movement and the environmental movement should merge as the regional reform movement. The issues of social stewardship and environmental stewardship are inextricably interwoven. The connecting link is America's environmentally and socially destructive land development and housing patterns. To win today's civil rights battles as well as today's environmental battles one needs to change the same set of "rules of the game." Ultimately, the real question about creating livable communities is "Are we going to live—and learn—together?"

NOTES

1. A dissimilarity index measures the relative evenness or unevenness of the distribution of a target population across all census tracts, school attendance zones, etc. It is typically calculated by comparing the distribution of a given minority population (for example, blacks, Hispanics, poor persons) with the distribution of the dominant group (for example, whites, nonpoor persons, etc.). A score of "100" indicates total segregation—that is, all blacks (and only blacks) live in certain neighborhoods and all whites (and no blacks) live everywhere else. By contrast, a score of "0" indicates that every neighborhood has the same proportions of whites and blacks as the regional averages.

2. From 1970 to 1990, economic segregation increased in 70 percent of major metro areas. During the economic boom of the 1990s, the indices declined slightly as unemployment fell in inner-city neighborhoods by 1999.

3. Table 6.3 presents 27 of the 33 metro areas because I had not done the laborious calculations for the other six metro areas that I had not visited (nor have I updated calculations for Census 2000). The examples chosen were Detroit, as the U.S.'s most racially segregated; Milwaukee, as the United States's most economically segregated; Newark as typical of the minimal racial desegregation of the New York area; Atlanta, as the metropolis of the South; Charlotte, as having made greater progress on racial and economic integration than Atlanta;

and Oklahoma City, as having experienced the greatest improvement in racial segregation in the past three decades.

4. For a fuller discussion of city "elasticity" and its consequences, see the author's *Cities without Suburbs: A Census 2000 Update*, 3rd ed. (Washington DC, and Baltimore: Woodrow Wilson Center Press and Johns Hopkins University Press, 2003).

5. These urbanized areas in White America are Altoona, PA; Billings, MT; Binghamton, NY; Cedar Rapids, IA; Dubuque, IA; Eugene-Springfield, OR; Fargo-Moorhead, ND-MN; Great Falls, MT; Green Bay, WI; Huntington-Ashland, WV-KY-OH; Johnstown, PA; Manchester, NH; Portland, ME; Provo-Orem, UT; Sioux Falls, SD; Spokane, WA; Springfield, MO; and Wheeling, WV.

6. Of 57 White America metro areas, these 18 were the only ones with data for urbanized areas dating from 1960. It is clear that the metropolitan regions in White America (listed in note 5) are far smaller than are the most racially segregated regions with which they are compared (listed in note 7). The apples-to-oranges nature of the comparison counsels caution about the conclusions. However, the problem is inescapable. Few minorities are attracted to regions that, however valued by their inhabitants, are somewhat economic backwaters on the national scene. With its high-tech-driven dynamism, even Salt Lake City (which I had dubbed "the Capital of White America" in earlier writings) attracted a large Hispanic immigration in the 1990s.

7. In descending order (from most racially segregated to less economically segregated as measured by dissimilarity indices), these 19 urbanized areas of Diverse America are Detroit, MI; Chicago-Northwest Indiana, IL-IN; Milwaukee, WI; New York-Newark, NY-NJ-CT; Cleveland, OH; Buffalo-Niagara Falls, NY; Flint, MI; Cincinnati, OH-KY-IN; Saginaw, MI; St Louis, MO-IL; Stamford-Bridgeport, CT; Miami, FL; Birmingham, AL; Youngstown-Warren, OH; and Philadelphia, PA-NJ.

8. Technically, all income-related data in the 1990 census reflected 1989, the previous year. However, I will characterize all economic information from the 1990 census as 1990 data. Census 2000 has yet to release fully comparable data by which this analysis can be updated.

9. See my chapter, "Trends in School Segregation," in Richard D. Kahlenberg, ed., *Divided We Fail: Coming Together through Public School Choice: The Report of the Century Foundation Task Force on the Common School* (New York: The Century Foundation Press, 2002).

10. Both studies are available on my Web site (www.davidrusk.com).

11. Both these outstanding mayors stepped down in 2003 after multiple, successful terms of office.

7

Social Framework: Planning for a Civic Society—Investing in Social Infrastructure to Develop Social Capital

Meredith Cooper

Around the world, social capital researchers are committed to studying the many factors contributing to social capital decline. However, the diversity of community types, societal and cultural differences, and the variety of contributing factors pose great difficulty in the development of a single, concise explanation. The problem is not simply a matter of finding more time in a day or turning off the television, but in how we design our communities. It is time to look at communities from within, identifying existing opportunities for the development of formal and informal community networks, cultivating those networks that currently exist, and ensuring that available infrastructure nurtures the creation of new connections.

Community planners and experts in related disciplines currently give little consideration to aspects of their communities that support social connections. Instead, traditional planning has tended to focus on isolated aspects of communities such as how to move automobiles around the city or increase jobs by bringing in new industry, rather than taking into account the correlations between the physical, environmental, social, and economic components. The result is often an alarming disconnect between citizens and their communities. At the same time, as Americans become increasingly individualistic, some question whether or not "community" still exists in modern America. In light of this shift toward individualism, many experts are starting to see that now is a critical time for development professionals to begin intentionally incorporating opportunities for social interaction into design regulations under the rubric of making visible a "social infrastructure" that is as critical to successful community functioning as the physical infrastructure that underpins traditional planning.

With municipal populations increasing in recent years and America's rural landscape giving way to standard subdivisions, traditional centers of activity such as the general store or community center have all but disappeared. Opportunities for social interaction within communities or neighborhoods are more limited today, and the development of social connections often requires the intentional and ongoing effort of committed individuals. A lack of informal social interaction discourages the development of relationships between old-timers and newcomers and hinders the ability of newcomers and children to fully develop a sense of place within their communities. Fortunately, emerging approaches to community design are beginning to highlight the importance of maintaining and creating infrastructure that supports social interaction, often as a means to other ends including health and well-being, environmental protection, crime reduction, and other goals.

The work of experts such as Robert Putnam, who has laid much of the foundation for explaining how social capital develops, and Ray Oldenburg, who has studied and evaluated the places people gather, has led to critical insights into community-based social interaction. Though statistical and empirical evidence clearly reflect a decline in civic engagement, Putnam and others struggle to attribute the decline to particular changes in lifestyle. Investigation of potential contributing factors reveals that there is no single factor causing this trend. Instead, trends in civic participation must be considered individually due to the vast number of interconnected factors impacting American lifestyles.

This chapter considers the correlation between intentionally designing communities to create opportunities for social interaction and the subsequent rates of civic participation in communities, by bringing together four core themes: social capital theory, sense of place, community social interaction, and social infrastructure. The first section provides an analysis of social capital theory as well as perspective on the many factors contributing to the undeniable disconnect between people and their communities. The second section establishes a framework for understanding the relationship between the individual and one's connection with place, to provide a context for considering the value of daily social interaction. Third, a discussion of spatial analysis of community social interaction and a supporting case study exhibit a process for measuring and assessing municipal-scale social interaction. And lastly, reflection on the role of social infrastructure in community development confirms the underlying assertion that the community design process must begin to incorporate an assessment of existing or potential opportunities for social interaction and identify actions for improving social conditions.

DEFINITIONS

For readers unfamiliar with some of the concepts discussed throughout this chapter, the following definitions may be helpful.

Social Capital

Robert Putnam, author of *Bowling Alone: The Collapse and Revival of American Community*, explains that "social capital," a concept closely related to "civic virtue," refers to "connections among individuals—social networks and the norms of reciprocity and trustworthiness that arise from them."[1] In the context of social capital theory, Putnam further explains that social networks refer to both personal and professional relationships and the connections to others that develop from those relationships. Similarly, norms of reciprocity are generated through the development of trust which, through the course of time, is nurtured by a successful give-and-take process that ultimately leads to "generalized norms of reciprocity."[2]

Third Places

Ray Oldenburg, author of *The Great Good Place: Cafés, Coffee Shops, Bookstores, Bars, Hair Salons and Other Hangouts at the Heart of a Community*, defines "third places" as "informal public places . . . [that] serve community best to the extent that they are inclusive and local." According to Oldenburg, third places follow first places (home) and second places (work).[3]

Social Infrastructure

The New Hampshire Minimum Impact Development Partnership (NHMID), a collaboration between The Jordan Institute and Audubon Society of New Hampshire, describes social infrastructure as "the network of human relationships which form the basics of our private lives, our work lives, and our lives as members of our local communities. Part of this network includes employment, public health, education, the arts, recreation, and similar activities in our communities which contribute to—or detract from—our quality of life."[4] According to NHMID, social infrastructure can be either formal (e.g., community or church meetings, a yoga class) or informal (e.g., chance encounters at a local store, park, library).

SOCIAL CAPITAL THEORY

In modern communities, organizations such as church groups, municipal boards/committees, parent/teacher organizations, youth athletic leagues, Boy Scouts, Girl Scouts, and many other community-based associations contribute to the success of local municipalities. Participation in groups enables individuals to develop and nurture relationships with fellow neighbors, parents, activists, town government, volunteers, and others, while working together to achieve desired outcomes. Yet as exemplified by the case study described above, research shows that many societal factors currently contribute to the decline of participation in these civic groups and community activities. Though researchers debate the nature and extent of the decline, evidence strongly supports the belief that communities are growing and changing and that those changes are impacting collective action and the development of community-based relationships created through civic participation.

Defining Social Capital

According to modern-day social capital expert Robert Putnam, "the core idea of social capital theory is that social networks have value."[5] Putnam explains that while physical capital refers to objects and human capital refers to individual knowledge or "properties," social capital is imbedded in "social networks and the norms of reciprocity and trustworthiness that arise from them."[6] Lochner et al. (1999) describe social capital as a concept that "originated in the fields of sociology and political science."[7] Community-based problems such as poorly funded public schools, crime, and teen pregnancy cannot be solved individually but instead require political and environmental reform. Yet reform requires cooperation among neighbors and others to overcome inhibiting barriers and successfully create change. Social capital has both geographic (place-based) and relational (person-to-person) aspects, which must be holistically understood if such social ills are to be effectively and completely addressed.

Social capital is critical to the success of communities. In *Bowling Alone*, Putnam writes, "we are still more civically engaged than citizens in many other countries, but compared with our own recent past, we are less connected."[8] It is as if people are seeking methods for being involved without actually getting their hands dirty.

What is causing this proposed decline? Putnam suggests that the trend is not limited to one or even several components of American society, but rather impacts everyone. Similarly, the work of social capital theorists shows there is no single societal factor contributing to the decline. With limited methods for measuring each factor, researchers debate the extent to which different factors contribute to declining civic participation. In *Bowling Alone* Putnam exemplifies the challenge researchers face when he offers this list of possible factors:

> Business and time pressure; economic hard times; the movement of women into the paid labor force and the stresses of two career families; residential mobility; suburbanization and sprawl; television, the electronic revolution, and other technological changes; changes in the structure and scale of the American economy, such as the rise of chain stores, branch firms, and the service sector, or globalization; disruption of marriage and family ties; growth of the welfare state; the civil rights revolution; the sixties (most of which happened in the seventies), including Vietnam, Watergate, and disillusion with public life; and, the cultural revolt against authority (sex, drugs, and so on).[9]

To some extent, all of these factors ultimately contribute to the decline. Benjamin Barber, author of *Strong Democracy: Participatory Politics for a New Age* (1984), supports the notion that civic participation is on the decline. Though his discussion focuses more on developing an argument for reinstating the democratic process than on the statistical evidence proving factors of decline, Barber supports Putnam's more recent work when he suggests that since World War II voting rates for presidential elections tend to hover around 50 percent. This, he says, is "lower than every other noncompulsory democracy in the West."[10] Machinery, bureaucracy, and technology, among other factors, are decreasing participation and impacting the ability of leaders to lead and govern this democratic nation. Barber's discontent with this societal dropout is evident when he compares the social decline to an economic condition—bankruptcy.

In *Bowling Alone*, Putnam explains the importance of social capital by outlining its many functions. First, he posits that cooperative efforts ensure that one person is not left to complete the work of the whole. Social norms and networks subsequently alleviate process failure by reducing potential for "tragedy of the commons" and "the free-rider problem" scenarios. Second, Putnam suggests that social capital "greases the wheels," relying on the trust that comes from working in close proximity to and being reliant on others in the network. People are less willing to jeopardize their societal position when daily or frequent interactions are required to maintain trust and connectedness. Third, we become ever more aware that our success and failure depends on "the kindness of strangers" and friends alike. Participation in clubs and groups builds connections and tolerance, reduces cynicism, and encourages empathy of others. Give-and-take becomes an inherent and necessary process, thus reducing the need to get ahead while putting others down in the process.

Why is individual participation in community life so critical? Putnam suggests, that like the pebble in the pond, the impact radiates far beyond the "point of initial contact." In other words, changing trends act like a wave influencing the actions of others. For example, decreasing participation in a fraternal club might subsequently lower the participation in women's groups as women choose to stay home with their boyfriends or husbands rather than join their girlfriends for an evening out. Over time, decreased participation can lead to serious personal or societal consequences such as the breakdown of trust between neighbors or development of a sense of disillusionment with political processes.

As infrastructure that supports social interaction continues to disappear from modern communities, the gap in participation widens. For example, the potential is greater that younger generations raised in isolated residential environments will further remove themselves from their communities rather than become more engaged. If current trends continue, communities will face serious social, economic, and political consequences as a result of this increasing individualization. Data are frequently presented in today's research, suggesting that social disconnect in communities is ever-present and seriously in need of being addressed by planners and others.

Factors of Social Capital Decline

There are many factors potentially contributing to the decline in civic engagement. However, because of our interest in community planning, the discussion here focuses on two factors: (1) time and time constraints and (2) mobility and sprawl. With each factor we discuss how they are impacted by social infrastructure.

Time and Time Constraints

One of the most prevalent factors contributing to people's declining participation in community life is the limited time available for doing so. For most people, daily schedules are generally planned well in advance, with little flexibility for dealing with broken-down cars, sick children, or leaking roofs. Ironically, many attend workshops focused on time management, while wishing to be part of yet another social circle, involved in another club or committee, or attending another entertaining event.

In a survey conducted for a case study for the Northeast Earth Institute, whose workbooks encourage voluntary participation in discussions around sense of place, living a simple life, and similar topics, lack of time was resoundingly identified as a constraint on the ability of participants to engage in community life, despite a desire to be involved in their communities.[11] Ideally, most of those surveyed would have preferred more hours in a day if the option were given. However, much to the dismay of those seeking to ease their schedules, time does not necessarily increase for people just because they resign from a board or quit a team. Rather, most people's experience shows that this so-called *extra* time gets quickly taken up by those many other activities filling each person's days and nights.

While some people find themselves overcommitted, every community has people who choose not to participate in community life at all. For the most part, those who choose to be involved are very involved in more than one activity, while those who choose not to participate are often disengaged to the point of being considered *isolates*. However, perhaps people's isolation is due less to personal choice and more to a lack of opportunity, or infrastructure, which allows for voluntary participation. A lack of social infrastructure hinders people's ability to easily and efficiently participate in community life.

To gain a clearer understanding of the role and complexity of time constraints in the lives of today's average American, social capital researchers have asked whether people are really busier today than they were 10, 20, or 50 years ago. For example, Putnam suggests that though still up for debate, the "best guess is that there has not been much change" in the number of hours people work.[12] He references the work of John Robinson and Geoffrey Godbey whose research reflects a "6.2-hour-per-week *gain* in free time between 1965 and 1995 for the average American."[13] Putnam adds that although the actual number of available free-time hours may not have increased, "there is surely no evidence that we have *less*."

Juliet Schor, author of best-selling books *The Overworked American* and *The Overspent American*, disputes Putnam's conclusion that leisure time has increased, or even remained stable. In an unpublished paper prepared for a presentation at the Conference on Civic Engagement in American Democracy, Schor (1997) sheds new light on Putnam's conclusions and the research used to make his assessment. Specifically, she considers the variety of data sources recording and assessing the proportion of work versus leisure hours among the American public, which include business surveys, household surveys, and time-diaries. Schor's assessment focuses largely on the discrepancy in the results of the latter two data sources. She concludes that the variety of household surveys "show evidence of rising [work] hours," though the actual percent increase is not conclusive.[14]

According to Schor, many factors, including differences in time periods, populations surveyed, level of detail in surveys, and so on, may provide some explanation for this dispute. She maintains that discrepancies in data collection must be addressed in order for work/leisure time availability to be accurately assessed.

Though Schor insists that Putnam's explanation is in fact deeper than it appears, one thing seems clear: Time for participating in community life is limited for most. If this is true, where does our time go? Putnam offers several explanations. First, additional free time might come in moments or spurts that do not necessarily allow for engagement in organized activities or completion of significant tasks. Second, the proportion of accumulated free time is disproportionately dispersed; with less-educated Americans gaining free time while college-educated Americans have lost it. Third, there are a growing proportion of dual-income families whose earners spend more time at work than was previously the norm. Lastly, difficulty in coordinating available free time with the busy and conflicting schedules of others burdens the system and the ability to collectively rather than independently work toward achieving a desired goal.

Although the extent to which time constraints truly impact people's ability to participate in civic life is largely debated, time clearly plays a role in where and how people engage in leisure activities. Because today's community planning practices locate social arenas outside of what most would consider reasonable walking distances, people are forced to make choices between community participation and social events. In traditional communities, public and private engagements would have occurred within a reasonable distance of one another, enabling people to participate in community life and social events, while simultaneously reducing the commuting time required for accessing opportunities. When combined with other factors such as lengthier commutes to work, services, and public events, time and time constraints further impact people's ability and willingness to participate in community life.

Mobility and Sprawl

A second factor impacting people's ability to participate is the increasing amount of time spent in cars commuting to and from work, shopping, and social events. As the automobile became more reliable and infrastructure was designed and built to accommodate cars, Americans quickly developed a dependence on them. Americans today are more mobile than ever. With 20 percent of the U.S. population moving every five years, there would seem to be a correlation between mobility, being rooted in a community, and people's level of engagement (Sale, 2000).

Though Putnam recognizes the likely correlation between mobility and participation, he refutes it. Instead, he provides evidence to show that although we are seemingly a residentially mobile culture, mobility has not actually increased in the last 50 years. In the 1950s, for example, "20 percent of Americans changed residence each year, 7 percent moving to a different county or state."[15] Yet during the 1990s, these numbers are comparable to 16 percent and 6 percent respectively. Homeownership at the end of the twenty-first century was at an all-time high—67 percent in 1999—with only one in four homeowners expecting to move in the next five years.

With this strong evidence that American society is not as mobile as it appears, Putnam considers other explanations. He quickly rules out possible factors such as people moving to less congenial places, or people moving to metropolitan areas being "predisposed against civic engagement." Eventually, this train of thought leads him to consider the possibility of a connection between participation and suburbanization. After all, suburbanization is linked with increased distance between home and work as well as greater segregation by race and class.

Through further exploring this possibility, Putnam identifies an undeniable correlation between suburbanization and declining participation in community life. Surprisingly, the so-called social homogeneity, or segregation of the white and educated, that develops in the suburbs, actually reflects low rates of civic engagement. In part, these low rates of participation are attributed to the shift from downtown focal points, such as mom-and-pop stores on Main Street, to big-box stores on the edge of town that serve a regional rather than a community-based clientele. Larger, regional shopping complexes reduce chance encounters and opportunities for informal conversation with neighbors. Yet such informal encounters contribute to the development of networks and trusting relationships among neighbors, upon which community-based organizations depend.

Ray Oldenburg (1999) describes the typical American connection to place as follows:

> The typical suburban home is easy to leave behind as its occupants move to another. What people cherish most in them can be taken along in the move. There are no sad farewells at the local taverns or the corner store because there are not local taverns or corner stores. Indeed, there is often more encouragement to leave a given subdivision than to stay in it, for neither the homes nor the neighborhoods are equipped to see families or individuals through the cycle of life. Each is designed for families of particular sizes, incomes, and ages. There is little sense of place and even less opportunity to put down roots.[16]

Oldenburg is merely reflecting on the result of years of poorly planned communities.

Development and availability of the personal automobile has also significantly contributed to people's inability to participate in their communities. According to Putnam, Americans today spend an average of 72 minutes per day behind the wheel. Not only are we driving more, but increasingly this time is spent alone in the car. Perhaps Putnam's most compelling statistic reflecting the decline in civic engagement is the insight that "each additional ten minutes in daily commuting time cuts involvement in community affairs by ten percent."[17]

Suburban sprawl and an increasing dependence on the personal automobile clearly contribute to the decline in civic engagement. However, this trend is not limited to suburban communities. It extends to urban and rural areas across the country. Suburban sprawl is causing urban fragmentation and blurring the boundaries of rural communities. As a result, relationships traditionally established among neighbors are being seriously disrupted.

Mobility and sprawl, as well as time and time constraints, are factors of decreasing community participation. However, the role of many other factors including disruptions of marriage and family and technological and communication advances, must also be considered and assessed. Studying these factors in combination with one another, rather than as isolated sources, will ultimately enable communities to understand the complexities, and begin taking steps toward reversing the trend of declining participation. Additionally, planners will better understand the critical links between social infrastructure and healthy, viable communities and have a clearer foundation from which to explain these benefits to the communities with which they work.

SENSE OF PLACE

Without the presence of place-based social infrastructure that allows all members of a community to participate in civic life on a variety of levels, children and adults alike struggle to build a connection not only with other people, but also with the community itself. Understanding one's *sense of place* and a healthy connection with one's surroundings depends largely on a person's social experiences in that place.

The United States was founded on the premise of freedom. However, political separation and religious nonconformity were merely the beginning of a culture that would come to be dominated by the success of the individual rather than the common good. Inevitably, practices of individualism have led to a serious disconnect between Americans and the communities in which we reside. Though the freedom that came with America gaining its independence provided opportunity previously undreamed, the ultimate degree of individual separation from society is an unintended consequence of this fundamental value in our society.

Much of today's writing about sense of place focuses on our connection with the environmental conditions of the landscape including soils, climate, water, plants, and animals. But equally important in establishing a sense of place is the ability to identify with infrastructure such as historical buildings, parks, trails, or a general store. Indeed, it is unlikely a person can know a place without investing time to develop a connection with the social as well as the physical aspects of that place.

According to researcher Leanne G. Rivlin (1987), the first major developmental stage for a child is the separation of self from the world. The experiences a child has once reaching that stage become part of the child's conceptions of him or herself and those around him. The experience is therefore social, emotional, and cognitive; and one that provides a "sense of connection to place" such as home or neighborhood. She further explains that development of both sense of self and sense of place do not end with childhood, but rather continue throughout one's lifetime even when one's place changes or one moves.

As adults, says Rivlin, there is a common search for "home." While some leave the home of their parents and begin right away to settle into what will become home for them and their new family, others spend part of their adult years searching for their place to call home. Eventually, most settle for a place that "feels like home." The process of developing a sense of place and identifying with a neighborhood or community is highly dependent on an individual's sense of self and psychological development and is a struggle individuals have faced for hundreds if not thousands of years.

The inevitable growth impacting communities today also impacts our relationships and sense of place. Rapid growth is increasingly separating neighbors and neighborhoods and significantly altering the identity of the individual with place, be it in childhood or adulthood. Our mobile culture, in which "20 percent of [the] population moves to a new home every five years," has not considered the implications of the increasing disconnect of people from their communities.[18] We are less and less involved in our communities; civic participation rates are dropping, volunteerism has plummeted, and subsequently, we have fewer encounters with neighbors and our physical surroundings. Community centers, parish halls, recreation halls, if they exist at all, are usually run-down or underutilized and no longer provide the sense of community they once did. If local public infrastructure does not exist to support active social networks, the struggle to identify with place will be even greater.

Beyond considering individual connections to place, be it neighborhood or community, it is also important to understand the role of traditional communities in our changing culture. Arthur Mehrhoff (1999) argues that the need for community is not just theoretical, but is actually an inherent human desire. Traditional communities, he says, are defined as "physical places where basic human needs are met and primary relationships maintained."[19] Mehrhoff takes a *systems* approach to community design, looking at the modern community as a complex social system. His analysis of traditional communities identifies several components necessary for traditional communities to function as collective systems. First, community "always implies groups of people and their demographic characteristics," though many communities, and particularly rural towns, are experiencing rapid demographic transition. In today's communities, residents may be of the same ethnic and racial background, or share kinship with other residents, but these ties are becoming less common.

A second component in Mehrhoff's analysis suggests that community "has typically been characterized by a high level of social interaction," which implies that community must provide opportunities for interaction. Mehrhoff acknowledges that, for better or worse, small towns with strong social ties have the potential to be either supportive or suffocating. What is key, he argues, is the presence of supportive relationships when times of need arise.

Historic patterns reveal the shifts of social connections in traditional communities. For example, postindustrialization had serious impacts on the development and sustainability of strong social ties within traditional communities. The repercussions of this mechanization of American society have similarly impacted social ties in modern communities. The more recent breakdown of social ties can be, according to Mehrhoff, attributed to several factors, including the increasing specialization of labor, extension of the market economy, increased influence of government bureaucracy, more differentiated interests (e.g., cable TV, Internet), and growth of metropolitan regions. As Mehrhoff seems to suggest, if historical and current trends toward the breakdown of social ties continue to persist, the few remaining traditional communities will likely become obsolete or isolated beyond relevancy. A third component of Mehrhoff's functioning community system is that its social ties and shared demographics produce shared values. In any community, and particularly smaller, rural towns, common values develop through participation in a local church or other organization that defines and supports those values. But again, postindustrialization, which created communities of mixed demographics, experiences, and cultural perspectives, has posed difficulty in the establishment of common value systems.

Lastly, Mehrhoff claims that a functional community "implies a shared territory" or, in other words, has common interest in a shared resource or occupation such as farming, mining, or timber harvesting. Postindustrialization and the development of the automobile have enabled both a diversity of occupation and people's ability to work farther from home. For the most part, communities no longer have compact urban centers or pedestrian-friendly downtowns, so people have become separated and disconnected from what was once a "shared territory." The result is that in most communities today, sense of place has all but disappeared. While Mehrhoff places little emphasis on the need for designing built or natural infrastructure to support social connections, his insistence that community development in modern America requires a balanced, whole-systems approach supports the basic premise that social development will not occur unless community design intentionally integrates opportunities for social interaction.

Based on the discussion above, it is clear to me that the presence of social infrastructure in communities not only creates a sense of place and a traditional community sentiment, it also serves a practical function. Human-scale, walkable communities with efficiently located social infrastructure support economic function by keeping dollars in the community. They enable people to shop at mom-and-pop stores on Main Street rather than regional shopping centers. Similarly, social infrastructure in the natural landscape, such as community parks or other recreational areas, contributes to environmental protection by eliminating the need for people to drive miles out of town to fulfill an inherent desire for connecting with nature. Local opportunities for meeting daily social, economic, natural, and physical needs will contribute to the development of healthy communities and will lead to benefits such as an increase in human health and well-being.

As communities grow in size and identifying shared values becomes more challenging, understanding why and how individual sense of place develops can play an important role in facilitating social connections. People's intrinsic desire to share with those around them should lead planners to consider sense of place needs in the development of common ties.

COMMUNITY SOCIAL INTERACTION

Spatial analysis of community social interaction can reveal significant information about where and how residents interact with one another. For example, in communities lacking a designated community center or with a vaguely defined town center, it can be difficult for residents to find common ground for casual interaction and to nurture a sense of place. A process for measuring and mapping social interaction (see case study) can reveal hubs of activity or activity centers for both formal and informal networking and can also provide information regarding usage rates of particular community infrastructure. Activity centers then become a priority for planning boards or others as the community grows and changes.

As important as identifying where people go is learning where people do not go. Identifying usage rates through spatial analysis can help planners and others identify underused social infrastructures and can help answer questions about the potential for usage rates to increase if, for example, additional meeting space were added to increase capacity in a particular infrastructure. Similarly, measuring and evaluating municipal social interaction can reveal the accessibility of destinations via various modes of transportation including walking, biking, public transportation, or driving. While most social interaction is located in a central area, other social interaction probably takes place in locations scattered throughout a city or town. By knowing the location of significant social interaction in a given community, surveys on social interaction can ask:

1. Would locating additional social infrastructure outside of the activity center increase automobile traffic along residential roads?
2. Would locating social infrastructure outside of the activity center encourage people to participate who otherwise might not?

Another critical dimension addressed through spatial analysis of social interaction, particularly as communities grow, is the regional impact of municipal social infrastructure. For residents who live in one town but work in another, or whose children do not go to school in the town in which they reside, the social interactions in a surrounding community may actually be more relevant. Regional consideration should raise planning and other town decision-making questions such as:

1. Why do people travel to other communities to access services?
2. Would residents prefer to have these services located in town?

3. Would locating these services in town reduce travel time?
4. If services were located in town, would residents have increased opportunities to interact and build social networks?

Currently, no tool exists for identifying community-based social interaction and measuring its usage. A tool for identifying social interaction and its supporting infrastructure seems a necessary component in order to ensure that desired civic engagement is supported by available infrastructure. The case study demonstrates a process that residents of local communities can use to identify existing social infrastructure and to consider additional formal and informal opportunities that would support community-wide social interaction.

ASSESSING SOCIAL INFRASTRUCTURE: A CASE STUDY

Community Profile

Canterbury, New Hampshire, a community of approximately 2,000 people, is centrally located, bordering the state's capital city of Concord. Incorporated in 1741, the town has primarily served as a farming community. Canterbury looks much like a traditional New England community, comprised of a small village with a general store, church and parish hall, town center with gazebo, fire station, historical society, town offices, and library. Residences surround the village center, reaching to all corners of the town's 43.9 square miles of land area.[20] Farm types include a variety of dairy, vegetable, orchards, and homesteads. The community has its own elementary school, but the middle school and high school are cooperatives located in neighboring communities requiring students to be bussed or driven to school.

Canterbury faces growth issues similar to other New Hampshire communities, such that incoming residents continue to decrease the proportion of long-time residents. With rising numbers of newcomers, Canterbury has only recently been named a bedroom community, or a place where people live, eat, sleep, and send their children to school, but do not work and where they have little involvement in community affairs and local politics.

In small New Hampshire communities such as Canterbury, things get done because volunteers commit their time to local efforts. However, in many cases, the same residents volunteer again and again while others participate little, if at all.

As Canterbury works to address its growing population, residents are having to make decisions about the community's future. For example, expansion of the library has been an ongoing debate for the last several years. While most residents admit the library could use an expansion, some adamantly oppose changing its location from the historic Elkins home. Others feel there is no solution other than to construct a larger facility within the town center. A major reason for expanding the library is the need for additional public meeting space, which could support more social interaction. Other meeting spaces in the village include rooms in the town offices and the Parish Hall.

It was anticipated that by identifying existing social infrastructures used for conducting business, both formal and informal, the community of Canterbury would better understand the frequency of use of existing services and the demand for additional infrastructure.

Research Design and Methods

Through the distribution of a townwide newsletter, Canterbury residents were given the opportunity to respond to questions related to community participation and social interaction. The survey included questions about boards or committees they belong to within the community, locations in town where they meet with neighbors, either formally or informally, whether or not they volunteer in the community, what, if any, social infrastructure is missing from the community, and whether or not they feel the community is well supported by volunteers.

Once collected, survey results were compiled and summarized. From the results, a map was created to reveal the formal and informal infrastructure residents identified as significant for uniting neighbors and friends for town meetings, church meetings, informal gatherings, or chance encounters.[21] With enough survey responses, both formal and informal infrastructures would be compiled into a single map and designated in a graduated color scheme to reflect usage rates.

Case Study Conclusions

Although the Canterbury survey yielded few responses, those that were returned provided valuable insight regarding committees that receive the most support, where additional volunteers are needed, and which infrastructures are most critical to the town's formal and informal social networking. Additional space for gatherings, opportunities for recreation, and reaching out to the more isolated residents were identified as priority concerns that, if addressed, would likely increase interaction and build social networks.

Careful analysis of the results revealed the various desires of residents for meeting both current and future social infrastructure needs. Responses to several questions listed lack of time as a significant factor in levels of interaction. The availability of a centrally located local pub, deli, tearoom, coffeehouse, and/or counter space with no scheduled time for gathering was mentioned by several respondents as a possible solution to time constraints. An infrastructure such as a pub or coffee shop with flexible hours that allows residents to stop on the way to work, after dinner, or at any time of day, might even encourage so-called "isolates" and "bedroom community types" to get involved.

Although additional research would be necessary for identifying the underlying vision for Canterbury's social needs, this brief summary exemplifies the value residents place on local opportunities for interacting with friends and neighbors. With growing numbers of new residents, it is becoming increasingly important to understand where and how residents, new and old alike, can establish and maintain trusting relationships through casual and organized interaction within the community while simultaneously nurturing a personal sense of place.

SOCIAL INFRASTRUCTURE

Social capital is inherently associated with other community capital including natural, economic, political, and human. Intrinsically, social capital extends beyond the horizontal theory that it is simply about networks of formal and informal relationships between individuals, and rather, should be understood as being of a vertical nature in which most, if not all, aspects of community capital are impacted and influenced by those relationships.[22] Therefore, the presence of infrastructure that allows for and subsequently supports social capital development is critical to the creation and success of political, personal, economic and other community ties.

Civic Participation and Third Places

Third places, which refer to those places in communities that are not home (first places) or work (second places), and which provide a space for informal gatherings with friends, neighbors or strangers, are in essence the community-scale social infrastructures that encourage social capital (Oldenburg, 1999). However, by referring to such places as social infrastructure, rather than third places, the language remains consistent with that used by planners and other community development professionals. These audiences need to understand the importance of locating human-scale opportunities for social interaction in modern communities.

Lisbeth B. Schorr (1997) explains that community conditions influence a number of factors including youth violence rates, school failure and dropout rates, and teen pregnancy. Not surprisingly, this burden falls hardest on the poorest members of the community. It takes a strong sense of community to believe that people can improve their situation. Schorr acknowledges that many societal conditions including high delinquency rates, educational failure, infant mortality, child abuse, adolescent substance abuse, and gang violence are all linked to the lack of social infrastructure at the neighborhood level. Design practices that eliminate institutions and other settings that facilitate social networking pose serious consequences to sustainable community function.

Schorr explains that traditional neighborhood and community connections have eroded over time. Programs have been established to address growing needs and to prevent the social consequences of declining social capital. Some of these efforts have included settlement houses, welfare, and the beginning of formalized social services. Each of these programs, Schorr suggests, sought to address poverty by integrating the educated with the poor; advocating for better social services; providing jobs, shelter, housing, and food; and promoting self-improvement for local residents. Programs either offered support or established themselves in the lives of the poor by acting as extended family to assist in time of need.

Research shows, however, that family and neighbor connections, and the ability of an individual or family to turn to other community members for support, has all but disappeared. Traditional neighborhoods and communities have changed with the times becoming more individualized, secluded, or separated. As a result, new approaches were developed for improving societal conditions. These new approaches reject the traditional methods of addressing social issues (poverty, crime, etc.) on a case-by-case basis, and instead emphasize a more holistic method of community-based strategies which integrate traditional community planning and development with social services and educational enhancements. Schorr's work describes how collaborative efforts of community members, local corporations, nonprofit organizations, and elected officials often result in advocacy for better health care, education, and employment.

In communities throughout the world, social infrastructure (i.e., third places) performs many community-building functions. First is the ability to unite neighbors and neighborhoods. Second, they serve as "Ports of Entry" for visitors and newcomers to connect with the community. Third, they serve as sorting areas through their allowance for broad-scale association of people with varying experiences and interests. Fourth, third places function as staging areas from which neighbors and friends can provide assistance in time of need. Fifth, they provide public characters, or those most likely to keep an eye on what's happening. Sixth, third places unite youth and adults, thus decreasing the segregation of youth and increasing the understanding of both parties of the other. Seventh, third places serve the elderly by keeping them connected with community and the community aware of their day-to-day needs. Eighth, third places provide a forum for political discussion and process. Ninth, they serve as a basis for intellectual development. And lastly, third places provide office space for neutral business transactions (Oldenburg, 1999).

Certainly, the list extends well beyond those listed here. What is key to their success, however, is that we enjoy these networks. They are voluntary networks built on our desire to belong and to be included rather than through any obligatory demands.

While social infrastructure ensures a high quality of life through formal and informal gathering, celebration, meeting, and so on, one must remember the critical role they play in a functioning democracy. Although day-to-day civic participation is voluntary, being able to participate in civic life is a necessary and key component of community process. Yet in order for people to become and remain involved, we must insure that we intentionally create and/or preserve places where we can interact.

In *The Great Good Place*, Oldenburg declares, "houses alone do not a community make." In doing so, he draws on the link between suburbanization and involvement in public life. But Oldenburg is taking Putnam's work a step further, highlighting the relationship between the increasing fragmentation of the landscape and lack of opportunity for building connections. He points to the experience of the suburban housewife of the 1950s and 1960s who became increasingly isolated without an automobile. The problem has grown with residential development, and today there is little opportunity for spontaneous interaction that builds and sustains social capital. Ultimately, we have created suburbs that guarantee the isolation of individuals in a world fragmented by the ubiquitous automobile.

With growing populations and increasing demands for workforce housing, industrial employment, and material goods, big-box retail and chain restaurants are replacing the coffee shops, cafés, bookstores, and barber shops that once lined America's Main Streets. Encounters with neighbors or friends at these large service centers are, at best, rare. Rather than make visits to common places on Main Street as parents and grandparents experienced, Americans today spend most of their time trying to get away from the essentials of community life (Oldenburg, 1999).

What has been the result of this disappearance of public life? To start, expectations on work and family have escalated, with those institutions having great difficulty meeting the many social, psychological, and emotional needs of individuals that used to be met through various social networks. Where those expectations are not met, Americans turn to individualistic pursuits which guarantee that we will not have to associate with others. Americans have become so consumed with the goal of achieving individual freedom that we are seemingly oblivious to the many benefits of well-developed public life.

Beyond providing any number of psychological and physiological benefits, the significance of social infrastructure becomes additionally apparent when one considers the world's social history. By looking at the contribution of social arenas to the success of ancient civilizations, the need for similar infrastructure in modern communities becomes clear. For example, in Greek and Roman societies ancient architecture clearly emphasized the worth of the public or civic individual rather than the private or domestic individual. Involvement in public life was inherent in historic cultures and supported in ancient design in which "few means to allure and invite citizens into public gatherings were overlooked. The forums, coliseums, theaters, and amphitheaters were grand structures, and admission to them was free."[23] Most modern planning practices must be modified if the desired outcome is healthy, sustainable communities that foster social capital.

In *The Death and Life of Great American Cities*, Jane Jacobs illustrates the many changes burdening communities and provides a framework for a discussion of the shortcomings of modern planners, developers, and architects in designing communities that celebrate social connections. Almost 50 years after its first publication, the planning community continues to apply practices that likely receive discouraged sentiments from Jacobs. Although she focuses primarily on urban communities, Jacobs's reference to the importance of individual responsibility in community life applies to all community types. She describes this responsibility as a learned process developed through personal experience. Her discussion emphasizes the role of adults in the development of all children, not just one's own, in community life. Today, most communities are designed to put our residences away from the rest of the community, thus limiting the presence of adults on the street to help maintain order and silently teach the lesson of public responsibility.

Although she assesses the role of the automobile from the perspective of planners and architects, Jacobs explains that the automobile has too often and too conveniently been "tagged as the villain." Instead, she suggests that automobiles are "less a cause than a symptom of our incompetence at city building." She explains:

> Of course planners . . . are at a loss to make automobiles and cities compatible with one another. They do not know what to do with automobiles in cities because they do not know how to plan for workable and vital cities anyhow—with or without automobiles. The simple needs of automobiles are more easily understood and satisfied than the complex needs of cities, and a growing number of planners and designers have come to believe that if they can only solve the problems of traffic, they will thereby have solved the major problem of cities. Cities have much more intricate economic and social concerns [than] automobile traffic.[24]

To their credit, Jacobs admits that planners had an unavoidable lack of knowledge regarding the impact that planning for autos rather than people would ultimately have on modern society. However, many planners today continue to design communities to accommodate the needs of the automobile. Rarely can people access necessary services or drink a beer with neighbors at a local bar without driving to get there.

Communities are not human in scale, and the pockets of social infrastructure that do exist are largely inaccessible.

Today, whether urban or rural, a community with a healthy public life integrates work, commerce, and residences to the best extent possible. As Oldenburg asserts, it engages a diversity of people, creating opportunities for social interaction among a wide range of classes, ages, and economic or educational status. Communities are human in scale, enabling people to walk, and pedestrians and automobiles are appropriately accommodated. There are ample places to sit and children can play in the streets.

Third places provide a forum for local decision making and information sharing to occur. Some people will choose not to participate. But perhaps some of those people have chosen to remain isolated because they do not want to sit on a board or committee to be involved. In most communities, informal opportunities for voluntarily participating are today limited if they exist at all. Therefore, residents must begin demanding the integration of infrastructure that encourages the participation of *all* residents in public life. And planners must begin meeting those demands.

Community-Based Social Infrastructure

Sadly, American communities today generally discourage and even prohibit third places. However, one emerging effort geared toward improving this situation has recently been created by the New Hampshire Minimum Impact Development Partnership (NHMID), a collaborative project of The Jordan Institute and Audubon Society of New Hampshire. In an effort to design more effective, efficient, and integrated land-use planning and development practices, NHMID has developed the Three Infrastructures Approach to Land Use Planning. The Three Infrastructures Approach proposes that design supporting a balance of green, built, and social infrastructure will not only be more effective, efficient, and integrated, but will also produce a higher quality of life. Built infrastructure, which has traditionally been the primary focus of planners, architects, and the like, is defined by NHMID as "the many constructed elements that transport and shelter people, goods, and information."[25] Green infrastructure, a component of communities gaining increasing attention in the planning process, encompasses "the natural life support system of interconnected lands and waters upon which human life and economic activity, as well as other forms of life, depend."[26] Social infrastructure, defined as "the opportunities within a community for organized and informal social connection," supports the notion of third places described above and has received the least consideration in the planning process.[27]

Communities would not exist without people (social) and people would not survive without shelter (built) and basic resources including air, water, and sunlight (green). NHMID's Three Infrastructures Approach is innovative. In addition to the traditional focus on built and green infrastructures, NHMID suggests communities that incorporate social infrastructure into the design will promote "public health, safety, and general quality of life." This is because social infrastructure supports opportunities for social interaction and subsequently the development of social connections required for a healthy community.

For the most part, consumers as well as some professional planners are comfortable with modern planning practices, and the thought of placing additional requirements on planning and zoning causes people to cringe. Multi-acre lots that promote a sense of privacy have become the norm. But as populations grow and demand for housing increases, traditional approaches are not sustainable. Clearly, market demand for these planning practices has driven the decision making of local officials and some planning professionals to support inefficient planning. Market demand combined with the willingness of developers and others to meet those demands have together created communities designed for cars, not people.

As the proportion of easily developable larger lots diminishes in the wake of growth, planners face new challenges in designing communities. Already they are being asked to design neighborhoods smaller in scale to accommodate more housing while still maintaining a sense of privacy for homeowners. Innovative planning approaches such as that proposed by NHMID provide planners with sustainable alternatives. Additionally, once consumers begin to understand the multifaceted benefits of more innovative approaches, they will begin to perceive them less as regulations and more as desired norms.

While planners can change their practices, they alone cannot change market demand. Therefore, it is critical that the lay community begin to understand the foreseeable long-term impacts that current demands for housing, transportation, and commercial development will have, should it continue. With this in mind, NHMID's voluntary practices have been developed with the support not only of planners and architects, but also realtors, conservationists, public health professionals, and others. This and other multidisciplinary approaches will ensure that proposed design practices consider the contributions of all factors when planning for healthy, sustainable communities. Similarly, a spatial analysis created through a process for mapping community social infrastructure, such as that described earlier, will provide a forum through which residents of a given community can share their thoughts and concerns about impending growth and their vision for social interaction within the community.

Because organizations focused specifically on building community social capital are rare if they exist at all, it is crucial that stakeholders from all disciplines begin to encourage growth patterns that support social interaction. Opportunities for social interaction are critical to the development of social networks, and ultimately the level of civic action.

In addition to providing forums for local decision making, social infrastructure serves other functions as well. Comparable to those functions identified by Oldenburg regarding third places, NHMID recognizes these functions of social infrastructure: support, safety, bonding, connection, information, governance, education, service, and commerce. The combination of these functions reflects the holistic process though which social capital contributes to healthy communities.

Social infrastructure can exist both formally and informally, but only if we have the places—whether built or green—to interact. At the community scale, organized or formal social infrastructure refers to event-based opportunities for gathering such as Town Meetings, scout meetings, conservation commission meetings, or a yoga class. Informal social infrastructure refers to place-based chance encounters with neighbors or friends, possibly occurring at a town store, along walking trails, or at a town park.

The mere presence of social infrastructures will not ensure the participation of all community members. Nor should it be expected to. Instead, the availability of voluntary, informal places to meet, gather, stop-in, purchase a snack, visit with neighbors, or just plain hang out, must be in place for those who do choose to participate. In small-scale communities, social infrastructure will support even those members of a community choosing to remain isolated, because a forum is provided in which people can check in with local shopkeepers or others to be sure the isolates are safe and healthy. Social infrastructure enables people to express care for neighbors, because it allows them to develop trust of others in the community, and to engage in reciprocal giving and sharing. Furthermore, social infrastructures strengthen a person's sense of place, because the experiences in such places support the many emotional needs not met at home or work.

Through their research on social capital, Ian Falk and Sue Kilpatrick (2000) support this differentiation between social capital and social interaction processes. They conclude that in order for social capital to exist, it must be able to be produced. Social capital, they suggest, is an outcome of social interaction. To understand how this works, they distinguish between two types of learning—formal and informal—which enable the development of knowledge and values. Traditionally, social capital research has emphasized the development of social capital through formal, or institutionalized, learning. But in fact, there is significant value in the more informal learning—mundane conversation—that takes place in communities. Informal learning takes place naturally in our normal routines and may not be considered "learning" in the normal sense.

Planners need to consider the critical role of social infrastructure in communities but generally lack the tools necessary for identifying social infrastructure and measuring its usage. The process described earlier for identifying and assessing social infrastructure through spatial analysis, though still in its infancy, provides a basis from which to begin measuring existing social infrastructure and planning for the future. By inventorying and mapping social infrastructure, professional planners, volunteer planning boards, and community members would have a basis from which to consider the potential implications of new development on social connections and participation within communities. Additionally, communities would have a clearer understanding of where and how people participate, enabling planners to design infrastructure based on actual rather than perceived needs.

CONCLUSION

As communities grow, opportunities for hearing and sharing stories of local traditions disappear. But community is about "real people with real names."[28] For the sake of what Ronald J. Hustedde (1998) refers to as the "saving power of relationships" and the ability of relationships to "sustain us" in time of need, communities must begin to demand design practices that provide opportunities for building social connections. Social infrastructure is critical to the development and sustainability of community-based relationships and subsequent civic action.

Because the mere presence of social infrastructure cannot be expected to rebuild public life, the many societal factors contributing to the apparent decline in civic participation must simultaneously be addressed. To begin this shift, Oldenburg predicts the eventual change in American attitude in three areas. First, current understanding of convenience will move from auto dependency to walking and the use of nearby facilities. Second, social isolation caused by self-help models will be realized and people will begin to understand the emotional benefits and healing powers of social connections. And third, the "tyrannical force of the physical environment" will be revealed, instilling in people the desire to connect with the place they call home.[29]

Ultimately we must strive to create healthy communities that strike a balance between social, economic, and political structures while meeting the educational, psychological, and physiological needs of individuals. The American appeal toward independence must begin to shift toward a demand for development practices that integrate local, human-scale opportunities for social interaction and establish a foundation for public life. In communities, this shift will create opportunities for people to share information and engage in experiences that build connections, form relationships, and develop an unyielding sense of trust among neighbors and friends.

Social infrastructure is the foundation of healthy, sustainable communities. Until municipal design practices support sufficient, accessible social infrastructure, communities can expect increases in time constraints, mobility, and auto dependence, and an inevitable decrease in social capital.

NOTES

1. Putnam, 2000, p. 19.
2. Ibid., p. 21.
3. Oldenburg, 1999, p. xvii.
4. http://www.nhmid.org/infrast.htm#social.
5. Putnam, 2000, pp. 18–19.
6. Ibid., p. 19.
7. Lochner et al., 1999, p. 259.
8. Putnam, 2000, p. 183.
9. Ibid., p. 187.
10. Barber, 1984, p. xiii.
11. Cooper, 2001.
12. Putnam, 2000, p. 190.
13. Ibid.
14. Schor, 1997, p. 2.
15. Putnam, 2000, p. 205.
16. Oldenburg, 1999, p. 4.
17. Putnam, 2000, p. 212.
18. Sale, 2000, p. x.
19. Mehrhoff, 1999, p. 19.
20. *New Hampshire Community Profiles*, 2003.
21. Additional information specific to data layers within the mapping component was gathered through my participation in the *Environmental Education Institute: Community Mapping 2002* course offered by the University of New Hampshire Cooperative Extension. Maps specify data sources for individual map layers.
22. Christian Grootaert (1998) asserts that Putnam's "horizontal" theory that social capital is limited to associations between people is "narrow," and suggests that in a more "vertical" view, social capital has deeper effects on community and economic development—that it is

through networks and norms that people "gain access to power and resources" and "decision making and policy formulation occur."

23. Oldenburg, 1999, p. 17.
24. Jacobs, 1993, pp. 10–11.
25. Foss et al., 2002, p. 5.
26. Ibid.
27. Ibid.
28. Hustedde, 1998, p. 161.
29. Oldenburg, 1999, pp. 286–88, 291–96.

BIBLIOGRAPHY

Agrawal, A., and C. C. Gibson. 1999. "Enchantment and Disenchantment: The Role of Community in Natural Resource Conservation." *World Development* 27: 629–49.

Barber, B. R. 1984. *Strong Democracy: Participatory Politics for a New Age.* Berkeley: University of California Press.

Brewer, Gene A. 2003. "Building Social Capital: Civic Attitudes and Behavior of Public Servants." *Journal of Public Administration Research and Theory* 13: 5–26.

Coleman, J. S. 1988. "Social Capital in the Creation of Human Capital." *American Journal of Sociology* 94 (supplement): 95–120.

Community Culture and the Environment: A Guide to Understanding a Sense of Place. 2002. U.S. EPA (EPA 842-B-01-003), Office of Water. Washington, DC: National Center for Environmental Publications and Information.

Cooper, M. 2001. An Evaluation of the Northeast Earth Institute's Effectiveness in Building Social Capital in New Hampshire Communities. Unpublished case study.

Crocker, J. P., Jr., and W. R. Potapchuk. 1999. "Exploring the Elements of Civic Capital." *National Civic Review* 88(3): 175–96.

Etzioni, A. 2000. "Back to We" (excerpts from *The Spirit of Community* [1993]). In *Discussion Course on Discovering a Sense of Place* (pp. 6-5–6-8). (Available from the Northwest Earth Institute, 505 SW Sixth, Suite 1100, Portland, OR 97204.)

Evers, A. 2003. "Social Capital and Civic Commitment: On Putnam's Way of Understanding." *Social Policy and Society* 2: 13–21.

Falk, I., and S. Kilpatrick. 2000. "The Role of Social Capital in Rural Development: What Is Social Capital? A Study of Interaction in a Rural Community." *Sociologia Ruralis* 40: 87–110.

Fischer, C. S. 1982. *To Dwell among Friends: Personal Networks in Town and City.* Chicago: University of Chicago Press.

Flora, C. B. 1997. "Innovations in Community Development." In *Rural Development News* 21: 1–2. (Available from the North Central Regional Center for Rural Development.)

Flora, C. B., and J. L. Flora. n.d. *Measuring and Interpreting Social Capital on the Community Level: The Difference and Similarities between Social Capital and Entrepreneurial Social Infrastructure.* Retrieved August 9, 2002, from http://www.worldbank.org/poverty/scapital/library/flora2.htm.

Flora, J. L. n.d. *Social Capital and Communities of Place.* Retrieved August 9, 2002, from http://www.worldbank.org/poverty/scapital/library/flora1.htm.

Fodor, E. 1999. *Better Not Bigger: How to Take Control of Urban Growth and Improve Your Community.* Stony Creek, CT: New Society Publishers.

Ford, L. R. 2000 *The Spaces between Buildings.* Baltimore: Johns Hopkins University Press.

Foss, C., K. Hartnett, and M. Cooper. 2002. "A Three Infrastructures Approach to Land Use Planning in New Hampshire." *New Hampshire Audubon* 38: 5–12.

Francis, M. 1989. "Control as a Dimension of Public-Space Quality." In I. Altman and E. H. Zube, eds., *Human Behavior and Environment: Advances in Theory and Research* (pp. 147–72). New York: Plenum Press.

Friedman, J. 1987. *Planning in the Public Domain: From Knowledge to Action*. Princeton, NJ: Princeton University Press.

Gladwell, M. 2000. *The Tipping Point: How Little Things Can Make a Big Difference*. Boston: Little, Brown and Company.

Glaeser, E. L., D. Laibson, and B. Sacerdote. 2002. "Social Capital: An Economic Approach to Social Capital." *The Economic Journal* 112: 437–58.

Gottlieb, R. 1993. *Forcing the Spring: The Transformation of the American Environmental Movement*. Washington, DC: Island Press.

Grootaert, C. 1998. *Social Capital: The Missing Link*? Retrieved August 9, 2002, from http://www.worldbank.org/poverty/scapital/wkrppr/sciwp3.pdf.

Hall, E. T. 1951. *The Hidden Dimension*. Garden City, NY: Doubleday.

Hauser, S. M. 2000. "Education, Ability, and Civic Engagement in the Contemporary United States." *Social Science Research* 29: 556–82.

Hayward, J. 1989. "Urban Parks: Research, Planning, and Social Change." In I. Altman and E. H. Zube, eds., *Human Behavior and Environment: Advances in Theory and Research* (pp. 193–216). New York: Plenum Press.

Hiss, T. 1991. *The Experience of Place: A New Way of Looking at and Dealing with Our Radically Changing Cities and Countryside*. New York: Vintage Books.

Homan, M. S. 1999. *Promoting Community Change: Making It Happen in the Real World*. Pacific Grove, CA: Brooks/Cole Publishing.

Hustedde, R. J. 1998. "On the Soul of Community Development." *The Journal of the Community Development Society* 29(2): 153–65.

Jackson, W. 1997. "Becoming Native to This Place." In H. Hannum, ed., *People, Land, and Community* (pp. 133–41). New Haven: Yale University Press.

Jacobs, Jane. 1993. *The Death and Life of Great American Cities*. New York: Modern Library.

John F. Kennedy School of Government, Harvard University, Saguaro Seminar. 2002. *Social Capital Community Benchmark Survey Short Form*. Cambridge, MA: Harvard University Press.

Kemmis, D. 1990. *Community and the Politics of Place*. Norman: University of Oklahoma Press.

Landolt, P., and A. Portes. n.d. *Unsolved Mysteries: The Toqueville Files II: The Downside of Social Capital*. Retrieved August 9, 2002, from http://www.prespect.org/print/V7/26/26-cnt2.html.

Lochner, K., I. Kawachi, and B. P. Kennedy. 1999. "Social Capital: A Guide to Its Measurement." *Health & Place* 5: 259–70.

Magdol, L., and D. R. Bessel. 2003. "Social Capital, Social Currency, and Portable Assets: The Impact of Residential Mobility on Exchanges of Social Support." *Personal Relationships* 10: 149–70.

Marston, S. A., and G. Towers. 1993. "Private Spaces and the Politics of Places: Spatioeconomic Restructuring and Community Organizing in Tuscon and El Paso." In R. Fisher and J. Kling, eds., *Mobilizing the Community: Local Politics in the Era of the Global City* (pp. 75–102). London: Sage Publications.

McAdam, D., and R. Paulsen. 1993. "Specifying the Relationship between Social Ties and Activism." *American Journal of Sociology* 99: 640–67.

McClaughry, J. 1997. "Bringing Power Back Home: Recreating Democracy on a Human Scale." In H. Hannum, ed., *People, Land, and Community* (pp. 133–41). New Haven: Yale University Press.

Mehrhoff, W. A. 1999. *Community Design: A Team Approach to Dynamic Community Systems*. London: Sage Publications.

Meurs, H., and R. Haaijer. 2001. "Spatial Structure and Mobility." *Transportation Research Part D: Transport and Environment* 6: 429.

Mier, R. 1995. "Economic Development and Infrastructure: Planning in the Context of Progressive Politics." In D. C. Perry, ed., *Building the Public City: The Politics, Governance, and Finance of Public Infrastructure* (pp. 71–102). London: Sage Publications.

Morrow, V. 2001. "Young People's Explanations and Experiences of Social Exclusion: Retrieving Bourdieu's Concept of Social Capital." *International Journal of Sociology and Social Policy* 21: 37–63.

New Hampshire Community Profiles: Canterbury. Retrieved March 8, 2003, from New Hampshire Employment Security Economic Labor and Information Bureau Web site: http://www.nhes.state.nh.us/elmi/htmlprofiles/pdfs/canterbury.pdf.

Oldenburg, R. 1999. *The Great Good Place: Cafés, Coffee Shops, Bookstores, Bars, Hair Salons, and Other Hangouts at the Heart of a Community*. New York: Marlowe and Company.

Olson, M., Jr. 1965. *The Logic of Collective Action: Public Goods and the Theory of Groups*. Cambridge, MA: Harvard University Press.

A Plan for Tomorrow: A Comprehensive Long-Range Plan. 1989. (Available from the Town of Canterbury, NH.) Presented by the Canterbury Planning Board.

Platt, R. H. 1996. *Land Use and Society: Geography, Law, and Public Policy*. Washington, DC: Island Press.

Ponting, C. 1991. *A Green History of the World: The Environment and the Collapse of Great Civilizations*. New York: St. Martin's Press.

Poplin, D. E. 1979. *Communities: A Survey of Theory and Methods of Research*. New York: Macmillan.

Porta, S. 1999. "The Community and Public Spaces: Ecological Thinking, Mobility and Social Life in the Open Spaces of the City of the Future." *Futures* 31: 437–56.

Portes, A. 1998. "Social Capital: Its Origins and Applications in Modern Sociology." *Annual Review of Sociology* 24: 1–24.

Putnam, R. D. 2000. *Bowling Alone: The Collapse and Revival of American Community*. New York: Simon and Schuster.

Richardson, J. 2000. *Partnerships in Communities: Reweaving the Fabric of Rural America*. Washington, DC: Island Press.

Rivlin, L. G. 1987. "The Neighborhood, Personal Identity, and Group Affiliations." In I. Altman and A. Wandersman, eds., *Human Behavior and Environment: Advances in Theory and Research* (pp. 1–34). New York: Plenum Press.

Roseland, M. 1998. *Toward Sustainable Communities: Resources for Citizens and Their Governments*. Gabriola Island, BC, Canada: New Society Publishers.

Rudd, M. A. 2000. "Live Long and Prosper: Collective Action, Social Capital and Social Vision." *Ecological Economics* 34: 131–44.

Sale, K. 2000. *Dwellers in the Land: The Bioregional Vision*. Athens: University of Georgia Press.

Sanders, S. R. 2000a. "Homeplace." From *Orion* (1992, Winter). In *Discussion Course on Discovering a Sense of Place* (pp. 2-8–2-10). (Available from the Northwest Earth Institute, 505 SW Sixth, Suite 1100, Portland, OR 97204.)

Sanders, S. R. 2000b. "Web of Life." (From *The Georgia Review* [1994].) In *Discussion Course on Discovering a Sense of Place* (pp. 6-3–6-4). (Available from the Northwest Earth Institute, 505 SW Sixth, Suite 1100, Portland, OR 97204.)

Schor, J. B. 1997. *Civic Engagement and Working Hours: Do Americans Really Have More Free Time than ever Before?* Paper presented at the Conference on Civic Engagement in American Democracy, Portland, ME, September.

Schorr, L. B. 1997. *Common Purpose: Strengthening Families and Neighborhoods to Rebuild America*. New York: Doubleday.

Stegner, W. 2000. "The Sense of Place." (From *Where the Bluebird Sings* [1992].) In *Discussion*

Course on Discovering a Sense of Place (pp. 1-3–1-6). (Available from the Northwest Earth Institute, 505 SW Sixth, Suite 1100, Portland, OR 97204.)

Suzuki, D., and A. McConnell. 1997. *The Sacred Balance: Rediscovering Our Place in Nature*. Vancouver: Greystone Books.

Wade, J. L. 1996. *Windows on the Future: The Two Worlds of Development*. Presidential address at the annual conference of the Community Development Society, Melbourne, Australia.

White, L. 2002. "Connection Matters: Exploring the Implications of Social Capital and Social Networks for Social Policy." *Systems Research and Behavioral Science* 19: 25–269.

8

Political Framework:
The Politics of Sprawl

David C. Soule

The management of growth in states and metropolitan areas waxes and wanes as a political issue. The intensity and timing of development, market forces, environmental threats, and the rapidity of change in a region are all indicators of the strength of "smart-growth movements." In other sections of this volume, we have discussed the legal and policy responses of states and localities to these forces (see chapters 3 and 4 in this volume). As a complement to the chapter on metropolitan politics (see Chapter 11 in this volume), which uses data and information to identify stress indicators (municipal and county fiscal capacity, poverty, racial segregation, etc.) to determine which types of communities might align themselves together to build a coalition to change laws and regulations, this discussion takes a look at traditional political theory and how these principles lend themselves to an analysis of the politics of sprawl.

This chapter explores the alignment of power to meet the conflicts that sprawl engenders. In its simplest iteration that is the nature of politics. Is there a conflict of significant enough proportions to require that governments create a new regime of laws and or regulations?

According to Janda et al., government is fundamentally:

the legitimate use of force . . . to control human behavior within territorial boundaries. Every government requires citizens to surrender some freedom to obtain the benefits it provides. There are three principal purposes of government:

1. *Maintaining order*: Preserving life and protecting private property
2. *Providing public goods*: Instituting projects that benefit all individuals but are not likely to be produced by the voluntary acts of individuals
3. *Promoting equality*: Redistributing income to promote economic equality or regulate behavior to promote social equality.[1]

ISSUES IN POLITICAL THEORY THAT AFFECT SPRAWL

While this volume makes no pretense of addressing the complexities of political theory, there are several important concepts that help frame sprawl in a political context. The first is *sovereignty*, defining the extent to which the regime (in this case local, county, and state governments) has the capacity to govern its own affairs without depending on another layer of government to empower them. As we have discussed in other chapters, in the American system, local (municipal/county) governments are creatures of the state and may, in most cases, only exercise powers specifically granted to them by their respective states. States on the other hand, have considerably more freedom under the U.S. Constitution to exercise broad powers in the system we call "federalism."

The second concept is *access* to the political process and to political leaders. Sprawl is essentially a local phenomenon, overseen by the land-use authorities defined in state law and local charters. Hence, since the power of these local agencies is exercised in town halls and county offices, citizens have considerably more access to the decision making and decision makers. Officials live and often work in the communities they serve, making them substantially more visible and accessible than state or federal officials.

Interest groups perform an important function in the American political system. They are "organized bodies of individuals who share some political goals and try to influence public policy decisions."[2] A number of groups have formed around the sprawl issue to compete with more established constituencies of business and development interests. Some of the groups specialize in land use concerns while other general interest groups including many environmental organizations have embraced sprawl as part of a larger (e.g., environmental) problem.

The political *agenda* is drawn from the set of issues that generate *conflict* between disparate groups. Competing groups seek to assert their solution to the conflict by proposing specific actions that can be taken to resolve the conflict in favor of their policy prescription.

Power is the capacity to impose a solution on a conflict. In the sprawl framework, as we has seen, there are significant constellations of forces and interests that engage in various aspects of the transactions that lead to changes in the landscape. More importantly, as we see in the sovereignty question, power is diffused throughout the intergovernmental system. Also, because sprawl is the result of thousands of small, incremental decisions by land owners and development interests, it is difficult to define the "levers" where power can be exercised.

Values and *ideology* affect individual and organizational responses to issues, conflict, the use of power, and the definition of "success." Values are the "lens" through which we perceive issues and evaluate policy responses. While deeply held, in many cases, their measurement is difficult. For example, many people would perceive that "quality of life" is an important value and improving it is an important policy. However, one person's definition of quality of life (a vibrant urban setting with 18 hours of active "street life") might be directly opposite to another's. Ideology is the organized assembly of values applied to a political strategy or philosophy. Our traditions tend to consolidate ideological positions into "liberal" and "conservative," but many issues in the sprawl debate are not easily isolated into one of these large "baskets." Ideological positions are likely to focus on the role of regulation, the rights and responsibilities of business, particularly the development sector, and the legitimacy of intensifying human settlement as a competitor to agricultural use or wildlife habitat.

Civil rights and *civil liberties* are important constitutional protections that override many other interests and prerogatives of citizens. In a sprawl context, the rights of property owners are a critical component of any regulatory regime. In the larger context, racial, ethnic, and income distinctions are important equity considerations that override, on occasion, the majority opinion on issues of exclusion, separation, and protection of property values. Paul Davidson, a noted city planner in the 1970s, questioned how the "police power" of the state can be used to promote wealth creation and racial segregation in local zoning regulations.[3]

Laws created by legislative bodies must be *enforced*. The land-use laws and regulations have the force of law and individuals may face sanctions for inappropriate uses of their property as defined by local ordinances. Equally important, local land-use decisions can be appealed to the courts by any party with standing. On rare occasions, these decisions make their way to the U.S. Supreme Court, particularly around issues of due process or overly aggressive regulation which is perceived as a "taking" under the Fifth Amendment.

Finally, the questions of *legitimacy* and *authority* are important political concepts that have resonance in the sprawl debate. Many of the forces affecting sprawl (economy, environment, social equity, and tax and infrastructure policy) operate at a level between the "layers" of government. They are regional, often spilling over political boundaries of states and localities. Therefore, there is a problem of governance that has not been worked out effectively in most states. There are several notable "experiments" in Oregon, Minnesota, Florida, and Maryland (see Chapter 3 in this volume). However, in the majority of cases, there is no "legitimate" government entity with the "authority" to deal comprehensively with these forces. That leads to a number of conflicts that cannot be resolved within the established regimes. The question of whether sprawl is a strong enough concern to create a new regime is discussed below.

URBAN POLITICAL THEORY

According to Harrigan and Vogel (2003), there are several theories in urban politics which might explain growth dynamics in metropolitan regions and the interests and forces that shape the debate. These include: the Growth Machine, Unitary Interest Theory, and Regime Theory. These theories consider various alignments among and between business and political leaders and citizen/civic groups within the community.

The Growth Machine

Espoused primarily by the sociologist Harvey Moltoch, much of what drives the economic and political interface in urban politics is the desire to grow rather than face decline. The business sector is bifurcated between firms doing business in the area—both export (basic) industries primarily doing business outside the local area and local (service) industries serving the local economy—and real estate/development businesses which make money converting land from one use to another. In "growth-machine theory" developers run the "place." The primary economic goal is to "grow our way to the future." This set of transactions—converting land from one use to another—takes place in the local (municipal, county) political environment under a legal regime primarily enabled by state government (see chapters 3 and 4 in this volume). The political conflict, therefore, is between the economic forces driving changes in land use and those seeking protection from these changes. While these "interests" may take traditional forms—development interests vs. neighborhoods—they are often more complex.

Unitary Interest Theory

Offered by Paul E. Peterson in 1981 in his book *City Limits*, Unitary Interest Theory posits that three sectors (business, government, civic) have a common (unitary) interest in making sure "export" industries grow and thrive. In this case, the focus is on jobs by growing the local economy and keeping it viable in an increasingly competitive environment. The real estate/development interests are a service function to the firms doing business outside the area. From this perspective, the land/real estate transaction is only one part, and often a small part, of the cost of doing business in a local area. Real estate interests align themselves with the larger economic interests to advocate land-use strategies emphasizing cost reduction (e.g., streamlining regulations, low taxes) as a way to "help" the overall regional advantage.

Regime Theory

Clarence Stone advocates a notion of "informal arrangements" between public and private interests that are in constant flux, depending on local conditions, particular issues, and the necessity of mixing the alignment of forces to accomplish a particular objective. As applied to urban/city politics, Regime Theory focuses on downtown development applying a progressive strategy to engage neighborhood interests in supporting a strong core, keeping the pressure off residential neighborhoods and, more importantly, keeping taxes lower on residential property.

TOWARD A POLITICAL THEORY OF SPRAWL

While urban political theory is helpful in identifying the constituencies and policy perspectives, it needs to be modified to deal with a land-use effect (sprawl) which crosses municipal boundaries and needs a regional or metropolitan geography to be measured and, presumably, managed. State geography is often too large and heterogeneous (urban, suburban, rural) to provide a proper context for a sprawl-management regime. However, states are the logical battleground for the political forces in conflict over the incremental effects of changing land use. Further, key infrastructure systems (highways, transit, water, and sewer) are laid out, built, controlled, and managed by state agencies or quasi-public authorities. Therefore, the politics of sprawl arc best understood as an interplay between state and local government regimes which, when effectively managed, might lend themselves to better outcomes.

Borrowing from the urban theorists, it is possible to create a hybrid theory of the politics of sprawl by defining a unitary interest in a regime that encounters, responds to, "regulates," and, consequently, successfully interacts with the growth machine by creating a governance system that balances competing claims for the use of power to resolve conflicts. This is, in effect, the strategy that is emerging in many regions around the country (see Chapter 19 in this volume). To begin to construct this theory, it is necessary to define the competing interests and then to determine an effective alignment of interests to change the outcomes of current land use practice and therefore to manage sprawl.

POLITICAL ISSUES AND CONFLICTS IN THE SPRAWL DEBATE

As we indicated above, conflict is the essence of politics. Conflict is engendered by competing responses to issues of public policy. In the sprawl debate, there are a number of issues that emerge. Since they are covered in detail in other sections of this volume, this discussion will simply identify the issue and the main themes.

Each of the issues discussed in other sections provides a rich mix of conflicts and an array of actors and interest groups that are engaged in developing and implementing strategic responses to the issues.

Loss of Land

One of the driving forces in the current sprawl debate is the consumption of land which would otherwise be available for agriculture or wildlife habitat. Over the past half-century, human settlement patterns have pushed denser residential, commercial, and industrial development beyond the fringe of metropolitan areas. Fueled by expanded highway access and cheaper land prices, more and more farms and natural areas are transformed into residential subdivisions, shopping malls, or office and industrial parks. While the land is not literally "lost," its previous use (agriculture, forestry, habitat) is transformed in a way that is irrecoverable. This leads to a perception of threats ranging from endangered species to loss of family farms to environmental threats (water, air, etc.) (see Chapter 13 in this volume).

Agricultural Issues

One of the most active interest groups in the sprawl debate is the American Farmland Trust (AFT). Partnering with a number of federal agencies such as the U.S. Department of Agriculture, AFT monitors the encroachment of urban and suburban development on rural and agricultural lands. AFT Vice President Edward Thompson Sr. argues:

> Not only does agricultural protection further smart growth, integral to smart growth is the protection of urban-influenced farmland. Sustainability begins— although it does not end—with the land that feeds us. The farmland closest to our cities and suburbs—the very land threatened by sprawl—is as important to American agriculture as any land in the nation.[4]

Environmentally Sensitive Issues

The integration of greenspace into the urban fabric is a long-standing principle of city and regional planning. Frederick Law Olmsted and many others understood the synergy between the natural and built environment. Blossoming in the United States at various times and in various ways (see Chapter 21 in this volume), buffering urban settlement and natural settings is a key strategy which helps shape urban growth and simultaneously protects environmentally sensitive lands. According to Blaha and Hamik, "Land conservation is an attractive complement precisely because it is non-prescriptive, market-based and enthusiastically supported by the public."[5] A fundamental underpinning of the modern environmental movement has been the identification and protection of wildlife habitat from human encroachment. Wetlands protection, coastal zone management, watershed management, biodiversity, and numerous other federal and state initiatives were created in response to the urbanization of the American landscape and have the externality of also defending against sprawl.

Pace of Development

Development in and of itself may not be of direct concern. In fact, properly managed, development is essential to the economic livelihood and prosperity we hold as an essential value in American society. However, as the economy cycles through periods of growth and the demand for land and labor increase, the sprawl debate intensifies. Further, with the accumulation of wealth, the preferred residential setting for families continues to be detached single-family houses on large lots. This places significant pressure on land, particularly near highways and in "greenfields" to be transformed. More significantly, the pace of land consumption in the last 50 years has accelerated at an alarming rate. According to one study:

> The conversion of raw land continued at such a pace, the land defined as "urbanized" in one region of Massachusetts grew at a rate 300% greater than experienced in all the years from Plymouth Rock to the atom bomb.[6]

Density

Nineteenth-and-twentieth-century planning, particularly in the United States, has linked density of development with unsavory adjectives such as unsafe, overcrowded, unhealthy, and even dangerous. Clearly, the early tenements in many urban settings legitimately met and exceeded these descriptions. The urban renewal programs of midcentury were built around bulldozing "slums" and eliminating concentrations of people, particularly poor people, in favor of opening large tracts of urban and suburban land for lower-density development. According to Robert Grow, architect and founder of Envision Utah and winner of the 2003 American Planning Association's award for excellence in planning:

> Americans have a problem with the concept of density. In other contexts, the word "dense" means crowded or, more importantly, "stupid!" We need to change our language if we are going to convince people that large lot subdivisions are not the only answer to family residential choice. In Utah, we never talk about density. Instead we reframe the discussion pointing to traditional family residential settings in neighborhoods where people meet each other on sidewalks, observe life from porches facing the street, and walk to neighborhood services including shopping, libraries, post offices, and even work.[7]

Transportation

The rational nexus between transportation access and land use is a well-established construct in local, regional, state, and, most recently, federal policy. In the past, transportation officials were often unwilling to accept that new or expanded transportation capacity would transform adjacent land uses. Transportation facilities performed a "service function" to land-use decisions made by local officials interacting with development interests. "Give me a land-use plan and I'll give you a transportation plan to serve it" was the norm. However, with the passage of the Intermodal Surface Transportation Efficiency Act (ISTEA) in 1990, the linkage between transportation and land use became a matter of federal law and policy. Richard Moe, in an address to city leaders in Boston in 1997, said:

> The decentralization was made possible by the development of new transportation and communication technologies. These new technologies have enabled twentieth-century America to do something unique in the history of Western civilization: We've turned our cities inside out, releasing industry, commerce and population from the core, leaving ruin and wasted investment behind. Henry Ford once said, "We shall solve the city problem by leaving the city." That was bad advice, but we're still following it.[8]

While planners struggle with the complexities of planning requirements that pit highway investments against mass-transit facilities and do battle with auto-dependent land uses, new opportunities for transit-oriented development give at least some practical strategies for sprawl opponents to introduce into the political debate.

Property

One of the strongest contrarian arguments in the sprawl debate focuses on the rights of private property owners. The constitutional protection of private property against "takings" by government entities without just compensation has led to a number of court cases, which question the validity of land use regulations. These court cases are summarized in Chapter 3 and point to a series of critical questions in the politics of sprawl.

Values

Property has value, which is enhanced (or diminished) by a variety of circumstances. Some governmental decisions increase the value of the land (infrastructure improvements, especially transportation access). That incremental value accrues primarily to the landholder. Several new taxation regimes (tax increment financing, value capture taxation) attempt to capture a portion of this value increase to finance additional improvements. However, overzealous land-use controls have met with aggressive challenges. One of the most recent is a ballot initiative passed in November 2004, which could roll back the benefits of the urban growth boundary in Oregon (see Chapter 3 in this volume). William Fischel argues that the municipal corporation is uniquely structured to protect property values because the people who are affected directly by the corporations actions—home owners—are the voters who decide how the corporation will act (Fischel, 2001).

INTEREST GROUPS

From this brief overview of issues, we can identify a set of interest groups who attempt to influence the decisions of the local, regional, and state officials who exercise some level of control, management, or regulation over land use. Local property owners and taxpayers drive much of the reaction to sprawl-management efforts. Concern over property values, tax rates on that property, impact of major budget items (especially public schools) drive the debate. Until recently, many advocates for smart growth and sustainable development have ignored this dynamic. This volume is the first compendium to bring the property tax nemesis to the fore as a key strategic component of the sprawl debate. Several states are beginning to take this one. In 2003, Connecticut issued a report of a legislative commission which was the first major report linking property tax issues to sprawl. In Massachusetts, a new law, Chapter 40-r of the statues, passed in 2004 and was signed into law by a Republican governor. It is the first attempt to tackle school-cost burden of housing in local communities reliant on the property tax. By tying state subsidies into smart-growth overlay districts, the state takes away a major argument for bringing affordable housing into suburban locations. By the state using transit-oriented development and village-center zones, strategies begin to emerge which make smart growth more realistic.

Business

As we discussed above in the outline of various political theories, the business community plays important and strategic roles in the sprawl debate. The general business community, chambers of commerce, and various sectoral business organizations (high-tech, etc.) are likely to be only peripherally engaged in the land-use discussion. As one business leader suggested in a private conversation, "The real estate decision is only about 4 percent of our cost structure. Labor, access to capital, regulatory costs, and access to transportation networks are more important to us."[9]

The more significant players in the business community are the development interests who make their living transforming the land from one use to another. The real estate interests interact with the sprawl debate from a straightforward analysis of the costs and benefits of growth management. These interests will engage immediately and aggressively if their economic well-being is threatened. They will perceive many of the sprawl prescriptions as antithetical to their interests. However, given the opportunity for nonideological debate, real estate interests can be a very positive force for re-investment in older industrial areas. These interests have lobbied for and supported brownfield revitalization, tax credits for renovation of historical properties, and tax increment financing.

Smart-Growth Advocates

Over the last five years, an impressive network of planners, environmentalists, community activists, and other organizations have banded together to expand and refine the "smart growth" message. A number of states have nonprofit organizations acting as consortia and alliances across this broad spectrum. A national group has formed—Smart Growth America—which has linkages to many national interest groups with a diverse constituency. The philanthropic community formed The Funders Network for Smart Growth and Livable Communities to assist in disseminating information to advise foundations on the effectiveness of various arguments. As noted above, The Funders Network has commissioned a series of "translation papers" that link smart growth to a series of other philanthropic initiatives including agricultural protection, greenspace acquisition, and social equity. Finally, a group has formed which monitors ballot initiatives across the country on state and local "smart growth" decisions. This inherently political action of bringing propositions to the voters is a key metric that has moved sprawl forward as an increasingly visible political issue.

Land Owners

Everyone who owns real property is concerned about other people or jurisdictions putting restrictions on the use of their land. Those same owners are equally concerned about noxious or nuisance uses on abutting land.

The constitutional protections against the taking of land by regulatory "confiscation" sets a boundary around legislation. There must be a reasonable connection (rational nexus) between the external effect of the use of land and the regulation of that activity (Kaiser et al., 1995).

Land Developers

Land developers have a different interest. They purchase raw land with the intent of converting it to more intense use (Diamond and Noonan, 1996). This activity produces significant wealth in the American society. Because land is bought and sold in private transactions, our legal framework favors the owner of the land (Galaty et al., 1994).

The legal basis of the entire planning and development system anticipates a continuing segregation of land uses (zoning) and a continuing division of land into smaller parcels (subdivision). If the policy prescriptions do not account for this fact, they will fail.

Abutters

Zoning is built around the "nuisance doctrine" and enforced by the police power of the state (Downs, 1973). The law gives the right to manage land use to the municipal corporation. The various boards seek opinions of abutters. Although abutters often have little legal standing beyond appearance and testimony, the Boston region is replete with intense responses by abutters to unwanted land uses.

The Role of the State

According to the U.S. Constitution, multiple powers are reserved to the states. Land use, although not specifically mentioned, is one of those powers. Through various structures, the state oversees the registration of land records (deeds, conveyances, etc.) and manages welfare, public safety, and courts and jails. However, by far the most important activity of the states, for this volume, is the creation of large infrastructure systems, most particularly the layout of major highways and transit systems. These decisions, as posited in the definition of sprawl used in this analysis, are critical to the types and rates of change in population and employment in the cities and towns.

Regional Governance Systems

Sprawl is a metropolitan dynamic. Cities and towns in the region are subjected to different pressures as intraregional migration takes place. Therefore, it is appropriate to consider whether greater than local management systems are in place to assist the state and the municipalities with this pressure. Counties are used in many parts of the country to create a more regional context for development. However, counties are weak (or nonexistent) in New England and, where they do exist, their geographies are so anachronistic that they are under pressure to dissolve. However, other regional structures are traditionally used to respond to greater than local concerns. Special-purpose districts such as port authorities, turnpike authorities, and metropolitan water and sewer commissions oversee major infrastructure systems. Regional councils (regional planning agencies, Councils of Governments, etc.) were established in the 1960s to allow for intermunicipal cooperation among cities and towns. For the most part these agencies are voluntary associations of local governments in a metropolitan region and are advisory. Several parts of the country (Cape Cod, Vermont, Florida, Oregon—see above) have created sophisticated regional land-management systems.

Nature of Local Government

Sprawl happens on the ground at the municipal level. The municipality or county is the smallest general-purpose governmental unit in most states. There are smaller (and larger) special-purpose districts which meet one particular need (fire, school, etc.), but local governments are the local taxing and legislative authorities. Municipalities are the building blocks of public safety, K–12 education, public works, tax assessment and collection, and other sundry functions. More important for this volume, local government is authorized to plan for and manage the use of land within its boundaries.

NOTES

1. Janda, 2001.
2. Ibid.
3. Private conversation.
4. Thompson, 2001, p. 1.
5. Blaha and Hamik, 2000, p. 4.
6. "Vision 2020" slide show for Southeastern Massachusetts.
7. Robert Grow, Speech to Alliance for Regional Stewardship, 2002.
8. Richard Moe, Speech to Boston 400, November 1, 1997.
9. Soule et al., 2004.

BIBLIOGRAPHY

Blaha, Katherine, and Peter Hamik. 2000. *Opportunities for Smarter Growth: Parks, Greenspace and Land Conservation.* Miami, FL: The Funders Network for Smart Growth and Livable Communities and The Trust for Public Land.

Chapin, F. Stuart, and Edward J. Kaiser. 1979. *Urban Land Use Planning.* 3rd ed. Urbana: University of Illinois Press.

Diamond, Henry L., and Patrick F. Noonan, eds. 1996. *Land Use in America.* Washington, DC: Island Press and Lincoln Institute of Land Policy.

Downs, Anthony. 1973. *Opening up the Suburbs: An Urban Strategy for America.* New Haven, CT: Yale University Press.

Fischel, William A. 2005. *The Homevoter Hypothesis: How Home Values Influence Local Government Taxation, School Finance, and Land-Use Policies.* Cambridge, MA: Harvard University Press.

Galaty, Fillmore W., Wellington J. Allaway, and Robert C. Kyle. 1994. *Modern Real Estate Practice.* 13th ed. Chicago: Real Estate Education Company.

Harrigan, John J., and Ronald K. Vogel. 2003. *Political Change in the Metropolis.* 7th ed. New York: Longman.

Janda, Kenneth, Jeffrey M. Berry, and Jerry Goldman. 2001. *The Challenge of Democracy: Government in America.* Boston: Houghton Mifflin.

Judd, Dennis R., and Paul Kantor, eds. 2002. *The Politics of Urban America: A Reader.* 3rd ed. New York: Longman.

Kaiser, Edward J., David R. Godschalk, and F. Stuart Chapin. 1995. *Urban Land Use Planning.* 4th ed. Chicago: University of Illinois Press.

Moltoch, Harvey. 1976. "The City as a Growth Machine: Toward a Political Economy of Place." *American Journal of Sociology* 82 (September): 309–32.

Peterson, Paul E. 1981. *City Limits.* Chicago: University of Chicago Press.

Soule, David, Joan Fitzgerald, and Barry Bluestone. 2004. *The Rebirth of Older Industrial Cities: Exciting Opportunities for Private Sector Investment.* Boston: The Center for Urban and Regional Policy at Northeastern University.

Stone, Clarence N. 1989. *Regime Politics: Governing Atlanta, 1964–1988.* Lawrence: University of Kansas Press.

Thompson, Edward J. 2001. *Agricultural Sustainability and Smart Growth.* Miami, FL: The Funders Network for Smart Growth and Livable Communities and The American Farmland Trust.

PART II

SPRAWL DYNAMICS

9

Real Estate Markets and Property Law

David C. Soule

REAL ESTATE MARKETS

Land use in whatever manifestation—sprawl or otherwise—is a complex phenomenon involving sophisticated land economics. Land markets are different for residential development than they are for commercial and industrial development. Land values are influenced by transportation access, by taxation, by regulatory regimes. These factors may restrict the supply of land available for development that will impact price. They may also make land that has greater access to infrastructure more desirable and therefore more valuable.

The price/value relationship is obvious in the purchase of a home—"I want to buy a home where, in addition to meeting my need for shelter, this asset will appreciate in value." People choose their residences based on their stage in the life cycle (single, married, parents, etc.). The residential real estate market is sensitive to the value of land, the cost of construction, the cost of money, and the various tax considerations packaged into federal (e.g., mortgage deduction), state (e.g., K–12 education subsidies), and local (e.g., property tax) systems (Case, 1986; Case and Cook, 1989).

This dynamic also operates in the location of businesses. Suburban and exurban land is cheaper than urban land, making it desirable if transportation access exists. Firms need to get their goods to market and their employees to work.

The two markets, housing and commercial development, intersect around one critical factor, the commutation requirements of workers—the jobs/housing balance (Cervero, 1989). This intersection provides an analytical framework for understanding how to intercede to change outcomes.

PROPERTY LAW

Real estate and property laws are inherent underpinnings of any land-management system and any land-use regulatory scheme. The transfer of property and its conversion from one use (forest, agriculture) to other uses (residential, commercial, or industrial) is the essence of a complex debate. It is important to understand property and real estate laws as separate from land-use regulation (see Chapter 3 in this volume).

Under the U.S. Constitution, numerous powers are reserved to the states. While property and real estate are not specifically itemized in the Constitution, the colonial mechanisms for owning and subdividing land were well established at the state level long before 1789 and continue to operate under state laws and regulations. Local governments, however, are creatures of the state. Under "Dillon's Rule" local governments (municipalities and counties) exercise only the powers explicitly granted to them by the states. Local ordinances and regulations must be developed under grants of power enabled by state legislatures and governors as interpreted by state courts.

Someone always owns the land. If an individual (or corporation) does not own it, then it is in the public domain, owned by one or more government agencies or corporations. Government has the right to dispose of its land holdings, which it does through a variety of mechanisms (Haar and Kayden, 1989). Throughout colonial America, the British government retained the right to confiscate real or personal property deemed necessary for government use. One example of this is the "king's arrow" burned on large pine trees and therefore reserved for the British Navy. However, the nature of the American Revolution requires us to insert one additional premise that protects in a unique way. As we discussed in Chapter 2, on federal policies, the Fifth and Fourteenth amendments create significant protections for the owners of private property that gives the real estate market significant permanent and speculative value.

Several other legal concepts expand the definition of private property in important ways. First, property comes with a bundle of rights. These include the "right to use," the "right to rent or sell," the "right to include in one's estate." More sophisticated rights include air rights (building height, sunlight access/restriction, and even viewscape), mineral rights (oil, coal, natural gas, and minerals underground), and timber harvesting. Other laws constrain these rights. Zoning and health laws restrict rights to use. Antidiscrimination laws restrict certain rights to rent or sell. Probate laws restrict inheritance. Further, some of the bundle of rights may separate from the property through restricted covenants, easements, and transfers of development rights (Galaty et al., 1994).

Land and buildings on the land as property are "real" assets, distinct from other "personal" property (furnishings, vehicles, etc.). They are a measure of wealth that is included is the estates of individuals. Real estate can be bought or sold as an asset, leased or rented, used as collateral to secure debt, and, subject to land-use regulations, used for residential, commercial, or other purposes.

Real estate regulation operates under a separate legal regime overseen by state laws but largely managed at the municipal or county level. *Deeds* are the legal instrument used to specify ownership (title) of the land and associated buildings on the land. Deeds are legal documents and public records "registered" with the appropriate recording office. Other legal documents may also exist to support various aspects of the land and buildings including surveys, plot plans when the land has been subdivided, location of structures and associated facilities (wells, septic systems, etc.), and easements. If the real estate has been used as collateral for debt, a *mortgage* is registered as well on behalf of the lien holder.

Residential Property

Ownership and transfer of property, which is used primarily for residential purposes, is a relatively simple transaction. In this country, it is the principal asset of most individuals and families. Throughout the last century, it has been the primary builder of personal wealth. Home ownership is the American dream widely touted by a broad coalition of homebuilders, real estate professionals, and government agencies at all levels. Owning a home is advocated as providing stability and "permanence" or at least longevity within a community. Generous tax deductions for mortgage interest and local property taxes provide significant subsidies to homeowners.

However, because of a number of flagrant abuses among unscrupulous financial institutions abusing consumers, and because of significant federal financial support and subsidies of the residential market, particularly in the postwar period, there are a number of federal laws that are used to supervise the transfer of residential property. Nondiscrimination, truth in lending, appraisals and structural inspections, and floodplain and property insurance are all required because federal agencies underwrite or guarantee the bulk of the residential mortgages in this country. While real estate licenses to realtors and brokers are issues by state authorities, all licensing exams require a working knowledge of these legal regimes.

Commercial Real Estate

Commercial transactions are more complicated. Land may be owned and developed by one party while the commercial enterprise is operated by another party. Multiple additional parties may be involved in the financing, providing the basis for a substantial and lucrative industry in this country. The basics are the same—deeds, other legal documents (surveys, inspections, appraisals, etc.), mortgages—and are public documents registered with the appropriate authorities. However, because the property is used to generate *income*, another sophisticated set of considerations is in place.

Many residential properties are, in fact, commercial enterprises because their sole purpose is to lease or rent the living space to generate income rather than to occupy it as an owner. Numerous state and local laws oversee the relationship between landlord and tenant, such as the health and safety considerations of the units (e.g., building codes, lead paint, etc.), eviction for nonpayment of rent or other abuses, and rent control. Some residential properties become hybrids between owner-occupied and rental units. The classic triple-decker in many cities allowed families to get a start by owning the entire structure, living in one unit and renting the others. During the later part of the twentieth century a number of rental properties converted to condominium ownership to reap the financial rewards of such conversions. Investors bought many units in these complexes as income-generating property.

The balance of the commercial real estate market is properties developed for retail, office, or industrial use. Each of these segments has specialized requirements too numerous to itemize here. A working knowledge of the "business" of commercial real estate is essential to understand the economic forces in land-use conversion. Without that, it is impossible to intervene in the sprawl debate and change the course of the discussion generically, or more importantly, on a specific site in play.

Development and Speculation

Real estate markets are regional in context. Commercial real estate markets are regional, but they are also segmented into "downtown," "suburban," and "speculative." The sprawl debate is essentially about the speculative market. Communities on the outer edge of the current urban/suburban definition often have large tracts of land in agricultural, forest, or other low-impact current use. Many states allow significant tax breaks to owners of parcels larger than 10 acres as a subsidy to retain the land in that current use (use value taxation). However, these laws also allow the owner to declare an intention to change the use, declining the continuing tax break and, occasionally, repaying a portion of or the entire subsidy. The land nearest the urban edge in a metropolitan region begins to increase in value as the laws of supply and demand begin to make it more advantageous to grow houses or shopping malls than corn or sugar maples. Public investment intended to service the additional demand, including roads, water, sewer, and schools, further increases the value of the land and the rate of conversion to more intensive uses.

As the market ripens, commercial real estate interests also monitor other changes in the area. The location of transportation systems, particularly highways, substantially increases the value of properties if there is an access point (curb-cut, highway interchange, transit station, rail freight capacity, and certainly a general aviation facility) or one can easily be created. Monitoring the properties receiving "use value" tax breaks and near these transportation connections gives insight into which lands might be most ready for purchase by commercial interests for development or speculation. As the properties come on the market, communities may choose to intervene through public purchase or restriction, or securing a private benefactor to place the land in trust.

Once the land changes hands to a developer or speculator, there is an entirely different motivation in using the land other than agriculture, forestry, or preservation. The land is now a commodity that must be converted to a higher or "better" use to reap the financial reward expected from developing the property. In most cases, this involves a change in local land-use regulation to allow the change in use. In some cases, communities have sent a signal to the market that they want and encourage this change. However, in other cases, current local residents perceive this development initiative as a hostile takeover and an imminent threat to the quality of life. This "battle" cost is a risk/reward calculation for the developer, which, properly calculated, is part of normal "due diligence" in the conversion process.

Because there are significant costs, but greater potential rewards, real estate investors have created a variety of legal instruments to capitalize this initial stage. Some combination of owner equity and commercial lending, similar to an individual purchasing a home, might create the initial framework for financing. However, a more common strategy is to create a pool of investors, frequently including institutional investors (e.g., pension funds) organize them into a real estate investment trust (REIT), and use multiple sources of capital to spread the risk and harvest the reward. The returns on these investments often outpace other investment strategies (stocks, bonds, etc.), and therefore real estate constitutes a component of many fiduciary investment vehicles.

Finally, because the real estate market is speculative, a great deal of the outcome depends on external factors beyond the control of the developer/owner. Many buildings are created in office parks or retail districts to meet a current demand. As the market changes, these complexes increase or decrease in value based on the commercial activity of the tenants. Leases are structured to accommodate these changes and balance the rent/income to meet current market conditions. Commercial indices read out these values in various segments of the market (downtown, suburban, "class A" office space, etc.) on a regular basis based on vacancy rates and square-foot costs of leases. As vacancy rates decline, lease costs rise, sending a signal that new construction may be appropriate. During the boom cycles significant overbuilding of speculative office and retail structures can take place that then lie fallow during the absorption periods that follow. Predicting these cycles is an art, not a science, but the prevailing wisdom is that there will be cycles.

Unfortunately for planners and smart-growth advocates, the public interest in "managing" growth is countercyclical. When things are heating up, people want to slow things down. When everything is slowing down, people, fearing for their jobs and livelihoods, demand a loosening of restrictions on development.

Public Interventions

There is often a public interest in maintaining land in its current condition, either as open space or as a means of retaining "community character" as development pressure builds. This may be for aesthetic or recreational purposes, and in more sophisticated land management systems this is a critical growth management tool. However, because of the constitutional protections against taking land without compensation, there are significant restrictions on the public's right to preservation.

Eminent domain is a process of securing private property for a valid public purpose. Money changes hands as the property comes under public control, but the public purpose overrides the private interest. Used extensively by urban pioneers such as Frederick Law Olmsted and Robert Moses, land was taken out of the private market for parks, roads, public buildings, and other public purposes. However, during the 1950s and 1960s, this strategy was used by urban renewal advocates such as Edward Logue, first director of the Boston Redevelopment Authority, for wholesale slum clearance for commercial development and highway construction. A public outcry arose leading to a substantial change in this strategy. The West End of Boston, an urban ethnic enclave destroyed in this period and memorialized in Herbert Gans's *The Urban Villagers* (1962), led to changes in the rights of neighborhood residents facing the bulldozers. The use (or threat of its use) of eminent domain to encourage private development is under new political scrutiny after a recent Supreme Court decision upheld the right of government to use this power to support private development.

Modern preservations of either neighborhoods or countrysides must now rely on raising the funds to purchase the property at fair market value. In recent years, this has been the strategy of choice of many states and localities seeking to preserve open lands as open space into perpetuity. It is the safest and most secure strategy available. However, it is expensive, and funds may be required when other equally compelling demands are placed on the public resources. Moreover, the properties for which funds are available are not necessarily those that best contribute to smart growth, as motivations (such as economic exclusivity) may be at work.

An alternative is to use gifts and philanthropic resources to purchase the land in trust. Tax laws are used to provide a level of return to the current owner that partially offsets the market value of the property. The land trust movement is one of the oldest and most successful land preservation movements in the country. Organizations like the Trust for Public Lands assemble capital through contributions and donations to purchase land protecting it by placing it into trust, conveying it to a government agency.

Another strategy used for various purposes includes creating an easement on the property. This removes one of the bundle of rights (right of exclusive use) and places a covenant on the land for a specific purpose. Used extensively by utility companies to locate a pipeline or catenaries for overhead wires, these easements allow access to land owned by others to maintain these utility systems. However, this strategy is also used to create conservation easements on private land to protect wetlands, wildlife habitat, and other environmentally sensitive land without requiring the public to purchase to property for protection.

NOTE

I would like to express my sincere appreciation to William G. "Buzz" Constable, Esq., of the A. W. Perry Company for his thoughtful editing of this chapter.

BIBLIOGRAPHY

Bowman, Ann O'M., and Richard C. Kearney. 2005. *State and Local Government*. 6th ed. Boston: Houghton Mifflin Company.

Case, Karl. 1986. *Economics and Tax Policy*. Cambridge, MA: Lincoln Institute of Land Policy.

Case, Karl, and Leah Cook. 1989. "The Distributional Effects of Housing Price Booms: Winners and Losers in Boston, 1980–88." *New England Economic Review, Federal Reserve Bank of Boston* (May/June): 3–12.

Cervero, Robert. 1989. "Jobs-Housing Balancing and Regional Mobility." *Journal of the American Planning Association* 55(2): 136–50.

Galaty, Fillmore W., Wellington J. Allaway, and Robert C. Kyle. 1994. *Modern Real Estate Practice*. 13th ed. Chicago: Real Estate Education Company.

Gans, Herbert J. 1962. *The Urban Villagers: Group and Class in the Life of Italian-Americans*. New York: The Free Press.

Geltner, David, and Norman G. Miller. 2001. *Commercial Real Estate Analysis and Investments*. Mason, OH: South-Western Publishing.

Haar, Charles M., and Jerold S. Kayden, eds. 1989. *Zoning and the American Dream: Promises Still to Keep*. Chicago: Planners Press of the American Planning Association.

Haar, Charles M., and Lance Liebman. 1985. *Property and Law*. 2nd ed. Boston: Little, Brown, and Company.

10

Transportation Systems:
Market Choices and
Fair Prices—Five Years of
Twin Cities Research

Curtis Johnson

SURPRISING ANSWERS ON CONGESTION AND SPRAWL

The Twin Cities metropolitan area of Minnesota emerged in the 1990s as a leading laboratory in which to study the effects of substantial growth in both commercial and residential development. As growth consumed land and spurred daily vehicle miles driven well beyond the rate of population increases, some obvious research questions were begging for clear answers. Could transportation infrastructure keep pace with or adapt to this pattern of growth? What investments would produce the most benefits and be affordable in view of expected public revenues? What are the social and environmental implications of the present pattern? And what are the policy options worth considering?

From 1997 to 2002 the Center for Transportation Studies at the University of Minnesota sponsored a series of 16 research projects, titled The Transportation and Regional Growth Study (TRG). These reports were designed to analyze the relationship of transportation and land use in a region approaching three million in population and to lay out policy alternatives that seem well supported by that research.

The TRG study—summarized in this chapter—explored the linkages between land use, community development, and transportation in the Twin Cities metropolitan area. It investigated how transportation-related alternatives might be used in the Twin Cities region to accommodate growth and the demand for travel while holding down the costs of transportation and maximizing the benefits. The costs of transportation are construed broadly and include the costs of public sector infrastructure, environmental costs, and those costs paid directly by individuals and firms. Benefits are also broadly construed. They include the gains consumers accrue from travel, the contribution of transportation and development to the economic vitality of the state, and the amenities associated with stable neighborhoods and communities.

These research studies, taken together, suggest two promising paths for new state and regional policy—moving toward truly honest pricing of transportation services and land development, and providing more choices than exist today for community development and travel modes.

New Growth Strains Old Policies

Serious traffic invaded the Twin Cities region in the 1990s. For a 40-year interlude, Minnesotans had the luxury of thinking of traffic the way winter residents in Arizona think of snow—as someone else's problem. As congestion on the metropolitan region's freeways and major roads increasingly undermined the region's long-enjoyed easy mobility, people began asking why this has happened and what can be done about it.

When people hear that today's traffic is merely the leading edge of an emerging future, one in which the residential population will swell by at least 700,000 over the next 20 years—over a million more within 30 years—they put tough questions to government officials: How did this problem get to this level? And what are you going to do about it?

Twin Cities residents are acquiring an attitude about traffic. This should not surprise anyone. The region has long been an easy place to get around. Land and water seemed in almost endless supply. Median income for a four-person household has soared, rising by 2000 to $70,500. That is, 13 percent above the national average and 64 percent higher than 1990. The region ranked seventeenth in the nation on this measure in 1990; today the rank is fifth.

Many families, feeling affluent, found the region's former farms and forests bursting with large new houses on spacious lots, a crop they eagerly harvested. Bargain-hunting families found more house for the buck at the edge, too. The result: a general spreading out, farther and farther from traditional employment centers.

Yet the region remains organized as though the metro area were only the seven counties designated in 1967. The actual region is somewhere between 19 and 24 counties, three or four of which are in Wisconsin. Applying the standard of including counties where 5 percent or more residents commute back inside the beltway, 24 counties would be in the metro orbit. Urbanization is spreading where it was never contemplated, resulting in increasing traffic on roads back to employment and commercial centers.

In its 2002 report on Urban Mobility, the Texas Transportation Institute said the Twin Cities is tied for second with the Atlanta region for the fastest rate of congestion growth. No one is saying the Twin Cities area has become Bangkok, or even Boston, but the Minnesota Department of Transportation (MnDOT) says 65 percent of freeway travel in the region now occurs under congested conditions. Worse, MnDOT says that vehicle miles traveled will increase by at least a third over the next 20 years, which will double today's experience in traffic delays.

The people of this region already know all this. Today's drivers may not be able to recite the number of congested lane miles, or ratios of travel delays, but they know they are stuck in traffic—a lot. And they don't like it.

The suburbs are home to the worst of more than two dozen bottleneck zones, where, nearly every workday, serious congestion is routine. Most bottlenecks are design problems, usually the result of limited original construction funds. Most have plausible cures. But current funding levels, MnDOT officials say, make it possible to take on only a third of those bottlenecks.

Meanwhile, the march outward continues. More business and commercial centers are built in the developing suburbs and beyond. Housing starts are highest farther from the metropolitan center, even as single-family detached home production recently became less than half the annual production. In general, though, the pattern remains vaguely true to the stereotypical American dream—as much house as a family can get, on as much ground as possible, for the lowest possible price.

Surveys over the last decade suggest a majority of households still prefer newer, low-density housing in middle-class suburbs to older, higher-density housing in mixed social-class neighborhoods close to the metropolitan center. The majority prefer detached houses to apartments or condominiums. They choose patterns that rely on automobile travel rather than public transit or walking. That said, it is equally true that this real estate model has been the predominating product in the market for the past half-century. Developers produced what experience suggested would sell best, and people bought what was available. The low-density, single-family subdivision, with all other land uses but churches and schools banned, became the norm. Mortgage financing and local zoning lined up to make it the way to go (Adams et al., 1998).

Three generations have experienced this pattern, with the effect that it seems like the way the world was meant to be. It's the norm now. And, in recent years, this development pattern has spread to rural counties surrounding the metro area, producing pockets of suburbanization that soon require services, from roads to sewers to schools.

The Builders Association of the Twin Cities, in a 1996 report that focused on 13 of the region's counties, called this spreading out "the random development of unsewered large lots and the non-contiguous, leapfrog development of sewered subdivisions that create physical and social barriers to the orderly and economical extension of urban services." The BATC report finds that this pattern raises the costs of urban services that are passed first to the developer but then shared with the housing consumer—and the public at large. The builders say this leapfrogging is the direct result of running out of land with access to urban services within the seven-county Metropolitan Council area. So builders and buyers push out to find affordable land friendly to development and let the consequences pile up for the next generation (Adams et al., 1998). The first taste of those consequences is today's traffic.

While the benefits of travel for most residents of the region continue to outweigh the burdens, congestion has undermined the expectations of enough people to become a major political issue. The legislature has already concluded that something must be done.

So, surely, something will be done. And that probability is the calling card for this body of research. Because even if legislators agree on what the problem is, they part paths on what has caused it and over what remedies would work. Did the state fail to keep up on road building? Were transit investments postponed too long? What solutions would now make any difference?

Getting to any plan of action fast runs into politics that demands quick and simple judgments, often at the expense of complex realities. Land-use choices and transportation investments are rather permanent decisions, the effects of which are difficult to reverse. The costs of transportation investments are usually very high and lead times very long; policymakers have to persuade citizens to pay for something long before the benefits can be demonstrated.

Yet the whole idea of urban planning, rather than leaving every decision to a presumably pure market, is that there are better and worse ways of organizing how land is developed and how people move around. The TRG research sought to cut through the fog of competing claims and inform the choices facing policymakers who must decide how to preserve the region's livability and competitiveness for the next generation.

What's the Problem?

Congestion, while it confirms the popularity of the Twin Cities area, poses a growing threat to the region's way of life and points to controversial issues in the community development system.

In one respect road congestion is a success story; it is visible evidence that a growing population has the money and motivation to go many places. Congestion—too many vehicles trying to pass through the same stretch of road at the same time—delivers daily confirmation that the region is growing, not declining.

Many of the most envied urban regions anywhere are congested places, and this has always been true. Congestion is a positive signal when long lines form for a great concert or museum exhibit, or crowds throng a retail and entertainment complex, or wonderful restaurants require advance reservations. Congestion outside on sidewalks is a good sign. Inside shops and restaurants, it's all *ka-ching* and merchants smiling.

On roads, however, congestion always attracts criticism. People forget that there was congestion before there were freeways. It used to take much longer to get from place to place. The addition of the freeway system dramatically expanded access for more people to more destinations. While occupying only 3 percent of the land in the region, the freeways now carry eight times the number of vehicle miles than the region transported before the freeway era.

Nonetheless, today's growing congestion challenges the region's competitiveness and its reputation as a good place to live. By 1970, 25 percent of the region's traffic converged daily on the 2 percent of its roads that were freeways. A quarter-century later, freeways were still just 2 percent of the region's roadway capacity, but they carried 44 percent of total traffic (Barnes and Davis, 1999).

Much of the region's economy depends on the efficiency of freight movements. More firms than ever rely on just-in-time inventories of parts and supplies, not to mention perishable goods. In this sector, time is money. If a UPS driver's route slows to half the usual efficiency, the company needs twice as many trucks and drivers to maintain the same level of service. The costs are not just a hit to the UPS budget; they spread over the economy. Over time, the region, which needs higher productivity to be competitive, finds itself with a comparative disadvantage (even though UPS volumes may reflect more ordering by phone or Internet and fewer shopping trips by car).

Or consider the possible plight of Fridley-based Medtronic—one of Minnesota's most successful research and manufacturing firms. If medical devices cannot be transported reliably and efficiently to MSP Airport, it becomes a growing cost to the company; if the situation becomes critical, why would Medtronic continue to manufacture these devices here? Since new road infrastructure is not keeping pace with growth, congestion strikes employers and citizens like a darkening cloud over the region's prosperity.

By 1997, during peak traffic periods, 35 percent of the freeway miles and 55 percent of the principal arterial miles in the seven-county area had traffic volumes exceeding the designed capacity (Barnes and Davis, 1999). Miles of congested freeway have grown from 72 in 1984 to 102 in 1994 and are expected to increase to 220 by 2020. Re-engineering bottleneck zones would bring some relief, and some roads seem clearly to need more lanes. But today's official 20-year transportation plans suggest that few government officials see massive new road construction as a cure for congestion.

Congestion is only a symptom. The problem is the "system" that sponsors a spread-out growth pattern coupled with nearly total dependence on personal vehicles. Today's problem is complex but not mysterious. A list of what the region has more of than before tells the story (Adams et al., 1999b):

- A rapid rise in number of households—reflecting everything from higher incomes and personal preferences to divorces.
- The trend toward more vehicles per household—the effects of multiple work destinations and teens owning cars (1.1 vehicles for every Minnesotan over 16).
- The increase in number of trips and length of trips—reflecting relative prosperity and the sheer distances between destinations resulting from a spreading out of the region.

Between 1970 and 1990 almost all the increase in automobile trip rates was attributable to more trips taken by women and by older men. Women joined the work force, men could drive into their later years, but both groups were generally discriminating in their use of automobiles. By contrast, succeeding generations have grown up in an atmosphere of easy use of cars, now the universal trip tool for most people and most trips. Retail centers, once fairly concentrated, spread with the region's growth. The shopping day got longer, and Sundays became yet another shopping day.

Further stimulating this dramatic increase in daily miles traveled each day was the sheer expansion in the number of jobs. Growth in jobs directly translates into more people with a need to get to work. As this created more income, more mobility was demanded. Car ownership continued to expand. And where there are cars, they will be used (Barnes and Davis, 1999).

The same period saw a dramatic decentralization in where work was done. Firms contracted for services to do accounting, clean buildings, or manage computer information. Services went to clients rather than the old way of clients traveling to service places. In sum, travel went up.

The initial freeway system, once completed, made 10-mile trips seem like five-mile trips. Speeds were fast and no stop signs interfered. People drove significantly more miles, but did not spend substantially more time doing it. Freeways seemed like pure pathways to progress. Time spent traveling became more important than miles, and it still is.

Bus service, always caught in the vagaries of legislative appropriations, cannot keep pace with the development pattern. And though proposals for rail or light-rail routes to provide alternatives in certain corridors came and went for 30 years, nothing was approved until the mid-1990s, when the legislature agreed to matching federal, county, and airport authority funding for a light rail-line extending from the Mall of America to downtown Minneapolis along Hiawatha Avenue. In general, though, funding for transit fell behind the pace of development.

Today's traffic scene looks like this (Barnes and Davis, 1999):

- Work trips are longer, when measured in miles, though only slightly longer when measured in minutes.
- Transit works best headed for downtowns or other major employment centers. Because auto use has increased so much, the share of trips served by transit has dropped to roughly the national average—2.5 percent of all trips, 5.2 percent of work trips, and 25 percent of all trips into central business districts. Walking and biking to work claim about 4 percent. The number of people per car at peak times, 1.12, is only slightly higher today than in 1948, suggested that driving alone has long been a Twin Cities habit.
- Work trips are complicated by trip "chaining," as people add stops to pick up children at day care, to collect the dry cleaning, to mail a package (though these are minor miles compared with work trips).
- The size and duration of the evening peak, by 1990, was higher than the highest point of the morning rush time, and the majority of trips are not work-related.

That portion of trips that are not work trips carry important policy implications, if there is potential for spreading them out across the day and evening. Certainly, when congestion reaches a tipping point, drivers seem to find other routes or other times of day. Before long, though, that mid-day trough, when congestion traditionally took a break, will just disappear.

While travel into the central business districts has continued to grow, the growth rate to suburban destinations has been faster. In one sense, the market registered the central business districts as "full," while the suburbs seemed still relatively empty. Growth goes to places not already full.

A "chicken-and-egg" type debate rages among analysts as to whether accommodating the automobile has led to inefficient land uses (such as spread-out office or commercial centers, and relatively few houses on large tracts of land) or whether inefficient uses of land have generated the longer, less direct trips. What seems undeniable, though, is that decisions about where to live and work and shop all have something to do with the travel equation. People are responding to the implied incentives in the land-use and transportation system.

The market, among developers and buyers, drivers and riders, is always incentive-driven. The evidence is transparent in every major decision about land-use and transportation investments. Interacting back and forth, they form a continuing process of "circular and cumulative causation" (Adams et al., 1999b). The land development/transportation problem has no simple cure.

Regardless of cause, this region is headed toward a point where the difference in traffic between peak times and nonpeak times will be insignificant. Roads will fill and stay filled. Once a highway is full, it cannot really get fuller—it can only stay fuller longer (Barnes and Davis, 1999).

First people sense "diminishing returns." Their trip times are less certain. Then it feels like the system has hit the wall, with seeming suddenness. To illustrate this, assume that lily pads in a pond, consuming water and space, tend to reproduce by doubling each day. On one inevitable day, they cover up half the pond; the next morning, it's the entire pond. And it seems like a surprise (Ward et al., 1998).

Of course most people assume that if a road is full, lanes can be added, and if that proves insufficient, more roads can be built to take the excess demand. Back when the freeways were built, expectations of an easy mobility were permanently packed into the new and wide roadbeds. Low fuel prices still make auto travel seem inexpensive. So, naturally, many people conclude that expanding road capacity is a sure cure.

Increasingly, transportation officials representing the region and the state advise against this convenient optimism. They cite problems with acquiring right-of-way for expansion, now enormously more difficult in the already built-up areas. And the cost of acquisitions, compounded by the regulatory steps through which any construction must navigate, produces staggering estimates for significant expansion of road capacity. They point out that almost every dollar now projected over the next 20 years to MnDOT may well be needed just to care for the system already in place. The interstates, built between the 1950s and the 1970s, have a working life of about 30 years. It is obvious that many sections of this system are wearing out.

Even if money were not a problem, officials say, adding lanes and roads is no panacea for the congestion pain ahead. Almost at the moment that new capacity shows up, so do a host of drivers who have been using other routes or other modes of travel (such as buses or vanpools), or who have been traveling at other times of day to avoid the jams. A new road also attracts "new" drivers, seeing opportunities for travel not seen before. For some period of course, this behavior must be releasing capacity elsewhere, making it easier to travel other routes. But in the zone of greatest concern—on major freeways—it is now common for people to wonder why adding lanes did not deliver as much relief as people expected.

There are only three classic remedies (Barnes and Davis, 1999):

1. *Add more lanes, more roads.* Case in point: spend the one to two billion dollars it will take to add a lane to the I-494/694 beltway. The trouble is, the effects are not simple. If two lanes run each way and two more are added, twice the lanes should be twice the throughput; but often, this increase has the hydraulic effect of building a greater mass, which transfers the congestion to another stretch not designed to handle it. Or it induces so many people to use the road who had not previously that the remedy is nullified.

   On the other hand, it is undeniable that at present the metro areas in the United States with the least congestion are the ones with the greatest number of lane miles per capita (think Kansas City or San Antonio), suggesting that, at least technically, it is possible to "build your way out of congestion." Others say those regions merely have excess capacity awaiting the impact of serious growth pressure and that the Twin Cities region would not have today's problem if it had not become a growth center.

2. *Restore the capacity for faster travel.* Redesign the use of existing freeways and major arterials for higher speeds, either by grade separations or reducing access points so that only longer-trip users qualify. Either of these interventions, when proposed, generates considerable controversy, even for a freeway corridor.

3. *Reduce demand.* This approach turns the issue on its head by suggesting demand for using the road capacity, at least at certain times of day, can be substantially reduced. Here an increased investment in transit has a role. By building convenient transit choices in zones of the region's highest densities, those who prefer riding to driving might switch, for some trips. New choices, however, constitute no warranty against congestion, as the road capacity released may fill up rapidly. And, if the transit service is popular, it becomes its own zone of congestion.

So perhaps the fundamental issue is not to reduce congestion, but to provide choices and improve accessibility. Congestion, in large part, has to do with the number of people trying to access popular destinations, whether for work trips, errands, or pleasure. Transit provides another means of access to major destinations.

A policy of "value pricing," charging a fee to use uncongested lanes in traffic-clogged corridors, is slowly spreading in regions around the world that are coping with rising peak traffic loads, with the fees collected often dedicated to redesigning bottleneck zones or for improved transit, or both.

A major issue for continuing research also lingers here. In a policy environment that encouraged and rewarded closer grouping of these destinations (often described as "higher densities"), would the market respond with more people living in and near these zones and making a significant share of trips without using an automobile? This research suggests that activity-rich commercial zones have that potential (Barnes and Davis, 1999).

Transit can be used surgically to provide choices and strategically to induce new development patterns, but it will not significantly reduce congestion.

When measured in 1990, 90 percent of all trips in the region were made using automobiles, which is roughly at the national average for metropolitan areas. As noted earlier, transit carried 2.5 percent of all trips, though, significantly for the congestion challenge, 5.2 percent of all work trips and 25 percent of all work trips headed for the central business districts (Barnes and Davis, 1999).

Transit, at its peak share, carried 25 percent of all trips back in 1949 (about a third of which consisted of school buses). In raw numbers, transit has held its own, but the population has tripled. The Metropolitan Council current policy features a commitment to double transit capacity in the next 20 years. If that is done, depending on how and where that capacity is deployed, it is conceivable that transit could, if not significantly alleviate congestion in the zones of greatest urban density, at least provide better choices than people have today for getting where they want to go.

Transit advocates point to two primary assets: efficiency—more carrying-capacity than cars—and equity—a minimal provision of accessibility to critical destinations for people who do not own a car. The "efficiency" point is generally persuasive for peak-hours conditions, if the service is convenient and frequent and goes where the demand is. However, when the service does not meet those standards, and attracts few riders, the efficiency argument falls flat. Transit run as a public service is often forced to provide a large vehicle for a small number of people at the edges of the travel day, as an equity policy. It is not clear that bus or rail service is an efficient response to this need.

Rail is the subject of long-running Twin Cities debate, made all the more lively by the approval and current construction of the Hiawatha light rail line. Advocates point to lower energy costs and emissions for operating rail, and, in the case of the Hiawatha line, to potential community redevelopment impact. Critics point to the capital costs per rider and to energy consumption during construction and say it will take 50 years to break even on energy (Barnes and Davis, 1999).

Commuter rail, passenger cars on regular heavy-gauge train tracks (usually shared with freight traffic), can claim lower capital costs, but operating costs are sufficiently significant as to require large subsidies, and hence, produce troublesome politics. Supporters point to places such as Chicago, where commuter rail is a popular option for suburban communities, many of which have residential densities comparable to those in the Twin Cities region.

Carpooling, theoretically a slam-dunk success, runs headlong into preferences for privacy and real needs for scheduling flexibility. Lanes reserved for carpools are underutilized and thus under constant criticism.

The ultimate low-capital approach is, of course, more facilities friendly to walking and biking. Here weather is the big discourager, despite resurgent attention to the health effects of more exercise. Support for these facilities is passionate but pales beside the dominant car culture. While walking and biking claim 20 percent or more of commute trips in some cities (mostly smaller ones) of northern Europe, for example, they generate less than 1 percent of commute trips in the Twin Cities region (Barnes and Davis, 2001).

Buses, given a dedicated right-of-way, can compete even with rail at providing superior service, and could play a significant role in expanding choices for mobility and accessibility. The region has become richer, on average, but it is also a proven magnet for immigrants, many of whom take the most menial jobs and need public transportation. The historic problem has been a steady reluctance to build and operate a significantly better bus service. Playing the dark-horse role in this script of uncertainties is something called PRT—Personal Rapid Transit. PRT, neither an auto nor a train, but a small vehicle running on a single elevated rail, might play a circulation role in defined zones. But it is as yet an unproven technology.

Despite these prospects, the forecast for travel growth is a formidable factor. By 2020, there will be at least 29 percent more trips taken daily in the core seven counties of the region, at 14 percent greater average length. Multiplying these two variables produces a forecast of 46 percent more daily vehicle miles traveled than was true in 1995 (Barnes and Davis, 1999). These forecasts are, of course, assumptions, not facts. But they are assumptions rooted in the tenacious trends of the past half-century, which suggest that development densities will continue to decline while population grows. If so, trip lengths and miles traveled will continue its march up the charts.

The future impact of greater congestion on this trend is the key issue to debate, however. The prospect of higher speeds, and the ease of getting to farther-away places, have given us today's land-use and travel patterns. As more roads fill up and traffic slows down, will the incentives shift toward working and shopping closer to home? Even so, there is no basis on which to project more people using transit unless transit service becomes something that it is not today. Should transit service become more extensive and more convenient to users, the balance of trips could shift. But the pessimists will win this argument if the preponderance of new jobs continues to show up in outlying metropolitan locations (Neckar, 2003).

Research also shows that, while they are necessary and useful in data analysis, averages can mislead, forming a statistical mask over important differences. Averages on road congestion projections might seem unduly optimistic, mixing in many roads not yet under traffic pressure with a few critical corridors choking on traffic. Conversely, averages might understate the potential for transit to play a significant role. To the degree that exclusive corridors for rail or buses form an integrated pattern within the densest zones of the metro area, they might serve not only as serious alternatives on transportation but provide incentives for more employment and commercial locations, thus altering the historic land-use pattern. Recent experience in other regions shows high densities building up around effective transit corridors. Obviously, zoning policy that forces separation of housing and employment and shopping forces the number of vehicle trips higher. Zoning changes toward mixed use create opportunities and choices. In any event, without an unprecedented investment in transit, the forecast becomes self-fulfilling. By 2020, the zone served by the circumferential freeways will be fully congested.

"Negative Externalities": Another Bundle of Bad News

If you are a driver enjoying abundant accessibility to all those places you want to go in as efficient a time as possible, you may declare the system a success. However, if you live near a roaring concrete canyon of cars whose drivers are enjoying their rights of efficiency, you may appreciate it less. The noise is irritating and the emissions worrisome. It's that old principle again—that one person's opportunities are another's burden.

Economists and transportation planners define these adverse effects, these by-products of a benefit enjoyed by those who use a service, as "negative externalities." In the road system, that includes noise, pollution, sometimes just the visual sacrifice of seeing a crowded roadway where once there may have been trees and tranquility. (It is worth remembering, of course, that horses on dirt roads also generated negative externalities.)

Nearly every one identifies these downsides to the automobile and roadway system. But there is another one, particularly sensitive to Minnesotans, for whom lakes and rivers are virtually a sacred resource. As development covers more of the region's land, the danger to water may loom as the largest threat. Research reveals how much the "DNA" of the conventional suburban development necessitates large commitments of concrete and asphalt for principal arterials, collector roads, neighborhood roads, and, of course, driveways. The by-product is chemical pollution from engine emissions and road maintenance products, even dust particles from tire wear.

Large residential lawns are kept green by chemicals laden with organic and toxic residues that run off when it rains. In addition, development brings the strip malls, the clinics and car shops, schools, and fast-food establishments—all surrounded by large parking lots. The spreading infrastructure covers surfaces, reducing the porosity of the ground, and diminishes the recharging of the underground aquifer supply. And when it rains and water runs off or through storm drainage systems, it carries the chemistry of modern living—nitrogen, geneterovirals, and road salts—straight into the surface-water system of the region. The Mississippi River watershed supplies 75 percent of the region's drinking water. Minneapolis, St. Paul, and several suburbs draw all their drinking water from surface sources. More than 100 other suburban communities compete for a share of the Prairie du Chien aquifer, on which the region also relies to replenish the streams that feed principal rivers (Neckar, 2003). It is now common also to see newspaper articles citing nanoparticles from diesel emissions as likely causes of the surge in the incidence of asthma and other pulmonary diseases.

So there are multiple burdens borne by everyone, by-products of the benefits enjoyed by users of the system. By what means could these externalities be met? There are three main ways (Barnes and Davis, 1999):

1. *Reduce access.* Limit the number of places easy to get to, with the result that fewer miles (theoretically) are driven. Politically, this is a nonstarter. And, like many solutions, it is too simple. Externalities are not mere functions of how many miles are driven. For example, a new car might be driven dozens of miles and produce less pollution than an old one with worn-out emission controls in just one mile. "Where" also matters. Slow, congested driving in a densely populated zone has more negative impact than getting up to speed in the countryside.

2. *Rely on technological innovation.* A second approach has demonstrated more potential for impact: technological innovation. Go to Mexico City or San José, Costa Rica, or any number of metropolitan areas where the vehicle fleet is not technologically up to date. The difference is palpable. Forty years of innovation makes it possible to have cars in U.S. cities and still breathe the air. Even in the United States, though, technology has not guaranteed good air. For example, pollution in the Atlanta region in the 1990s, along with severe congestion, forced a radical reform in regional planning for transportation and land use.

3. *Soften the impacts.* A third way is to use all sorts of mitigating measures. Noise barriers on freeways, for example, reduce the sounds emanating from the traffic. In neighborhoods, though often controversial, traffic-calming devices such as speed bumps or small roundabouts at intersections reduce speeds as well as noise.

Air and water quality are likely to become increasingly sensitive subjects on the Twin Cities political scene. Occasionally there are rumblings about this region skirting the edge of the Environmental Protection Agency's nonattainment threshold for air quality. And while the connection between spreading, low-density development and water quality does not seem firmly set in the minds of most Minnesotans, it is an issue whose time is coming.

Reaching the Limits of Current Conditions

Congestion, something that Twin Cities area residents could for so long conveniently associate with other places, has taken up permanent residence in this region. Even with more roadway capacity, congestion will get worse.

Major investment in transit might have some mitigating effect, but only if it offers trip times competitive with the automobile; if you have to wait longer for a ride than it takes to drive, most people will drive. Transit's largest role may be to provide choices about ways to get around in some parts of the region. Think of the urban regions with effective transit services; they are still congested places. But like good and bad cholesterol, it matters whether you have the "good" congestion.

Land-use practices also have consequences and limits. The spread-out, low-density pattern of development—especially commercial development—brought some costs

Figure 10.1
Limits to Growth

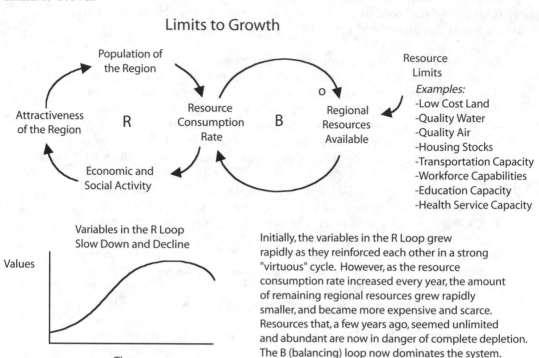

Limits to Growth

Variables in the R Loop
Slow Down and Decline

Initially, the variables in the R Loop grew rapidly as they reinforced each other in a strong "virtuous" cycle. However, as the resource consumption rate increased every year, the amount of remaining regional resources grew rapidly smaller, and became more expensive and scarce. Resources that, a few years ago, seemed unlimited and abundant are now in danger of complete depletion. The B (balancing) loop now dominates the system.

Options to sustain high levels of overall attractiveness include: (a) Raise or eliminate the limits, (b) reduce or stall the population of the region by deciding how to make the region less attractive to residents that have or will have a relatively high resource consumption rate, or (c) reduce the level of economic and social activity by imposing regulations or policies that make it more difficult to do marginal business or sustain pleasant social interchange.

that were not advertised. Beyond congestion, there are now serious threats to air and water quality. All the mitigating measures imagined by planners today are costly. Even the system as it stands cannot be afforded into the future on the financing model the state and region has today. People have not changed their travel behavior significantly, largely because the time it takes for daily journeys has not yet exceeded their tolerances. But that may soon change.

Perhaps the region is finding its own version of limits to growth. Of the million more people expected in the next 30 years, most of those would be the sons and daughters of existing residents. So, whether to grow is not the question (Adams et al., 2002). The "limits" question is whether the region, because of its past decisions on development and transportation patterns, now faces a choice among inherently unattractive options. By analogy, if the region were a business, one might say there is a problem with the convenience or attractiveness of the product. Shall we improve the product and raise prices to pay for the improvement, on the grounds that our customers will appreciate and pay for the solution? Or do we advertise that it isn't perfect but it's not very expensive? None of these choices is very appealing.

As Figure 10.1 illustrates, at some tipping point a combination of conditions start to drag down the quality of life. It is at the point that the hardest choices have to be made (Ward et al., 1998).

WHAT ARE THE UNDERLYING CAUSES?

Anyone listening to the political debate over land use and transportation will surely hear the claim that today's pattern is the result of natural market forces. People made choices about where to live and how they would get from place to place. Developers produced housing where they could make a profit, delivering products experience taught them would sell. People buying homes chose from what was available and that reinforced the "wisdom" of the market.

Underneath that superficial rendering of market behavior, however, is a serious subterranean set of causes. The incentives in the tax code, the influence of zoning ordinances, and the myriad land- and housing-development rules and regulations compose a system that encourages additional development of low-density suburban areas and discourages investment in the redevelopment of the older parts of the region. Despite the modest effects of Minnesota's tax-base sharing law and the highly redistributive character of the state's fiscal policies, this incentive system wages a strong and durable influence over development patterns. Money for roads seems consistently tilted toward high-speed arterials. It is doubtful that state and regional policies were built as an intentional strategy for low-density development. But neither are the effects accidental. They are the direct result of the composite policies of the state and region (Adams et al., 2003).

The Twin Cities area has a history of low density. Today's larger lots and spread-out development are not a trend shift, but a continuation of historical patterns.

Low density, ironically, has its roots in the best transit era the region has known. In a long stretch of Twin Cities' history, from the late 1880s to the 1920s, streetcar service operated on more than 500 miles of tracks (Adams et al., 2003). Streets were lined with shops and offices, producing enough density around streetcar stations to make transit a popular service. So successful was this service that its owners, then private parties, developed extravagant expectations for the system. They overbuilt. In the wake of this overbuilding, landowners sold larger-lot parcels, locking in a land-use destiny for the region as a lower-density place.

Soon after, of course, came the surging dominance of the automobile as the principal mode of travel. Money flowed to road building. The interstate system emerged and freeways arrived in the Twin Cities, vastly increasing the commuting reach of Minnesota's workers and setting off a dispersal of major employment centers. People moved for opportunity, and employers followed. Commercial and retail investments followed where people went. Everyone enjoyed the near-term benefits of cheaper land and easy commutes. For a long time, this formula worked well enough.

REGIONAL POLICIES: ENCOURAGING LOW-DENSITY AND SPREAD-OUT DEVELOPMENT

The relative absence of natural barriers such as mountains or an ocean, combined with an abundance of good roads, gave nearly ceaseless encouragement to the outward spread of homes and jobs. Besides, it was the driving force in the development culture. From the corporate boardroom to the priorities of "highway" departments to the images in *House Beautiful* magazine, the larger home on the spacious lot away from other activities was the goal that drove growth (Neckar, 2003).

Since the formation of the Metropolitan Council in 1967, it has been a regional responsibility to manage this growth in an orderly fashion. The Council's tools have principally been the rate at which sewer interceptors are provided to deliver urban wastewater treatment service; and the power to determine the allocation of federal highway money that comes to the region. For about 20 years, this produced a slow but steady expansion of what was called the Metropolitan Urban Service Area, with most of the growth added contiguously. However, still relatively inexpensive fuel prices, combined with rising prices for land inside the MUSA, stimulated a market for urban development beyond the seven-county jurisdiction of the Council. Where river crossings slowed growth, new bridges were added. In recent years, this farther-out development in so-called collar counties accounted for a rising share of the new building permits. By 2001 permits for new housing in outlying counties were 25 percent of the total for the 19-county area.

The real estate market shows that a majority of people in the home-buying market still prefer newer, larger houses on bigger lots. A minority prefer smaller, older, denser situations. As is often said, this market is a quest for closets and bathrooms (bigger and better ones) combined with the will to drive farther to qualify for loans. But when three submarkets were subjected to a 25-year analysis of how housing prices change, it turns out that property value increases greater than inflation accrue disproportionately to the newer/larger home model (Adams et al., 1998). To be sure, demographic shifts, such as an influx of immigrants, change the patterns, as does an outflow of retirees. And other conditions influence home-location decisions, such as perceptions of the quality of schools or the safety of neighborhoods. But if property taxes for a similarly situated home in a newer, outer area are lower than its cousin in the center of the region, is that not a "capitalized" tax differential that is simply not fair?

A similar question applies to charges for basic infrastructure. If the charge to join the wastewater treatment system for new users is less than the marginal cost to the public to provide the service, is that fair? Compared to what, one might ask? Previous regional research has concluded that houses—and businesses—in the core of the region actually pay more than the marginal costs for providing sewer services. So if data also indicate that newer, larger homes on larger lots are enjoying appreciation in property values more rapid than those which are smaller and older nearer the region's center, then state and regional policy would certainly appear to be punitive to the latter group and to be giving a break to homebuyers who, on average, appear to be among the most affluent (Adams et al., 1998). That these policies and practices have influenced the development pattern in the Twin Cities seems clear enough.

Local governments play the predominant role in land development. Their zoning ordinances and development rules favor a low-density, generally homogeneous pattern in which homes are separated from all other uses except for churches and schools and lower-priced housing is discouraged.

Local communities, while they create comprehensive land-use plans that are reviewed (by the Metropolitan Council) for compatibility with the prevailing regional framework, still hold most of the cards in determining development patterns. But no community can develop in a way that avoids impact on other communities. The location of commercial activity affects traffic patterns. Communities draw on common and finite sources of capital for schools, sewers, and roads (Neckar, 2003).

Local governments also draw commercial and industrial operations from older locations to newer ones. Since commercial enterprises pay higher rates of property taxes than do homeowners, having a healthy mix of commercial property owners in the tax base is a prized objective in all but the wealthiest communities of the region. Cities that still have land supply and the political will to develop it deploy a formidable arsenal of assets, such as:

- Still abundant stretches of land that are easier and cheaper to develop than tackling tight sites, brownfields, and sometimes excessive bureaucracy in core cities.
- The relatively higher costs of rehabilitating existing structures compared with starting freshly, compounded by even more costs if any properties have "historic" designation (though sometimes mitigated by tax credits).
- Environmental regulations that are often more flexible in the developing suburbs.
- A market preference for suburban amenities, coupled with a majority preference for living in newly developed communities nearby.
- Free (or at least not directly charged to the user) parking.
- The increasing number of enterprises not requiring proximity to their suppliers or customers.
- Public subsidies—ranging from provision of tax-exempt industrial revenue bonds to uses of Tax Increment Financing.

The steady decentralization of commercial, light industry, and retail enterprises scatters the major employment sites in a pattern nearly guaranteeing more scattering of the population and more driving in total to access necessary daily destinations. These commercial-industrial zones are powerful centrifugal development forces, more so than building housing subdivisions at the edge.

Then there are zoning ordinances. These local "laws" directly affect, as they are intended to, the physical impact of development on the land patterns and the affordability of homes in that community. Zoning ordinances often specify a long list of constraining requirements, designed in sum to produce predictability to the nature and quality of development the community experiences. These ordinances now typically spell out minimum lot widths and sizes, minimum floor areas for a single-family residence, and minimum number of garage spaces. Then add the standardization of product imposed by the mortgage financing industry. The visual result is a pattern of homes that look very much alike in size if not style; and, a relative scarcity of homes that are affordable to people making less than median household incomes. While land prices in some areas of the region have constrained lot sizes, in general the low-density ratio retains its tenacious hold on the region's housing pattern.

City officials, when they get pressure for more diversity of pricing in houses, characteristically point out that they have to rely on the property tax source for most urban services and that lower-valued homes tend to cost a city more for services than the city can collect in taxes. (And, for school districts, this tax math can be even harsher, if the average household has one or more school-age children on whom several thousand local dollars must be spent each year.) So, in some communities, this revenue-effect becomes a stubborn standard for maintaining minimum specifications and giving a clear preference to developing upper-bracket homes.

Enabling this pattern is of course the provision of sewer capacity, the capital cost of which were, for a generation starting in the mid-1960s, paid in large part by the federal government as part of the effort to improve water quality. But since the last decade or so, the costs fall entirely to the region and sometimes the state. That the dollars are regional puts a decidedly different edge on the equity question: if it costs more per unit to provide sewer services in a low-density development pattern, are those marginally higher costs recouped? If they are not, why is the region subsidizing this more costly form of development?

Roads are often the initial "enablers." Built from funds that federal, state, and county taxpayers have provided, they essentially open up areas for profitable development and homeownership opportunities. Publicly provided sewer pipes often run right along the same right-of-way corridor. When buyers realize a gain on their properties that exceeds the rate of inflation in these newer areas, they are in essence pocketing a wealth transfer from their fellow taxpayers, some of whom may not be so fortunate (Adams et al., 1998).

On all these infrastructure questions, state and regional policies seem driven by "averages." Indeed, it is into the realm of averages that policymakers take quick refuge, because by definition they smooth out differences. Most economists, though, argue that the best and most relevant measure of the cost of adding services is the "marginal" cost. Marginal costs will show when additional capacity is efficient by adding scale; conversely, they unmask inefficient or exceptionally expensive costs per unit of growth. They reveal certain "lumpy" expenditures, such as when an entire additional school must be built. And, importantly, marginal costs, when taken from the pockets of beneficiaries, send an accurate "market" signal about what this growth actually costs. The charges then force a discussion about what is a public good, with costs justifiably shared, and what is a private good that merits no subsidy (Ryan and Stinson, 2002).

To the degree that averaging costs produces unfair results, it is not just a suburban/ urban conflict. Marginal costs can exceed average ones quite dramatically when growth prompts expensive retrofitting of existing facilities in older parts of the region. And government is not alone in practicing pricing by averages. Providers of natural gas, electricity, and telephone service in the region do substantially the same thing. In applying average costs for installations, the more expensive transactions become unearned bargains to users.

Minutes Matter, Not Miles

The conventional way of measuring the growth in traffic is the annual count of vehicle miles traveled, often expressed as "VMT." This measure makes a case for faster cycles of road maintenance and replacement needs. But counting VMTs is no help at all in explaining the behavior of citizens in their role as regional motorists. The reason: it is the time it takes to get from where you are to where you are going that matters. No one counts miles. And that "time budget" for commutes has grown from 20 minutes in 1980 to 21 minutes in 1990 to 23 minutes in 2000—in other words, not much.

To explain even the modest rise, some analysts point to residential land-use practices; but it is not clear from research data that any other patterns of land use would have reduced travel times. No one would look at a blue Neon and a black Porsche and conclude that black paint costs more than blue paint. Like paint, land uses are easily seen; because they are, they attract disproportionate attention compared with underlying causes like fundamental changes in the economy (Barnes and Davis, 2001).

A glance back a half-century is useful. The Twin Cities' urbanized area in 1958, compared with 1990, covered about a fourth of the land area, was two to three times as dense, had nearly no purely residential zoning, and had transit serving almost all the built-up area (albeit at a 7.5 percent share of trips). Yet travelers in 1958 spent substantially the same amount of time per day getting around as travelers of 1990 did. The 1958 crowd didn't cover as many miles, because speeds were slower, but they spent as much time.

Now again, averages inform but can also mislead. Drilling down for differences among travelers, and looking for any variation that exceeds 10 percent, one finds that people traveling from outlying exurban or rural areas—no surprise—have longer trips in times as well as miles. They are on the road 80 minutes a day, compared to 68 for a person living closer to the center of the region. All the variation in time is related to commutes. None of it is for trips not related to getting to work. People in Minneapolis or suburban Apple Valley are spending about the same amount of trip time going to the grocery store, the dry cleaners, or the movies.

But what about transit users? Certainly, proportionately more people live in the center cities who do not use automobiles for the work trip. A concentration of employment in a district significantly affects use of transit. Best examples are the two downtowns and the University of Minnesota area. These zones, while constituting less than 1 percent of the total land area of the region, claim 60 percent of all transit trips (as well as a majority of the walking and biking trips). These zones attract in excess of 15 percent shares for transit from many supposedly transit-hostile suburban locations. Parking costs, good bus service, and personal calculations about convenience go a long way in explaining this behavior (Barnes and Davis, 2001).

It makes more sense to focus on problem travel than all travel generally. And research shows that work trips are the key. So, instead of designing a policy framework that strives to build higher densities everywhere, including residential neighborhoods, the odds would seem to favor concentrating on major employment and commercial destinations. In these areas, transit service becomes feasible.

Think about it: congestion, peaking at work-trip times, shows up almost entirely in areas around commercial destinations, not residential zones. These commercial zones, while congested, are also the zones in which people who decide they want a less auto-intensive lifestyle may create a market for housing (implications both for immigrants and the surging crowd of boomers who are rethinking their options for grayer years).

In these approaches there are serious possibilities to reduce automobile travel. But no one should imagine housing markets producing less auto travel or more transit travel quickly or easily, or that congestion will be erased from daily experience. An increase of 1000 people per square mile yields about 1 percent increase in transit share of work trips and about 1 percent decrease in overall daily driving per person. In other words, the region would have to boost density by 50 percent over the current average of 2000 people per square mile—a formidable prospect considering the densest residential areas of the entire metro area have only 10,000 people per square mile.

Most of the costs for automobile travel are borne by users themselves, out of their personal and family budgets. In a climate of relatively low prices for fuel, the potential for incentives to change modes or other travel choices is limited.

The amount of travel each day is immense. On a typical day, in 1998, 2.6 million people made 9.1 million trips. Ninety-four percent of those trips used a personal vehicle. Two and a half percent of the trips were by transit and another 3.5 percent by school bus. The total result that day was 71 million miles of travel (Anderson and McCullough, 2000).

Obviously, people see benefits in taking all these trips. They are worth what they cost. But two troubles are poised to ambush these benefits. One is that the amount of travel is expected to grow significantly, as the population swells. And second, too little consideration is given, anywhere, to the full costs of these trips. The total cost per person was $9000 in 1998 (which would be at least $11,200 a person by 2020). Travelers themselves pay 84 percent of the total in fixed costs (vehicles, driveways, garages, etc.) and variable costs (fuel, insurance, maintenance). Those costs are considered "internal." Since a car seems essential in today's culture, most people do not spend time calculating or worrying over these costs.

But in addition, there are costs paid by government at every level, about 9 percent of the total, which are funded through property, sales, fuel, and income taxes. Sixty percent of these costs are related to building and maintaining streets and highways, the rest going for services such as transit, law enforcement, emergency medical, environmental protection, and parking. Finally, there are "external" costs, 7 percent of the total, and these are also not borne directly by the user imposing them. They produce effects that translate to significant publicly shared costs. These kinds of costs are the most difficult to estimate but some, such as costs associated with congestion (pollution, productivity), have significant potential to rise. Congestion produces additional, obvious costs to drivers and riders caught in it, but that cost is mostly accounted for as "internal."

That people are routinely willing to spend such sums is clear evidence that the benefits of travel in the region greatly outweigh the costs. Any policy initiative narrowly aimed at reducing driving is likely doomed, given the percentage of costs borne by users. Policy is likely better focused on specific issues that pose more threat to the region's future—the work trip, congestion zones, and vehicles with faulty emission systems (Barnes and Davis, 1999).

GOVERNMENT AND TAXPAYER COSTS

The costs borne by government or taxpayers are only 16 percent, but, in absolute terms, these costs are large and likely to grow. Minnesota taxpayers contributed $4.5 billion in the 1998 study year and are projected to contribute $6.9 billion by 2020. These are both big numbers. But consider the underlying story: revenue constraints have driven down spending on roads to the point that it no longer correlates to household wealth, as tracked by the rise in personal income. What is spent on transit, while it continues to rise, also falls short of the growth in demand.

Law enforcement and safety costs associated with transportation will likely rise at a rate 33 percent faster than the growth in population. The costs of environmental protection and cleanup—covering everything from leaking gas tanks to auto emission effects to providing noise barriers—will continue to rise, at least as rapidly as the general economy.

Few people ever think about energy security costs as a part of the region's transportation system. But these costs, which cover the region's share of protecting foreign oil shares to the costs of the Strategic Petroleum Reserve to the more localized costs of ethanol subsidies, are real and are expected to rise by 60 percent by 2020.

Parking costs are substantial and headed higher. Just the parking provided for directly by government agencies, subtracting any fees paid by parkers and totally ignoring all other parking costs, will generate cost increases somewhere between 80 and 120 percent faster than the general economy, if present trends hold.

The "external" costs of transportation, at a midrange projection, will rise by almost 70 percent by 2020. Air pollution may benefit from continued technological progress on emissions, and noise, while irritating, is a relatively small part of the total cost. But crashes and congestion will rise much more significantly. Crashes are likely to rise by 50 percent while congestion costs actually triple in their impact. Nonetheless, even a doubling of all government spending (through a rise in taxes) would make scarcely more than a 10 percent dent in the transportation budgets of users (Barnes and Davis, 1999).

What Are the Policy Choices?

The context for any policy changes is what current politics makes possible. At least for the near term, the political scene will be swamped by the struggle to rebalance budgets around slower-growing revenues. In the longer term, though, the politics of congestion will likely predominate, as the trend toward too many people using the same road at the same time persists.

The region's growing congestion results in part from the number of potential destinations accessed from a given road. Obviously, more destinations generate more traffic. But does land-use policy have any effect on transportation behavior? If the region succeeded in raising the density levels of housing, would trips be shorter on average? Would there be more use of public transit?

The converse question carries equal weight: would a change in transportation patterns make a measurable change in the market for land development and housing preferences? The disquieting conclusion from most research is that surprisingly little is certain about these interactions. People decide on housing locations for a variety of reasons. Where roads or rail lie may influence commercial locations, but transportation has not dominated residential decisions in a long time. People choosing residential locations seem to have shared a key assumption with businesses locating office and commercial facilities: that government will extend the transportation and other infrastructure to those locations. It is an assumption not yet overturned.

This ambiguous state of affairs may, however, be on its last legs. People still believe they can get just about anywhere in about 20 minutes. While the trip-time averages haven't moved much, that 20-minute traditional commute time is now enjoyed by less than half of commuters. Commutes of 40 minutes or more have increased by

32 percent since 1990, reflecting the proportion of people living farther from major employment centers.

Ever since the streetcar bred desire to move outward, the Twin Cities region has been on a steadily spreading-out growth curve. If it were not for today's traffic, undermining expectations of convenient mobility, most people would not think there was any problem with this low-density spread-out pattern. But there is. The costs of maintaining the system are growing.

Think of it like a house the region's citizens own. Rather than live too close to each other, people added wings and rooms. Then, one day, the wake-up call is a list that says the whole thing needs painting and the roof needs replacing and all the landscaping is worn out. No one seems to have contemplated the costs of keeping up something more spread out than it needed to be.

Another analogy is the accountant's balance sheet. We are naïve if we think that just spending more chasing a problem produces an asset. Assets have to be compared with liabilities to show whether the "net" is positive. If we spend more on health care, while ignoring prevention of disease, is that progress? We could generate a lot of cash flow with a big prison system and find we had not advanced any social progress. The same is true with transportation. Increasing the system's volume, if we are adding to the liability side of the ledger, neither tames congestion nor produces any alternatives (Adams et al., 1999b).

So here is the fundamental question: What are the policy changes that would make a difference? The answer appears to lie in two, and only two, categories: adopting policies of honest pricing of transportation services and land development, and providing more choices than exist today for community development and travel modes.

Honest Pricing: Letting the Market Work

Honest pricing? That simply means full disclosure of true costs. How would that work? In theory, the estimated costs from land development impacts and transportation services could be more directly reflected in the hierarchy of decisions that now govern investor, developer, and buyer behavior (Ryan and Stinson, 2002). An honest price might slow the conversion of fresh land for development, stimulate more creative redevelopment in existing communities, and provide resources and incentives for investment in transportation alternatives.

First, recall how that decision chain generally works today. Investors look for land where they see potential for pricing value that exceeds rural or agricultural use. Developers come along, if they are not the investors, and assess the land's potential for a particular class of buyers; if that assessment is favorable, they seek to acquire or control the land to develop a market for those buyers. Developers then evaluate the available land against the total supply that may be available for development. They size up the zoning scenarios that will likely apply, what demands there may be for developer-provided infrastructure, and what sort of regulatory environment development will occur in.

They must also take demand into consideration, estimating how buyers will intuitively see the net benefit of buying, how many such households there might be in the demand pool, how rapidly housing units would sell, and whether supportive retail and commercial development will follow. Somehow the market keeps all these measures in equilibrium. If the rate of demand goes up and supply is not keeping up, values and prices rise. If, however, prices rise too much, demand drops back.

When buyers enter this scenario, they have their own mental calculations to make. Buyers typically look at what principal and interest will cost, how this purchase will affect their property tax bill (modified by effects on income tax liability). Most buyers are also looking for long-term impact. They assume that if they buy a new house in a good development there will also be good schools and a safe environment and their house value will rise faster than inflation (Adams et al., 1998).

Buyers apparently do give some thought to transportation costs associated with buying a new home, especially if a new location requires adding another vehicle. With fuel still relatively cheap, though, variable costs do not seem to get much respect with the possible exception of the "time" cost. Only if the time required for trips from this new location is seen as beyond what seems reasonable is the buyer's sense of the "net relative benefit" of the home damaged.

Honest Pricing of Transportation Costs

Transportation, research shows, both leads and lags development. But there is surely an interaction between the two, particularly when transportation decisions have the effect of promoting inefficient land development. And sometimes there is a fiscal impact on communities from a transportation decision, even if that decision cannot be technically considered a "cost" of transportation (Adams et al., 1999a).

Shelter and mobility may start out as very separate concerns for most people. But in economic systems, they inevitably become entangled. Economists remind us that when the demand for any "good" increases, the price of a complementary "good" is likely to fall. If the perceived price of buying a car goes down, the demand for automobile-oriented destinations goes up. So as people conclude that owning and operating vehicles is cheap, relative to other costs, their demand for homes and job locations becomes less sensitive to distances they will have to travel.

So, what would it take for pricing to slow the rate of new land conversion (Ryan and Stinson, 2002)? The simple answer: Expose the users of the road system to a larger share of the public costs. Today, state aids to local governments, local property taxes, and motor vehicle registration taxes handle 70 percent of those costs. Total Minnesota state and local public expenditures for the road system are $2.4 billion a year; at today's rate of driving, 52 billion miles a year, that is 4.8 cents per mile of travel. Much of that cost is borne by low-mileage households or people who do not drive at all.

Without changing the total revenue collected, that 70-percent ratio could be reversed. To illustrate, suppose that the state income and sales taxes now going for transportation in local aid formulas were eliminated and that the property tax and motor vehicle registration tax (which are not sensitive to how often a vehicle hits the road) are cut in half. Instead collect that revenue through the motor fuels tax. This tax, currently set at 20 cents, would rise by 30 cents, with the result that 70 percent of system costs would be borne by those using the roads. (One immediate result might be interest in more fuel-efficient vehicles.)

Another means of focusing cost on the user would be a tax on miles driven. Assuming the same cuts in income, sales, and property taxes, a three-cents-per-mile charge would replace lost revenue. (One hundred miles of travel at three cents per mile would cost a motorist three dollars. A 50-cent-a-gallon tax—assuming the

18 miles-per-gallon fleet average—would cost a motorist $2.89 for the same 100 miles—roughly the same.)

So, taxing either miles or fuel asks users to finance the marginal costs of the system. The first reactions to proposals of this sort almost always suggest they are too complex to administer, or just too radical. On the other hand, the system as it stands rather radically hides the true costs from users. In addition to largely hidden general public costs, if the "external" costs of the road system were loaded on to users through the motor fuels tax, the price per gallon would rise by 67 cents (Ryan and Stinson, 2002).

Today's tax system for transportation is only partially driven by use. Based on 1996 data, a family with a modest home and a five-year-old Taurus automobile pays at least $400 in road-related property tax whether they drive or not (Ryan and Stinson, 2002). This is also true for transit.

The threshold of a tax shift that would translate into measurable market behavior change is probably relatively high. Road system costs would have to be more visible and directly paid by users for their impact to change buying-decision behavior. For developers, it is estimated that a rise of $5,000 in annual commuting costs would push the development premium for land acquisition past the feasibility point. Up to a point, buyer behavior might be merely to trade for more fuel-efficient vehicles.

Technology will likely continue to be a wild card in this analysis. Once Intelligent Transportation Systems technology hits the mass market, and people can equip their cars for computer-controlled spacing in traffic, this option may actually seem to insulate commuters from some effects of a congested commute. Conceivably, under conditions of persistently dangerous congestion and rising numbers of crashes, some roads might be open only to vehicles equipped with ITS.

Nonetheless, a policy of honest pricing appears to be a potentially effective tool. But can it gain a political foothold in today's environment? Recent experience in the Twin Cities region with efforts to price use of roads generates very little optimism. In the late 1990s the state authorized a proposition to cooperate with the Federal Highway Administration in testing driver behavior incentives and revenue potentials by charging tolls—a "value pricing" demonstration. This proposal would have shifted more costs to users and made creative use of the private sector in getting the long-awaited Highway 212 built faster. To leave no democracy stone unturned, the enabling statute set up an approval process resembling the decision rules of the United Nations Security Council—any member city affected by the road could veto the approach. One city, Eden Prairie, did.

In 1997, MnDOT proposed allowing motorists caught in the increasing congestion on I-394 to buy into the lanes reserved by agreement with the federal government for high occupancy vehicles (a standard currently set at two persons per car). The public reaction was fast and ferociously against the proposal, which was summarily withdrawn. Some critics said these were lanes for the rich. The evidence, however, from a prior demonstration in San Diego on a similar stretch of freeway, is that all income groups pay tolls for access to a faster road, tolls which, by the way, average about what transit fares are. Recent local surveys indicate receptivity may be increasing for this approach.

One way in which transportation costs are already "priced" is through the ramp-meter access system on the region's freeways. The Twin Cities is among 11 such regions in the United States that make extensive use of meters to manage freeway flow. The objectives are to move more vehicles through these corridors, at higher average speeds and lower trip times, with greater predictability and a lower incidence of crashes.

The ramp-meter system does yield these benefits, but over time, as congestion has grown, it has also irritated many motorists stuck in queues, waiting longer than they felt to be reasonable. Hearing those voices, the legislature ordered a shutdown period in late 2000, around which MnDOT conducted a major analysis of effects and later a market study of users. While results were uneven from area to area, average volumes went down by 9 percent and travel times went up by 22 percent. More important, crashes went up by 26 percent.

Based on the study of the shutdown period, however, and experiments in managing the meter system in the year thereafter, important changes were set for the fall of 2002 to use metering somewhat more selectively, to make the system more directly responsive to real-time congestion, and to assure motorists that wait times in the queue would not be excessive.

Clearly, any serious plan to shift more costs directly to users will have to come wrapped in a better explanation to citizens than any initiative seen so far. But progress will come slowly or not at all without shifting to full cost accounting that is more transparent and better tied to user behavior. Even tied more to users, pricing is unlikely to make a discernible dent in congestion levels. People pay more to buy and use cars in Europe, where support is balanced between roads and transit, and yet there is congestion in nearly every successful urban region. But charging directly for road use may still be sensible. Minnesota transportation revenues will have to exceed current rates just to sustain today's level of service (Ryan and Stinson, 2002).

Honest Pricing of Land-Development Impacts

Cities have to build and support adequate infrastructure and assure a flow of revenue sufficient to provide local services. So their power to tax and to regulate land presents them with a constant balancing challenge. As costs have risen, so has the popularity of charging development-impact fees, exactions, and special assessments in order to pay for improvements.

Impact fees as practiced in many states have become rare in Minnesota, a casualty of the *Country Joe* decision in 1997, which stopped the city of Eagan from charging new developments for road access. But "exactions" continue as charges to developers for on-site capital improvements such as hook-ups for sewer and water (in addition to a regional access charge for reserve capacity of the wastewater treatment system), stormwater management, or sidewalks and local streets. This pay-as-you-go approach is beginning to stir some reaction as fees in some communities have risen to eye-popping levels (Adams et al., 1999a).

To avoid litigation, cities generally exercise considerable care that such charges are relevant to the new development and are exacted proportionately to the size of the project. But research indicates that, in the complex tangle of finance of development and taxation, the cost may not actually fall on the developer (much less on the buyer market). The anticipation of the exaction may see more than half the cost translated into a lower market price to the landowner. As the sale proceeds anyway, it is difficult to see how the exaction is a tool for equity or for slowing the rate of development, if that is the objective.

If the fairness of forwarding a share of the real costs of development to the presumed beneficiaries is the objective, then special assessments that fall directly on the buyers of the housing units are a more direct and likely effective tool.

A policy of choices—realistic alternatives to driving and residential options closer to major employment and commercial amenities—would make the region a more competitive market economy.

Today's political rhetoric runs at a high temperature over transit. Transit skeptics see proposals for rail and rapid busways as punitive to automobiles. They suspect that congestion is manufactured by undernourished road budgets. They charge transit advocates with "social engineering." This is, of course, a reversible canard, just as easily assigned to a half-century of policies that favored single and segregated land uses and nearly total dependence on automobiles to get to necessary destinations. Meanwhile, congestion continues to get worse. So, if the problem is that this spreading out pattern is indeed not sustainable—environmentally, logistically or financially—then the challenge would seem to be one of rebalancing policy back toward a market of choices.

But how can this be done, with any assurance of impact on the travel and location decisions people make? Most past research indicates that changes in residential land use, such as increasing densities, returning to mixed uses, adding jobs or retail, have little impact on decisions about travel—unless somehow all those tools are applied together. People are going to travel, whether the road is fast or slow. And they will take jobs and pick places to live for a complex set of reasons. The challenge of daily travel is but one of those factors.

But three serious prospects do shine through the TRG research statistics and analyses.

Commercial Centers—The Key to Transit Success

Research shows that the densest sectors in the region, namely the two downtowns and the University of Minnesota district, prove to be significant in influencing the mode of travel people choose. People who live in these districts or near them and work within them have multiple choices. They can drive (if they are willing to pay what parking costs), take transit, bike, or walk.

But, it is equally true that even suburbanites who live a considerable distance away, if they work in one of these zones, are much more likely to use transit to get there every day. These three destinations have many employers, multiple activity centers for meetings, restaurants, cultural events, and medical and other professional services, as well as sports and entertainment. They are compact enough that arriving by transit (or parking once) encourages walking from place to place. Could these characteristics of these three activity-rich zones be replicated? Almost certainly, increasing the density of commercial development is much more likely to have a beneficial impact on travel behavior than higher suburban residential densities is ever likely to have.

Major employment and commercial concentrations, once fairly centralized, are spread all over the region today. If zoning codes were liberalized to encourage mixing employment and housing and shopping and entertainment, how many of these districts might become major activity centers? Would paths for walking be demanded and delivered? And, just as both downtowns experienced in recent years, would a market for housing and supporting amenities follow? Research findings certainly suggest this is a plausible scenario.

There are other zones, smaller than most major employment centers, but with potential to create the good kind of congestion. All over the Twin Cities area's mature suburbs, the enthusiasm grows today to restore or create town centers. From Burnsville to Mendota Heights, Hopkins to Maple Grove, the trend has set in. People want a *there* there. Local officials are hearing the demand for a walkable town center with civic spaces along with the shops, cafés, and offices.

It turns out that higher densities, if they produce a high-quality environment, are popular. Just crowding things together is not, and never will be. Higher densities also produce more taxable property and more capacity to provide services—up to a point. Up to that point, every additional property-owning citizen is another payer toward relatively fixed costs. But, beyond a certain density of population, the actual per-capita costs of a city begin to rise. Law enforcement becomes a 24/7 proposition. Demand for emergency services rises. Everything wears out more rapidly (Barnes and Davis, 2001).

Neighborhoods—The Intersection of Community Development and Transportation

Trip-making behavior within neighborhoods and between neighborhoods actually can change, provided that local land-use planning is tied closely to transportation policy locally and regionally.

The evidence comes from an intense analysis of development and redevelopment sites in the communities in the North Metro I-35 Coalition. This coalition includes Arden Hills, Blaine, Circle Pines, Mounds View, New Brighton, Roseville, and Shoreview. These cities cover the full suburban range of development—from the tightly planned industrial suburb of the late nineteenth century to residential subdivisions with cul-de-sacs to agricultural land primed for development (Swenson and Dock, 2003). Despite the coalition's name, these communities generally do not lie in one of the major transportation corridors.

Weaving together a fine-grained picture of the infrastructure, economic activity, and demographics of this stretch of communities, "modeling" research shows the potential of a higher density of jobs (more jobs than a lower-density commercial pattern would yield) in a physical pattern that makes transit commutes an option, facilitates circulation within the zone without the use of cars, and encourages walking. While the potential is there, the prospects of shifting to a more compact commercial form depend entirely on zoning, economic development, transportation, and community infrastructure decisions being planned and implemented together, not separately (Swenson and Dock, 2003). This sounds like a sensible thing to do, but it is rarely done. Perhaps local officials see higher densities in Manhattan or Chicago terms, instead of the modest seven-units-an-acre threshold that makes transit service feasible.

Commuter rail—or any other means of providing a transit alternative—somehow gets debated all by itself, with capital and operating costs arrayed in newspapers, alongside estimates of a potential ridership. This is not a useful market analysis without linking it to land uses. If local governments become believers in choices, and open their zoning codes to densities and a mixture of land uses that might be supported by a robust market of residents and business investors, then transit access becomes a feasible option. Neither Portland nor Boston is all high density. But there are zones of choice and that is what is missing in the Twin Cities region, outside of the urban core (Neckar, 2003).

Some communities—inner suburbia—either have or will have a chance at all-day transit service within the next 20 years. Outer suburban communities have only peak-hour service to major employment destinations such as the core cities. But neighborhoods in all of these communities could be designed with a higher density of destinations connected with walking and biking paths—a plan that sounds both sensible and simple. But today's practices starkly contradict this pattern.

The common human experience in most suburban commercial centers is the necessity to use a vehicle to go from place to place, even if the second destination, not really very far away, can be seen from the first. The design of these areas assumes an automobile for every movement. Some of these centers are actually dangerous places to be a pedestrian.

But for policymakers, the message is optimistic. The key is an environment with incentives for more people to live and work in or near a commercial zone, with a reasonable balance of jobs and housing, where a majority of daily needs can be satisfied with a short trip, where community design facilitates walking or biking, and where a serious investment in transit accessibility is visible to everyone living there.

Could markets for more efficient use of land by employers and homebuyers be affected by providing commuter-passenger rail service to major destinations? Research suggests this is also a winning strategy if local governments change their zoning to welcome a dense mixture of employers, services, amenities, and residential developments in 12-minute proximity to rail stations. Families just might choose smaller lots and homes in return for better amenities and more choices for transportation. The question is whether other communities can succeed without transit. If costs for automobile dependence soar, why would not the market for alternatives rise too?

New Markets for Housing—A Push from Changing Demography

The third prospect that seems to make the numbers stand up and salute is simply the differences in people. Not everyone is looking for the same life experience in the region. While a large market may still be attached to the twentieth-century version of the American dream, there are population groups developing decidedly different preferences.

Immigrants continue to stream toward the core city areas, in part because most of the housing that is affordable to lower-income families is nearby. Many students see advantages in living near the University of Minnesota campus. Some people from a wide range of population groups who work in downtowns have decided to avoid the daily road commute. They prefer to live in the downtown district or nearby.

And here is the bonus: the boomers. In a trend that was just beginning to accelerate as these research studies were being conducted, boomers, people born between 1945 and 1963, began to move. The oldest boomers are turning 50 at the rate of one every eight seconds. From real estate trend reporting, at least one in five are opting out of the large lot and big house with the long commute. In most of their households, the kids are gone, and as it's often put, the dog has died. They're prime candidates for high-amenity, low-maintenance living near the places they like to go. Hence the rush to townhouses and condos in not only Minneapolis and St. Paul, but also in a growing set of suburbs now tapping the trend.

Any policy interventions that the state might authorize for the Twin Cities region will carry a significant price tag, whether it is funding for local communities trying to expand choices for residents and business, or resources for an integrated system of transit. The somewhat surprising reminder from this entire body of recent research on the region is how important markets are. They determine locations for commerce, preferences about housing, choices of mobility. This research suggests that policies of honest pricing of land development and transportation services, along with expanded choices about places to live and work, offer the best chances to improve the competitiveness, the mobility, and overall livability of the region for the next generation.

NOTE

This chapter is adapted from the report "Market Choices and Fair Prices" (see http://www.cts.umn.edu/trg/research/reports/TRG_17.html) with permission from the Center for Transportation Studies at the University of Minnesota. The author, Curtis Johnson, is a principal and senior writer with the Citistates Group. The entire TRG report, which is a summary of the interdisciplinary research and outreach study conducted by the Center for Transportation Studies at the University of Minnesota, can be viewed and downloaded at www.cts.umn.edu/trg.

BIBLIOGRAPHY

Adams, John, Mark D. Bjelland, Laura J. Hansen, Lena L. Laaken, and Barbara J. VanDrasek. 1998. *The Role of Housing Markets, Regulatory Frameworks, and Local Government Finance*. CTS 98-01. www.cts.umn.edu/trg/research/reports/TRG_01.html.

Adams, John S., Julie L. Cidell, Laura J. Hansen, Hyun-joo Jung, Yeon-taek Ryu, and Barbara J. VanDrasek. 1999a. *Development Impact Fees for Minnesota? A Review of Principles and National Practices*. CTS 99-04. www.cts.umn.edu/trg/research/reports/TRG_03.html.

Adams, John S., Julie L. Cidell, Laura J. Hansen, and Barbara VanDrasek. 1999b. *Synthesizing Highway Transportation, Land Development, Municipal and School Finance in the Greater Twin Cities Area, 1970–1997*. CTS 00-01. www.cts.umn.edu/trg/research/reports/TRG_04.html.

Adams, John S., Julie L. Cidell, Laura J. Hansen, and Barbara J. VanDrasek. 2002. *House Price Changes and Capital Shifts in Real Estate Values in Twin Cities–Area Housing Submarkets*. CTS 02-01. www.cts.umn.edu/trg/research/reports/TRG_07.html.

Adams, John S., Joel A. Koepp, and Barbara J. VanDrasek. 2003. *Urbanization of the Minnesota Countryside: Population Change and Low-Density Development Near Minnesota's Regional Centers, 1970–2000*. CTS 03-01. www.cts.umn.edu/trg/research/reports/TRG_10.html.

Adams, John S., and Barbara J. VanDrasek. In press. *Case Studies of Development in the Minneapolis–St. Paul Metropolitan Region*.

Anderson, David, and Gerard McCullough. 2000. *The Full Cost of Transportation in the Twin Cities Region*. CTS 00-04. www.cts.umn.edu/trg/research/reports/TRG_05.html.

Anderson, David, and Gerard McCullough. 2003. *The Distribution of Transportation Costs in the Twin Cities Region*. CTS 03-03. www.cts.umn.edu/trg/research/reports/TRG_15.html.

Barnes, Gary, and Gary Davis. 1999. *Understanding Urban Travel Demand: Problems, Solutions, and the Role of Forecasting*. CTS 99-02. www.cts.umn.edu/trg/research/reports/TRG_02.html.

Barnes, Gary, and Gary Davis. 2001. *Land Use and Travel Choices in the Twin Cities, 1958–1990*. CTS 01-01. www.cts.umn.edu/trg/research/reports/TRG_06.html.

Johnson, Curtis. 2003. *Market Choices and Fair Prices: Research Suggests Surprising Answers to Regional Growth Dilemmas*. CTS 03-02. www.cts.umn.edu/trg/research/reports/TRG_17.html.

Neckar, Lance M. 2003. *Urban Design and the Environment—Highway 61/Red Rock Corridor*. CTS 03-04. www.cts.umn.edu/trg/research/reports/TRG_13.html.

Ryan, Barry, and Thomas F. Stinson. 2002. *Road Finance Alternatives: An Analysis of Metro-Area Road Taxes*. CTS 02-04. www.cts.umn.edu/trg/research/reports/TRG_09.html.

Scott, Thomas M., and Barbara Lukermann. In press. *Public Policy, Transportation, and Regional Growth*.

Smith, Laura J., John S. Adams, Julie L. Cidell, and Barbara J. VanDrasek. 2002. *Highway Improvements and Land Development Patterns in the Greater Twin Cities Area, 1970–1997: Measuring the Connections*. CTS 02-03. www.cts.umn.edu/trg/research/reports/TRG_08.html.

Swenson, Carol, and Frederick Dock. 2003. *Urban Design, Transportation, Environment and Urban Growth: Transit-Supportive Urban Design Impacts on Suburban Land Use and Transportation Planning*. CTS 03-06. www.cts.umn.edu/trg/research/reports/TRG_11.html.

Ward, M., K. Brown, and D. Lieb. 1998. "National Incentives for Smart Growth Communities." *Natural Resources & Environment* 13(1).

11

Atlanta Metropatterns: A Regional Agenda for Community and Stability

Myron Orfield

METROPATTERNS

Atlanta has been one of the most dynamic regions in the United States in recent years. It gained more than 640,000 new jobs during the 1990s—representing a 42 percent increase in employment in one decade. Its population grew by nearly 40 percent, three times faster than the nation as a whole.[1] However, the benefits of this growth have not been spread evenly across the region. Gains in jobs and population occurred disproportionately in the northern and northeastern suburbs.[2] Concentrated poverty, on the other hand, continued to destabilize schools and neighborhoods in Atlanta, nearby suburbs to the south and further afield in places like Douglasville and Conyers. Even parts of relatively well-off counties like Gwinnett and Cobb, including Marietta, Norcross and Lilburn, experienced growing poverty in the last decade (see Maps 11.2, 11.4, and 11.5).

The social, educational, and economic needs associated with concentrated poverty dramatically limit the life opportunities of residents, discourage investment by families and businesses in these neighborhoods, and place a significant burden on the resources of these areas. Ultimately, people living in these high-poverty neighborhoods become isolated from the educational, employment, and social opportunities available to residents in other parts of the region—a trend that makes it extremely difficult for them to participate fully in the metropolitan economy.

A related consequence of uneven population and job growth in the Atlanta region is sprawl. Concentrations of poverty in the inner part of the region contribute to sprawling development patterns at the edges of the region, as the core communities become less desirable places to live or to locate businesses. The resulting pressure to accommodate population growth elsewhere introduces a host of social and fiscal pressures. In the 1990s, population grew by more than 50 percent in nine of the region's 20 counties.[3] All are on the fringes of the region where infrastructure is least likely to already exist. Many of these areas must accommodate this growth with only modest fiscal resources.

The same patterns of metropolitan growth that lead to especially poor and isolated neighborhoods in the central city are also creating significant fiscal and social stress in some inner suburbs and in older incorporated towns on the urban edge. While the social problems in these areas are generally not as severe as in the poorest city neighborhoods, they reflect growing instability that could lead to rapid social decline.

In particular, inner suburbs—lacking a central business district, older neighborhoods with strong housing stock capable of gentrification, and arts and cultural amenities—can be even more vulnerable than the central city. For this reason, as poverty and social instability cross the city limits, problems often accelerate and intensify. Increasing social stress in schools and neighborhoods, the loss of local businesses and jobs, and the erosion or slower-than-average growth of the local tax bases are symptoms of this decline. Parts of DeKalb, Clayton, and south Fulton counties show signs of these stresses.

Many outer suburban communities in the region are also struggling with lower-than-average fiscal resources. In places like Spalding, Carroll, Bartow, and Newton counties, this problem is combined with pockets of poverty to create significant stress. In others, including places like Henry, Paulding, Coweta, Barrow, Gwinnett, Fayette, and Walton counties, low or modest fiscal capacity combined with high growth rates creates a different kind of stress. As these suburbs grow, they initially seem to offer an alternative to the distressed and declining communities at the core of the region. Still allowing relatively easy access to the jobs and cultural amenities of the central city, they can also offer higher-achieving schools, lower land costs, new homes, more space, less congested streets, and lower taxes.

Eventually, however, the costs of growth can exceed the ability of local taxpayers to pay for it. Many communities experience fiscal stress as they struggle to keep up with the demand and the costs of new schools, roads, sewers, parks, and many other public services. The fiscal stress associated with the costs of rapid, low-density residential growth frequently forces local governments to engage in wasteful competition with one another, as each attempts to add lucrative residential, commercial and industrial properties to its local tax base. Generally, only a few communities are successful in this competition, while most fall further and further behind in their attempts to get ahead.

The winners of this competition, which include communities in Forsyth and north Fulton counties, enjoy plentiful local resources and bear few of the region's social costs. It is in these places where the most expensive homes are built, where commercial and industrial development is most lucrative, and where the social strains associated with poverty are practically nonexistent. Eventually, however, these winners become victims of their own success. Open spaces that first drew people are soon lost to development and traffic congestion rises as the concentration of regional shopping and employment centers increases. These communities soon resemble the urban centers that its residents and businesses were attempting to avoid. Further, many employees of the businesses in these new employment centers cannot afford to live in expensive local housing, forcing them to drive long distances or look elsewhere for work. In fact, in 2001, residents of the region had the longest daily vehicle-miles traveled per capita after the residents of Houston—35.6 miles.[4] Moreover, the Atlanta

The Local Effects of Unbalanced Regional Growth:
The Pittsburgh Neighborhood

Atlanta's historic Pittsburgh neighborhood, located just south of downtown, is the quintessential loser of regional patterns that concentrate poverty and fiscal stress in core areas. Despite pockets of stability, the neighborhood faces a variety of challenges, including high levels of poverty, low incomes, and deteriorating housing stock. These indicators help illustrate how even impressive local efforts to revitalize struggling core communities have limited long-term success unless they are accompanied by regional policies that break the pattern of economic and physical decentralization.

Population and Poverty

Decline in the Pittsburgh neighborhood goes back decades. The neighborhood was hardest hit in the 1970s, when it lost 44 percent of its population and the poverty rate skyrocketed from 29 to 48 percent (Table 11.1). (The regional poverty rate was steady at about 12 percent during the 1970s.)

Despite more favorable regional economic conditions in the 1980s and 1990s, the neighborhood continued to decline. Population continued to shrink, though at a slower rate. The losses were especially significant in a period when the population of the Atlanta metropolitan area boomed. In the 1990s, for example, the neighborhood lost 10 percent of its population, while the region grew by 40 percent. During the same period, the city of Atlanta grew by 6 percent.

Likewise, the neighborhood's poverty rate dipped slightly during the 1980s and 1990s, but still remained above 40 percent, a common threshold for extreme poverty.[5] The problems associated with concentrated poverty make it difficult for residents to interact with mainstream society, undermine their employment opportunities, and limit their educational achievements.

Reflecting trends in the neighborhood as a whole, Pittsburgh's remaining elementary school shows a disproportionately high share of poor students. The percentage of elementary school students who qualified for free lunches—82 percent—was almost 2.5 times the percentage for the entire Atlanta metro area in 2000, and slightly higher than in the city of Atlanta as a whole.

Concentrated poverty in Pittsburgh disproportionately harms people of color, who have made up more than 95 percent of students enrolled in the neighborhood's elementary school since the 1990s and more than 97 percent of the neighborhood population since the 1970s.

Educational Attainment and Employment

Along with high levels of poverty have come low levels of educational attainment and employment. In fact, in 1990, the percentage of people in the Pittsburgh neighborhood with less than a ninth-grade education—22 percent—was more than twice the corresponding percentage in the city of Atlanta, and almost three times the percentage in the entire metropolitan area. The discrepancy remained in 2000. Similarly, the percentages of people with high school and college degrees in the city of Atlanta and the Atlanta metropolitan area far exceeded the percentages of people with similar degrees in the Pittsburgh neighborhood in both years (Table 11.1). As a result of these and other factors, by 2000, the unemployment rate in Pittsburgh was almost four times higher than the regional unemployment rate.

The decentralization of jobs in the metro area exacerbates these patterns. From 1990 to 2000, the neighborhood lost 22 percent of its jobs, and the number of jobs in the city of Atlanta grew by just 3.6 percent. Once again, these changes in the core came in a decade when the Atlanta metro area as a whole gained jobs at an impressive rate of 37 percent.

The employment opportunities of Pittsburgh residents are further restricted by their limited access to suburban job centers. Residents of the Pittsburgh neighborhood are almost 10 times more likely to use public transportation to go to work than the average resident of the Atlanta metro area.[6] However, the public transit network in the Atlanta metropolitan area does not quite extend to the growing job centers in the outlying suburbs of Atlanta.[7] The limited scope of the public transit network thus makes it harder or even impossible for Pittsburgh residents to access suburban jobs.

Revitalization Efforts

The Pittsburgh neighborhood's struggles in recent decades come despite significant revitalization efforts. Recently, for example, the Pittsburgh Community Redevelopment Plan laid out 27 redevelopment projects including civic and transportation improvements. The plan also included economic-development, land-use, and rezoning plans.[8] In addition, the neighborhood has been included in a variety of other government and philanthropic efforts.

These efforts—many well designed and executed—are important steps in improving social and physical conditions in the neighborhood. But they are simply not enough to fundamentally change its prospects because they do not address the regional imbalances that put core communities at a competitive disadvantage. For example, local efforts to attract businesses to the neighborhood are undermined by city-suburb tax rate differentials. Efforts to revitalize the neighborhood's housing stock are hurt by a fragmented system of local governance that creates incentives for growth on the urban edge rather than the reuse of previously developed land. Difficulties in obtaining employment are exacerbated by regional transportation policies that provide few opportunities for inner-city residents to reach growing suburban job centers and by struggling local schools. Local efforts to improve the performance of the neighborhood's schools and increase local job opportunities for residents are hindered, in turn, by concentrated poverty that makes education much more difficult to provide while depressing local demand for the products of local businesses.

metropolitan area experienced the highest increase in median travel time in the entire country—a jump from 24.8 minutes in 1990 to 29.5 minutes in 2000.[9] As a result, an increasing number of businesses in these areas are finding it difficult to fill positions as they grow.

Competition among cities and counties for a larger tax base also creates strong incentives for local governments to limit their supply of affordable housing. In their attempt to attract high-end residential and commercial developments, many local governments resort to exclusionary zoning practices that limit affordable housing within their borders.[10] Aggregated over the entire region, this process creates very uneven distributions of affordable housing and often results in absolute shortages.

Both problems are evident in the Atlanta region. The distribution of affordable housing is very uneven. The fastest growing job centers in the northern and northeastern parts of the region contain little affordable housing, even for moderate-income households. Most of the existing stock of affordable housing is clustered around the city of Atlanta, the communities to the immediate south of the city, and in

Table 11.1. Pittsburgh Neighborhood Characteristics Compared to the City of Atlanta and the Metropolitan Area

	Pittsburgh					City of Atlanta			Atlanta Metropolitan Area		
	1970	1980	1990	2000	% Change 1990–2000	1990	2000	% Change 1990–2000	1990	2000	% Change 1990–2000
Population	7,430	4,199	3,624	3,261	−10	394,017	416,474	6	2,959,950	4,112,198	39
White	361	155	70	37	−47	122,363	138,352	13	2,136,171	2,616,482	22
Black	7,063	4,044	3,554	3,167	−11	264,213	255,689	−3	746,441	1,216,230	63
Jobs	—	—	1,699	1,328	−22	422,295	437,572	4	1,545,505	2,189,470	42
% of Workers Using Public Transportation	—	—	40	34	−14	20	15	−25	5	4	−19
Unemployment Rate	4	—	15	19	26	9	14	53	5	5	6
Median Household Income	—	5,366	10,095	16,759	66	22,275	34,770	56	35,646	51,948	46
Poverty Rate	29	48	43	41	−5	27	24	−11	10	9	−6
% of Housing Units Vacant	5	13	18	24	32	15	10	−32	10	5	−47
% of Population with:											
Less than 9th Grade	58	50	22	14	−35	11	7	−34	8	5	−30
High School or higher	21	29	42	55	31	70	77	10	79	84	7
College Degree or higher	—	3	2	4	122	27	35	30	26	32	22
Elementary School Data*											
% of Students Eligible for Free or Reduced Lunch	—	—	86	82	−5	72	78	7	30	34	12
% of Students Non-Asian Minority	—	—	100	96	−4	89	91	3	36	46	25

*Elementary school data are for 1992 and 2000.

Sources: Atlanta Regional Commission (job data); National Center for Education Statistics (elementary school data); U.S. Census Bureau.

a few parts of the outermost suburbs. This distribution reinforces existing patterns of racial and income segregation.

The spatial mismatch between jobs and affordable housing contributes to the growing socioeconomic isolation of many minority residents, who find it increasingly hard to access the job centers of the north and the northeast due to limited affordable housing alternatives and lack of public transportation. The mismatch also exacerbates the problems of traffic congestion and lengthy commutes—problems that reduce the quality of life of all the region's residents.

Uneven growth also hurts the overall performance of the regional economy. A growing body of research shows the interconnectedness of central cities and suburban areas within metropolitan economies. One study of 78 metropolitan areas, for instance, found that median household incomes of central cities and suburbs move up and down together in most U.S. metropolitan areas and that the strength of this relationship appears to be increasing.[11] Another study of 48 metropolitan areas found that metropolitan areas with the smallest gap between city and suburban incomes had the greatest regional job growth.[12] These and other studies argue that cities and suburbs within a metropolitan area are interdependent and that when social and economic disparities are minimized, the region is stronger.

SOCIAL SEPARATION AND SPRAWL

Atlanta's population has almost tripled since 1970.[13] As in most American metropolitan areas, much of the growth is occurring in the region's outer suburbs. Population grew by more than 50 percent during the 1990s in nine of the region's outermost counties—including Forsyth, Henry, Paulding, Gwinnett, Coweta, Pickens, Walton, Cherokee, and Barrow. In contrast, the core of the region, including the city of Atlanta and the counties to the south of the city, lagged behind other parts of the region (see Table 11.2).

Job growth in the region also showed a highly decentralized pattern during the 1990s. Although the job densities (jobs per square mile) remained high in the core areas, these areas experienced the lowest rates of growth in the entire region. A snapshot of job density in the region in 2000 shows a clustering of jobs around major highways and reveals the extent to which transportation choices impact the distribution of jobs in the region (see Map 11.1). However, many neighborhoods in the city of Atlanta and Fulton, De Kalb and Clayton counties lost jobs while the region as a whole was gaining jobs at an average rate of 36 percent (see Map 11.2).

Job growth was greatest in outer areas, especially in the suburbs to the north of I-20.[14] During the 1990s, employment more than doubled in Forsyth (215 percent), Paulding (130 percent), and Cherokee (123 percent) counties (see Map 11.2 and Table 11.1).

Fueled by the decentralized growth of jobs and population, the physical bounds of the region have been expanding rapidly for decades. Low-density development has been a defining characteristic of the Atlanta region since the 1970s. Between 1970 and 2000, the amount of urbanized land in the Atlanta region grew by 316 percent, while the region's population grew by just 182 percent (see Map 11.3). Measured another way, the region doubled in size during the 1990s alone—from 65 miles measured north to south to an astounding 110 miles.[15]

Table 11.2. Population and Jobs by County, 1990 and 2000

	Population			Jobs		
County	2000	1990	Percentage Change 1990–2000	2000	1990	Percentage Change 1990–2000
City of Atlanta	416,474	394,017	5.7%	437,572	422,295	3.6%
Barrow County	46,144	29,721	55.3	11,612	8,538	36.0
Bartow County	76,019	55,911	36.0	30,627	20,078	52.5
Carroll County	87,268	71,422	22.2	31,714	27,128	16.9
Cherokee County	141,903	90,204	57.3	33,161	16,041	106.7
Clayton County	236,517	182,052	29.9	135,900	102,794	32.2
Cobb County	607,751	447,745	35.7	312,092	207,663	50.3
Coweta County	89,215	53,853	65.7	26,906	17,579	53.1
DeKalb County (excl. Atlanta)	636,090	512,298	24.2	339,985	275,037	23.6
Douglas County	92,174	71,120	29.6	33,650	19,672	71.1
Fayette County	91,263	62,415	46.2	32,882	18,246	80.2
Forsyth County	98,407	44,083	123.2	33,987	11,268	201.6
Fulton County (excl. Atlanta)	429,307	288,473	48.8	300,243	164,158	82.9
Gwinnett County	588,448	352,910	66.7	292,000	151,725	92.5
Henry County	119,341	58,741	103.2	31,424	13,423	134.1
Newton County	62,001	41,808	48.3	17,561	11,348	54.7
Paulding County	81,678	41,611	96.3	11,869	5,440	118.2
Pickens County	22,983	14,432	59.3	5,387	3,922	37.4
Rockdale County	70,111	54,091	29.6	34,600	21,369	61.9
Spalding County	58,417	54,457	7.3	22,734	18,861	20.5
Walton County	60,687	38,586	57.3	13,564	8,920	52.1
Regional Total	4,112,198	2,959,950	38.9	2,189,470	1,545,505	41.7

Source: U.S. Census Bureau.

These patterns meant that population density in the urbanized portions of the region declined by 32 percent, from 4.1 people per acre in 1970 to 2.8 people per acre in 2000. Compared to moderate- and high-density development, low-density development intensifies the need for roads and other infrastructure, provides few opportunities for effective mass transit, and threatens air and water quality. It is also associated with increased per-person costs for some public services including schools, police and fire, and often, with higher housing prices.

The growth of population and jobs in low-density outer suburbs has other important implications. Rapid growth often burdens growing communities with significant public costs. The flight of jobs to outer suburbs undermines the core areas, further reducing their ability to fund public services and support local businesses. Growing discrepancies between the core and the outer suburbs deepen regional patterns of social stratification.

Map 11.1
Atlanta Region: Total Jobs per Square Mile by County and the City of Atlanta, 2000

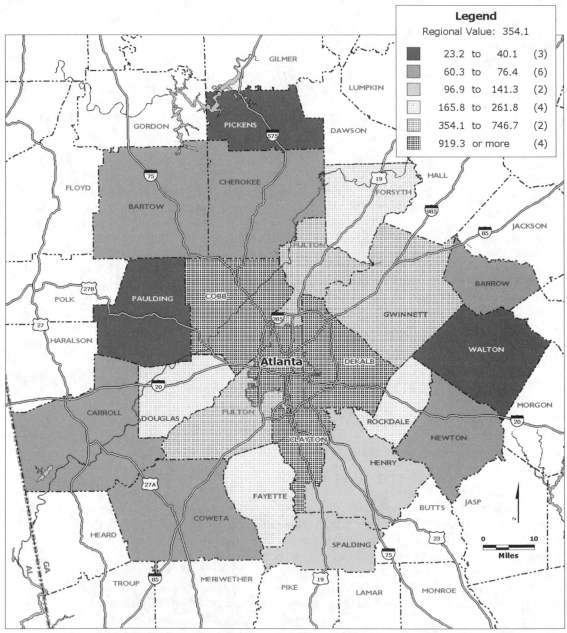

Data Sources: Atlanta Regional Commission; Department of Labor. Cartography by Ameregis.

Map 11.2
Atlanta Region: Percentage Change in Total Jobs per Square Mile by County and the City
of Atlanta, 1990–2000

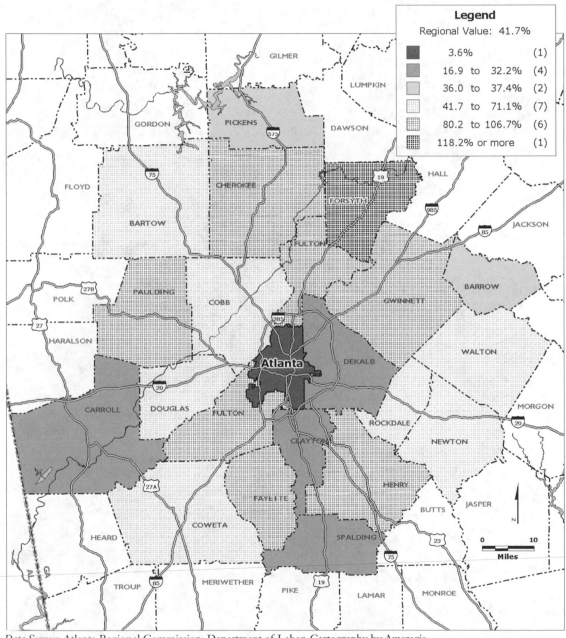

Data Sources: Atlanta Regional Commission; Department of Labor. Cartography by Ameregis.

Map 11.3
Atlanta Region: Housing Development by Census Tract, 1970–2000

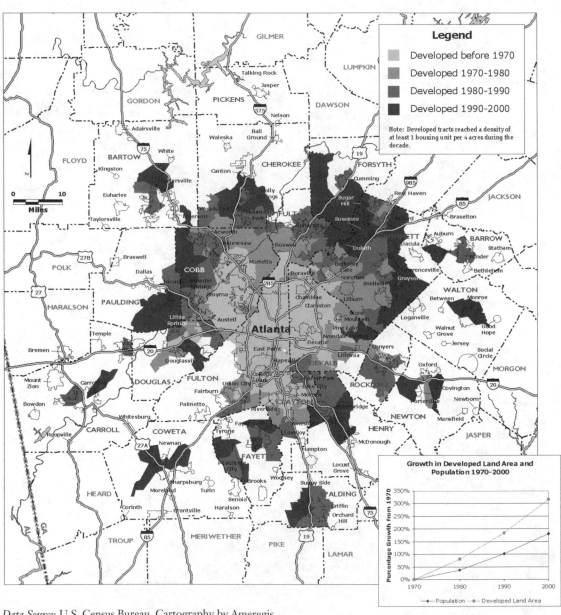

Data Source: U.S. Census Bureau. Cartography by Ameregis.

Racial and Income Segregation

One of the most harmful consequences of this sprawling development is a devastating pattern of social stratification that divides the region by income and race. Communities in the Atlanta area are highly segregated, with poor households and people of color disproportionately located in the city of Atlanta and south Fulton, Clayton, and DeKalb counties.[16] This divide is most clearly reflected in the region's schools.

School demographics are a powerful prophecy for communities. Deepening poverty and other socioeconomic changes show up in schools before they do in neighborhoods and in elementary schools before junior and senior high schools. When the perceived quality of a school declines, it can set in motion a vicious cycle of middle-class flight and disinvestment.[17]

Schools in the Atlanta region are highly segregated by income. In 2000, 52 percent of poor students in the Atlanta region would have had to change schools to achieve an identical mix of poor and nonpoor students in each building in the region. That's up 2 percentage points from 1992.[18] Moreover, poor students are disproportionately concentrated in the core areas (see Map 11.4). Most of the schools in the city of Atlanta have extremely high percentages of elementary students eligible for free lunch. The district's average free-lunch rate, 78 percent, is more than twice the regional average. Similarly, inner-suburban school districts, such as those in DeKalb and Clayton counties, house higher than average rates of poor students—51.2 percent and 48.7 percent, respectively. These core areas also have the highest concentrations of child poverty in the region (see Map 11.5). However, even school districts in the outer suburbs such as those in Spalding County are not exempt from student poverty in schools. For example, Spalding school district had the region's third highest rate of poverty in its schools, 49.5 percent, after the Atlanta and DeKalb county school districts.

Concentrated poverty constitutes a serious social problem because schools enrolling many poor students often suffer from risk factors—everything from inexperienced teachers to unstable enrollment—that lower educational achievement among students and diminish their prospects for the future.[19]

This pattern of concentration especially harms people of color, as racial segregation interacts with prevailing patterns of income segregation to further widen social discrepancies in the region. In part due to subtle discrimination in the housing market, people of color are much more likely than whites to live in high-poverty areas and to attend high-poverty schools (see Maps 11.4 and 11.6).[20] The percentage of white students in the region who attended high-poverty schools was only 9 percent in 2000, while the corresponding percentage for non-Asian minority students was 66 percent—seven times higher (see Map 11.7). The concentration of minority children in poor schools and poor neighborhoods deepens the socioeconomic gulf dividing the Atlanta region.

Racial segregation in the region remains quite high. In 1990, 65 percent of the non-Asian minority students in elementary schools would have had to change schools in order to achieve a balanced racial distribution in the region's schools. This percentage remained the same in 2000, reflecting the persistence of racial segregation

Map 11.4
Atlanta Region: Percentage of Elementary Students Eligible for Free Lunch by School District, 2000

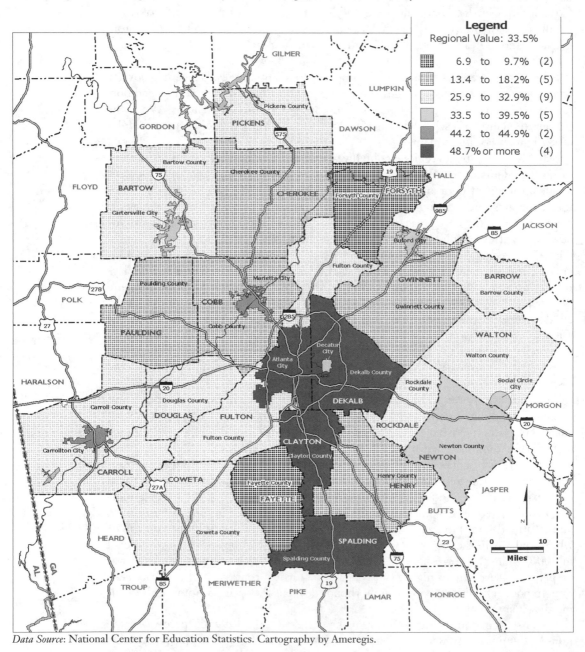

Legend
Regional Value: 33.5%

6.9 to 9.7%	(2)
13.4 to 18.2%	(5)
25.9 to 32.9%	(9)
33.5 to 39.5%	(5)
44.2 to 44.9%	(2)
48.7% or more	(4)

Data Source: National Center for Education Statistics. Cartography by Ameregis.

Map 11.5
Atlanta Region: Percentage of Children Ages 5–17 in Poverty by Census Tract, 1999

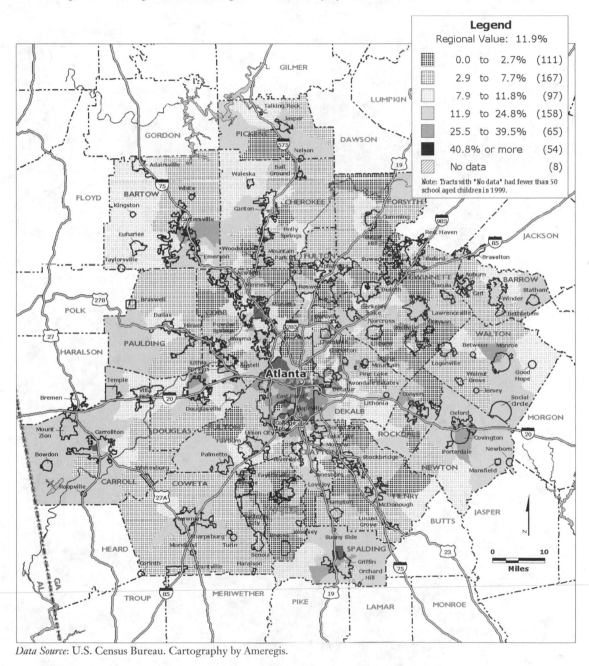

Legend

Regional Value: 11.9%

	0.0 to 2.7%	(111)
	2.9 to 7.7%	(167)
	7.9 to 11.8%	(97)
	11.9 to 24.8%	(158)
	25.5 to 39.5%	(65)
	40.8% or more	(54)
	No data	(8)

Note: Tracts with "No data" had fewer than 50 school aged children in 1999.

Data Source: U.S. Census Bureau. Cartography by Ameregis.

Map 11.6
Atlanta Region: Percentage of Non-Asian Minority Elementary Students by School District, 2000

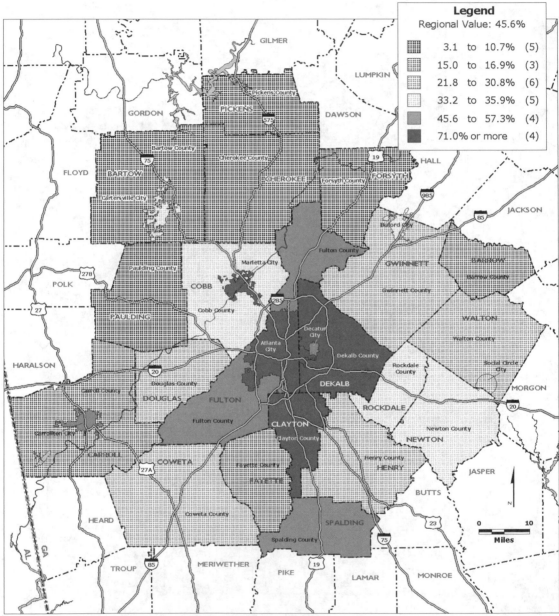

Data Source: National Center for Education Statistics. Cartography by Ameregis.

Map 11.7
Atlanta Region: Change in Percentage of Non-Asian Minority Elementary Students by
School District, 1993–2000

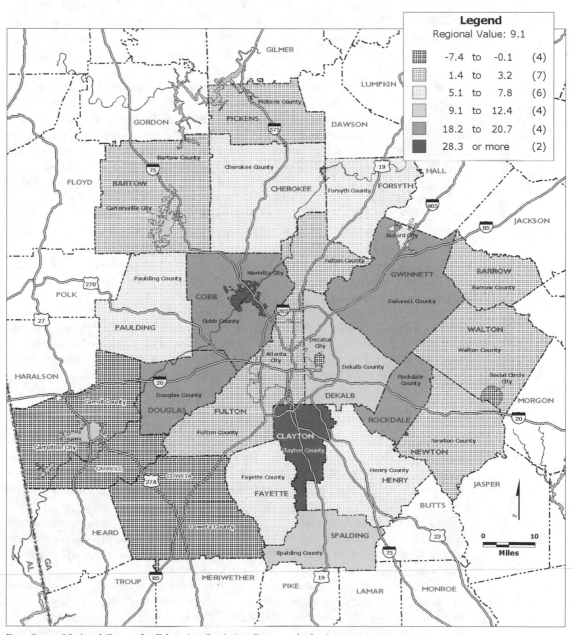

Data Source: National Center for Education Statistics. Cartography by Ameregis.

despite rapidly changing demographics in the region. This degree of racial segregation compares poorly to those of other metropolitan areas—in 1997, Atlanta was the 10th most segregated region among the 25 largest metropolitan areas.[21]

Many schools in older suburbs such as those in Cobb, Douglas, and Gwinnett counties, for example, are now starting to show the same patterns of social change that occurred a generation ago in the core areas of the region (see Map 11.8). This socioeconomic shift has serious effects. Eventually, when schools reach certain thresholds of poverty, middle-class families with children—those of all races—will leave the community, and they will eventually be followed by other middle-class segments of the housing market.

The departure of the middle class from a neighborhood strains both old and new communities. In fast-growing communities at the edge of the region, the middle class is streaming into increasingly overcrowded schools. For example, Gwinnett County suffers from the worst student-overcrowding problem in the state. Over 80 percent of the county's schools are overcrowded, and the school system can only accommodate its students with the additional capacity of 850 mobile classrooms.[22] The outward flight of middle-class families strain fiscal resources and disrupt lives.

But the more powerful harms of this flight accrue to the people left behind in communities of concentrated poverty. High concentrations of poverty affect individual residents and their families as well as the community as a whole. Studies have found that poor individuals living in concentrated poverty are far more likely to become pregnant as teenagers,[23] drop out of high school,[24] and remain jobless[25] than if they lived in socioeconomically mixed neighborhoods. These types of outcomes dramatically diminish the quality of life and opportunity.

Similarly, the concentration of poverty and its attendant social isolation make education, job search, and general interaction with mainstream society difficult. The impact of concentrated poverty also extends into the larger regional economy by reducing the regional pool of skilled workers and otherwise creating a less attractive environment for economic growth and development.

FISCAL INEQUALITY

The Atlanta metropolitan area has a highly fragmented system of local government, and its municipal governments rely very heavily on locally generated revenues to pay for public services.[26] Together, these factors place tremendous pressure on most communities to compete for development that will expand their property tax bases.

This can drive local land-use planning decisions, encourage sprawl, and increase economic and social stratification. Much of this competition simply shifts economic activity from one part of the region to another, contributing no net gains to the region as a whole.

To win the most profitable land uses, local governments may offer public subsidies or infrastructure improvements. But perhaps the most common approach is "fiscal zoning"—making land-use decisions based not on the intrinsic suitability of the land or the long-term needs of the region, but on the tax revenue development can generate right away. For example, a region as a whole benefits when most communities contain a mix of housing choices because workers have a choice of communities to live in.[27] But individual localities can reap short-term fiscal benefits by

Map 11.8
Atlanta Region: Change in Percentage of Elementary Students Eligible for Free Lunch by School District,
1993–2000

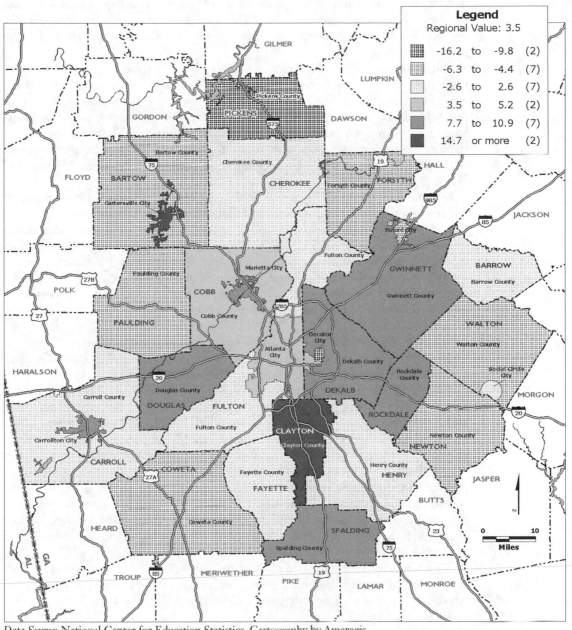

Legend
Regional Value: 3.5

-16.2	to	-9.8	(2)
-6.3	to	-4.4	(7)
-2.6	to	2.6	(7)
3.5	to	5.2	(2)
7.7	to	10.9	(7)
14.7	or more		(2)

Data Source: National Center for Education Statistics. Cartography by Ameregis.

severely limiting the land zoned for multifamily development or by requiring very large (and therefore more expensive) homes and lots.

The competition for tax base among local governments creates the potential for a vicious, self-reinforcing cycle of decline in places that "lose" the competition early in the game. As a municipality loses tax base, it faces a choice—it can levy high tax rates in order to provide competitive public services or provide relatively few, or low quality, services at competitive tax rates. Either choice puts it at a disadvantage in the competition for jobs and residents, leading to further losses and further declines in its ability to compete.

Older communities in the region are doubly hurt by these trends. These places must contend with aging infrastructure, high concentrations of poverty, higher crime rates, and other factors that strain their limited resources. With their modest property values, they have few resources to provide for their great needs. The city of Atlanta, for example, has to deal with disproportionate costs of poverty—78 percent of the city's elementary students were poor in 2000 compared to a regional average of 33 percent—with a tax base that is less than 1 percent greater than the regional average.

Communities that face high social needs with low or moderate tax resources cannot reinvest to rebuild sewer systems and roads, rehabilitate housing, maintain parks, or clean up polluted land without state or federal aid. Those burdens make it even more difficult for these communities to remain competitive with newer communities that offer cheaper land, newer homes, and more open space. In addition, the resulting concentration of public services most necessary for low-income populations—public transit or homeless shelters, for instance—encourages further concentration of poverty in a few areas. This increases the total regional costs of dealing with concentrated poverty.

Meanwhile, places that "win" the most lucrative homes and businesses can provide high-quality services at more reasonable rates, in turn attracting even more economic activity. But there are actually few winners in this competition.

For many communities on the urban edge, all is not well, either. The same patterns that hurt older, struggling communities also discourage long-term planning that would allow growing communities to develop in an orderly and efficient way. Because competition for certain land uses can be so intense—and the impact of losing so severe—communities often feel they have to grab all the development they can before it leaves for another place. That is especially true in newly developing communities, trying to build an adequate tax base to pay for their growing needs and to pay off debts on new infrastructure. But these low-capacity places are rarely in a good position to win the competition for the most "profitable" land uses, ending up instead with moderately priced single-family housing that generates more costs—for schools, roads, and sewers—than they produce in revenues.

These challenges are evident in many of the outlying suburbs, such as those in Bartow, Barrow, Paulding, Carroll, Coweta, Spalding, Newton, and Walton counties, which have to deal with booming population with lower than average property tax bases (see Map 11.9).

The overall result of fiscal zoning and the other strategies communities embrace to attract tax base is the concentration of households with the greatest need for public services in communities that are the least able to generate the revenue to provide them.

Map 11.9
Atlanta Region: Property Tax Base per Household by Municipality and County Unincorporated Area, 2000

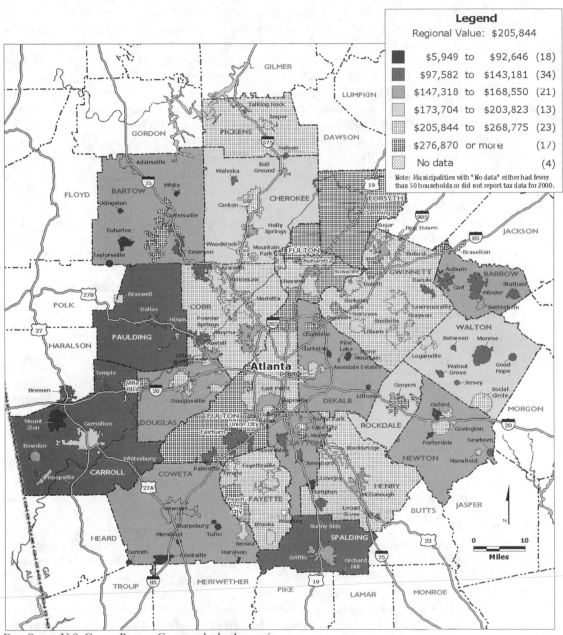

Legend

Regional Value: $205,844

$5,949 to $92,646	(18)
$97,582 to $143,181	(34)
$147,318 to $168,550	(21)
$173,704 to $203,823	(13)
$205,844 to $268,775	(23)
$276,870 or more	(17)
No data	(4)

Note: Municipalities with "No data" either had fewer than 50 households or did not report tax data for 2000.

Data Source: U.S. Census Bureau. Cartography by Ameregis.

Municipal Finance

The effects of this competition are evident in the dramatically different abilities of Atlanta's local governments to finance public services. The strongest tax bases in the region are concentrated in rapidly growing job centers such as Forsyth and suburban Fulton counties. The weakest tax bases, on the other hand, are concentrated in outlying counties and older incorporated suburbs across the region (see Map 11.9).

One way to measure the disparities among communities is to calculate the ratio of tax base in a high-capacity place (the one at the 95th percentile) to the tax base in a low-capacity community (the one at the 5th percentile). In 2000, if all the municipalities in the region had levied the same tax rate, the revenues (per household) coming to the 95th percentile municipality would have been 5.6 times the revenue of the 5th percentile municipality. Put another way, for all residents of the region to receive equal levels of public services, municipalities with the lowest tax bases would have to tax residents at nearly six times the rate of those with the highest tax bases—something that no place can afford to do if it hopes to succeed in the competition for businesses and residents.[28]

State and federal aid does little to reduce these disparities. For municipal services, the ratio stays roughly the same when state aid is included. Federal aid actually worsens these disparities, as the 95th-to-5th percentile ratio increases from 5.6 to 5.9 when federal aid is included.

The pattern of change in tax bases shows a clear pattern of relative decline in the core of the region (see Map 11.10). Tax base grew more slowly than average in much of Clayton, Fulton, and DeKalb counties.

School Finance

Schools are another very important component of greater Atlanta's local fiscal landscape. In fact, the bulk of local property taxes go to school districts—72 percent of municipal and school property-tax revenues in 2000. The state of Georgia also contributes much more aid to local school districts than to municipalities. State funds represented 52 percent of total school financing in the late 1990s, compared with just 3 percent of municipal expenditures.[29]

Together, state and federal aid in Georgia also do a much better job of equalizing resources available for schools than for municipalities. In 2000, the 95th-to-5th ratio of local tax base per pupil for public schools was 3.2, compared with 5.6 for municipalities. State and federal aid reduced the ratio for school districts to just 1.4, meaning that fiscal capacity in the 95th percentile district exceeded that in the 5th percentile district by 40 percent. The equivalent ratio for municipal services was 5.9, meaning that fiscal capacity in the 95th percentile municipality exceeded that in the 5th percentile place by 490 percent.

However, the fiscal story for schools is not all positive. Districts' fiscal conditions are decided not just by their financial resources, but also by the costs they face in providing a given level of service. To examine the relationship between fiscal condition and service costs in public schools, this study first grouped districts by revenue capacity per pupil. That is the revenue a district would generate for each student if it assessed the state's average tax rate on its own tax base, plus state and federal aid. Districts with capacities per pupil at least 10 percent above the regionwide average

Map 11.10
Atlanta Region: Percentage Change in Property Tax Base per Household by Municipality and County
Unincorporated Area, 1993–2000

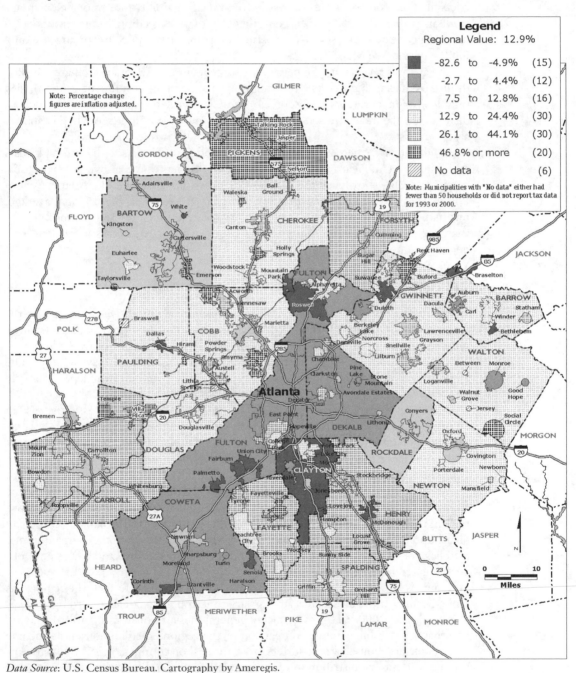

Legend
Regional Value: 12.9%

-82.6 to -4.9%	(15)
-2.7 to 4.4%	(12)
7.5 to 12.8%	(16)
12.9 to 24.4%	(30)
26.1 to 44.1%	(30)
46.8% or more	(20)
No data	(6)

Note: Municipalities with "No data" either had fewer than 50 households or did not report tax data for 1993 or 2000.

Note: Percentage change figures are inflation adjusted.

Data Source: U.S. Census Bureau. Cartography by Ameregis.

were classified as high capacity. Those with capacities at least 10 percent below average were classified as low capacity. The remaining districts were considered moderate capacity.

School districts were then categorized as either low- or high-cost. High-cost districts fit at least one of three criteria—a free-lunch-eligibility rate among elementary students greater than 40 percent, enrollment growth exceeding 30 percent (about 4 percent per year) over a seven-year period, or an enrollment decline of any size during the period (see Map 11.11).[30]

The analysis reveals that 56 percent of students in the Atlanta region are enrolled in districts facing high costs (from high poverty or rapid enrollment growth) with only low or moderate fiscal resources. The Clayton, Coweta, and Paulding school districts are the most stressed districts in this group, facing both low fiscal capacity and high costs.

An additional 22 percent of students are enrolled in districts with both high costs and high revenue capacity. Although these districts have above-average fiscal resources, some show even greater signs of stress. For instance, the Atlanta School District has revenue capacity that is 17 percent greater than the regional average, but its poverty rate (measured by eligibility for free lunch) is 132 percent greater than the average, and the districts must cope with the extra costs associated with declining enrollment as well.

AFFORDABLE HOUSING

The realities of local-government finance create strong incentives for local governments to limit the amount of affordable housing within their jurisdiction. Localities must pay attention to the net effect that any new development will have on local revenues and expenditures—on whether the proposed development "pays its way." The amount of revenue that local governments can generate on their own depends largely on the value and types of land uses within their boundaries.

When the property tax is the primary source of local revenues, as is the case in Georgia, localities have a strong incentive to maximize the value of property by limiting development to high-end residential or commercial developments that augment tax base by more than the cost of the local services they require.

In their attempt to attract high-end residential and commercial developments, many local governments resort to exclusionary zoning practices that limit the amount of affordable housing within their borders. When aggregated over the entire region, this process often results in regionwide shortages of affordable housing and distributions of affordable housing that hurt the regional economy—creating mismatches, for instance, between where workers can afford to live and where new jobs are being created.

Atlanta is known as a relatively affordable housing market. In fact, the region was ranked fourth most affordable among large metropolitan areas according to U.S. Census data in 2000.[31] However, such a general measure of housing affordability—one that is based on a simple comparison of the region's median household income with its median house value—suffers from three shortcomings. First, it fails to capture the geographic distribution of affordable housing and how this relates to other factors like the regional distribution of jobs. Second, it masks the wide disparities that exist in the amount of affordable housing available to people at different income

Map 11.11
Atlanta Region: School District Classification

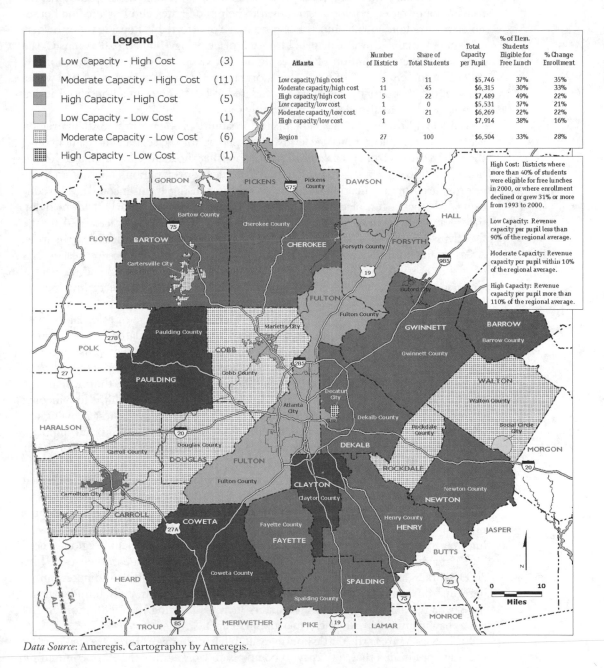

Legend

■	Low Capacity - High Cost	(3)
■	Moderate Capacity - High Cost	(11)
■	High Capacity - High Cost	(5)
▨	Low Capacity - Low Cost	(1)
▦	Moderate Capacity - Low Cost	(6)
▦	High Capacity - Low Cost	(1)

Atlanta	Number of Districts	Share of Total Students	Total Capacity per Pupil	% of Elem. Students Eligible for Free Lunch	% Change Enrollment
Low capacity/high cost	3	11	$5,746	37%	35%
Moderate capacity/high cost	11	45	$6,315	30%	33%
High capacity/high cost	5	22	$7,489	49%	22%
Low capacity/low cost	1	0	$5,531	37%	21%
Moderate capacity/low cost	6	21	$6,269	22%	22%
High capacity/low cost	1	0	$7,914	38%	16%
Region	27	100	$6,504	33%	28%

High Cost: Districts where more than 40% of students were eligible for free lunches in 2000, or where enrollment declined or grew 31% or more from 1993 to 2000.

Low Capacity: Revenue capacity per pupil less than 90% of the regional average.

Moderate Capacity: Revenue capacity per pupil within 10% of the regional average.

High Capacity: Revenue capacity per pupil more than 110% of the regional average.

Data Source: Ameregis. Cartography by Ameregis.

levels. Third, it doesn't reveal how the availability of affordable housing across the region has changed over the last decade.

For this work, the availability of affordable housing in the Atlanta region was examined in 1990 and 2000 for households at three income levels—30 percent, 50 percent, and 80 percent of the regional median income. The price of a home affordable to a household at each income level was calculated using a formula developed by Fannie Mae, a nonprofit corporation established to help moderate- and low-income households achieve homeownership.[32] The percentage of affordable housing units (owner- and renter-occupied) was calculated for each place using 1990 and 2000 census data that details the distribution of homes by market value and apartments by monthly rent. The combined cost of a monthly mortgage and property taxes associated with a home at the affordability cutoff was considered to be the amount a household at that income level could afford to pay in monthly rent.

Maps 11.12 through 11.14 show that affordability problems in the Atlanta region are most severe at lower income levels. At 30 percent of the regional median income, the region suffers from an overall affordable housing shortage—11 percent of households have incomes in this range, but only 6 percent of the region's housing units are affordable to them.[33] In addition, most affordable housing at this income level is concentrated in just a few places—the city of Atlanta, a few inner suburbs, and the older, incorporated centers of the outlying suburbs. The problem is exacerbated by the fact that shortages are most dramatic in the region's most economically active areas. Areas in and around the region's fastest-growing job centers in the northeast (parts of Cobb, Forsyth, Gwinnett, Cherokee, and north Fulton counties) and the southwest (south Fulton and Fayette counties) are largely unaffordable to low-income households.

Although the region does not suffer from an overall shortage of affordable housing at higher income levels, the distribution of housing affordable to these households is very uneven. In 2000, 21 percent of households in the region had incomes less than 50 percent of the regional median, and 25 percent of the region's housing units were affordable to them. For households at 80 percent of the median, the equivalent figures were 39 percent and 63 percent. However, as with the low-income group, housing for these groups is most limited in the region's fastest growing job centers. As a result, even many people with moderate incomes—police, firefighters, and teachers among them—have difficulty finding affordable housing in the areas of the region with the strongest local economies.

The costs associated with mismatches between where new jobs are being created and where low- and moderate-wage workers can afford to live hurts businesses as well as workers. Workers who cannot afford to live near their jobs face longer commutes, increasing costs to themselves and to other users of the region's congested highway system. This is clearly a significant problem in the Atlanta region, where 79.8 percent of the region's workers in 2000 drove to work alone in their cars.[34] By 2000, workers in the region experienced a median commute of 29.5 minutes, up 19 percent from a median of 24.8 minutes in 1990.[35] One recent study found that the time penalty paid by rush-hour commuters increased during the 1990s more in Atlanta than in any other American metropolitan area.[36]

Businesses in areas with little housing suitable for their workforce are also hurt by the wage premiums they must pay to compensate workers for the extra commuting costs associated with working in their location rather than in areas closer to home.

Maps 11.15 through 11.17 show that affordability problems increased during the 1990s. The regionwide availability of affordable housing declined for each of the three income groups during the 1990s. The decline was greatest (3.5 percentage points) for moderate-income households (those with incomes at or below 80 percent of the regional median income). The percentage of housing stock affordable to people with

Map 11.12
Atlanta Region: Percentage of Housing Units Affordable to Households at 30 Percent of the Regional
Median Income by Municipality and County Unincorporated Area, 2000

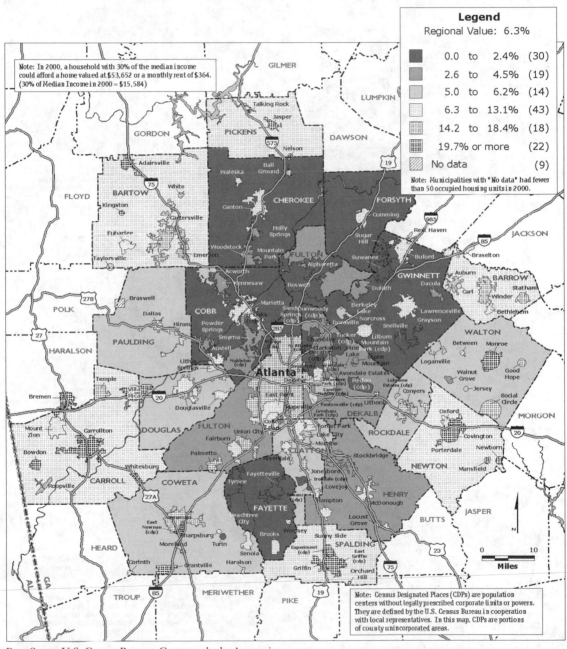

Data Source: U.S. Census Bureau. Cartography by Ameregis.

Map 11.13
Atlanta Region: Percentage of Housing Units Affordable to Households at 50 Percent of the Regional
Median Income by Municipality and County Unincorporated Area, 2000

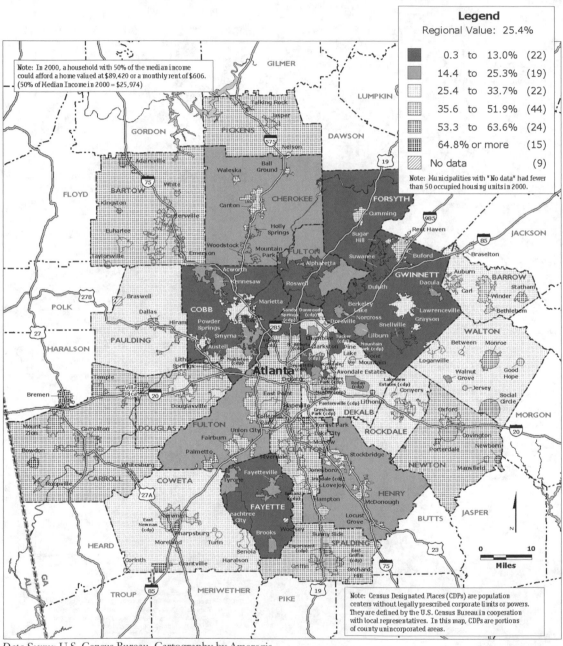

Note: In 2000, a household with 50% of the median income
could afford a home valued at $89,420 or a monthly rent of $606.
(50% of Median Income in 2000 = $25,974)

Legend

Regional Value: 25.4%

	0.3 to 13.0%	(22)
	14.4 to 25.3%	(19)
	25.4 to 33.7%	(22)
	35.6 to 51.9%	(44)
	53.3 to 63.6%	(24)
	64.8% or more	(15)
	No data	(9)

Note: Municipalities with "No data" had fewer
than 50 occupied housing units in 2000.

Note: Census Designated Places (CDPs) are population
centers without legally prescribed corporate limits or powers.
They are defined by the U.S. Census Bureau in cooperation
with local representatives. In this map, CDPs are portions
of county unincorporated areas.

Data Source: U.S. Census Bureau. Cartography by Ameregis.

Map 11.14
Atlanta Region: Percentage of Housing Units Affordable to Households at 80 Percent of the Regional
Median Income by Municipality and County Unincorporated Area, 2000

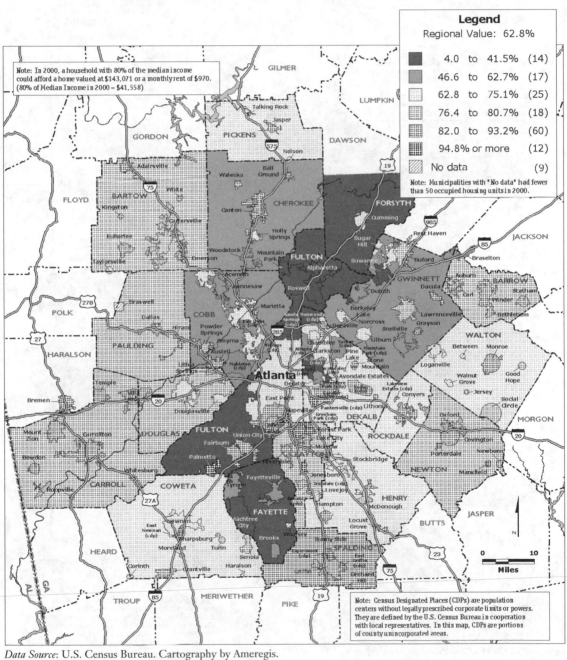

Legend
Regional Value: 62.8%

	4.0 to 41.5%	(14)
	46.6 to 62.7%	(17)
	62.8 to 75.1%	(25)
	76.4 to 80.7%	(18)
	82.0 to 93.2%	(60)
	94.8% or more	(12)
	No data	(9)

Note: Municipalities with "No data" had fewer
than 50 occupied housing units in 2000.

Note: In 2000, a household with 80% of the median income
could afford a home valued at $143,071 or a monthly rent of $970.
(80% of Median Income in 2000 = $41,558)

Note: Census Designated Places (CDPs) are population
centers without legally prescribed corporate limits or powers.
They are defined by the U.S. Census Bureau in cooperation
with local representatives. In this map, CDPs are portions
of county unincorporated areas.

0   10
Miles

Data Source: U.S. Census Bureau. Cartography by Ameregis.

Map 11.15
Atlanta Region: Change in Percentage of Housing Units Affordable to Households at 30 Percent of the
Regional Income by Municipality and County Unincorporated Area, 1990–2000

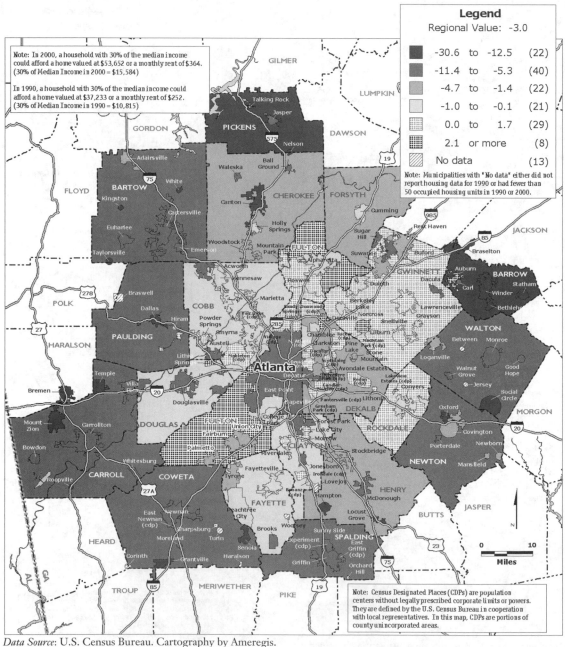

Legend

Regional Value: -3.0

■	-30.6 to -12.5	(22)
▨	-11.4 to -5.3	(40)
▨	-4.7 to -1.4	(22)
▨	-1.0 to -0.1	(21)
▨	0.0 to 1.7	(29)
▨	2.1 or more	(8)
▨	No data	(13)

Note: Municipalities with "No data" either did not report housing data for 1990 or had fewer than 50 occupied housing units in 1990 or 2000.

Note: In 2000, a household with 30% of the median income could afford a home valued at $53,652 or a monthly rent of $364. (30% of Median Income in 2000 = $15,584)

In 1990, a household with 30% of the median income could afford a home valued at $37,233 or a monthly rent of $252. (30% of Median Income in 1990 = $10,815)

Note: Census Designated Places (CDPs) are population centers without legally prescribed corporate limits or powers. They are defined by the U.S. Census Bureau in cooperation with local representatives. In this map, CDPs are portions of county unincorporated areas.

Data Source: U.S. Census Bureau. Cartography by Ameregis.

Map 11.16
Atlanta Region: Change in Percentage of Housing Units Affordable to Households at 50 Percent of the
Regional Income by Municipality and County Unincorporated Area, 1990–2000

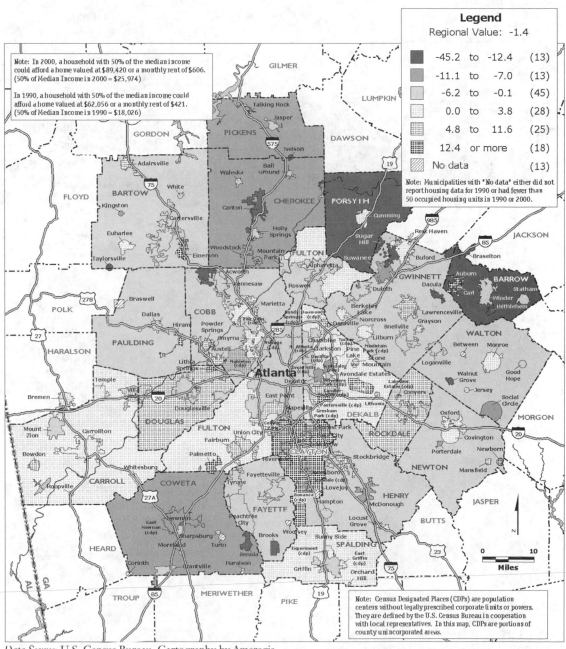

Legend

Regional Value: -1.4

-45.2 to -12.4	(13)
-11.1 to -7.0	(13)
-6.2 to -0.1	(45)
0.0 to 3.8	(28)
4.8 to 11.6	(25)
12.4 or more	(18)
No data	(13)

Note: Municipalities with "No data" either did not
report housing data for 1990 or had fewer than
50 occupied housing units in 1990 or 2000.

Note: In 2000, a household with 50% of the median income
could afford a home valued at $89,420 or a monthly rent of $606.
(50% of Median Income in 2000 = $25,974)

In 1990, a household with 50% of the median income could
afford a home valued at $62,056 or a monthly rent of $421.
(50% of Median Income in 1990 = $18,026)

Note: Census Designated Places (CDPs) are population
centers without legally prescribed corporate limits or powers.
They are defined by the U.S. Census Bureau in cooperation
with local representatives. In this map, CDPs are portions of
county unincorporated areas.

Data Source: U.S. Census Bureau. Cartography by Ameregis.

Map 11.17
Atlanta Region: Change in Percentage of Housing Units Affordable to Households at 80 Percent of the
Regional Income by Municipality and County Unincorporated Area, 1990–2000

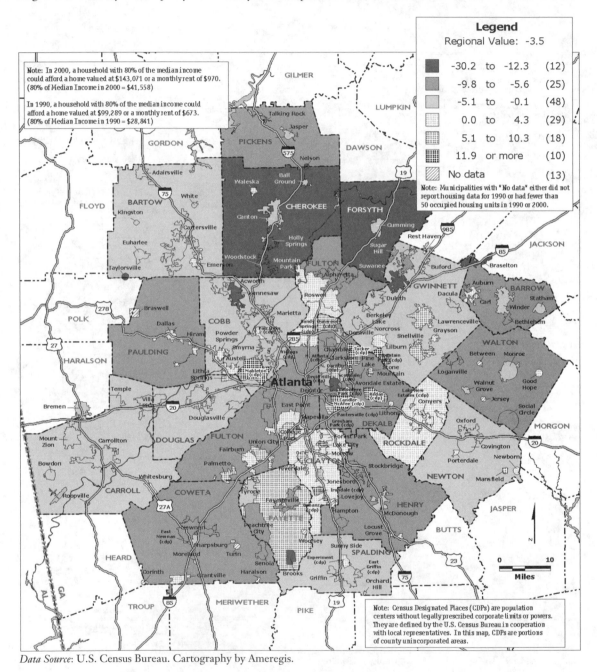

Legend

Regional Value: -3.5

■	-30.2 to -12.3	(12)
■	-9.8 to -5.6	(25)
▨	-5.1 to -0.1	(48)
▨	0.0 to 4.3	(29)
▨	5.1 to 10.3	(18)
▨	11.9 or more	(10)
▨	No data	(13)

Note: Municipalities with "No data" either did not report housing data for 1990 or had fewer than 50 occupied housing units in 1990 or 2000.

Note: In 2000, a household with 80% of the median income could afford a home valued at $143,071 or a monthly rent of $970. (80% of Median Income in 2000 = $41,558)

In 1990, a household with 80% of the median income could afford a home valued at $99,289 or a monthly rent of $673. (80% of Median Income in 1990 = $28,841)

Note: Census Designated Places (CDPs) are population centers without legally prescribed corporate limits or powers. They are defined by the U.S. Census Bureau in cooperation with local representatives. In this map, CDPs are portions of county unincorporated areas.

0   10
Miles

Data Source: U.S. Census Bureau. Cartography by Ameregis.

30 percent of the regional median income declined by nearly as much—3 percentage points. The declines were widespread, with no parts of the region showing consistent gains across the income categories.

Map 11.18 summarizes the distribution of affordable housing shortfalls for the three income levels. A place is considered to have a shortfall of housing affordable to households of a particular income if the share of its housing stock that is affordable to that group is less than the portion of the region's households that fall in that income range. For instance, 11 percent of the region's households had incomes below 30 percent of the regional median income in 2000. A place was therefore considered to have a housing shortfall for that income range if less than 11 percent of its housing stock was affordable to households in that group. (The equivalent cutoffs for 50 percent and 80 percent of the median income were 21 percent and 39 percent, respectively.)

Overall, affordable housing shortfalls are greatest in Forsyth, Fulton, and Fayette counties. Large tracts of these counties show shortfalls for all three income categories. The unincorporated portion of Cherokee County and a few other municipalities east of Atlanta show shortages in both of the lower income categories, while much of the rest of the region has shortfalls for the lowest income category. Only the city of Atlanta, a few inner suburbs, and outlying incorporated areas meet the affordability standard for each income group.

Not surprisingly, these patterns correspond with many of the other trends revealed elsewhere in this work. In particular, affordable housing shortfalls tend to be greatest in areas with the highest tax bases, greatest job growth, and lowest poverty in schools. These areas could therefore absorb significant amounts of affordable housing without risking damage to their fiscal condition. The clear implication is that the region is in a position to reap the significant economic and social benefits from distributing affordable housing more evenly—including shorter commutes and lower costs of dealing with the effects of highly concentrated poverty—without injury to areas that accept more affordable housing.

LOOKING FORWARD: STRATEGIES FOR REFORM

Regional competition for tax base and uncoordinated growth are hurting almost every city and suburb in the Atlanta region—leading to concentrated poverty and abandoned public facilities in the central city, growing social and fiscal strain in older suburbs, and traffic snarls, overcrowded schools, and degraded natural resources on the urban fringe.

The fragmented nature of the region's political system—20 counties, 129 municipalities, and 29 school districts—makes it unlikely that reform at the local level will solve these complex problems. Solutions must focus on regional initiatives. Broad policy areas where regional reforms are most needed to combat social separation and wasteful sprawl include:

- *Greater tax equity* to equalize resources among local governments,
- Smarter *land-use planning* to support more sustainable development practices,
- New *affordable housing initiatives* to expand opportunities for low- and moderate-income residents and promote integrated schools and neighborhoods,

Map 11.18
Atlanta Region: Affordable Housing Shortfalls by Municipality and County Unincorporated Area, 2000

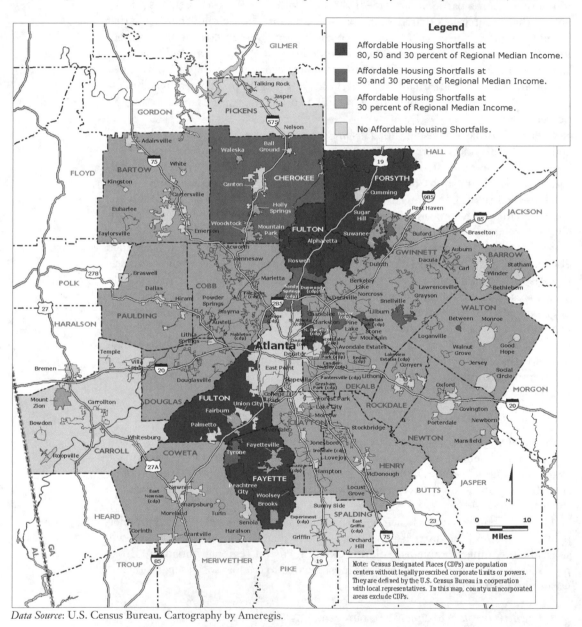

Data Source: U.S. Census Bureau. Cartography by Ameregis.

- Strengthened *metropolitan governance* to give all communities a voice in regional decision making.

In addition to addressing individual problems, these strategies are mutually reinforcing. Successfully implementing one makes implementing others much easier, both substantively and politically.

Tax Equity

One area ripe for reform is Georgia's local government tax system. In the state's system, residential and commercial development largely determine a community's local tax base. As a result, there is wide variation in the ability of local governments to generate revenue from their tax bases.

Reducing disparities among local governments is important because it helps reduce the incentives for communities to compete against their neighbors for tax-generating developments, regardless of how they would best fit into regional land-use patterns. It also provides a boost to places struggling with weak tax bases and great social and physical needs, and it assures that all residents enjoy at least a minimum standard of service for important local public services.

There are regional policies that can both reduce the inequalities between local governments and decrease the incentives for them to engage in wasteful competition for tax base.

Implement Tax-Base Sharing

One possible strategy involves moving from reliance on locally generated tax revenues toward a form of tax-base sharing. In such a system, a portion of regional tax base is pooled and redistributed on a more equitable basis.

Since the early 1970s, the Minneapolis–St. Paul region and the New Jersey Meadowlands have had tax-base sharing programs. Each year, the Twin Cities program collects 40 percent of the growth in commercial-industrial property-tax revenues from the region's local governments. This pool of funds is then redistributed based on local per-capita tax base. Another program in New Jersey, the Meadowlands program, operates on a smaller scale. It collects 40 percent of growth in all property tax revenues in the Meadowlands district, which encompasses portions of 14 communities and redistributes the funds based on the share of the area's property value that falls in each of the communities.[37]

In both cases, this process has a redistributive effect—tax-base-poor communities get back more than they paid into the pool, while tax-base-rich communities get back less. Because all communities keep a majority (but not all) of the growth within their borders, the program also reduces the incentives to compete for tax base while still allowing communities to cover the local costs of development.

Other Policy Alternatives

Tax-base sharing is just one way to create more equitable fiscal relationships among local governments. Disparities can also be significantly reduced by reforming the state's municipal-aid program. In its current form, the program does little to ease disparities among local governments. A reformed state-aid program could be modeled after Georgia's school-aid program, which is designed to increase equity among school districts. State aid for municipalities can ensure that all places have the resources to support services that, like education, many would consider essential—among them public safety, streets, and sanitation services.

In addition, in areas where development is desired, the property tax can be improved by allowing for differential taxation of land and what is built on it. Used most extensively in Pennsylvania, the "two-tier" property tax can encourage more intensive use of land by taxing land more heavily than improvements.[38] By shifting the tax burden from the improvements to the land itself, this type of tax encourages development of abandoned or underdeveloped land in already developed areas. In addition, when combined with other measures to protect farmland or open space, it encourages more efficient use of land in developing areas.

Regional Land-Use Planning

Tax policies are only part of the reason for the inequitable and inefficient growth occurring in the Atlanta area. The localized nature of planning also contributes to unbalanced growth. This arrangement makes it very difficult to implement coherent policies in areas with regional implications, such as housing, transportation, economic development, or environmental protection. A variety of reforms are possible in this area.

Strengthen the Georgia Planning Act

Developing a cooperative land-use planning framework that encourages places to consider the regional consequences of local decisions is an essential aspect of a regional reform agenda. Increasingly, officials around the country are turning to smart growth, an efficient and environmentally friendly development pattern that aims to preserve open space and agricultural lands, ease traffic congestion by creating a balanced transportation system, and make more efficient use of public investments. Smart growth provides people choice in where they live and work and how they get around.

The Georgia Planning Act, adopted by the state general assembly in 1989, embraces smart growth principles, but lacks ways to enforce its goals. The state has a variety of tools at its disposal to give the plan more teeth: technical assistance, streamlined permitting, and, most importantly, a broad spectrum of state spending and monetary aid. Any of these could be dispensed on a priority basis, favoring municipalities that enact planning and zoning rules consistent with the planning act. Such incentives would encourage local governments to consider more of the costs and benefits to the entire region when making development decisions.

Regional land-use planning efforts, like those required in Oregon's statewide program, help officials coordinate investments in roads, highways, sewers, and utilities. Concurrency requirements like those in Florida mandate that infrastructure be online by the time development takes place. In addition, there are also a variety of agricultural and open-space preservation programs available.[39]

In addition to its social and environmental benefits, emphasizing compact development and community reinvestment can save money. Analysis of New Jersey's State Development and Redevelopment Plan, which emphasizes smart growth, found that implementing the plan would reduce the fiscal deficits of local governments caused by growth by an estimated $160 million over 20 years and save an estimated $1.45 billion in water and sewer infrastructure.[40]

Adopt a "Fix It First" Policy on Infrastructure

Land-use policies cannot be separated from decisions on infrastructure investments—sewers, roads, bridges, and schools. These facilities have powerful effects on development patterns. State subsidies of such facilities in previously undeveloped areas have encouraged low-density sprawling development at the expense of existing communities.

Particularly in an era of tight budgets, Georgia officials should focus limited dollars on existing facilities. Lawmakers could, for instance, follow the lead of New Jersey legislators, who in 2000 approved a "fix it first" policy that gives funding priority to maintaining roads and bridges in existing communities. In Michigan, officials are considering a similar policy that would reserve 90 percent of state infrastructure funding for existing facilities and would require developers to pay impact fees to cover the full cost of water and sewer extensions to their developments.

Affordable Housing

Ensuring that all communities in greater Atlanta, particularly those fast-growing suburbs with new jobs and good schools, strengthen their commitment to affordable housing is an essential component of a reform agenda because it helps reduce the consequences of concentrated poverty and racial segregation on core communities. It allows people to live closer to work and provides them with real choices concerning where they live.

There are several types of fair-share housing efforts that may have a place in greater Atlanta.[41] New Jersey's Mount Laurel program is perhaps the most developed and best known. Based on decisions issued by the New Jersey Supreme Court, Mount Laurel requires all communities in the state to provide "realistic opportunities" for affordable housing. A state agency calculates the number of units each community must allow using a complex formula that takes into account the community's existing housing stock, median income, availability of land, and other factors. Participation is voluntary, but communities that submit a plan for meeting their housing goals are protected from Mount Laurel-related lawsuits by developers.

Massachusetts's fair-housing act, referred to as the Anti-Snob Zoning Act, allows affordable-housing developers to appeal the denial of a local zoning application to a statewide appeals committee. This committee may overrule the decision of the local board if subsidized affordable housing represents less than 10 percent of the community's housing stock or covers less than 1.5 percent of land zoned for residential, commercial, or industrial use, or if the proposed development remains within certain size limits. This appeals process is combined with finance programs to encourage affordable housing construction.

Other states have enacted other strategies. In the Portland, Oregon, area regional officials aim to reduce the cost of land by requiring local communities to zone residential land using minimum, instead of maximum, density requirements. In Connecticut, the state offered incentives that encouraged local governments in the Hartford region to negotiate an affordable housing compact that established affordable housing goals for each community.

Each of these models has both strengths and weaknesses. For example, the New Jersey program defines the number of affordable units needed in each community based on a complex formula that takes into account a wide array of community characteristics, but requires a team of employees to calculate. Massachusetts's program uses a much simpler formula to decide whether a community has met its affordable housing obligation, but the uniform requirement does not take into account the breadth of factors the New Jersey program does.

Other methods to expand the supply of affordable housing in economically stable communities include a state multifamily housing tax credit and a "moving to opportunity" program that assists low-income families relocating to low-poverty communities. Programs like these can help reduce housing segregation and increase opportunities for very low-income people.

An expedient way of introducing affordable housing to areas that lack such housing is building developments that are heterogeneous in terms of income. These mixed-income communities are less likely to elicit NIMBY reactions from communities and local governments and tend to make zoning approvals more politically feasible.[42]

Moreover, mixed-income communities create a number of economic and social benefits that make them attractive.[43] Because they also enable higher-quality housing with smaller amounts of public subsidy, they make affordable housing more viable, and, thus, can be important in getting additional affordable units built. In addition, mixed-income communities help alleviate the social ills associated with concentrated poverty by offering role-modeling to children of poor families and job-networking opportunities for adults.

Although mixed-income communities can also present unique managing and marketing challenges to developers,[44] these communities could be an effective way to address the skewed regional distribution of affordable housing in the Atlanta region.

Metropolitan Governance

As in most places, the fragmented nature of local government in greater Atlanta has discouraged coordinated strategies for dealing with regional problems. That is unfortunate, because many of the challenges are simply too large for any one local government to address alone.

Effective, efficient regional efforts strike a balance by allowing local control over issues best addressed by local governments, while promoting cooperation on larger issues affecting the entire region, such as highway and sewer investments, affordable housing, transit, land-use planning, air and water quality, and economic development.

Intergovernmental cooperation in the Atlanta area can be improved both by strengthening existing regional bodies and by creating incentives for communities to cooperate on planning efforts and service provision.

Strengthen Regional Institutions

The Atlanta region already has two important regional bodies, the Atlanta Regional Commission (ARC) and the Georgia Regional Transportation Authority (GRTA). GRTA has fairly broad powers to improve transportation in the region, including the ability to finance projects that alleviate air pollution, to approve land transportation plans, and to operate transit systems. ARC oversees a variety of regional activities, including land use, water supply and transportation planning, employment services, and regional data analysis. In addition, ARC serves as the region's metropolitan planning organization, a body empowered by the federal government to make planning and funding decisions for the region's transportation systems.

These organizations have many accomplishments to their credit, but their powers to enact significant regional reforms are still limited. Armed with greater powers, they could make more headway on a whole host of regional issues, such as land-use planning, housing and redevelopment efforts, and the protection of farmland and other open spaces. Greater powers should be accompanied by reforms making these organizations directly accountable to constituents.[45]

In addition, these bodies must be appropriately scaled. While the legislation that created GRTA allows it to expand its jurisdiction to new counties if they exceed certain air quality measures, ARC's boundaries have remained static as the region has grown considerably. The agency serves only 10 counties within a metropolitan area that, based on its housing and labor markets, now covers 20 counties. For ARC to become a more effective regional body, its jurisdiction should be expanded to cover the entire metropolitan area.

If not crafted carefully, regional efforts like these can potentially dilute the political power of minority and other underrepresented communities.[46] To avoid such an undemocratic outcome, elements of local and regional governance should be balanced very carefully to ensure fair representation for all communities. Specific institutional arrangements to achieve such a balance have already been suggested by numerous scholars.[47]

It is also important to remember that local and regional governance are not mutually exclusive. Indeed, examples of fruitful cooperation in Atlanta demonstrate that local and regional entities can successfully reinforce each other in dealing with regional problems. One example is the cooperation between the Atlanta Neighborhood Development Partnership, Inc. (ANDP)—a local advocacy group—and the Atlanta Regional Commission. Thanks to efforts by ANDP, ARC made the distribution of regional transportation funds to local governments contingent on their accommodation of mixed-income housing developments.

Encourage Municipal Cooperation

There are many opportunities for local governments to participate in alliances and joint planning activities without changes in regional governance structures. In Pennsylvania, for example, "smart growth" legislation passed in 2000 authorizes local governments to work together to plan and to implement plans and provides several tools to help, including transfer of development rights and tax-base sharing programs. It also authorizes state agencies to provide funding priority to these cooperative efforts.[48]

Montgomery County, Ohio, home to Dayton and 29 other localities, has established a program to share some of the benefits of new economic development.[49] The ED/GE program provides both a countywide funding pool for economic development projects and a "government equity" fund that shares a portion of growth in municipal property- and income-tax revenues. Although small in scale, the voluntary program is a mechanism for local governments to share the benefits and the responsibilities of economic development and growth.

There are also examples of communities banding together around shared interests. The First Suburbs Consortium—an organization of older suburbs in several Ohio metropolitan areas—has undertaken a variety of activities to improve their health, including lobbying for changes to state laws that currently emphasize building new infrastructure instead of maintaining existing facilities. They also established a low-interest home-improvement loan program for residents of member communities.[50]

Organize and Mobilize

Meaningful regional reform will not occur by releasing a report. Nor will it will be achieved simply by the goodwill of politicians. Real change will require a broad coalition of elected officials who are motivated by political self-interest and the social and fiscal health of the communities they represent.

But there are communities where opponents—waving the banner of local control—are sure to resist reform. In these places, reformers can help counter resistance by mobilizing support from the religious community and civil-rights, environmental, labor, and business organizations—groups that can appeal to both self-interest and ideals.

Such changes will offer relief to all communities. For cities, they mean enhanced opportunities for redevelopment and for the poor. For fiscally stressed suburbs, they mean stability, community renewal, lower taxes, and better services. For developing bedroom communities, they offer sufficient spending on schools and clean air and water. Affluent suburban communities also stand to gain from regional efforts that preserve open space and reduce traffic congestion.

NOTES

Editor's Note: Atlanta Metropatterns is a joint project of Metropolitan Area Research Corporation, Ameregis, and Atlanta Neighborhood Development Partnership. It is funded by a grant from the Annie E. Casey Foundation. Published by the Metropolitan Area Research Corporation in August 2003. It is reprinted here with permission.

Ameregis is a research and geographic information systems (GIS) firm that documents evolving development patterns in U.S. metropolitan regions and the growing social and economic disparities within them. Ameregis is dedicated to integrating GIS mapping and traditional research methods to inform decision-making. Metropolitan Area Research Corporation is a research and advocacy organization that participated in this project. These two organizations assist individuals and groups in fashioning local remedies that address these concerns. Both were founded by Myron Orfield, a nationally recognized leader in promoting reform around issues of land use, social and fiscal equity, and regional governance.

Atlanta Neighborhood Development Partnership (ANDP) is a nonprofit organization established in 1991 to develop and rehabilitate very low- and low-to-moderate-income housing, develop other neighborhood services, and empower Community Development Corporations (CDCs). The Partnership is among a select group of housing intermediary organizations in the United States that leads and supports grassroots efforts by connecting community residents with resources, funding opportunities, expertise, training, and other services to stabilize and revitalize neighborhoods.

1. In this study the Atlanta region is defined as the Atlanta Metropolitan Statistical Area. It currently includes the following 20 counties: Barrow, Bartow, Carroll, Cherokee, Clayton, Cobb, Coweta, DeKalb, Douglas, Fayette, Forsyth, Fulton, Gwinnett, Henry, Newton, Paulding, Pickens, Spalding, Rockdale, and Walton.

2. Only three of the existing 18 job centers in the Atlanta region are located to the south of I-20—a freeway that historically divided the region racially and geographically. Similarly, only one of the five newly emerging job centers in the region is located to the south of I-20. For a map illustrating the geography of employment centers in the Atlanta region, see Figure 2 in Robert D. Bullard et al., *Sprawl Atlanta: Social Equity Dimensions of Uneven Growth and Development* (Atlanta: Clark Atlanta University, The Environmental Justice Resource Center, January 1999), available at http://www.ejrc.cau.edu/sprlatlexcsum.html.

3. See Table PHC-T-4 in U.S. Census data, 2000.

4. Computed from the U.S. Department of Transportation, Federal Highway Administration, Highway Statistics Table HM-72, October 2002. The table is available at http://www.fhwa.dot.gov/ohim/hs01/hm72.htm.

5. See Paul A. Jargowsky and Mary Jo Bane, "Ghetto Poverty in the United States, 1970 to 1980," in Christopher Jencks and Paul E. Peterson, eds., *The Urban Underclass* (Washington, DC: The Brookings Institution, 1991), pp. 235–73; John D. Kasarda, "Inner-City Concentrated Poverty and Neighborhood Distress: 1970 to 1990," *Housing Policy Debate* 4(3): 253–302.

6. In 2000, 34 percent of Pittsburgh residents in the workforce used public transportation to get to work, while only 3.7 percent of the workforce in the Atlanta metro area went to work by public transit.

7. *Moving Beyond Sprawl: The Challenge for Metropolitan Atlanta* (Washington, DC: The Brookings Institution), available at http://www.brook.edu/dybdocroot/es/urban/atlanta/consequences1.htm.

8. Urban Collage, Inc., Huntley & Associates, Altamira Design and Common Sense, CHJP and Associates, *Pittsburgh Community Redevelopment Plan*, September 2001.

9. Computed from U.S. Census data, 1990 and 2000.

10. For examples of such exclusionary zoning practices in Henry and Fayette counties, see Janet Frankston, "Sprawl Linked Back to Lack of Affordable Housing," *The Atlanta Journal-Constitution*, September 30, 2002.

11. Larry C. Ledebur and William R. Barnes, *All in It Together: Cities, Suburbs and Local Economic Regions* (Washington, DC: National League of Cities, 1993).

12. William R. Barnes and Larry C. Ledebur, *City Distress, Metropolitan Disparities, and Economic Growth* (Washington, DC: National League of Cities, 1992).

13. U.S. Census data, 2000.

14. See Figure 2 in Bullard et al., *Sprawl Atlanta*.

15. See www.sierraclub.org/sprawl/whitepaper.asp.

16. In 2000, the percentage of nonwhites in the overall population of the Atlanta region averaged 40.2 percent. The corresponding percentages were 65.1 in Clayton, 67.8 in DeKalb, 54.7 in Fulton, and 68.7 in the City of Atlanta in the same year. U.S. Census data, 2000.

17. See James S. Coleman, *Equality of Educational Opportunity* (Washington, DC: Government Printing Office, 1966); Gary Burtless, ed., *Does Money Matter? The Effect of School Resources on Student Achievement and Adult Success* (Washington, DC: Brookings, 1996); James Traub, "What No School Can Do," *New York Times Magazine*, January 16, 2000.

18. These percentages are dissimilarity indexes, commonly used statistics to measure the degree to which two groups are evenly distributed in a given geographic area. In this case, they can be interpreted as the percentage of one of the groups that would have to change for all schools to have the same racial or income mix. For more information on school and residential segregation in U.S. metropolitan areas, see John R. Logan, "Choosing Segregation: Racial Imbalance in American Public Schools, 1990–2000" (Albany, NY: Lewis Mumford Center for Comparative Urban and Regional Research, State University of New York at Albany, 2002), available at www.albany.edu/mumford/census/.

19. Gary Orfield and John T. Yun, *Resegregation in American Schools* (Cambridge, MA: The Civil Rights Project, Harvard University, 1999).

20. For a general discussion of housing discrimination, see John Yinger, "Testing for Discrimination in Housing and Related Markets," in *A National Report Card on Discrimination in America*, ed. Michael Fix and Margery Austin Turner (Washington, DC: The Urban Institute, 1998). High-poverty schools are those with free lunch eligibility rates of 40 percent or greater.

21. See Table 3-2 in Myron Orfield, *American Metropolitics: The New Suburban Reality* (Washington, DC: Brookings Institute Press, 2002), p. 52.

22. Richard W. Williamson, "Busting at the Seams: Gwinnett Schools Are Overcrowded and Getting Worse," *Creative Loafing*, January 27, 2001, available at http://atlanta.creativeloafing.com/2001-01-27/comment.html.

23. Jonathan Crane, "The Effects of Neighborhoods on Dropping Out of School and Teenage Childbearing," in *The Urban Underclass*, pp. 299–320; Susan E. Mayer, "How Much Does a High School's Racial and Socioeconomic Mix Affect Graduation and Teenage Fertility Rates?" in *The Urban Underclass*, pp. 321–41; Douglass S. Massey and Nancy A. Denton, *American Apartheid* (Cambridge, MA: Harvard University Press), pp. 169–70; Dennis P. Hogan and Evelyn Kitagawa, "The Impact of Social Status, Family Structure, and Neighborhood on the Fertility of Black Adolescents," *American Journal of Sociology* 90(4) (1985): 825–55; Frank F. Furstenburg Jr., S. Philip Morgan, Kristen A. Moore, and James Peterson, "Race Differences in the Timing of Adolescent Intercourse," *American Sociological Review* 52 (1987): 511–18; Elijah Anderson, "Neighborhood Effects on Teenage Pregnancy," in *The Urban Underclass*, pp. 375–98; Sara McLanahan and Irwin Garfinkel, "Single Mothers, the Underclass, and Social Policy," *The Annals of the American Academy of Political and Social Science* 501 (1989): 92.

24. Crane, "The Effects of Neighborhoods," pp. 274–320; Mayer, "Graduation and Teenage Fertility Rates," pp. 321–41; Massey and Denton, *American Apartheid*, pp. 169–70.

25. Massey and Denton, *American Apartheid*, pp. 180–82.

26. Among the 25 largest metropolitan areas in the country, Atlanta was the ninth most politically fragmented region in 1997. Georgia ranked 49th out of 50 states in the percentage of municipal expenditures financed by state aid. See Orfield, *American Metropolitics*, Tables 5-1 and 7-2.

27. See this chapter's "Affordable Housing" section for a further discussion of why this is the case.

28. This assumes that a dollar of spending generates the same amount of services in all parts of the region. In reality, however, the areas with the lowest capacities are also likely to be the places with the highest service costs, implying that the actual disparities are even greater than this simple comparison indicates.

29. See Orfield, *American Metropolitics*, p. 87.

30. These measures reflect a range of factors that increase costs. A high rate of free-lunch eligibility, a commonly used proxy for poverty, generates greater needs for services and increases the cost of reaching a given level of service. Enrollment declines increase costs per pupil because fixed costs are spread over fewer students and because some variable costs are often difficult to reduce over relatively short time periods. Quickly growing enrollments increase costs because it is often difficult to spread the associated capital costs over the full lifetime of the assets.

31. Tinah Saunders, "Atlanta Ranked as Fourth Most-Affordable Housing Market," *The Atlanta Journal-Constitution*, July 1, 2002.

32. The formula assumes that housing costs should not exceed 28 percent of gross income. A calculator available at www.fanniemae.com was used to calculate the affordability cut-offs assuming an mortgage rate of 7 percent, a 10 percent down payment, and local property taxes equal to the region-wide average in the relevant years.

33. U.S. Census data, 2000.

34. This percentage is slightly higher than the percentage of commuters who drove to work alone in Georgia, which had the 15th highest share of commuters driving to work alone in the nation in 2000. U.S. Census data, 2000.

35. Computed from U.S. Census data, 1999 and 2000.

36. David Schrank and Tim Lomax, *2001 Urban Mobility Report* (College Station: Texas Transportation Institute, Texas A&M University 2001), Table A-3, p. 39.

37. See Thomas Luce, "Regional Tax Base Sharing: The Twin Cities Experience," in Helen F. Ladd, *Local Government Tax and Land Use Policies in the United States* (Northhampton, MA: Elgar Publishing, 1998) and New Jersey Meadowlands Commission, "Tax Sharing in the Meadowlands District," available at www.hmdc.state.nj.us/tax.html.

38. See Alanna Hartzok, "Pennsylvania's Success with Local Property Tax Reform: The Split Rate Tax," available at www.earthrights.net/docs/success.html and Wallace E. Oates and Robert M. Schwab, "The Pittsburgh Experience with Land Value Taxation," in Ladd, *Local Government Tax and Land Use Policies*.

39. See Orfield, *American Metropolitics*, for more discussion of land-use planning tools.

40. "The Costs and Benefits of Alternative Growth Patterns: The Impact Assessment of the New Jersey State Plan" (New Brunswick, NJ: Center for Urban Policy Research, Edward J. Bloustein School of Planning and Public Policy, September 2000).

41. This summary of state fair-share housing policies is from Charles E. Connerly and Marc Smith, "Developing a Fair Share Housing Policy for Florida," *Journal of Land Use and Environmental Law* 12(1) (1996).

42. Charles S. Wilkins Jr., "Concept Paper: Mixed-Income Rental Housing" (Millennial Housing Commission Preservation and Production Task Forces, n.d.), available at www.mhc.gov/papers/cpmirh.doc.

43. The following discussion of the positive social and economic externalities associated with mixed-income communities is based on Alastair Smith, *Mixed-Income Housing Developments: Promise and Reality* (Cambridge, MA: Joint Center for Housing Studies of Harvard University Neighborhood Reinvestment Corporation, October 2002) and on Charles S. Wilkins Jr., "Concept Paper."

44. Smith, "Mixed-Income Housing Developments."

45. See, for example, note 44.

46. John Powell, *Racism and Metropolitan Dynamics: The Civil Rights Challenge of the 21st Century* (Minneapolis, MN: Institute on Race and Poverty, August 2002), p. 25, available at http://www1.umn.edu/irp/publications/racismandmetrodynamics.pdf.

47. An important concept that focuses on protecting minority interests within a regionalist agenda is John Powell's notion of "federated regionalism." For an elaboration of this concept, see John Powell, "Race and Space," *Poverty and Race*, January/February 1999, available at http://www.prrac.org/topics/jan99/powell.htm; and Powell, "Racism and Metropolitan Dynamics."

48. See Joanne R. Denworth, "Growing Smarter Legislation—New Options for Multi-Municipal Planning and Implementation" (Philadelphia: 10,000 Friends of Pennsylvania, May 2001), available at www.10000friends.org.

49. Montgomery County Economic Development/Government Equity (Ed/Ge) Handbook, 2001–2010.

50. See www.firstsuburbs.org.

PART III

WHAT'S WRONG WITH SPRAWL?

12

Shared Freedom: A Dynamic Standard for Equity in the Sprawl Debate

John Moynihan

Recognition of the inherent dignity of the equal and unalienable rights of all members of the human family is the foundation of freedom, justice, and peace in the world.

United Nations Universal Declaration of Human Rights,
December 10, 1948

AGREEING ON THE MEANING OF EQUITY

Hard-nosed developers and real estate investors will tell you that residential development is about legal, financial, and political deals. They will tell you that it is a tough, confrontational business in which developers get trapped between regulatory permitting needs and community mitigation costs. These costs are viewed as the "equity" issue by "constituent oriented" local politicians, but beyond the limited value structures of developers, investors, and politicians, equity is more than mitigation costs and extra-low income housing squeezed out of development profits. It is the fundamental requirement for sustained economic and social growth. It is the ethos of a people. The development pattern of a region, especially the assortment and suitability of the housing available, are visible indicators of equity. It is what makes communities authentic, livable, and civilized with the variety of housing needed over a lifetime by most people. Communities either contribute to—or detract from—the ability of present and emerging generations to live lives that they value, and attempts to explain the absence of equity in housing as a result of market demands put the issue of equity on the sprawl agenda.

The values debate regarding equity has come alive these days thanks to Neo-traditionalist initiatives.[1] Unfortunately, their approach to it centers on a false choice between either the quest for an "efficient society" or the quest for a "human community," as if fundamental logic prohibited the achievement of both. In reality, the upward progress of human development is not a selection between these false alternatives, but, in fact, only moves forward when both are included. Real estate development portrayed as a conflict between either developing or acquiring properties, and the intelligent planning of livable communities, is a simplistic and false divide. The premise of this article is that anything that does not serve the human needs of both efficient society and human community cannot, as a matter of historical reality, survive.

SCHOOLS OF THOUGHT REGARDING EQUITY

While equity or ethical theories about fairness may constitute a large part of the history of philosophy, there is very little agreement about what we mean by equity even though there are only about four schools of ethical thought that inform current policy debates. At times aspects of these systems blend and at other times lead to opposing conclusions.

The *rights-based* approach to ethical thinking started with the Platonic worldview of the English philosopher Thomas Hobbes, who saw every individual as being at war with every other individual and therefore viewed the ethics of interpersonal relationship as the rules of engagement for war. Endless struggle between conflicting individual rights is resolved by forming contractual agreements that become the "Leviathan" or the government. In this way, autonomous individuals are able to address common needs. It prioritizes principles (human rights) over policies (societal goals). As the opening quote from the United Nations indicates, human rights are a universal approach to ethical policy.

Utilitarian ethical standards take things in the opposite direction and measure actions by the final result rather than the starting principle. The central issue for the early nineteenth-century English philosopher Jeremy Bentham was that the rightness of actions depends on their "utility," meaning the benefit, pleasure, or happiness produced by the action. The utilitarian school measures moral action in terms of consequences. Actions are good if they produce a good result (societal goal), and bad if they do not. One formulaic presentation of this is to claim that ethical policies are those that lead to the greatest happiness for the greatest number. While there are certainly "rights" theorists (Hollenbach) who support the quest for the "common good," it is "utilitarianism" that forms the core thinking of "common good" efforts.

A third and intriguing school of ethical thought is captured in the phrase *categorical imperative*. It originated with Emmanuel Kant. The "categorical imperative" school struggles for footing these days for the same reason that "art for sake of art" struggles to stay alive in a pragmatic world. It is an "intuitive" sense of what is right, and is most clearly understood through analogy with genius rather than piety. Ethical standards are set and raised by those few who, similar to an artistic virtuoso or mathematical savant, live ethical lives with a genius that cannot be acquired. In doing so, they set the standard to be emulated by others.

Finally, like an old coat that will not wear out, we have *situation ethics*. Situation ethics does not lend itself to easy review because it is based on a fresh examination of discovered facts and not on a set of established principles. A suitable analogy would be the television series *CSI* (Crime Scene Investigation), where the system relies on the meticulous rigidity of accurate fact accumulation and the application of collective common sense to what is actually known rather than what is commonly believed. It is a refreshing approach to equity because it overcomes the tendency to characterize what cannot be factually alleged. When facts are unknown, assumptions stand in for the missing evidence as if these assumptions were a legitimate addition to the fact-accumulation process. We see this repeatedly in the media, in litigation, and in policy disputes; probably it is most evident in congressional hearings.

This mini-overview of a few streams of ethical thought is deliberately concise and intended only to place the equty issues of sprawl in a larger context. Equity is often demoted to a nonessential in the jargon of development industry shoptalk by the simple act of elevating it to the level of an esoteric, academic, or even a pious concern. Equity, however, impacts everyone, and humans have been talking about it since the days of Aristotle, for whom philosophy was shoptalk. Every story has to begin someplace. This one starts in the seventeenth century. The historical thought that has informed modern debate is helpful because ethical standards are only complicated by unexamined approaches that ignore history. Neotraditionalists, for example, promote a "common good" solution to a development crisis caused by an "individualist culture." There is a historic validity to common-good ethical thinking. Added to this, the smart-growth ideas forming the policy debates about sprawl today have sound common sense and regional economic development needs attached. That however, does not mean that everyone who opposes common-good ethics is a greedy, selfish obstructionist. There is historic validity to "individualism" also. It has an ethical base that considers human freedom to be a fundamental value that overrides any quest for the common good. It has a special wariness about valuing the common good over individual interests. It is a prudent awareness constitutive to the very meaning of the "New World" and the human aspiration for freedom represented by that world.

Narcissism as Public Policy

It is no easy task, therefore, to blend the needs of individual autonomy and common good public policy. There is no question that in this society, we tend to keep the reality of "the other person's needs" outside the gated community of rabid individualism. We relegate those who talk about equity to the status of background musicians who step into target range if they attempt to assume the role of conductor. The fierce individualism inherent in rational liberalism has given low priority to public issues ranging from public schools that sadly can't serve all comers to public toilets that actually *do*.

Because of this, common-good land-use policy ideas, such as the desirability of directing growth to older cities, tax revenue sharing, urban growth boundaries, or compact development, are all uphill endeavors. All of these "common sense" ideas are driven by someone's vision of the "common good." Regardless of how beneficial any of the ideas might be, capitulation to any of them is inconsistent with the idea of freedom and individualism at the heart of this democracy.

As a consequence, it isn't exactly a surprise that the normative ethical standard for suburban residential development has been unadulterated, often arrogant individualism. One consequence of the American belief that everyone has an inherent right to act exclusively on the basis of self-interest is that this nation has become a marketing fantasyland. It is fitting irony that free, financially unencumbered, self-reliant consumers oblivious to all external conditioning will buy anything they're told to buy. The only thing better than a house in the suburbs is a bigger house in the suburbs.

It may not have been his intention, but the unrefined, naked contractual theories of Thomas Hobbes provided the mechanism for making narcissism work as public policy. He made the commonwealth the Great Leviathan, the "artificial animal" that we freely create to cope with the common needs that won't go away while we are being self-centered. It works. It is a methodology for avoiding communal responsibility, and more importantly for avoiding the deliberative process of democracy. It was a stroke of genius. Ethical responsibilities are dumped on a service industry, similar to having a contractual agreement to take out the garbage, do the taxes, or clean the apartment. Rational liberalism makes the state the "service agency." The bourgeoisie only do what they choose to do, and deliberating with Plato about the complexities of equitable development is not something that they choose to do. Conflict avoidance rather than conflict resolution is the name of the game, and tolerating the diversity of the world from a safe, uninvolved distance is preferable to being deeply involved in the *sturm und drang* of working out urban diversity.

Sprawl is not an accident. It didn't happen because we were not paying attention. It will not go away because we keep insulting it. It sells because it is an effective escape mechanism from the democratic responsibilities of deliberation and participation. Freedom is about both rights and responsibilities.[2] Democracy is the "no rest" deliberative process that takes care of the working end of the deal, meaning that the end goals of human happiness, dignity, freedom, and human solidarity are accomplished only through the daily task of dealing with our diversity, and making the difficult accommodations that eventually make human solidarity or the "common good" possible. As a matter of fact, the preamble of the Constitution faces up to this common obligation. It lays out the tasks that await the new nation of self-sufficient individualists. It states that we created this government to "form a more perfect union, to establish justice, to insure domestic tranquillity, to provide for the common defense, to promote the general welfare, and to secure the blessings of liberty for ourselves and for our posterity."

A SIMPLE ANALOGY

More than anything else that can happen to a self-centered individual, being in love demonstrates the truth of Michael Sandel's statement, "We can know a good in common that we cannot know alone."[3] Anyone who has ever been lucky enough to have a great love affair knows that the self is not diminished by attunement with another. Nevertheless, the process of achieving solidarity with another runs counter to the insight of liberalism, and that is why the Leviathan on these shores is still called "The Great American Experiment." The unsettling reality about any experiment is that failure is one of our possibilities. This nation can still revert to the uncivilized state of ritualistic murder and primitive religious rites described by William Golding in *Lord of the Flies*. The preamble to our Constitution tries to offset this, but the preamble is similar to wedding vows that are easier to make than to live. The key to making freedom work is the same as the key to making love work. It is called accommodation:

Thus the relationship between a married couple regarded independently of family networks and related social forces must be maintained chiefly by accommodation to each other, if the relationship is to be moulded (molded) into one of permanent mutual affirmation.[4]

One of the reasons that housing is a continuing issue in this nation is that it is a constant test of this unresolved aspect of democracy. John Rawls, until his recent death, was the leading authority on blending the "common good" declarations of our constitution and the inherent individualism of our people. Because Rawls was the respected giant on the issue, his work winds up being very bad news for Neotraditionalists. Neotraditionalism is used in this setting to represent the ideas promoted by both smart-growth enthusiasts and The Congress for the New Urbanism.[5] The intention of Neotraditionalism is to select and promote whatever is environmentally best, supports the common good of society, is politically and economically sustainable, and is somehow traditional. It is a product of the new information age elite that David Brooks calls the bourgeois bohemians, or the "Bobos."[6] They prefer to be called "New Urban," but given the general concerns of the movement, Neotraditionalist is more appropriate. Basically, their concern is that government has gone overboard supporting individual rights over the common good and the time for a correction has arrived. Rawls, to the contrary, held that the goal of a common good "is no longer a political possibility for those who accept the constraints of the liberty and toleration of democratic institutions."[7]

Equity in Economic Terms: Equality, Parity, and the Free Market

Ethics is about rules of conduct between people, and Rawls recognizes this with "rules of reciprocity." He does it, however, with dry formulas that remind me of my grandmother making mathematically certain that none of the grandchildren could complain that their piece of apple pie was smaller than the rest. This is a far cry from establishing a new plurality with relationships that are enriching, meaningful, and worth pursuing. The Rawls body of work is extensive and significant and does address the issue of fairness by prioritizing the weakest. It does not, however, address the reality of systemic capacity deprivation, organized interests, institutional injustice, and structural inequities that deny both the weak and the strong of an opportunity to grow in civility, grace, and decency.

Despite theoretical positions that seem to make everything impossible, flesh and blood humanity continues to develop and grow. In the world of reality beyond the narrowness of mathematical equality, political power, and philosophical reasoning, there is an entire universe of dynamic new pluralities with social, political, and growth-inducing complexity found in neighborhoods, in business, in research, in the arts, in medicine, and even in jurisprudence. The logical goal of dynamic groups is constructive, collaborative, trusting relationships. This is the paramount requirement for human advancement in the direction of increased civility and still unknown freedoms. In this real world, inequitable and exclusionary residential production policies not only violate human rights; they also splatter common-good ideals by doing as much harm to as many people as possible. Human development means working to end the deprivations that make it impossible for people to live long, healthy lives, to acquire a basic education, to share in the comfort and technological standards of modern civilization, and especially to participate, as equals, in human community and in the politics, ideas, and civic life of the commonwealth. Using situational ethics alone, the facts are staggering:

> Across the world we see unacceptable levels of deprivation in people's lives. Of the 4.6 billion people in developing countries, more than 850 million are illiterate, nearly a billion lack access to improved water sources, and 2.4 billion lack access to basic sanitation. Nearly 325 million boys and girls are out of school. And 11 million children under age five die each year from preventable causes— equivalent to more than 30,000 a day. Around 1.2 billion people live on less than $1 a day (1993 PPP US$), 2.8 billion on less than $2 a day. Such deprivations are not limited to developing countries. In OECD countries more than 130 million people are income poor, 34 million are unemployed, and adult functional illiteracy rates average 15%.[8]

The tranquilizing argument that gives pause to everyone who is appalled by this kind of disparity is the seemingly irrefutable laissez-faire claim that logic demands that the hard reality of economic efficiency be taken care of before the soft concerns of disparity can be brought to the policy table. The free market operates on the premise that there can be no outside common-good concerns that impede the free working of the system. Robert Kuttner calls this the "the economic illusion," which he says is

> the vision of static tradeoffs; the idea that we must sacrifice well-being in the present for investment in the future; social justice for economic rationality; work satisfaction for labor discipline; decent wages for international competitiveness.[9]

Kuttner and the other liberals have been loosing this argument ever since the Bretton Woods Agreement went down in flames over a half-century ago. In a very interesting parallel to the current Congress of New Urbanism (CNU), Smart Growth Network (SGN), and the environmental "Green" movement, the Bretton Woods Agreement in 1944 set fixed exchange rates in an effort to put economic common good controls on the free-world markets. Milton Friedman, who has dominated modern economic theory, ended this failure half a decade later when he called for flexible (uncontrolled) rates. A free market can't be controlled. The principle of prosperity for Friedman starts with individualism. He and Friedrich August von Hayek make the interest of the free individual the basis of order. Since the market can only be reasonably predictable if political interests do not manipulate it, the absence of outside force becomes the supreme condition of economic and human development.

With this basic conviction, free trade is the essential means of interaction, and social policy aimed at the common good through state intervention will only impede economic development. The self-regulating market only works if it is not manipulated by an imposed vision of the common good that inevitably distorts it. This lesson has been coming across with the clarity of Lesson #1 in flying: "That is the sky, and this is the ground. Don't confuse them!"

Milton Friedman demonstrated that freedom is essential but not that it is solitary. Equity is also an essential that must inform all development, but it is synonymous with "civilized behavior," not with "equal distribution." In addition, freedom from outside force is only a human right in a civilized, equitable world. Equality which gets subordinated to freedom is an exact measurement applied inappropriately to a variable world. All of this gets lost with the liberal strategy of seeking equality through redistribution rather than equity through justice. Inequality is not the issue. If inequality results from systemic deprivations, it is the deprivations that are the issue. Inequalities, in general, are natural. I am taller than Yana Klochkova from the Ukraine, who won both the 200-meter and 400-meter medley in the 2000 Olympics, but I can only go a few laps before I reach the limit of my skills as a swimmer. People are not equal in knowledge, skill, strength, size, or any other way. People are equal only in their dignity bestowing rights, freedoms, and responsibilities and this is something that is never put on a back burner.

SOCIOLOGICAL CONCEPTS HELP DEFINE THE "REAL" PROBLEM

The "efficiency orientation," therefore, is not a substantive base to which an accidental formula for equity taken from Rawlsian or utilitarian ethics is applied to color in the picture. Any truly applicable norm must embrace the orientations of both equity and efficiency. The historic norm that does this was established at the dawn of sociology with the pivotal distinction between *Gemeinschaft* ("community") and *Gesellschaft* ("society") by Ferdinand Tonnies, who demonstrated that these are not opposing or separate groupings but rather aspects of the same thing. Humans have societal and communal responsibilities at the same time. The modern volunteer army of the United States, as one example, is a family army in that the soldiers are also husbands, wives, moms, and dads. Society and community do not represent alternative choices but rather a constant conflict. Community has a relationship obligation demonstrated with family ties and obligations, and society has a task obligation that can be demonstrated through military, team, or business responsibilities. In *Gemeinschaft*, the interdependence of the members is the imperative factor. An elder or a child is more important to a family than the attainment of an outside objective. In *Gesellschaft*, a purpose-oriented team works toward the accomplishment of a goal, and the members have a value in relation to that goal. Productive human beings are necessarily both. "In *Gemeinschaft* they stay together in spite of everything that separates them; in *Gesellschaft* they remain separate in spite of everything that unites them."[10]

The Tonnies distinction is basic. It gave birth to the discipline of sociology and, as Francis Fukuyama points out, it is a key distinction that cannot be ignored:

> Virtually all the social thinkers at the end of the nineteenth century—including Tonnies, Maine, Weber, Emile Durkheim and Georg Simel—devoted their careers to determining the nature of the transition. Indeed the American sociologist Robert Nisbet, once described the entire subsequent thrust of his discipline as one long commentary on gemeinschaft and gesellschaft.[11]

The politically liberal insistence on redistribution formulas to make the world a fair place only gives false priority status to the idea of efficiency. Unfortunately, it also gives churches and foundations funds. Politicians get a moral issue tied to votes and resources. The artificial supremacy of "efficiency" makes wealth and property appear sacrosanct even though, in most cases, both were obtained by means other than efficiency, and it places those without either wealth or property on the outer margins of society. Hell for the avaricious is a final termination of their tilted game where all the rules work to their benefit. Systems without equity are all headed for that certain termination. It is only this awareness that brings a realistic turn to the illusion that efficiency is a solitary or primary need. Strict accounting alone demonstrates that it is stupid to deny the bargains of long-term positive sum tradeoffs.

For our discussion, this has an immediate relevance. In the suburbs today, we see an emphasis on the short-term advantages of zoning, driven by fiscal pressure to optimize tax revenue to local governments, that, effectively, makes sprawl happen. The fact that fiscal zoning is, in terms of actual long-term gain, economically disastrous is the bottom line awareness that makes the path to a more equitable world a reality.

Instant solutions to inequity don't exist, but a realistic path, based on equity, does. What is more important, everything that is alive and growing with determination to be around for another sunrise is on that path. We start down that path by respecting the human dignity of the person in front of us and ultimately realize that open-armed acceptance of the human rights of all people is inevitable. This leads to an increasing awareness of interdependence, solidarity, and our final common destiny in freedom. Because of global awareness, and the exploding information technology, we are rapidly loosing our convenient capacity for profound interpersonal ignorance.

Efficiency without equity is a limited-notion destined for entropic demise. Equity, in the sense of the ethos of a just and civilized people, is the dynamic that lets efficiency live. It *is* the categorical imperative of Emmanuel Kant, meaning that there is a built-in need for equity. As a matter of fact, it was Adam Smith who expressed equity as the "rule of unintended consequences." The selfish and the rapacious are led, argued Smith, by "an invisible hand" to "advance the interest of the society," and this they achieve, "without intending it, without knowing it."[12] If the course of human events is in the direction of increased equity, it is not because there is some divine light guiding it. It is simply because nothing else works. That is why Adam Smith, John Stuart Mill, and John Maynard Keynes, as well as moderns from John Kenneth Galbraith and Amartya Sen to Barry Bluestone, have all recognized the functional obsolescence of inequity.

A Conflict in Religious Circles?

I went into the mall at the Prudential in the Copley District of Boston one time looking for aspirin. When I didn't spot a drugstore, I stopped at one of the posh kiosks and asked a teenage attendant where I might go. "Oh you can't find anything that you actually need in this mall," she replied. Equity is a fallible, deliberative, and constantly changing process of cultural reconstruction that values common sense about individual human interests, respects differences, and seeks direction, growth, consensus, and value in the choices made. Only involved practitioners of life, and informed fallibilists with the patience to slowly study human patterns and an operational dedication to genuine reciprocity, can make the case for equity. These are not qualifications that bring the organized religion immediately to mind.

With apologies to rationalists everywhere, I am indelibly a medieval Catholic. It is, as someone once joked, "like being in the Book of the Month Club. There is no way to get out of it." Equity is thought to be a moral value involving fairness. This involves religion, and I am so medieval that religion equates to Catholicism. That is because there is a perennial reality about Catholicism that lives in a modern, pragmatic world. That perennialism is not the organizational genius of popes like Innocent III, who gave the Church a coherence in space and a continuity in time required by the centuries, but rather it is the simplicity, humility, poverty, and faith of Francis of Assisi who remained faithful but disorganized. He marveled at the complexity of creation without giving a thought to any need for organization. The following story could be about the meeting near Perugia in 1209 between Francis of Assisi and the organizational man, Pope Innocent III.

A stone wall standing between a priest on a stroll and a farmer illustrates this divide. The cleric called over the wall to the farmer to tell him that he and God had done a wonderful job. The farmer responded, "You should have seen the place when He was running it by Himself." The cleric, standing outside the wall of root-smashing, boulder-removing, knuckle-bruising labor, had a masterful overview, but no realistic concept of the laborious process involved. The farmer let his individual labors find their place in a creative design that he had no need to control.

For the past 30 years, Rev. David Hollenbach at Boston College has written on social justice and the Church, bridging the divide between the simplicity of faith and the organizational complexity of a legalistic, centralized, and politicized institutional Church. He says, "Human dignity can only be respected and realized within society when the essentially moral call to mutual interdependence is heeded."[13] He would disagree with me that equity is basically an economic necessity built into the design of the universe and independent of theological definition. He argues that equity is essentially moral, and treats religion as "orthopraxy," or doing the right thing, rather than "orthodoxy," or "believing" the right thing.

You can find Hollenbach's point of view backed up by the rich literature of church social teachings over the past century, but not in the operational politics or pronouncements of Rome. This is tempered by the realization that even Saint Francis failed to curb the headstrong needs of an imperial Rome. Freedom was paramount for Saint Francis. If he was "not to put himself in an attitude of revolt toward the Church hierarchy, he also would not compromise his freedom."[14] He didn't win because he wasn't looking for a win. He looked rather for the positive sum possibilities of a new awareness in the faith that the essential key to spiritual growth is the constant expansion of bargaining power, not the elimination of freedom and responsibility. The road to Assisi and the path to equity are the same. If he is right, and the call to mutual interdependence is essentially a moral call, then this is an interesting awareness for sprawl managers.

Unlike Descartes, Charles Sanders Pierce saw inquiry as a collaborative venture that begins when a previously held belief is disturbed. He advanced New England pragmatism according to Louis Menand's *The Metaphysical Club*, as the statistical reasoning of contrite fallibilists. Menand gives exhilarating life not only to Pierce, Oliver Wendell Holmes Jr., William James, and John Dewey but also gives life to the emergence of the modern American mind committed to openness, change, and the never-ending search for truth as community. Hollenbach, cited above, articulates the more promising points of convergence between the imperial mindset of Rome and this version of American pragmatism. The slowly evolving collective awareness that developed in the American mind is foreign to the institutional church. It is very sobering for example, to realize that in July of 1870, while the truly significant development in responsible human growth and thought described by Menand was taking place here in New England, Pope Pius IX, under the pressure of losing the Papal States and in fear of rational liberalism, declared the Doctrine of Papal Infallibility. This may have been the catalyst that brought about the clearly explicit pragmatic realization of Pierce and the Metaphysical Club that cognitive advance requires the humble acceptance of errors to be corrected over time by additional input from multiple sources.

The contribution of Oliver Wendell Holmes Jr. to American pragmatism is the most devastating to systems of autocratic dominance. As Chief Justice he based the law of this nation on the "experience of precedent" rather than on power-manipulated "principles," as it is with Church Cannon Law. He doesn't eliminate the need for logic, but he bases the law on actual experience, and he demonstrated his point by arguing both sides of legal disputes using the same legal principles. The foundation of "experience" or "precedence" is the vital key that enables the law of this land to defend human freedom rather than be manipulated by selective interpretations of principle by power interests. Another great teacher, in a more distant time, did exactly the same thing when the Pharisees called for an authoritative interpretation of the Sabbath that would either condemn his own disciple's actions, or contradict the established law of the Sabbath. Jesus used the very same legal premise as Oliver Wendell Homes Jr. He used the simplicity of historical precedent by reminding the Pharisees that King David, whom they did not dare condemn, did the same thing, and for emphasis added, "I am the Lord of the Sabbath."[15]

David Hollenbach has dealt sensitively for years with the conflict between the need to seek the common good and the commonsense need of individualism to fear anyone with a "common good" plan. He brings these opposing streams together by recognizing the shared need of both for freedom and solidarity. The divide between those in this nation who see freedom as open ended or without direction and those who see freedom as open to an unknown but unfolding transcendent reality moves closer together in the awareness that David Hollenbach shares with Amartya Sen. Freedom is the goal of human development.

HOUSING AS A LITMUS TEST FOR EQUITY

With that stated—who cares? Housing in American society is not the leading candidate for human deprivation in the world, but for those of us who live here, it is the immediate issue of overwhelming ethical significance. We are not doing well, and neither piety nor pragmatism is helping. With all the caution of a two-year-old armed with crayons let me color in the self-serving residential development policy that forces millions of low-income workers to be dependent on redistribution and charity. The blunt and unfortunate truth is that most suburban churches talk about charity, not justice.

Those who do not make above 30 percent average median income (AMI) need some kind of charity, but working families above this level should be able to find a home that they can afford. That is an injustice that is treated in churches with silence.

The policy to exclude low-level working people from most communities obliterates their fundamental human right to survive and grow through participation in community. Only murder and slander surpass the disrespect for individuals and human dignity demonstrated by the exclusion of working families through suburban fiscal zoning. To counterbalance this abuse, we have designed governmental affordable housing programs that stigmatize the excluded as needy, incompetent, helpless, and worthless by confining them to urban catchment areas.

Animals in the wild have a better chance of selecting a safe abode protecting them from the dangers of *their* world than the housing-deprived in this society have of doing the same thing for themselves and their children. The poor are frequently those who work hard but earn below market salaries. If they cannot afford to live in a community of choice, we corral them into designated catchment areas, or urban blocks without basic protection, services, opportunities, amenities, or the economic diversity needed by all of us, but especially by those who are just starting or have limited capacity and resources. Concentrated poverty, crime, drug abuse, violence, inadequate educational opportunities, and lack of resources replace the helpful relationships that come with a more normal, and quite easily achievable, economic distribution. The evolution of this nightmare housing paradigm is perfectly normal to those who view human history as a zero-sum confrontation of "every man against every man" and human evolution as aimless, cutthroat, and devoid of justice.

The rock-bottom basics of human existence for self-respect, dignity, and participation in community are programmatically eliminated by federal and state funding sources of housing affordability and by the regulatory, fiscal-oriented laws of communities. We have created, instead, a number of well-meaning intermediate agencies that, unfortunately, need many of these same state and federal funds to continue their "advocacy." If a machine produced three malformed squeegees out of every five, the logical solution would be to repair the malfunction, not start a charitable "squeegee warehouse" for malformed squeegees. When housing prices and rents rise 20–40 percent faster than incomes, and every increase in family income is met with an even faster rise in housing costs, the existing system is intentionally structured to be inequitable. The system itself is designed to cause deprivation and a reduction of social capital. The cynical logic of the system is that the disparity will keep increasing between median income and median cost, leaving more and more people housing deprived and dependent upon governmental subsidies to meet housing costs.

All of this takes place against the claim that Americans are a tolerant and generous people. Unfortunately, the passive, remote, easy-going, conflict-free, self-serving virtues of toleration and generosity do nothing for anyone. That is why they are so common, so quickly praised, and so easily and publicly practiced. But equity is about what we do, about action and about results. It is about accepting the reality of human conflict as something to work through fairly with integrity and courage.

Both planners and preachers like to pretend that system failure is the fault of modernity and that they have the solutions mined from the graciousness and virtues of tradition. It is a masterful and sinister delusion to pretend that all we have to do to return to a better time is to follow instructions. The best for humanity lies in the future, and it belongs to those who retain control and believe in individual freedom. "Where did things go wrong?" is a trick question. When have they been right? Only individuals who have retained bargaining power and are free, can contribute to the development of community.

THE PAST AS PROLOGUE TO OUR CURRENT POLICIES

The portrayal of historic Boston as a city that sprawl destroyed by eliminating refinements like the mansard-roofed homes that made Boston rival Paris for beauty demonstrates the delusion of Neotraditionalism. The end of the nineteenth century, known as the Gilded Age, was a time when people dressed formally and both people and buildings wore hats. It was a polite time. Milton Friedman aside, the free market operating in the exclusive interests of the powerful is brutal in any age to those who live on the margins, but the selective awareness of planners and preachers applies to history as well as current events.

They will tell you that in 1890, Chauncy Street in Boston was a graceful, tree-lined street. Today, as a consequence of the sprawl development policies of this century, it is a service road for a department store and a hotel. Before and after photographs of Chauncy Street could provide the perfect setting for a "Neotraditionalist" sermon on the need to return to the values and gentility of a previous generation. This is a controlled, selective interpretation, and a realistic examination of historical precedent reveals a more truthful picture.

Everything was not gilded in the Gilded Age. A New York reporter named Jacob Riis, who brought about the development reforms (misguided, in my judgement) of this century, used the information technology available to him as a police reporter. He published shocking photographs of destitution that he got by going into tenements in the late evening when the population was hardly at its best for public presentation. The photographs were a sensation and his 1890 book, *How the Other Half Lives*, brought the inhuman reality of nineteenth-century development practices out into the open.

One of the stories that Riis tells is about Daniel Murphy. "Old Dan" had made a fortune running "Blind Man's Alley," a colony of blind beggars. Because his tenants were blind, he never bothered to clean the place. The Board of Health finally ordered him to clean up the filth, which was so thick on the walls that police claimed the building could not burn down and called it "The Dirty Spoon." In court he made a passionate plea based on his condition. He had gone blind himself in old age. Old Dan protested the court's order to renovate his pigsty based on his knowledge and total distrust of his own kind among the developers and builders in the real estate industry. Knowing how easy it is to take advantage of the blind, he protested to the court, "Do you want me to get skinned?"[16]

Housing policy in the nineteenth century left little to be emulated. Thousands of "Swamp Angels" lived in the New York sewers and 100,000 lived in rear tenements on Cherry Street, in Hell's Kitchen, on Battle Row, and the Mulberry Street Bend. They lived and died with the stench of airshafts, squeaking pumps that held no water, watching their children die from deprivation, lack of air, and freezing cold. Tenement dwellers were almost certain fatalities every time there was an epidemic. These people lived and died thinking that "such as we" deserve no better. The dream of freedom and solidarity that the immigrants brought with them has taken root on these shores in spite of—not because of—the development standards of nineteenth century.

A Lesson from Physics: The Second Law of Thermodynamics and a Thoughtful Alternative

New Urbanism is therefore, new only in relationship to the last bad architectural idea. The 1928 *Congres Internationaux d'Architecture Moderne* (CIAM) took care of disorganized complexity in turn-of-the-century cities with Le Corbusier's free-standing buildings connected by motorways. That idea was so bad that SGN has gone way beyond the traditionalism of CNU and all the way back to organic life with the idea of "growth." Organic life is a matter of capturing and processing energy through thermodynamics to form new life and new structure. There is, however, a second law of thermodynamics that SGN doesn't mention. Organisms consume more order than they create, indicating that growth leads to entropy. The word "smart" in "smart growth" should refer to some awareness of what constitutes "order" and what constitutes "disorder." It doesn't! As Robert Wright tells us in *Nonzero: The Logic of Human Destiny*, "The key to staying alive is to hang on to the order and expel the disorder."[17] He makes the distinction between order and disorder quite memorable by using the analogy of the before and after states of a four course meal.

Diana Eck makes this very same point in a less visceral way. She makes the insightful observation that diversity becomes pluralism through a change process that creates something new and discards something old. Beyond superficial engagement, there is an accommodation or an attunement to a new energy and a new existence:

> First—pluralism is not just another word for diversity. It goes beyond mere plurality or diversity to active engagement with that plurality. Diversity alone is not pluralism. Pluralism is not a given, but must be created. Pluralism requires participation and attunement to the life and energies of another.[18]

The choice for what goes and what stays does not matter to the individual if it does not include the "self." Neotraditionalists ask that individuals give up individual preference for the common good. If you can picture someone holding his wallet above his head as the tide rises, you get the picture of what Neotraditionalists are proposing. From the smallest organism to the most complex group on earth, the key to dealing with the second law of thermodynamics is attunement to the life of another and new collaborations, but always taking the self along. Collaboration that ends in elimination is identical to a Hobbesian confrontation that ends in defeat. This is why Hobbes saw life as warfare and why power and force are central to historical development. In zero-sum encounters there are only two entities—a winner and a looser. Robert Wright makes a powerful case for the pragmatic significance of human evolution through combinations worked out in mutual collaboration that he calls, "non-zero-sumness." Nonzero is not a termination of life, but a new and larger life. Nonzero is the predominant path of development that replaces mastery with equity.[19]

Mergers have always taken place. They are the same as zero-sum encounters in the sense that things go and things stay. The difference is that there are no longer losing and victorious entities. There is a single new and larger entity. The key is making sure that you are a conscious part of the new entity. Non-zero-sum development is accelerating because of technology, higher educational standards, and easier movement throughout the world. According to Wright, this introduces a sense of crisis. It is in the nature of authors to put their themes into the center stream of historical development and see the opening or termination of ages, and Robert Wright is no different:

> We are indeed approaching a culmination of sorts; our species seems to face a kind of test toward which basic forces of history have been moving for millennia. It is a test of political imagination—of our ability to accept basic necessary changes in structures of governance- but also a test of moral imagination.[20]

I am more at ease with the overall brutal calmness of his writing. Robert Wright, for the most part, approaches the epic of humanity from the patient slopes of practical observation and in doing so finds ongoing information technology at the center of the game. The key to staying alive is both knowing where the emerging order is and having the ability, power, and capacity to be able to choose it.

> In societies, in organisms, in cells, the magic glue is information. Information is what synchronizes the parts of the whole and keeps them in touch with each other as they collectively resist disruption and decay. Information is what allows life to defy the spirit, though not the letter of the second law of thermodynamics (entropy). Information marshals the energy needed to build and replenish the structures that the entropic currents of time tirelessly erode. Information is a structured form of matter or energy whose generic function is to sustain and protect structure. It is what directs matter and energy to where they are needed, and in so doing brushes entropy aside, so that order can grow locally even as it declines universally—so that life can exist.[21]

Years ago, Ted Brameld told us that order, process, and goals are the basic elements of reconstruction.[22] The emerging order comes out of agreed-upon goals, and when the new order forms, if you are outside the process, you are also outside newly developed goals and consequently left out of the new order. That is the true brutality of life. The arrow of history may be upward, but there is no guarantee that you have a ticket. You either work at the game of life or kiss your enemies goodbye. Organic life grows. It must continue the dynamic of creation. Whatever life is, it is the opposite of institutional sepsis, stagnation, and entropy. Life demands open-armed acceptance of human pluralism and a genuine awareness of human interdependence. This is not hopeful altruism; it is the fundamental logic of destiny.

Both the sprawling development patterns of the twenty-first century and Neotraditionalist solutions are equally shortsighted. The only systems that have survived throughout history increased the distribution of bargaining power. If a system is premised on either excluding people or asking individuals to relinquish their self-interest in the interest of the common good, that system is a power grab by elitists who use domination to consume non-zero-sum surplus for their exclusive use. Bargaining power is taken away from individuals and groups who passively accept proposed arrangements, designs, schemes, and plans either because they believe that "such as we deserve no better" or simply because they believe that it is best for the common good.

The basic trend is this: new information technologies open up new vistas of non-zero-sumness. But typically the transmutation of non-zero-sumness into positive sums depends on granting broad access to those new technologies, along with the freedom to use them well. And over the long run, polities that fail to respect this liberating logic tend to get punished with relative poverty. Far from being new, this is to some extent the story of history.[23]

COMMON DELUSIONS

Urban planners, churches, and advertising hype artists claim that they are dealing with "disorganized complexity" in need of their saving plan. People who are free from delusion, including Jane Jacobs, Diana Eck, Amartya Sen, and Robert Wright, know that complexity already has order. Wisdom respects existing organization, not hype. The reason that information technologies are at the center of the game is that the task of separating emerging order from the delusions and disorder of hype artists gets trickier by the day. As mentioned earlier, extreme individualism has made this nation a marketing fantasyland.

Automobile manufacturers have taken full advantage of this for years and don't show any signs of diminishing. The opening line of the commercial for the 210hp Saab 9-3 Sports Sedan reads as follows, "There is a state that is utterly free. It is a place with no borders, where the pursuit of happiness is the only law and the national pastime is the game of 'What if?'" This new automotive hype line competes not with the reality of our clogged highways, but with a host of creative illusions selling the freedom, power, rebellion, and independence offered by today's muscle cars. The 210hp Saab bragged about in this advertisement becomes a wimp next to the new 300hp S60 R Volvo. Never mind new urbanist opposition to our automotive culture; without leaving the slick pages of your favorite magazine, you can view the cult of Americana over the past half-century on the road with Thelma and Louise in a 66 T-Bird preparing to make like an airplane over the Grand Canyon. There is a real need to have a serious talk with the American public about reality, but the Congress for the New Urbanism (CNU), unfortunately, doesn't currently provide a realistic framework for this debate.

No group understands more clearly the slim chances that exist for changing the automotive culture of the nation than urban politicians, especially mayors. The CNU vision, or delusion, in my eyes, is one where everyone walks everywhere if they are not sitting on their humanly scaled front porch having a civilized conversation with sidewalk strollers undisturbed by cars crawling at the top speed of a Citroen 2 CV because of the humanly scaled street. This wipes out whatever may be true in the Neotraditionalist pitch. Genuine, realistic human progress requires a conscious union of opposites and an insightful awareness of parallel interests that enable opponents to appreciate inevitable contradictory perspectives producing an improved new reality, and an improved common vision of solidarity that is freely chosen.

Deciding how to proceed—how to retain value as we seek upward progress in a changing world, where the tasks and the appropriate procedures keep changing—takes constant, collaborative effort and active deliberation. Commandeering insightful prophecies, master plans, lists of principles, and ingenious visions vested with political and economic power do not take humanity toward the upward slopes of reason when the price is "freedom." Whenever there is a master plan that takes away choice, no matter how pretty the pictures may be, the authorship is not the invisible hand of human destiny. It is the discernible script of power politics. Power is the domination of some human beings by other human beings. The coerced imposition of someone else's fantasy of the "good life" is always a delusion.

Whenever we have a group of people running around with the answers to social questions rather than with the questions, coercion is not far behind. Politicians operate on such short-term contracts that they never have time for the slow cooking that quality and substance require and are always trying to force-feed something. They really hate questions that do not have clear majority answers. The temptation to break the grip of sprawl with the simplistic imposition of a development plan that is the result of an economic or political power alliance is understandable. Unfortunately, capitulation to an abstraction adorned in political and economic power that only limits the decision-making circle of inclusion is regressive. True human progress can only take place in the framework of freedom of association of speech and the full inclusion of those involved as equals in human dignity and human destination.

There are many examples of the common-good need to put order before human freedom in current policy prescriptions for sprawl. One emerging concept being used in Massachusetts at the moment is the creation of an omnibus agency overseeing housing, transportation, energy, and the environment. The smart-growth agenda of the administration is both welcomed and blessed by every rationalist around except those who are being trampled. The unprecedented power alignment of state agencies has the resources to control all aspects of regional and state development. The immediate target is to direct development to built-up urban areas, meaning that, for the moment anyway, towns with affluent standing are safe. Opportunities to implement admittedly very rational plans in dense urban centers are promoted to serve the entire region. The problem is not with the rationality, but with the coercive power of the governors of states.

As frustrating as disorganization may appear to be, coerced order—i.e. implementing plans not endorsed by the local population—is anathema in a free society. This is particularly true for this society. The citizens of this nation established the definition of freedom in both the Revolutionary and Civil Wars, and it is a vital distinction that can never be overruled, no matter how rational, or well intentioned those in power believe themselves to be:

> Never was freedom's protean and contested nature more evident than during the Civil War. "We all declare for liberty," Lincoln observed in 1864, "but in using the same word, we do not mean the same thing." To the North, freedom meant "each man" to "enjoy the product of his labor"; to southern whites, it conveyed mastership—the power to do "as they please with other men and the product of other men's labor." The Union's triumph consolidated the Northern understanding of freedom, and the identity of those entitled to enjoy its blessing were themselves transformed.[24]

Neotraditionalists make a sound case for "place-making" over "land-use" planning. Their planning ideas expand the range of choices available and increase mixed income production. They return to the civility of pedestrian living and raise our hopes for full-service transit systems, and most importantly, they reverse the damage caused by urban disinvestment reducing the probability of pockets of poverty. In contrast, sprawl and our automotive culture have long lists of rational shortcomings and bad public policy consequences. There is one vital flaw to Neotraditionalism: plans! Public-good plans do not recognize the liberal bias that space is to be protected for private autonomous choice, and you can count me in with the bad guys. My own home is in a curvilinear cul-de-sac intended to discourage cruising by strangers and eliminate the "cut through" traffic. It has 60-foot-wide streets to allow two fire engines to pass in opposite directions and the 90-foot circle so that they can turn around and do it again.

Andres Duany is right (Duany et al., 2001). In a cul-de-sac without a fire station, there isn't even a source of response for the second engine. Nevertheless the neighborhood is not the disaster that Duany wants it to be. My daughters learned to roller skate and ride bikes in the circle. It is a pleasant, quiet leafy-lawn kind of place that has more than its share of social capital. Living with contradictory principles is more normal than admitted and not as hypocritical as presumed. Hypocrisy is promoting something without believing it. I believe in both retaining my individual freedom and in seeking the common good. What I do not believe in is abandoning my right to decide.

It is unfortunate that current responses to the "sprawl problem" have gone for hype over deliberation and claim to be the answer for everything from providing social capital to being the ultimate "fat farm" because they have everyone walking. If a single development needs discussion to resolve conflicts, certainly a generalized new development approach requires the same open, full scrutiny, and not simply publicity and marketing. Terry Szold, at the Center for Urban Policy Research at MIT, has outlined the problem. She says that there is a need for confluence between the stream of development thinking with a focus on place making and the process stream with a focus on "equity, and inclusiveness."

> They (Neotraditionalists) have shown us some models and examples of alternative futures for the American landscape, while also racing downstream in a powerful and highly visible way. Unfortunately, as they race in the 'place making' stream, they offer little in the way of process to help the profession navigate the challenges left in their wake.[25]

Human Solidarity and Freedom

The bottom line is that genuine smart growth requires an expansion of individual freedom because survival demands an increase in the distribution of bargaining power (solidarity), not a diminishment. Even though I disagree with Hollenbach's morality premise, he offers the only dynamic standard that does this. "Shared freedom" prioritizes both freedom and interdependence.

> The solidarity of shared freedom is an essentially dynamic standard. It sets us on a transformative path rather than leading to an all-or-nothing call for utopia. This is because it is a normative standard that takes history seriously, and presumes that the internal link between the good of persons, and the common good is itself historical and dynamic. Invoking the norm of solidarity in

shared freedom therefore means starting from where we are and seeking to move toward a common life in which more people are free and active participants.[26]

Zero Mostel is supposed to have said, "The freedom of any society varies proportionately with the volume of its laughter." If it is true, then it is because freedom, like laughter, is infectious. Through it we are bonded to each other not through strands of intellectual rope that restrain us but through absurdities, contradictions, and vulnerabilities that make us more human in our togetherness than we are alone. It is a circumstance that increases with the growing convergence of worldwide diversity, presently being dramatically pushed forward by the explosion of information technologies and the growing reality of global situational awareness demonstrated by the recent wars.

The climate of lawlessness at Abu Ghraib was seen as atrocious but doesn't begin to compare with the performance of the highly civilized Greeks at the time of Socrates, who killed all male prisoners. You have to concede that some improvement has taken place. Our reasons for not emulating ancient Greece in regard to the treatment of prisoners, in addition to the fact that these days cameras record things, is that we live in globally interactive times. There are higher ethical standard today, but there are unsentimental, nonpious, pragmatic reasons for those higher standards:

> Respect for people's basic humanity—that is viewing people as people, worthy of decent treatment—may not extend much further than practical considerations dictate. But practical considerations dictate a much larger moral sweep now, because interdependence has grown further. You simply cannot do business with people while executing their male citizens, and increasingly we do business with people everywhere. The growth of non-zero-sumness, a growth driven by technological change but rooted more fundamentally in human nature itself, has in this one basic and profound way improved the conduct of humans. In fully modern societies, people now acknowledge, in principle at least, that other people are people too.[27]

The growing reality of "non-zero-sumness" in our world expands the contract theories of Hobbes from simple confrontation to a cooperative dimension of interaction that Hobbes never considered. This does not mean that the reality of a Hobbesian "zero-sum" confrontation evaporates because public officials speak with great optimism about the equitable spread of burdens, the quality of open space, their love for renewable energy, and the need for regional coordination.

The imposition of ready-made solutions on other people removes the fundamental dynamic of nonzero interdependence because the alternative to defeating our opposites in (zero-sum) power confrontations is joining them, through (non-zero-sum) deliberation. The pragmatics of non-zero-sum unions is key to everything. Non-zero-sum unions increase in capacity. The zero-sum approach to opposites leaves the victor the same size. The only difference is that now the victor has non-zero-sum neighbors who have joined with others to be much bigger and therefore much more dangerous. Logic strongly dictates that the zero-sum, warfare approach has diminishing returns leading to eventual extinction.

Robert Bellah, in *Habits of the Heart*, claims, "We are beginning to see now that the race of which he (Hobbes) speaks has no winner, and if power is our only end, the death in question may not be merely personal, but civilizational."[28] The more prudent path is that of shared freedom. Ethics is not "so much a matter of having exact rules about how precisely we ought to behave, as of recognizing the relevance of our shared humanity in making the choices we face."[29]

This is not a new and radical idea. The advance of civilization by means of positive sum agreements has always taken place by finding a standard of reasonableness that accommodates conflicting values and discards whatever has become mutually irrelevant. Every time this has happened in history, existing arrangements have become expendable. Issues of value have been retained and waste identified as waste.

If freedom is the imperative of those who believe in efficiency, it is also the imperative of those who dream of equity. Equity in housing as in human development itself does not have any saving vision known to mortals. It has only a process or a path known by all who listen, work, collaborate, retain the freedom of their bargaining power, and are open to new unions and the eventual inclusion of all. The need for deliberation and democratic involvement is a tough sell for those of us who prefer to let others do the deliberating. If, however, the choice is to either actively participate in my own evolution or be extinguished by the manipulative visions of others, then working to achieve equity has a compelling allure. The bad news is that we all have to really go to work—or as that great humanitarian, Jerry Garcia, used to say, "Something has to be done! It is a damn shame that we are the ones who have to do it."

NOTES

1. Neotraditionalism is a current theory of community planning that embraces concepts like "town and village centers" mixed-use development (residential, commercial, etc.) as a way to overcome the impacts of sprawl.

2. United States Constitution, http://www.house.gov/Constitution.

3. Sandel, 1992, p. 183.

4. Tonnies, 2001, p. 23.

5. New Urbanism is a design concept which favors a reintegration of zoning to allow a return to denser urban development. The Congress for the New Urbanism maintains a Web site at www.cnu.org.

6. Brooks, 2000, p. 1.

7. Rawls, 1993, p. 201.

8. *United Nations Human Development Report 2003*, http://hdr.undp.org/hd/.

9. Kutner, 1989, p. 8.

10. Tonnies, 2001, p. 52.

11. Fukuyama, 1992, p. 9.

12. Smith, 1976 [1776], p. 26.

13. Hollenbach, 1979, p. 82.

14. Sabatier, 2003, p. 89.

15. Matthew 12: 1–8.

16. Riis, 1997, p. 29.

17. Wright, 2000, p. 244.

18. Eck, 2001, p. 70.

19. Wright, *Nonzero*, p. 257.

20. Ibid., p. 6.

21. Ibid., p. 250.

22. Brameld, 1957, pp. 15–20.

23. Wright, 2000, p. 198.
24. Foner, 1998, p. 97.
25. Szold, 2000, p. 40.
26. Hollenbach, 1979, p. 85.
27. Wright, 2000, p. 208.
28. Bellah et al., 1996, p. 295.
29. Sen, 1999, p. 283.

BIBLIOGRAPHY

Bellah, Robert N., Richard Madsen, William M. Sullivan, Ann Swidler, and Steven M. Tipton. 1996. *Habits of the Heart, Individualism and Commitment in American Life*. Updated ed. London: University of California Press.

Bluestone, Barry, and Bennett Harrison. 2000. *Growing Prosperity, The Battle for Growth with Equity in the Twenty-First Century*. Boston: Houghton Mifflin.

Brameld, Theodore. 1957. *Cultural Foundations of Education, An Interdisciplinary Exploration*. New York: Harper and Brothers.

Brooks, David. 2000. *Bobos in Paradise: The New Upper Class and How They Got There*. New York: Simon and Schuster.

Duany, Andres, Elizabeth Platter-Zyberk, and Jeff Speck. 2000. *Suburban Nation: The Rise of Sprawl and the Decline of the American Dream*. New York: North Point Press.

Eck, Diana L. 2001. *A New Religious America: How a "Christian Country" Has Become the World's Most Religiously Diverse Nation*. New York: HarperSanFrancisco.

Foner, Eric. 1998. *The Story of American Freedom*. New York: W. W. Norton and Company.

Fukuyama, Francis. 1992. *The End of History and the Last Man*. New York: Free Press.

The Great Disruption: Human Nature and the Reconstitution of Social Order. 2000. New York: Simon and Schuster.

Hobbes, Thomas. 1958 [1651]. *Leviathan, Parts One and Two*. Indianapolis, IN: The Liberal Arts Press.

Hollenbach, David. 1979. *Claims in Conflict: Retrieving and Renewing the Catholic Human Rights Tradition*. New York: Paulist Press.

Hollenbach, David. 2002. *The Common Good and Christian Ethics*. Cambridge: Cambridge University Press.

Kuttner, Robert. 1984. *The Economic Illusion: False Choices Between Prosperity and Social Justice*. Boston: Houghton Mifflin.

Matthew, Confraternity Edition.

Menand, Louis. 2001. *The Metaphysical Club*. New York: Farrar, Straus and Giroux.

O'Connor, Thomas H. 2001. *The Hub, Boston Past and Present*. Boston: Northeastern University Press.

Putnam, R. D. 2000. *Bowling Alone: The Collapse and Revival of American Community*. New York: Simon and Schuster.

Rawls, John. 1972. *A Theory of Justice*. Cambridge, MA: Harvard University Press.

Rawls, John. 1993. *Political Liberalism*. New York: Columbia University Press.

Riis, Jacob. 1997 [1890]. *How the Other Half Lives: Studies Among the Tenements of New York*. New York: Penguin Books.

Sabatier, Paul. 2003. *The Road to Assisi: The Essential Biography of Saint Francis*. Edited by Jon M. Sweeney. Brewster, MA: Paraclete Press.

Sandel, Michael. 1992. *Liberalism and the Limits of Justice*. New York: Cambridge University Press.

Sen, Amartya. 1999. *Development as Freedom*. New York: Random House.

Smith, Adam. 1976 [1776]. *An Inquiry into the Nature and Causes of the Wealth of Nations*. Edited by R. H. Cambell and A. S. Skinner. Oxford: Clarendon Press.

Szold, Terry S. 2000. "Merging Place Making and Process in Local Practice." In Lloyd Rodwin and Biswaprina Sanyal, eds., *The Profession of City Planning: Changes, Images, and Challenges 1950–2000*. New Brunswick, NJ: Center for Urban Policy Research.

Tonnies, Ferdinand. 2001. *Community and Civil Society*. Edited by Jose Harris. Cambridge: Cambridge University Press.

Wolfe, Alan. 2000. *Moral Freedom: The Search for Virtue in a World of Choice*. New York: Oxford University Press.

Wright, Robert. 2000. *Nonzero: The Logic of Human Destiny*. New York: Pantheon Books.

WEB SITES

Rivlin, Alice. 2000. "The Challenge of Affluence." Adam Smith Award Lecture, National Association of Business Economists, Brookings Institution, September 11. http://www.brook.edu/es/urban/speeches/challengesof.

United States Conference of Mayors, http://www.usmayors.org/uscm/hungersurvey/hunger2001.pdf.

United States Constitution, http://www.house.gov/Constitution.

13

The Impact of Sprawl on the Environment and Human Health

Sarah Gardner

As houses and shopping centers are scattered in ever-expanding circles around cities and towns, the impact on the land is devastating. As farmland is paved and natural habitat converted to lawns, the ecological damage is permanent. Many environmental problems have remedies: air and water pollution can be reduced through pollution control technology, contaminated land can be remediated and reused, but sprawl causes irreversible damage to the landscape. Sprawl's attendant environmental impacts—air and water pollution, carbon dioxide emissions, and habitat loss—are as persistent and intractable as sprawl itself because they arise from a pattern of land development that is, by definition, unsustainable.

The ambition of owning a single-family home with an expansive lawn—as promised in an advertisement for the second Levittown, "every house will have its own 'park,'" [Rome, 2001, p. 122]—has led to widespread development of open space. The conversion of natural vistas of meadows and woodlands to suburban landscapes of pavement, clapboard, and concrete has undermined the ability of the dream to deliver the promise of a pastoral utopia. Changes in patterns of land use are the most obvious effects of sprawl, but the impacts of sprawl development extend beyond the aesthetic misery of suburban strip malls, the anomie of large-lot subdivisions, and the pang of nostalgia when the last farm in town succumbs to the bulldozer. Sprawl causes a myriad environmental problems that have seriously endangered public health. This chapter presents findings from the literature on the consequences of sprawl on seven topics: open space; air quality; climate; water quality; wildlife; ecosystems; and human health.

LOSS OF OPEN SPACE

Open space is being lost at a precipitous rate. About 15 percent of all the land in the nation was developed between 1992 and 1997 (Hirschhorn, 2001). Land consumption rates are increasing much faster than population growth as average house and lot sizes have gotten bigger. Even metropolitan regions such as Cleveland, with shrinking populations, are expanding the amount of developed land area (Benfield et al., 1999). The suburbs of the early 1900s contained about eight lots per acre, using considerably less land per family than the contemporary subdivisions of two- to five-acre lots. These early suburbs, known as streetcar suburbs, were dense enough to be served by mass transit, unlike those of today. In contrast, suburbs built since 1960 have consumed an average of an acre for every two residents. House and lot sizes in conventional suburban developments have been increasing since the 1960s. Populations are spreading out: the density of urban settlement decreased by 23 percent between 1970 and 1990 (ODLCD, 1992).

"Mansionization," the act of tearing down an existing house and replacing it with one that is bigger and oversized relative to the surrounding houses in the neighborhood, is becoming common in many areas. In Massachusetts, for example, household sizes are shrinking while houses are becoming larger all the time; the average size of a new house in 1950 was 800 square feet, in 1970 it was 1,500 square feet, and in 1998 it was 2,190 square feet, and in 2000, when the average household contained 2.5 people, 18 percent of the new houses built were over 3,000 square feet (Breunig, 2003; U.S. Bureau of the Census, 2000). The average lot size has increased proportionately, growing 47 percent since 1970 (Breunig, 2003). A land-use study of Chester County, Pennsylvania, found that every acre of single-family housing development results in the loss of 1.56 acres of open space (Clarion Associates, 2000).

There are numerous collateral effects. Large houses consume more energy. They also require more extensive road networks. And they pollute more: Contaminated runoff from lawns, driveways, parking lots, and roads is the leading cause of water pollution. Suburban development also leads to increased automobile use, a leading source of air pollution. Suburban houses have been found to consume more energy than urban households, even if constructed according to energy efficient standards, primarily because of increased driving (Browning, 1998).

This trend in housing consumes land at tremendous rates. Between 1985 and 1999, Massachusetts lost 40 acres of open space per day to development; 65 percent of this was for large-lot housing construction (Breunig, 2003). Other New England states are undergoing similarly rapid suburbanization that outpaces population growth. In Vermont land is being developed at about 2½ times the rate of population growth (Vtsprawl, 2003). New Hampshire's developed land increased by 36.9 percent between 1982 and 1992, while in Maine it increased 16.4 percent while the population grew 8.6 percent (Vtsprawl, 2003).

This pattern is being repeated throughout all regions of the country. Arizona lost 403,000 acres to development between 1982 and 1997 (USDA, 2000). Population grew only 4 percent in Chicago between 1970 and 1990, but land under residential development increased 46 percent. During the same period, Atlanta developed 8 times more land than it added population.

The rapid rate of land consumption cannot be solely blamed on the American appetite for increasingly large houses. Population growth is a basic contributing factor as well. Southeast Florida, for example, where drainage of the wetlands for development has shrunk the Everglades to half its original size, is expected to gain 2.5 million more residents by the year 2025. California has similar rapid population growth: net annual growth (minus deaths) is 600,000 people (creating a need for 200,000 new housing units each year). The state's population doubled since the mid-

1960s (Bank of America et al., 1996, 4). Per-capita land consumption does not fully explain the rate of sprawl, according to a study of land use in California. Researchers found that population growth is also a key contributor to sprawl development: Between population increases and per capita land use increases, the landscape is being developed at a record pace. Contrary to research in other states, Kolankiewicz and Beck (2001) found that land consumption rates per resident decreased in most urbanized areas in California, including new urbanized areas (ibid., p. 2). The study concluded that 95 percent of sprawl in all 28 of California's urbanized areas is related to population growth, while only 5 percent is due to increased per-capita land consumption (ibid., p. 4). In fact, while it is quite simple to measure the rate of development with orthophotos and GIS mapping programs, attributing the precise cause of sprawl to either land consumption or population growth is a much more tenuous proposition.

Much of the land being consumed by sprawl is prime farmland lost to food production forever. Florida loses about 10,000 acres of cropland per year; at that rate all agricultural land will be gone in 50 years. Developers favor farmland because it tends to be relatively flat or gently sloping and cleared. Urban sprawl leads to the destruction of farming as outward growth and real estate demands increase the value of land. A study by the American Farmland Trust estimates that the United States loses about 50 acres an hour to sprawling developments, or 1 million acres per year (AFT, 1998; Benfield et al., 1999, p. 65). The losses include the most productive farmland in the country, including California's Central Valley, which lost over a half-million acres between 1982 and 1987, including microclimates that support unique crops that cannot be replaced by land in other places (Bank of America et al., 1996). Sprawl makes farming less profitable than selling to developers, and as each farm sells out, the critical mass of farms necessary to sustain agricultural services shrinks away until farming in the region ceases to be economically viable. Housing sprawl heightens uncertainty for local agricultural economies, and farmers are often tempted by the prospect of selling rather than continuing the risky business of farming on the edge of residential developments.

Sprawl threatens the future of farming in America. Over half of the fruit, vegetable, and dairy producing farmland faces development pressure (Cieslewicz, 2002, p. 26). Farms in New Jersey, where development pressures are especially intense, are steadily becoming smaller, less profitable, and fewer in number. According to the agricultural census, 40,000 acres of farmland and 108 farms were lost in New Jersey between 1997 and 2002; of those that survived, only 19 percent made over $25,000 in annual sales, which is down 24 percent from five years earlier (Olanoff, 2004). Pennsylvania lost 20 percent of its farmland between 1969 and 1992 (Clarion Associates, 2000). As prime agricultural lands are lost to sprawl, less suitable land for farming must be brought into cultivation, which often require more chemicals or irrigation, both of which create further environmental problems.

AIR QUALITY

Low-density development with single-use residential zoning and branching cul-de-sac street systems mandate auto dependency: Sprawl leads people to drive more, consume more fossil fuels, and produce more greenhouses gases and air pollution. Sprawling development of housing, shopping malls, and business parks pushes new construction to the periphery of towns, increasing the distance between housing and other destinations such as school, shopping, and work. As more than one observer has noted, "modern suburbia is a creature of the automobile and could not exist without it" (John Rae quoted in Jackson, 1985, p. 247).

Commuting time has been steadily increasing with the pace of development. The farther out of town people live, the more they drive. The percentage of people working outside their counties of residence increased by 200 percent between 1960 and 1990, and the proportion of workers commuting within their counties declined (Jackson and Kochtitzky, 2001, p. 6). According to the Sierra Club, the average American driver spends 443 hours each year driving (Jackson and Kochtitzky, 2001, p. 6). Vehicle miles traveled annually in the United States increased 140 percent between 1950 and 1990 although population increased only 40 percent during those four decades (Cieslewicz, 2002, p. 24; OMS, 1993). The increases are attributed to an increase in the average trip length (as housing becomes farther away from work and shopping) and in the number of trips per person, combined with decreases in vehicle occupancy and in usage of other modes of transportation (U.S. DOT, 1992). Researchers have documented how vehicle miles driven per person increase as household density decreases; as development becomes more compact, more trips are made by walking, bicycling, or mass transit (Dunphy and Fisher, 1996). Newman and Kenworthy (1989) found that residents of a suburban fringe development consume 12 times as much gasoline as residents of Manhattan do. An average suburban household has 2.3 cars and takes 12 vehicle trips per day (Calthorpe, 1993). Not surprisingly, all this driving has led to congestion. The average driver wastes 51 hours a year stuck in traffic, a four-hour increase over five years ago. The same study found that highways are congested an average of seven hours a day, which is up from 4.5 hours in 1982 (Howlett, 2003).

Increased vehicle use is due not only to greater distances between destinations but also to the design of new suburbs, whose wide roads and few sidewalks are not conducive to walking. At least one-third of all urban development is devoted to motor vehicle infrastructure: roads and parking lots (Ben-Joseph, 2002, p. 112). A study of Chester County, Pennsylvania, found that every 100 acres of single family residential development was supported by an additional 38 acres of roads and 18 acres of utilities (Clarion, 2000). The shocking statistic that 25 percent of trips are less than one mile long prove that something is amiss in the design of the contemporary suburb (Oge, 1995).

Residential sprawl, shopping malls, and business "park" sprawl all generally preclude alternative transportation; the roadways linking suburban settlements are usually hostile to pedestrians and bicyclists. Mass transit is designed to move commuters to and from central cities, where jobs were once concentrated; transit cannot easily capture the dispersed suburban population. Commuting patterns have changed in recent decades as employment densities have declined and businesses have left cities for suburban office parks. Leapfrog developments—scattered developments that leave large areas undeveloped—create isolated pods surrounded by lawn and connected by major arteries and do not lend themselves to service by mass transit. Today many jobs are in suburban office parks and as many as half the commuting trips are between two suburbs (Cervero, 1989). Usage of mass transit is much lower in the United States than any other industrialized nation (Benfield et al., 1999), and the relationship between sprawl and a decline in transit usage is well documented (Newman and Kenworthy, 1989).

Auto dependency is both a quality of life issue and a health issue. The average car burns 550 gallons of gasoline per year, producing 8,800 pounds of carbon dioxide (CO_2); SUVs and minivans, which have captured over half the vehicle market, burn about twice as much gasoline, emit two to three times as many nitrogen oxides, and produce twice as much CO_2, yet are exempt from air quality regulations (Benfield et al., 1999, p. 51). Perhaps because people now spend more time in their cars, they are choosing roomier (but more polluting) vehicles. Autos account for one-third to one-half of carbon monoxide, nitrogen oxides (NOx), and volatile organic compound (VOC) pollution, posing a substantial risk to public health (GAO, 2002). Specifically, vehicles produce 62 percent of carbon monoxide emissions, 26 percent of VOCs, 32 percent of NOx, and about 9 percent of particulate matter (EIA, 1996; U.S. DOT, 1996; Jackson and Kochtitzky, 2001). Automobile emissions, especially benzene and formaldehyde, account for half of other toxic air pollutant emissions (OMS, 1994).

These airborne pollutants exacerbated by sprawl pose serious health risks. NOx, for example, impairs the respiratory system. Regions of New Jersey with higher concentrations of NOx have an increased number of asthma episodes (N.J. DEP, 2003, p. 151). A chemical reaction that occurs between NOx and VOCs in the presence of sunlight generates ground-level ozone, which singes the lungs when inhaled and which causes such respiratory problems as asthma, acute and chronic bronchitis, chronic obstructive pulmonary disease (COPD), reduced lung function, and premature death (Goldberg, 1999; N.J. DEP, 2003, p. 156). Emergency-room visits for asthma attacks have been shown to increase as much as 36 percent on high ozone days, which are primarily in the summer but can occur anytime between April and October (Goldberg, 1999). Ozone has ecological effects as well. It can suppress the growth of plants and increase their susceptibility to insects and disease and causes significant damage to crops (*National Air Quality*, 1995). Studies of plants in nonattainment areas have shown that ozone causes visible injury to most plant species and reduces the productivity of crops (Cieslewicz, 2002, p. 31).

Particulate Matter (PM) refers to pollution caused by solid or liquid particles from airborne smoke, dust, ash, or condensed vapor. Fossil fuel combustion, particularly by diesel cars and trucks is the principle source of PM pollution. When inhaled, fine particles can become lodged in the lungs interfering with respiratory function (N.J. DEP, 2003, p. 157). They also aggravate respiratory and cardiovascular disease and damage lung tissues, and impair lung function (*National Air Quality*, 1995). Research has also linked increased polycyclic aromatic hydrocarbons (PAHs) with vehicle emissions. PAHs are carcinogens that collect in reservoirs polluting the water. Since the 1970s, the predominant sources of PAHs in reservoirs were from auto exhaust, ties, soot, and road asphalt, indicating a link between sprawl PAH contamination of surface water (Van Metre et al., 2000).

Air pollution in most U.S. urban regions exceeds the health standards set by the U.S. EPA: Over 90 metropolitan areas regularly exceed the ozone standards (OMS,

1993). A recent European study found that vehicle emissions are responsible for 6 percent of the total mortality in Austria, France, and Switzerland, or more than 40,000 deaths per year, which is twice as many deaths due to car accidents (Jackson and Kochtitzky, 2001).[1] In America, the number of children with asthma has doubled since 1980, from 3.6 percent to 8.7 percent, and in the same period, deaths from asthma have increased more than 75 percent (Dionne, 2004). Although car engines have become cleaner, polluting 90 percent less than the cars of 25 years ago, the number of vehicle miles driven has increased so dramatically to have cancelled out the gains from clean vehicle technology (CARB, 1994). Auto emissions continue to increase about 1 percent per year (EIA, 1996). Cars are not the only sources of air pollution in suburbia—a few hours of lawn mowing produces more pollution than running a car for a few days (Associated Press, 2003). Paul Lioy, Director of the Environmental and Occupational Health Sciences Institute, said, "The new sources [of air pollution] of biggest concern are not the old chemical plants, but us" (Associated Press, 2003).

CLIMATE CHANGE

Tip O'Neill famously remarked that all politics is local. The same is true for most pollution: suburban excess produces global effects. The increase in driving necessitated by sprawl has led to more greenhouse gas emissions, more than a third of which come from vehicles (Heart et al., 2002, p. 5). Clearing forests and fields for new roads, driveways, and building sites destroys carbon sinks—areas of forested land that are large enough to absorb substantial amounts of carbon dioxide from the earth's atmosphere. They are replaced with lawns, which are a much less absorptive substitute, exacerbating the effects of increased auto emissions. Carbon dioxide, the principle contributor to climate change, has risen 30 percent since the preindustrial era (N.J. DEP, 2003). The earth is warmer now than it has been in the past 2,000 years. The United States already accounts for 34 percent of global CO_2 emissions (BTS, 1996). Global temperatures have already increased between 0.5 and 1.1 degrees Fahrenheit since the late 1800s, and the 1980s and 1990s were the warmest decades in recorded history (IPCC, 1995b).

Many scientists around the world, including those associated with the Intergovernmental Panel on Climate Change (IPCC), have assessed the future implications of global warming and climate change. Among the myriad environmental impacts are (1) rising sea levels, which will affect fresh water supplies and may cause contaminants from landfills and septic systems to enter waterways; (2) fisheries and biodiversity will be affected as up to 43 percent of the coastal wetlands could be destroyed; (3) forests will be affected as the vegetation changes, which could cause increases in forest fires, diseases, and forest pests; (4) wind patterns will generate more intense damaging storms; (5) the remaining glaciers will melt, affecting water supplies and agricultural production; and (6) as the polar regions warm and the ice caps melt, arctic species will be at risk. The anticipated public health impacts include increased incidence of vector-borne tropical diseases from the northern migration of disease-carrying insects such as malaria, dengue, yellow fever, and viral encephalitis; severe heat waves; disease caused by contaminated water supplies; and increased death from violent storms (IPCC, 1995a). While sprawl development is not solely responsible for greenhouse gases and climate change, low-density development and the increased amount of driving it engenders is a major contributor to greenhouse gas emissions.

WATER SUPPLY

Sprawl affects the water supply in two ways. First, population growth increases the demand for water. The cleanest water flows off forested land and the 192 million acres of national forests are a major source of drinking water. Converting forest land to developed land therefore reduces the national supply of pure drinking water. About 40 percent of Americans get their water from underground aquifers. Groundwater also supplies half of the water in rivers and lakes that provides water for everyone else (Doggett, 2002). When more is withdrawn from the aquifer than is replenished through precipitation, a water shortage occurs. Shortages can compel municipalities to rely on surface water which is often contaminated. For example, during the drought of 2002, which affected half of the continental United States, 98 percent of the drinking water withdrawn from the Passaic River in New Jersey was treated sewage (Pringle, 2002). Overdevelopment—creating a substantial increase in impervious surfaces—causes rainwater that could be recharging groundwater supplies to sluice into streams and storm drains. Pavement and buildings block billions of gallons of rainwater from seeping through the soil to replenish groundwater. Estimating the loss of water through runoff, one report found that Atlanta loses between 57 and 133 billion gallons a year, enough water to supply the needs of 3.6 million people a year (Doggett, 2002).

Not only does suburban sprawl development reduce the supply and the quality of groundwater, but water consumption increases in large-lot housing subdivisions where larger lawns are watered (Snyder and Bird, 1999). Metropolitan areas, especially in the western states, have expanded far beyond the capacity of their water resources. Los Angeles, for instance, consumes almost 3 million acre-feet of water per year,[2] or 1 trillion gallons of water. Only one-quarter of this supply is derived from local water resources while three-quarters of it is imported from three distant watersheds (*Sprawl Hits the Wall*, 2001). Water planners in California estimate annual water shortages by the year 2020 to be between 2 million and 8 million acre-feet (Bank of America et al., 1996, p. 12). In New Jersey, one-third of the water planning regions have water supply deficits; if population growth continues, a statewide deficit is predicted by 2040 (N.J. DEP, 2003, p. 186). In fact, two-thirds of the world's population is expected to experience water shortages within the next 25 years (Dombeck, 2002).

Second, to the extent that sprawl converts forest land to developed land, it affects the quality of the drinking water supply. Forests absorb the most water while impervious surfaces, which prevent infiltration of water into the soil, have the highest runoff rates. The volume of runoff from a one-acre parking lot is about 16 times that of a one-acre meadow (Jackson and Kochtitzky, 2001, p. 13). Roads, driveways, and roofs account for most man-made impervious surfaces. The huge houses and large lots that dominate the contemporary housing market have long driveways and wide streets that create vast seas of impermeable surfaces whose runoff causes erosion and degrades habitat as it pollutes water bodies. Large lots were once thought to protect water quality by reducing the percentage of the lot covered by a building's footprint. However, it is now known that the more extensive road and driveway network necessary to connect the houses in large lot subdivisions actually increases the percent of impervious coverage to 10 to 50 percent above that of cluster developments or traditional town centers (SCCCL, 1995). The trend of overbuilding roads and parking lots to account for maximum capacity causes extensive damage to watersheds.

Suburban developments often encroach and destroy wetlands, which are hydrologically important because they store floodwaters, recharge groundwater, and filter water. Paving wetlands and floodplains increases the risk of flooding. Regions that preserve wetlands and floodplains are less prone to damaging floods. Scientists studying flooding in Delaware found that urbanization has significantly increased the state's vulnerability to flash flooding (Montgomery, 2003).

Nonpoint source water pollution—contaminated runoff from roofs, driveways and roads, building sites, and chemically treated lawns—presents the main challenge to water quality. As it flows, stormwater runoff from rain or melting snow collects and transports contaminants such as oil and grease, salt, litter, soil, silt, pet waste, and lawn chemicals. This polluted water drains directly into streams and rivers without the benefit of treatment. Unlike factory effluent pipes or sewage plants, runoff is not easily regulated through pollution control technology. Sixty-seven toxic pollutants have been found in runoff from urbanized areas (Thompson, 1998). Each year an estimated 2,300 tons of sediment erode from building sites during construction (Koch, 2000). Vehicles contribute to water pollution as emissions and fluids from cars contaminate roadways. Ten percent impervious cover is the threshold at which fish populations begin to decline, and at 30 percent impervious cover many more species disappear and watersheds are considered to be "generally degraded" (Arnold et al., 1996). A subdivision of one-acre lots typically has 10 to 20 percent impervious surface.

New residential subdivisions are frequently located in areas that are not connected to municipal water or sewer and instead use private septic systems and wells. On-site septic systems are used in 37 percent of new housing developments. New systems are known to leach pollutants into groundwater, but old and failing systems are in wide use and constitute a substantial source of water pollutions. Most municipalities lack laws requiring septic systems to be pumped out regularly. Between 10 to 30 percent of septic systems fail each year, threatening the integrity of groundwater (Rubin et al., 2000, cited in Daniels and Daniels, 2003, p. 104). In Florida, for example, an estimated 450 million gallons of partially treated wastewater is discharged from septic systems. When located too close to wells and drinking water aquifers, septic systems increase the levels of nitrates, fecal coliform, and fecal staphylococcus bacteria in drinking water (Daniels and Daniels, 2003, p. 103).

Lawn chemicals represent another important source of contamination. Treated lawns are not ecosystems but are environmental hazards. The prevalent development pattern of large houses with expansive lawns leads to increased use of fertilizers, herbicides, and pesticides. A 1999 poll by *U.S. News* showed that the number of Americans who chemically treat their lawns increased from 55 percent to 67 percent in the 1990s (WED, 2004). Nitrogen fertilizer runoff enters streams and rivers where it causes algal blooms that reduce oxygen levels and harm aquatic, estuarine, and marine ecosystems. Nitrogen may also seep into groundwater, affecting drinking water supplies. When lawn chemicals runoff into streams and lakes they harm insects and fish and disrupt the entire food chain. Pesticides are ubiquitous: every major chemical class of pesticide has been detected in the ground and surface waters of New Jersey, for example, and lawn and garden use is a major source (N.J. DEP, 2003, p. 162). Pesticides pose a risk to human health when they are present in drinking water, especially likely in private wells, which are not monitored. Many lawn chemicals are known carcinogens and hormone disrupters (see www.wsn.org/pesticides/health/). The use of lawn chemicals accounts for the majority of wildlife and bird poisonings reported to the U.S. Environmental Protection Agency (MARC, 2004).

HABITAT AND WILDLIFE

Suburban lawns make ideal habitat for Canada geese, and their population has increased dramatically in recent decades to the detriment of other species of waterfowl that compete for food and nesting sites. White-tailed deer have become more abundant in suburbia and public parks where they thrive in edge habitats and have no natural predators and there is little or no hunting. The population of deer in New Jersey, for instance, has doubled in the last 20 years (N.J. DEP, 2003).

Overpopulation of these adaptive species causes other problems. Excessive fecal matter from Canada geese leads to nutrient loading in waterways and ecological damage from excessive algae growth. A deer density of 20 per square mile damages native plant communities and can reduce bird and mammal breeding habitat. Studies indicate that some bird species disappear in areas of high deer concentration (Cieslewicz, 2002, 35; N.J. DEP, 2003). Dangers to human health include increased incidence of Lyme disease—there were 1,722 cases in New Jersey in 1999—and auto collisions with deer, of which about 20,000 occur annually nationwide (N.J. DEP, 2003, p. 118). About 150 people die each year in auto accidents involving deer (Ashton, 2003). Research on deer-car collisions in Wisconsin found that the deer population explosion is not solely at fault; because of sprawl, the amount of driving on rural highways has nearly doubled since 1983. The increase in rural miles driven better explains almost three times as many deer-auto collisions as does the herd size (Cieslewicz, 2002, 34). Significant numbers of other animal species are killed by cars every year; excluding deer, approximately 18,000 animals are killed each year in New Jersey alone (N.J. DEP, 2003, p. 136).

As subdivisions encroach onto habitat there is less room for wildlife, and wild animals become more prevalent in suburbia and on the suburban fringe. There has been a dramatic increase in wild animal sightings and attacks on humans; in the 1990s there were more injuries from bear, alligator, and cougar attacks than any point in American history (Lowy, 2001). Most recently, two cyclists were attacked by a mountain lion in Whiting Ranch Wilderness Park in Southern California where suburban developments border the wilderness area (Associated Press, 2003). Alligator attacks are also on the rise in the Everglades. Bison, which are not usually violent towards humans, have injured at least 56 people in the past 15 years; most attacks result from provocation or from people getting too close (Acerrano, 1997).

ECOSYSTEM SERVICES

Ecosystem services are the goods and services provided by natural systems such as forests, rivers, wetlands, and estuaries which sustain human life. Not only does sprawl increase pollution and threaten biodiversity, it also degrades the integrity of the land, impairing its ability to filter water and air and absorb carbon dioxide. Open space is not an amenity. It is necessary to the health of all species. Forests, wetlands, estuaries, beaches, and other ecosystems provide essential services that sustain human life, filtering pollutants, cycling nutrients, purifying water, and limiting the destructiveness of floods. These natural functions are compromised when land is developed. Small reductions in open space can cause a ripple effect through the food chain and in adjacent habitats (Kane, 1997). A 12 percent loss of forest cover in a watershed will have an impact on the life of a stream, which is the habitat of many creatures at the bottom of the food chain. Salt marshes are especially productive habitats. One acre of salt marsh is equal in biomass to 10 acres of farmland (biomass refers to biological matter: plants and animals and the materials they produce [Kane, 1997, p. 13]). The ecosystem impact of development is broader than the direct impact on the developed land.

Forests purify the air as well as the water. Forests in watersheds and surrounding reservoirs protect the water against nonpoint source pollution (runoff) and cleanse the water supply as it flows downstream. Grasslands, which support many raptors, waterfowl, and upland species, have been called the most endangered habitat in the world due to development and desertification. Farmland and airports are virtually the only expanses of grasslands that remain in the Northeast United States (Kane, 1997, p. 14).

Environmental economists have calculated the economic value of the free services provided by nature in fiscal terms.[3] The financial worth of wetlands, for example, have been estimated at tens of thousands of dollars per acre per year (Maltby, 1986). By absorbing water, wetlands prevent flooding. Between 1993 and 2001 floods killed more than 850 people in the United States and caused at least $89 billion in property damage. Much of the flooding occurred in areas where development had been allowed in floodplains and where wetlands had been drained for development (Jackson and Kochtitzky, 2001, p. 14). The incidence of damaging floods has been increasing. In the Seattle-Puget Sound area of Washington State, for example, floods that once occurred four times a century now occur every year (Goldberg, 1999). In Massachusetts, the Charles River Basin prevents $18 million in flood protection services each year. The natural cleansing of the water by the protected lands surrounding the Quabbin and Wachusett Reservoirs has been valued at $180 million, or the cost of a filtration plant. And the urban forests in the state are valued at $300 million for their service of storing and absorbing carbon (Bruenig, 2003, p. 20). Trees provide ecosystem services as well. A study by the North American Forestry Association found that a 50-year old tree provides annual benefits of $75 for stormwater and soil erosion control, $75 for wildlife shelter, $75 for air cooling, and $50 for air pollution control. Capitalized at a rate of 5 percent, the market value of a 50-year-old tree would be over $55,000 (Clarion Associates, 2000, p. 11).

While not considered an ecosystem service, working landscapes obviously contribute to human sustenance as well. Farmland provides more than pretty scenery: locally grown food is fresher and more nutritious, is more energy-efficient than transporting fruits and vegetables across the country, and is important for food security. The average U.S. supermarket food item travels 1,400 miles (USDA, 2002, p. 5) and the environmental costs of industrial agriculture are significant, including groundwater contamination, soil erosion, and loss of biodiversity. The food security movement is a grassroots effort to promote local self-reliance through sustainable local food systems. Their goal is to develop alternatives to agribusiness and to the concentrated ownership of farms in order to counteract the centralization of food production that undermines regional self-sufficiency. By promoting local agriculture, providing markets for local produce, and protecting family farms and farmland, the food security movement aims to build up communities' food resources so they can better supply their own needs (Fisher, 1997). As sprawl devours farmland, opportunities for local agriculture become increasingly limited.

The most desirable farmland is level or gently sloping, with well-drained soils and few trees. Regrettably, these are precisely the same attributes that make land suitable for profitable development. With the exception of the rare steadfast farm, most farmland near cities and towns has been erased by development. Growth pressures are now pushing construction onto marginal lands, wetlands, floodplains, and steep slopes, which are geologically and ecologically unsuitable for building sites. Wetlands provide habitat for many species and also absorb and retain water like a sponge, providing floodwater storage that minimizes damage to developed areas. Urbanization increases the percent of impervious cover, which increases stormwater runoff and flooding and decreases aquifer recharge. Wetlands also filter water and serve as groundwater recharge areas.

Technological developments have enabled development on these vital lands. Dredging and draining has permitted such projects as a 106-house complex in a mangrove swamp in Florida, a summer resort on a New Jersey marsh, and a residential development on a tract of water in Ohio (Rome, 2001, p. 167). In the 1960s, one-third of the wetlands on Long Island were drained or filled to create developable land (Rome, 2001, p. 163). Developers attempt to mitigate the damage through controversial practices such as wetlands replication, the engineering of new artificial wetlands to replace destroyed natural basins. The success of this practice—whether or not new wetlands are equal in quality to old wetlands—is subject to debate among wetlands experts.

If it were not for the occasional devastating deluge, floodplains would be ideal building sites. Because they are flat, site preparation is easy and profitable for developers. Floodplains were popular subdivision sites through the 1950s when realtors were not required to disclose the risks and before most cities and counties had restrictions on floodplain development (Rome, 2001). After countless destructive floods in the 1950s and 1960s, hydrologic plans are now required for drainage swales and retention ponds to slow and store stormwater runoff. Such engineering solutions have become the norm in new developments.

Steep slopes and hillsides began to be developed on a large scale in the 1950s. Hillsides were bulldozed and contoured to created steplike plateaus and level building sites. The first large, terraced development was a 652-house Coyote Hills project in Monterey, California, for which over a million cubic yards of dirt were moved (Rome, 2001, p. 166). Because of steep grades and lack of vegetation, bulldozed slopes are prone to erosion as soil slips downhill and silt and mud contaminate the downstream waters. Landslides are a risk with hillside development. Suburbs in Washington, Cincinnati, and Pittsburgh, and several in California, have had serious landslides. Landslide disasters of the 1950s and 1960s led to more careful site planning, drainage swales, and engineering of hillside developments. These techniques have allowed this type of hillside development to continue. At the same time, SUVs have enabled access to mountaintop houses with their steep driveways—house sites that previously would have been inaccessible.

HUMAN HEALTH IMPACTS

Though they may appraise the worth of a tree, cost-benefit analysts cannot assess the value of human life. "How you build things influences health in a much more pervasive way than I think most health professionals realize," said Dr. Richard Jackson of the Center for Disease Control (Neergaard, 2003). Sprawl-induced pollution causes disease and fosters a sedentary lifestyle that contributes to obesity, hypertension, heart disease, diabetes, asthma, and mental disorders such as anxiety and depression.

The air pollution that results from sprawl causes respiratory disease. Even relatively low ozone levels can aggravate any respiratory illness such as asthma, bronchitis, or emphysema. Small particulate matter from diesel car and truck emissions, and from coal-burning power plants, exacerbates preexisting lung disease. The Comparative Risk Project found that in New Jersey, where over 600,000 people have asthma, all residents are potentially exposed to hazardous levels of ozone and PM, as well as Nitrogen Oxides and Sulfur Oxides (N.J. DEP, 2003, p. 73). Everyone is affected by air pollution, but children are at a higher risk because they inhale more air per body mass and tend to be more active outside in the summertime than adults. Nationally, asthma rates have increased 75 percent since 1980. Over the past decade, childhood asthma has increased by 87 percent (Pringle, 2002).

Human health is also affected by water pollution generated through the increase in impervious surface. A study of New Jersey drinking water found that the water supply for over 4 million state residents is contaminated with sprawl-induced runoff and sewage discharge containing arsenic, radium, mercury, volatile organics, pesticides, and toxic byproducts (Pringle, 2002). A 2001 study by Johns Hopkins University found that outbreaks of waterborne illness from surface water contamination follow extreme rainfall events in which stormwater runoff flows directly into surface waters (Jackson and Kochtitzky, 2001, p. 13).

In addition to these direct assaults, sprawl also engenders many insidious attacks on public health. For example, sprawl necessitates more driving, and as people drive more their risk of traffic injuries and fatalities increases (Ewing et al., 2000). Traffic congestion causes stress and can result in aggressive driving or road rage, which resulted in 28,000 deaths between 1991 and 1996 (Squires, 2002, p. 1). Unlike American cities, many European cities are designed to facilitate walking and cycling. A recent study found that pedestrians and bicyclists in America are three to six times more likely to be killed or injured than those in Holland or Germany (Fox, 2003).

Modern development patterns, which have designed physical activity out of community plans, play a role in the current obesity epidemic. Obesity is unhealthy, increasing the risk of many diseases, including adult type 2 diabetes, which can lead to blindness, amputations, kidney failure, and heart disease. According to the National Institutes of Health, the prevalence of obesity has doubled in the past two decades. Half of Americans are overweight, and one-third are obese (Gordon, 2003). The number of obese children has doubled in the past 25 years. The Health Promotion study, a collaboration of the *American Journal of Health Promotion* and the *American Journal of Public Health*, reviewed research on over 200,000 people living in 448 U.S. counties. They found that "U.S. adults living in sprawling counties weigh more, are more likely to be obese and are more likely to suffer from high blood pressure than their counterparts in compact counties" (Fox, 2003). Much of this is due to sprawl. Ewing et al. (2003) found that each extra degree of sprawl translates into extra weight, less walking, and higher blood pressure, and residents of sprawling suburbs weigh on average six pounds more than city dwellers (Ewing et al., 2003). A follow-up study found that "having shops and services near to where you lives was the best predictor of not being obese" (Lawrence Frank quoted in Stein, 2004).

Walking is one of the best forms of exercise: studies have shown that as little as 40 minutes of walking per day, even in 10-minute increments, provides significant health benefits (Montgomery, 2001). The Health Promotion Study (Ewing, 2003) found that daily physical activity, such as running errands on foot, is more essential than formal exercise (e.g., attending a gym) to maintaining a healthy weight. In mild cases of anxiety and depression, physical activity has been found to be as effective as commonly prescribed medications (Jackson and Kochtitzky, 2001). Studies of exercise behavior found that environmental variables play a major role. Research by the Centers for Disease Control found that the main reasons given for not exercising were lack of structures (e.g., sidewalks, paths) and facilities (e.g., parks) and fears about safety (Jackson and Kochtitzky, 2001, p. 8). Low-density residential subdivisions generally lack sidewalks or destinations within walking distance, and residents therefore get little or no exercise as part of their daily routine unless they consciously seek it out.

The driving imperative also robs people of their freedom of movement and association. The wasted time stuck behind the wheel, an average of 1 hour per each 8 waking hours, diminishes the quality of life and family time (Forbis, 1998). Among the victims of sprawl are "cul-de-sac kids . . . bored teenagers, stranded elderly, and weary commuters" (Duany et al., 2000, p. 115). As traffic increases, walking and cycling become more dangerous and suburban parents become chauffeurs for their children; the modern phenomenon of the soccer mom who spends her days shuttling children to and from their activities is a product of suburban sprawl. In 1969, 69 percent of children walked to school; today that figure is only 10 percent (Kranz, 2003).

The new suburbs have been characterized by cultural critics as enclaves of anomie that breed loneliness and isolation. As urban immigrant groups gained economic power in the post–World War II period, their goal was to escape their densely settled, gritty urban neighborhoods for suburban single-family houses with expansive lawns and garages for the family car. These suburban immigrants traded urban neighborhoods for suburban privacy, and in so doing unwittingly exchanged community for social isolation. New residential developments are typically marked by a dearth of sidewalks and common areas, leading to "a depleted public realm," where neighbors may never meet or interact (Duany et al., 2000, p. 41). A study of Seattle found that people living in communities built before 1947, which tend to be high-density mixed-use neighborhoods with gridlike streets, traveled by bike or foot more than three times every two days, whereas people living in areas built after 1977 walked or bicycled barely once every two days (Montgomery, 2001). This particularly affects the elderly who are trapped in suburban developments where, with no street life or common space or shopping within walking distance, they have little or no opportunity to socialize. It is no coincidence that the average American child spends 6 hours and 43 minutes per day in such sedentary and solitary activities as watching television and playing video games.

The low-density pattern of settlement favors privacy over connectedness. By separating residents from each other, the new suburbs undermine a sense of community, cooperation, and "a feeling of concern and responsibility among families for the neighbors" (Jackson, 1985, 272). The absence of community undermines civic engagement (Putnam, 2000). In the HBO series *The Sopranos*, it is no wonder that Carmen, wife of Tony the mobster, is depressed and lonely living in their modern mansion in a large-lot subdivision on a curlicue cul-de-sac in New Jersey. Suburban housewives, who spend the most time in such enclaves, especially experience loneliness and depression from the lack of social interaction in these developments. A recent study suggests that traditional village development patterns meet women's needs in ways that suburban sprawl-type housing does not. Responding to a survey, women said they want to live in communities designed for "social interaction and convenience"; housing that is near grocery stores and parks, that is safe, and in which they feel like they are part of what is going on. They want living environments that enable them to come into contact with people. Women-friendly developments are housing clusters with grocery stores nearby, child care features, reliable maintenance, and environments suitable for teenagers. Researchers found that the surrounding community and the proximity to work, not the price or size of the home, is the key factor for women in deciding a home purchase (Paoli, 2003).

Suburban dwellers suffer from a loss of contact not only with other people but also with nature. Several studies have documented the health benefits of connecting with the environment, both passively, by observing a view, and actively, by walking or hiking (Henwood, 2002; Pretty et al., 2003; Maller et al., 2002). Contact with natural places also contributes to physical and mental well-being. Nature is a stress reducer and has a restorative effect. It provides "cognitive quiet": a state of mind that allows relief from the directed attention needed in every day activities (Kaplan and Kaplan, 1989). Studies have shown that people respond favorably to images of natural areas and respond negatively to images of sprawl development (Arendt et al., 1994). In contrast, the visual clutter of "ugly" development has been found to elevate blood pressure, increase muscle tension, and have a negative impact on mood (Benfield et al., 1999, p. 75). Views of nature, in contrast to urban scenes, have been found to have a positive impact on postoperative recovery: Fewer pain killers are needed and recovery is quicker (Ulrich, 1984). Recent research on children living in a Chicago housing project found that views of nature and greenery, even in small amounts, make a big difference in the children's ability to concentrate and control impulsive behavior (Taylor, 2003).

Open space is also important for children who have few natural places where they may explore and play in natural surroundings. Humans form bonds to the land. A study of University of California students found that over 80 percent listed wild or undeveloped places as their favorite childhood place (Arendt et al., 1994). The loss of beloved places to development can have a significant impact on individuals or communities. Converting open space to housing developments and shopping centers changes a town's character, which can have a profoundly negative effect when residents' sense of place is tied to the landscape of the town. While it is difficult to quantify this effect, there are innumerable accounts in local newspapers throughout the United States about the anguish residents experience when favorite natural areas are transformed. If dispersed development continues to be the norm and keeps up the current pace, open space and natural areas will be inaccessible to most urban and suburban dwellers.

CONCLUSION

As each single-family house lot promises privacy in a bucolic setting, it undermines the ability of the land and its resources to sustain such dispersed human settlement. The big house in the suburb and the supersized car promise easy living, but Americans have become pathologically dependent on their vehicles and prisoners in their isolated castles. Sprawl development is environmentally unsustainable. Suburbs cause more environmental damage per person than dense urban development. As wetlands are destroyed, floodplains are built on, and aquifer recharge areas are paved, the water that sustains human life becomes degraded. As the land is paved for the roads and driveways to support suburban housing, habitat is lost, and driving becomes mandatory, the quality of our air becomes compromised. As open space is lost, wildlife is endangered and biodiversity wanes. As a result of sprawl, people are getting sicker, fatter, more depressed, and less active physically and socially. Suburban zoning is a recipe for environmental degradation, not a safeguard against it; it does not protect but endangers public health. Sprawl is unsupportable in the long run.

William Whyte noted in 1968, "People have to live somewhere . . . and if there is to be any hope of having open space in the future, there is going to have to be a more efficient pattern of building" (Whyte, 1968, p. 199). One person's dream house is another person's sprawl, but the mainstream builders, realtors, planners, and politicians have yet to acknowledge the irrefutable fact that there is simply not enough buildable land for each American to achieve the dream of single-family homeownership. New urbanist developers and environmental planners have been campaigning for density by promoting urbanism: a return to cities and downtowns and the creation of village centers that are walkable and transit oriented. This approach solves the environmental and public health problems associated with sprawl while preserving open space for farming, ecosystem services, and for its aesthetic and recreational value.

NOTES

1. That said, vehicular homicide due to increased auto travel and residential roads that encourage fast driving, remains a perennial problem. The wide, curving streets of the new suburbs encourage fast driving and rarely have sidewalks, making walking hazardous. Pedestrian fatalities and injuries from traffic crashes are on the rise: In 2001 4,882 pedestrians were killed; one-fifth of these were children. Another 78,000 pedestrians, or one every 7 minutes, were injured in traffic crashes (U.S. DOT, 2001).

2. An acre-foot of water refers to the volume of water necessary to cover one acre to a depth of one foot.

3. Ecosystem services include climate regulation, freshwater regulation and supply, waste assimilation, nutrient regulation, habitat refugium, soil retention and formation, disturbance prevention, pollination, and recreation and aesthetics (Breunig, 2003, p. 20).

BIBLIOGRAPHY

Acerrano, Anthony. 2002. "Wild Animal Attacks Appear on the Rise." *Sports Afield*, February 20.

AFT (American Farmland Trust). 1998. *Farming on the Edge*. Washington, DC: Author.

Arendt, Randall, Robert Yaro, Elizabeth A. Brabee, Harry L. Dodson, and Christine Reid. 1994. *Rural by Design: Maintaining Small Town Character*. Chicago: American Planning Association.

Arnold, Chester L., Jr., and C. James Gibbons. 1996. "Impervious Surface Coverage: The Emergence of a Key Environmental Indicator." *Journal of the American Planning Association* 62(2): 243–58.

Ashton, Adam. 2003. "Deer Related Accidents Cost $1.1 B." Associated Press, November 4.

Associated Press. 2003. "Officials Blame Air Pollution in Worsening Asthma Epidemic." December 17.

Associated Press. 2004. "Suspected in Death, Mountain Lion Is Shot in California Park." *Berkshire Eagle*, January 10, A3.

Bank of America, California Resources Agency, and Greenbelt Alliance. 1996. *Beyond Sprawl: New Patterns of Growth to Fit California*. San Francisco: Authors.

Benfield, F. Kaid, Matthew D. Raimi, and Donald D. T. Chen. 1999. *Once There Were Greenfields: How Urban Sprawl Is Undermining America's Environment, Economy, and Social Fabric*. New York: Natural Resources Defense Council with the Surface Transportation Policy Project.

Ben-Joseph, Eran. 2002. "Smarter Standards and Regulations: Diversifying the Spatial Paradigm of Subdivisions." In Terry S. Szold and Armando Carbonell, eds., *Smart Growth: Form and Consequences*. Cambridge, MA: Lincoln Institute of Land Policy.

Berkshire Eagle. 2004. "Unsafe at any Speed." January 19, A6 [editorial].

Breunig, Kevin. 2003. *Losing Ground: At What Cost? Changes in Land Use and Their Impact on Habitat, Biodiversity, and Ecosystem Services in Massachusetts*. Lincoln, MA: Mass Audubon.

Browning, Richard. 1998. "Impacts of Transportation on Household Energy Consumption." *World Transport Policy and Practice* 4(1).

BTS (Bureau of Transportation Statistics). 1996. *U.S. Department of Transportation, Transportation Statistics Annual Report*. Washington, DC: Author.

Calthorpe, Peter. 1993. *The Next American Metropolis: Ecology, Community, and the American Dream*. New York: Princeton Architectural Press.

CARB (California Air Resources Board). 1994. *The Land Use-Air Quality Linkage*. Sacramento, CA: Author.

Cervero, Robert. 1989. *America's Suburban Centers: The Land Use–Transportation Link*. Boston: Unwin Hyman.

Cieslewicz, David J. 2002. "The Environmental Impacts of Sprawl." In Gregory D. Squires, ed., *Urban Sprawl: Causes, Consequences & Policy Responses* (pp. 23–38). Washington, DC: The Urban Institute Press.

Clarion Associates. 2000. *The Costs of Sprawl in Pennsylvania*. Philadelphia: 10,000 Friends of Pennsylvania.

Daniels, Tom, and Katherine Daniels. 2003. *The Environmental Planning Handbook for Sustainable Communities and Regions*. Chicago: Planners Press of the American Planning Association.

Dionne, E. J. 2004. ". . . But First, an Earthly Idea." *Washington Post*, January 16, A19.

Doggett, Tom. 2002. "Suburban Sprawl Blocks Water, Worsens U.S. Drought." Reuters News Service, August 29.

Dombeck, Mike. 2002. "Securing the Land Beneath Us." *Seattle Post Intelligencer*, March 31.

Duany, Andres, Elizabeth Plater-Zyberk, and Jeff Speck. 2000. *Suburban Nation: The Rise of Sprawl and the Decline of the American Dream*. New York: North Point Press.

Dunphy, Robert, and Kimberly Fisher. 1996. "Transportation, Congestion, and Density: New Insights." Transportation Research Record No. 1552. Washington, DC: Transportation Research Board.

EIA (Energy Information Administration). 1996. *Annual Energy Outlook*. DOE/EIA-0383 (96). Washington, DC: U.S. Department of Energy, January.

Ewing, Reid, Tom Schmid, Richard Killingsworth, Amy Zlot, and Stephen Raudenbush. 2003. "Relationship Between Urban Sprawl and Physical Activity, Obesity, and Morbidity." *American Journal of Health Promotion* (September).

Fisher, Andy. 1997. "What Is Community Food Security?" *Urban Ecology* (Spring).

Forbis, Jeanne. 1998. Quoted by the Associated Press regarding Intel's new "Internet car," January 7.

Fox, Maggie. 2003. "Urban Sprawl Makes Americans Fat." Reuters News Service, August 29.

GAO (General Accounting Office). 2002. *The Federal Government Could Help Communities Better Plan for Transportation that Protects Air Quality*. John B. Stephenson, Director, Natural Resources and Environment. Testimony before the Committee on Environmental and Pubic Works, U.S. Senate, U.S. General Accounting Office.

Gardner, Sarah S. 2004. "Review of *Urban Sprawl: Causes, Consequences & Policy Responses*, by Gregory D. Squires, ed." *Journal of Regional Science* 44(2).

Gordon, Debra. 2003. "Sprawling Environments Contribute to Sprawling Waistlines." *Advances (pamphlet series)*. Princeton, NJ: The Robert Wood Johnson Foundation.

Heart, Bennet, Elizabeth Humstone, Thomas Irwin, Sandy Levine, and Dano Weisbrod. 2002. *Community Rules: A New England Guide to Smart Growth Strategies*. Boston: Conservation Law Foundation and Vermont Forum on Sprawl.

Henwood, K. 2002. *Issues in Health Development: Environment and Health: Is There a Role for Environmental and Countryside Agencies in Promoting Benefits to Health?* London: Health Development Agency.

Hirschhorn, Joel S. 2001. "Environment, Quality of Life, and Urban Growth in the New Economy." *Environmental Quality Management* 10(3): 1–8.

Holtzclaw, John. 1994. *Using Residential Patterns and Transit to Decrease Auto Dependence and Costs*. San Francisco: Natural Resources Defense Council; Costa Mesa, CA: California Home Energy Efficiency Rating Systems.

Howlett, Debbie. 2003. "Study Finds Traffic Congestion Bad and Getting Worse." *USA Today*, October 1.

IPCC (Intergovernmental Panel on Climate Change). 1995a. *Second Assessment Report, Summary for Policymakers*. New York: Author.

IPCC (Intergovernmental Panel on Climate Change). 1995b. *Summary for Policymakers of the Contribution of Working Group 1 to the IPCC Second Assessment Report*. New York: Author.

Jackson, Kenneth T. 1985. *Crabgrass Frontier: The Suburbanization of the United States*. New York: Oxford University Press.

Jackson, Richard, and Chris Kochtitzky. 2001. *Creating a Healthy Environment: The Impact of the Built Environment on Public Health*. Washington, DC: Sprawl Watch Clearinghouse, www.sprawlwatch.org.

Kane, Richard P. 1997. "The Ecological and Biological Benefits of Open Space." In *The Benefits of Open Space*. Morristown, NJ: The Great Swamp Watershed Association.

Kaplan, R., and S. Kaplan. 1989. *The Experience of Nature: A Psychological Perspective*. New York: Cambridge University Press.

Koch, Stella. 2000. *Taming the Sprawl Monster: The Costs of Suburban Sprawl*. www.bewell-naturally.net/dcsprawl/costs.

Kolankiewicz, Leon, and Roy Beck. 2001. *Population, Immigration, and the Environment: Why Green Groups Abandoned the Goal of Population Stabilization*. Washington, DC: Center for Immigration Studies.

Kranz, Laura. 2003. "The Deadly Impacts of Sprawl." *Boston Globe*, January 21.

Lowy, Joan. 2001. "Predator Attacks Escalate as Americans Encroach on Wildlife Habitat." *National Geographic News*. news.nationalgeographic.com/news, August 27.

Maller, C., M. Townsend, P. Brown, and L. St. Leger. 2002. *Healthy Parks, Healthy People: The Health Benefits of Contact with Nature in a Park Context: An Annotated Bibliography*. Victoria, Australia: Deakin University and Parks.

Maltby, Edward. 1986. *Waterlogged Wealth: Why Waste the World's Wet Places*. Washington, DC: International Institutes for Environment and Health.

MARC (Mid-America Regional Council). 2004. *The Facts About Lawn Chemicals*. www.marc.org.

Montgomery, Jeff. 2003. "Sprawl May Make Flooding Worse." www.delawareonline.com.

Montgomery, Lori. 2001. "Life in the 'Burbs: Lack of Good Walking Sites Can Weigh Heavily." *Washington Post*, January 30.

National Air Quality: Status and Trends, Six Principal Pollutants-Particulate Matter. 1995. Washington, DC: Office of Air and Radiation, U.S. Environmental Protection Agency.

Neergaard, Lauran. 2003. "Sprawling Suburbs May Foster Obesity." Associated Press, August 29.

Newman, Peter W. G., and Jeffrey Kenworthy. 1989. *Cities and Automobile Dependence: A Sourcebook*. Aldershot, UK: Gower Publishing.

N.J. DEP (New Jersey Department of Environmental Protection). 2003. *Final Report of the New Jersey Comparative Risk Project*. Trenton, NJ: Author, March.

ODLCD (Oregon Department of Land Conservation and Development). 1992. *Indicators of Urban Sprawl*. www.uoregon.edu/~pppm/landuse/sprawl.

Office of Technology Assessment. 1994. *Saving Energy in U.S. Transportation*. Washington, DC: Author.

Oge, Margo. 1995. *Automotive Emissions: Progress and Challenges*. Presentation to Automotive Management Briefing Session, Traverse City, MI. August 9.

Olanoff, Lynn. 2004. "Farms Grown Smaller, Poorer." (Newton) *New Jersey Herald*, February 5.

OMS (Office of Mobile Sources, U.S. Environmental Protection Agency). 1993. *Automobiles and Ozone Fact Sheet*. Washington, DC: Author.

OMS (Office of Mobile Sources, U.S. Environmental Protection Agency). 1994. *Transportation Air Quality: Selected Facts and Figures*. Washington, DC: Author.

Paoli, Richard. 2003. "Survey Reveals What Women Really Want." *San Francisco Chronicle*, November 16.

Peet, Bill. 1970. *The Wump World*. Boston: Houghton Mifflin.

Pretty, J., M. Griffin, M. Sellens, and C. Pretty. 2003. *Green Exercise: Complementary Roles of Nature, Exercise and Diet in Physical and Emotional Well-Being and Implications for Public Health Policy*. Brighton: University of Sussex.

Pringle, David. 2002. *Environmentalists Launch Anti-Sprawl Blitz*. Trenton, NJ: Garden State Clean Water Action.

Putnam, R. D. 2000. *Bowling Alone: The Collapse and Revival of American Community*. New York: Simon and Schuster.

Rome, Adam Ward. 2001. *The Bulldozer in the Countryside: Suburban Sprawl and the Rise of American Environmentalism*. Cambridge: Cambridge University Press.

Romm, Joseph J., and Charles B. Curtis. 1996. "Mideast Oil Forever." *Atlantic Monthly* (April): 57–74.

Rubin, A. R., S. Hogye, and J. Hudson. 2000. "Development of EPA Guidelines for Management of Onsite/Decentralized Wastewater Systems." 2000 National Organization of Water Resources Administrators (NOWRA) Proceedings. Washington, DC: NOWRA.

SCCCL (South Carolina Coastal Conservation League). 1995. "Getting a Rein on Runoff: How Sprawl and the Traditional Town Compare." *South Carolina Coastal Conservation League Bulletin*, no. 7 (Fall).

Sierra Club. 1999. *Stopping Sprawl*. www.sierraclub.org/sprawl/report99/openspace.

Snyder, Ken, and Lori Bird. 1999. *Paying the Costs of Sprawl: Using Fair-Share Costing to Control Sprawl*. U.S. Department of Energy, www.sustainable.doe.gov.

Sorenson, Ann A., Richard P. Green, and Karen Russ. 1997. *Farming on the Edge*. DeKalb, IL: American Farmland Trust.

Sprawl Hits the Wall: Confronting the Realities of Metropolitan Los Angeles. 2001. Los Angeles: The Southern California Studies Center; Washington, DC: The Brookings Institution Center on Urban and Metropolitan Policy.

Squires, Gregory D. 2002. "Urban Sprawl and Uneven Development." In Gregory D. Squires, ed., *Urban Sprawl: Causes, Consequences and Policy Responses*. Washington, DC: Urban Institute Press.

Stein, Rob. 2004. "Car Use Drives Up Weight, Study Finds." *Washington Post*, May 31, p. A02.

Stone, Dave. 2003. *Addressing Health Inequalities in Rural Communities Through Nature*. Paper to Rural Affairs Forum.

Taylor, Andea Faber. 2003. "How Nature Heals Us: New Evidence that Natural Beauty, even in Small Doses, Reduces Stress." *Utne Reader* (November/December).

Thompson, Boyce. 1998. "Growing Smart: Whether You Call It Smart Growth or Sprawl, It's an Important Issue that We All Need to Address." *Builders*, National Association of Home Builders, July.

TNC (The Nature Conservancy). 1998. *The 1997 Species Report Card: The State of U.S. Plants and Animals*. Arlington, VA: Author.

Ulrich, Roger S. 1984. "Views Through a Window May Influence Recovery from Surgery." *Science* 224: 420–21.

Ulrich, Roger S., and Robert F. Simons et al. 1991. "Stress Recovery During Exposure to Natural and Urban Environments." *Journal of Environmental Psychology* 11: 201–30.

U.S. Bureau of the Census. 2000. *American Housing Survey, 1999*. http://www.census.gov /hhes/www/housing.

USDA (U.S. Department of Agriculture). 2000. *Summary Report: 1997 National Resources Inventory (revised December 2000)*. Washington, DC, and Ames, IA: Natural Resources Conservation Service and Statistical Laboratory, Iowa State University.

USDA (U.S. Department of Agriculture). 2002. *Urban Agriculture and Community Food Security in the United States: Farming from the City Center to the Urban Fringe*. Washington, DC: Author.

U.S. DOT (U.S. Department of Transportation). 1992. *National Personal Transportation Survey: Travel Behavior Issues in the 90s*. Washington, DC: Author.

U.S. DOT (U.S. Department of Transportation). 1996. *Transportation Air Quality: Selected Facts and Figures*. FHWA-PD-96-006. Washington, DC: Author.

U.S. DOT (U.S. Department of Transportation). 2001. *Fatality Analysis Reporting System*. National Center for Statistics & Analysis. Washington, DC: Author.

Van Metre, P. C., B. J. Mahler, and E. T. Furlong. 2000. "Urban Sprawl Leaves its PAH Signature." *Environmental Science & Technology* 34 (October 1): 4064.

Vtsprawl (Vermont Forum on Sprawl). 2004. "Exploring Sprawl." Retrieved January 23, 2004, at www.vtsprawl.org.

WED (Wisconsin's Environmental Decade). 2004. "Poison in the Grass." Pesticide Use Reporting and Reduction Project. Retrieved January 12, 2004, at http://www .clean wisconsin.org/.

Whyte, William H. 1968. *The Last Landscape*. Garden City, NY: Doubleday.

14

The Cost of Sprawl

David C. Soule

Sprawl spreads human settlement and economic activity out over the countryside rather than concentrating development in compact nodes. As a result, the conversion of raw, or rural, land to more intensive use requires the creation of more sophisticated infrastructure systems (transportation, water, wastewater, etc.), and expanded public facilities (schools, municipal services, sidewalks, etc.). Each of these has a fiscal impact on the governmental sector, particularly at the municipal or county level. Quantifying these impacts, however, is a formidable task. Paying for these impacts creates a considerable burden on the various levels of governments, which must absorb the costs of expanding public goods and services.

By 1974, various attempts had been made to address this complex phenomenon by trying to measure the "cost of sprawl." The most significant of these was sponsored by the Council on Environmental Quality, the U.S. Department of Housing and Urban Development, and the U.S. Environmental Protection Agency. Prepared by The Real Estate Research Corporation (RERC), the study titled "The Costs of Sprawl" attempted to assemble the known factors of development and quantify the multiple fiscal impacts of accelerating suburban development into the hinterlands of growing, or at least geographically expanding metropolitan areas. These "externalities" of the development system were not included directly in the private cost of purchasing a home or creating a new shopping center. However, they would become a burden on the taxpayers, current and future.

The report's research team created a research paradigm for quantifying the impact of development into specific terms to which policy makers could respond. The analysis compared six different densities of development from single-family homes on separate lots to high-rise (six stories) apartment buildings, all containing 1,000 dwelling units. By placing all of these development types in similar sites without any existing infrastructure, the framework controlled for some of the more significant variations in cost. Further, by aggregating various combinations of these "neighborhoods" into communities of 10,000 units, the study design allowed for the assembly of costs at a large enough scale for significant differences to appear and to be measured. By using different "mixes" in the development types, three scenarios were finally compared:

1. Low Density—entirely single-family, 75 percent in traditional subdivisions with the rest clustered;
2. Combination—equal shares of the 5 different types of units, 50 percent in traditional subdivisions and 50 percent clustered; and
3. High Density—all units clustered, with 40 percent in high-rise apartments, 30 percent in walk-up apartments, and 10 percent in single-family.

Anticipating a number of future considerations in the sprawl debate, particularly social and environmental consequences, the cost analysis included both economic costs and consequent effects—environmental, visual, and personal. Among the economic costs identified are schools, streets and roads, land consumption, utilities (water and sewer, as well as energy—gas and electric—and phone), and public facilities. Effects included environmental degradation—water, air, erosion, noise, vegetation, and wildlife—"visual" (visible) effects such as energy and water consumption, and personal effects—time (see Chapter 7 in this volume), traffic accidents, and crime. The study concludes that high-density residential development, planned in a tight configuration (i.e., clustered), is substantially less costly than traditional single-family low-density development. Some costs (crime, psychological effects) increase, but overall, the traditional suburb is costly to create and costly to maintain.

ACCLAIM AND CRITIQUE

The RERC report was the first comprehensive examination of the sprawl "problem" to appear in the United States and, for that matter, in the world. Other studies and disciplines had quantified the impact on specific components—water and sewer systems, transportation, and real estate. Some studies had discussed the social consequences of the suburban life-style. Others focused on triggers to metropolitan expansion including federal subsidies of highways, low-cost mortgages to returning veterans, race (white flight), and personal mobility (automobiles). Still others considered the health effects of urban densities. However, until 1974, there was no attempt to create a multifactor framework which would allow reasonable comparisons.

Alan Altshuler wrote a critical analysis of the first U.S. Department of Housing and Urban Development attempt to measure these costs. It appeared in 1977 in the *Journal of the American Planning Association*.[1] His conclusion was that the study inappropriately tried to measure the environmental and psychological impact of different residential types rather than sprawl. These are not quantifiable and therefore lead to unjustifiable conclusions. More importantly, he suggests that RERC underestimates the costs of servicing high-density development.

Expanding on Altshuler's critique, the editor of this volume suggests that several other key components are missing. First, the study focuses only on residential development. A significant portion of the twenty-first-century sprawl problem is the distribution of commercial and industrial activity into the suburbs in low-density, auto-dependent locations. In fairness, it took some time for the suburban shopping malls and the campus-style office parks to dominate the countryside. People moved to the outlying areas first. Jobs followed, complicating the transportation networks with suburb-to-suburb commutes and an intensification of home-based work and nonwork trips. Nevertheless, as the twentieth century ended and the new millennium approached, several new efforts would begin to create a demand for strict cost accounting of various development types, and a greater demand to "fix" the externalities of sprawl by placing the true burden of development impacts on the creators of the demands for new services. Policy makers in the states with the highest level of growth and change responded with a series of new fees and exactions which have had limited success and have generated court challenges from the development community. Determining the "rational nexus" between the development and its impact would prove increasingly difficult. More importantly, the cumulative effects of prior development might place the burden of the "fix" on the last one in whose activity would "break the system," rather than the community as a whole. Finally, the argument that the taxes are paid on improved real estate represents the fundamental building block and fairest revenue source for paying for increased public goods and services.

In 1989, the Urban Land Institute, an independent research organization established to conduct practical research in the field of real estate, commissioned James Frank to review the literature in a monograph entitled "The Costs of Alternative Development Patterns." Citing the RERC study as a significant contribution to the understanding of impacts of development, Frank reaches back, citing earlier works including Wheaton and Schussheim (1955) funded by the U.S. Housing and Home Finance Agency, which focused on the fiscal impact of residential development on municipal budgets. Based in Florida, Frank was particularly concerned about creating alternative revenue streams for local government as a way to offset these costs. He suggests that Wheaton and Schussheim developed an important distinction among primary facilities serving new development, secondary direct facilities serving the neighboring area but not the entire community, and secondary indirect facilities serving the entire community. This framework laid the groundwork for studies, which would follow, but also provided an important methodology for discovering the "rational nexus" of development and its impact. A further distinction was made categorizing the costs themselves into capital, operating, precipitated (brought on by new development), and full (precipitated and a share of "inherited" costs of existing facilities) costs. This seminal typology allows a discussion of the "marginal" costs of adding new development and the average cost for each user now and in the future. The burden for providing extensions of infrastructure falls on the public sector. Therefore, a level of precision for determining the fair allocation of those costs became possible. Most importantly for this study, while the private development costs were relatively constant regardless of location, the public sector costs varied dramatically if new development was discontinuous with existing development requiring significant extensions of infrastructure. While this study did not consider some costs that would be factored into later discussions (e.g., public safety), it provided an important beginning.

Frank cites another early study by Isard and Coughlin (1957), which focused on growth at the fringes of existing development and included industrial as well as residential development. A 1958 study by the Urban Land Institute compared the costs of developing large lots for residential use, differentiating between on-site septic systems and central sewer systems. It concludes that a reduced standard for services (reduced road width and road surface treatment, open swale drainage vs. pipes, etc.) might be appropriate if lots were large enough.

An unpublished monograph by John Kain is mentioned which clearly distinguishes between patterns of development—urban (compact) vs. low-density—and the justification of large-scale infrastructure systems, particularly wastewater treatment. Servicing low-density development with extensive central disposal is hardly cost effective. Such systems require an economy of scale, which is only available with a more compact development pattern.

Frank notes one further early study in the United Kingdom (Stone, 1973). Using a traffic model to compute the cost of producing roads to service different development patterns, Stone determined that a tight settlement pattern is approximately 15 percent cheaper to service than one dispersed throughout the countryside.

Turning then to the RERC study, Frank summarizes the findings described above and then cites Windsor's critique (1979) of the study. He suggests that the study was also flawed because the dwelling units were inconsistent in the different development models (floor space, students generated, etc.) and a limited cost model, which did not adequately account for the creation of trunk lines to noncontiguous (leapfrog) new development.

COSTS OF SPRAWL REVISITED (1998)

It would take a full quarter of a century from the RERC study for a comprehensive update. Robert Burchell at the Center for Urban Policy Research at Rutgers assembled a team that included Anthony Downs, noted sprawl watcher (now of the Brookings Institute) and an initial participant in the RERC study, to construct a new analytical framework (Burchell et al., 1998). Funded by the Federal Transit Administration through the Transportation Research Board, the study looked back to the RERC study and then forward to the future, providing a state-of-the-art synopsis of the quarter of a century of developments in analytical techniques.

This study is a "must-read" for anyone attempting to understand the phenomenon of sprawl and its costs to individuals and society. Going far beyond Clark's presentation, the Burchell team surveys over 500 studies looking at sprawl and suburban development in general: quantitative and qualitative studies, engineering as well as social and quality-of-life considerations, primary and secondary studies, and pro and con discussions. The exhaustive review produces a new analytical framework, which allows for affirmative and normative conclusions in five impact areas:

1. Public and private capital and operating costs;
2. Transportation and travel costs;
3. Land/natural habitat preservation;
4. Quality of life; and
5. Social issues.

At the conclusion of the study, more than 40 measures are identified, two-thirds negative and one-third positive, sorted into the five areas. The methodology corrects the previous limitation of analyzing only residential development. Suggesting that almost every county in the United States is experiencing some limited amount of sprawling development, only 20 percent of the counties are faced with "serious" sprawl pressure. Sprawl shouldn't be a surprising outcome, since our land-use regulations signal the market that that's what is expected and what should be proposed for expedited approval. Moreover, this pattern of development has broad support because (until recently) it keeps traffic down, increases property values, and promotes a supportive educational environment for our children.

Burchell begins to paint sprawl's dark side as he suggests that the accelerating costs of maintaining this idyllic vision is being corrupted as the bill comes due for servicing the suburban dream. The costs of roads alone will require significantly more spending than education, health care, public safety, environmental protection, and recreation. The cost for deferred maintenance of our existing system is expanding exponentially. He concludes that the current emerging consensus that "something must be done" is that we can't afford this much longer.

Jumping back to early studies to trace the origins and current "face" of the sprawl mindset, Burchell cites Tocqueville's observation that Americans don't want boundaries. Instead, as John Delafons pointed out in 1962, we have a "prairie psychology" that lets us interpret our desires and dreams with a frontier vision. Land is cheap and in great supply. Property rights are protected in the Constitution. Our regulatory framework allows development "to wander." (Delafons, 1962). Enhanced by Adam Smith's "invisible hand" of the market, we are victims of Pogo's dilemma—we are the enemy.

Defining sprawl is like grabbing soap in the shower. Burchell suggests that the elusive definition must include low-density, but also noncontiguous (leapfrog) and "ribbon" (e.g., strip commercial vs. downtown) development patterns. Agricultural lands are particularly vulnerable because they are cleared, flat, and relatively cheap. Environmentally sensitive lands, which provide critical natural habitats, are also at risk. And, of course, the ubiquitous automobile must be accommodated.

Because the automobile is such a crucial factor in the sprawl equation, the study identifies several studies that attempt to quantify the interaction between transportation and land use. Citing Robert Cervero's important metric of jobs/housing balance (1989), Burchell finds that a pernicious effect of sprawl is the depletion of jobs from the central city where employment needs are the greatest.

Burchell, to his credit, includes a discussion of the benefits as well as the costs. These include reduced congestion (at least temporarily) from intersuburban commuting, and more affordable housing in the periphery with increased chances of home ownership and increasing family wealth through real estate appreciation. He also makes an important distinction between costs to the individual, to the immediate community, and to the society at large. Citing the contributions of Peter Gordon and Harry Richardson, he points to consumer demand and satisfaction as a key driver in the continuing quest for more of what we have.

Finally, Burchell takes note of the emerging equity debate as essential to the conversation. A continuing legacy of sprawl and suburban development in general is the limitation of choice to racial and ethnic minorities. Even the New Urbanist prescriptions risk promoting gentrification of urban neighborhoods, driving the poor from even that limited choice.

2000 STUDY

In 2000, Burchell and others released a new major analysis of the costs of sprawl and alternative development patterns based on the framework and methodology of the 1998 study. Again, the study was funded by the Federal Transit Administration. The three-volume work of more than 600 pages analyzes all 3,100 counties in the country. Counties are defined as urban, suburban, rural, and undeveloped based on previous land-use activity. A 25-year forecast of development under alternative patterns is applied. Under one major scenario, growth is unconstrained. Under the other, significant controls on development are modeled. These empirical results are then presented for individual county and statewide discussions.

> Sprawl as defined is taking place in 740 of 3,091 counties and 160 of 172 EAs nationwide. . . . Sprawl is taking place to a much greater extent in the South and West regions of the United States, especially in counties in Florida, Texas, and California, than it is in other locations. These locations consist of [areas] that will show the largest absolute growth increments during the next 25 years (Los Angeles-Riverside, CA) and those whose growth will be much more modest (Austin-San Marcos, TX); [and areas] that encompass close to 90 counties (New York-Northern NJ-Long Island, NY-NJ-CT-PA-MA-VT) and those that contain few counties (Tucson, AZ); [and areas] that exhibit significant amounts of sprawl but are able to accommodate most of it (Atlanta, GA) and relatively little sprawl and difficulty accommodating it (Lexington, KY-TN-VA-WV EA); [areas] with large core areas that serve as receiving locations (Chicago-Gary-Kenosha, IL-IN-WI) and those that have small cores wherein little growth can be absorbed (Tucson, AZ); and [areas] that have existing planned responses to growth control (Portland-Salem, OR-WA, and Lexington, KY-TN-VA-WV) versus those that have unbridled growth with little control (Los Angeles-Riverside, CA-AZ and Las Vegas, NV-AZ-UT). (Burchell et al., 2002, 117–18)

STATE STUDIES

Even before the release of Burchell's 2000 study revisiting the costs of sprawl, a number of states with emerging growth-management programs commissioned their own studies quantifying the impacts of sprawl. These include Pennsylvania, Rhode Island, Maryland, Maine, and Delaware. Different groups commissioned the studies in different states. Other states, including New Jersey, South Carolina, and Florida, had Burchell's team perform his basic analysis.

While each state comes to the conclusion that sprawl is an expensive form of development, different methodologies and procedures were used to perform the analyses. In 1997, the state planning office in Maine conducted an internal study. Taking a 30-year retrospective, the focus is on the cost to taxpayers for new schools, roads, police, and other expanded services. While the research also identifies environmental costs, it highlights a theme that would resonate around New England and, for that matter with most states—the loss of community character. More importantly, the authors point to the real culprit—thousands of individual decisions to create a healthy and safe environment for their children. But not everyone has that choice. The poor and the elderly become increasingly isolated in this development pattern. This results in further stresses on the fabric of a civic society, built around the tradition of town and village centers, community values, and grassroots participation in the purest form of democracy in the world—the open town meeting.

Also in 1997, the Sierra Club assisted the State of Maryland, a frontrunner in the new "smart growth" movement, in producing a monograph entitled "Sprawl Costs Us All." This title would be used in a later, national policy document released by the Sierra Club in 2002 (see below). By suggesting that there were externalities in the sprawl system that affected everyone, the report helped to broaden the appeal of the arguments beyond planners and environmentalists. The short (16-page) report devoted a short section to quantifying the impacts with a traditional recitation of the costs identified in other studies, but turns quickly to the inadequacy of even one of the best state regimes to control the problem.

The Rhode Island study was released in 1999. Prepared for Grow Smart Rhode Island, a nonprofit public interest group, the report had an interesting perspective, placing suburban sprawl and urban decay side by side as different aspects of the same set of land-use policies. The authors of the study, H. C. Planning Consultants, Inc., and Planimetrics, LLP, created a cost structure that differentiated between one-time costs (capital) and recurring costs (operation and maintenance), creating an "equation of cumulative impact" to predict the long-term consequences of development. With only 39 municipalities in the state, the research team was able to create a typology of four kinds of communities—urban core, urban ring, suburban, and rural/emerging suburban. The analysis determines the differential impacts on each. The cost structures are based on 40 years of historical data and are projected into 2020. The study tracks the impact of sprawl particularly on the rural/emerging communities and the urban core. By including opportunity costs (loss of agricultural products from converted farm land and loss of economic productivity from abandoned industrial areas), the methodology allows an extension of the impacts to the real costs of sprawl.

The Delaware study, prepared by the Delaware Chapter of the Sierra Club, was released in 2000. Once again, the report is short (19 pages), but focuses the bulk of the presentation on a qualitative presentation of the arguments—loss of farmland and open space, local public services, environmental degradation, with the major part of the discussion on costs of transportation facilities to support auto-dependent land uses.

A BIGGER TENT

With the loss of farmland at an accelerating and alarming rate, the American Farmland Trust (AFT, 2002) developed a cost model with a specific policy goal in mind: Farmland in active agricultural use has a significantly smaller impact on municipal budgets than that land converted into suburban and urban uses. Focusing on states in the Northeast including Massachusetts, Connecticut, and New York, the AFT cost model suggests that residential development costs $1.15 in services for every $1 in tax revenue it generates. Commercial and industrial development are less expensive, $.36 in cost vs. $1 in revenue. However, active farmland is at the bottom of the list with $.34 in cost to $1 revenue. Sprawl is gobbling up farmland at a particularly aggressive pace in the fringes of metropolitan areas. The conclusion is that this is bad public policy and, even worse, unsustainable and unaffordable.

In 2002, the Sierra Club took up the gauntlet, very much on the offense, with the issuance of its monograph *Sprawl Costs Us All*. Building on the themes of its earlier state-based studies, this monograph, while adding nothing new to the analytical framework, renewed the call for an expanded discussion of sprawl and its ubiquitous impacts and stimulated extensive discussions, particularly within the environmental advocacy community.

Finally, in an early battle, affordable housing advocates initially perceived smart growth as an elitist and antagonistic force, keeping land off the market in a preservation strategy designed to relieve recalcitrant suburbs from providing their fair share of housing supply, driving the cost of land higher and making building lots less affordable. By the start of the millennium, new coalitions were forming to bring these divergent positions together. In one of the boldest strategies, a task force in Massachusetts has proposed legislation that would use state revenues to facilitate smart-growth development in town and village centers and near transit stations by providing subsidies in perpetuity for school-age children generated by increasing the housing supply in these locations. The rudimentary framework for this legislation passed both houses and was signed by the governor in 2004, but the subsidy portion was stripped as a fiscal measure in the final days of the session.

LIMITATIONS

The debate continues to rage over the relative costs, and now benefits, of sprawling development patterns. While the analysts have refined their methodologies and sharpened their pencils, many of the costs continue to be difficult to quantify. Advocates for a continuation of expanding development, such as the homebuilders and real estate organizations, indicate that the principal cause for cost increases is the extensive regulatory environment of local government. These barriers not only add real costs (pavement, sidewalks, infrastructure) and impact fees where permitted, but they add to the risk/reward threshold developers must build into their cost structures to anticipate the costs of delay and unpredictability. Further, local regulatory boards, responding to the sentiments of local voters, are unwilling or unable to grant flexibility and density upgrades to developers, which would reduce costs. Opting instead for traditional subdivision patterns, municipalities regularly resist smarter proposals, which would increase density and therefore traffic, schools, and infrastructure requirements.

The Maryland experiment, under Gov. Parris Glendening, focused on restricting the use of state subsidies for transportation, water and sewer, open space, and location of public buildings to promote sprawl. While this policy is contained in rudimentary form in the Twin Cities Metropolitan Framework Plan, the Oregon Urban Growth Boundary strategy, and the New Jersey State Plan, Governor Glendening was able to focus state policy in smart ways. His message to local and county officials was "sprawl if you want, but we won't bail you out with roads and other infrastructure." A different governor is in Annapolis. It will take time to see if the retargeting of subsidies will manifest itself in a permanent change in state policy.

FUTURE RESEARCH

Burchell's latest study lists a 12-part research agenda still in front of us, including an ongoing effort to define and measure the very concept—sprawl—under discussion. These include the development of a consistent definition of sprawl and the creation of a database to allow more exacting interregional comparisons. The team recommends an aggressive interaction with market advocates to isolate those forces, which contribute to sprawl, and those which could be harnessed to rechannel supply and demand to achieve a better outcome. Planners and public officials need greater precision in their definitions of environmentally sensitive lands and tools to protect farmland and silvaculture, such as models used for predicting the use of, demand for, and cost of infrastructure, particularly transportation facilities: Concerns about the interaction between transportation and land use need to be responded to with tools and models that expand our knowledge of and capacity to respond to traffic congestion. Finally, policies developed to control and manage sprawl need to aggressively protect the choices and opportunities of every citizen and their capacity to achieve success and prosperity. This is the primary basis of the social contract between the government and its citizens of all income, racial, and ethnic backgrounds.

NOTE

1. Alan Altshuler, "Review of *The Costs of Sprawl*," *Journal of the American Planning Association* 43(2) (1977): 207–9.

BIBLIOGRAPHY

AFT (American Farmland Trust). 2002. *Farming on the Edge: Sprawling Development Threatens America's Best Farmland*. Washington, DC: Author.

Altshuler, Alan. 1977. "Review of *The Costs of Sprawl*." *Journal of the American Planning Association* 43(2): 207–9.

Burchell, Robert W. et al. 1998. *The Costs of Sprawl—Revisited*. Washington, DC: National Academy Press.

Burchell, Robert W. et al. 2002. *Costs of Sprawl—2000*. Washington, DC: National Academy Press.

Cervero, Robert. 1989. "Jobs-Housing Balancing and Regional Mobility." *Journal of the American Planning Association* 55(2): 136–50.

The Cost of Sprawl. 1997. Augusta: Maine State Planning Office.

The Costs of Sprawl: Detailed Cost Analysis. 1974. Washington, DC: Real Estate Research Corporation and U.S. Government Printing Office.

The Costs of Sprawl in Delaware. 2000. Wilmington: The Delaware Chapter of the Sierra Club.

The Costs of Suburban Sprawl and Urban Decay in Rhode Island. 1999. Prepared by H. C. Planning Consultants and Planimetrics. Providence: Grow Smart Rhode Island.

Davis, Judy, and Samuel Seskin. 1997. "Impacts of Urban Form on Travel Behavior." *Urban Lawyer* 29(2).

Delafons, John. 1962. *Land-Use Controls in the United States*. Cambridge, MA: MIT Press.

Downing, Paul B. 1973. "User Charges and the Development of Urban Land." *National Tax Journal* 26: 631–37.

Frank, Jerome E. 1989. *The Costs of Alternative Development: A Review of the Literature*. Washington, DC: Urban Land Institute.

Isard, Walter, and Robert E. Coughlin. 1957. *Municipal Costs and Revenues Resulting from Growth*. Wellesley, MA: Chandler-Davis.

Muro, Mark, and Robert Puentes. 2004. *Investing in a Better Future: A Review of the Fiscal and Competitive Advantages of Smart Growth Development Patterns*. Washington, DC: The Brookings Institution Center on Metropolitan and Urban Development.

Persky, Joseph, and Wim Wiewel. 2000. *When Corporations Leave Town: The Costs and Benefits of Metropolitan Job Sprawl*. Detroit: Wayne State University Press.

Speir, Cameron, and Kurt Stephenson. 2002. "Does Sprawl Cost Us All? Isolating the Effects of Housing Patterns on Public Water and Sewer Costs." *Journal of the American Planning Association* 68(1): 56–70.

Sprawl Costs Us All. 2002. Washington, DC: Sierra Club.

Sprawl Costs Us All: A Guide to the Costs of Sprawl and How to Create Livable Communities in Maryland. 1997. Leonardtown, MD: Sierra Club.

Stone, P. A. 1973. *The Structure, Size, and Costs of Urban Settlements.* Cambridge: Cambridge University Press.

Wheaton, William L., and Morton J. Schussheim. 1955. *The Cost of Municipal Services in Residential Areas.* Washington, DC: U.S. Department of Commerce.

Windsor, Duane. 1979. "A Critique of *The Cost of Sprawl.*" *Journal of the American Planning Association* 45(3): 279–92.

PART IV

MEASURING AND ANALYZING SPRAWL

15

Measuring Change: Databases, Build-Out Analysis, Scenario Planning, and Models

David C. Soule

Sprawl is a phenomenon that transforms the landscape over time. As we have seen, incremental changes in land use make the management of sprawl a difficult planning and regulatory issue. Further, it is difficult to gain public attention for a problem that is slow moving and is, generally, the result of demographic and economic forces that become a "problem" only when it is too late to do much. However, there are a number of measurement tools available, including many that provide a predictive analysis allowing planners, policy makers, and citizens to see where they've come from and where current policies will take them. This chapter explores various components of the data and modeling issue. Several other chapters discuss tools for civic engagement and the interface with the legal regimes of planning and zoning (see chapters 3 and 4 in this volume).

One of the most significant challenges to researchers exploring the sprawl problem is identifying and then agreeing on a set of factors that adequately describe the phenomenon and then establishing a set of measures that can be used to monitor change over time. Recent research has moved us closer to a satisfying set of measures, but even defining the geography that is used for interregional comparisons becomes a concern. Further, as this chapter attempts to demonstrate, there are complexities in the sprawl debate that resist a common set of metrics. If we are measuring density, how can we also measure social equity and environmental justice? If we are measuring economic changes, how can we also measure highly localized governance systems with unique and highly competitive political regimes? If we are measuring environmental changes, how do we also measure residential markets?

While this chapter will draw no comprehensive conclusions to these questions, we will explore the current state of data archives available to researchers and discuss ongoing efforts to establish a set of metrics that allow at least a common ground for analysis. Further, we will briefly discuss how these data are traditionally modeled for decisions on regional infrastructure systems.

TECHNIQUES FOR MEASURING SPRAWL

Current Studies

Many regions assume that other parts of the country experience sprawl more than they do. However, several studies offer new insight into that assumption. A recent Brookings Institution study based on the single factor of density—persons per urban acre—reveals that the Boston region sprawls more than Los Angeles, New York, and San Francisco[1] (see Table 15.1). A low score indicates more sprawl—more people spread out over a given land area. The Brookings study is based on a comparison of Consolidated Metropolitan Statistical Areas. The authors conclude that areas that have greater political fragmentation sprawl more than those that do not.

David Rusk, a contributor to this volume (see Chapter 6), and Joel Garreau have conducted studies of sprawl, comparing cities with one another. Many cities, as noted by Rusk, used annexation to adjust the city boundary to accommodate spreading human density (Rusk, 1993). However, many cities cannot. For example, Boston did annex several communities prior to 1910. However, there is a deep rich colonial history of municipal governments in New England; many were set up by the King of England. With the purest form of democracy in the world (town meeting), small towns fiercely defend their boundaries against urban encroachment. This is very different in other parts of the country. Rusk posits that "elastic" cities—those that can and do annex—do better that their "inelastic" counter parts, hemmed in on all sides by incorporated municipalities. Garreau's study of "edge

Table 15.1. Who Sprawls the Most

Rank	Metropolitan Area	Persons/Urbanized Acre
1	Honolulu	12.36
2	Los Angeles–Anaheim–Riverside	8.31
3	New York–Northern New Jersey–Long Island	7.99
4	Reno, NV	7.99
5	San Francisco–Oakland–San Jose	7.96
6	Miami–Fort Lauderdale	7.93
7	Provo–Orem, UT	7.78
8	San Diego	7.50
9	Visalia–Tulare–Porterville, CA	7.39
10	Modesto, CA	7.31
11	Phoenix	7.20
12	Salinas–Seaside–Monterey, CA	7.08
13	Stockton, CA	6.82
14	Las Vegas	6.67
15	Chicago–Gary–Lake County	6.02
16	Providence–Pawtucket–Woonsocket, RI	5.93
17	Washington, DC	5.88
18	Buffalo–Niagara Falls, NY	5.74
19	Boston–Lawrence–Salem–Lowell–Brockton	5.65
20	Santa Barbara–Santa Maria–Lompoc, CA	5.56

Source: The data is drawn from the Natural Resources Inventory developed by the Natural Resource Conservation Service of the U.S. Department of Agriculture.

cities" is primarily anecdotal and qualitative. He points to an observable phenomenon, akin to location theory, that communities on the fringes of metropolitan areas are becoming important in their own right. This causes metropolitan areas to develop multicentric or "poly-nucleated" configurations where edge cities compete for jobs, people, infrastructure funds, and other resources against traditional central cities (Garreau, 1988).

Recent work (Galster and Hanson, 2001) expands the conversation by defining multiple parameters for measuring sprawl and separating them from the consequences. They suggest factors that should be taken into consideration when considering the existence and extent of sprawl. The following eight factors are offered:

1. *Density* (average number of residential units per square mile),

Low Sprawl   High Sprawl
/---/
High Density/Urban Acre   **Low Density**

2. *Continuity* (land is built upon at urban densities in an unbroken fashion),

Low Sprawl   High Sprawl
/---/
High Continuity   **Low Continuity**

3. *Concentration* (disproportionately in one area rather than spread out),

Low Sprawl   High Sprawl
/---/
High Concentration   **Low Concentration**

4. *Clustering* (development is tightly bunched to minimize amount of land developed),

Low Sprawl   High Sprawl
/---/
High Clustering   **Low Clustering**

5. *Centrality* (development is close to central business district),

Low Sprawl   High Sprawl
/---/
High Centrality   **Low Centrality**

6. *Nuclearity* (single nucleus of development),

Low Sprawl   High Sprawl
/---/
High Nuclearity   **Low Nuclearity**

7. *Mixed uses* (two different land uses in same small area), and

Low Sprawl   High Sprawl
/---/
High Mixed Use   **Low Mixed Use**

8. *Proximity* (different land uses are close to each other).

Low Sprawl   High Sprawl
/---/
High Proximity   **Low Proximity**

Sprawl exists to the extent that a region scores high on these factors. Galster and his team apply this definition of sprawl to 13 metropolitan regions,[2] with an indication that further research is needed to expand the database and refine the analysis.

In 2004, Smart Growth America, a policy institute focused on developing quality research and specific policy recommendations to those interested in managing sprawl, released a report creating a four-factor index for measuring and defining the impact of this complex phenomenon. The factors include residential density; neighborhood mix of homes, jobs, and services; strength of activity centers and downtowns; and accessibility of the street network. The report analyzes 83 metropolitan areas and creates a substantive and reasonably satisfying index. From these data, which are publicly accessible on the Smart Growth America Web site (www.smartgrowthamerica.org) and consistent with the organization's mission, a series of insights and policies are developed. Volume 1 of the report provides a summary of the index, its metrics, rankings of the metropolitan areas, and recommendations. Appendix 1 of the report provides a summary and critique of other indices, including the Brookings and Galster studies discussed above. Volume 2, the technical report, can also be downloaded.

It is beyond the scope of this chapter to undertake a critical review of each of these efforts, but they are presented to expose the level of interest in creating a satisfying measurement system. Further, the complexities of geographical definitions (Metropolitan Statistical Area [MSA], Consolidated Metropolitan Statistical Area [CMSA], Primary Metropolitan Statistical Area [PMSA], etc.), particularly when making comparisons over time, make it difficult to even be sure that we are talking about the same analytical basis when moving from study to study. Finally, as we shall see in the discussions below, there are multiple databases, measurement systems, and tools and models that expand these limited indices significantly.

DATA FOR ANALYSIS

Time Series Data

The primary method of measuring change is to compare the same area over discreet time periods. From this basic analysis, areas can be compared to each other in various ways. A simple calculation allows you to determine the rate of change in numerical terms (e.g., total population increase/decrease between periods). Comparisons can be made between areas (for example, ranked based on the rate of change). Calculations can then proceed in complexity by changing from numerical increase to percentage increase, increasing the number of variables in the comparison, etc. Sophisticated analyses apply statistical procedures (regression, cluster, and factor analysis, etc.) and other higher orders of mathematics to determine the interrelationship of multiple variables, to develop trend lines, and ultimately to develop sophisticated models to predict future relationships.

For the purposes of this volume, it is readily apparent that the studies discussed above have used a variety of these procedures to measure the changes linked to sprawl. Each of the studies uses at least one variable to measure change and the most useful employ the more sophisticated multivariate analysis. As we shall see, the advanced tools that are now in use throughout the country have added significant complexity. These models, however, are not necessarily used for interregional comparisons. Usually, because of the data requirements, generic models are used in specific regions and calibrated to local conditions. The models used by government agencies, such as the Bureau of Economic analysis, will take significant economic performance indicators and conduct periodic analyses of the entire country with information packaged for specific regions.

As useful as time series data are, there are a number of problems that require manipulations and adjustments to be sure that the measurements are accurate. A few of these are discussed below.

Establishing Boundaries

To conduct a regional analysis, it is necessary, first, to define the region. One would expect that boundaries would be easily established. In fact, many federal and state agencies accomplish this task by aggregating smaller, substate political subdivisions (such as municipalities, counties, etc.) into groups. In most areas of the country, county boundaries are the norm. However, in New England, because of the historical primacy of the municipality over the county, various configurations are utilized. County boundaries do exist, but sometimes simply as a geographical artifact rather than as a governmental unit. Definitions included later in the next section lay out the various common characteristics of these regional boundary definitions.

Changing Boundaries

While political boundaries at the state and county level (and in New England at the municipal level) are reasonably fixed over time, regional boundaries used for statistical definitions and comparisons are regularly transformed after each significant measurement period (e.g., decennial census). This makes abundant sense from an analytical perspective. Common census definitions measure urban, urbanized, and metropolitan areas, not necessarily political subdivisions. However, city boundaries change as well. Therefore, it is not possible to assume that the land area for a city is the same in 1790 as it is in 1950 or 2000. The ability of cities to annex unincorporated areas in the surrounding county creates a dynamic urban environment. This is much more the norm outside the northeast region of the country. David Rusk, mentioned earlier in this chapter, uses this concept of an "elastic city" to account for and discuss regional differences. Throughout most of the country, municipal corporations are annexing unincorporated land in the surrounding county all the time. While this is less of a historical problem in the six New England states because of the relative importance of cities and town over counties, and therefore, produces a very small number of annexations, it is still a major problem for maintaining the validity of the units of measurement over time.

As regions grow and change, the sphere of influence of the central city on the surrounding area expands or contracts. Census definitions for regional (mainly metropolitan) areas are constructed to specifically measure those changes and, hence, the geography encompassed by these definitions changes over time. Similarly, census data is used to apportion districts for local, state, and national elections. These definitions, while not directly linked to sprawl, impact the distribution of power throughout the political system, which can impact the attention that regional growth and change receives.

Microlevel data (e.g., census tracts and blocks) is also collected and measured to monitor changes. Each of these definitions has a rigorous set of empirical criteria behind them. One would expect these boundaries to change as neighborhoods within cities and towns change. Therefore the geography encompassed by the definitions of census blocks and tracks may change as well.

Having established that changing boundaries makes time series data difficult, multiple analytical frameworks have been developed throughout the research community to overcome this issue. Using techniques analogous to indexing cost of living data for inflation adjustments, geographers and other analysts "work around" these anomalies and assure that comparisons are valid.

Databases

A vast amount of information is available to assist researchers in exploring changes in human settlement patterns over time. Much of the current data is available in electronic form. Historical data is often available electronically for earlier periods, as long as one remembers that the geography of the measurement area changes over time and adjusts accordingly. In sprawl research, this is helpful because it actually measures the expanding (or declining) influence of central cities on their surrounding areas. The point is, the researcher must use caution to maintain the integrity of the measurement system before the results can be accurately determined.

Census: Standard Definitions

The Census Bureau of the U.S. Department of Commerce provides the richest reservoir of demographic information. The census has also collected data in various forms with increasing sophistication over time. In Article 1 Section 2, the U.S. Constitution provides for a decennial enumeration of population. The original intention, of course was to provide a method for determining the proportion of the population for representatives to the House of Representatives. Data thus exists for each state in the union and enumeration district from 1790 forward. Minor civil divisions (often, but not always, municipalities or counties) are valuable substate geographies.

The most common boundary definitions used in regional analysis are those developed by the Census Bureau of the U.S. Department of Commerce. The current definitional parameters are summarized below.

Defining Metropolitan and Micropolitan Statistical Areas

The 2000 standards provide that each Core Based Statistical Area (CBSA) must contain at least one urban area of 10,000 or more population. Each metropolitan statistical area must have at least one urbanized area of 50,000 or more inhabitants. Each micropolitan statistical area must have at least one urban cluster of at least 10,000 but less than 50,000 population.

As of June 6, 2000, there were 362 metropolitan statistical areas and 560 micropolitan statistical areas in the United States. In addition, there are eight metropolitan statistical areas and five micropolitan statistical areas in Puerto Rico.

Principal Cities and Metropolitan and Micropolitan Statistical Area Titles

The largest city in each metropolitan or micropolitan statistical area is designated a "principal city." Additional cities qualify if specified requirements are met concerning population size and employment. The title of each metropolitan or micropolitan statistical area consists of the names of up to three of its principal cities and the name of each state into which the metropolitan or micropolitan statistical area extends. Titles of metropolitan divisions also typically are based on principal city names but in certain cases consist of county names. (Reprinted from www.census.gov)

Older Definitions

Consolidated and Primary Metropolitan Statistical Area (CMSA and PMSA)

If an area that qualifies as a metropolitan area (MA) has 1 million people or more, two or more Primary Metropolitan Statistical Areas (PMSAs) may be defined within it. Each PMSA consists of a large urbanized county or cluster of counties (or cities and towns in New England) that demonstrate very strong internal economic and social links, in addition to close ties to other portions of the larger area. When PMSAs are established, the larger MA of which they are component parts is designated a Consolidated Metropolitan Statistical Area (CMSA). CMSAs and PMSAs are established only where local governments favor such designations for a large MA.

Metropolitan Statistical Area (MSA)

Metropolitan statistical areas (MSAs) are metropolitan areas (MAs) that are not closely associated with other MAs. These areas typically are surrounded by non-metropolitan counties (or county subdivisions in New England).

Census Tract

Census tracts in the United States, Puerto Rico, and the Virgin Islands of the United States generally have between 1,500 and 8,000 people, with an optimum size of 4,000 people. Counties and statistically equivalent entities with fewer than 1,500 people have a single census tract. Census-tract boundaries are delineated with the intention of being maintained over many decades, so that statistical comparisons can be made from decennial census to decennial census. However, physical changes in street patterns caused by highway construction, new developments, and so forth, may require occasional boundary revisions. In addition, census tracts occasionally are split due to population growth or combined as a result of substantial population decline.

Census Block

Census blocks are areas bounded on all sides by visible features, such as streets, roads, streams, and railroad tracks, and by invisible boundaries, such as city, town, township, and county limits, property lines, and short, imaginary extensions of streets and roads. Generally, census blocks are small in area; for example, a block bounded by city streets. However, census blocks in sparsely settled areas may contain many square miles of territory. All territory in the United States, Puerto Rico, and the Island Areas has been assigned.

Metropolitan Areas

Because sprawl is a regional phenomenon, the standard comparative technique is to compare metropolitan areas throughout the country. Most of the studies referenced in this volume have used this geography. These definitions have changed over time as well. Beginning with the 1950 census, the Bureau created the first definitions of Standard Metropolitan Statistical Areas (SMSAs). The SMSA definitions did not adequately describe the dynamic changes underway in the second half of the twentieth century, particularly as the interstate highway neared completion. There were numerous multistate metropolitan areas and, for logical reasons, it became important and necessary to monitor changes across state lines. Because numerous federal programs use census data to determine eligibility for grants, data structures were needed to allow the president and Congress to allocate funds to governors and legislatures to distribute to their constituent political subdivisions. Two new categories of statistical geography were introduced. Primary Metropolitan Statistical Areas (PMSAs) were aggregated into Consolidated Metropolitan Statistical Areas (CMSAs). These definitions were used through 1999 and for initial data generated in the 2000 census.

In 2003, the Census Bureau again restructured the metropolitan definitions. The older CMSA/PMSA definitions are now simplified and described as metropolitan statistical areas. In an unusual step, an entirely new statistical definition—Micropolitan Areas—was added to accommodate smaller towns and cities throughout the country. No significant research has been released using these new boundaries or definitions. However, microeconomic studies are already using the micropolitan definitions to site retail establishments. Both metropolitan and micropolitan definitions are considered Core Based Statistical Areas (CBSAs) because they are built around a core city. According to a study by Brookings (Frey et al., 2004), 93 percent of the population of America and 46 percent of the land is now included in one of these areas leaving a much smaller portion of the country defined as "rural."

Local Market Areas (LMAs)

Not all analysis is conducted using census geography. The U.S. Department of Labor defines Labor Market Areas (LMAs) by aggregating counties within states. LMA definitions are constructed to encompass a geography that reasonably satisfies the following criteria—the area within which one would expect a person to reside who is employed in a firm or establishment within the same geography. However, these definitions are widely used to measure changes in key employment factors (e.g., unemployment rates) and for the allocation of federal grants for training displaced or underskilled workers. From a social equity standpoint, these definitions can be important in determining race-based employment solutions such as affirmative action and equal opportunity. However, census definitions are more often used to make these judgments because of the more sophisticated "journey to work" analysis developed each decade from census data.

Bureau of Economic Analysis

The Bureau of Economic Analysis consolidates counties into 172 Economic Areas. These definitions are currently underutilized as regional geographies because census boundaries are more easily compared on a number of characteristics that are important to understanding the dynamics of sprawl. However, significant economic data is processed on a regular basis, including sophisticated input/output models for each region. One important researcher, Michael Porter at the Harvard Business School, uses these regions as well as census boundaries for metropolitan areas and state boundaries to conduct his "cluster analysis" (see Appendix I at the end of this book), which has become the dominant paradigm for economic development specialists around the country.

Zip Codes and Area Codes

While not necessarily a dominant definition in sprawl circles, the zip codes created by the U.S. Postal Service and the area codes used by phone service providers (a state function), are important to mention in passing. Numerous market studies are conducted using zip codes rather than census tracts and blocks. These boundaries are less likely to change over time and usually morph by adding additional digits to the traditional five-digit system. They can be easily linked to streams of address-based data (such as customer lists) and are cross-tabulated to other data sets, including census information, by numerous commercial services. Until the explosion of the cellular telephone industry, area codes also provided a stable platform for marketing consultants when the distinction between local and long-distance service was more meaningful.

Local and State Systems

There are numerous state and local geographies that use either standard aggregations of political subdivisions and/or census tracts and blocks. Legislative districts, precincts, and wards, are the most obvious examples. However, many state agencies use unique geographies to create administrative districts and to monitor activity. Environmental programs often use watershed or airshed boundaries for collecting data and creating pollution mitigation requirements. Most states have created regional planning boundaries for areawide coordination of large-scale infrastructure systems.

Summary and Research Implications

This discussion was included primarily to alert the casual reader to the complicated environment in which research on the complexities of sprawl must currently take place. Multivariate analysis requires the correlation of different information.

Multiple extra steps must be undertaken to be sure that the same geographies are used (e.g., labor force changes using labor market data and commuting patterns using journey to work information from the census). When time series are needed and the data-collection period is different (e.g., annual vs. decennial), even more complex calculations are necessary. Fortunately, these parameters are well understood by sophisticated researchers and this is a research concern that is usually overcome. However, media reports and advocates of specific policies, based on these studies, may not be as sensitive. Further, as we discussed in the opening section, different studies come to very different conclusions about the extent and rate of sprawl based on the number of variables included.

INDICES

One traditional use of data is to create simple indices like the ones discussed above to measure sprawl. The research draws conclusions about various relationships between sets of data and inherent or explicit policies. In the sprawl indices, the goal is to determine "who sprawls the most" and why. As we have seen in other discussions in this volume, there is no clear policy regime available to manage sprawl. Consequently, the index is helpful in calling attention to the aggregate consequences of a lack of policy. There are two other indices available, used in Myron Orfield's work, which are useful to introduce. While they don't measure sprawl, they measure two other social equity issues that are important concerns in the sprawl debate—racial segregation and income disparity.

Segregation

The segregation index, developed by researchers at the Mumford Center at the University of New York at Albany, looks at microlevel data to determine the extent of racial and ethnic segregation in an area by analyzing the number of persons in one race (e.g., black) who would have to move into an area (neighborhood, census tract, municipality, etc.) to provide racial (or ethnic) balance to the area.

Graphic Interface

One of the most dramatic ways to demonstrate the impact of human settlement patterns on the surrounding countryside is to create a graphic portrayal of that change. A variety of techniques make this possible.

Maps

Cartographers are skilled interpreters of changes in the landscape. A review of the historical geography of an area is possible by comparing maps from different time periods. Because many of these changes associated with sprawl are relatively slow moving, it is necessary to have maps from different decades to demonstrate the impact of changes. If the maps can be collected to correlate with the decades of census, then a story can be woven linking population dispersal to changes in the map. Using highway maps before and after the creation of the interstate highway system will amplify the story.

Aerial Photography

Most areas have current and historical aerial photography that can be used to make reasonable comparisons in the countryside over time. In recent years, many of these have been created in digital form, which allow integration with computer cartography. Several systems use satellite imagery to provide sophisticated analytical capacity.

Geographic Information Systems (GIS)

Geographic Information Systems (GIS) integrate computer cartography with data connected with the geography. Multiple layers of graphical information can be overlain to generate complex maps. With the data linked to the layers, the high-end GIS software systems allow calculations based on geographic areas (e.g., percentage of race, ethnicity in census tracts) and allow these analyses to be graphically portrayed on a new map layer. These systems also allow aerial photographs and copies of paper maps (digitized) to be included as data layers.

BUILD-OUT ANALYSIS

An example of the use of these tools for sprawl research is a technique known as build-out analysis. The procedure predates current technology but is made substantially easier with GIS technology. Build-out analysis starts with the zoning ordinance in a community. Current development in each district is catalogued. Undevelopable land (wetlands, protected open space, etc.) is netted out. Projected uses are calculated on the remaining developable land creating the anticipated impact in the community when it is "built out." From these data, further analyses allow projections of the new development on infrastructure, schools, water supplies, and other services.

INTERPRETING RESULTS

Data and information are often presented as "neutral" information without bias or normative interpretation. Unfortunately, choosing what gets measured is a policy decision based in values of both the researcher and the policy analyst. If statistics on municipalities are generated on issues such as crime, pollution, or school performance, cities often suffer when compared to their suburban counterparts. However, many regions have undertaken "report cards" that focus on the positive dynamics for cities and regions including economic performance, education and training, entrepreneurial activity, and now, several metrics have been created that include the "smart growth" performance of regions and projects within regions (see Fleissig and Jacobson, 2002). Therefore, a careful researcher will explore the fine print of the analytical framework before interpreting the results.

MODELING

Vision/Goals Based

Many regions are moving to a vision-driven policy plan that describes an ideal future and then focuses on a policy regime that will guide the region to that future. Pioneered by Peter Calthorpe and Richard Fregonese, these visioning exercises have been used in places as diverse as Salt Lake City, Los Angeles, Chicago, and Boston. Citizens are given a series of "chips" that allow them to allocate densities into various parts of the city or the region; alternative policies are then generated using the outputs of these various scenarios and citizens can see, graphically and visually, the consequences of their choices. "Envision Utah," the most widely celebrated process using this technique, recently received the award for excellence in planning from the American Planning Association.

Infrastructure Capacity

Another technique for measuring or, in fact, metering change is the use of infrastructure capacity as a change agent. Clearly, if the sewers back up or the well runs dry, there are serious implications for human health and safety. When the highway is congested, people may be willing to tolerate delays, but human health does suffer through air pollution, injuries and death in traffic accidents, and stress and road rage. More importantly, urban infrastructure systems are expensive and require long lead times for planning and implementation. Consequently, there are sophisticated planning and engineering models used to make these determinations.

Transportation

One of the earliest efforts to apply complex econometric modeling to transportation systems was undertaken by Alan Voorhees in the Chicago Area Transportation study in the late 1940s. A set of traffic zones was created on a map of the area, which acted as both sending and receiving areas for trips. The criteria for how many trips would be generated or attracted to a specific zone was the land use in the zone. If the zone had high-density residential uses, more trips would be generated than a rural single-family subdivision. If the area was an employment center, then more trips would be attracted to it than an open space reserve. Using a concept from physics, the model then calculated the relative attraction and generation between zones based on distance between the zones and size of the trip generators. This "gravity model" mimics the relationship between planetary bodies in the solar system, which have gravitational fields based on size and distance.

From these initial measures, trips were assigned to networks and distributed throughout the network based on access, capacity of the network, time of day, and other characteristics of travel behavior. This model, with several refinements, is still the industry standard for predicting the demand for new transportation infrastructure. Applets of the model are used in more local conditions to predict traffic generation for new land uses (shopping centers, residential subdivisions, office parks, etc.) on local streets and roadways. Traffic mitigation requirements (additional lanes, turn-outs, traffic signals) are then required to maintain tolerable levels of service in neighborhoods and communities.

Land Use as an Input to Transportation Models

One example of importance to sprawl researchers is the way models are constructed to predict transportation demand into the future. The basic model design takes existing land use and the regulatory framework for land use (i.e., zoning) as an input into the transportation demand analysis. Trip-generation rates (i.e., the number of daily trips a particular land use will add to the traffic pattern) for various land uses (residential, commercial, industrial) are calibrated based on national standards and then used as critical components of the models which distribute these trips to the existing transportation network. Sophisticated models allow traffic assignments to be allocated to different modes (transit, highways, rail, etc.). However, by using land use as an input, the models are biased toward allocating a greater and greater number of trips to the network. The models do allow the network to be degraded by congestion by indicating a level of service for each link (A=best, F=worst). However, the model then calls for more capacity to be created to relieve congestion. In recent years, policies have created demand management alternatives (congestion pricing, flexible work hours, and ridesharing).

What is really needed is to run the models backwards. This would require us to describe the optimum traffic network and tolerable conditions on that network and then solve for the land-use densities that would be necessary to accomplish these conditions. If local governments, which are the stewards of land use and its regulation, were given the consequences of the various choices of their decisions, perhaps they would choose tighter development patterns. This would, of course assume, that better transit services were available to meet the increased demand. Advocates of transit-oriented development are moving in that direction.

Water Supply

Adequate and safe water supply is a critical component of human settlement. Throughout human history, water bodies have been prime locations for intensified development. As density increases, individual private water supplies (wells, etc.) are no longer adequate to sustain the community. Public water supplies require large holding areas (reservoirs, aquifers, etc.) to provide the daily demands. These systems also require treatment facilities, pipes to distribute the supply, and pressurization to insure that water can flow uphill as well as down and maintain safe yields for fire suppression and other uses. These metrics can be calculated and are part of the planning and engineering available to communities as they build out. However, water supplies are particularly vulnerable to contamination for pathogens and harmful chemicals. Surface water systems are more easily protected than groundwater aquifers because contamination sources are more likely to be observed and cleaned up. During the last half of the twentieth century, scientists and engineers have refined their understanding and analytical processes to provide planners with better tools for protecting existing and future water supplies and for predicting the average safe yield of existing systems. More importantly, these analyses are critical to determining whether new development will require additional water supply capacity to be created.

Wastewater Management

Wastewater management systems are also a critical infrastructure component of complex urban regions. Low-density residential and commercial uses can often safely dispose of wastewater through on-site septic systems. As density increases, some states and localities permit multi-unit systems (package treatment plants) that can accommodate larger volumes of waste but process the effluent on-site in a technology similar to smaller scale septic tanks and leach fields. However, urban densities require full-scale wastewater treatment plants. Effluent arrives at the plant through pipes that receive the wastes from residential, commercial, and industrial facilities and is treated through a variety of biological and chemical processes before being discharged into lakes or rivers.

In the past, industrial discharges may have mixed with human waste before arriving at the treatment plant. However, aggressive state and federal regulations have curtailed and substantially eliminated these discharges. Stormwater, however, is often mixed with sanitary sewage wastes, creating substantial surges in volumes arriving at treatment plants during storm events.

Sophisticated planning and engineering models are available to planners as they anticipate development. Since long lead times are required to add capacity to large-scale urban systems, excess capacity is often designed into treatment plants to handle expected growth.

From a sprawl perspective, density requires an intensification of wastewater management. Therefore, one significant sprawl management strategy is to monitor the sewer service area as a potential "urban service/urban growth" limitation. Growth management systems in Oregon and in the Twin Cities have applied this concept as a mechanism for managing sprawl by allowing development within the area served by sewers but restricting it on the periphery.

Scenario Planning

The most sophisticated modeling and management systems incorporate an analytical framework that allows a comparison of alternative development scenarios to accommodate different densities for projected growth. While the Calthorpe/Fregonese process described above creates a visual and interactive methodology for this type of planning, a rigorous analytical capacity must exist to support scenario planning to have an impact on the infrastructure systems required to serve the preferred development densities. A variety of models are in place to assist planners as they explore alternative scenarios. The U.S. Environmental Protection Agency has conducted a review of these tools with an excellent comparison to the cost, complexity, and presentation tools, such as visual simulations, available. This report can be downloaded from EPAs website at the following address: www.epa.gov/tools.pdf.

LIMITATIONS

Equity Problems

One of the common critiques of growth management systems and planning in general is that social equity is inadequately addressed. Planners are criticized for serving the local populations in their communities without addressing the needs of other residents in the region. As the sprawl debate emerged from the twentieth century, a new emphasis is being placed on serving low-income and minority populations. As one official commented, "Smart growth should not be about soccer moms in SUVs talking on cell phones and drinking Starbucks coffee. To be truly smart, people in my district need to access the benefits that growth brings to the region. We need to include everyone in this discussion or we will continue to exclude people who need to achieve their share of the American dream."

Choice Limitations

One of the best metrics for measuring change from an equity standpoint is to determine who has accessed past growth opportunities and who has been denied choice by law or circumstance. Decennial demographic data from the census offers a consistent framework for analysis. Legal challenges, such as the NAACP case against Mount Laurel, New Jersey, demonstrate that planning must respond to the needs of everyone in the region to pass muster with the courts. New court challenges continue around school finance based on the property tax, which inherently benefits richer communities over poorer communities.

OUTCOMES

Data, the use of data to measure change over time, and the analysis of past data to predict future changes allows planners, officials, and, increasingly, citizens to affect growth management policies. If the systems are designed properly, then future data collection will allow others to determine whether the outcomes fit the projections and to adjust policies to better accommodate the needs of all citizens.

NOTES

1. Fulton and Pendall, 2001, p. 6.
2. Galster et al. include the following 13 regions: Atlanta, Georgia; Boston, Massachusetts; Chicago, Illinois; Dallas, Texas; Denver, Colorado; Detroit, Michigan; Houston, Texas; Los Angeles, California; Miami, Florida; New York, New York; Philadelphia, Pennsylvania; San Francisco, California; and Washington, D.C.

BIBLIOGRAPHY

Ewing, Reid, Rolf Pendall, and Don Chen. 2004. *Measuring Sprawl and Its Impact.* Washington, DC: Smart Growth America.

Fleissig, Will, and Vickie Jacobsen. 2002. *Smart Scorecard for Development Projects*. Washington, DC: Congress for New Urbanism and the U.S. Environmental Protection Agency.

Frey, William H., Jill H. Wilson, Alan Berube, and Audrey Singer. 2004. *Tracking Metropolitan America into the 21st Century: A Field Guide to the New Metropolitan and Micropolitan Definitions*. Washington, DC: The Brookings Institution.

Fulton, William, and Rolf Pendall. 2001. *Who Sprawls the Most? How Growth Patterns Differ Across the U.S.* Washington, DC: Center on Urban and Metropolitan Policy, The Brookings Institution.

Galster, George, and Royce Hanson. 2001. "Wrestling Sprawl to the Ground: Defining and Measuring an Elusive Concept." *Housing Policy Debate* 12(4): 681–717.

Garreau, Joel. 1991. *Edge City: Life on the New Frontier*. New York: Doubleday.

Projecting Land-Use Change: A Summary of Models for Assessing the Effects of Community Growth and Change on Land-Use Patterns. 2000. Washington, DC: Office of Research and Development, United States Environmental Protection Agency.

Rusk, David. 1993. *Cities without Suburbs*. Washington, DC: The Woodrow Wilson Center Press.

16

Taking Democracy to Scale: Tools for Planning at the Speed of Change

Ron Thomas

> There can be no public without full publicity in respect to all consequences
> which concern it. Whatever obstructs and restricts publicity limits and distorts
> public opinion and checks and distorts thinking on social affairs. Without free-
> dom of expression, not even methods of social inquiry can be can be developed.
> For tools can be evolved and perfected only in operation; in observing, report-
> ing and organizing actual subject matter; and this cannot occur save through
> free and systematic communication.
>
> John Dewey, The Public & Its Problems, 1927

A tool is generally defined as something to help someone do something. To look
into the topic of planning tools, we must also consider how they will be used, what
they are to do, and what they will produce. Too often, the answers to these questions are assumed and a detailed treatise ensues on the technicalities of support
mechanisms, much like an owner's manual. With the rapid changes in technology,
the concepts, values, and purposes of how and why we use tools can be more important to understand than describing any one tool.

   For us the general topic is urban planning, with a strong leaning to the large- and
regional-scale issues of sprawl being addressed under the banner of smart growth.
To begin, it is safe to say that smart growth is growing out of an advocacy movement
to affect the type, location, and scale of urban development, especially on the fringes
of metropolitan regions, which has acquired its own broad label of *sprawl*. While
smart growth champions intensification and redevelopment of traditional urban
centers, its cause, to date, has been the development at the haphazard expansions at
the urban edges, and its countering strategies have often seemed to vacillate between aggressive political activism and supportive education, with communication

gaps often existing between the advocates and the institutional leaders, often elected officials, who are the message targets of antisprawl, smart-growth proponents.

As smart-growth activities have continued to strike public and political nerves and address issues of significant economic and environmental import, the label continues to grow in acceptance by an increasing number of national organizations and institutions: American Planning Association, Urban Land Institute, and Brookings Institution, to name a few, in addition to the several national organization founded with a antisprawl mission.

In its evolution, antisprawl advocates can learn from other initiatives in planning practice such as historic preservation that, in a few decades, has grown from fringe activist concerns to an established component of comprehensive planning practice. Other issue areas also continue to evolve such as gentrification of older urban neighborhoods and fair housing. A look back for context is especially important for antisprawl activities that are often being initiated by motivated activists not familiar with earlier, relevant planning activities.

Underlying the legacy and context of the last several decades in urban planning and development is that many of the innovative experiences, their methods and tools have not yet been authenticated by the standard planning texts, and in too many texts on new planning, writers keep rediscovering (reinventing) well-established methods and tools. For example, the design workshop activity called "charrettes" has been used continuously as a participatory tool in planning activities for the last four decades, yet planning literature exists in every decade since the 1960s that declares it has invented the charrette as a new planning tool. But not only are some of the most important and effective planning tools not documented in the core planning literature, the practice of planning itself has evolved in basic ways still not taught in most planning curricula.

Context is also important in order to understand differences between past efforts and the challenges of antisprawl campaigns under the smart growth banner, which in many ways has broken the bounds of traditional planning and entered into a realm of issues and scale of geography that demands an essential transformation of planning practice to succeed.

A final impediment to using new tools are core values about the nature of planning held by professional planners within most governmental, social, and economic systems. Often these assumptions remain unarticulated truisms that the professional planner hardly ever communicates to politician or public alike. Often they are so ingrained that that they become almost a professional set of religious convictions, as described by the management consultant Joel Barker on the theory of paradigms,[1] and originally explored by Thomas Kuhn:

> Paradigm . . . a constellation of concepts, values, perceptions and practices shared by a community which forms a particular vision of reality that is the basis of the way a community organizes itself.

And to paraphrase Barker:

> A paradigm is a set of beliefs, held by an individual, a group, or a civilization which they hold to be true and precludes them from seeing any other possibilities.

A short story may explain this phenomenon. In our look into planning tools for smart growth, the recognition of these underlying values is essential if the array of new tools and technologies available to us is to be put to effective use.

While working on an important highway plan and redesign, the power of these professional mind-sets was pointedly demonstrated by a veteran highway engineer. This particular corridor had been in legal conflict for 25 years, and a new project team was charged with creating a public, participatory planning process to move the project forward to resolving the deteriorating levels of service and safety along the existing highway. While the team was charged by both the governor and state director of transportation to work with their appointed advisory board as the surrogate project client, this particular planner was visibly upset that we might talk with the Advisory Committee about information before it had been signed off on by the state's department of transportation. "We don't do it that way!" was his admonishment, even as the empowered advisory group was moving the project forward by consensus and state planning money was again flowing to his consulting firm. It is these usually unspoken beliefs that have a much greater influence than admitted on planning practitioners, who usually share a professional pride in "scientific objectivity" while engaged in a practice that is highly situational, political, and values-based. What is liked usually succeeds over what is right. The successful practitioner's challenge is to seek and facilitate alignment between the "like" and "right." Tools, techniques and methods can assist with achieving this alignment.

DRIVING VALUES

The core assumptions here about tools are that, first, public land-use based planning is (should always be) a democratic process and must be managed as an open and inclusive exercise of democratic governance. However, planning at any scale that shapes and directs decision making affecting the future of human settlement and the natural systems that support us also requires the knowledge and expertise of collaborating professionals from disparate practices and a break with the established public paradigm. Also, the inclusion of responsible decision makers is key. Much planning literature tends to address one or the other of these sectors of practitioner, politician, or public and assumes that one sector has full planning responsibility over the other sectors, if they are even recognized. In other words, we find much of the literature aimed at either the professional expert planner, the policy political decision maker as planner, or the activist advocate planner.

A core value here is that effective smart growth planning requires the active participation and partnership of at least these three core sectors of decision makers, expert professionals, and civic activists. In addition, the public-at-large (as the electorate) needs to be informed, provided the opportunity for input, and invited to participate.

Another assumption is that tools are not only technological things; tools are also activities, skills, and methodologies shaped by the intentions of the people who use them.

TOOLS FOR WHAT?

What and who changes a city, a neighborhood, or a region and how? Is urban change intentional or random? Is planning a civic exercise in democratic intentions, or a futile exercise against market-driven circumstance? How can we plan for urban change in ways that respond to people's current preferences while addressing the large urban systems that support today's complex urban structures going beyond the borders of even the largest cities? What is the time horizon that we should envision in planning? Generally, today's paradigm of neighborhood-scale planning seeks action in a geography of personal experiences of the participants and in a time frame of the present to perhaps five years out. City comprehensive plans tend to address a 5- to 10-year period. The practice of regional planning, driven by the requirements of transportation planning, considers 30- to 50-year horizons and at a geography that few people (including experts and officials) have personally experienced. This challenge of democratic regional planning calls for new tools and techniques to affect the scale of sprawl.

Along with scale, smart growth has introduced the notion of immediacy and action into the process of regional planning. Smart growth has taken the position that change must happen now to land-use activities that immediately begin to alter significant core economic, political, and social practices, including development patterns, public financing priorities of transportation and other infrastructure, consumption of open space and other natural resources in nonrenewable ways, and equity consideration, especially in the housing market. These and other land-use practices including development design qualities, as fostered by the New Urbanists, are the types of immediate action issues that have, for the first time, entered into the long-range purview of regional planning. This new complexity of short-range actions across jurisdictional lines and considerations beyond the current generation demands new types of technical, communication, and decision support tools that began coming on-line with the millennium in the public planning arena. All these tools, though, have their origins in earlier precedents, origins, and evolution of postwar twentieth-century planning practice.

LOOKING BACK

Smart growth seems to have reversed two planning trends for the last 50 years. First, it has embraced large-scale geographies for the first time since the era of urban renewal and interstate highway construction 40 years ago, but it has done so as a populist, activist movement. Historically, these two—large scale and activism—have been antithetical, as the large scale has been the domain of the expert-driven establishment and activists have aimed at the known, familiar, immediate neighborhood, building, or site scales.

To address sprawl, smart-growth campaigns are advancing planning policy at scale in new ways. The considerations for the quality of life and environment issues are largely new in the regional planning arena. These are the issues which, in turn, resonate with the public at large. Then as the public expresses their irritations at the perceived loss of these valued qualities—such as a new big box in the middle of a former farm field—they act on these feelings at election time, even if the farm field was in another jurisdiction.

A dominant trend in urban planning for 30 years, since the failures of many massive urban-renewal projects and dislocation such as those caused by urban interstate highway construction, has been to open planning to ever more public participation, especially at the neighborhood, special district, and municipal scales.

While there is much to be done in researching the methodologies and effectiveness of these practices, public participation is well established in these frameworks that have defined jurisdictional geography and foreseeable time frames. But, what of the emerging importance of multijurisdictional, multigenerational, regional planning to control sprawl? How do we bring democratic planning to scale in major metropolitan regions? Can the public contribute? Do they want to contribute? How can they contribute? A barrier often cited by officials and public alike is the irrelevance to people's daily lives of the long time frame to plan and implement change of regional systems. The challenge at hand is to make the geography and time frame have meaning and importance to the lives of individuals, their families, and communities.

Emerging from the Back Room

"Make no small plans" was Daniel Burnham's clarion call to a rapidly urbanizing nation 100 years ago, and, energized by its growing place in the world market, the young nation carved bold new cities out of forest, prairie, and plains. Not far behind the Burnham-inspired City Beautiful Movement came large systems building of dams, highways, and power utilities to support the burgeoning urbanization. With the Depression, a large-systems focus continued to dominate national policy with the New Deal for economic recovery. Without a break, we were at war and everyone pulled together to weld, rivet, and fight, while urban migration especially from the rural South and recovering Dust Bowl were affecting a midcentury transformation of cities.

During this first half of the twentieth century, "We the People" were the background to this national ascendancy. A few voices such as Jacob Riis[2] and Jane Addams[3] fought for safety and welfare of the disenfranchised. Others brought these same concerns into the national culture through their art, such as Upton Sinclair's *The Jungle*, John Steinbeck's *The Grapes of Wrath*, Eudora Welty's *One Time One Place: Mississippi in the Depression*, and Ralph Ellison's *Invisible Man*. But in the first half of the twentieth century neither culture nor art nor even politics was seen as germane to the big-systems goals of the urban planner. At their root, these early planning and development policies were ones of wealth and power over worker, orchestrated by the expert using the resources of both wealth and worker for a greater national good. By the 1950s this top-down system was about to change or at least to begin a change in ways that are still unfolding.

Dream Interrupted

The 1933 World's Fair with its Century of Progress exhibit projected a future vision that may have then seemed fantastically remote, coming as it did in the middle of the Depression. But it created a vision so powerful and resonant that it would incubate nearly 20 years as the nation recovered from the Depression, fought a world war, and emerged as the solidified world center for hope and the future: we could do anything, we believed.

Much as been written about the Levittown American dream,[4] the GI Bill, and the Home Loan Bank Board that fostered postwar suburbanization. Suffice it to say, it resonated with the American public in many ways as a new domestic migration wave staked a claim on the suburban fringes as a new inalienable right for a family home on a piece of land away from the cities the culture had demonized even before Sinclair, Steinbeck, and the Muckrakers and going back to Jefferson's agrarian idealism. The postwar dream has grown from $3,000 for a 1,000-square-foot cottage in Levittown to the MacMansions of today with the $400,000 to $800,000 price tag for an acre or two or five with 5,000 square feet or so under roof.

At the outset of the Depression in 1929, the nation's population of 122 million was generally either urban residents (80%) or rural residents (20%). The suburban population was insignificant. In the two decades following the war, *suburban* became a census category in 1950; by 1970 the suburban population had become the largest category, and by 2000 it accounted for more than 50 percent of the total population.

This represents a population redistribution of historic proportions, for not only was the population changing location, it was changing culture and establishing a new values system of home, family, community, and territory in a nonurban, nonrural, and new suburban pattern.

The dream of the 1933 World's Fair was the push, but urban renewal and the interstate highway system were the pulls. These two national public works initiatives articulated the shadow side of the dream of the slum city (tracing back to Dickens) and the new auto technology to escape it quickly on the transplanted German-style *autobahn* of the new interstate highway system. These two activities, renewal and highway building, simultaneously tore down as much as to 30 percent of the urban American fabric in some cities and involuntarily relocated nearly 20 million Americans—virtually all poor and mostly black, but the white, poor working class was not spared.

Needless to say, the people were not consulted in the process. It was the halcyon days for the technocrat, and the politicians listened to ideas for big plans, which stirred some men's souls but put terror in the hearts of others.

Enough Is Enough

The era of big-systems building and excesses also catalyzed reactions with the simultaneous rise of the public voice on a number of fronts, the most notable of which was the Civil Rights Movement. At the same time, urban planning began to evolve a new and energized focus on people, the environment, and urban community, stimulated and articulated by writings such as Michael Harrington's *The Other America*,[5] Rachel Carson's *Silent Spring*,[6] and Jane Jacobs's *The Death and Life of Great American Cities*.[7]

Often it was the civil rights organizations and the emerging ecumenical, urban, faith-based organizations that rallied to say, "Stop! Enough!" The techniques and tools, in addition to the Gandhi/King nonviolent resistance, were formulated by activists like the Chicago organizer Saul Alinsky,[8] who counseled people to "embarrass them and they will stop." Around the country, a new, young generation of urban–planner activists took to the streets and urban neighborhoods to organize and resist top-down change, legitimized by professional voices such as Paul Davidoff.[9] The purpose and energy of the times gained institutional support from federal programs such as VISTA and civic support such as the Community Design Centers[10] sponsored by the American Institute of Architects. Historic preservation[11] gained the legal tools to stop a lot of the destruction in the name of history; many of these organizations continue to operate at varying strengths today. But taken together, these efforts created the basic tool kit for community-based planning that is still evolving today.

Time to Make Some Small Plans

While Alinsky was forming the activist's tools for grassroots resistance in a postwar America, several voices began to articulate the need and tools for collaboration and participatory change. Also in Chicago, ecumenical organizations working with the legacies of Jane Addams saw that reactive resistance stops actions, but collaboration was needed to make positive change. This effort to foster collaboration continues internationally today with organizations such as The Institute for Cultural Affairs.

Tools like brainstorming, preference ranking, and collaborative problem-solving techniques were bringing new planning tools from such disparate sectors as military war gaming and new business management practices espoused by W. Edwards Deming, another Chicagoan who had to go to Japan to implement his new management idea for customer-driven total quality. Concurrently, other management theories were emerging, supporting interactive group work and team models[12] for business organizations.

Two early documented uses of these participatory planning practices were the neighborhood-planning program in the Mantua neighborhood[13] in Philadelphia and the Neighborhood Charrette organized by James Rouse's urban designer, Morton Hoppenfeld,[14] in the Fells Point neighborhood of Baltimore.

The Charrette can be traced back over 100 years[15] as an intense architectural workshop, but it was a professional activity. Innovators like Hoppenfeld and Davidoff democratized the concepts and brought them to the people in the spirit of the 1960s' activism and recognition of cities as communities of people as well as built systems exemplified by the Hartford Process[16] (arguably the first participatory, urban goals setting program).

Participation Becomes a Norm . . . Sometimes, in Some Places

As the activism efforts of civil rights and antiwar protest gained in effectiveness, so did the public's abilities to stop things, from highway construction to historic building tear-downs, such as the pioneering preservation organizations like Don't Tear It Down in Washington, D.C. With this demonstrated interest in public action, a network of socially active, innovative planners, designers, and architects, joined by academics, journalists, and politicians, entered into the activist fray of the 1960s. These innovator leaders were reinventing planning methodology and including the likes of Lawrence Halprin, Ian McHarg, David Lewis, Morton Hoppenfeld, and Wolf von Eckardt among others. Their personal ideas and actions have led the way to today's continuously emerging planning tools, methods, and strategies—which remain by and large outside the mainstream of the academic planning paradigm.

Some examples for these trendsetters and planning innovators include the following people and their contributions to the values, methods, and tools for

		Tool Tips 1	
Tool	*Function*	*Application*	*Example*
Recording group work	Collecting, exchanging, and delivering information	All face-to-face collaborations	Flip Chart & Markers, http://www. grove.com/

planning. Lawrence Halprin—one of the most important landscape architects of the mid–twentieth century—synthesized planning and design as a creative, participatory experience. Working with his wife, Anna Halprin, they went far out into the creative spheres in interactive workshopping, and from their experiments at Eslen, Halprin brought back the Take Part Workshops[17] that became the foundation of his planning scale urban work, such as the 1975 Cleveland Downtown Plan. These hands-on interactions around sensing place and intuiting actions presaged the learning research that is only now emerging around the concepts of "multiple intelligences"[18] beginning to have major influence on communication and education practices. Take Part Workshops made the planning process a way to heal the wounds of urban renewal, white flight, and highway riffs by being open, participatory, and democratic and at the same time showing that planning can be energizing, rewarding, and engaging. The take part process also anticipated by two decades the later work of John Kretzmann and John McKnight at Northwestern University and their articulation of "assets-based planning."[19] While much of planning theory has been framed to address problems (deficits) such as substandard housing, traffic congestion, and flooding, for instance, Assets-based planning begins with the assumption that any place and community contains bountiful resources embodied in its people to be marshaled to move to an even better future. David Cooperrider has formulated an accompanying facilitation method of Appreciative Inquiry.[20]

Halprin's landscape architect colleague, Ian McHarg,[21] while making great contributions to the analytical approaches to large scale, ecologically-based landscape design, made another great contribution to systems thinking in planning with the environmental layers concept in his design with nature approach, which provided a way for all, professionals and public alike, to understand complex information sets. McHarg's environmental layers predated and clearly laid out a conceptual framework for later graphical information systems and tools that are the core of today's newest, emerging computer-based tools.

TAKING PLANNING TO SCALE IN THE THIRD DIMENSION

American urban planning, in contrast to contemporary European planning, has been based more on two-dimensional, categorical planning and land-use policies than three-dimensional and urban design. To a large extent, the bridge between building architecture and urban planning has eroded in the United States since Daniel Burnham's plan for Chicago. David Lewis has been a strong, but one of too few, voices for the importance for planning in the third dimension. One of the most powerful outcomes and benefits of three-dimensional planning is the resulting visualizations that are much more accessible and readable to the general public with approaches recently published in an urban design guidebook series by Lewis and his colleagues.[22]

Lewis's other driving contribution to planning and architecture has been his fervent conviction that the users of the professional experts' work must also be participants in its creation. Out of this relationship and understanding between professional and public/client collaboration brings the needs of the user and the expertise of the professional to create a truly responsive and effective result.

In his project approach, Lewis has practiced and demonstrated the application of the charrette in his lay and professional collaborations. Beyond his professional practice, Lewis was one of the founding champions and inventors of the American Institute of Architects Regional/Urban Design Assistant Teams—a precursor to similar technical assistance workshop programs of the Urban Land Institute, the American Society of Landscape Architects, and the American Planning Association. A milestone program at the U.S. Department of Housing and Urban Development (HUD), championed single-handedly by Andy Euston, in the 1970s, partnered with the National League of Cities to establish urban planning and design as a core municipal service.[23] The Urban Environmental Design Program, chaired by Charleston Mayor Joe Reilly, set the stage for the Mayors Institute for City Design and other design-related planning initiatives. The program was articulated is a series of publications and materials such as *Cities by Design*[24] and *Design for Low Income Neighborhoods.*[25]

Another, and less-recognized, contributor to public planning practice, is that of Morton Hoppenfeld, James Rouse's principal urban designer and planner. Out of the fray of the Civil Rights Movement and community activism, Hoppenfeld emerged as a young Baltimore activist committed to neighborhood-based approaches. James Rouse himself has recognized Hoppenfeld as the person who opened Rouse— initially a conventional suburban shopping center developer—to the possibilities of urban redevelopment, new communities, and great design. Behind Rouse's business, developments and leadership can be found Hoppenfeld's commitment to great design, cities, and social activism.

It was Hoppenfeld who weighed in with Baltimore's neighborhood leaders, organizing to stop the new Interstate 95 corridor from coming directly through the city and destroying their neighborhoods as had happened in other urban areas across the country. Hoppenfeld not only helped organize an effective Alinsky-style resistance, he introduced one of the first applications for the professionally assisted, community-based design charrettes that began to break down the barriers between expert and community.

From these urban activist professionals over the intervening three decades, a new model of applied research has evolved into an academically accepted research methodology of action research that makes the object of the research a knowing and contributing subject to the outcomes of the expert's practice. It is a model clearly relevant to the practice of the public planner at every level and by and large should replace the scientific research model that keeps ordinary people in the dark. A definition of action research follows.[26]

Action research can be described as a family of research methodologies, which pursue action (or change) and research (or understanding) at the same time. In most of its forms, it does this by using a cyclic or spiral process, which alternates between action and critical reflection, and in the later cycles, continuously refining methods, data, and interpretation in the light of the understanding developed in the earlier cycles.

It is thus an emergent process, which takes shape as understanding increases; it is an *iterative* process, which converges towards a better understanding of what happens.

In most of its forms it is also participative (among other reasons, change is usually easier to achieve when those affected by the change are involved) and qualitative.

A growing number of planning practitioners such as Ken Reardon, known for his community-based work with East St. Louis, and John Forester,[27] both now at Cornell, have articulated the application of action research[28] to urban and regional planning. Nevertheless, it is curious that action research theory and methods have not penetrated urban and regional planning curricula as thoroughly as they have programs in education, health care, and business programs. The case is made here that urban planning and action research should be synonymous in a democracy except in rare and clearly defined instances.

During these three decades of the 1950s, 1960s, and 1970s, few academic planning programs were effective or even seemingly interested in a pedagogy that related and integrated urban-scale planning, three-dimensional design, social activism, participatory collaboration methods, and public communications into the mainstream programs in the established architecture or urban planning paradigms.

At the same time, however, a number of planning theorists, architecture critics, and journalists filled in the void of academics. The prime example is Jane Jacobs with her seminal *Death and Life of Great American Cities*. Upon reflection, some of the most important works in planning theory have come from journalists like Jacobs and other uncredentialed planners such as journalist Neal Peirce in writings such as *Citistates*,[29] Joel Garreau's *Edge Cities*,[30] critiques of Ada Louise Huxtable in the *New York Times* and her *Will They Ever Finish Bruckner Boulevard?*,[31] and Wolf von Eckhardt's *A Place to Live*.[32] Consistently and increasingly these leading theorists and critics have reported on, called for, and expected real participation and effective communications to and from the public. Their contributions as journalist go to the point that most often paradigm shifts come from those close to but outside the member holders of the main paradigm, to the point that journalists may have contributed more to advancing new planning theory than professional planning practitioners—at least during these transformational decades.

THE PUBLIC TRUST: MEGATRENDS IN PLANNING

Argument is often heard about the constitutional nature of our government that is established on a representative republic form of government. Without doing a major historical discourse, let us here recognize that from the penning of the words "We the People . . ." the public values of the nation's history have continued to increase the expectation in the individual's right and opportunity to have direct access the systems and processes of governance at every level from federal to neighborhood.

By 1978 a federal General Accounting Office publication identified 176 federal program requirements for public participation. Every state has established extensive requirement for public hearings around public actions, especially those affecting public taxing, financing, and expenditures. Sunshine laws for opening public meetings and Freedom of Information Acts have firmly established the public's constitutional and legal rights to know and to have a voice.

For the last three decades the leading national associations directly and indirectly related to public planning activities, such as the American Planning Association, National League of Cities, International City Management Association, and those as diverse as the Urban Land Institute and the National Trust for Historic Preservation, have all espoused open, inclusive best practices to successful urban development. At the same time, these same organizations continue to award projects annually for approaches to open participation and inclusion as exceptional innovations. Old ways change slowly and even with the demonstrated successes, action research–driven participatory planning is still regarded as the exception in planning and development practices.

While planners and designers were hard at work devising less intrusive, environmentally friendly impact mitigations, public interest advocates in such organizations as the Kettering Foundation[33] and Harvard Mediation Project[34] were bringing international and labor mediation practices and tools into the public planning arena. These new sets of tools indicated recognition that careful negotiation methods were increasingly needed to resolve differing public interests. In this era of urban development moving into the 1980s, many of the land-use conflicts were also shifting from city to suburbs around undesirable but necessary public land uses such as landfills, power plants, prisons and even in some cases educational facilities catalyzing the birth of NIMBY ("Not in My Back Yard") as a new planning force. Too often the mediators, facilitators, and participatory planners are brought in only after the NIMBY organization has been catalyzed by a confrontational public initiative—if not consciously confrontational, then often dismissive, which generates most unfortunate reactions. The implication here is that in most cases the public planning officials have created their own worst enemies in NIMBYs as reactionaries and not initiators.

This paradox of success, with open planning on the one hand and the hesitancy of acceptance by planning institutions on the other, reflect an unfortunate state of affairs. While practical experience demonstrates the value and effectiveness of open, participatory methods, yet their practice is still the exception and not the norm of public planning. Even where experts and officials recognize that officials must keep the public informed on needs, problems, and issues, the approach often used involves arm's-length tools to conduct safe, anonymous opinion surveys and eliminate the anticipated discomfort of meeting people face to face—especially if they might be unhappy. Pollster Daniel Yankelovich, in *Coming to Public Judgment*,[35] has been warning of the fallacy of this seemingly risk-free approach from several vantage points:

- The public does not feel included by arms-length surveys.
- The information from opinion polling is quick responses and not informed judgments.
- Professional experts stand as a filter between the public and official decision makers as interpreters of the tools.

Surveys, Yankelovich argues, have their place in public planning and policy making, but they are not tools for authentic democratic engagement. (A totalitarian leader would be as best advised to use polling as a democratically elected leader, for instance.) While many public officials would like to jump to conclusions about public opinion rather than face the mounting controversies and conflicts from hostile constituents, political safety is found behind the legal authority of elected, representative government. Somehow, over the evolutionary practice of public planning, officialdom has increasingly sought to hide behind the constitutional definitions of representative government; all the while the public activists have expected and the courts have ruled for the rights of the citizen and their advocate organizations to participate in the planning process. The antisprawl advocates have embraced and practice these values to the fullest.

Returning to our issues and sprawl, a case could be made that the practice of *regional planning* at the end of the twentieth century was evolved from and based on the big-systems rational planning method of the urban renewal days, a system, on one hand, perpetuated by federal and state transportation planning regulations while at the same time being in conflict with federal and state guidelines for public participation. Consequently, regulations trump guidelines, and the regional planning process until very recently viewed public participation as inconsequential, add-on events and not core planning practice.

As general urban planning practice has evolved over the last 40 years, engagement and participation practices have become more effective and planning strategies have become more interactive and responsive, especially in the smaller geographic land-use planning arenas from neighborhoods to municipalities. However, except for the individual academics here and there, even these widely used planning practices remain outside the mainstream of normal planning pedagogy in the standard planning curriculum.

The last 30 or 40 years of public planning and development have dramatically demonstrated that people will get involved and take every means of action when public policy and projects are perceived to be bad for their families, their property values, their quality of life, and their community (and perhaps in this order of priority action). A summary look at some milestones in citizen action around land-use issues has also seen a growth in scale of interest.

- *Destruction of neighborhoods (1950s and 1960s)*—Urban renewal and urban interstate highways unquestionably rallied community activists to stop the wholesale destruction of more and more urban neighborhoods from Baltimore to San Francisco. Often, the organizers were civil rights groups allied with ecumenical faith-based groups in the Saul Alinsky mold.
- *Destruction of major landmark structures (1960s and 1970s)*—Related and unrelated urban development overlapping the urban renewal period showed little regard for the tradition urban fabric and history. (It was Gropius who held that "History is bunk!" for the International School modern designer.) The now standard podium high-rise architecture style was meeting the economic and image aspirations for government, business, and design style makers alike with lukewarm to negative public appeal. When loved but

Tool Tips 2

Tool	Function	Application	Example
Keypad polling	Collecting information	Face-to-face opinion polling	Option Finder, http://www .option finder.com Ortek, (503) 626-0171

often forgotten historic landmarks were slated for demolition, like Penn Station and Grand Central Station, the upper-middle class were activated with champions like Brandon Gil, who then rallied to join the working class to stop the destruction. With the gentry now active even they were winning some but losing many.

- *Siting of major noxious public facilities like power plants and landfills (1970s and 1980s)*—Even before the Three Mile Island disaster, increasing numbers of public voices began to organize around the impacts of negative but basic public works such as power plants, treatment facilities, landfills, and most recently nuclear waste dumps. A now sophisticated public-interest network had learned to use the legal system and with concerted effort stop about anything, and NIMBYs were born with nonnegotiable conflicts for public planners.

- *Destruction and encroachment on open space and valued environmental assets (1980s and 1990s)*—Green spaces were slipping from the public's experience, from the national attention focused on the traffic congestion and air pollution in Yosemite National Park to the development in rural green-fields that had been unprotected but expected to remain for generations past.

- *Perceived erosion of "Quality of Life" across traditional boundaries (1990s—New Millennium)*—Sprawl has catalyzed smart-growth campaigns that have emerged in the last decade as headlines in every major metropolitan region send warnings about sprawl, congestion, and cultural erosions that seem to present these as peculiar to that one metropolitan area that is actually a national trend or crisis, depending on one's point of view. Increasingly, a growing number of local elections are voting officials in and out of office for problems no one jurisdiction (not even the major city center) can solve alone.

As we have seen, the two earlier activist movements for urban neighborhood renewal and historic preservation succeeded in establishing these assets of our cities and towns as important planning components, which they clearly had not been for public planning officials and business since the big systems projects of the New Deal.

SPRAWL—THE MILLENNIUM'S PLANNING CHALLENGE

What has been changing? National surveys since the mid-1990s continue to point to public attitudes ranging from concern to anger rising around three growing issues:

- Traffic congestion
- Loss of open space and other quality-of-life assets including historic resources
- Housing accessibility and affordability issues

At the same time the market (people making individual decisions) continue to move farther out to greenfields that are consumed by bigger homes, while this same public is expecting public officials to fix the resulting problems that cross jurisdictional lines with resources diminishing from continued taxpayer revolt against tax increases.

In this climate, as articulated by James Kunstler in *The Geography of Nowhere*,[36] it is understandable why public officials and staff alike would prefer to stay at arm's length from the public with scientific surveys, trends analysis, and legal requirements, but the level of public emotions place-to-place across the country is throwing these same officials out of office. At the same time, the antisprawl advocates have seen that Alinsky-type strategies can stop some things and possibly "throw the rascals out," but the scale of the sprawl issues will not be addressed, much less solved, with adversarial strategies; hence, the emergence of "smart growth" as a national political, planning, and development strategy initially advanced most actively by the Sierra Club[37] and joined by an increasing number of advocate and planning organizations.

The problem in many places is that the same people and organizations who began as Alinskyesque, antisprawl campaigners have attempted to switch to a more educational smart-growth strategy but remain identified with their former adversarial beginnings. Moreover, many of the regional agencies traditionally responsible for the cross-jurisdictional, infrastructure, and environmental systems had neither the authority to enforce actions, the experience with diverse advocacy groups, nor the resources to engage in a more interactive public planning process. With the continued lag in academic planning theory to close the gap with the evolution of successful practice, little remedial help seemed available or directly applicable on the regional scale to the sprawl challenges.

Meanwhile the parallel universe of university department research and applied planning practice were finally reversing their diverging courses between planning theory and practice. With emerging tools, technologies, and methods, theory and practice have begun to converge to address the complexity, scale, and politics of sprawl with crossover methodologies from areas such as computer science, social sciences, business management, and design.

What follows is a short recounting of ideas and applied research that has been published mostly by practitioners (often journalists) that traces some paths that have reinvented planning. These efforts have shaped a new planning practice that has eclipsed the scientific-research-based rational planning model that still dominates the planning textbooks (but not successful planning practice).

Over the last three or four decades much of planning practice has shifted as leaders, professionals, and the public have become involved and brought disciplines, practices, and experiences from other fields. While not intending to be a treatise on planning methods and their history, some mythological context needs to be defined to understand the purpose and application or the new and evolving planning tools.

Method—From War of the Worlds to Land-Use Games

Ironically, one of the fields to have a most profound affect on planning practice comes from the Cold War gaming at the Pentagon. In working through possible war games, military strategist such as Herman Kahn[38] looked into the future by *thinking the unthinkable* but also began to think in sequences and relationships that could be used by the new mainframe computers to analyze possibilities such as John Nash's "Nash Equilibrium" for strategic noncooperative games (popularized in the movie *A Beautiful Mind*), and others such as Harold Kuhn,[39] then creating the new discipline of cybernetics.[40] Today cross-discipline scientists such as Margaret Wheatly are bringing new concepts like Chaos Theory into management and planning.[41] At its most basic, game theory allows for multiple possibilities and responses in a variety of ways to a range of identified variables, whereas much of urban planning theory since the City Beautiful movement had been utopian idealism that projected the best future end plan.

It was the Eisenhower-labeled military-industrial complex that was laying the foundations for today's interactive computer tools. While the Eisenhower era gave us the rationale of national defense for the interstate system; and it was this same Pentagon-based complex that was pushing the edge of new, emerging, relativity-based systems theories of cybernetics for Cold War applications to the new computer technologies of sophisticated game theories.

In an unlikely marriage, the military-driven cybernetics field has been woven with the democratic social activism founded in the Civic Rights Movements. The resulting process-based planning in both the public and business sectors is more prominent in its application, successful in its results, and perfected in its tools, technology, and theory than is widely recognized by the mainstream planning institutions.

From End Game to Road Mapping

Closer to home professionally, applications to planning and design began to emerge in animated and accessible publications, such as Don Koberg and Jim Bagnall's *The Universal Traveler*,[42] that presented a simplified systems theory to apply to design and planning problems. Even more systematic and far reaching was the work of Christopher Alexander, beginning in 1967 with the seminal *Notes on a Synthesis of Form*, that continues nearly 40 years later.[43] Close by in the Bay Area, Landscape Architect Lawrence Halprin was creating his Take Part workshop process and seeking to systematically convey the creative, intuitive process in the RSVP Cycle.[44] As mentioned earlier, one of the most profound and lasting efforts to bring system thinking into planning and large-scale urban design is Ian McHarg's *Design with Nature*. Not only did McHarg's holistic concept of the environment resonate with the times, but his introduction to design analysis with landscape layers could be said to have created the systems thinking that would make GIS possible in their evolving, accessible, and user friendly forms such as the ArchView application and Community Viz.[45]

Method—Getting from Here to There

Over the last two decades the laboratories for democracy have been in the leading-edge companies with their new team-based management practices and not in the public sector with public contact only through surveys and increasingly restrictive public-hearing requirements. This transformation can be instructive for changes underway in public planning.

Resistance to broad participation in planning has not only come from the planning establishment, but also from the countervailing methods of organizational management in practice throughout the twentieth century. With a long legacy, the scientific method came not from today's technocrats but from the Age of Enlightenment in the eighteenth century and philosophers and scientists such as Descartes. The scientific method has been institutionalized in the organizational and management practices for nearly two centuries of industrialization in America.

Most notably Frederick Taylor[46] and Henry Ford were the thinker and doer combination to put scientific management to work at an unprecedented scale by approaching the worker as a production machine and eliminating individual initiative, creativity, and responsibility from the production line. This testimony by Frederick Taylor in 1902 captures the essentials of scientific management theory:

> The first of these . . . duties taken over by the management is the deliberate gathering in on the part of those on management's side of all of the great mass of traditional knowledge, which in the past had been in the hands of the workman, and which he has acquired through years of experience. The duty of gathering in all this great mass of traditional knowledge and then recording it, tabulating it and, in many cases, finally reducing it to laws, rules, and formulae are applied to the everyday work of the workman in the establishment, through the intimate and hearty cooperation of those on management's side, they inevitably result first, in producing a much larger output per man, as well as an output of a better and higher quality; and second, in enabling the company to pay much higher wages to their workmen; and third, in giving the company a larger profit.

Today's participatory team-based management is truly a revolution in management theory that reverses much of Taylor's theory that was in place for most of the twentieth century. While the books on the new paradigm began a flood in the 1990s, this work on engaging, empowering, and entrusting the worker began with the early work of Kurt Lewin[47] in the 1940s beginning with the National Training Lab,[48] was exported to Japan by W. Edwards Deming[49] with his Total Quality Management (TQM) theory and has been launched into the twenty-first century by Peter Senge in *The Fifth Discipline*.[50] The interactive methods for collaborative and group work have been the innovations of management "change agents"[51] who began using the now ubiquitous flip charts, dot ranking, and facilitation skills, more than those in government and activists' arenas.

Tool Tips 3

Tool	*Function*	*Application*	*Example*
Visualization	Exchanging information	Presentation	Keyhole, http://www. keyhole.com /?promo=gd l-en Graphics software: Photoshop, Illustrator

TECHNIQUE—THE HOW

Computer technology is beginning to provide significant breakthroughs with tools for planning and other civic interactions. However, none of these tools are shrink-wrapped and ready for use off the shelf. Neither are they meant to be free-standing, problem-solving push-button tools. They are intended as support tools for understanding the complexities of planning related information and of assistance in problem-solving interactions. The key word here is interaction—how people work together to understand, evaluate, arrive at, and agree on solutions. Interactive work under various labels such as creative problem solving, groupwork, and teamwork has become a highly refined set of professional tools developed jointly in the worlds of teamwork in the corporate setting and collaborative work in social service–type organizations, and the facilitator has become an essential professional to guide interactive group work.

The 1976 publication *How to Make Meetings Work*,[52] by Michael Doyle and David Strauss, provides an accessible bridge from management theory to practical use in the public and civic arenas. This book remains the first read for anyone venturing into collaborative and participatory work by laying out clear guidance for the process planner, group facilitator, and organizational manager. These process skills in facilitation are the foundation for successfully using the new technology-driven tools to be described shortly. The facilitator is to the new tools what a skilled carpenter is to a hammer, saw, and plane. Other important contributions to developing process skills and tools for planners include Susan Carpenter and W.J.D. Kennedy's *Managing Public Disputes*,[53] Lawrence Susskind and Jeffrey Cruikshank's *Breaking the Impasse*,[54] and Roger Schwarz's *The Skilled Facilitator*.[55] These cover the range of interactive management from dispute resolution and mediation to practical problem solving and creative collaborations.

A MEDIA TOOLS BOX TO DELIVER THE MESSAGE

Prior to the emergence of the Internet, one of the more underrecognized and underutilized tools to take public planning to scale was the wide range of communication media available to the planner. The professional planner was (and still is) often resistant to simplifying planning issues and ideas into clear, concise messages

Tool Tips 4			
Tool	*Function*	*Application*	*Example*
GIS remote sensing	Interpreting information	Presentation	Blueline Group, http://www.blueline-group.com

compatible with communication media that do live by headlines and sound bites. A very small subset of the planning profession, such as Moore Iacofano Goltsman, Inc.,[56] and Ted Becker,[57] has championed and pioneered the use of mass media and communications as planning tools. A special issue of the *Journal of Architectural Education*,[58] guest-edited by the author in 1978, summarized the potential of communication tools for designers and planners.

While planners might mistrust the brevity constrains of the media, process facilitators likewise have not been comfortable with the remoteness of the media, trusting only face-to-face interactions instead of media "packaging." Consequently, the use of television (along with newspaper and radio) in regional planning programs for electronic town meetings have remained isolated, yet documented innovative demonstrations have proved successful in places such as Roanoke, Virginia, as early as 1978 and Savannah, Georgia, Houston, Texas, and Albuquerque, New Mexico, in 1999 with the Rio Grande Council of Governments Regional Planning, which won an Emmy in the process. The effectiveness of the media was demonstrated, but the costs where usually a deterrent to others. Often as challenging in marshaling the media for planning has been the cultural differences between the professional planner and their politician bosses on one side and the press and media professionals[59] on the other. Bridging these communication gaps remains a barrier to consistently and effectively reaching and engaging the public through mass media.

Communication tools continue to be used as innovative planning tools but an exception to normal practice. However, the Internet and its protocols may be changing this old mindset. Nevertheless the Internet, while capable, still lags as an interactive tool in public planning, serving primarily as a tool for information delivery. An early innovative Web site designed to support Berkeley's plan update was deemed illegal by the state and operated independent of the city's public input process. But, breakthrough Internet tools, such as MyRegion.org[60] in Orlando, developed by Neighborhood America,[61] and the Full Circle Project at the Northeastern Illinois Planning Commission,[62] are growing. These and related innovators are setting the stage for a new generation of public planning tools and technologies.

A NEW PARADIGM

Along with the activism of the Civil Rights Movement in the 1950s and related actions to stop the destruction of large-scale urban renewal and interstate highways, a new 1960s generation of architects, designers, and planners went into the field to work at the grassroots community level. Venues abounded internationally in the Peace Corps, domestically in VISTA, and in any number of service organizations and federally funded community action programs. Most specifically for planners (especially those with design roots) was a network of Community Design Centers sponsored by American Institute of Architects' chapters around the country, legacies of which still thrive,[63] such as Ron Schiffman's Center for Community and Environmental Development at Pratt Institute[64] in Brooklyn. Their operating principles were—and continue to be—community based, participatory, democratic, and process oriented.

In these cases, the community people involved knew their own local problems, had ideas of what they did and didn't like, wanted action, and had little time between work life and family life to have the patience for a lot of speculation by professional experts. What they did need was help in problem solving, actionable project design, and implementation expertise.

New professionals with community-based methods, such as Paul Davidoff at MIT, Rich Ridley and John Weibenson in Washington, Susan and Michael Southworth in Boston, Morton Hoppenfeld in Baltimore and Annette Anderson at the Eastern Tennessee Community Design Center in Knoxville, were weighing in across the country. Most jumped into problem solving in the spirit of the *Universal Traveler* with action questions like, "What do we want?" "What don't we want?" "How can we get there?" and "What could get in our way?" What was emerging was a strategic approach to planning and community design that was a radical break with the Rational Planning Model that researched all possible "feasible" alternatives, analyzed them, and prioritized them with detailed research methods. The community action planner worked with shared experience, best available information, and creative intuition. Often these grassroots efforts were in conflict with and blocked by the systematically driven official agencies with a resulting distrust by community activists for numbers driven analytical experts.

A similar evolution of strategic thinking can be found in other results-oriented areas such as business management, education, and health care. Over the next two decades strategic planning would emerge as the predominant action-oriented planning method, but, while eclipsing the rational planning method in the field, urban and regional planning curricula seldom include strategic planning in the lesson plan except for those creative, iconoclastic few within academia.

By the early 1980s, the large federal funding for local planning, such as the HUD 701 Program, had disappeared and local community-based planning was left to be eked out of limited Community Development Block Grant funds, and with these, only for distressed neighborhoods.

The resulting decline in the urban planning field was leading to the emergence of public/private action efforts such as downtown revitalization and the Main Street program often led by business and community leaders and not the local planning agency. The International City/County Management Association (ICMA) began receiving requests from its membership for planning assistance in the late 1980s, and director Don Bourrit asked the author and his colleagues Mary Means and Margaret Grieve to author a publication on current, successful, local planning practices. Having just completed a two-phase, seven-year community-based planning program in Roanoke, Virginia, we were seeing the success of other community-based strategic type programs. We began *Taking Charge: How Communities Are Planning Their Futures* by surveying ICMA membership built around a basic question: "What are you doing to plan for the future that is working?" As a membership survey, we received a very high return of nearly 50 percent of ICMA's more than 5,000 members. The findings were very revealing on the state of local planning. About 75 percent of the respondents said they did not have time or resources to plan and that day-to-day maintenance of zoning, permitting, and codes overburdened their current capacities.

For the 25 percent who had a positive response, virtually every one described some kind of open, action-oriented, strategic planning process. While the word was not used in the survey, a large majority responded with the "vision thing" described somewhere in their response. These results exactly paralleled our Roanoke experience that a new community-based strategic planning approach to urban planning was emerging.[65]

ANIMATING IDEAS, VISUALIZING CHOICES

The pioneers of community-based, participatory strategic planning made another significant contribution to democratic planning practice: graphics. The highly precise engineering and architectural drawings of the day in the 1960s were at the same time too technical, intimidating, costly, and time-consuming to be responsive to the interactive, quick-response mode of the community action milieu that sought to explore and visualize many ideas before settling on one. The answer emerged as lively, humor-infused, three-dimensional cartoons. The poster plan for Lowell, Massachusetts, by Michael and Susan Southworth is an icon of the era. Others, such as those by the late Rich Ridley and John Weibenson with his Archihorse comic strip in Washington, D.C., continued to develop the style well into the 1980s and in Weibenson's work until his death in 2003. The tradition continues in Washington with Roger Lewis's weekly column in the *Washington Post* in which he often reports on and illustrates today's regional sprawl problems.

These innovators broke through the paradigm of graphics that impress and sell and created integral communication based visualization tools that were used to inform and explain in personal and amusing ways. This spirit has carried into many of the graphic and visualizations tools flourishing in today's cyberdesign world.

"Welcome. Did you have difficulty finding us?" In the *Washington Post* column ("Shaping the City") by Roger K. Lewis, FAIA, University of Maryland.

NEW CONCEPTS TO GUIDE THE FUTURE

With interactive, democratic process planning well demonstrated and documented in an action research mode, several conceptual tools have been evolving that can be applied to make public planning even more effective. These include the following: strategic planning, scenarios, dialogues, future searches, and learning organizations. These can be further explored from the brief references below.

- *Strategic Planning* is the core methodology of process planning. By its name it focuses efforts on the key (strategic) issues, looks internally and externally at current and future influences, and then identifies "How, what, when, where, and who" for action. Visioning drives strategic planning but is often used as an end without exploring external threats and opportunities or internal strengths and weakness that frame strategic action plans. John Bryson's work[66] on strategic planning is a clear guide for the public and civic sectors.

- *Scenarios* are an approach to strategic thinking by considering different possible futures formed by pulling information from all sources to form stories about possible futures in order to plan for their potential consequences. Peter Schwartz provides the most accessible description of scenario planning in *The Art of the Long View*.[67]

- *Dialogue* is a methodology that has been developed by a group of practitioners as disparate as family therapists and pollsters. Dialogue, according to Daniel Yankelovich,[68] takes on a counseling role between the engaged parties. Dialogue facilitates not only information exchange, but also mutual learning and understanding between participants. Dialogue breaks with the normal demands of public planning participation and is unbounded by time constraints or agenda content—the principal drivers of usual public participation and often the cause of process failure. The purpose of dialogue is to first foster understanding between participants and then to cultivate trust leading to understanding. Dialogue assumes that these are the prerequisites to successful problems solving.

- *Future Search* is a crossover approach to large-scale civic visioning championed by management consultant Marvin Weisbord.[69] The Future Search Network describes the process as "an interactive planning process used world-wide in diverse cultures to achieve shared goals and fast action. Future search leads to cooperative planning that lasts for years." Weisbord and his network of colleagues are marshaling the best practices that have reinvented business organizations and applying them to civic initiatives. Future search is an example of why the recent laboratories for democratic practices have not been with legally bound public activities like public hearings.

- *Learning Organizations* is another breakthrough management concept that has been most effectively articulated by Peter Senge in *The Fifth Discipline*. Learning organizations are the result of engaged, interactive participatory systems in which all members are valued and expected to bring ideas, information, and motivation into the success of their shared mission. This is the complete reversal of outdated scientific management theory where

Tool Tips 5

Tool	Function	Application	Example
Interactive real-time GIS	Generating information	Participatory scenario building	Paint the Town (Index), http://www.crit.com/about/PLACE3S Community Viz, http://www.communityviz.com/

a worker was divorced from thinking and contributing other than scripted routines. Customer service is an underlying value and has been applied to government by writers such as John Osborne and Ted Gaebler in *Reinventing Government*.[70]

TOOLS FOR USE WHERE?

Public participation practices run the gamut in today's civic arena from legally bound and regulation-dictated public hearings with no anticipated change in the presented information to open shared responsibilities between formal authorities and citizens in collaborative planning workshops. The wide range of possibilities in this governance continuum is at the heart of the debate about the American system that polarizes the Federalists against the Jeffersonian in an academic debate about representative government or participatory democracy.[71] This polar debate is academic in that over two hundred years of evidence in the evolution of the American system is that we have both. We do have a constitutional representative republic, but we also have a participatory civic value system that has now been institutionalized in federal, state, and local government laws establishing a range of mechanisms from open meeting laws, freedom of information acts, public hearing regulations, and public participation requirements.

Today's complex multitiered public planning must design its public participation structure to balance the required government's legally bound requirements with citizens' expected level of public involvement. Without the right mechanisms and tools in place, the participation may become inconsequential, and without the expected openness to public participation citizen opposition can be expected. Such a citizen reaction will often find its outlet at the polls if not satisfied by the planning process itself.

Increasingly in today's "Information Age" economy and culture, highly educated workers are learning participatory practices in their workplaces and expecting them to be practiced by their representative democratic governments. The contract, evolved through history, has categorically established every citizen with this inalienable right.

There are few citizen and voter frustrations that don't find expression in the gap

Tool Tips 6			
Tool	*Function*	*Application*	*Example*
Web Conferencing	Exchanging Information (Any Time)	Participation across time and distance	Web Council, www.webcoun cil.com

that exists between expectation for inclusive civic involvement and exclusive government practices. Unfortunately, even many of the mechanisms in place under the banner of public participation are, in truth, ways to control the public and not encourage and empower authentic participation.

Public Participation Typology

Public Participation might be generally categorized into one of two general methodologies: managed and collaborative. The well-established methodology for managed group work is *Robert's Rules of Order*. This is a nearly universal form of group work used by committees, councils, and other organized groups.

The field of Organization Development (OD) is an eclectic field of endeavor dealing with effectiveness, productivity, performance, and worker satisfaction, which draws from fields such as psychology, education, and management. The OD field is pioneering group process methodologies, and there are well-established principles of group dynamics that are known but not yet integrated into the public arena of democratic governance. These are a set of participatory practices yet to be universally legitimized in the public administration arena to support a recognized standard as an option for doing public business in a more creative, interactive, and collaborative way than allowed under *Robert's Rules*.

The following definitions are taken from common usage in the field and provide an overview of the assumptions and expectation to each tool. The use of tools should be driven by the activity planned for their use. The job of the planning process manager is to design a process that sequences and coordinates activity goals with a series of interactions, using the most effective tools to achieve the desired results with an understanding of how people take in information, process it, and apply it to creative or decision making activities.

Robert's Rules Managed Formats

- *Meeting*: An established convening of an identified group to conduct specific work in a set time frame. While meetings have traditionally been conducted under *Robert's Rules*, there are increasing trends to use more interactive formats in normal meetings.
- *Public Hearing*: A mechanism that is required to allow for conducting public business in public view and voice. While public hearings are often identified as the structure for public participation, many studies have identified the public hearing format as a negative methodology of meeting citizen expectation for a real role in governance when it is the sole venue for pub-

311

Tool Tips 7			
Tool	*Function*	*Application*	*Example*
Electronic Flip Chart	Build Information	Group Brainstorming and ranking	Council (Mac), http://www.covision.com/ Ventana (PC), http://www.groupsystems.com/

lic participation.[72] When coupled with interactive participation opportunities, public hearings are a useful, formal final review before taking decision votes.

FACILITATED COLLABORATIVE RULES

- *Town Meeting*: An open public congregation with both officials and citizens in which there is an equal opportunity for all to participate in a democratic manner.
- *Forum*: A more structured process than a town meeting in which there is an expectation for a more structured agenda in relation to purpose. An additional characteristic of a forum is to embody a level of importance in the conduct of public business.
- *Workshop*: A more informal activity than either a town meeting or forum. Training, other learning, and skill-building activities are appropriate at workshops. A workshop implies a real opportunity for exchange without the encumbrance of official action.
- *Vision and Strategic Planning*: Coming from first the military and then business management world of fast response, vision and strategic planning has supplemented analytic, long-range planning as a mechanism for organizational planning. While long-range planning continues as an important activity for research and financial management, *Vision and Strategic Planning* has emerged as a core leadership activity. In the public sector, vision and strategic planning is most often a public participation process.
- *Charrette*: A specific workshop type (still with somewhat limited recognition in the civic arena) that includes design professionals engaged in various ways in a creative informal exploration of the physical implications of a public issue in a short, set time frame. Drawings, pictures, and other visualizations are an expected result from this activity. Charrettes are a form of design-driven strategic planning. In addition, Charrettes most often include a learning workshop aspect with students and/or "citizen interns" participating with professional designers. A principle of the charrette is that the expert does not own the pencil and any participant can put lines on paper. Below are several methodologies for organizing the charrette process.

CHARRETTE

Charrette, or "Little Cart" in French, has its architectural heritage in nineteenth-century Paris at the École Des Beaux Arts, where carts were wheeled through the design studios to collect the students' architectural projects due at midnight. Students would jump on the carts furiously adding their-last minute touches to their drawings. Charrettes have come down to through the century to mean intense, hectic, deadline-driven design activities.

In the last 25 years the term has developed with a more specific definition. Three venues were developing the charrette into a new design process in the 1960s. The American Institute of Architects Urban Design Committee, led by David Lewis, began to develop its Regional Urban Design Assistance Teams (RUDAT) to provide opportunities for designers to conduct intense, pro-bono design workshops addressing the range of urban issues the emerging.

A charette gives participants tools and opportunities to create a model of an alternative design and development strategy in an intense workshop session.

During this same period, Morton Hoppenfeld, urban designer with the Rouse Company, made a personal commitment to bring design assistance into-inner city Baltimore and combined two concepts: the charrette and participatory design. Hoppenfeld believed in demystifying design and invited the community participants to pick up pencil and pen and draw their ideas along with the architects.

The third formative force was the emerging interest in community action (Civic Rights, Model Cities, and the Great Society), providing the climate for many cities to establish pro-bono, cause-driven community design centers. In the intervening years, the charrette has come to have several defining characteristics.

- A charrette is a design-focused workshop.
- A charrette is time bounded, ranging from a day to up to a week. Two or three days are the average.
- A charrette addresses public design issues, often with pressing social or environmental concerns.
- A charrette is a design "brainstorm" to generate multiple ideas (scenarios), not technical studies or concrete solutions.
- A charrette often has some pro-bono attributes and participation by accomplished designers visiting from outside the charrette community.
- A charrette often includes student or intern participation.
- A charrette has public involvement and media aspects.

THE TOOLS TEST

While the adage that "you need the right tools to do a job" is well established, the converse is equally true that "you need the right job for the tool." This chapter has explored the origins, values, and methodologies for regional-scale, interactive planning on an action research model. Any use of the new technology-based tools should be carefully considered as compatible enhancements and supports to the overall intentions of the planning process they are to assist. Using GIS when a paper map will do, for instance, or keypad polling when dot ranking on a flip chart is more immediate, can be counterproductive. The following are considerations in selecting and employing the tools. More thorough explorations of evaluative criteria can be found at the Web sites of AmericaSpeaks and PlaceMatters.

- *Is it in scale with the purpose?* Use tools that will seem appropriate to and comfortable for the participants. (Don't show off.)
- *Does the tool support the values of face-to-face deliberation?* Direct, personal participation is at the core of successful planning. Tools should be selected that simulate or otherwise enhance the vales of face-to-face deliberations. (Don't use tools to keep people at arm's length.)
- *Is the tool neutral but balanced and accurate in information delivery?* Neutral facilitation is a core value in participatory planning, but participants, especially in regional activities, need clear, accurate, and balanced information in many forms. Most tools are neutral on information delivery, but the research and programming of the data and information is a challenge to the sponsors. (Don't use tools to sell your position or if you do, give fair warning that what follows is delivering a positional message.)
- *Will the tool capture and record the process?* As with current controversies about electronic voting machines, make sure you have tools that will capture and record the process. (If you don't have a decision trail and can't recall the decisions, the results are lost in the digital ether.)
- *Does the tool extend the process beyond the place event?* When focusing on face-to-face engagement, consider other interested and vested stakeholders and publics. Consider tools to reach beyond the confines of the event itself and leverage the value of extended outreach. (Don't assume that others not in attendance will accept the surrogate participants as representative if there was no other communication.)
- *Will the tool maximize the inclusion of diverse voices?* At the heart of the facilitated process is the commitment to hear and include all voices. By its nature, a skilled facilitator will ensure that a few voices and positions do not dominate. Use tools to actuate this value.
- *Does the tool provide interactive feedback and complete the communication cycle?* Plan every activity with the tools for a full communication cycle: message formulation, message delivery, response, and conclusion. (Don't design a slick PowerPoint presentation with no mechanism in place for people to respond and affect the results.)
- *Is the tool transparent in its functioning?* The earlier computer modeling tools ingested loads of data and delivered results that often were taken on faith that the program was doing the right thing. (Don't hide in black boxes.)
- *Is the tool cost beneficial?* Tools DO have costs—and many not insignificant. Evaluate the costs of doing without verses the direct and indirect benefits of bringing in new technology, which can have its own excitement level. (Evaluate the cost of doing without as well as doing with.)

Tool Tips 8

Tool	Function	Application	Example
Electronic Town Meetings	Delivering Information	Reaching general public	Electronic Town Meetings, https://fp.auburn.edu/tann/tann2/index.htm http://www.planning.org/bookservice/description.htm? BCODE=AGCV

- *Will using the tool become "ho-hum"?* New tools can bring high-user engagement to new participants. Conversely, users can become bored or impatient with the tools when they become routine and standard in the way of public engagement. (Use tools for a purpose and not an end.)
- *Is support capacity available?* In virtually all planning interactions as described here, the engagement sponsors will need to facilitate the interactive process, will want to deliver planning information, and will need to manage the tools technology. These are three distinct full-attention roles that require at least three activity managers at any planning event in addition to the technical planning team. The number will increase from there, depending on the nature of the planning work, the size of the group, and the political significance for the process. While it should go without saying, experience shows that any use of these technologies takes experienced competencies of staff, consultants, or trained volunteers. (Test the technology *and* the people before opening the doors.)

Rules of Engagement

Engaging the public, processing complex information, and maintaining an agenda and schedule are the usual drivers of the public planning process, but there are also sets of expectations people bring into an activity. Somehow, these expectations are usually played out in scale with expectations, outcomes, and levels of the involvement. (The larger the results, the greater the expectations brought to the table.)

For the process manager, any group can be expected to go through a learning cycle[73] that has been characterized as:

- *Forming*: Begin every engagement with introduction time and never give short shift to being clear on purpose, schedule, roles, and ground rules of the interaction. If managing a series, repeat the forming activity every time. People have a strong need for clarity, especially when on strange turf. Forming is the first step in collaborative work and team building.

Tool Tips 9

Tool	Function	Application	Example
Interactive Town Meeting Web Site	Maintaining Involvement	Providing information with query menus and response surveys	Full Circle, http://www .NIPC.org

- *Storming*: If forming is a time for the group, whether a few or hundreds, then storming time is needed to bring in the human nature for establishing identity and individuality. Everyone wants to be known and recognized, some more than others. Storming stakes out the "Me" among the "We." Roles, such as leaders, creatives, skeptics, supporters, and quiet observers, will emerge.
- *Norming*: After forming and storming people will *almost* be ready to go to work . . . but not quite. Norming is establishing the verbal and nonverbal expectations, agreements, and practices of how the group will function. Here the ground rules are accepted or changed and put into practice. The group has hit its norm when, for instance, a member will speak out to a late arrival that "*We* expect everyone to be on time!"
- *Performing*: Finally, work begins. Allowing and facilitating the right balance of forming, storming, and norming will ultimately contribute to successful work collaboration.

A facilitator will understand the need for this cycle to play out, and attempts to short-circuit the process to "get on with the agenda" will usually result in a negative group response that will consume even more time. On the other hand, not sensing when a phase has played out and letting individuals keep the group unproductively in a phase can also lose the group's support in what is seen as a waste of time. Understanding and managing these "off-agenda" but necessary activities is the domain of a skilled facilitator.

A CHANGING CATALOGUE OF TOOLS

We live in a time of continuously changing technology. New tools emerge daily and familiar ones become obsolete. Place Matters (http://www.placematters.us/) is an information center and peer network of tools developers and users tracking the changing technology of tools. For a network of tool-savvy process designers, managers, and users visit the AmericaSpeaks site, www.americaspeaks.org/.

Many of the emerging tools for planning, especially large-scale planning, are, in one form or the other, communication tools—collecting, interpreting, depicting, relating, exchanging, and disseminating information as well as analyzing information. The following defines the basic tool groups available to planners:

- *The Flip Chart*: Low-tech, high-touch paper pad on easel is a basic recoding tool essential for group work with or without computer support. The paper flip chart remains in front of the group for referral and updating as work progresses. So, keep your magic markers handy. They are not obsolete yet. David Sibbett of Grove Consulting[74] has taken the recorder's role to a graphic art form.

- *Key pad polling*: Developed for market research work, the hand-held keypad has become available as wireless systems and within the range of public planning programs. Keypads are best used to measure levels of opinions and preferences around choices in order to further discuss and refine the choices. As an interactive planning tool, keypads should not generally be used for final Yes/No votes. Input and feedback is immediate, anonymous, and digitally captured.

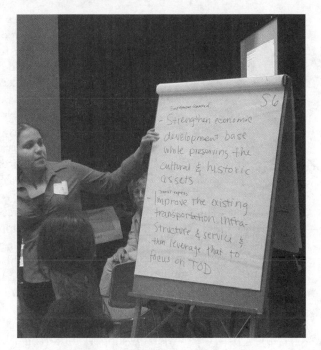

Capturing the issues and insights on newsprint or other media frees participants to engage in the discussion while providing a real-time visible record of their work.

- *GIS*: Graphical information systems have evolved to finally bridge the gap that has long separated data research experts from public planning activists and ordinary people—including most public officials, who have long been baffled by conventional planner-speak. With GIS outputs, complex information is visual and understandable to all and relationships even previously indecipherable to the expert can be explored. GIS is making complex data understandable to all and is helping to close the long-standing trust gap between the experts and the community.

- *Real-time, interactive GIS (INDEX and PLACE3S)*: A new, essential core set of tools especially useful to smart growth planning are on-line and at work. These tools allow small group work to input physical planning ideas into a GIS system that, on its face, is a computer paint box replacing Magic Marker drawings on paper maps. They only begin with input capture in that they can first relate the input to any number of graphical data layers and also evaluate the input in terms of built-in indicators. A recent innovation for these tools is to run from a Web site instead of individual computers so that all input is assembled at a central source for comparison and integration. The Web source can then make the results available to anyone with Web access. Applications of these tools in regional planning include the Sacramento Area Council of Governments' (SACOG) Blueprint and the Northeastern Illinois Planning Commission's (NIPC) Common Ground.

Using keypads connected to a computer, which analyzes responses to questions or proposals, gives ranked instant feedback to participants to guide collaborative work as opposed to "Yes/No" voting.

- *GIS modeling*: Computer modeling is another evolving tool set applicable to antisprawl activities. The hope for these models 20 years ago was that they would provide predictive results to complex planning problems; however, it seems that the expectations have been lowered to a more realistic level. These models are still mostly backroom input/output operations that are bought into a presentation and reporting mode in planning projects. A number to the promising modeling tools include Urban Sim at the University of Washington and LEAM (Land use Evolution and impact Assessment Model) at the University of Illinois. Such models are now being developed more in the mode of "What if" scenario builders to consider strategic planning choices and not black-box deliveries of "The Answer." These tools are most effective when planned into the overall program process and require significant time, skill, and funding.

- *A word about Land-Use GIS Modeling*: These are definitely exciting new tools to support long-range, large systems planning. They analyze large amounts of data against land-use determinants such as market dynamics, commute patterns, environmental factors, and other selected variables and depict the outcomes in GIS maps. These programs are in developmental phases, they require huge amounts of data input (at great costs), and they also must be put in place by a few knowledgeable experts. They are being applied in beta testing by a number of regional planning agencies. While very promising, their future and general availability is uncertain.

- *Visualization tools*: These are fast growing, still developing, and relatively costly in both time and technology. They are generally of three types:

1. *Image making software* such as Illustrator, Photoshop, and Flash for picture and video simulation.
2. *Remote sensing* such as those found at http://elwood.la.asu.edu/grsl/UEM/ and link http://ces.asu.edu/csrur/.
3. *Presentation enhancements* are programs such as Keyhole, for instance, which gives dimensionality to maps and animates presentations with fly-overs from one area to another.

These tools can both aid in seeing and understanding planning and design proposals and add the "Wow!" factor to gain attention, interest, and participation.

Conferencing

Tools are entering the market daily that assist in information exchange between participants in a program, project, or process as a one-time event or ongoing activities.

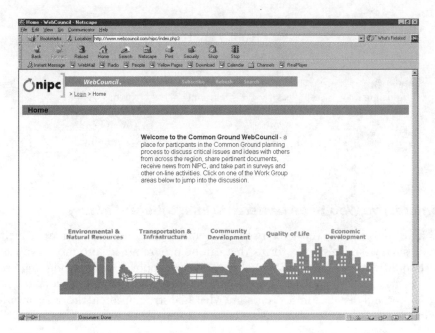

New electronic tools allow people to participate in scenario planning even when they are not present and continue working between face-to-face sessions.

Meeting Support Groupware (Same Time, Same Place)

These computer-based systems are used in face-to-face meetings where each participant or small group can generate and input ideas (brainstorm) or rank responses over the course of the meeting. Two systems tested in the public planning arena are Council (Mac based) and Ventana (PC based). These systems come with staffing and technical demands but are very effective when working with very large groups or highly charged, conflict-laden issues. Groupware Web information can be found at: http://www.usabilityfirst.com/index.txl. AmericaSpeaks is a national source, founded by Carolyn Lukensmeyer, for information, advice, and support of large scale, tools-supported participation as demonstrated in the Listening to the City forum in post–9/11 New York. Information can be found at http://www .americaspeaks.org.

Web Conferencing (Same Time, Different Place)

A larger number of programs are on the market to assist in remote conferencing either by telephone, interactive Web site, video, or a combination. The most useful for work groups and other conferencing activities allow for several capabilities: support for presentation information such as a PowerPoint or video, ongoing on-screen recorder note taking, polling, and ranking capability. Such programs of the many on the market include Assemble Conferencing, eCollaborate, iLinc, Mshow, NetTogether Presenter, Present Online; an information source is at http://www .thinkofit.com/webconf/.

Tool Tips 10

Tool	Function	Application	Example
Land use modeling	"What if" Analysis	Generating regional plans	Urban Sim, http://www.urbansim.org/ LEAM, http://www.leam.uiuc.edu/

Interactive Web Sites (Different Time, Different Place)

These tools make Web sites two-way communication tools. Features include simple surveys and response forms that can be programmed into most Web sites. More sophisticated supplier provided systems can support extensive ongoing group work such as CoVision's *WebCouncil* where remote participants can work together across time and distance in forums somewhat like structured chat rooms; an information source is http://www.covision.com/services/online.htm.

Internet Town Meetings

Internet Town Meetings draw participants, usually with a recognized name moderator and "hot topic" issue. Examples of these can be found in real-time and anytime formats. Simple chat room and response form Web site design tools can structure the use for the Web for these interactive conferencing that again are aimed at niche audiences for open participation or reconvening of subscribed participants. Organizations like Web Lab (http://www.weblab.org/home.html), Publicus (http://www.publicus.net/), and Information Renaissance (http://www.info-ren.org/) can assist in creating Web forums. e.democracy, e.government, and others support ongoing, on-line communities. Their Web sites are good resources for public interest planners.

Electronic Town Meetings (ETMs)

As defined here; Electronic Town Meetings have been used for 20 years, applying television as a support to the planning process. ETMs are best used as a special event within a planning program. Proponents warn of long, real-time, C-Span type coverage of public events and advocate using magazine, public affairs, and call-in formats to use television as a compelling and effective communication tool in concert with other available technology. Media partners supporting the principles of civic journalism can be most constructive in forging planning/media partnerships.[75]

Make These Core Planning Values

Planning a planning process is another skill with little documentation but is the underpinning of the successful practitioner. Tools exist to support the planning process and should be selected with a full understanding of the contribution they will make and the limitations they bring. The following are some basic process-planning principles to guide tool selection.

- *Begin at the beginning*: Plan and begin outreach and engagement as early as professionally and politically possible and then back up a couple of steps and actually begin there. One of the hardest trust factors for the professional planner it seems, is to go public before all the answers are known. Managers and politicians should open the door at the beginning with questions like, "What is the problem?" Or, "Should we do this?" Or, "What would you like to see if . . . ?"

- *Be inclusive*: Limits are often arbitrarily imposed in planning participation around perceived limitations of time, resources, or even room sizes. The first evaluators should be questions like, "Who needs to be involved?" and "Who wants to be involved?" Then ask the resource and logistic question of "how." If there are identified resource gaps, be realistic that the lack of commitment and/or resources to meet the external expectations is the first indicator of potential failure. Another rule of thumb is to ask the questions about who might be against the plan or who could stand in the way of implementation and then make sure they are on the recruitment list.

- *Be clear*: The next most frequent cause of failed planning processes is the lack of clarity on the part of the sponsor. Often experts and politicians alike must always project certainty. Being honest trumps posturing every day. People generally also respond well to clarity in what they are asked to do and *not do*. Overpromising paints a metaphorical target on the process. Too often the public will be told that "We are going to do what you want," when everyone knows that city council will have to make the ultimate decision and evaluation will need to ensure feasibility. Clearly communicate these intentions up front. "We need your thoughts and ideas to help us make the best plan to take to city council in six months. We will be using the information from the next three monthly workshops to help us measure financial cost related to community preferences." (Note the inclusion of time and schedule.) Ask for agreement and formalize the agreement to the extent necessary. Consensus head nodes are often fine, but in conflict-laden areas a signed agreement may help gain clarity and then buy-in.

FACILITATION REMINDERS

Ensure that any public planning process has a skilled facilitator who serves as the champion of the participants. The facilitator should have no precommitment or vested interest in predetermined outcomes, which is one reason that the expert planner may not be the best person to facilitate a public process. The role of the facilitator as described in *How to Make Meetings Work* and *The Skilled Facilitator* clearly define these values. A few reminders should become constant watchdogs throughout any program or project.

- *Be fair*: There are always several potentially competing demands for fairness that challenge any project manager and even the most skilled facilitator.

These might include being fair to each individual participant while also being fair to the group as a whole. The expectations and demands of both individuals and the group must also be balanced with the integrity of the process as defined at the beginning and guided by the agreed-on ground rules.

- *Use it*: Don't invite participation and interaction without a clearly defined plan for how public input will be used. If you are not or cannot use new ideas or different opinions, don't ask.
- *Take steps forward*: Continuously cycle back at every step to show how the participation is contributing to the progress of the program.

Public engagement at the regional scale brings several challenges of a different scale from programs working at the more local, neighborhood scale. The biggest challenge is that regions by their very nature are large areas, and the best time for most public meetings brings people together during the weekly rush hour. Asking people to come together at some central point puts a time and travel burden on participants that can be a real disincentive. Regional initiatives also cross jurisdictional and territorial borders, which bring additional challenges to instill a sense of ownership and relevance for many participants. Often people will be considering issues for some areas they have never visited. Little work has been done on the peculiar and unique characteristics of participatory regional planning dealing with sprawl. The Common Ground Regional Plan of the Northeastern Illinois Planning Commission has been learning from its three-year process that included some

Use all available means to keep communications open and accessible, as in this newspaper insert form for Imagine Houston.

272 municipalities, covering 3,400 square miles with a population of over 8 million people. Some of these lessons include:

- *Make it easy*: Metropolitan regions are challenging to move around in. Centralized gatherings in one place are more challenging for participants. The greater the distance a regional program covers, plan on holding multiple meetings around the region at every step. Common Ground has zoned the greater Chicago region into outreach districts with groupings of 7, 14, and 38 clusters for differing intensities of engagement.
- *Take bigger steps*: Unlike neighborhood planning, regional planning participants may expect the program staff to do more analysis, modeling, or other professional work between meeting sessions, whereas the norm in neighborhood planning is that participation will be in the room at every step. This can mean fewer gatherings than in more localized planning programs. In short, those planning regional scale participatory planning programs can expect to hold fewer meetings with more work accomplished between gatherings.
- *Use best available technology*: With complex information, diverse participants, and large numbers participating over extended periods of time, the new technology tools are becoming an essential to antisprawl-oriented regional planning and should be budgeted from the beginning of the program.
- *Keep the lines open*: These types of regional programs are often very concerned with representation, diversity, continuity from one gathering to the next, and decision-making responsibilities. Program managers should expect that all events are open public meetings, allow for late arrivals to be included in the process, and design open and responsive communication channels, including interactive Web sites, local print, and electronic media.

A ROLE, NOT A LABEL; A PROCESS, NOT AN ACTIVITY

The emergence of new tools and technology promises to take planning to regional scale with open engagement, delivery of timely, understandable information, and tools that help evaluate the choices for informed decision making.

These principles define a planning process where tools support a different kind of planning process and with professionals who see their role as facilitators ensuring open engagement and informed judgments. These professional facilitators use surveys as background checks to the face-to-face dialogues and eschew nonengaged public actives such as the walk-around Open House popular with many large-scale projects with public participation requirements. In addition to the established roles for planners as research analysts, creative problem solvers, policy advisors, land-use experts, and other technical capabilities, several other roles should be considered for regional planning teams with professional skills including:

- *Facilitator*: The skilled manager of a group's work ensures participation, fairness, effectiveness, and relevance of collaborations and interactions.
- *Conflict mediator*: Facilitation with training in managing interactions containing conflict between participants.

- *Cultural anthropologist*: Skills to assess and understand social and cultural values are at the core of international community development, but seldom used within the United States. Differences around issues such as land tenure, market practices, cultural values, and micropolitics can vary greatly in major metropolitan regions, and understanding these can be supported by anthropological skills.
- *Historian*: Similar to the anthropologists, the historian can help surface long-established values, practices, and norms that are at the core of land-use, development, or conservation activities within ever smaller geographic units down to neighborhoods and villages.
- *Illustrator*: From cartographer to cartoonist, regional planning calls for a full complement of visualization skills at every step to visualize everything, including photography.
- *Events manager*: Success will be in the details. A regional program will take at least one year and can be continuous over multiple years. With literally hundreds of events to plan, arrange, and manage, someone, preferably with professional skills, may be working constantly on events such as board meetings, workshops, media events, presentations, and major forums.
- *Media specialist*: Like the events manager, a regional program will have and should use many channels of targeted and public communication. Crafting and producing these communication vehicles for Web, print, broadcast media, and special events will be a constant and professional need.

Common Ground: A Case Example

The Northeastern Illinois Planning Commission (NIPC) is the regional planning agency covering the six-county region around Chicago. The region includes six counties, the city of Chicago, and 272 other municipal governments, with a population of over 8 million people. Increasing growth pressures with accompanying congestion and loss of open space had created the mounting public concerns about sprawl. Along with these concerns came the political will to launch a new regional planning process. Common Ground was the brand name of the regional planning process launched in 2001.

Begin at the Beginning

Common Ground began by holding a series of listening sessions at 14 locations around the region to ask what should be addressed by the new regional plan. To begin, staff and volunteers were trained as neutral facilitators. A regional portrait was presented in PowerPoint. Keypad polling was introduced to rank issues and choices and futures scenarios were used to stimulate dialogue on possible futures.

Large Convening to Open the Process

The next stage took a summarized issue report to an open Town Hall–type forum. Extensive work was done to invite and deliver representative participants from minority, immigrant, and special-interest communities (including youth). Nearly 1,000 participated in an AmericaSpeaks-designed large group process, with

Carolyn Lukensmeyer acting as room facilitator. Each round table of eight participants included a trained neutral facilitator, keypad polling tools for each participant, and CoVision Council groupware computers on each table. During the forum day, running from 9:00 on a Saturday morning until 3:00 in the afternoon, each dialogue cycle included first a PowerPoint presentation of an ideas or issues set followed by individual priority polling with instant feedback. A 45-minute facilitated table discussion followed to conclude the cycle, with table consensus entered into the Council computer to be summarized by the Theme Team for feedback to the room.

By the end of the day, a set of prioritized regional issues had been formed for the whole region and individuals were recruited for strategic planning teams for five topical work groups.

With careful planning, supporting tools, and an experienced room facilitator, very large groups can have productive participations.

Coming to Public Judgment

For the next seven months, these five work groups met monthly with a planner and facilitator supporting each group. Using conventional flip charts and ranking methods, these work groups crafted strategic planning goals for the five topical areas (transportation, economic development, housing, environment, and quality of life). To facilitate participation, these monthly meetings were held at four different locations. Groups could share work progress across geography, issues, areas, and time using a WebCouncil-supported Web conferencing program.

To move from issues to goals, a series of rank SWOT (strengths, weaknesses, opportunities, and threats) analysis were conducted with the groups where issues were framed as possible futures that were in turn categorized into one of four quadrants that included:

- Desirable and likely
- Desirable and unlikely
- Undesirable and likely
- Undesirable and unlikely

The issues entered into one of these categories were then ranked by participants by importance for planning actions. For example, "Unlikely and Desirable" may need stimulations and "Likely and Undesirable" may need action to counter. Scatter diagrams produced a frequency analysis diagram of the results. A similar interactive survey was put on the Common Ground public Web site for public input.

A final session convened all participants regionwide to consolidate goals into a single set for each topic and together craft a vision statement.

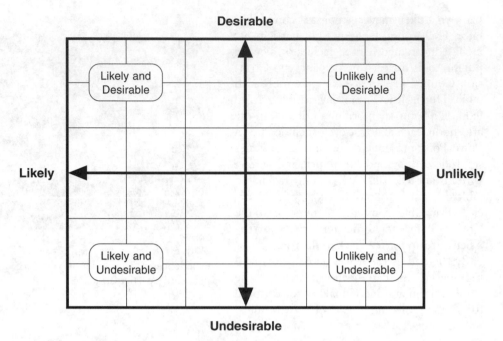

Creating a typology to analyze various weighted outcomes allows participants to assign alternative strategies into categories that facilitate better choices tied to critical actions and resource allocations.

Putting Goals on the Ground

NIPC developed an interactive GIS tool it branded as Paint the Town, which the agency used to finalize population forecasts with each jurisdiction in the region. This tool supports real-time land use "sketching" (ideally with touch-pad screens) into a GIS systems with based data layers with built-in evaluative indicators. The system was built on the INDEX platform with Criterion Associates.

For Common Ground regional planning application, Paint the Town was developed into a regional paint box to identify a palate of different kinds of regional centers, transportation corridors, and environmental areas. Another innovation was to run Paint the Town from NIPC's server, where all input was collected for reporting and consolidation into a synthesized result at 14 Paint the Region workshops to identify Centers and Corridors around the region.

Participants worked at facilitated round-table discussions. Each table also included a Paint the Region GIS facilitator who entered the group's ideas onto Paint the Town's Web servers, and each table also had a LCD projector and screen so the table could follow all computer entries. Ideas were recorded at each table's flip chart.

Constructing the Framework

From nearly 100 worktables of Paint the Town input, the computer could record hundreds of ideas, but the synthesis required old-fashioned brainwork first

Ideas are generated and presented for keypad polling and instant feedback on polled results.

by the staff to put together a less cluttered mapping of centers and corridors. Then professional and agency planner work groups were convened from each area in the region to help synthesize the input into a coherent centers and corridors scenario.

Adding the Flesh

The synthesized framework was then filtered through several scenario screens. First, stakeholder, leadership, and professional groups reviewed and commented on the framework. Other topical scenarios were used to evaluate potential development strategies. The scenarios included the following:

- Green Infrastructure vision created by NIPC with Chicago Wilderness— an environmental coalition;
- A Macro regional Economic Framework development for the state by Michael Gallis;
- A Housing Accessibility Plan developed by an advocacy organization, Chicago Metropolis 2020;
- The adopted Regional 2030 Transportation Plan; and
- NIPC 2030 population and jobs forecasts.

The scenarios were used to establish benchmarks and choices of each center. Further, sustainable development urban design concepts were attached to each center type. Together, the scenarios and development guidelines presented a set of choices for each center that provided guidelines for local planning actions to achieve the vision and goals of Common Ground. A supporting planning guide was produced as a detailed implementation plan. The Web site with an interactive response survey was used throughout the process along with a concise summary action report.

Reengaging for Implementation

The final phase of Common Ground before entering into implementation was to conduct a final input and public information activity coupling a Town Hall forum with an Electronic Town Meeting. The Common Ground plan was presented in three optimized scenarios around economic futures, community livability futures, and environmental futures. Transportation models were run to depict the implications of choices on future transportation systems, and the University of Illinois ran these scenarios through its "What if" LEAM land-use model. These scenario choices were animated in flyover visualization using Keyhole software.

In addition to the forum convening, partner organizations throughout the region held simultaneous local Town Hall meetings with volunteer facilitators to deliberate on the preferences and priorities of the various scenarios for the proposed centers and corridors. Input from the forum and local town halls fed into a live, real-time Web conference open to public participation.

With the intensive input from the Town Hall day, the final plan was published on NIPC Web site, in a CD version, and in conventional publications, including a tabloid newspaper insert.

Common Ground now provides a land-use framework for other regional planning programs such as the regional transportation plan. Together the regional land-use and transportation plans and the related scenarios provide a context and priorities for local land-use plans.

NOTES

1. Joel Barker, *Discovering the Future: The Business of Paradigms* (St. Paul, MN: ILI Press, 1985).

2. Jacob Riis, *How the Other Half Lives: Studies Among the Tenements of New York* (New York: Penguin Books, 1997 [1890]).

3. Jane Addams, *Twenty Years at Hull-House: With Autobiographical Notes* (New York: Macmillan, 1910).

4. Herbert J. Gans, *The Levittowners: Ways of Life and Politics in a New Suburban Community* (New York: Columbia University Press, 1982).

5. Michael Harrington, *The Other America: Poverty in the United States* (Baltimore: Penguin Books, 1962).

6. Rachel Carson, *Silent Spring* (Boston: Houghton Mifflin, 1962).

7. Jane Jacobs, *The Death and Life of Great American Cities* (New York: Random House, 1961).

8. Saul Alinsky, *Rules for Radicals: A Practical Primer for Realistic Radicals* (New York: Random House, 1971).

9. Paul Davidoff and Thomas Reiner, "A Choice Theory of Planning," *AIP Journal* (1962).

10. Association for Community Design, http://www.communitydesign.org/.

11. National Trust for Historic Preservation, http://www.nationaltrust.org/help/save_historic_buildings.html; Preservation Action, http://www.preservationaction.org.

12. Marvin Weisbord, *Productive Workplaces: Organizing and Managing for Dignity, Meaning, and Community* (San Francisco: Jossey-Bass, 1987).

13. "Mantua," *Design Quarterly* (1969).

14. Morton Hoppenfeld, "A Sketch of the Planning-Building Process for Columbia, Maryland," *Journal of the American Institute of Planners* 33 (1967).

15. National Charrette Institute, http://www.charretteinstitute.org/.

16. The American Cities Corporation, *Hartford Process* (n.p., 1970).

17. Lawrence Halprin and Jim Burns, *Taking Part: A Workshop Approach to Collective Creativity* (Cambridge, MA: MIT Press, 1974).

18. David G. Lazear, *Seven Ways of Knowing: Teaching for Multiple Intelligences* (Palatine, IL: Skylight Publishing, 1991).

19. John P. Kretzmann and John L. McKnight, *Building Communities from the Inside Out: A Path Toward Finding and Mobilizing a Community's Assets* (Chicago: ACTA Publications, 1997).

20. David L. Cooperrider, Peter F. Sorensen Jr., Diana Whitney, and Therese F. Yaeger, eds., *Appreciative Inquiry: Rethinking Human Organization Toward a Positive Theory of Change* (Champaign, IL: Stipes Publishing, 1999).

21. Ian McHarg, *Design with Nature* (New York: John Wiley & Sons, 1992).

22. Ray Gindroz et al., *The Architectural Pattern Book: A Tool for Building Great Neighborhoods* (New York: W. W. Norton, 2004) and *The Urban Design Handbook: Techniques and Working Methods* (New York: W. W. Norton, 2003).

23. Ronald Thomas, *Cities by Design: A Guide for Public Officials* (Washington, DC: National League of Cities, 1981).

24. Ibid.

25. Ronald Thomas and Margaret Grieve, *Design for Low Income Neighborhoods* (Washington, DC: National League of Cities, 1979).

26. Action Research Resources, http://www.scu.edu.au/schools/gcm/ar/arhome.html.

27. John F. Forester, *The Deliberative Practitioner: Encouraging Participatory Planning Processes* (Cambridge, MA: MIT Press, 1999).

28. Chris Argyris, Robert Putnam, and Diana McLain Smith, *Action Science* (San Francisco: Jossey-Bass, 1985).

29. Neal R. Peirce, Curtis W. Johnson, and John Stuart Hall, *Citistates: How Urban America Can Prosper in a Competitive World* (Washington, DC: Seven Locks Press, 1993).

30. Joel Garreau, *Edge City: Life on the New Frontier* (New York: Doubleday, 1991).

31. Ada Louise Huxtable, *Will They Ever Finish Bruckner Boulevard?* (Berkeley: University of California Press, 1989).

32. Wolf von Eckardt, *A Place to Live: The Crisis of the Cities* (New York: Delacorte Press, 1974).

33. Kettering Foundation, http://www.kettering.org/.

34. Harvard Mediation Project, http://www.law.harvard.edu/students/orgs/hmp/index.php.

35. Daniel Yankelovich, *Coming to Public Judgment: Making Democracy Work in a Complex World* (Syracuse, NY: Syracuse University Press, 1991).

36. James Howard Kunstler, *The Geography of Nowhere: The Rise and Decline of America's Man-Made Landscape* (New York: Simon & Schuster, 1993).

37. Sierra Club, http://www.sierraclub.org/sprawl/.

38. Herman Kahn, *Thinking about the Unthinkable* (New York: Horizon Press, 1962).

39. H. W. Kuhn and A. W. Tucker, eds., *Contributions to the Theory of Games*, vol. 1 (Princeton, NJ: Princeton University Press, 1950).

40. David P. Barash, *The Survival Game: How Game Theory Explains the Biology of Cooperation and Competition* (New York: Times Books, 2004).

41. Margaret J. Wheatley, *Leadership and the New Science: Discovering Order in a Chaotic World*, rev. ed. (San Francisco: Berrett-Koehler, 2001).

42. Don Koberg and Jim Bagnall, *The Universal Traveler: A Soft-Systems Guide to Creativity, Problem-Solving, and the Process of Reaching Goals* (Los Atlos, CA: Kaufmann, 1974).

43. Christopher W. Alexander, *Notes on the Synthesis of Form* (Cambridge, MA: Harvard University Press, 1964).

44. Lawrence Halprin, *The RSVP Cycles: Creative Processes in the Human Environment* (New York: G. Braziller, 1970).

45. The Orton Family Foundation, *Making Community Connections: The Orton Community Mapping Program* (Steamboat Springs, CO: Author, 2004).

46. Frederick Taylor, *The Principles of Scientific Management* (New York: Harper & Brothers, 1911).

47. Kurt Lewin, *Resolving Social Conflicts: And, Field Theory in Social Science* (Washington, DC: American Psychological Association, 1997).

48. NTL Institue, http://www.ntl.org/about.html.

49. Mary Walton, *The Deming Management Method* (New York: Dodd, Mead, 1986).

50. Peter M. Senge, *The Fifth Discipline: The Art and Practice of the Learning Organization* (New York: Doubleday, 1990).

51. Dick Axelrod and Emily Axelrod, *You Don't Have to Do It Alone: How to Involve Others to Get Things Done* (San Francisco: Berrett-Koehler, 2004).

52. Michael Doyle and David Straus, *How to Make Meetings Work: The New Interaction Method* (New York: Wyden Books, 1976).

53. Susan L. Carpenter and W.J.D. Kennedy, *Managing Public Disputes: A Practical Guide for Professionals in Government, Business and Citizen's Groups*, 2nd ed. (San Francisco: Jossey-Bass, 2001).

54. Lawrence Susskind and Jeffrey Cruikshank, *Breaking the Impasse: Consensual Approaches to Resolving Public Disputes* (New York: Basic Books, 1989).

55. Roger Schwarz, *The Skilled Facilitator: A Comprehensive Resource for Consultants, Facilitators, Managers, Trainers, and Coaches*, 2nd ed. (San Francisco: Jossey-Bass, 2002).

56. Moore Iacofano Goltsman, Inc., http://www.migcom.com/flash.html.

57. Ted Becker, https://fp.auburn.edu/tann/tann2/project4.html.

58. Ronald Thomas, "Designing with Communications," *Journal of Architectural Education* 7(3) (1978) (special issue).

59. Michael Hollinshead and Ronald Thomas, *Electronic Town Meetings: Planning for the Information Age* (Chicago: Planning Commissioners Service, n.d.) (videocassette).

60. East Central Florida Regional Planning Council, http://www.myregion.org/myregion/.

61. Neighborhood America, http://www.neighborhoodamerica.com/.

62. Full Circle, http://www.chicagoareahousing.org/FC/Index.htm; Northeastern Illinois Planning Commission, http://www.nipc.org/.

63. Association for Community Design, http://www.communitydesign.org/.

64. Pratt Institute Center for Community and Environmental Development, http://www.picced.org/.

65. Lynda H. Schneekloth and Robert Shibley, *Placemaking: A Collaborative Approach to Creating Community* (New York: Wiley, 1995).

66. John M. Bryson, *Strategic Planning for Public and Nonprofit Organizations: A Guide to Strengthening and Sustaining Organizational Achievement* (San Francisco: Jossey-Bass, 1995).

67. Peter Schwartz, *The Art of the Long View: Planning for the Future in an Uncertain World* (New York: Doubleday, 1996).

68. Daniel Yankelovitch, *The Magic of Dialogue: Transforming Conflict into Cooperation* (New York: Simon & Schuster, 1999).

69. Marvin R. Weisbord, *Discovering Common Ground: How Future Search Conferences Bring People Together to Achieve Breakthrough Innovation, Empowerment, Shared Vision, and Collaborative Action* (San Francisco: Berrett-Koehler, 1993).

70. David Osborne and Ted Gaebler, *Reinventing Government: How the Entrepreneurial Spirit Is Transforming the Public Sector* (Reading, MA: Addison-Wesley, 1992).

71. Richard K. Mathews, *The Radical Politics of Thomas Jefferson: A Revisionist View* (Lawrence: University Press of Kansas, 1986).

72. Kettering Foundation, *Citizens and Politics: A View from Main Street America* (Dayton, OH: Author, 1991).

73. Bruce W. Tuckman and Mary Ann C. Jensen, "Stages of Small Group Development Revisited," *Group and Organizational Studies* 2 (1977): 419–27.

74. David Sibbett, Grove Consulting, http://www.grove.com/.

75. Jay Rosen, Davis Merritt Jr., and Lisa Austin, *Public Journalism Theory and Practice: Lessons from Experience* (Dayton, OH: Kettering Foundation, 1997).

PART V

CROSS-CUTTING ISSUES

17

Sprawl and Local Government Taxation Regimes: Cause and Effect

Ari Bruening, James Hlawek, and David C. Soule

Like each of us, municipal governments must balance the expenditures and revenue in their budgets. The more revenue a municipality takes in, the better the services it can provide, from education to police protection. Local governments obtain revenue from many sources, including the property tax. The nature of the property tax is such that many municipalities can affect the amount of revenue they receive by structuring the land uses within their jurisdiction in certain ways—ways that lead to sprawl.[1]

There are a number of studies that have emerged in recent years which identify a critical nexus between local government revenue sources, particularly the property tax, and sprawl. The most recent is the report of a Blue Ribbon commission in Connecticut that identifies the property tax as the principle cause of sprawl in that state. A recent analysis (Soule, 2004) suggests that traditional policy prescriptions for managing sprawl focus on traditional land-use controls, ignoring the fundamental interaction between the use of land and the mechanisms that local governments have available to raise revenue for critical local services (K–12 education, public safety, etc.). Other studies have made similar causal suggestions.

The 87,000 local governments in the United States receive revenues from multiple sources, not just the property tax. Some of these sources, particularly state aid, are designed to level the playing field regarding differential tax capacity. However, it is also important to understand that 46 states have passed Tax and Expenditure Limitations (TELs), which restrict the capacity of local governments to raise the revenues they need to provide basic services. The result is that the importance of land-use planning to revenue sources is magnified.

While the constitutionality of the property tax to provide general municipal services has not been challenged, there are a number of court decisions and pending cases which directly challenge the property tax as the basis of providing K–12 education. Since public education is one of the principal factors in residential choice of persons with school-age children, the linkage to land-use policy is not a difficult case to make. Sooner or later, the broad question of land-use policy, taxation, and sprawl management will come together in the policy systems at the state and local level.

In this article, we explore the link between municipal revenue sources and land use, focusing on the property tax and, to a lesser extent, the sales tax. We argue that the property and sales tax are important causes of sprawl and that TELs actually exacerbate the problem. We first briefly describe the sources of revenue available to municipalities. We then examine more closely the effect that two of these revenue sources, the property tax and the sales tax, have on land use in general and specifically on sprawl. In this section, we analyze this effect through using two states, Massachusetts and Utah, as case studies. Finally, we discuss the implications of local sales and property tax for transit-oriented development, the most prominent alternative to sprawl.

LOCAL REVENUE SOURCES

There are dozens of types of local governmental revenue, which can be categorized in many different ways. For this discussion, we have classified the types based on the entity responsible for transferring the revenue to the local government. Most local revenue is received either from other governments or from individuals and businesses. Figures in this section are from the United States Census Bureau.

Revenues Received from Other Governments

In 2000–2001, local governments received approximately 35 percent of their revenue from other governmental entities: the federal government, state governments, and other local governments. Over 90 percent of this intergovernmental revenue comes from state governments, which provide a variety of different types of revenue to local governments. Examples include direct aid for public schools, state highway aid for county or city roads, local governmental shares of lottery proceeds, library assistance, and state property tax replacement credits, which are payments intended to reduce local governmental reliance on the property tax.

The federal government also provides some assistance directly to local governments, although the amount is quite small in comparison to the amount of revenue that the federal government provides to state governments: in 2000–2001, the federal government provided eight times as much revenue to state governments as to local governments.

Finally, local governments can receive revenue from other local governments, such as when one local governmental entity is compensated for assuming responsibility for a service typically provided by another local government. For example, a county government may take over police jurisdiction within a city.

Revenues Received from Individuals and Businesses

Local governments typically receive the majority of their revenue directly from individuals and businesses. The funds received from individuals and businesses consist of two general types of revenue: taxes and fees.

Taxes

A tax is a compulsory assessment against an individual or a business. Taxes usually do not have any direct relationship to the amount of governmental services provided to or consumed by individuals or businesses. Instead, taxes provide governments with a general source of revenue. Since the tax assessment usually does not have a direct relationship to a corresponding governmental expenditure, the taxation power is subject to abuse. Accordingly, the power of taxation is usually limited: As creatures of the state, local governments typically cannot assess a tax unless it is authorized by state legislation, the state constitution, or home-rule authority. Still, local governments have the power to assess several different types of taxes.

The most common type of tax assessed by local governments is the property tax, which is a major focus of this article. Used in all 50 states, property taxes provide more revenue to local governments than any other source other than state government transfers. Taxes levied on property typically consist of ad valorem and non–ad valorem assessments. Ad valorem taxes are assessed in proportion to the value of the taxpayer's property and are usually used for local governmental services such as public schools. Non–ad valorem taxes are not assessed in proportion to the value of the taxpayer's property, and non–ad valorem tax revenue is usually used for general services such as fire protection and waste removal.

Other common types of local taxes include local income taxes, which are significant sources of revenue in cities and towns in Ohio, Indiana, Michigan, Maryland, Missouri, New York, and Pennsylvania, among other states (approximately 14 states authorize local governments to assess income taxes). Another significant local tax is the local sales tax, which is authorized in approximately 34 states. Local governments may assess a general sales tax, or they may assess a local tax on specific items, such as gasoline, tobacco, or alcohol. In some states, the local sales tax generates minimal amounts of revenue and is intended to provide modest reduction in property tax assessments. In other states, such as Alaska and Alabama, where the local sales tax can be as high as 7 percent, the local sales tax is a significant source of revenue.

In addition to these general taxes, local governments may have authority to assess many other types of taxes. A thorough listing of these types of taxes is beyond the scope of this article. Some examples of these types of local taxes include motor vehicle excise taxes, corporate excise taxes, hotel and motel taxes, property transfer taxes, and tourist taxes. (Florida, for example, taxes anyone who rents or leases any accommodation for less than six months.)

Fees

Unlike taxes, fees are revenue sources that are assessed in proportion to the cost of providing a service or regulating an activity. Indeed, the local government typically cannot charge fees that significantly exceed the cost of providing the service or regulating the activity. If the fee is assessed for the cost of regulating an activity, the activity usually has to be within the local government's home-rule authority or within its police power to regulate general health, safety, or welfare.

Local governments may assess dozens of different fees. One category of fees consists of licenses and permits. For example, a local government may assess an occupational license fee on all businesses as a way of recouping the costs of regulating business activity, or a municipality may charge annual fees for liquor licenses to balance the expenditures necessary to monitor alcohol sales. Also, local governments may require fees for permits that are necessary for individuals to conduct disruptive activities, for example, those that disrupt traffic.

Another category of fees involves user charges for the cost of services provided by local governments. Utility services, such as sewage, water, electricity, and natural gas, provide a higher portion of total local governmental revenue than any other service: 8 percent in 2000–2001. Another example is local telecommunication service, such as 911 emergency assistance. Additional examples of revenue-generating services include transportation, such as public transit or municipal airports; recreation, such as public stadiums or swimming pools; health care; trash removal; and parking, including both municipal parking lots and parking meters. A final example is educational services: Local governments commonly receive revenue from municipal institutions of higher education or from incidental services in primary or secondary education, such as hot lunch programs.

A third category of fees is impact fees, which are charges assessed against property developers for the costs of services and infrastructure that become necessary because of the development. Local governments have increasingly used impact fees to prevent or to reduce the costs of suburban sprawl. Although developers have challenged the authority of local governments to charge impact fees on several occasions, the authority to assess such fees has generally been upheld in courts, as long as there is a relationship between the fee and governmental land use concerns.[2]

A final category of fees are special assessments, which are charges levied against individuals within an area for capital improvements, public services, or facilities provided to individuals within that area. Examples of special assessments include neighborhood sidewalk construction fees or the fees of constructing flood prevention walls. The ability of local governments to raise revenue through special assessments is often authorized by home rule charters.

Revenues Received from Miscellaneous Sources

Local governments may also receive some revenue from sources other than governments, individuals, and businesses. A primary example is interest from investments, from which local governments received almost 4 percent of their total revenue during 2000–2001. Another example is payments from municipal employees for funding public retirement funds.

MAKING THE SPRAWL CONNECTION

Opponents of sprawl often assume that local government land-use decisions are the product of unfettered choice and that sprawl results from local attempts to insulate communities from disliked land uses and residents. In response, some scholars correctly point out that background legal rules structure the choices that localities can and will make.[3] One of the background legal structures that affects local choice is the system by which localities obtain revenue. Property taxes and sales taxes, it is hypothesized, create strong incentives for municipalities to favor certain land uses over others, thereby contributing to sprawl.

Does the system of local government taxation affect local land-use decisions? The answer is a resounding yes. The property tax leads to sprawl by incentivizing low-density uses and disincentivizing housing, whereas the sales tax promotes sprawl by incentivizing retail. This section discusses the various ways in which the property and sales tax contribute to sprawl.

We first examine the mechanisms through which local governments in two states, Massachusetts and Utah, obtain revenue through taxation and the land-use incentives that those mechanisms create for local governments. We chose these states because they have both had TELs in effect since the 1980s, but they have responded in different ways to the constraints the TELs place on local budgets. Massachusetts offers essentially a "pure property tax" regime for most locally raised discretionary revenues, whereas Utah provides a local-option sales tax as a TEL relief. California and a number of other states follow the Utah model and, we discover, this policy incentivizes retail land uses, further intensifying the sprawl problem.

Our analysis demonstrates not only that the property tax encourages sprawl but also that TELs exacerbate the problem. The exceptions to the property tax caps in the two states incentivize sprawl, as does the TEL relief of the local option sales tax in Utah.

Massachusetts: The Property Tax

Massachusetts is an example of a state that forces local governments to rely on the property tax for most of their discretionary revenue.[4] In the 1980s, however, Massachusetts limited the amount of revenue that local governments can generate through the property tax. In this section, we discuss the implications of Proposition 2½'s tax limitation provisions on the ability of municipalities to raise local revenue through the property tax and illustrate the sprawl-producing incentives that Massachusetts's property tax system creates. We then demonstrate the effect of these incentives—sprawl—by analyzing the characteristics of those communities that have been able to "win" under Proposition 2½.

What Is Proposition 2½?

During the late 1970s, Massachusetts voters had some of the highest state and local tax rates (including property taxes) in the nation. In response, an initiative entitled "An Act Limiting State and Local Taxation and Expenditures" was placed on the November 1980 ballot and subsequently approved by the voters of the Commonwealth. The initiative became effective for fiscal year 1981. Because the initiative bore some similarity to the Proposition 13 property-tax limitation measure approved by California voters in 1978, the initiative became commonly known as Proposition 2½.

Proposition 2½ contains several provisions that significantly affected the fiscal policies of local governments.[5] Among the most significant provisions are two limitations on the amount of property tax that a municipality can levy. Under one provision, municipalities are limited to levying 2.5 percent of the total "full and fair cash valuation" of all taxable real and personal property (the fair cash value of all real and personal property as certified by the Commissioner of Revenue) within a municipality for a given year. This maximum amount that a municipality can levy is known as the municipality's levy ceiling.

The second significant property tax provision limits the rate by which a municipality's levy limit can increase annually to 2.5 percent. Note that a municipality's annual levy limit is different from the municipality's levy ceiling. The levy ceiling represents the maximum total amount that a municipality can levy in a given year based on the total "full and fair cash valuation" of taxable real and personal property during that year. The levy ceiling is calculated independently each year and incorporates increases in the market value of existing property. The levy limit is calculated based on a 2.5 percent increase in the levy limit from the previous year without considering any increases in the assessed value of existing property.

The 2.5-percent cap on the growth rate of a municipality's levy limit does not include new growth within the municipality. New growth includes any increase in the full and fair cash value of real property because of new development or significant changes to existing property, the value of exempt real property that becomes taxable property, the value of condominium conversions, and the value of new subdivisions. New growth does not include increases in the market value of existing and unchanged property.

The 2.5-percent annual growth limit also can be bypassed by a municipality's voters in one of two ways. First, voters can pass an override, which permanently increases the levy limit base by any amount up to the levy ceiling. Municipalities typically submit overrides to voters when they wish to increase their funding for general ongoing operating expenditures or more specific operating expenditures, such as expenditures for schools or police, beyond what the levy limit can provide. Second, voters can pass an exclusion, which temporarily increases the levy limit by any amount necessary to fund a capital project or to pay debt service costs. Exclusions can fund a capital project (capital outlay expenditure exclusions) or payment of debt service costs related to a capital project (debt exclusions).

Proposition 2½ does not allow municipalities to relieve themselves of their statutory responsibilities, such as the obligation to provide public education. Thus, as Proposition 2½ constrained the amount of revenue that municipalities were able to collect,[6] the initiative had an immediate impact on the quality of services that municipalities were able to offer.

Proposition 2½ clearly accomplished one of its primary objectives: reducing Massachusetts property tax rates, which are now only slightly above the median tax rate in the other 49 states. However, as described below, Proposition 2½ also had a profound impact on land-use decisions made by local governments.

Municipal Response to Proposition 2½

As Table 17.1 shows, Proposition 2½ levy limits appear to have constrained many municipalities during each of the 20 years for which data is available (FY 1985 through FY 2004).[7] Throughout its lifetime, Proposition 2½ levy limits have served as a handcuff for a significant number of municipalities. During the height of the Commonwealth's fiscal crisis in 1991, over 81 percent of Massachusetts municipalities (285 out of 351 municipalities) levied taxes within 99.5 percent of their levy limit. Without Proposition 2½, these municipalities almost certainly would have raised more revenue by increasing their property tax rates.

Table 17.1. Annual Number of Municipalities Whose Levies Are Within 99.5% of Their Levy Limit

Fiscal Year	Number of Municipalities Whose Actual Levies Are Within 99.5% of Their Levy Limit	Fiscal Year	Number of Municipalities Whose Actual Levies Are Within 99.5% of Their Levy Limit
1985	117	1995	230
1986	120	1996	171
1987	102	1997	171
1988	140	1998	160
1989	117	1999	138
1990	278	2000	146
1991	285	2001	149
1992	275	2002	169
1993	254	2003	193
1994	254	2004	180

Identifying the "Winners" and "Losers" of the Proposition 2½ Era

Proposition 2½ Objectives

Because Proposition 2½ constrains municipalities in their ability to generate revenue through property taxes, local governments have few options in seeking to increase revenue. As a result, the property tax limitations of Proposition 2½ have created a new category of municipal fiscal objectives. Using these objectives—increasing their ability to generate revenue through increasing the levy limit, increasing their levy limit without increasing the number of service-demanding residents, and attracting new growth—to gauge municipal success under Proposition 2½, we sought to identify whether Proposition 2½ creates "winners" and "losers" among the 351 municipalities in Massachusetts. The following describes these objectives along with our findings in more detail.

Increasing the Levy Limit. In response to Proposition 2½ constraints, municipal managers are likely to focus on increasing their capacity to generate revenue through property taxes by increasing their levy limit in any possible way. The levy limit automatically increases each year by 2.5 percent. However, given its small size, this automatic increase effectively serves as nothing more than an inflationary adjustment. Still, municipalities have the capability to increase the levy limit beyond 2.5 percent through new growth, exclusions, or overrides. The ability to increase the levy limit beyond the automatic adjustment is especially important to municipalities that may be in need of additional revenue for an expansion or improvement in municipal services or in anticipation of a fiscal crisis, such as a reduction in state aid. We discovered that a number of municipalities have been relatively successful in finding ways—whether through new growth, overrides, or exclusions—to increase their capacity to generate revenue through the property tax.

Maximizing Levy Limit Per Resident. As the municipalities seek to increase their levy limits, municipal managers are likely to seek to stabilize municipal population. Increasing the levy limit may be fiscally irresponsible if the increase arises from new growth that creates a substantial increase in residents who require additional municipal services, the cost of which exceeds the increase in the levy limit. Accordingly, the fiscally prudent means of increasing the levy limit is to achieve new growth without a corresponding increase in population.

We found that success in maximizing levy limit per resident varies significantly among the 351 municipalities. Thus, although Proposition 2½ places handcuffs on nearly all of the Commonwealth's 351 municipalities, the handcuffs have become much tighter on some municipalities: those municipalities that have a substantially lower levy limit per resident than other municipalities. The municipalities with low levy limits per resident face significant constraints in raising local revenue sufficient to provide adequate municipal services to their residents. Proposition 2½ has allowed a municipality like Weston (a wealthy suburb) to raise more than six times the amount of property tax revenue per resident than a municipality like Lawrence (an older industrial city).

Attracting New Growth. Municipalities can achieve new growth by developing open space, making significant additions to or redeveloping existing property, revising the tax status of exempt real property, converting rental property into condominiums, or creating subdivisions. The cumulative dollar value of new growth over time is a measurement of the success of municipalities in adding to their levy limits without having to seek voter approval.

We again found significant disparity in the ability of municipalities to attract new growth. Location or other inherent advantages may allow certain municipalities to attract more new growth than other municipalities are able to attract. Larger urban and suburban areas in the Commonwealth have the most new growth while the smaller rural areas have the least new growth. Many of the new-growth "winners" are located along Interstate 495 the outer beltway around the Boston Metropolitan Region, whereas many of the new-growth "losers" are located closer to Boston. For those municipalities that are unsuccessful in attracting new growth, the only other option for increasing the property tax capacity beyond the annual adjustment is to seek voter approval for overrides or exclusions.

Characteristics of the Proposition 2½ "Winners" and "Losers"

After analyzing relative success under these Proposition 2½ objectives, we identified those municipalities that achieved relative success in achieving each of these objectives, and we classified them as Proposition 2½ "winners."[8] In a similar manner, we classified those municipalities that were relatively unsuccessful in achieving these objectives as Proposition 2½ "losers." We analyzed various characteristics of the "winners" and "losers" to determine what they have in common. We found similarities among the "winners" and the "losers" in their location, wealth, and land use.

Location

There are several pockets of either "winners" or "losers" throughout Massachusetts. The Boston metropolitan region is one prominent example that provides strong support for the conclusion that "winning" or "losing" is related to location. A significant number of municipalities located within the Route 128 ring around

Boston were identified as Proposition 2½ "losers." On the other hand, a significant number of Boston suburbs located outside of Route 128 were identified as Proposition 2½ "winners." The predominance of Boston area "winners" outside of the Route 128 ring becomes especially clear along Interstate 495—especially to the immediate west of Interstate 495.

The relationship between location and Proposition 2½ success is that municipalities that had open space during the early days of Proposition 2½ were easily able to attract new growth and expand their levy limit. In addition, these municipalities had the flexibility to alter their land-use policies to attract the right type of new growth—presumably the type of low-density development consistent with sprawl—to fill those open spaces.

Wealth

A second characteristic that appears to be related to "winning" or "losing" is a municipality's wealth, as measured by per capita income. Table 17.2 demonstrates clear correlation between a municipality's per capita income and their success or lack thereof under Proposition 2½. The "winners" are comprised largely of wealthy municipalities, and the "losers" are comprised largely of poor municipalities.

Many of the wealthy municipalities may not need to be Proposition 2½ "winners." These municipalities have such historically strong tax bases that they do not need revenue beyond the standard yearly increase—or perhaps residents of these municipalities only demand limited municipal services. For example, only a minority of children in a wealthy municipality may attend public schools, thereby allowing the municipality to maintain a low education budget that does not require additions to the levy limit.

On the other hand, the correlation between poverty and lack of success under Proposition 2½ is quite strong. This correlation suggests that poor municipalities—those municipalities that most need to attract new growth to provide services to their needy residents—are unable to attract, or have been unsuccessful at attracting, new growth or otherwise expanding their levy limits. The burden of Proposition 2½ falls disproportionately on the poor. Proposition 2½ appears to have placed handcuffs on most municipalities. However, many of the wealthy municipalities have been able to slip the handcuffs through new growth or smart growth, whereas very few of the poor municipalities have been able to do so.

Land Use

A third characteristic that appears to have some relationship with "winning" and "losing" is a municipality's land use. For example, there is a relationship between

Table 17.2. "Winners" and "Losers" Separated by Wealth Quartile

Wealth Quartile	"Winners"	"Losers"
1 (Municipalities ranked 1–88 in per capita income)	38	15
2 (Municipalities ranked 89–176 in per capita income)	20	11
3 (Municipalities ranked 177–265 in per capita income)	14	16
4 (Municipalities ranked 266–351 in per capita income)	6	38

success or lack of success under Proposition 2½ and the percentage of total parcels in a municipality that are single-family detached homes. A municipality that consists predominantly of single-family detached homes is almost three times more likely to be a "winner" than a "loser." Similarly, a municipality that consists primarily of other land use, such as multifamily homes or commercial parcels, is more than three times more likely to be a "loser" than a "winner."

Municipalities that consist of a relatively large proportion of multifamily dwellings are more than twice as likely to be "losers" than to be "winners." However, the converse does not appear to be true. Municipalities that have low proportions of multifamily dwellings are only slightly more likely to be "winners" than to be "losers." Excluding or discouraging multifamily housing is not alone a guarantee of success under Proposition 2½. Such a municipality likely still needs to attract *large* single-family homes—or be in the right location or have wealthy residents—to succeed. On the other hand, pursuing or allowing multifamily housing does appear to be detrimental to a municipality's ability to succeed under Proposition 2½.

We also found a strong relationship between dense housing and lack of Proposition 2½ success. Municipalities with the densest housing are nearly three times more likely to be Proposition 2½ "losers" than they are to be Proposition 2½ "winners." On the other hand, there does not appear to be any correlation between sparse housing and success under Proposition 2½. There might actually be a relationship between sparse housing and *lack* of Proposition 2½ success.

Nevertheless, some municipalities with significant amounts of multifamily housing units or with dense housing can succeed under Proposition 2½. Holyoke, a municipality located near Springfield in western Massachusetts, is one such example. Attracting low-density, single-family housing is not a guarantee of Proposition 2½ success. Hingham, located along the South Shore area near Boston, is just one example of a Proposition 2½ "loser" that is dominated by low-density, single-family housing.

We discovered a slight relationship between Proposition 2½ success or lack thereof and whether a municipality is overwhelmingly residential or maintains more of a residential/commercial mix. Municipalities that have the highest percentage of occupied parcels that are commercial or industrial are more likely to be "losers" than "winners," but the relationship is not strong. Municipalities apparently can be "winners" as bedroom communities or by pursuing more of a mix of commercial development. However, overemphasis on commercial or industrial development may coincide with a lack of Proposition 2½ success.

Planning decisions *may* affect a municipality's ability to succeed under Proposition 2½. Unlike the other characteristics that appear to contribute to Proposition 2½ success—location and resident wealth—municipalities can feasibly influence this factor through zoning, tax abatements, and so forth. Pursuing a land-use strategy that features more single-family homes and less multifamily housing or heavy commercial and industrial development, to the extent such a strategy is feasible, may help some "losers" to become "winners." Focusing on land-use changes may provide hope to some Proposition 2½ "losers" that the Massachusetts General Laws have not sentenced them to a lifetime of fiscal hardship. However, characteristics such as geography and residential wealth may trump the ability of many municipalities to escape the handcuffs of Proposition 2½ through land use policy.

Even if planning alone is not enough to turn a loser into a winner, a municipality's objective of slipping the handcuffs of Proposition 2½ may cause the municipality to shun smart growth. Municipal planners seeking to combat sprawl through building higher-density housing developments may have difficulty selling their ideas to elected officials, who understand that a municipality that plans for dense development will have a lower likelihood of fiscal success given the tax limitation constraints imposed by Proposition 2½. Sprawl is unavoidable as long as the ability of municipalities to generate local revenue is dictated by Proposition 2½.

Findings

Proposition 2½ was enacted to protect property owners from skyrocketing property taxes. In accomplishing this objective, the initiative appears to have been a success and is undoubtedly praised by property owners. But this success has not come without inflicting significant burdens on other stakeholders, such as municipalities throughout Massachusetts. Some municipalities have been much more successful than others in overcoming these burdens.

Many of those municipalities that were not successful never really had a chance to overcome the Proposition 2½ constraints. These municipalities were on the wrong side of the tracks: they had little open space that could be rezoned or redeveloped, or they had poor residents who made attracting significant new growth nearly impossible. For many of those municipalities, exclusions or overrides have not been an option because the constituency is not likely to approve an increase in their taxes.

Although Proposition 2½ may have equitably distributed benefits to all property owners, the initiative did not equitably distribute the associated burdens to all municipalities. Proposition 2½ may be a boon for the Commonwealth's wealthiest residents—large property owners—but it appears to have placed insurmountable obstacles in the path of some municipalities attempting to raise local revenue to provide services to its neediest residents. Proposition 2½ has placed handcuffs on nearly all of the Commonwealth's 351 municipalities. But some of those municipalities were barely bound and were easily able to shed their handcuffs, while some were tightly bound.

In addition, Proposition 2½ has forced municipalities to alter their land-use decisions in a way that has led to sprawl. Proposition 2½ leads to sprawl in four ways:

1. Localities will favor low-density land uses because the value of the property is more likely to pay for the services required. For example, large-lot housing is more likely to generate enough money to pay for the educational expenses required by the housing's occupants than is dense housing. Because of increased low-density development, the geographical size of the metropolitan area becomes much larger than it would otherwise be.
2. The new-growth exemption may also lead to rapid turnover in land use because municipalities enable high-value uses to leap to new areas very easily. Thus, as an area grows older, land uses are more likely to leap to the newer, more rural, and booming suburbs, contributing to rapid geographical expansion of the urbanized region.

3. Property tax incentives lead to increasing wealth disparities. As municipalities disfavor dense housing and restrict development to high-end housing, affordable housing will be scarce and will be located primarily in older, poor areas that can attract little new growth. The result is a geographical separation of rich and poor. In addition, wealthier communities will be more likely to attract desirable commercial land uses, thereby leading to geographical separation between poor residents and jobs. Because poor residents are unable to find easily accessible jobs, the geographical wealth disparity increases—as does the wealth disparity of municipalities, as property values and tax revenue continue to increase in the wealthy areas while decreasing in the poor areas.

4. Competition for new growth undermines any regional cooperation that is necessary to combat sprawl. Rather than plan together to manage regional growth, localities will compete for desirable land uses. Some communities will obtain those land uses, while other communities will be stuck with either no new growth or undesirable new growth.

Although most of these sprawl-creating impacts are inherent in the property tax structure itself,[9] Proposition 2½ exacerbates them by limiting municipal revenue-generating options. Financially strapped localities are given few options other than to seek new growth that will provide a net revenue gain.

Utah: TEL Relief Through the Sales Tax

In 1985, the Utah legislature passed the Tax Increase Disclosure Act (more commonly known as Truth-in-Taxation), which creates a property tax cap similar to that mandated by Massachusetts's Proposition 2½. Like Proposition 2½, Truth-in-Taxation mandates a levy limit that is based on the previous year's levy limit. Unlike Massachusetts, however, Utah does not automatically increase the levy limit from year to year.

Instead, localities that wish to increase their property tax revenue (for example, to counteract inflation) must either go through a Truth-in-Taxation process or attract new growth. The Truth-in-Taxation process involves publishing, in the newspaper and a public meeting, the intention to increase taxes. Most public officials have been reluctant to undergo such a process. Effectively, then, the only way that Utah municipalities can increase their property tax revenue is to attract new growth. Like the system in Massachusetts, this system pushes municipalities to pursue land uses that pay for themselves: retail, office, and perhaps low-density residential.

In addition, Utah exempts 45 percent of the value of primary residences (including rental properties) from taxation.[10] Thus, Utah provides a huge disincentive to plan for residential housing; the property taxes received from the housing in most cases will not pay for the increased services required.

In Utah, however, localities can also influence their revenue by attracting retail. In the last 30 years, the local-option sales tax has overtaken the property tax as the dominant source of local government revenue. The local-option sales tax is a 1-percent sales tax that municipalities can opt to levy on purchases. Every municipality in the state has opted to levy the tax.

As of 1989, 50 percent of the local-option sales tax dollars are distributed to local governments based on population, while the other 50 percent are distributed according to point of sale.[11] To attract point-of-sale revenue, local governments compete for retail stores.

A survey of local government officials in California, where the sales tax provides the largest source of local discretionary revenue, confirmed that localities consciously seek to maximize sales tax revenue. In fact, sales tax revenue was cited by local officials as the primary factor influencing the desirability of land uses, and commercial uses were considered the most desirable.[12]

Although the sales tax loosens the handcuffs of the property tax TEL and removes the pressure on municipalities to attract new growth that pays for itself, the sales tax generates its own incentives that alter land-use choices in extremely important ways.

1. Municipalities allow retail companies to build and move wherever they want, leading to a large and rapid turnover in retail, which in turn leads to excessive land use whenever a retail establishment moves (for example, because the home community or a neighboring community managed to attract a larger competitor).

2. The necessity of attracting retail dominates all other land use planning goals. A locality that would otherwise plan for compact, smart-growth development will bend to the wishes of a big-box retail establishment that wishes to locate in a certain place.

3. Retail tends to gather around freeway interchanges. This type of land use again alters the planning that cities would otherwise do. Where freeways do not cut through the center of town, this growth creates low-density sprawl by pulling other land uses away from the dense urban core.

4. Municipalities disfavor housing—particularly high-density housing—and are increasingly forced to turn to residential impact fees to gather revenue. This leads to a lack of affordable housing.[13] What affordable housing exists is located in older, poor areas, again creating spatial wealth disparities.

5. Cities are more likely to focus on attracting big-box retail rather than smaller stores, because a single big-box retail store can generate substantial retail sales; although smaller stores may generate similar sales in the aggregate, the return for the location of one store is much higher for big-box retail.

6. Wealthier suburbs are able to provide incentives for retailers that attract more retail than the population of the suburb would otherwise warrant.[14] This leads to a decentralization of retail as stores move away from the central city to the suburbs, decreasing metropolitan density and further attracting wealthy residents to the suburbs.

7. Competition for sales tax, like competition for property tax, undermines regional cooperation. A single Wal-Mart's decision to locate on one side of a municipal boundary rather than the other (or to move from one city to another) can significantly impact municipal revenue while generating that revenue from the same taxpayers' wallets.

The sales and property taxes provide significant incentives for localities to encourage sprawl by planning for commercial and low-density land uses and by discouraging high-density housing. The result is rapid land consumption, increasing congestion and pollution, and spatial wealth disparities.

TAXING TRANSIT-ORIENTED DEVELOPMENT (TOD)

The most prominently advocated alternative to sprawl is transit-oriented development (TOD). TOD generally involves mixed-used, dense development in close proximity to transit stations. As an alternative to sprawl, TOD has been much lauded and promoted in urban planning and new urbanism[15] circles. New urbanists try to sell TOD principles to states and localities, arguing that TOD will reduce automobile travel, improve air quality, promote community, limit land consumption, and create a more aesthetic urban environment. This chapter assumes that these benefits of TOD are desirable and achievable, but questions whether the local government revenue regime effectively closes the door on TOD for most communities. Whereas most research has focused on the costs and benefits of TOD, this chapter questions whether TOD will occur at all given our current systems of local government finance.

Peter Calthorpe, one of the leading proponents of TOD, recommends that urban TODs contain 20–60 percent housing and that neighborhood TODs contain 50–80 percent housing.[16] Municipalities can influence the types of land use that occur around transit stations in several ways: by rezoning the land, by influencing the siting of the station itself,[17] and by providing incentives (e.g., density bonuses) to developers. Given the analysis above, it initially appears that the common property tax systems, such as those in Massachusetts and Utah, will discourage municipalities from siting high-density land uses, particularly housing, near transit stations (or anywhere). Upon further reflection, this initial conclusion appears to be correct, although it may be the case that a municipality that builds a well-balanced TOD will not incur more service costs than revenue generated. The sales tax, on the other hand, will encourage communities to build transit-accessible retail in the vicinity of transit stations, again reducing the amount of transit-oriented housing.

In a system with a pure property tax, localities may be able to balance their budgets while planning for TOD, but those localities that favor retail and office uses near transit stations will fare even better. In a system that includes the sales tax, TODs will likely be skewed towards retail use. Thus, the property tax and sales tax not only encourage sprawl, they discourage the most prominent alternative to sprawl.

The Property Tax and TOD

Generally, the property tax discourages dense development because high-density land uses do not pay for themselves. Several mitigating factors, however, may make dense, mixed-use TOD feasible in a system that relies entirely on property taxes for local government revenue.

1. Because TOD is by definition mixed-use, the actual housing per square mile does not differ much from a detached-home bedroom community; thus, a municipality would not generate significantly less property tax per capita through TOD than it would by building low-density housing.

2. Because property values increase near transit stations for all types of uses (including housing, commercial, and office uses),[18] the disincentive to build dense housing is not as strong as initially appears; the property values of the housing units are more likely to pay for increased services than in the absence of a nearby transit station.

3. Mixed-use neighborhoods have higher property values than do bedroom communities, when all other factors are controlled for. Siting housing and office uses close to retail may moderately increase commercial property values by making the retail more conveniently accessible.[19] Similarly, residential and office property values will increase because of the accessibility of nearby retail.[20] In addition, proximity to single-family housing actually reduces property values, creating a disincentive to place residential housing in bedroom communities.[21]

These findings mitigate the disincentives that the property tax generates for housing in TODs, but it is not clear that they overcome them. Although it may be the case that dense housing in mixed-use areas has higher property values than housing of a similar density in a bedroom community, it does not follow that high-density housing in mixed-use areas has higher property values than low-density housing in bedroom communities. When a municipality faces a choice of land uses around a transit station, it may very well conclude that the highest aggregate land value would result from a concentration of retail and office space around the station, surrounded by low-density housing. Nevertheless, it is very possible that a municipality will conclude that the property tax generated by a TOD will pay for all services required, even if mixed-use dense development is not the highest revenue generating use. Thus, although the property tax does not preclude TOD, it incentivizes retail- and office-heavy TOD.

The Sales Tax and TOD

The sales tax certainly incentivizes retail development around transit stations, assuming that transit-oriented retail is viable. Retail development costs, however, are significantly higher near transit stations because of higher property costs; greater governmental regulation in central urban areas, where most transit stations are located; likelihood of brownfield pollution problems; and inability to build large stores.

Nevertheless, a municipality, when choosing among land uses near transit stations, will likely encourage those uses that will generate the most sales tax. The transit station, like a freeway interchange, provides added accessibility that the locality can exploit. Given the right marketing and encouragement, transit-oriented retail appears to do fairly well.[22] In fact, rents and property values for transit-oriented retail are very high and increase in proportion to transit system ridership and to retail accessibility from the transit station.[23] Thus, cities face incentives not only to build retail near transit stations, but to orient the retail toward the transit station. Essentially, the more accessible the retail, the more sales it will generate.

Certainly, some types of retail generally will not flourish near transit stations: appliance and home improvement stores, for example. On the other hand, other retail stores—those with more pedestrian-friendly products, such as convenience and specialty stores—can do very well, particularly if conditions are right. If there is nearby office space, commuters may frequent the transit-oriented retail because of its convenient location. Indeed, a factor affecting the property value of transit-oriented retail establishments is their proximity to other uses, such as services and office space.[24]

Thus, the sales tax encourages municipalities to site retail near transit stations, and municipalities, if they make the right efforts, will probably be successful at attracting that retail. On the other hand, it is also possible that the sales tax will motivate cities to site auto-oriented retail uses in close proximity to the TOD. These retail establishments may compete with and reduce the viability of the transit-oriented retail.[25]

Existing studies of transit stations in California, where local governments rely predominantly on the sales tax for revenue, confirm that retail dominates housing near transit stations. For example, Marlon Boarnet and Nicholas Compin visually surveyed transit station areas in San Diego County and concluded that residential housing was a dominant use near only 17 of the 48 stations in the county.[26] Only 18 of the stations had been zoned for residential use on more than 20 percent of the land within a quarter mile of the station and only seven had been zoned more than 50 percent residential, whereas 23 had been zoned less than 5 percent residential.[27] In contrast, "at forty-three of the forty-eight stations, dominant nearby uses include a commercial or industrial component."[28]

A study of existing and proposed stations throughout Southern California reaches a similar conclusion: "Municipalities behave as if they prefer to use rail transit stations for economic rather than residential development."[29] After analyzing the amount of land zoned for particular types of land use within a quarter-mile of transit stations and comparing it the percentage of land zoned for that use in the municipality as a whole, the study concludes that municipalities overwhelmingly zone for more commercial use than residential use near transit stations (as measured by the ratio of the percentage of land use near the station to percentage of land use outside the station area).[30] Although new urbanists would encourage siting of retail near transit stations rather than far from them, the overwhelming tendency to zone for commercial use near transit stations does not bode well for transit-based housing.

Findings

Although a locality that wishes to build a well-balanced TOD may be able to do so while balancing municipal revenue and expenditures, the property tax and sales tax incentivize municipalities to encourage commercial and office uses near transit stations at the expense of housing—particularly high-density housing. The result is TODs that are not as well-balanced as new urbanists urge.

The net result of a disproportionate siting of commercial uses near transit stations is a glut of "destination" stops and a scarcity of "origin" stations.[31] Too few housing units near transit stops could significantly reduce ridership, undermining the goals of the mass-transit system. In addition, a lack of transit-oriented housing, by reducing ridership, could actually lead to the economic failure of the retail destination stops. Municipalities are thus caught in a vicious prisoner's dilemma: It is in each locality's individual self-interest to site retail near transit stops, but a collective decision to site too much retail will harm all municipalities.

CONCLUSION

Local government taxation regimes create important incentives regarding land use. Municipalities, like people, must balance their expenditures and revenue, and land-use decisions can significantly affect both. Whether municipalities would choose sprawl in the absence of taxation regime incentives is an open question, but localities do not operate autonomously; they face constraints created by background legal regimes, including revenue generation regimes.

The local property tax and sales tax incentivize municipalities to discourage dense housing and to encourage commercial and office uses, thereby producing sprawl. These incentives may prevent the widespread construction of TODs, and where TODs are built, they are likely to be unbalanced. Given the local government taxation system, municipalities are likely to build more retail and office space and less high-density residential housing than may be desirable near transit stations.

Unless and until local government taxation regimes are modified to eliminate sprawl-producing incentives, it is unlikely that the current trends of rapid geographical expansion of metropolitan areas, increased automobile use, and shocking spatial wealth disparities will end. The transit-oriented developments that many envision as an alternative to sprawl are unlikely to come to fruition—at least in the way advocates envision—without serious reforms in the ways municipalities gather revenue.

NOTES

1. For purposes of this chapter, sprawl is defined as rapid land consumption, spatial wealth disparity, jobs-housing mismatch, and excessive auto use.

2. See, e.g., *Coulter v. City of Rawlins*, 662 P.2d 888 (Wyo. 1988).

3. See, e.g., Gerald E. Frug, *City Making: Building Communities Without Building Walls* (1999).

4. Massachusetts also provides significant state aid to cities and towns based on complex formulas. The incentives this state aid creates for localities are beyond the scope of this article.

5. In *Boston Water & Sewer Commission v. Metropolitan District Commission*, the Supreme Judicial Court held that Proposition 2½ applies only to cities and towns and does not apply to local governments that are formed by special legislation, such as water districts.

6. To balance the adverse fiscal impact of the provisions described above, Proposition 2½ also includes provisions designed to protect municipalities from additional expenditures. One such provision, known as the Local Mandate Provision, bars any state rule or regulation that results in the imposition of unreimbursed costs to a city or town after January 1, 1981. The Local Mandate Provision serves to protect municipalities from some, but certainly not all or even a significant portion, of the sting of the Proposition 2½ property tax provisions.

7. The Massachusetts Department of Revenue Web Site (http://www.dor.state.ma.us) contains extensive information for all 351 municipalities in Massachusetts for each year starting in FY 1985 and continuing through FY 2004.

8. We identified "winners" as those municipalities that were ranked in the upper quartile among the 351 municipalities for a majority of the Proposition 2½ objectives, whereas

"losers" were considered to be those municipalities that ranked in the lower quartile for a majority of the Proposition 2½ objectives.

9. Some argue that the property tax may actually *increase* density by increasing the cost of housing, thereby decreasing home size. See Robert W. Wassmer, "The Influence of Local Fiscal Structure and Growth Control Choices on 'Big-Box' Urban Sprawl in the American West," in *The Property Tax, Land Use and Land Use Regulation* (Dick Netzer, ed., 2003); Jan K. Brueckner and Hyun-A Kim, *Urban Sprawl and the Property Tax*, http://www.igpa.uiuc.edu/publications/workingPapers/WP84-sprawltax.pdf (unpublished manuscript at 3) (2000). The property tax could have such an effect in the absence of governmental regulation—although it also might *decrease* density by increasing the cost of capital improvements, see *id.* at 2—but it also creates sprawl-producing incentives for government regulators that lead to alterations of normal market activity.

10. *Utah Code Ann.* § 59-2-103(2).

11. See Utah Foundation, *Financing Government in Utah: A Historical Perspective* 88 (2000).

12. See Paul G. Lewis and Elissa Barbour, *California Cities and the Local Sales Tax*, Public Policy Institute of California, at 87 fig.5.1, 89 tbl.5.5 (1999), available at http://www.ppic.org/content/pubs/r_799plr.pdf.

13. See *id.* at xv.

14. Wassmer reports that "the percentage of statewide discretionary municipal revenue from general sales taxation exerted a significant positive influence on . . . non-central retail activity. For every 1 percent increase in sales tax reliance, real retail sales in non-central metropolitan places in the West rose by 0.24 percent." Wassmer, *supra* note 9, at 115. This effect was even greater for retail types that tend to be big box. See *id.*

15. New urbanism is an urban planning movement that gathered many supporters in the 1980s and 1990s. It advocates walkable communities, mixed housing types, and balancing of jobs and housing. See Congress for the New Urbanism, *About New Urbanism*, http://www.cnu.org/about/index.cfm (last visited April 30, 2004); see also Congress for the New Urbanism, *Charter of the New Urbanism*, http://www.cnu.org/about/index.cfm (last visited April 30, 2004).

16. Peter Calthorpe, *The Next American Metropolis: Ecology, Community, and the American Dream* 63 (1993).

17. Boarnet and Crane, for example, argue that municipalities in California, where the sales tax is the largest source of local discretionary revenue, influence the siting of stations so that they are located in economic, rather than residential, centers: See Marlon Boarnet & Randall Crane, "L.A. Story: A Reality Check for Transit-Based Housing," 63 *Journal of the American Planning Association* 189, 197 (1997).

18. See, e.g., Robert Cervero and Michael Duncan, "Transit's Value-Added Effects: Light and Commuter Rail Services and Commercial Land Values," in *Transportation Research Record* 1805, at 8, 15 (2002) ("Being within walking distance of an LRT station in Santa Clara County increased [commercial] land values on average . . . by about 23%"); Roderick B. Diaz, *Impacts of Rail Transit on Property Values*, http://www.apta.com/research/info/briefings/documents/diaz.pdf, at 1 (surveying studies of the impact of rail transit on residential property values and concluding that "proximity to rail is shown to have positive impacts on property values"); Rachel R. Weinberger, "Light Rail Proximity: Benefit or Detriment in the Case of Santa Clara County, California?," in *Transportation Research Record* 1747, at 104, 111 (2001) ("The analysis demonstrates overwhelmingly . . . that the presence of the light rail system has, in fact, conferred a rental premium on office properties that lie within its catchment or service area."); Bernard L. Weinstein and Terry L. Clower, *An Assessment of the DART LRT on Taxable Property Valuations and Transit Oriented Development* (September 2002), http://www.apta.com/research/info/briefings/documents/dart2002.pdf, at i (concluding that light rail stations in Dallas significantly increased property values for residential

and office properties but not for retail and industrial properties). But see Robert Cervero, "Rail Transit and Joint Development: Land Market Impacts in Washington, D.C. and Atlanta," 60 *Journal of the American Planning Association* 83 (1994) (asserting that studies show that "urban rail transit will significantly benefit land use and site rents only if a region's economy is growing and a number of supportive programs are in place").

19. See Cervero, *supra* note 18, at 89 ("[M]ixed-used projects have outperformed single-use office buildings, leasing new space more quickly and at higher rents."); Cervero and Duncan, *supra* note 18, at 15 (finding that proximity to labor markets and services increased commercial property values).

20. Robert Cervero and Michael Duncan, "Neighborhood Composition and Residential Land Prices: Does Exclusion Raise or Lower Values?," 41 *Urban Studies* 299, 307, 309 (2004) (finding that single-family and multifamily home values are higher in mixed-use neighborhoods and that nearby retail activities significantly increase mixed-use housing property values). On the other hand, racial diversity and low-income residents generally decrease property values, see *id.* at 312, inviting one to question whether the property value benefits of multifamily housing and mixed-use development are not outweighed by the property value impacts of the types of residents who tend to live in dense housing.

21. See *id.* at 307, 310–11.

22. Before a transit stop becomes a popular destination, nearby retail may not benefit much from the transit stop, but once a few businesses successfully attract transit riders, other businesses will begin to benefit from the increased number of potential customers who frequent the area. Thus, a sort of snowball effect occurs: it may be difficult to get the ball rolling, but once it rolls it will grow rapidly larger.

23. See Cervero, *supra* note 18, at 87 ("[O]ffice rents near stations tended to increase as systemwide transit ridership increased."); Diaz, *supra* note 18, at 4 ("[T]hose systems with the highest rates of ridership and that reached more locations within their respective regions . . . experienced the most significant association between distance from transit stations and property values.")

24. See Cervero and Duncan, *supra* note 18, at 14.

25. See Calthorpe, *supra* note 16, at 82 ("New competing retail uses should be strictly limited within one mile of the core [TOD] commercial area.").

26. See Marlon G. Boarnet and Nicholas S. Compin, "Transit-Oriented Development in San Diego County: The Incremental Implementation of a Planning Idea," 65 *Journal of the American Planning Association* 80, 85 Tbl.1 (1999).

27. See *id.*

28. See *id.* at 83.

29. Boarnet and Crane, *supra* note 17, at 189.

30. See *id.* at 195–96.

31. See Boarnet and Crane, *supra* note 17, at 200.

18

Immigration: Friend or Foe

Alexander von Hoffman and David C. Soule

Are immigrants a major cause of sprawl in the United States? Some people think so. A recent study issued by the Center for Immigration Studies (CIS) suggests that all of the smart-growth prescriptions offered by respected planning and environmental organizations ignore the principle driving force behind the rapid consumption of land in the United States—population growth, especially expanding immigration. Drawing on the database used by many other studies of sprawl—the U.S. Department of Agriculture's National Resources Conservation Inventory of nonfederal land—the CIS report suggests that you can't be smart about growth without facing the immigration question.

The report has generated significant controversy among environmental and social advocacy groups, which consider immigration policies and population controls harkening back to the xenophobic days of the "Know Nothing" Party. Antiforeign sentiments aside, the increasing diversity in the American metropolis is a widely touted and often celebrated fact of twenty-first-century demographics. However, the study points out that, while we are a nation of immigrants, ironically, immigration has always caused anxiety in some Americans. Although some, including Dowell Myers and a number of city mayors who have been trying to attract immigrants, have extolled the virtue of the newcomers, others have blamed them for a variety of ills, now including sprawl.

During the last part of the twentieth century, immigration bifurcated into two main streams. Many low-wage jobs were open to immigrants from Latin America, the Caribbean, Africa, Southeast Asia, and Eastern Europe. These immigrants were often victims of political persecution and economic exploitation, arriving as generations of others had before them to take whatever menial work was available.

However, a different set of factors led a wave of highly skilled migrants to enter the country with numerous economic and social advantages available immediately. American institutions of higher education have a long tradition of welcoming foreign-born students. During the second half of the twentieth century, many countries subsidized their educated young adults to consume the college and university programs established to attract them. After their student visas expired, many talented immigrants, faced with returning to less prosperous and less safe conditions in their countries, found ways to remain in the United States.

As the high-tech boom surged through the 1980s and 1990s, a number of companies sought workers from many places outside the United States to meet the demands for the skill sets the technology sector required. One company spokesman commented that "you can hear 20 languages spoken in our lunchroom and our caterers have had to respond with meals to meet all palates and requirements from kosher to Thai and all gradations in between."

As this new era continues to unfold, the long-term effects on the United States are unclear. However, several trends are apparent which, for this volume, require a closer inspection.

THE 2000 CENSUS AND IMMIGRATION

The 2000 census declares that for the first time many American cities and their regions are becoming a majority of minorities. A number of cities, such as Los Angeles and Miami, crossed that threshold 10 years ago. Dowell Myers, based at the University of Southern California, discusses the dynamic forces that are shaping the metropolitan regions of this country in a positive context. Many urban theorists focus on "place-based" strategies, which monitor changes in geographic areas (census blocks and tracks, cities, counties, and MSAs). Myers argues that this places too much emphasis on the geography and misses the demography. His study of Los Angeles, Chicago, New York, and Washington, D.C., suggests that the impact of demographic forces is stronger, and more optimistic, than traditional insights into metropolitan regions identify.

Myers suggests that immigration, a traditional source of new "blood" in this country, continues to be a vital and dynamic force. Since the 1950s, the urban dialogue has focused almost entirely on the seemingly intractable problem of race, specifically black/white relations. Asian and especially Hispanic migration into the four regions in his study is dramatically transforming the complexity of urban regions. The diversity of these American regions is expanding exponentially.

Myers is intensely critical of place-based studies, which miss the significant dynamic of upwardly mobile immigrant populations. "Immigrants arrive poor but they quickly build economic strength."[1] This insight into the demographics of the metropolitan regions is particularly useful in gauging the success of regions over time. As individuals and families increase their personal economic well being, they move up (and usually) out of their "geography of entry." They may or may not stay in their region. In fact, Myers's data suggest that many move to other regions.

For central cities, which are often the gateways for immigration, this may be bad news. When people get an economic foothold, they have more choice and can access alternate locations for jobs and housing. This choice may still be constrained by race and income, but inner cities can still empty out.

Audrey Singer of the Brookings Institution has explored these trends in the 2000 census with longitudinal analysis through the entire twentieth century. According to Singer, "the share of the U.S. population that is foreign-born is lower (11.1%) at the end of the twentieth century than at the start (13.6% in 1900 and 14.7% in

355

1910)." In 1900, 10 percent of the immigrants were from Latin America and over 86 percent were from Europe. By the end of the century, Latin American immigrants made up half of the foreign-born population, with Europe contributing 13 percent, Asia 34 percent, and Africa 3 percent. Mexico contributes the largest number of immigrants (over 58 percent of the Hispanic population).[2]

Not surprisingly, cities did well in the 2000, census but all early indications suggest that this is due to continuing foreign immigration. In fact, according to Alan Berube, "if not for immigration, several of the nation's largest cities including New York, Minneapolis/St. Paul, Chicago, and Boston would not have grown during the 1990s. Cities will continue to be gateways for the world's population to enter and take a chance on achieving the American dream."[3]

Singer notes, however, that different cities are acting as gateways in twenty-first-century America. "Established Gateway" cities, including Chicago (61%), Los Angeles (19%), Miami (31%), New York (37%), San Diego (41%), and San Francisco (26%), experienced far less metropolitan growth in foreign-born population between 1990 and 2000 than "emerging gateway" cities including Atlanta (262%), Charlotte (315%), Fort Worth–Arlington (131%), Las Vegas (248%), Orlando (140%), and Salt Lake City (174%).[4] Further, according to Berube, "in the emerging gateways, the locus of immigration is the suburbs, not the central city."[5] Singer takes the "gateway" concept further, positing that there are actually six major types of U.S. immigrant "gateways":

1. *Former gateways* (e.g., Cleveland and Buffalo): attracted immigrants in the early 1900s.
2. *Continuous gateways* (e.g., New York and Chicago): long established points of entry.
3. *Post–World War II gateways* (e.g., Los Angeles and Miami): high attraction over the last 50 years.
4. *Emerging gateways* (e.g., Atlanta and Dallas): fast immigrant growth over the last 20 years.
5. *Reemerging gateways* (e.g., Seattle and Twin Cities): waned as destinations in the middle of the century but now important again.
6. *Preemerging gateways* (e.g., Salt Lake City and Raleigh-Durham): attracted significant immigration in the 1990s.

Pressure will continue on cities and, more significantly, on "first tier" cities/suburbs, which abut central cities to accommodate the new arrivals. Housing supplies are constrained in cities.

Either as a result of this constraint or the process of spatial assimilation of newcomers, scholars have found, immigrants have increasingly sought homes in America's suburbs. According to Clark and Patel, who analyzed public-use microdata samples (PUMS) for the Los Angeles area, residential choices of the newly arrived foreign-born has changed from 1985–1990 to 1995–2000. Their concentration in the inner core (central city) has decreased, resulting in a wider dispersion of the newly arrived foreign-born. In addition, professional immigrants are seen to be settling away from the inner core but across an increasingly wider region of the suburban area.[6]

Logan examined 69 metropolitan areas between 1990 and 2000 and found "strong evidence that immigrants are now a major contributor to suburbanization."[7]

Combining these calculations with additional data from the period between 1970 and 2000 led Singer to conclude that "by 2000 more immigrants in metropolitan areas lived in suburbs than cities, and their growth rates there exceeded those in the cities."[8]

Suburbs are not noted for their friendly attitude toward the development of multifamily and small-tract starter homes. Consequently, urban policies, especially strategies in metropolitan regions, need to factor equity and social condition into their framework.

Immigration as a Factor in Sprawl

One way of testing whether immigrants have contributed to sprawl in the United States is to identify where immigrants have been settling in the nation's metropolitan areas. One of the authors, Alexander von Hoffman, investigated this possibility in research conducted at the Joint Center for Housing Studies of Harvard University. The research examined the location of immigrant residences, as recorded in census data, in 1970 and 2000 in 14 metropolitan areas: Atlanta; Boston; Chicago; Dallas–Fort Worth; Houston, Los Angeles; Miami; Minneapolis–St. Paul; New York; Phoenix; Portland; St. Louis; San Francisco; and Washington, D.C. To trace the movement of people, both foreign and native born, the metropolitan areas were divided into concentric circles at intervals of 10 miles from the major city's city hall, so as to be able to compare the populations of the resulting mile-rings (0–10, 10–20, 20–30, and beyond 30 miles) in 1970 and 2000 (see Table 18.1).

The research summarized in Table 18.1 shows that in 1970 immigrants concentrated extremely heavily in the area closest to the center. In all 14 metropolitan areas, the largest share of the foreign-born lived in the inner ring (0–10 miles from city hall). Moreover, in 11 metropolitan areas, immigrants residing within 10 miles of city hall made up a majority of the total foreign-born population, and in the remaining three, just a little less than a majority of all foreign-born residents (New York, 49%, and Los Angeles and San Francisco, 44%) lived in the inner ring. Remarkably, in nine metropolitan areas, the inner-ring claimed more than two-thirds of the foreign-born.

Over the next 30 years, the foreign-born spread out from the center, but mainly to developed suburbs, as opposed to the far-flung exurban areas. The inner ring's share of all immigrants fell dramatically in all the metropolitan areas, except Boston and New York, where it declined only slightly. Between 1970 and 2000, the number of metropolitan areas with a *majority* of foreign-born residents in the inner ring fell from 11 to 4. Yet the inner ring still claimed the highest portion of the foreign born in eight metropolitan areas, down from 14 in 1970, but still the majority of the metropolitan areas in the study. In the four remaining metropolitan areas, the largest share of metropolitan foreign-born residents had shifted to the 10–20-mile bands, an area composed mainly of cities and established suburbs. In the Atlanta region, famous for its vast sprawling pattern, the suburban band held half of all the foreign-born. In the Los Angeles metropolitan area, inner and suburban rings (0–10-mile and the 10–20-mile) held the same share, 30 percent of the foreign-born population.

Thus, by 2000, the foreign-born population had spread out mainly to suburban areas. In all but one of the 14 metropolitan areas, the majority of immigrants could be found in the inner and suburban rings (between 0 and 20 miles from city hall).

Table 18.1. Composition of Percent Foreign-Born in Varying Distances from Central Cities, 1970 and 2000

	Atlanta	Boston	Chicago	Dallas	Houston	Los Angeles	Miami	Minneapolis	New York	Phoenix	Portland	St. Louis	San Francisco	Washington, D.C.
% foreign-born 1970														
0–10 miles	66.4%	52.4%	59.3%	74.7%	67.5%	44.0%	70.3%	81.3%	49.4%	71.1%	73.5%	69.2%	43.6%	77.7%
10–20 miles	30.5%	16.0%	23.3%	19.1%	15.8%	32.0%	19.2%	16.5%	29.9%	24.7%	11.2%	26.2%	20.8%	19.5%
20–30 miles	2.8%	11.1%	9.9%	2.3%	6.0%	11.1%	6.2%	2.2%	8.3%	3.6%	5.6%	3.1%	12.1%	2.0%
>30 miles	0.3%	20.5%	7.5%	4.0%	10.7%	12.9%	4.3%	0.1%	12.3%	0.6%	9.6%	1.5%	23.5%	0.7%
% foreign-born 2000														
0–10 miles	20.8%	50.7%	44.0%	48.1%	36.7%	30.4%	37.5%	65.0%	46.7%	54.9%	54.5%	41.2%	23.1%	42.5%
10–20 miles	50.3%	15.3%	22.1%	41.8%	47.0%	30.4%	39.6%	30.1%	29.6%	35.6%	24.0%	42.8%	17.4%	39.4%
20–30 miles	23.0%	15.7%	18.4%	6.4%	10.6%	17.0%	12.4%	3.4%	9.7%	5.1%	7.2%	11.5%	17.0%	14.6%
>30 miles	5.9%	18.4%	15.5%	3.8%	5.6%	22.3%	10.5%	1.6%	14.0%	4.4%	14.3%	4.5%	42.5%	3.5%

In 13 of the metropolitan areas, the share in these two rings was a striking two-thirds or more of the total foreign-born population.

In one metropolitan area, that of San Francisco, the majority of the foreign-born lived in the outermost ring, but this is the exception that proves the rule. The areas beyond 30 miles from San Francisco include several counties that increased population between 1970 and 2000. In particular, Santa Clara County, located far to the southeast of the city of San Francisco, experienced tremendous growth in population, adding 600,000 residents, to reach a total of a little under 1.7 million. In fact, the county had become an urban area largely independent of the older Bay Area cities, San Francisco and Oakland. Most of the population growth, moreover, took place in the city of San Jose, whose population increased by almost 450,000 to reach 895,000. In Santa Clara County, as elsewhere, immigrants clustered in central locations. By 2000, the county's central city of San Jose contained 330,000 immigrants, a group which made up 58 percent of the total of the county's 573,000 foreign-born residents. Thus, what appears to be exurbia in the San Francisco statistics is in fact an urban area in which the foreign-born concentrated in the center.

To summarize, during a period of significant sprawl, immigrants—like native-born Americans—departed the central city. While some moved to the far reaches of metropolitan areas, by far most either stayed in central cities or moved to areas of established suburbs. A fair assessment would be that immigrants probably contributed to American urban sprawl, but only in a minor way.

The Regional Context

Exurban communities, those on the outer fringes, are undergoing rapid transformation, as they become the affordable housing for their regions. Ron Thomas, executive director of the Northern Illinois Planning Commission in Chicago and a contributor to this volume, suggests that major portions of the metropolitan development in the next 20 years will take place outside of the geography of the six county Northeastern Illinois region. Los Angeles is discussing the "fifth ring" of development in the "Inland Empire" miles outside of the central core. These rapidly growing fringe areas, according to Myron Orfield, are under as much fiscal stress as inner areas as they struggle to provide basic services (roads, schools, public safety, etc.) to their residents.

Where from Here

The CIS study raises the question of whether there are more immigrants coming than we can/should absorb. The CIS proposition summarized in Table 18.2 that current immigrants have a higher birthrate than other current population groups in the country is confirmed by Singer. However, cultural factors, especially religious and ethnic influences, are significant in this discussion.

The normative argument—is this a good or bad thing?—yields different answers, based on current trends. From a sprawl perspective, we are constantly pushing the urban edge. One preliminary study indicates that, if the population/immigration trends continue for the next 50 years, the largest metropolitan areas in the country,

Table 18.2. Total Fertility Rates by Race/Ethnicity, 2001

	Total Fertility Rates (Average Number of Children a Woman Gives Birth to in Her Lifetime)
Hispanic	3.2
Black	2.1
Native American	2.1
Replacement Level	**2.1**
Asian	2.0
White	1.9

Source: Singer, 2003.

assuming they continue their gateway status, will push these edges into each other, creating what geographer Jean Gottman called "megalopolises" over 40 years ago.[9] In fact, the U.S. Census bureau, when it created micropolitan areas in 2003 based on the 2000 census, flirted briefly with simultaneously creating this category.

Some policy analysts would see these trends as the basis for re-introducing immigration quotas while others would see this as a continuation of necessary, essential, and perhaps inevitable requirements for balancing national and global requirements. What sprawl analysts need to resist is becoming a shill for anti-immigrant bias, based on mean-spirited xenophobic interests. A constructive debate includes at least one consideration that 1990–2000 immigration has an urban salvation result: Thank God for immigrants or our cities would be emptying out. More importantly when diversity is seen in a global context, American economic and social policies require a recognition that our workforce, our economy, and even our ability to keep the promise of Social Security must allow for significant and continuing immigration.

In a political context few elected officials reflect the diversity demands that arise from higher concentrations of Asian and Hispanic populations. The suburban transformation described by Singer and others further demands recognition that a new politics is necessary. While we enjoy Thai and Brazilian restaurants on Main Street, we need to build pathways into city, town, and county commissions, boards, and elected office for the emerging majorities in our society.

NOTES

1. Myers, 1999.
2. Singer, 2004.
3. Berube, 2003.
4. Singer, 2004.
5. Berube, 2003.
6. Clark and Patel, 2004, p. 10.
7. Logan, 2003, p. 8.
8. Singer, 2004, p. 10.
9. Gottman, 1964.

BIBLIOGRAPHY

Beck, Roy, Leon Kolankiewicz, and Steven A. Camarota. 2003. *Outsmarting Smart Growth: Population Growth, Immigration, and the Problem of Sprawl*. Washington, DC: Center for Immigration Studies.

Berube, Alan. 2003. *Census 2000: Key Trends & Implications for Cities*. Presentation to the Knight Center for Specialized Journalism "Cities, Suburbs, and Beyond," October 30. Washington DC: The Brookings Institution, Center on Urban and Metropolitan Policy. Powerpoint Presentation downloaded from brookings_metropolitan_policy_program@lyris.brookings.edu.

Clark, William A. V., and Shila Patel. 2004. *Residential Choices of the Newly Arrived Foreign Born: Spatial Patterns and the Implications for Assimilation*. Los Angeles and Irvine: University of California, Los Angeles and University of California, Irvine.

Gottman, Jean. 1964. *Megalopolis: The Urbanized Northern Seaboard of the United States*. Cambridge, MA: MIT Press.

Logan, John R. 2003. *America's Newcomers*. Albany, NY: Lewis Mumford Center for Comparative Urban and Regional Research at the University at Albany.

Myers, Dowell. 1999. "Demographic Dynamism and Metropolitan Change: Comparing Los Angeles, New York, Chicago, and Washington, D.C." *Housing Policy Debate* 10(4): 919–54.

Singer, Audrey. 2004. *The Rise of New Immigrant Gateways*. Washington, DC: The Brookings Institution.

PART VI

POLICY PRESCRIPTIONS

19

Governing Complexity: The Emergence of Regional Compacts

Douglas Henton, John Melville, and John Parr

The modern metropolitan region is a picture of complexity. We see fragmented local government structures with multiple jurisdictional boundaries, dynamic businesses riding endless waves of "creative destruction," and ever-changing patterns of civic leadership driven in part by the new demographics of age and ethnicity. Somehow, we need to find new ways to govern this complexity as we try to manage for growth and promote community well being, while sustaining regional economic prosperity and ensuring that everyone participates in economic and social opportunities.

Thomas Homer-Dixon, in *The Ingenuity Gap* (2000), asks the fundamental question of whether our world is simply becoming too complex and fast paced to effectively manage change. He argues that because challenges facing society are often beyond our understanding, a critical "ingenuity gap" is growing between the need for practical and innovative ideas to solve our complex problems and our actual supply of those ideas.

There appears to be an ingenuity gap in the current thinking and practice of regional governance around critical issues of managing growth, preserving quality of life, and promoting economic vitality. These challenges spill over city and county boundaries. Communities working alone can not effectively address critical issues such as sprawl, job training, housing, traffic, air quality, and water supply. These problems do not respect local political boundaries. Moreover, their resolution are not limited to government action, but also involve business and nonprofit organizations. They require a "regional community" collaborating on a cross-sector regional basis. The need for new regional approaches stands in sharp contrast to current realities of government fragmentation.

Allan Wallis, of the University of Colorado in Denver, has described the dilemma faced by most metropolitan regions: "Expanding the power of the metropolitan region runs counter to the cultural preference for keeping government as small as possible with power exercised close to the people affected. The inherent conflicts between ends and means have made achieving effective regional government or governance extremely difficult" (Wallis, 1996, p. 15).

Resolving this dilemma requires creative thinking about governance and how we manage the inherent complexity of regions. Fortunately, across America we see a series of experiments that involve networks of regional stewards working in their metropolitan or rural areas who are influencing regional direction through ad hoc approaches, rather than new formal government structures. Regional stewards—leaders committed to the long-term well-being of place—are integrators who cross boundaries of jurisdiction, sector, and discipline to address complex regional issues such as sprawl, equity, education, and economic development. They see the connections between economic, environmental, and social concerns and they know how to "connect the dots" to create opportunities for their regions. This has been called "ad hoc regionalism" or "pragmatic regionalism."

In particular, many regions are experimenting with new multisector approaches to these challenges, which are based on networked governance that seeks a middle way between traditional top-down hierarchy and private market solutions. Underlying most of these regional approaches is an understanding that regional stewardship emphasizes a commitment to place rather than to a single issue and broad coalitions of business, civic, and government leaders to develop a shared regional vision to guide specific actions (see Henton et al., 2003).

Increasingly, key components of these approaches are compacts among local governments evolving from the long-used intergovernmental agreements (IGAs) and joint powers agreements/authorities (JPAs). These compacts vary dramatically, but all include some sharing of power among governmental entities. This sharing ranges from land-use decisions to providing services. Moreover, some private sector and nonprofit entities are entering into agreements to work collaboratively on regional issues. This chapter explores governing complexity in rural and metropolitan regions with a focus on the role of compacts.

GOVERNANCE CHALLENGES FOR THE TWENTY-FIRST CENTURY

Governance is how people come together to address common problems. It is more than government. At the regional level it involves citizens, businesses, nonprofit organizations, and educators as well as government working in various ways to set direction, solve problems, and take action.

Regional governance in the United States requires solving problems across multiple jurisdictions—cities, townships, and counties. The evolution of regional governance has gone through three phases. The first involved attempts at *government consolidation*—creating unitary governments from several jurisdictions. While this started in the 1800s there was a flurry of mergers in the 1960s and 1970s; examples included Indianapolis—Marion County and Nashville—Davidson County. A second phase, starting in the late 1950s, focused on *regional planning and coordination of local government activities*. This phase was stimulated by federal government requirements in the housing, transportation, and other development arenas. It also included the creation of regional agencies such as the Metropolitan Council in the

Twin Cities of Minnesota. The third phase, starting in the 1980s, has involved *regional public-private cooperation* involving a variety of partnerships and alliances among business, government, and community groups. This third phase is often called *civic regionalism* to distinguish it from prior efforts focused primarily on efforts to create regional government.

Metropolitan regions face a number of governance challenges in the twenty-first century:

- *Scale*: As regions grow, they continue to expand beyond traditional political jurisdictions. Many regions now encompass several cities, towns, and counties. How to deal with this political fragmentation in the face of growing economic regions is a challenge to most regions.
- *Speed*: The innovative economy is based on speed. Governance institutions are having trouble keeping up with the pace of change. Few institutions have learned how to operate on "Internet time," but they are being asked to respond more quickly to economic changes.
- *Participation*: How much civic engagement is possible in regional governance? The challenges of scale and speed combine with a lack of trust of ineffective institutions to discourage participation in regional governance. However, without civic engagement, regional governance will not be responsive to citizen needs. According to Robert Dahl, a leading thinker on democracy, "Scale, complexity and greater quantities of information impose ever-stronger demands on citizen's capacities. As a result, one of the imperative needs of democracy is to improve citizen's capacities to engage intelligently in political life"(Dahl, 1999).
- *Accountability*: How are public and private leaders, working in a variety of public-private partnerships and hybrid institutions, held accountable to citizens for outcomes? If there is a growth of new regional organizations not directly elected by the people, how is the leadership in these organizations selected and replaced?
- *Effectiveness*: In the end, what matters is how well regional institutions respond to the changing needs of the region. Fragmentation of responsibility and the increasing pace of change have made it difficult for institutions to meet those needs. Worse, a lack of effective regional governance leads to conflict and competition among jurisdictions and between the public and private sectors, which leads to gridlock.

ALTERNATIVE APPROACHES

Just as regional economies have been changing, so too must our institutions for regional governance. As Dahl says, "Perhaps our institutions created in democratic countries during the nineteenth and twentieth centuries are no longer adequate. If this is so, then democracies will need to create new institutions to supplement the old" (Dahl, 1999). A variety of approaches can be used to address the regional governance challenges in the twenty-first century. David Walker, of the University of Connecticut, Storrs, developed a typology that highlights the levels and degrees of difficulty of different approaches to regional governance.

The Easiest Eight

1. *Informal cooperation* generally involves collaborative and reciprocal actions between two local jurisdictions, does not usually require fiscal actions, and only rarely involves matters of regional or even subregional significance. While reliable information on the extent of its use is generally absent, anecdotal evidence suggests that informal cooperation is the most widely practiced approach to regional governance.

2. *Interlocal service contracts* are voluntary but formal agreements between two or more local governments and are widely used. Metropolitan central cities, suburbs, and counties generally rely on them to a greater extent than nonmetro municipal and county jurisdictions.

3. *Joint powers agreements (JPAs)* are agreements between two or more local governments to provide for the joint planning, financing, and delivery of a service for the citizens of all the jurisdictions involved.

4. *Extraterritorial powers* permit cities to exercise some of their regulatory authority outside their boundaries in rapidly developing unincorporated areas. A number of states do not authorize extraterritorial powers, and because this approach does not apply to cities surrounded by other incorporated jurisdictions, it is less used than other techniques. Moreover, less than half the authorizing states permit extraterritorial planning, zoning, and subdivision regulation. This tends to make effective control of fringe growth difficult.

5. *Regional councils/councils of governments (COGs)* rely heavily on interlocal cooperation, and they assumed far more than a clearinghouse role in the late 1960s and 1970s. Federal grant programs with a regional thrust sometimes used COGs for their own integral parts of a strong, state-established substate districting system as well. Rural COGs tend to take on certain direct assistance and servicing roles for their constituents, while the more heavily urban ones usually serve a role as regional agenda-definer and conflict-resolver.

6. *Federal encouraged single-purpose regional bodies* are single-purpose regional bodies, which come into being when institutional strings are attached to federal aid programs. Single-purpose regional bodies now exist only in a few federal aid programs (notably economic development, Appalachia, Area Agencies on Aging, job training, and metro transportation). Continued federal funding makes them easy to establish, and they play a helpful, nonthreatening planning role.

7. *State planning and development districts (SPDDs)* are districts established by the states during the late 1960s and early 1970s to bring order to the chaotic proliferation of federal special purpose regional programs. A states own substate regional goals are a prominent part of the authorizing legislation or gubernatorial executive orders that established SPDDs. Although feasible, SPDDs are somewhat difficult, because special authorizing legislation is required, state purposes and goals are involved, and the establishment of a new statewide districting system can at least initially appear threatening, especially to counties.

8. *Contracting* with the private sector is the only form of public-private collaboration analyzed here and is the most popular of all such forms. Service contracts with private providers are now authorized in many states—fewer than their intergovernmental counterparts and usually with far more detailed procedural requirements. Their use has clearly increased from the early 1970s to the present with scores of different local services sometimes provided under contracts with various private sector providers. Joint powers agreements and interlocal service agreements, however, are both more popular than contracting with private firms.

The Middle Six

1. *Local special districts* are a very popular way to provide a single service, or multiple related services, on a multijurisdictional basis. Three-quarters of all local special districts serve areas whose boundaries are not coterminous with those of a city or country.
2. *Transfer of functions* is a procedural way to change permanently the provider of a specific service. This method saw a jump in use in the 1970s and 1980s. The larger urban jurisdictions are much more likely to transfer functions than the smaller ones. Cities are likely to shift services, first to counties and then to COGs and special districts. Despite its increased popularity, the difficulties involved in transfers of functions should not be overlooked. Few states authorize such shifts, and in half these cases, voter approval is mandated. In addition, the language of some of the authorizing statutes does not always clearly distinguish between a transfer and an interlocal servicing contract.
3. *Annexation* is the dominant device for properly aligning local jurisdictional servicing boundaries and expanding settlement patterns. Although the vast majority of annexations involve very few square miles, they are an incremental solution to closing the gap between governmental servicing boundaries and the boundaries of the center city. Annexation is limited by the nature of state authorizing laws (most do not favor the annexing locality) and a reluctance to use the process as a long-range solution to eliminating local jurisdictional, fiscal, and service fragmentation. Annexation, then, has limited geographic application and is usually used incrementally. However, when assigned a key role in a city's development, it can transform a municipality from a local to a regional institution. As a result of recent legislative reform, Local Agency Formation Commissions (LAFCO) may play a more significant role in California.
4. *Regional special districts and authorities* comprise the greatest number of regional governments in our metro areas. Unlike their local urban counterparts, these Olympian organizations are established to cope on an areawide basis to address a major urban challenge such as mass transit, sewage disposal, water supply, hospitals, airports, or pollution control. Relatively few large, regional units have been established because they (1) require specific state enactment and may involve functional transfers from local units; (2) are independent, expensive, professional, and fully governmental; and

(3) are frequently as accountable to bond buyers as to the localities and the citizen consumers.

5. *Metro multipurpose districts* differ from the other regional model in that they involve establishing a regional authority to perform diverse—not just related—regional functions. At least four states have enacted legislation authorizing such districts, but they permit a comparatively narrow range of functions. This option clearly ranks among the most difficult to implement. While multipurpose districts have a number of theoretical advantages (greater popular control, better planning and coordination of a limited number of areawide functions, and a more accountable regional government), political and statutory difficulties have barred their widespread use.

6. *The Reformed Urban County* is difficult to form because it transforms a unit of local government, a move frequently opposed by the elected officials of the jurisdiction in question. As a result, many states have enacted permissive county home-rule statutes, but few charter counties (generally urban) have been created.

The Tough Trio

All three of the following examples involve the creation of new areawide levels of government, reallocation of local government powers and functions, and, as a result, disruptions of the political and institutional status quo. All three options involve very rare and remarkable forms of interlocal cooperation.

1. *One-tier consolidations*, which expand municipal boundaries, have had a lean but long history. From 1804 to 1907, four city–county mergers occurred, all by state mandate. Then municipalities proliferated, but city–county mergers virtually stopped for 40 years. There have been fewer than two dozen city–county consolidations, most endorsed by popular referendum. Among the hurdles to surmount in achieving such reorganizations are state authorization, the frequent opposition of local elected officials, racial anxieties (where large minorities exist), an equitable representational system, concerns about the size of government, and technical issues relating to such matters as debt assumption. Most consolidations have been partial, not total, with small suburban municipalities, school districts, and special districts sometimes left out. However, the new county government generally exercises some authority over their activities. In addition, the metro settlement pattern, in some cases, has exceeded the county limits, so that the reorganized government may be the prime service provider and key player, but not the only one. This, of course, is another result of rigid county boundaries. One-tier consolidations have generally been most suitable in smaller nonmetro urban areas and in smaller and medium (ideally unicounty) metro areas.

2. *Two-tier restructurings* seek a division between local and regional functions with two levels of government to render such services. These and other features—notably a reorganized county government—are spelled out in a new county charter adopted in a countywide referendum. Metro Toronto,

which created a strongly empowered regional federative government to handle areawide functions and ultimately led to some local reorganization, is a model for this approach. The prime American example is Metro Dade County (Miami-Dade). Unlike the incremental reform approach of the modernized or urban county, a drastically redesigned county structure and role emerged from a head-on confrontation over restructuring.

3. *The three-tier reforms* are a rarely used approach. There are just two U.S. examples. However, they deal with the special problems of multicounty metro areas. The first example is the Twin Cities (Minneapolis-St. Paul) Metropolitan Council. The other three-tier experiment is Metro in Portland. Both examples illustrate how other multicounty metro areas might approach areawide service delivery and other metro challenges, but they are arduous to achieve and not easy to sustain.

Virtually all the various approaches described above have been on the increase. Since the early 1970s, the use of the eight easiest approaches has seen a net increase despite a reduction in the number of regional councils and federally supported substate districts. Meanwhile five of the six middling approaches grew markedly (the exception was the metro multipurpose authority). Even the three hardest approaches have grown in use. However, very few metro areas rely on only one or two forms of substate regionalism and instead employ multiple approaches.

The easier procedural and unifunctional institutional service shifts tend to be found more in larger metro areas, while the harder restructurings usually take place successfully within the medium-sized and, especially, the small metro areas. The expanded use of 10 of the 14 easiest and middling approaches is largely a product of local needs and initiatives, as well as a growing awareness of their increasingly interdependent condition.

While jurisdictional fragmentation has not been reduced as a result of restructuring, even incomplete forms of cooperation have been useful. Such approaches are used extensively; in a majority of metro areas they are the only feasible forms of regional and subregional collaboration. Like much else in the American system of metropolitan governance, the overwhelming majority of interlocal and regional actions to resolve servicing and other problems reflect an ad hoc, generally issue-by-issue, incremental pattern of evolution. Moreover, most of the major reorganizations were triggered, at least in part, by a visible crisis of some sort.

The intergovernmental bases of substate regional activities remain as significant as ever. The states, which always have played a significant part in the evolution of their metro areas, must move into a new primary role if the federal role in this arena continues to erode. Growth management is one of the key issues that is seeing different approaches being advocated and adopted. In general there are two divergent theories—a prescriptive approach that establishes state mandates and review procedures, and a collaborative approach that keeps intact local control, but uses consensus-building, collaborative planning and the creation of written agreements to guide implementation. Comparative analysis of these two approaches are inconclusive in determining which one has a greater positive impact on creating sustainable communities. States such as Florida, which passed prescriptive laws in the 1985, are now developing regional-based collaborative approaches. It also seems clear that property rights advocates and other interests that oppose state mandated approaches are much stronger political forces than they were a decade ago. Because it is generally easier to develop consensus about what should happen in a particular community, there started emerging in regions in the 1990s an approach that involves a variety of collaborative models with public, private, and community organizations working with networks based on voluntary agreements.

TOWARD REGIONAL COMPACTS

Written compacts or agreements can provide simple rules to guide complex behavior of individuals within regions. A key requirement is trust or agreement that reciprocity makes sense (if you abide by the rules and I follow the rules, we are both better off). This can often happen more easily in smaller communities where face-to-face interaction and trust relationship can be built than in larger areas.

The national "mainframe, one size fits all," centralized governance models need to give way to a more distributed intelligence through a series of regional networked compacts based on cooperation and consensus-building among leaders at the more decentralized level.

We are at a point were we need to reflect on the nature of new regional agreements. We need to help stimulate dialogue about new forms of "networked" regional governance based on compacts that better connect individual choice with regional visions. New models of networked regional governance are needed because traditional top-down hierarchies no longer achieve their intended purpose in addressing complex challenges. These networked approach models need to based on an understanding of the power of bargaining and social interaction as an alternative to traditional government hierarchies and markets. New regional compacts based on simple rules should be created using shared information to create the foundation of trust required for networked governance. Compacts that build trust require "face-to-face" interaction in decentralized environments where information can be shared through personal interaction within networks.

Ted Halstead of the New America Foundation has called for a "fourth American social contract." The first social contract helped found the nation; the second put it back together after the Civil War; and the third built a middle-class society through government social programs and economic regulation. The next social contract must be able to "reconcile competing demands of flexibility and fairness and will require new roles and responsibilities for all three parties to the contract: government, business and citizenry" (Halstead, 2003).

"Civic revolutionaries" in regions across America are now laying the groundwork for the nation's next social contract. In response to complex regional growth, transportation, housing, and public safety challenges, they are creating new "regional compacts" that provide both a plan of action and a framework of accountability. These agreements are examples of creative governance involving multiple parties and jurisdictions—addressing problems that are beyond the scope of local governments and defy "top-down" national solutions.

Robert Klitgaard and Gregory Treverton, in their report for the IBM Center for the Business of Government, "Assessing Partnerships: New Forms of Collaboration" (March 2003), pointed out that there are two drivers for these increased use of these collaborative approaches: (1) the communication revolution brought about by technology which makes collaboration easier, and (2) the shift in societal power to the "market state" which "respects neither the borders nor the icons of the traditional state."

Current experimentation with regional compacts is redefining how we govern ourselves. Two key examples are illustrative and deserve detailed description: The Mile High Compact in Denver, Colorado, and The Oregon Solution.

The Mile-High Compact

One example of how policy makers are rethinking metropolitan governance occurred in the 1990s in Denver, Colorado. Throughout the decade, the Denver Regional Council of Governments (DRCOG) had been working with its 49 member local governments to develop a regional growth and development plan. Its key vehicle was Metro Vision 2020, the long-range growth strategy for the Denver region. Metro Vision provided a regional context for local decisions regarding growth and development over a 20-year timeframe. It considered such issues as urban growth boundaries; higher density, mixed-use development; infill and redevelopment; and multimodal transportation systems. While a significant step forward for metropolitan Denver, actual implementation strategies became entangled in discussions over Metro Vision's four key tenets: It had to be voluntary, flexible, collaborative, and effective. Discussions were especially focused on the voluntary and flexible tenets of the plan. These western local governments were adamant that no one would tell their communities how to grow.

Toward mid-decade, the rapid growth of the region became a concern to an interesting coalition of environmental and business advocates. State legislation was drafted that incorporated much of Metro Vision's components; however, it made them mandatory. The ultimate failure of the legislation sent a strong signal to local government officials. By 1999, leaders from DRCOG and the Metro Mayors Caucus, along with city managers and senior planners, began meeting to draft an intergovernmental agreement that incorporated many of the principles of Metro Vision 2020.

The working group gave itself a deadline of 90 days to reach agreement on key issues related to growth and development decision making in the region. The result—the Mile High Compact—was a unique intergovernmental agreement among local governments in the Denver region to commit to use their comprehensive plans as the primary tools for decision making regarding growth and development in their communities. This approach shifted local comprehensive plans from purely advisory documents to the primary framework for local decisions regarding growth and development. Moreover, the Compact created a context for those decisions by acknowledging Metro Vision as the regional framework for local decision making. The Compact embodied Metro Vision and its core elements and outlined the critical elements to be included in local comprehensive plans.

On August 10, 2000, 26 of DRCOG's 49 member governments signed the Mile High Compact at a ceremony in Denver. These local governments represented the largest and fastest growing communities in the region. Soon after the ceremony, seven additional local governments signed the Compact. To date over 35 local governments have signed, representing over 80 percent of the region's population and over half of the state's population.

The significance of the Mile High Compact goes well beyond the issues of how regions and their local governments make decisions regarding growth or whether such decisions will be mandated by a "higher authority," i.e., the state legislature. The Compact serves as a model of how leaders in the Denver metro area can come together to frame and address complex and, often contentious, issues. As issues related to rapid growth have given way to current issues of hemorrhaging state and local budgets, the Mile High Compact remains revered as a product of collaborative problem-solving for critical issues. It is held in high regard by regional policy makers for its simplicity and its focus. The issues addressed by the Compact have gone on to be standard fare for more formal, legalistic intergovernmental agreements among communities in the Denver region. Its lasting legacy is the recognition by local officials that actions by one community have implications for its neighbors throughout the region and that mandated, "one size fits all" governance mechanisms, such as the results of legislation, are not the best models for regional governance. Moreover, it has shown that governance that occurs "offline;" i.e., outside the normal *Robert's Rules of Order* policy process, can be effective and sustainable and appropriate for the complex issues facing regions today.

Oregon Solutions

Oregon Solutions grew out of the State of Oregon's Sustainability Act of 2001. Initially inside the executive branch of state government, since January of 2002 it has been a program of the National Policy Consensus Center (NPCC) at Portland State University. Oregon Solutions has promoted a new style of community governance, one based on the principles of collaboration, integration, and sustainability.

Oregon Solutions works to develop sustainable solutions to community-based problems that support economic, environmental, and community objectives. It is the only statewide program of its kind. Based on Oregon Solutions' success, NPCC is working with other states to explore developing similar programs for addressing state objectives through on-the-ground, community-level projects. The NPCC model centers on the idea that many state agencies have program objectives that can only be met at the community level.

The aim of the program is to build solutions through the collaborative efforts of businesses, government, and nonprofit organizations. To date, Oregon Solutions has launched 20 community-based collaborative projects that have addressed a variety of environmental, social, and economic issues at the local level. Many of those projects are still underway, striving to achieve some combination of the state's Sustainable Community Objectives.

Oregon Solutions projects are implemented using a Community Governance System. Each project grows out of collaborative efforts of government, businesses, and nonprofit organizations and must support at least one of several sustainable community objectives established by the program. The process for initiating an Oregon Solutions project involves: (1) identification of a problem or opportunity defined by the community, (2) identification of a neutral community convener from the local community, appointed by the Governor, to lead a "Solutions Team" to address the challenge, (3) creation of an Oregon Solutions Team of federal, state, local, and other government entities, businesses, nonprofit organizations, and citizens who can contribute to a solution, (4) development of a draft integrated solution that leverages the resources of the Solution Team to meet the challenges at hand and sustainability objectives, and (5) creation of a "Declaration of Cooperation" signed by team members that commits their resources and time for an integrated action plan.

Oregon Solutions was initiated by Governor John Kitzhauber and has been continued by Governor Ted Kulongoski. The projects Oregon Solutions have organized range from creating a fund to purchase transportation-related carbon offsets to creating a technology center to connect low-income residents to high-tech jobs to a marking final segment of the Lewis and Clark trail. Partners to the agreements and participants in implementation have ranged from government agencies, to environmental groups and corporations, such as Intel and Weyerhauser.

A major impact of the compact approach has been a switch from debate and discord over who controls the decision-making process and abstract arguments about the positive and negative impacts of growth. This unproductive use of human energy is replaced by focused, problem-solving–oriented dialogue that leads to clear problem definition, delineation of roles and responsibilities, and concrete implementation plans.

There are lessons being learned through the process of developing and implementing compacts. The effort needs to begin with a vision of the future for the community. This vision must be developed by the community so there is ownership. This is accomplished by including community leaders in all levels and steps of process. While broad public participation is critical, the work needs to be leadership driven because the leaders will be the ones who have to inform, explain, defend, and implement. The leadership must be diverse and inclusive, not just elected officials, but also business, neighborhood, and environmental leaders. They must work to educate each other and to keep each other honest.

Work on compacts must be supported by valid research and data. Implementation must be action oriented, but incremental. It is important to pick the items around which there is consensus, implement the solutions, and build on these successes.

Regional compacts are not a replacement for the current system of governance; they can help redefine federalism for our time. Essential roles remain for local, state, and federal governments—as partners in funding infrastructure, delivering services, and providing legal and regulatory frameworks to ensure fair and effective markets. In fact, for a new form of governance to take root, it is critical that governments create a supportive environment for regional solutions, rather than pursue policies that reinforce local fragmentation or impose top down mandates. What this means is that every region needs a careful delineation of complementary roles and responsibilities among the local, state, and federal partners and mutual accountability agreements such as compacts to seal the deal.

As in the past, many of the ideas for the nation's next social contract may very well come from experimentation happening right now in communities and regions across America. As the late John W. Gardner suggested, "Periodically, throughout our history, 'the folks out there,' out around America, far from power but close to the good American earth, have shown not only their creativity but their capacity to move the nation. This is such a time. The next America will be forged in America's communities. That's where the fabric of society is being rewoven" (Gardner, 2002).

BIBLIOGRAPHY

Dahl, Robert A. 1999. *On Democracy*. New Haven, CT: Yale University Press.

Gardner, John W. 2002. *A New Spirit Stirring: Quotations from John Gardner*. Stanford, CA: Haas Center for the Public Service.

Halsted, Ted. 2003. "The American Paradox." *The Atlantic Monthly* (January).

Henton, Douglas, John Melville, and Kim Walesh. 2003. *Civic Revolutionaries*. San Francisco: Jossey-Bass.

Homer-Dixon, Thomas. 2000. *The Ingenuity Gap: How Can We Solve the Problems of the Future?* New York: Alfred A. Knopf.

Klitgaard, Robert, and Gregory Treverton. 2003. "Assessing Partnerships: New Forms of Collaboration." Washington, DC: IBM Center for the Business of Government, March.

Wallis, Allan. 1996. "Rebirth of City States and the Birth of the Global Economy." *National Civic Review* 85.

20

The Local Arena: Changing Regulations and Standards to Address Sprawl

Terry Szold

Communities around the nation are undertaking a variety of initiatives to address past regulatory and development practices that have resulted in sprawl. Sometimes regulations resulting in sprawl are caused by inadvertent rather than deliberate actions, and they can be opaquely concealed within general welfare promoting controls, such as standards for fire prevention, public health, and safety. Most typically, "sprawl-promoting" devices reside in local zoning regulations.

Of course, zoning itself is not to blame—it is simply the framework that accommodates the rules that we decide to apply to land and how it is used. That being the case, by targeting the "right" regulations for change, local communities, especially when combined with supportive regional, state, and federal polices, can take steps to foster better development outcomes.

While these efforts should be viewed as works in progress, particularly when compared with the long-established policies and development standards that they are intended to modify, such local initiatives and interventions—some to reduce traffic and better manage roadway infrastructure, some to encourage more compact and/or mixed use development, some to specify place-based rather than generic commercial design—are worthy of attention from the broader planning community and highlighting in a collection such as this.

Additionally, it is important that the planning profession not minimize the significance of what may appear in some cases to be relatively small gestures for curbing sprawl. Let's take the example of the requirements routinely applied to commercial development to ensure an adequate parking supply. For many years, such requirements mandated that a ratio of about five spaces per 1,000 square feet of gross floor area of retail be provided on-site by the developer. But by following this "tradition," these requirements create a surplus of parking spaces beyond what is needed to adequately serve the use. What one observes from even the most casual windshield survey across the nation's shopping malls is that while fierce competition exists for parking spaces closest to major openings in the mall, many vacant (and perpetually unused) spaces can be seen along the periphery of an always over-large lot, in locations too far away from central points of access to be practical.

Consider a proposed 100,000-square-foot retail development with the parking space ratio described above. Assuming an individual parking space of about 10 feet by 20 feet, along with a 10-foot maneuvering aisle (a total of 300 square feet per space), at least 500 parking spaces will be generated, creating about 150,000 square feet of impervious surface area or about 3.5 acres of parking. Adjusting the requirements ratio from five spaces to four per 1000 square feet of gross floor area and assuming the same spatial layout however, generates 120,000 square feet of impervious surface. This reduction in paving would in turn reduce stormwater runoff management requirements and provide more opportunity for preventing the existing vegetation from being removed as part of the site-planning process. Even more importantly, such a decision may result in a modest (if tacit) incentive for shoppers to drive-share when they visit this shopping area.

Burlington, Massachusetts, located in suburban Boston, applied the standard type of requirement that generated more parking than was actually needed. By visiting sites during peak periods, and engaging a transportation consultant who assembled empirical evidence and relevant studies to provide a basis for adjusting ratios downward, the Burlington Planning Board was able to adopt the new parking ratio requirements with almost no opposition; rarely did such reduced on-site parking generate many complaints. In fact, in retrospect, based on the lack of complaints, perhaps they did not reduce parking ratios enough. Nonetheless, the above example is illustrative of how typical suburban zoning requirements can be adjusted, often painlessly and sometimes seamlessly.

Other suburban zoning and site planning requirements can be changed and new tools and methods can be adopted without repudiating the sense of safety and responsibility in site planning that elected officials want to retain as they approve new development or redevelopment. This chapter explores some recent examples of these types of regulatory initiatives, which when taken collectively can be viewed as a significant movement away from the sprawl paradigm of development. Beyond simply citing examples from around the country, this chapter reflects some of the challenges and difficulties that are associated with this effort.

EMERGING TRENDS

A variety of trends are evident throughout the country, consisting of the methods used to mitigate the impact of sprawl and actively shape alternate development outcomes. There is a group of *primary interventions*. These are regulatory strategies that seek to fundamentally change or modify the standard (i.e., Euclidean—see definitions in Chapter 1) zoning concepts. Some of these regulations encourage mixed-use development and discourage single use or uses of the type that promote sprawl. Another category of primary intervention are "form-based" approaches to land use regulation. Here, the intent is to reinforce or shape development based on existing or desired "built form" in a community, rather than regulate by generic zoning districts.

Secondary interventions attempt to address consequences from sprawl promoting patterns of development. Examples of these include revising street standards and modifying access opportunities to existing roadways, thereby discouraging uncoordinated curb openings and encouraging shared access to property.

Primary Interventions

Mixed-Use Zoning

Mixed-use zoning, where commercial development is included with varying levels of residential density, is one of the tenets of the smart growth/antisprawl efforts. It is also frequently a hard sell in predominantly single-family use suburbs. That may be changing. There is increased openness to the idea of allowing commercial strip areas to become more densely developed mixed-use centers.

With suburban communities, it has become easier for planners to sell the idea of a mixed-use development, with a component of affordable housing, as an alternative to a major box store, for example. Additionally, in communities with a large inventory of light industrial land, planners may find it easier to make the case for higher density housing mixed with commercial use in such settings, since these areas are more remote from traditional single-family neighborhoods that are more risk averse and change resistant.

Critics may complain that allowing and concentrating such higher density housing in nonresidentially zoned areas forces the subsequent residents into a kind of exile from single-family neighborhoods and can be viewed as an exclusionary practice. However, it is more appropriate to view such change as another phase in the evolution of suburbia and a welcome tool that holds promise for creating the live/work environments, and will continue to be a significant intervention to address sprawl and encourage improved development outcomes.

Transit-Oriented Development (TOD)

Since Peter Calthorpe's publication of *The Next American Metropolis: Ecology, Community, and the American Dream* in 1993, in which he illustrated the concept of transit-oriented development (TOD) in a compelling way, communities around the country have adopted zoning regulations that allow for more compact, denser, and less parking-intensive development focused around transit stations. Communities now embrace TOD not because they are ideological adherents to Calthorpe's vision, but because they believe that promoting transit, pedestrian access, and mixed-use development near transportation nodes will enhance the quality of life and livability of places.

While many of TOD regulations are less than 10 years old and it is too early for them to be declared universally successful, the fact that communities are using these tools and techniques—or are at least interested in experimenting with them—is a welcome sign, and another trend that shows that prior zoning practices are being reconsidered.

In California, for example, both Los Angeles County and the City of Los Angeles have adopted various incentive provisions to nurture and encourage TOD. The State's Caltrans Web site contains substantial information on TOD development that has been built. Comprehensive TOD zoning regulations are about to be adopted by additional jurisdictions in the state. Pasadena has recently proposed major zoning provisions that would prohibit non-transit-oriented uses, including drive-through businesses, and other non complementary uses such as carwashes and car dealerships. Minimum parking requirements will be reduced by 25 percent and maximum parking allowances for both residential and commercial development are proposed to be established.

In a recent article by Marya Morris (2002), increasing the density of residential areas and employment centers is detailed as a key component for transit-oriented development to come to fruition. New zoning must be developed to generate the alternative development patterns desired, consistent to support and enhance transit and pedestrian-friendly design and mixed land use. In her article, Morris references a variety of cases where TOD is becoming a reality. Seattle's City Council, as part of its Station Area Planning Program, created and adopted a Transit Overlay District around a variety of light rail stations, with density appropriate for the rail use and walkability. Morris also notes Montgomery County, Maryland's, efforts to provide mixed-use zoning around transit stations, with the inclusion of a range of commercial and residential uses, and maximum floor area ratios (FAR) of 3.0. The Transit Station—Mixed Use (TS-M) zone, located closest to the transit station, provides for a variety of mixed uses. The Transit Station—Residential Zone, adjacent to the station area, allows a mix of residential uses with retail and service related uses by special exception, and permits a 2.5 FAR.

Communities in North Carolina have adopted these kinds of alternative development regulations as well. The city and county of Durham are about to adopt a comprehensive Interim Transit Oriented Development-Compact Neighborhood (ITOD-CN) Overlay District to establish complementary mixed-use development and appropriate design guidelines to encourage TOD. Minimum setbacks have been replaced with maximum setbacks, and open space reductions are authorized for those developments where street level and pedestrian amenities are provided. Up to 15 dwelling units are to be allowed in the core area one-eighth mile from the station area, and seven units an acre are to be provided in the support area located a half-mile away. Required parking space reductions are authorized as part of the site plan process. Finally, another North Carolina city, Raleigh, is set to adopt a TOD Overlay District. Their overlay district will prohibit traditional strip retail development, drive-through facilities, and other uses deemed not complementary with a transit-focused orientation.

Form-Based Planning

Another trend in suburban planning practice is form-based planning, which promotes a desired built form as the basis for regulation, rather than predetermined categories of land uses or standard zoning districts such as commercial, industrial, or residential. Regulation based on the *form* of proposed development rather than on generic use or dimensional categories provides an opportunity for communities to shape their physical and functional identity in a manner that is driven less by the conventional development market preferences than by the built form that a community wishes to nurture and protect.

Form-based planning embeds design considerations and prescriptions as a fundamental part of designating zoning districts, going well beyond traditional site-plan review that mainly centers on utility considerations, ingress and egress, vehicular circulation, and basic site layout. It also goes beyond mandatory or advisory design review that is sometimes only selectively applied to certain uses such as large-scale commercial or residential development. This trend is worth celebrating because it is the beginning of establishing "place making" as an integral part of the planning and regulatory process. Form-based approaches to regulation and planning deserve to be viewed as a sprawl reducing regulatory device because initial evidence suggests that the creation of some community form districts will be based upon compact, town-centered development and local vernacular rather than low density, generic designs. At a minimum, many of the emerging form-based districts are designed to preserve the virtues of more traditional neighborhoods and mixed-use development.

At the 1996 American Planning Association National Conference, attendees had an opportunity to hear a presentation from Christopher Duerksen, a consulting planner with Clarion Associates in Chicago, who presented a paper describing the efforts of several communities to substitute traditional zoning regulations with form-, character-, and context-based standards. He credited historic preservation ordinances and standards utilized in preservation-oriented residential districts with providing a foundation for an approach to regulation based on preferred design and development patterns. When compared to conventional zoning, which focuses on separating different types of land uses and often segregates places of work from residences and shopping areas, form-based planning focuses on the design of the built environment with regulatory emphasis on desired building form, vocabulary, and orientation, to ensure greater compatibility of differing land uses.

In his paper and presentation, Duerksen described the form-based approaches in Adams Township, Pennsylvania—two models of development that are based on existing patterns and small-town building styles:

- *Village Model*: This model is directed primarily at large-scale residential planned unit housing projects. It seeks to encourage compact development with the preservation of open space and to focus residential development around village activity centers. The standards associated with the village model define minimum parcel size, open space, and the distance of spacing between similar village developments.
- *Rural Commercial/Industrial Park Model*: This model envisions development closer to the interstate where there is pressure for retail, office, and industrial development. Design standards are tailored to preserve a more rural vocabulary of building form and site layout.

Also highlighted at the same conference session was the Community Form Plans of Louisville and Jefferson County (Kentucky) from its 1993 Comprehensive Plan, called Cornerstone 2020. Form districts are advanced in the Plan with several major goals, including using form districts as a tool for guiding land-use decision making; using form districts that respect the distinct patterns of development emerging from the county in the past; and using form districts to encourage more compact development as an alternative to the current sprawling suburban patterns that are excessively land consuming and too remote from shops, schools, and other pedestrian-centered activities.

In a departure from traditional zoning districts, the form districts are given names such as *traditional neighborhood, downtown, suburban neighborhood, Town Center*, and *Village*, each with its own characteristics and objectives. Each form plan contains examples of the development pattern preferred and specified in the different recommended districts. Regulations establish standards for each form district and are divided based on suburban or traditional form type. As may be expected, building height, design, and orientation as well as site planning, landscaping, sign regulations and lighting are the types of standards specified. In downtown and village districts, for example, buildings are oriented towards the street and parking is subordinated.

At a presentation to planners at the American Planning Association National Planning Conference in Washington, D.C., in 2004, the city planner from Louisville Metro presented the evolution and lineage of this city's form-based approach that began about a decade before. Cited as the precursors of the approach used in Louisville were the mixed-use Town Center in Hercules, California; the Columbia Pike Special Revitalization District in Arlington, Virginia; the Pleasant Hill California BART Station area; and the New Urbanist communities of Kentlands, Seaside, and Celebration, Florida.

After adoption of the Cornerstone 2020 Plan, in January 2003 the city of the Louisville and Jefferson County merged as a municipal entity called Louisville Metro, becoming the sixteenth largest city in the United States, with the population of almost 700,000 residents. Its form districts were ultimately adopted in March 2003, established and organized around the different land uses and desirable development patterns envisioned in the plan, including some of the more noteworthy:

- *Traditional Neighborhood*: focused predominantly on residential uses with streets organized in a grid pattern with sidewalks, situating higher density development near the neighborhood center and nonresidential uses at street corners or the center.
- *Downtown*: composed of commercial, office, civic, medical, and high-density uses, organized around a traditional street grid pattern, with on-street parking and buildings of greater volume and height than most other districts.
- *Traditional Marketplace Corridor*: located along major roadways, characterized by motor vehicle intensive uses, with buildings containing two or more stories offering second story residential or office uses. On-street parking and enhanced streetscapes are emphasized along with a connected street pattern including alleys.
- *Village*: a small-scale village center with mixed uses including median density residential use; that is pedestrian/bicycle/transit friendly; and has development patterns distinguished by open space.
- *Neighborhood*: designated as a predominantly residential use area with a diversity of housing styles and provision for connectivity between uses by automobile, pedestrian, bicycle, and transit.
- *Regional Center*: positioned for high-intensity uses such as a shopping, office, services, entertainment, and medium-to-high density residential use, within which pedestrian activity and shared parking is encouraged. The district is near to major arterials and interstate highway exits.

Ongoing research is needed to determine how influential the evolving form-based approach will be in shaping new settlement patterns and preserving traditional neighborhoods and centers. It is interesting to note that the Louisville-Metro model of form districts is not a "pure" form-based zoning model. Although its regulations were substituted for prior existing dimensional regulations, the underlying use regulations from pre-existing districts stayed the same. Essentially, Louisville-Metro created its form districts using an overlay district approach, superimposing new rules onto an existing zoning district model. Nonetheless, even this hybrid approach to form-based planning is one of the first of its kind to be applied on a city-wide or community-wide basis. Even New Urbanist models have not been applied this comprehensively; rather they have been applied on a project specific, or district specific, basis.

The Transect

Another new and promising approach to regulating the built environment is the concept of the transect. It enables all elements of the built and natural environment to be placed on an integrated scale or gradient, which acknowledges differences in form as one moves along a continuum—typically, from rural to more urbanized environments. It has similarities to form-based planning in that order and appearance are integral to its definition.

The transect, described and advocated by Andrés Duany and Emily Talen (2002), was inspired by environmental thinking; it allows a "slice" or section of a landscape to be viewed in terms of the changes along a continuum of differing habitats and characteristics. A major contribution of the transect is that it enables multiple considerations about built and natural form to be integrated in a manner that allows planners to think about regulatory decisions not as "human versus nature" choices, but rather via a new development guidance system where the built and natural environments are conceptualized as a single linked ecosystem.

Perhaps the most promising aspect of the transect is that it can easily be converted into a customized zoning system, within which different gradations or "transect zones" that move from rural to more urbanized forms. This new system enables communities to dispense with the predetermined, arbitrary, or often rigid hierarchies of Euclidean zoning, substituting transect zones or districts that are based on more form-based classifications.

There are a number of communities around the nation that have begun to experiment with the transect. The transect system is being applied to downtown Sarasota, Florida, as a strategy to address what the city's downtown plan described as "creeping suburbanization," particularly at its edge. Also, as an outgrowth of its comprehensive planning process in 2000, Saratoga Springs, New York, adopted as part of its zoning ordinance new transect categories within the city that were previously identified as special development areas suitable for mixed-use. Three urban transect categories have been adopted: Urban Neighborhood (T-4), Neighborhood Center (T-5), and Urban Core (T-6). Each of these categories has specialized design use and dimensional requirements that emphasize public realm, interconnecting streets, and public spaces, all intended to promote a gradation of an integrated, traditional urban fabric.

The town of Prescott Valley, Arizona, has applied transect-design concepts to its

Highway 69 Corridor. The town has established three distinct transect zones to provide increasing density, transitioning from more rural to more urban development patterns along the corridor. For example, the County Transect is intended to preserve natural features of the rural landscape, with emphasis on native plants, low land-use density, and preservation of public open space. The Town Transect recognizes more formal elements of public space and the design of man-made elements such as sidewalks and berms, signalized intersections, signage lighting, and channelized drainage, with an overall emphasis on visual character and pedestrian amenities. Moving to where building intensity is the highest, the Urban Transect is characterized by a major emphasis on design and pedestrian amenities and low driving speeds. As a result of this new system, Prescott Valley has amended its zoning code to reflect the three Transect Districts. New development standards, permitted uses, and signage regulations are expected to be devised and tailored to the different districts.

Because the transect is still a relatively new concept, it is too early to judge the value of the likely resulting form(s) of development or the Transect concept's contributions to sprawl reduction. Nonetheless, the immersive environment that this model provides, and the initial eagerness of a diverse set of communities to adopt such an approach—especially in areas that are prone to major redevelopment—portends well for multiple interpretations and manifestations of this approach.

Secondary Interventions

Revising Street Standards

A major critique of sprawl is that it involves the creation of unneeded roadway infrastructure. Significant activity is taking place in states, cities, and towns across the United States to develop alternative street standards. Many of these standards have been created to support Traditional Neighborhood Developments (TNDs) and New Urbanist communities, but even conventionally developed residential subdivisions are including reduced street widths.

In 2000, for example, the North Carolina Department of Transportation, Division of Highways, published a guidelines document for the creation of streets in TND developments. These guidelines include curb-to-curb cross-sections and renderings as well as standards for the creation of different street types, including alleys, lanes, streets, avenues, main streets, parkways, and boulevards. The importance of the document to North Carolina and to the local planning community is clear; these guidelines supersede established subdivision standards previously used.

Also in 2000, another guidebook sponsored by the State of Oregon addressed the creation of smaller streets, prepared by a group of stakeholders representing a diversity of design, planning, development, public works, and engineering interests. This effort was fueled in part as a result of a 1991 State Transportation Planning rule that required Oregon communities to attempt to minimize street width while still taking into account the operational needs of various street types. The guidebook includes a variety of reduced street-width scenarios and cross-sections and information on how to address emergency service and response concerns, such as fire response and snow removal. Included in the appendix of this document is a description of Oregon municipalities that have followed the guidebook and reduced their street widths since the inception of the 1991 rule.

While revising street standards in and of themselves will not change overall sprawl patterns of development dramatically, it does provide evidence that engineers, planners, public works officials, and public safety officials are coming together to ensure that this essential piece of American infrastructure does not always result in excessive impervious surface areas, or create environments hostile to pedestrian activity. Most importantly, these examples of revised street standards are a testament to the efforts of communities to make neighborhood livability as important as the utilitarian concerns of vehicular access.

Managing Roadway Access and Parking

Some suburban communities have begun to embrace giving zoning or development incentives to developers who propose projects that share access or reduce access points from their sites and parking lots onto major arterial roads. Some communities are also beginning to provide incentives for more pedestrian-friendly development or for creating access linkages between adjoining properties.

Another noteworthy recent effort linked to this is the effort to subordinate parking in relation to building form, particularly around town centers. In essence, subordination of parking requires that parking areas be placed to the rear and side of buildings, rather than in front-yard setback areas, a practice that frequently dominates the development pattern of commercial strip zones. Of course, this subordination of parking will not transform the predominant established pattern of auto-oriented development, but it can create more walkable environments in which the pedestrian is important.

Included below is a section of the City of Boyne City, Michigan's, 2001 access management requirements:

Section 24.90 Access Management Requirements.

A. Statement of Purpose.
The purpose of this section is to provide access standards which will facilitate through-traffic operations, ensure public safety along roadways, and protect the public investment in the street system, while providing property owners with reasonable, though not always direct, access. The standards are specifically designed for streets whose primary function is the movement of through traffic, as opposed to local streets whose primary function is access to adjacent properties.

Shared Access, Joint Driveways, Parking Lot Connections and
Rear Service Drives.
1. Shared use of access between two (2) or more property owners should be encouraged through use of driveways constructed along property lines, connecting parking lots, and rear service drives, particularly for the following: a) sites within one-quarter (1/4) mile of major intersections; b) sites having dual frontage; c) sites where frontage dimensions are less than three hundred (300) feet; d) locations with sight distance problems; and/or e) along roadway

segments experiencing congestion or accidents. In such cases, shared access of some type may be the only access design allowed.

The above regulation requires that vehicle access be restricted and guided to encourage shared access in areas experiencing congestion. The existence of these regulations clearly indicates that in this community, managing the number of "curb-cuts" becomes a critical management tool. While this paradigm shift does not exist everywhere around the country, and has only been experimented with on a limited basis in suburban locations, there is growing interest in this approach.

In 2002, the City of Junction City, Oregon, adopted its Access Management Ordinance Number 950. In concise and explicit terms, the city articulates the need to protect the substantial public investment in its existing transportation system, reduce the need for remedial measures, and discourage the unplanned subdivision of land that lead to uncoordinated access. Properties that are major traffic generators must provide cross-access drives and pedestrian access to allow circulation between sites. A system of joint-use driveways and corner access easements must be established wherever feasible. The ordinance also provides nonconforming status to existing access patterns within public rights-of-way as appropriate. However, in such cases, when new access or modified access to rights-of-way are requested—for changing or expanding a use that increases trip generation—such changes must be brought into compliance with the ordinance.

The town of Bedford, New Hampshire, adopted access management regulations for its primary commercial corridor (State Route 3). The Bedford ordinance includes detailed requirements for access standards, along with significant bonuses related to reducing impervious area and additional build-out opportunity for those properties that meet established performance standards. However, when Bedford attempted to apply some of the virtues of its performance-based approach used on Route 3, along with more form-based guidelines, to another roadway closer to its town center, significant obstacles were encountered. These obstacles are further detailed in the selected-cases section that follows.

In a related area, a number of communities around the country are embracing the notion that the character of neighborhoods and support for pedestrians should be placed higher in importance above considerations related to rapidly moving automobiles. To this end, communities have implemented traffic calming measures (see Glossary) within residential neighborhoods as well as along major arterial and commercial roadways.

All these provisions and initiatives are works in process. Nonetheless, these types of roadway and parking management initiatives are important measures, reflective of a general municipal awareness of the need to provide safe and adequate circulation and access for pedestrians and vehicles alike, linked to a larger need to not continuously expand infrastructure and increase low-density development at the expense of community character.

Selected Cases and What They Reveal

As communities attempt to inaugurate strategies to address sprawl, they face a wide array of challenges ranging from public fears about increased density to obstacles posed by well-intentioned but often inflexible environmental controls.

Planners working in communities that are in the process of developing antisprawl strategies are confronted with the often ubiquitous fear that changing or abandoning prior zoning controls will lead to uncontrolled development and limited protection for existing land uses. The three cases that follow are reflective of the challenges facing communities that are attempting to address the pervasive sprawl development paradigm.

Harvard, Massachusetts—Incentives Lead the Way to Mixed-Use

Today, local planners are faced with a diminished federal role in funding such important objectives such as the creation of affordable housing and enhancement of public realm. Equally challenging are the limitations on municipalities to raise additional revenue because of property tax caps and reliance on the local tax base to fund public education.

Zoning incentives, which have been in use in many jurisdictions for more than three decades, are likely to remain a method of choice for communities to achieve new and expanded infrastructure and to gain a wide variety of other amenities— such as improvement to the public realm—within the built environment. The smart growth/antisprawl movement has also led communities to explore ways in which zoning bonuses or concessions can promote preferred design and development objectives, including compact forms, mixed-use, and affordable housing opportunities.

While inclusionary housing incentives and requirements have been around for some time, incentives for the promotion of mixed-use development are still relatively new in suburban and exurban locations. In March 2004, the town of Harvard, Massachusetts, a small town of about 6,000 people located west of Boston along the Interstate 495 corridor, known for its pastoral landscapes and small-town atmosphere, adopted a Village Special Permit provision for its main commercial corridor. The provision, which I helped the town draft and revise, exempts mixed-use development from various dimensional and density requirements, while allowing additional floor area for such development. To achieve the benefits available under the new provision, a developer must undergo a variety of tests and demonstrate achievement of the following amenities (as is relevant): land preservation, preservation of unique built assets, and/or provision of low and moderate income housing.

It can be argued that had the town been serious about promoting mixed-use development, it should have enabled such development to occur by right instead of through a discretionary review process. However, that being said, it is important to recognize the enormous change that the town was willing to embrace via this effort. If the experiment is deemed a success by the local planning board and other public officials, and the rewards provided to developers are sufficient enough to yield a few attractive model development outcomes, the town could liberalize the approach within the next decade and allow such development by right instead of only by special permit.

Guilford, Connecticut—Maintaining the Historical Imperative

The town of Guilford, Connecticut, is a suburban community of approximately 21,000 about 30 miles north of New Haven. Over 90 percent of the town's housing stock is single family, and the community has a high per-capita income and well-educated population. The town has one of the largest collections of eighteenth-century homes in the United States, many of which are located near Guilford's Town Green.

In 1999, the town embarked on a project to prepare design guidelines and zoning regulations to help shape the built form of Route 1 East, known also as the "Boston Post Road," an arterial road that contains most of the Guilford's commercial land use and runs parallel to Interstate 95. The town's primary objective in preparing design guidelines and new zoning regulations for Route 1 East was to ensure that sprawl forms of development did not threaten or obscure the local historic resources and built form.

The firm of Icon Architecture from Boston, and Community Planning Solutions of Andover, Massachusetts, were selected by a special committee to assist the town in the effort. Icon assumed the lead role in preparing the design guidelines while Community Planning Solutions was tasked with the preparation of zoning amendments to help implement the planning goals that were established.

In December 2000, the Guilford Planning and Zoning Commission adopted four major amendments to the town's zoning code to help guide future development in accordance with the design and planning principles. The new amendments also included reference to the design guidelines that were prepared for the roadway and newly created zones.

The four major Zoning Amendments adopted by Guilford were the following:

- *Post Road Village Zone District (PV)*: This district established new use regulations, dimensional standards, and incentives to foster development compatible with the town's adjoining Historic District and its built form. Detailed Special Permit criteria were also established for utilization of bonus provisions.
- *Transitional and Service Zone District (TS)*: This district established new dimensional standards, aesthetic considerations, and incentives to foster development more compatible with the Town's traditional built form, but with greater allowance for a contemporary automotive orientation. It has fewer use and dimensional restrictions than the PV Zone.
- *Shopping Center Zone (SC)*: This district was essentially wrapped around a major shopping center area site as an attempt to foster high-quality design within this commercial area, which had become dated. New dimensional standards, aesthetic considerations, and incentives are included in the amendment.
- *Design Review Committee and Design Review Process*: This amendment established a Design Review Committee and Process, along with reference to the new design guidelines, all to be used in the development review process for the districts noted above.

In many respects, the regulations now in effect throughout Guilford's Route 1 East Corridor are an example of form-based approach described previously in this chapter. Over time, it will be interesting to evaluate how effective the regulations are in improving development outcomes along Route 1 East. To date, there is at least initial evidence that the new regulations prevented a large box "superstore" from being sited on the corridor. Also, redevelopment and aesthetic enhancement of a supermarket site in the shopping center zone, in accordance with the new guidelines, has been implemented.

Bedford, New Hampshire—Future Promise Facing Current Barriers

Even with the best intentions, communities undertaking initiatives and proposing implementation techniques to address the unwanted impacts of new development face significant obstacles. Some of these obstacles can pose what appear to be insurmountable barriers to achieve a more compact form of development. The experience of Bedford, New Hampshire, is a case in point.

In 2001, Bedford, a town of almost 20,000 people, set out to ensure that sprawl development would not totally consume the established form and function of the Route 101 corridor within the town, both in and moving away from its traditional town center. After several years of study, a consulting team working with a citizens' advisory committee proposed a new zoning initiative that was highly sympathetic to traditional neighborhood development and supportive of smart growth principles. Listed below are the goals of the new district devised:

The purpose of the Route 101 Performance Zoning District is:

a) To create a commercial district with a character and orientation towards shopping and business services to fill the needs of the local community rather than the regional market;

b) To encourage architecture that reinforces the traditional New England vernacular through the use of appropriate scale, design, materials, color, and detail;

c) To implement the traffic recommendations of the Route 101 Corridor Study 2002, including widening of Route 101 to four lanes, installation of a center vegetated median to restrict left turn movements, minimizing new driveway curb cuts, sharing access between adjacent parcels . . . [etc.]

d) To provide for generously landscaped areas along public rights-of-way that establish a visual pattern of tree-lined streets while calming traffic, and to provide ample screening of parking lots and objectionable features.

In addition, dimensional guidelines were developed to help subordinate parking in relation to buildings and to encourage more compact forms of development. An illustration of some of the dimensional requirements that were proposed is shown in Figure 20.1. Prior to their adoption, the town's Planning Director decided that it would make sense to apply the proposed regulations to sample sites in the targeted corridor. Two independent engineering consulting firms were engaged to ensure there would be more than one interpretation. What the Planning Director discovered as a result of this exercise was that the new ordinance would encourage forms of development that would directly conflict with state standards for wetlands and leach field requirements for subsurface disposal of sewage.

Figure 20.1
The Transect Illustrated: Built Environments

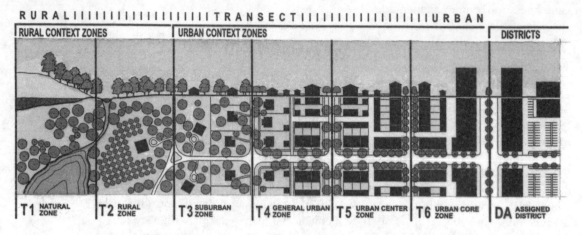

RURAL ||||||||||||||||||||||||| T R A N S E C T ||||||||||||||||||||| U R B A N

| RURAL CONTEXT ZONES | | URBAN CONTEXT ZONES | | | | DISTRICTS |

| T1 NATURAL ZONE | T2 RURAL ZONE | T3 SUBURBAN ZONE | T4 GENERAL URBAN ZONE | T5 URBAN CENTER ZONE | T6 URBAN CORE ZONE | DA ASSIGNED DISTRICT |

Specifically, state regulations mandate that structures be set back a minimum of 50 feet from wetlands, and that they further be set back 75 feet away from leach fields. Because of the presence of wetlands at the rear of lots along the commercial corridor, to be in environmental compliance parking areas would be required to be placed closer to the frontage of the properties, thus thwarting a key design objective of the proposed ordinance in the areas close to the town center. In essence, well-intentioned and scientifically based environmental regulations ran at cross-purposes with the "smarter" form-based regulations that were proposed. Ironically, had the town had public water and sewer available along the corridor, the regulations proposed to create and maintain a "traditional New England vernacular" of "tree-lined streets" and "a vegetated median" would have been workable.

This example is instructive, reminding us that when planners and citizens are looking to retrofit their zoning regulations to establish new development objectives—including sprawl-discouraging standards—it is important to be aware that a one-size-fits-all solution is not likely to work. The good news is that, even though the dimensional requirements proposed in Bedford's targeted zone may not be fully realized, it still is possible to implement a significant portion of the new design guidelines, such as bonus for shared access.

But a more important question arises from this example. Do we face the prospect that some percentage of the innovative regulations we propose will only make sprawl more passably attractive from a design perspective, and do little to change the underlying "genetic structure" of this type of development?

The answer drawn from these three cases and others like them is that higher density, cluster housing, and more concentrated commercial and mixed-use development face significant barriers in small suburban and exurban settings. Many of these barriers, as illustrated by the Bedford example, relate to rigid environmental standards designed to ensure that drinking water is not contaminated by subsurface sewage disposal. So yes, obstacles exist to fully realize smart growth and form-based zoning regulations in many communities that lack public water and sewer. To enable us to experiment and implement new antisprawl development regulations, new technology will be required in the form of environmentally sound treatment systems and other methods of sewage disposal. If this happens in the future, the only limitation to more sustainable development patterns may be any reluctance on the part of planners and/or the public to embrace the available alternatives.

The Challenges Ahead: Celebrating Incremental Change and Embracing Higher Density

It is important to reinforce that many of the efforts described throughout this chapter are "works-in-progress." The alternative regulatory models described can be more realistically and better categorized as examples of "improved development outcome methods" rather than part of a definitive "cure for sprawl."

With no magic bullet to rely on, planners and citizens have to demonstrate both resilience and patience in fostering alternatives to sprawl. As cited earlier, key aspects of the new zoning initiative within the town of Harvard's commercial area involved narrowing the range of permissible uses, encouraging more pedestrian activity and human scale interaction, and reducing automotive orientation, all the while establishing density bonuses and dimensional flexibility to encourage mixed-use development. Will these initiatives reduce automobile traffic or automobile-oriented commercial development entirely? Certainly not. But it is important to celebrate a community's efforts, no matter how small, to address concerns about sprawl and the inadequacies of Euclidean zoning. These early local efforts will provide a foundation for the evolution of like-minded communities away from large sprawling development that otherwise will continue to march unabated in many regions in the country.

This chapter covers only a selection of such planning efforts. It is far too early to gauge success. Major challenges remain for those municipalities that are in the midst of moving in this direction. Perhaps the greatest challenge relates to the issue of how to appropriately accommodate the higher density inherent in more compact forms of development in places reluctant to embrace it.

The planning community is going to have to do a lot more than point to traditional New England villages and places like Beacon Hill and Annapolis as standard-bearers of "good density" and thus, desirable places to live—because so few people can realistically afford to live in these places. We are going to be required, especially in most suburban locations, to identify alternatives to single-family development that will be seen as highly appealing. While it is easy to attack residential sprawl, it is very hard to sell new, high density as the preferred alternative. Working with suburban communities revising their zoning regulations, it is remarkably difficult to make a case for anything higher than 5 dwelling units per acre.

Recent research by Julie Campoli and Alex MacLean, supported by the Lincoln Institute of Land Policy (2002) and published as a working paper, represents a key attempt to help the public visualize different ranges of densities. This type of research-based portrayal is essential in providing citizens and public officials with fluency on the available choices and resulting patterns that come from alternative development practices. Most importantly, MacLean and Campoli draw a distinction between "measured density" and "perceived density" and through their use of aerial photographic images palpably show how alternative design techniques create different forms of neighborhood character and shape our perceptions. What is particularly important about this work is that it illustrates that density, in its variable forms, presents itself as being far from a monolithic pattern; it can be customized and fine-tuned to the context of the built form for each and every community.

Moreover, if state, regional, and local jurisdictions are going to be successful at promoting higher density and more compact forms of development, they need to undertake the following:

- Start with incremental recommendations for changing zoning and development regulations, including removing barriers to mixed-use development, encouraging housing to be developed in highway commercial zoning districts as a substitute for strip malls and megastores, and reducing high parking ratios that create excess impervious surface areas.
- Dispense with using the term "high density" as an all-purpose term for preferred development. Instead, agencies should advocate for context-sensitive design and density that builds upon existing models of development that can be viewed, touched, observed, and understood.
- Showcase outstanding examples of higher density development within the relevant region—or at least within a reasonable distance away—to illustrate how such new patterns are being advocated, so that members of the local community can to make their own judgments.
- Ensure that any new definition of growth that is advocated, such as transit-oriented development, does not get credit for being a smart-growth project simply because it involves higher density, when it offers no connection to transit and no accommodations for the disabled and maintains the high parking ratios that (at least implicitly) encourage auto dependency.
- Encourage local communities to nominate projects for smart-growth and other planning awards for development that is not only of comparatively higher density; select those projects that are land preserving and compatible with the development that it adjoins.
- Campaign for tax incentives or rebates for those who elect to reside in development that represents a viable alternative to sprawl forms of development.

The devil is in the details about smart growth and density. Unless good design is advocated and ensured as part of a new development, communities may occasionally be forced to accept higher density, but they certainly will not enthusiastically embrace or willingly pursue this alternative. And we need to acknowledge and nurture incremental changes in our settlement patterns without repudiating the prior form of development that many of our fellow citizens have elected to reside in.

In the meantime, city and town planners can take the lead role in showcasing where appropriate examples can be found of better development outcome. Most importantly, planners have the ability to craft regulatory interventions that can be strategically placed within conventional zoning codes that will help us embrace viable alternatives to sprawl. One need not say "let us begin" this important mission, since many communities have already inaugurated change. We need only to say, "Let us continue."

BIBLIOGRAPHY

Association for the New Urbanism in Pennsylvania. 2004. *What Is the Transect?* Retrieved April 7, 2004, from http://www.anupa.org/transect.php.

Calthorpe, Peter. 1993. *The Next American Metropolis: Ecology, Community, and the American Dream.* New York: Princeton Architectural Press.

Campoli, J., and A. S. MacLean. 2002. *Visualizing Density: Lower Density Catalog Images, 0.5–10.5 Units per Acre.* Cambridge, MA: Lincoln Institute of Land Policy.

Chael, Marice. 2003. "The SmartCode: A Weapon to Fight the Sprawl War." *The Town Paper* 5(2). Retrieved April 9, 2004, from http://www.tndtownpaper.com/Volume5/smartcode.htm.

City of Boyne City [Michigan]. 2001. Zoning Ordinance. Article XXIV Parking, Loading, and Access Management Standards. Boyne City: Author.

City of Louisville-Metro [Kentucky]. 2000. *Cornerstone 2020 Comprehensive Plan.* Louisville-Metro: Louisville and Jefferson County Planning Commission.

City of Louisville-Metro [Kentucky]. 2003. *Land Development Code.* Louisville-Metro: Louisville Metro Planning Commission, Department of Planning and Design Services.

City of Saratoga Springs [New York]. 2000. Zoning Ordinance. Saratoga Springs: Author.

Duany, A., and E. Talen. 2002. "Transect Planning." *Journal of the American Planning Association* 68 (3): 245–66.

Duerksen, C. J. 1996. "Form, Character, and Context: New Directions in Land Use Regulations." Paper presented at the American Planning Association Annual Conference, April.

Livable Places, Inc. 2003. *Encouraging Transit Villages.* Retrieved April 20, 2004, from http://www.livableplaces.org/policy/todincentives.html.

Morris, M. 2002. "Smart Communities: Zoning for Transit-Oriented Development." *Ideas at Work, Campaign for Smart Growth* 2 (4).

State of California. 2000. *California Transit Oriented Development Database (Caltrans).* Sacramento: Author. Retrieved May 9, 2004, from http://transitorienteddevelopment.dot.ca.gov/.

State of North Carolina. 2000. *Traditional Neighborhood Development (TND) Guidelines.* Raleigh: North Carolina Department of Transportation, Division of Highways.

State of Oregon. 2000. *Neighborhood Street Design Guidelines: An Oregon Guide to Reducing Street Widths.* State of Oregon: Neighborhood Streets Project Stakeholders.

Town of Bedford [New Hampshire]. 2003. Route 101 Corridor Performance Zone Ordinance (draft). Town of Bedford: Author.

Town of Bedford [New Hampshire]. 2003. Architectural Design Guidelines (draft). Town of Bedford: Author.

Town of Guilford [Connecticut]. 2003. Zoning: Chapter 273. Town of Guilford: Author.

Town of Harvard [Massachusetts]. 2004. Amendment to Protective Bylaw—Ayer Road Village Special Permit. Town of Harvard: Author.

Town of Prescott Valley [Arizona]. 2002. The Transect Design Concept. Retrieved April 7, 2004, from http://www.ci.prescott-valley.az.us/Development/PVParkway/transect.

Town of Prescott Valley [Arizona]. 2002. Town Code Amendments. Retrieved April 7, 2004, from http://www.ci.prescott-valley.az.us/Development/PVParkway/town_code.htm.

21

Greenspace and Natural Resource Preservation

Robert Yaro

WHY PRESERVE OPEN SPACE AND NATURAL RESOURCE SYSTEMS?

By its very nature, sprawl consumes open land and destroys its natural, scenic, cultural and recreational values. In response to escalating land consumption in metropolitan and natural resource regions, for more than a century planners have worked to protect open spaces and environmental systems they contain. This chapter briefly outlines the history of urban and metropolitan open space and natural areas protection in the United States. It then describes current approaches to open space protection, and techniques that are being used to protect open land and natural areas in metropolitan regions across the country. It closes with a discussion of what the next steps in efforts to protect these important places from sprawl should be.

BACKGROUND

Setting aside protected public open space is one of America's oldest traditions. In a departure from standard European practice, several early American cities, including New Haven, Philadelphia, Charleston, and Savannah, were designed around networks of squares or greens. William Penn's design for Philadelphia, for example, was organized around several large urban squares and blocks large enough to contain substantial home gardens. Penn's "green country town" was designed to avoid the urban ills that typified London and other seventeenth-century British cities, including overcrowding, congestion, and frequent epidemics.

At the heart of most seventeenth-century New England towns was a town common—land set aside for a range of public uses, from grazing cattle to training the militia. In the center of the region's largest city, the Boston Common was established in 1630, making this America's oldest urban park. Later in the seventeenth century, the Province Lands district on Cape Cod became the nation's first managed natural area, after clear-cutting of the area's ancient forests caused sand dunes to begin to migrate, threatening nearby Provincetown. Finally, the British colonial government practiced an early form of forest management, by prohibiting the cutting of large old growth pine trees. These trees were marked with "the King's Broad Arrow" and reserved exclusively for Royal Navy masts.

In the South most county seats were designed around courthouse squares, which became focal points for the lives of these communities. As the nation expanded in the nineteenth century, most Midwestern and Western county seats were also organized around courthouse squares.

STANDING ON THE SHOULDERS OF GIANTS: OLMSTED, ELIOT, AND MACKAYE

In the mid-nineteenth century, urban centers across the US began to explode around new steam-driven industries and new transportation modes. The rapidly expanding industrial economy attracted millions of immigrants who packed into dense urban neighborhoods, where extreme overcrowding bred crime, disease and vice. Middle- and upper-class residents escaped first to planned, lower-density expansions of urban centers, and then to the suburbs. Horse-drawn streetcars, and later suburban railroads, allowed for the rapid deconcentration of urban centers out into agricultural districts that were also the primary source of food for nearby growing cities. The nation's first planned suburbs, including Llewellyn Park in New Jersey and Riverside outside Chicago (designed by pioneering landscape architect and town planner Frederick Law Olmsted), were organized around protected open spaces. These spaces were not, however, accessible to the urban masses.

In 1850, in response to the city's rapid growth and overcrowding, progressive New Yorkers began a campaign to create a new Central Park which could relieve provide opportunities for recreation in fresh air and sunshine. Until then, none of America's growing urban centers had such a park. Historically, urban parks in British and European cities were the preserve of royalty and the gentry. Only in the nineteenth century did many of these parks become accessible to the general public. In 1833 the British Parliament enacted legislation authorizing the creation of a new generation of urban parks designed to promote public health and activity. In response, new parks in several large cities, including Liverpool's Sefton and Prince's Parks and nearby Birkenhead Park inspired young Frederick Law Olmsted to remark that "we have nothing like this in democratic America." Olmsted modeled his landmark "Greensward" plan for Central Park after these British precedents.

In 1876, Olmsted designed Boston's "Emerald Necklace" of parks and parkways, creating a green framework for Boston's growth. Over the next few decades, dozens of large cities, including Philadelphia, Chicago, Kansas City, Seattle, and San Francisco, emulated New York's and Boston's examples, and built large new urban landscape parks and park systems that continue to shape the development of these cities—many of them also designed by Olmsted's firm.

The rapid expansion of late nineteenth-century cities and overcrowding in inner-city neighborhoods led to several other open space innovations. A national playground movement promoted creation of thousands of these facilities in densely populated urban communities. And then, in the last decade of the nineteenth century, a number of innovations had a far-reaching influence on the shape of twentieth-century cities and suburbs. Olmsted's young partner Charles Eliot advanced two of these concepts. The first of these, in 1891, was Eliot's proposal to create the Massachusetts Trustees of Reservations, the world's first land trust and the model for national trusts all over the world. The Trustees, he envisioned, would "acquire, hold, protect and administer, for the benefit of the public, beautiful and historical places." Then, in 1893, Eliot proposed the creation of Boston's Metropolitan Park System, which would protect large landscapes, including beaches, watersheds, ridgelines, gorges, and other natural and scenic areas throughout the region. That same year, Daniel Burnham's White City plan for Chicago's Columbian Exposition inspired the creation of grand "City Beautiful" boulevards, squares, and esplanades across the country.

In this same era several innovations led to the protection of large rural natural areas. In 1885 New York State created the Adirondack Park, to protect this 5-million-acre area from clear-cutting. In 1905 Congress established the United States Forest Service and transferred the nation's forest reserves to the new agency. And under the leadership of President Theodore Roosevelt, the National Park system was expanded dramatically through the Monuments Act, which allowed presidents to protect important natural, scenic, and archeological sites by adding them to the national park system.

In 1925 Benton MacKaye proposed establishment of a greenbelt around Boston to serve as a "levee" to control expansion of the metropolitan "flood" even then spreading out across the landscape of eastern Massachusetts. In 1929, Charles Eliot II (the nephew of the pioneering landscape architect) further defined this concept into "the Bay Circuit," a greenbelt of trails and protected landscapes stretching in a broad arc around Greater Boston. Today, 150 miles of trails link 79 conservation areas in the Bay Circuit corridor, coordinated by the voluntary Bay Circuit Alliance of dozens of local trail and open-space groups.

POST–WORLD WAR II INNOVATIONS

The second half of the twentieth century brought a new era of innovation in open-space protection and natural area protection. In 1961 President Kennedy established the Outdoor Recreation Resources Review Commission (ORRRC), which proposed creation of the federal Land and Water Conservation Fund, a dedicated federal funding source for federal and state open space efforts.

In the late 1960s and early 1970s three books created a new environmental consciousness and changed the way the public and the planning profession looked at open space and the environment. Rachel Carson's *Silent Spring* focused the public on the threats of habitat destruction caused by human activity. Ian McHarg's *Design with Nature* demonstrated ways that metropolitan and rural development could be organized around natural systems, to both protect landscapes and resources and to improve community design. And William H. Whyte's *The Last Landscape* underscored both the threat that sprawl posed to important landscapes and the potential to marshal a new generation of conservation techniques to protect open spaces. The resulting environmental movement, embodied by Earth Day in 1970, resulted in a number of federal and state initiatives to protect open space and natural resources. These included:

- *Environmental Impact Statements*: The National Environmental Policy Act (NEPA) of 1969 requires that an environmental impact statement be prepared before any major action is taken requiring federal permits or funding. It also requires that alternatives to potentially damaging actions be identified in these statements. NEPA and similar legislation enacted in dozens of states have been used to protect important open spaces, such as New York's Storm King Mountain.
- *Wetlands Protection*: Section 404 of the Clean Water Act, first enacted in 1972, regulates the filling or destruction of important wetlands. Most states have adopted similar programs to protect these important natural areas, which now protect millions of acres of coastal and inland wetlands.
- *Endangered Species Protection*: The 1972 Endangered Species Act has been used to prevent destruction of important species and their habitats across the country. In several large natural resource areas, including the salmon habitat in the Pacific Northwest and the coastal heaths of Southern California, regional management plans have been developed that control development in these areas. State Natural Heritage programs in every state promote state actions to inventory and protect important natural areas.
- *Protecting Public Open Spaces from Intrusions*: Section 4F of the U.S. Department of Transportation Act of 1966 prohibits construction or expansion of highways in designated public parks or preserves, unless no "feasible or prudent" alternatives exist. Section 4F has been used to protect hundreds of parks from highway departments that had previously considered open spaces to be no more than reserved highway rights-of-way.
- *Coastal Zone Management*: The Coastal Zone Management Act of 1972 authorizes the states to prepare coastal zone management plans designed to balance conservation and economic development goals. Some states, including North Carolina, Oregon, and California, have used this authority to enact sweeping coastal preservation and public access programs.
- *Rails-to-Trails*: The National Trails System Act of 1983 authorizes preservation of unused rail corridors for trail use. The 1991 Intermodal Surface Transportation Efficiency Act (ISTEA) authorized use of federal funds to promote purchase and construction of rail trails. More than 12,500 miles of rail trails have been established, coordinated by the national Rails-to-Trails Conservancy.
- *State, County, and Municipal Open-Space Bonds*: Since the early 1960s, most states and a growing number of counties and municipalities have enacted bond issues for protection of important open spaces. New Jersey, Florida, Maryland, Massachusetts, and New York have led these efforts, each spending more than a billion dollars to purchase open space. In recent years, ballot measures at the state and local level across the country have protected millions of acres of open space.

In 2002, voters across the country approved 141 bond issues totaling more than $10 billion for open-space protection. Then again in the November 2004 election more than 125 communities in 26 states approved bond-issue measures totaling $325 billion. These initiatives are being funded from a wide array of sources, ranging from state general funds to new dedicated sales taxes. This widespread support for open-space protection suggests that even where voters are unwilling to support new smart-growth initiatives, they are generally prepared to support new taxes devoted to open space protection.

- *Regional Commissions, National Reserves, and "Greenline" Parks*: In the 1970s, several regional land-use regulatory commissions were established to protect large landscapes and resource systems. These were inspired by New York's "Blue Line" around the Adirondack Park, in which several million acres within a designated blue line received protection from inappropriate development and use within the state constitution.

  The most important of these were the Adirondack Park Agency and the New Jersey Pinelands, Lake Tahoe, Santa Monica Mountains, and California Coastal Commissions. These agencies adopt regional land-use management plans and regulate development and conservation activities. The Omnibus Parks Act of 1978 provided federal support for the New Jersey Pinelands and Santa Monica Mountains "national reserves," in what was anticipated to be a new national network of reserves and "greenline" parks. Several new federal greenline conservation areas, from Idaho's Sawtooth Mountains to the Florida Everglades–Great Panther Swamp area to the Northeast's Appalachian Highlands, have been established over the past two decades. Proposals for a new greenline National Park in the Northern Forests of New York, Vermont, New Hampshire, and Maine have languished, however.

  A second generation of regional land-use regulatory programs has emerged since the late 1980s, including the Cape Cod and Long Island Pine Barrens Commissions and the Columbia Gorge National Scenic Area (the latter administered by the USDA Forest Service and the several counties in Oregon and Washington State). In June 2004, New Jersey adopted legislation creating a regional land-use regulatory program for its Highlands region. Federal designation of a larger greenline preservation area stretching from Pennsylvania across New Jersey, New York, and Connecticut, was signed by President George W. Bush in November 2004.

- *The Contemporary Land Trust Movement*: Inspired by the success of the Massachusetts Trustees of Reservations and other land trusts, hundreds of new local and regional land trusts have been established in recent years. More than 1300 land trusts now operate in all 50 states, most of them established since 1980. These organizations have protected more than 6.5 million acres of open space, through purchase or donation of land or easements. The Land Trust Alliance serves as a national clearinghouse for information and activities among the nation's land trusts.

- *The Greenways Movement*: Since the 1970s a national greenways movement has emerged, with public and private organizations advancing protection of green corridors organized around trails, rivers, mountain ranges, and other resource systems. Many of these systems involve trail corridors linking protected lands. Since 1990 several states have established statewide greenway systems to coordinate planning and land conservation efforts. The most ambitious greenway proposal in the country is the East Coast Greenway, which will ultimately stretch along the urban corridor stretching from Florida to Maine.

- *Farmland Preservation*: In 1976 Suffolk County on Long Island began the nation's first program for the purchase of development rights for prime farmland. Since then, several states, including Massachusetts, Connecticut, New Jersey, Pennsylvania, and Maryland, and a number of counties have adopted similar efforts to protect prime agricultural lands, resulting in hundreds of thousands of acres of protected farmland in suburban and exurban areas threatened by metropolitan sprawl.

- *Land Banking and the Community Preservation Movement*: In 1985 the Massachusetts legislature established the Nantucket Land Bank, which was empowered to acquire open space on this offshore resort island financed by a 2 percent real estate transfer tax. In the years that followed, Martha's Vineyard and Cape Cod established similar programs. In 1998 New York State authorized five Eastern Long Island Communities to create Community Preservation Funds for open-space protection, also financed through real estate transfer taxes.

  Finally, in 2000 Massachusetts adopted statewide legislation empowering municipalities to create Community Preservation Funds, supported by local property taxes. This program requires that a portion of the funds go towards historic preservation and affordable housing in addition to open-space protection. The Commonwealth of Massachusetts has also initiated a statewide "build-out" analysis and has created a process to assist communities in integrating land-use planning with community preservation efforts. Community Preservation initiatives are now being considered in Connecticut, New York, and other states, suggesting that this could become a broader, and even a national movement.

BEST PRACTICES IN OPEN-SPACE PRESERVATION

Today, after more than a century of innovation in metropolitan and rural open-space protection, planners have a comprehensive set of tools needed to effectively protect critical open spaces from sprawl. The three key categories of tools in this toolbox are:

Intellectual and Planning Framework

The focus of open-space preservation has shifted from the parcel level (i.e., the protection individual parcels of land or individual parks) to the regional, or system level (i.e., the protection of regional networks or systems of open spaces and parks). While many open space initiatives are still organized around the goal of protecting individual parcels of land, their actions are more likely to be carried out in the context of a larger conservation objective, say the preservation of an entire ecosystem or landscape, which could be a watershed, estuary, river valley, or mountain range, or the landscape of an entire county or district.

Open-space preservation is also conducted in the larger intellectual and planning framework created by the smart growth, new urbanism, and limited development movements. Since the 1980s these movements have swept the country and fundamentally changed the way planners think about and manage sprawl and preserve land. These movements have created a new framework for planning at every level, from the state level to regional to the city to the neighborhood and subdivision level.

Smart Growth

More than 20 states now have some kind of state smart-growth or growth-management plan. The most effective of these, in such states as Washington, Oregon, Maryland, and Delaware, require that counties and municipalities designate development and conservation areas. A growing number of counties in these and other states have also adopted county plans that achieve the same goal. These plans, and consistent county and municipal zoning regulations, create a powerful framework for state, regional, and local open space protection plans.

Several states, including Washington, Oregon, California, and Minnesota, authorize or direct counties and municipalities to designate "urban-growth boundaries" identifying urban limits beyond which conservation zoning and rural uses will predominate. This movement was dealt a serious blow in the November 2004 elections, when Oregon voters adopted an amendment to the state constitution requiring compensation to property owners whose values were reduced as a result of the state's growth-management program.

In recent years, several metropolitan regions, including Salt Lake City, Austin, Chicago, Phoenix, Atlanta, and Los Angeles, have conducted regional "visioning" processes, in which thousands of citizens help shape regional growth strategies. These strategies are being used to underpin regional growth management strategies that include designation of large conservation areas at the metropolitan fringe and conservation corridors within built-up areas.

New Urbanism

While much of the New Urbanism movement has focused on the design of neighborhoods and new communities, several of the movement's leading proponents, including Peter Calthorpe and John Fregonese, are working at the regional scale to promote more compact, coherent, livable, and transit-oriented communities. Their plans for Sacramento, Salt Lake, and other regions are organized around the notion of limiting suburban sprawl through creation of urban growth boundaries and protection of conservation areas beyond these limits.

Limited Development and Conservation Subdivisions

Over the past generation a growing number of not-for-profit and for-profit conservation and development organizations have utilized limited development techniques to achieve both conservation and development goals. Since 1990, Randall Arendt and other planners have used the term "conservation subdivision" to describe development projects designed around the protection of important natural features. These subdivisions cluster development in areas with limited conservation values, and organize them around permanently protected natural features. These developments can achieve both the financial and conservation objectives of their proponents, creating a "win-win" situation for both environmentalists and developers. Some critics have maintained, however, that many of these projects represent a kind of "designer sprawl," cleaner and greener than conventional subdivisions, but sprawling nonetheless.

Local and regional land trusts and national conservation groups, such as the Nature Conservancy and the Trust for Public Land, and private, for-profit groups, such as New Hampshire's Lyme Timber and Florida's St. Joe's Forestry Company, are using limited development and conservation subdivision techniques to protect hundreds of thousands of acres of open space across the country.

The Open Space Protection "Toolbox"

A full range of techniques are now available to planners pursuing protection of individual parcels, landscape features, or entire ecosystems. These range from the oldest technique—the acquisition of a "fee-simple" interest in land (that is to say, all the rights and interests in a parcel of land) through purchase, donation, or bargain sale—to a range of "less-than-fee" techniques, including the purchase, donation, or regulation of a range of conservation easements. Less-than-fee conservation easements or restrictions include:

- *Conservation easements*, restricting the development potential on a piece of land;
- *Rights-of-way*, permitting public access to a trail corridor or natural feature, such as a beach or other resource;
- *Scenic or view easements*, preserving key vistas or outlooks for public enjoyment; and
- *Agricultural preservation restrictions*, limiting the use of a parcel of land to agricultural activities.

Institutions and Enabling Statutes

Whereas a century ago open-space protection might be carried out by a public park agency, today a broad range of public and private conservation groups are engaged in these activities. These range from special-purpose park districts and preservation groups to regional commissions to local, regional, or statewide land trusts or special-purpose groups, such as The Nature Conservancy or the Trust for Public Lands. Public land conservation agencies also frequently work in partnership with private advocacy groups or not-for-profit groups.

Over the past decade a number of sophisticated metropolitan and rural open-space and environmental protection initiatives have emerged that integrate the full range of the initiatives and techniques outlined above. Several large metropolitan regions, including New York, Philadelphia, Chicago, and San Francisco, have regional open space protection programs coordinated by non-profit planning and advocacy groups that incorporate all of these elements.

- *San Francisco's Greenbelt Alliance*. Established in 1969 as The People for Open Space, for nearly four decades San Francisco's Greenbelt Alliance has promoted land-acquisition and smart-growth efforts in the nine-county Bay Area region, focusing on protecting a permanent greenbelt around the urbanized portion of the region. In the late 1980s Greenbelt Alliance was one of the pioneers in promoting reuse of abandoned and underutilized "brownfield" sites throughout the Bay Area. In the 1990s the organization led campaigns in San Jose and several other municipalities to create permanent "urban growth boundaries" (UGBs) to constrain the region's voracious appetite for open land.

- *Chicago's Open Lands Project*. Established in 1963, Chicago's Open Lands Project has promoted the conservation of more than 43,000 acres of open space and advanced greenway and conservation projects across the six-county Greater Chicago region. Among Open Land's key successes have been creation of the Illinois and Michigan National Heritage Corridor, the first such designation in the country; protection and restoration of large areas of the former Joliet Arsenal; and creation of the Midewin National Tall Grass Prairie.

- The *GreenSpace Alliance of Southeastern Pennsylvania*. Established in 1992 by the Pennsylvania Environmental Council, the Greenspace Alliance is a coalition of more than 100 open-space advocacy groups in the Philadelphia metropolitan area. The Alliance has created a Greenplan to advance conservation of the region's most important open spaces and natural resource systems.

A NEW YORK REGION CASE STUDY: REGIONAL PLAN ASSOCIATION'S METROPOLITAN GREENSWARD

The oldest metropolitan Greenspace protection organization in the country is the Regional Plan Association (RPA), established in 1921 to create a long-range, comprehensive plan for conservation and development in the New York–New Jersey–Connecticut metropolitan region. RPA's first regional plan called for protection of a diverse set of urban, suburban, and rural parks, many of them connected by parkways that would make them accessible to metropolitan residents who increasingly had access to automobiles. Much of RPA's first plan was completed during the Great Depression through the actions of master builder Robert Moses and other public agencies funded by the Works Progress Administration and Civilian Conservation Corps. RPA also enlisted the support of wealthy private land owners and philanthropists, including the Rockefeller and Harriman families. As a result of these efforts, by the early 1960s the Tristate region had an open space system totaling more than one-half million acres, much of it linked by the nation's most extensive parkway system.

In the 1960s, as part of its Second Regional Plan, Regional Plan Association initiated a new campaign called "The Race for Open Space" to protect the region's dwindling supply of open land that was threatened by rampant suburban sprawl. In the process, RPA coined the term "open space" and initiated a multidecade campaign to protect several hundred thousand acres of open land across the New York metropolitan region. Under the leadership of biologist William Niering, RPA organized its regional open space protection strategy around the emerging concept of ecological systems. As part of this effort, RPA also led efforts to create the nation's first urban national park, Gateway National Recreation Area, and three other federal preserves: the Fire Island National Seashore, the Upper Delaware River National Recreation Area, and the Great Swamp National Wildlife Refuge. The goal of all these projects was to bring federal park and conservation areas into the heart of the nation's largest urban region. These actions inspired other national urban parks, including San Francisco's Golden Gate National Recreation Area, Cleveland's Cuyahoga Valley National Recreation Area, and the Boston Harbor Islands National Recreation Area. A number of state parks and preserves, notably Minnewaska State Park in upstate New York, were also established as a result of RPA's efforts.

As part of its "Race for Open Space," under the leadership of William H. White, RPA also promoted creation of a network of local land trusts, inspired by Charles Eliot's pioneering vision nearly 70 years earlier. The "Race for Open Space" resulted in the expansion of the region's open-space network to more than one million acres, through concerted action by local, state, and federal governments.

In the 1990s, as part of its Third Regional Plan, RPA took a fresh look at land consumption in the region and at the threat continued exurban sprawl was having on the region's "green infrastructure" of public water supply watersheds, rare plant and animal communities, estuaries, and recreational and scenic lands. These areas constituted literally millions of acres of land that could not be protected by traditional land acquisition techniques alone. At the same time, it was clear that there was no political will for the "top-down" land-use regulatory approach that had produced the Adirondack Park Agency, the Catskill Park, and the New Jersey Pinelands Commission a generation before.

For these reasons, RPA proposed the creation of a network of 11 large "regional reserves" constituting whole ecosystems and watersheds. RPA also proposed that these be managed through a new generation of "bottom-up" regional land-use regulatory commissions. Over the past decade three regional reserves have been designated, all encompassing important surface- and groundwater supplies.

New Jersey Pinelands

As noted earlier in this chapter, one of the largest regional reserves, the one-million-acre New Jersey Pinelands, located in Southern New Jersey, was protected since 1978 by the New Jersey Pinelands Commission, a state-mandated regional land-use regulatory commission. The Commission's management plan zones most of the Pines for exclusive forest and farm uses and permits only very low-density residential development outside of designated town centers.

Long Island Pine Barrens

The first of the new generation of regional reserves in the Tristate region is the Long Island Pine Barrens, a 100,000-acre area 60 miles east of New York City containing Long Island's most extensive groundwater resources and an extensive array of rare species and threatened ecosystems. The Long Island Central Pine Barrens Commission was established in 1993 after years of litigation over unplanned development in this district in Eastern Long Island. The Commission was established at the request of participating municipalities and is controlled by municipal and county governments. The state of New York provided important incentives for local governments to establish and participate in the commission, including state funds for land conservation and an indemnification process through which the state's Attorney General represents participating municipalities when they are sued over their land use regulations.

The Pine Barrens management plan zones areas into core preservation and compatible growth zones, permitting no development in the former and limited development in the latter. State, county, and municipal open-space funds are used to purchase easements or fee-simple interests in the core preservation zone. In addition, the commission operates a land bank that is used to transfer development rights from the core to the compatible growth zone and other nearby areas that have the infrastructure to support more intensive development.

The New York City Watersheds

In the mid-1990s RPA participated in a similar campaign to preserve New York City's public water supply watersheds, located as much as 120 miles north of the city, which were threatened by sprawl and urban and agricultural runoff. As a result of these threats, the United States Environmental Protection Agency threatened to require filtration of the city's water supply, which remained the only large unfiltered supply in the country.

To avoid filtration, the state and city of New York worked together to create a comprehensive management program for the city's watersheds, through accelerated land acquisition and land-use regulation in these areas. In 1997, the Environmental Protection Agency approved a filtration avoidance agreement. As a part of this program, the city also funds a number of programs to promote economic development and improve infrastructure in watershed communities and to improve land-stewardship activities in these places. The total cost of the program is roughly $1 billion—a lot of money, to be sure, but only a small fraction of the estimated $6 billion in capital expenses and the quarter-billion dollars a year in operating expenses that construction and operation of filtration plants would entail.

New Jersey–New York Highlands

Another regional reserve that is being protected as a result, in part, of RPA's advocacy is the Appalachian Highlands, straddling the New York–New Jersey border, which serves as the principal public water supply for Northern New Jersey. RPA began working with the USDA Forest Service and state agencies in the early 1990s to identify priority conservation areas. In the late 1990s, RPA and other conservation groups promoted the protection of the 25,000-acre Sterling Forest on both sides of the state border—the last remaining large conservation priority identified in RPA's first regional plan six decades earlier. In 2004, RPA and other participants in the Highlands Coalition—a broad alliance of environmental and civic groups—led a successful advocacy campaign to promote adoption by the New Jersey state legislature of the Highlands Water Protection and Planning Act. This law authorizes creation of a comprehensive management plan for the Highlands, and identifies priority conservation areas where development will be restricted. And then, in the fall of 2004, the U.S. Congress enacted the federal Highlands Conservation

Act, authorizing protection of the larger Highlands district stretching from Pennsylvania to Connecticut and authorizing expenditure of $110 million in federal funds for this purpose over a 10-year period.

Long Island Sound Stewardship Reserve

In 1999, RPA proposed the creation of another regional reserve, which would protect Long Island Sound, the region's largest estuary. In partnership with two other conservation groups, National Audubon and Save the Sound, RPA proposed creation of a Long Island Sound Stewardship system that would protect a network of hundreds of open spaces fronting on the sound and reclaims dozens more. RPA and its partners then convinced the states of New York and Connecticut and the U.S. Environmental Protection Agency to incorporate the Stewardship System into the federally authorized Long Island Sound Comprehensive Management Plan. Federal legislation designed to implement and help fund the Stewardship System was passed by the U.S. Senate in the fall of 2004 but failed to pass the House of Representatives. A renewed effort to enact this legislation will be made in the Congress in 2005.

New York–New Jersey Harbor

Since completion of its Third Plan in 1996 RPA has also led efforts to protect and reclaim another regional reserve, the New York–New Jersey Harbor. The harbor is distinguished from the other reserves in that it is located at the region's urban core, not its undeveloped periphery. Conservation efforts will, therefore, include both preservation of remaining open spaces as well as reclamation and restoration of bypassed and derelict waterfront sites. RPA's and other organizations' public efforts have been focused on creating a new network of state and federal parks and greenways throughout the harbor and promoting the creation of a conservation and restoration plan for the Harbor's estuarine resources.

Among the major new parks created over the past decade has been the Governor's Island National Monument, which will soon be complemented by a new 60-plus acre city-state park elsewhere on this historic 174-acre property. The National Monument is part of a newly established National Parks of New York Harbor, encompassing Liberty and Ellis Islands, the Gateway National Recreation area, and a dozen other historic parks in Manhattan.

A new Hudson River Park is being built in a joint venture between the city and state of New York along the length of Manhattan's West Side, from the Battery to 59th Street. From 59th to 72nd Street a new 34-acre, privately financed park is being built as part of Donald Trump's Riverside South project. From there north to Manhattan's northern tip, Olmsted's Riverside Park contains a new continuous bikeway along the Hudson Riverfront. On the Brooklyn waterfront, a new Brooklyn Bridge Park is being planned, along with a waterfront Greenway stretching from the Brooklyn Bridge to Coney Island.

Since 1995 all three states in the New York metropolitan region have been active in promoting open space protection through purchase and other means. Both New York and New Jersey have proclaimed the goal of protecting at least one million acres apiece, and more than $1.5 billion has been committed to this goal. RPA continues to strongly support these efforts, in partnership with a broad array of state, regional and local conservation groups.

CONCLUSION

Twenty-first-century open-space protection efforts can learn from more than a century of experience and innovation in the field. This experience suggests several key prerequisites for successful metropolitan open space protection strategies:

- *Clear priorities*: Protection priorities must be clearly defined and broadly supported.
- *The 3 "Ps"—patience, persistence, and perseverance*: A long-term vision and a persistent commitment to action are needed, and opportunities must be seized when they present themselves.
- *Long-term funding commitments*: Commitments to public and private funding must remain in place for decades and, in some cases, for even generations.
- *Creativity and entrepreneurship*: Innovative solutions will be needed to protect large landscapes, frequently involving a number of the techniques in the open-space protection toolbox.
- *Appropriate scale*: To protect significant natural resource systems and to shape metropolitan growth patterns, open-space protection must be carried out at the regional, not parcel, scale, encompassing thousands or even hundreds of thousands of acres.
- *Partnerships*: Increasingly, successful open-space protection efforts—particularly for large-scale landscapes—require partnerships between groups and sectors, as well as among different units of government.
- *Leadership*: Effective open-space protection initiatives require strong and effective leadership, whether from the public, civic, or business sectors, and, frequently, partnerships of all three sectors.

22

Regional Equity and Smart Growth: Opportunities for Advancing Social and Economic Justice in America

Angela Glover Blackwell and Radhika K. Fox

INTRODUCTION: EQUAL OPPORTUNITY IN THE TWENTY-FIRST CENTURY

The year 2004 marked the fiftieth anniversary of *Brown v. Board of Education*, the historic Supreme Court ruling that advanced the doctrine that separate is not equal in public education. This landmark decision is a cornerstone of civil rights laws that seek full inclusion and participation for all residents of the United States.[1] The Brown decision opened an important door to opportunity for the nation's children of color and helped usher in a full-fledged struggle for inclusion in other important areas—most notably voting, employment, and housing.

Reflecting on the past 50 years, it's clear that, despite impressive gains, the promise of the *Brown* decision—and what it signaled for America—remains unfulfilled. Because of *Brown*, segregation in public schools is illegal. Yet segregation and inequality continue. In metropolitan Boston, for example, 7 in 10 white students attend schools in the outer suburbs that are over 90 percent white, while almost 8 in 10 African American and Latino students attend schools in the city of Boston or in one of the urbanized satellite cities.[2] In the state of California, the problem of critically overcrowded schools disproportionately affects students of color who attend urban schools. Seventy-one percent of California's most severely overcrowded schools are located in large cities. Within these schools, 90.4 percent are students of color (68.2% Latino, 11.9% African American, 7% Asian).[3] As the more affluent members of our society move out of central cities and older suburbs, public investments in schools follow. Settlement patterns, and the development decisions and public policies that support these patterns, are systematically maintaining separate and unequal school systems across metropolitan regions.

The same dynamic is at work in housing. While housing discrimination has been outlawed, housing today is starkly divided by race and income. Historically, the Federal Housing Administration (FHA) restricted loans on a racial basis. It supported and encouraged the movement of middle-class, white households to the suburbs, moving population and resources out of central cities.[4] Current state and local practices continue to reinforce these regional disparities. For instance, suburban jurisdictions often enact exclusionary land-use policies (such as requiring expensive multicar garages or allowing only single-family homes on large lots) that make it very difficult for lower-income families to find places to live in newer developments.

Low-income people are stuck and concentrated in disinvested communities, which are more likely to be located in urban centers and older, declining, inner-ring suburbs. One telling indicator of this decline is the proliferation of vacant and abandoned properties. For example, in the city of Detroit, there are over 50,000 vacant and abandoned properties.[5] Concentrated poverty is high in many urban communities, and poverty rates are rising in older suburbs. The number of people living in suburban areas with high poverty concentrations shot up by more than 121 percent from 1980 to 2000.[6]

While laws have been established to promote equal employment, real access to jobs has diminished as employers have moved out of older urban areas to suburban office parks. As of 1996, only 16 percent of jobs in the average metropolitan area were within three miles of the central business district.[7] The challenge of regional access to jobs and services is further exacerbated due to limited public transit options, as public policy and funding continues to favor investments in roads over other transportation options.

Regional growth and development patterns also affect people's health. A recent study conducted in the lower-income, African American community of Harlem in New York City, found that 25.5 percent of the children have asthma, compared to the national average of 6 percent.[8] As a hub for regional movement of people and goods in New York, the Harlem community has a heavy concentration of diesel bus and truck traffic, and the tiny particles in diesel exhaust are thought to be a serious asthma trigger.

Clearly, many low-income people and communities of color are now isolated in neighborhoods that lack good schools, jobs, basic services, and social networks. Until relatively recently, the relationship between regional development patterns and inequality/inequity had not been widely addressed by social justice advocates, nor has it been deeply embedded in the search for solutions. Five years ago, in the first translation paper published by the Funders' Network, we asserted that development and growth patterns were a tremendous roadblock to fully realizing social and economic justice in America. Since then, the pursuit of regional equity has become an important and growing part of the work of advocates for social and economic justice and of proponents for better growth management. A growing number of advocates are employing a range of strategies to connect low-income communities and people of color to resources and opportunities available throughout metropolitan areas. Advocates for smarter growth strategies now have an opportunity to advance regional equity in policy and development decisions. This chapter, which examines the evolution of regional equity as an organizing framework for policy and practice, has three sections:

1. *The Concept, Appeal, and Use of Regional Equity* reviews the use of the regional equity framework by diverse groups across the country;

2. *A Framework for Action* considers four arenas for action—living near regional opportunity, linking people to regional opportunity, promoting equitable public investment, and making all neighborhoods stable, healthy, and livable—to realize the vision of regional equity; and

3. *The Way Forward* surveys the resources needed to deepen and strengthen the growing regional equity movement and strengthen alliances with important partners, such as those advocating for smarter choices about how communities grow.

THE CONCEPT, APPEAL, AND USE OF REGIONAL EQUITY

The previous discussion revealed how regional development patterns impact nearly every arena of potential opportunity for low-income people and communities of color. Current development patterns are not the natural result of the free-market economy. Rather, they flow from public policies that have provided powerful incentives for suburban growth, at the expense of central cities, older suburbs, rural communities, and their low-income residents.

In response to these patterns of regional growth and investment that have severely disadvantaged many families and communities, regional equity has emerged as an important goal or concept around which to organize advocacy and action to promote social and economic justice. At its core, regional equity seeks to ensure that individuals and families in all communities can participate in and benefit from economic growth and activity throughout the metropolitan region—including access to high-performing schools, decent affordable housing located in attractive neighborhoods, living wage jobs, and proximity to public transit and important amenities, such as supermarkets and parks.

In today's economy, the region is the backdrop against which opportunity and exclusion play out in America. When regional equity is prioritized as a goal, development and investment choices facing a community are evaluated in terms of how growth can create opportunity for all residents, helping to build a strong, healthy region.

It is increasingly apparent to advocates for social and economic justice that efforts to improve the quality of life in low-income communities of color cannot be successful without using regional analysis and action. Efforts seeking access to quality education, decent housing, jobs, and services will succeed only by changing the way resources, investments, and opportunities are allocated throughout regions.

When the concept of regional equity began to emerge in the late 1990s as a mechanism for understanding and changing opportunity structures in the United States, it was unclear if it would be embraced by social justice advocates. These advocates struggle to do the difficult on-the-ground work of protecting rights, rebuilding neighborhoods, and ensuring the availability of essential social services in low-income communities. In recent years, societal apathy and dwindling resources have made their work even more urgent and difficult. Would a regional equity framework help with these challenges? Additionally, to be effective in the regional arena, it is clear that expertise in planning, transportation, public finance, and zoning will be required—skills not traditionally associated with the social justice arena outside of community development. In the 1990s, many of the conversations about regionalism were driven by a smart-growth perspective, and rarely did these discussions lead with race and equity. Moreover, there had been limited participation from people of color in the smart-growth movement. Could meaningful coalitions be built between proponents for smart growth and advocates for equity who would necessarily introduce race and the tough challenge of inner-city disinvestment into the mix?

It is remarkable how quickly the regional equity framework has taken root in the minds and practices of change agents across the country. Many local and national organizations see that it offers a useful analysis of the structural roots of concentrated poverty in America. More importantly, regional equity ties that analysis to strategies and policies to more fairly steer development and investment.

As a vehicle for extending opportunity, regional equity has been inspired and informed by the movements for sustainable development, smart growth, and environmental justice. The quest for regional equity also builds on the vast experience and wisdom of other important social change movements. From the civil rights movement, regional equity advocates adopt a racial perspective for analyzing development and growth patterns. Building on neighborhood revitalization and community development efforts, regional equity efforts recognize that "place matters" and that revitalizing the physical environment of distressed communities improves outcomes for residents who live there. Drawing from the community building movement, the regional equity movement seeks holistic, comprehensive approaches to the needs of low-income communities, underscoring the connection between "people"- and "place"-based strategies.

The deep interest in this perspective was reflected in the enthusiastic response to Promoting Regional Equity: A National Summit on Equitable Development, Social Justice, and Smart Growth, held in the fall of 2002 and cohosted by PolicyLink and the Funders' Network for Smart Growth and Livable Communities. The conference drew over 650 community organizers; neighborhood, community, and faith leaders; public officials and academics; and representatives of foundations, regional agencies, and state and national policy organizations—half of whom were people of color and working on a range of issue areas. The summit created a rich exchange of strategies and the first major, public national coming together of regional equity and smart growth advocates.

Many smart-growth proponents recognize regional equity as an opportunity to connect to new constituents and bring an urgent human dimension to policy discussions focused on planning, density, and architecture. This recognition was reflected in the fourth annual 2004 New Partners for Smart Growth conference in Portland, Oregon. Participants focused on social equity through the opening plenary and a series of panel sessions that provided concrete tools and techniques for ensuring that equity concerns are at the forefront of the smart growth movement.

Adoption of Regional Equity

Indicators of the growing adoption of the regional equity framework include:

- Growth in research that documents regional inequities;
- Diverse constituencies and coalitions engaged in policy campaigns;

- Community organizing and base building; and
- Funder engagement and leadership.

Growth in Research That Documents Regional Inequities

A growing body of research documenting regional inequities has fostered broad dialogue and has served as a catalyst for action. Leading academics such as Myron Orfield, John A. Powell, and David Rusk[9] are framing these issues for a wide variety of audiences. Additionally, PolicyLink and other policy and advocacy organizations such as Working Partnerships USA, Strategic Concepts in Organizing and Policy Education (SCOPE), and the Atlanta Neighborhood Development Partnership (ANDP) have developed action-based research to inform policy campaigns. For example, ANDP just completed an extensive research and data project on regional housing disparities and has developed a set of policy recommendations for promoting mixed-income housing across the Atlanta metro region.

Diverse Constituencies and Coalitions Engaged in Policy Campaigns for Regional Equity

In the Boston metropolitan area, Action for Regional Equity (Action!) is advancing analysis and policy solutions to address the critical development challenges facing the region. The coalition consists of 20 Massachusetts organizations united to address continuing disparities in affordable housing, transportation investment, and environmental justice across the Boston region. Action! has initiated a campaign for a dedicated permanent revenue stream for affordable housing that meets specific equity criteria and is engaged in building the capacity of local leaders to advocate for equitable transit investments. Driving all of their work is a commitment to increased civic participation in policymaking.

In California, the Sustainable Communities Working Group, a collaboration of several statewide organizations, funded by The James Irvine Foundation, is advancing state policies for smart growth and regional equity. The Working Group comprises civil rights, social justice, and economic development organizations that are advancing a range of land-use and fiscal reform issues, including addressing the inequitable distribution of school construction dollars.

Community Organizing and Base Building

Regional equity will not fulfill its potential as a movement unless it connects to people in their neighborhoods and daily lives. This is beginning to happen through the work of a growing number of national organizing networks such as Association of Community Organizations for Reform Now (ACORN), Pacific Institute for Community Organization (PICO), and the Gamaliel Foundation. These groups are actively building a base of power in low-income communities to advocate for policies addressing the inequitable impact of regional development. New organizing tactics and alliances are emerging at both the community and regional level, with special attention on organizing across racial and geographic lines.

MOSES: Faith-Based Leaders Organizing for Regional Equity

Faith-based organizations have a unique ability to bring together diverse political constituencies on the common grounds of faith and community action, allowing them to mobilize large groups for change. The Metropolitan Organizing Strategy Enabling Strength (MOSES)—an interfaith community organization based in the Detroit region and dedicated to helping congregations and citizens gain greater influence in public policy debates—is an example of bringing community organizing strategies to the work of advancing regional equity.

Founded in 1998, MOSES realized that many of the neighborhood problems it was struggling to address in Detroit stem from political, economic, and social forces that are regional in nature. The centerpiece of MOSES's regional equity approach is transportation justice. It actively supports increasing funds for public transit and a range of land use reforms. A recent victory for MOSES was advocating for the inclusion of "Fix It First" land-use policies—mandates that prioritize repairing infrastructure and transportation in existing areas—as a central component of the recommendations that are part of Michigan Governor Jennifer Granholm's Land Use Leadership Council.

The work of MOSES is not an isolated example of faith-based leaders advocating for regional equity. It is an affiliate of the Gamaliel Foundation, a large national organizing network, whose American Metropolitan Equity Network (AMEN) recognizes sprawl as the driving force behind racial and economic segregation in the United States. The Ford Foundation and the C. S. Mott Foundation are key supporters of these efforts.

Funder Engagement and Leadership

The philanthropic community increasingly views regional equity as an important framework for assessing the systems and policy changes needed to connect low-income communities to opportunity. Over the past five years, the Funders' Network for Smart Growth and Livable Communities has worked to seed and promote philanthropic and community initiatives that integrate the goals of social equity and smart growth. Early on, the Network recognized that more conscious and deep attention needs to be paid to the social equity component. To build understanding of the importance of equity-centered smart growth, the Network convenes leaders from a range of sectors—philanthropic, nonprofit, academic, private, and public—at national meetings that serve as forums for developing common understandings about the relationship between smart growth and equity. Most recently, the Network launched the Regional and Neighborhood Equity Project (RNEP), a funder-initiated effort to identify, support, and replicate regional equity projects across the country.

A growing number of community and regional foundations are supporting their grantees in regional initiatives. For example, the McKnight Foundation in Minneapolis supports a People of Color Caucus to advance equity-centered smart growth policies. National funders like the Ford Foundation are supporting regional equity demonstration projects in such diverse places as Atlanta; Baltimore; Camden, New Jersey; Detroit; and Richmond, California.

All of this activity demonstrates the potential for building a broad-based social movement for regional equity. Fully realizing this potential will require deeper engagement from both social justice advocates and the smart-growth movement. Experience has shown that achieving authentic, sustainable progress requires that those who live in low-income communities and their advocates be fully engaged and in positions of leadership. Fortunately there are excellent examples of this in the work of leading advocates from across the country. The next section explores key arenas where communities, organizations, and institutions are embracing the regional equity framework and pursuing policies and strategies to realize its promise for achieving social and economic justice.

A FRAMEWORK FOR ACTION

To achieve regional equity, development policies that neglect central cities, older suburbs, and rural communities for the benefit of new suburban growth must be replaced with strategies that promote regional equity. This will improve the overall well-being of communities as opportunity in employment, education, transportation, and housing become more evenly available. As more people find paths to success, the entire region benefits from greater stability, security, and prosperity.

During the past five years PolicyLink, working with dedicated advocates for change, has promoted equitable development as a framework for achieving regional equity. Equitable development is guided by the following principles:

> **Promoting Regional Equity Collaboration in Greater Philadelphia: The William Penn Foundation**
>
> One of Philadelphia's largest philanthropic institutions, the William Penn Foundation, funds nonprofit organizations located and working in Greater Philadelphia. The foundation uses the theme of smart growth as the guiding framework for integrating its environmental and community development grantmaking throughout the region.
>
> The foundation's regional strategy for building livable communities hinges on the active role it plays as convener and facilitator and on a commitment to policy and system improvements. The foundation works with philanthropic organizations with similar interests and goals to identify common agendas and collaborative initiatives and supports a sophisticated network of organizations and funders throughout the region.

- *Integrate People- and Place-Focused Strategies.* Advance development and revitalization policies and practices that integrate people-focused strategies—efforts that support community residents and families—with place-focused strategies—those that stabilize and improve the neighborhood environment.
- *Reduce Local and Regional Disparities.* Craft solutions that simultaneously improve outcomes for low-income communities and build healthy metropolitan regions. Metropolitan areas that pay systematic attention to both regional growth *and* central city, suburban, and rural poverty issues are more likely to be competitive for national and international economic opportunities.
- *Promote Double Bottom-Line Investments.* Seek public and private investments that offer fair financial returns for investors and community benefits for residents (e.g., jobs, homes, businesses).
- *Ensure Meaningful Community Participation, Leadership, and Ownership.* For community residents and organizations to become fully engaged in impacting development decisions, they must have access to the tools, knowledge, and resources that can guarantee meaningful participation.

Using these equitable development principles as guides, advocates across the country are working in a number of different arenas including:

- Living near regional opportunity;
- Linking people to regional opportunity;
- Promoting equitable public investment; and
- Making all neighborhoods stable, healthy, and livable.

The examples below are illustrative of the many diverse actors and entry points for achieving regional equity.

Living Near Regional Opportunity

A home is more than shelter—when located in a community with resources and amenities it is a critical determinant of opportunity. Living in quality, affordable housing in an opportunity-rich neighborhood creates access to good schools, employment, social networks, quality public services, and opportunities for physical activity. Having a home at an affordable rent or mortgage leaves some resources available for other important needs such as health insurance, transportation, and investing in the education of one's children.

Owning a home is how most Americans build wealth. Yet, despite some closing of the gap, significant racial disparities exist in homeownership rates. According to the 2002 Census, 73 percent of white households own their home, compared to 47 percent of African Americans and 48 percent of Latinos. The bipartisan Millennial Housing Commission notes: "housing is inextricably linked to access to jobs and healthy communities and the social behavior of the families who occupy it."[10]

Given this fact, a key arena for promoting regional equity is ensuring that quality housing is affordable and available *throughout* metropolitan areas. Low-income families who reside in affordable housing close to good schools, employment centers, transportation systems, parks, grocery stores, civic institutions, and services are better positioned to succeed economically and socially. While large-scale public housing projects are no longer built in the most undesirable places and there exists an explicit goal of deconcentrating poverty through housing policy (Housing Choice Vouchers, Hope VI, Low Income Housing Tax Credits), the nation's housing markets remain starkly divided by race and income. This division is not simply an urban vs. suburban phenomenon. Many older, inner-ring suburbs are increasingly the destination for working families of color looking for affordable and safe housing choices. Often, these declining first-tier suburbs face many of the same challenges found in the urban communities being left behind.

Multiple forces conspire to prevent the production of more affordable homes and apartments in opportunity-rich communities. Discrimination and the practice of steering people of certain racial and ethnic groups to neighborhoods dominated by people of that same group limit housing choices, especially for people of color. A multifaceted approach is required to overcome the barriers these forces create.

Dismantling Exclusionary Land-Use Practices

Throughout the United States there are exclusionary land-use and zoning practices that function to maintain regional inequity. These regulations—such as minimum square footage, or large-lot and setback requirements—serve to deny whole groups and classes of people access to opportunity-rich neighborhoods. A survey in the 25 largest metropolitan areas showed that low-density zoning consistently reduced rental housing. The resulting shortage limited the number of African Americans and Latinos in those communities.[11]

Regulatory policies, if designed to increase regional equity, can open up opportunity-rich communities for development of homes and apartments that are affordable to a wider range of income groups. Such policies include fair-share housing agreements, inclusionary zoning, and zoning overlays that raise density and allow multifamily housing development.

Inclusionary zoning is being successfully adopted in many communities. Zoning rules are changed to require or provide incentives for private developers to create projects that include more affordable housing choices. In return, development costs are reduced through zoning variances, density bonuses, development rights, or expedited permits.

Montgomery County, Maryland, passed the first inclusionary zoning ordinance in 1974. Since then, numerous jurisdictions as varied as Sacramento, California; Santa Fe, New Mexico; Denver, Colorado; Boulder, Colorado; Cambridge, Massachusetts; and East Palo Alto, California have found inclusionary zoning to be an important tool in providing more affordable housing choices. From Los Angeles to Madison, Wisconsin, and Washington, D.C., diverse coalitions are calling for more inclusionary zoning to both produce and equitably distribute affordable housing in line with smart growth principles.

> **Thinking Regionally About Inclusionary Zoning in the San Francisco Bay Area**
>
> An innovative approach to thinking regionally about inclusionary zoning can be found in the San Francisco Bay Area. The Bay Area Inclusionary Housing Initiative is a unique partnership of community organizations and foundations advancing a multiyear, regional campaign to help Bay Area cities and counties accelerate adoption of inclusionary housing policies. Led by the Nonprofit Housing Association of Northern California, the goal of this regional initiative is to double the rate of inclusionary housing production. Communities that already have inclusionary zoning policies in place have demonstrated that it is a critical tool for providing much needed low- and moderate-income housing for working families.
>
> The participating foundations are S. H. Cowell Foundation, Fannie Mae Foundation, Evelyn and Walter Haas, Jr., Fund, Marin Community Foundation, Peninsula Community Foundation, The San Francisco Foundation, and Charles and Helen Schwab Foundation. The community partners include the Institute for Local Self-Government, Greenbelt Alliance, the California Affordable Housing Law Project, the Nine Country Housing Advocacy Network, and the Western Center on Law and Poverty.

Applying Regional Equity Criteria to Affordable Housing Funding Streams

Another important vehicle for achieving a more equitable distribution of affordable housing across regions is to apply regional equity criteria to public revenue streams that fund affordable housing production. For instance, by attaching requirements—such as locating affordable homes and apartments close to transit, new employment centers, and schools—to important capital streams like the Community Development Block Grant Program, Low Income Housing Tax Credits, and local/state housing bonds, jurisdictions are attempting to strategically place low-income people close to much needed structures and supports. More analysis, research, and policy proposals are needed to realize the full potential of such efforts.

The goal of distributing housing dollars based on regional equity criteria, however, should not lead to drawing limited resources away from communities in need. Rather, as jurisdictions consider the best ways to leverage existing resources, efforts must be made to expand the available pool of dollars for affordable housing. The following text box reviews how California and Massachusetts are attempting to leverage the use of their Low Income Housing Tax Credit dollars.

Regional equity criteria can also apply to the distribution of dollars for state housing trust funds or housing bond allocations. For example, Florida allocates housing trust dollars to counties on a per capita basis, ensuring affordable home ownership opportunities across the state and broad distribution of multifamily rental housing.

Linking People to Regional Opportunity

While development should equitably distribute housing choices across the region to reduce isolation and concentrated poverty, it is equally important to improve options and accessibility for low-income people and communities of color where they currently live. Regional equity advocates actively pursue strategies and policy changes that connect low-income people to employment and other opportunities through improved transportation options.

As of 1996, on average, less than 16 percent of jobs nationwide were within three miles of central business districts.[15] Given the movement of jobs away from cities, transportation systems consciously designed to link low-income communities to economic corridors and jobs are fundamental to advancing regional equity. Transportation advocates are working on multiple fronts to promote more equitable transportation policies. Two arenas are reviewed in this chapter: promoting transit-oriented development in low-income neighborhoods and engaging in policy campaigns to steer transportation dollars towards more equitable investment patterns.

Promoting Development and Investment around Transit Stations

Transit-oriented development (TOD) is development centered around transit stations as a way to improve transit accessibility and the surrounding community. In historically neglected neighborhoods, development near transit stations can spark revitalization, connecting more people in the area to jobs and creating (or, often, re-creating) a vital commercial center.

No longer the exclusive purview of planning agencies and private developers, TOD projects are increasingly being led by equity advocates, most notably community development corporations (CDCs). While transit-oriented developments in low-income communities can be a lifeline to opportunities across the region, such development can also fuel gentrification. The work of Chicago's Bethel New Life and Oakland's Spanish Speaking Unity Council are recognized national models of how to strike the balance between revitalization and preservation of affordability.[16]

While TOD projects have historically been planned around existing stations, regional equity advocates are also engaging in planning and decision making about where new transit lines and stations should be located. This planning is an opportunity to anticipate how such development can help achieve greater regional equity. As a result of community organizing and involvement, a regional development plan was created for the Interstate Avenue light rail line in Portland, Oregon. The plan cites *"benefit the existing community"* as a guiding principle and includes statements about preventing resident displacement in both the housing and economic development sections. Inclusion of such language is a notable step forward in planning for regional equity.

Immigrants: The New Dimension of Regional Equity

One of the big stories emerging from Census 2000 is that immigration was responsible for much of the nation's growth—and that this trend shows no sign of slowing. There are interesting shifts happening in settlement patterns: Immigrants who first settled in central cities are moving to the suburbs, but more recent immigrants are bypassing urban areas altogether and heading directly for suburbia. This shift is due in large part to sprawl-related job growth patterns. For immigrants to acquire new jobs that are increasingly located far from city centers, they must either live where the jobs are, though affordable housing is scarce, or utilize public transit, which is limited or lacking in many metro areas. This is a new dimension of a fundamental regional equity challenge known as "spatial mismatch" between jobs and housing.

Against this backdrop, in September of 2003, California Governor Gray Davis signed Senate Bill 60. The legislation, allowing undocumented immigrants to obtain a driver's license in California, was a pragmatic decision to respond to the realities of California's labor markets. It was repealed by Governor Arnold Schwarzenegger less than a month after he took office in November of the same year.

In the public debate, the bill was framed as an issue of equal rights for immigrants. Yet, at its heart was a workforce issue and could have had more universal appeal if it had been advocated for in terms of employer needs. Hope, and a chance to reframe the issue, still exists. Reborn as Senate Bill 1160, the driver's license legislation was recently approved by the California State Senate Transportation Committee and is winding its way through the legislative process.

Advocating for a More Equitable Use of Transportation Dollars

In addition to improving physical development around transit stops, growing numbers of robust coalitions are advocating for shifting transportation dollars to gain greater mobility for low-income people. Some coalitions, such as the Transportation and Land Use Coalition (TALC) in the San Francisco Bay Area, have succeeded in achieving a more equitable allocation of federal, state, and local transportation dollars.

Promoting Equitable Public Investment

Public investment decisions ultimately determine the quality of transit systems, the condition of public schools and facilities, and the presence of parks and open space.

Diverse Coalition Advocating for Transportation Equity

The Transportation and Land Use Coalition (TALC) is a partnership of over 90 groups working for an environmentally sustainable and socially just Bay Area. The coalition analyzes county and regional policies and works with member groups to develop alternatives. It usually kicks off grassroots campaigns with high-quality reports that generate headlines and outline their key recommendations. To date, TALC has been credited with a major shift in the Bay Area's transportation funding priorities with victories such as:

- Steering $375 million in the 1998 Regional Transportation Plan from highway expansion to maintaining public transit;
- Securing a commitment in December 2003 for the region to spend over $700 million of transportation funding to build transit-oriented housing, with bonuses for affordable units and safer streets; and
- Helping develop and then leading a campaign for a $1 toll increase on seven bridges that will generate over $100 million per year, in perpetuity, for public transit. Passed by the voters in March 2004, the measure includes major funding to connect low-income communities with job and education centers.

Too often, policymakers fail to consider the impact of investment decisions on low-income communities. Using public investments to promote regional equity is becoming an important strategy among social justice advocates. Advocates are taking a particular interest in the growing community benefits movement and in promoting equitable infrastructure investments at the state level.

Requiring Community Benefits

Large-scale economic development projects to build *regional* destinations—sport stadiums, entertainment arenas, hotels, office parks, and "big-box" retail services—often depend on taxpayer-supported public subsidies. The community benefits movement is based on the premise that public investments must yield defined public benefits, including good jobs, affordable housing, and child care. The movement is being driven by broad and diverse coalitions that include labor unions, community builders, housing developers, neighborhood advocates, and environmentalists.

The community benefits movement began in California when organizations in Los Angeles, San Diego, San Jose, and the East Bay began leveraging the potential of large economic development projects to benefit low-income communities. Perhaps the most comprehensive community benefits agreement to date was negotiated by the Figueroa Corridor Coalition for Economic Justice around the development of the downtown Los Angeles Sports and Entertainment District (Staples Center). This agreement included living wage jobs, local hiring requirements, job training, a 20 percent set-aside of affordable housing, and a commitment of $1 million for community parks and recreation, in exchange for organized community support of the project. Following this mutually beneficial agreement, one of the coalition members, the Los Angeles Alliance for New Economy, has been tracking development proposals in the broader Los Angeles region to determine when community benefits can be negotiated in exchange for support of a project.

The idea that communities must benefit from publicly subsidized development is spreading rapidly. It is being forwarded in metro regions across the country, including Milwaukee, Wisconsin; Atlanta; Boston; Seattle; New York City; and Washington, D.C.[17] In early 2004, a community benefits agreement was made for developments in the former Park East Freeway area of downtown Milwaukee. The Institute for Wisconsin's Future was a key advocate in this effort. The agreement ensures that affordable housing and union-level wages for construction workers will be part of all developments receiving public subsidies or built on public land.

Influencing Public Infrastructure Investments

Advocates are exerting increased influence on state public infrastructure investments through their focus on regional equity. Infrastructure dollars account for a large percentage of state spending and affect virtually every aspect of neighborhoods, cities, and regions. These decisions affect where housing is located, the variety and range of housing to be built, if and how people can get to jobs, the quality of education in the community, and maintenance of basic public health and safety. Equitable public infrastructure policies provide a path to real social and economic equity in, and between, communities.

Linking Economic Development Subsidies and Transit Access

A recent 50-state survey of economic development subsidy programs (e.g., loans, grants, and tax incentives) conducted by Good Jobs First[18] revealed that not one state effectively coordinates its economic development spending with public transportation planning. The survey also found that only four states—Ohio, Minnesota, Maine, and Connecticut—have any kind of system to collect even fragmentary data on corporate relocations that receive economic development incentives. In other words, only four states collect data that could help them determine if their economic development programs are reducing or increasing access to jobs for workers who cannot afford a car, or if they are harming or improving commuter choice when jobs get relocated. These are troubling findings, because in virtually all major metropolitan areas there is a spatial mismatch between jobs and housing. The study recommends that economic development subsidies should be granted in a manner that is "location efficient" by restricting subsidies to projects that have access to public transit.

Infrastructure issues are complex and highly technical; rarely the focus of public debate. This is likely to change, in part because a growing number of states are facing infrastructure crises stemming from long-term inattention to needed infrastructure improvements and flawed tax policies. Advocates for social and economic justice are focusing greater attention on these important regional equity issues.

School construction financing is an area of infrastructure investment that is uniting civil rights advocates and smart growth proponents around the issue of regional equity. Many state funding formulas for school construction promote sprawl by favoring construction of new schools in growing suburban areas over rehabilitation of older schools in the central city and closer-in suburbs. The following text box reviews efforts to reform state policy in this arena in Ohio, Maryland, and California.

Making All Neighborhoods Stable, Healthy, and Livable

Regional equity will be achieved when every neighborhood in the region has the essentials for healthy, productive living and is connected to opportunities throughout the region. This requires recognizing and meeting a minimum standard of livability below which no community falls.

According to the 2000 census, approximately one-quarter of all large cities (those with populations of more than 100,000) continue to face significant population decline and the disinvestment that follows. These cities are primarily located in the Northeast and Midwest and include such places as Cleveland, Detroit, Philadelphia, and Pittsburgh.[19] The Community Development Partnership

Promoting More Equitable Use of School Construction Dollars: Ohio, Maryland, and California

Ohio. In 1997, a state Supreme Court legal decision found Ohio's K–12 school system to be unconstitutional because students were not receiving a "thorough and efficient" education. The deficient physical state of the schools was cited as a major factor in the decision. As a result, Ohio has revamped its funding for school facilities so that schools in need are priorities, and the state has become a national model of how to more equitably distribute school construction dollars. The litigation behind this action was spearheaded by the Ohio Coalition for Equity and Adequacy of School Funding.

Maryland. Similar to Ohio's, Maryland's constitution contains a provision requiring the state to provide a "thorough and efficient" education. Maryland assessed all of its schools for health and safety standards as well as the ability to support educational programming. This survey covered 121,046,176 square feet of school space. The resulting inventory helped to establish minimum facilities standards, determine the level of need, and target resources to where they are most needed. The state currently increases its share of construction costs for low-wealth communities, with plans to increase the funds to low-wealth districts even further beginning in 2005 under the Guaranteed Tax Base Program.

California. In California, the Mexican American Legal Defense and Educational Fund (MALDEF) and Policy-Link are working with a range of equity advocates and smart-growth leaders to push for the redistribution of school construction funds so that overcrowded schools in low-income communities become more of a priority for state spending than greenfield school development. A new program, begun in 2002 and refunded in 2004, set aside $4.14 billion for new construction to relieve critically overcrowded schools.

Network (CDPN) is working to bring greater attention to the challenges that these "weak market" cities face, such as declining home values and equity, diminishing tax bases that lead to fewer public amenities, large-scale vacant and abandoned property, brownfields, racial concentration of poverty, loss of social networks, and lower median incomes.[20]

Rebuilding neighborhoods in cities with weak real estate markets so that they become or remain vibrant, supportive communities is a fundamental regional equity challenge. All communities in a region should be "places of choice," with the services and support individuals and families need in order to be economically and socially stable. Many distressed communities lack basic amenities (e.g., banks, grocery stores, neighborhood parks, and cultural centers) that families need to lead healthy, productive lives. Transforming distressed communities requires recognizing the competitive advantage of these places relative to the region and tailoring strategies to attract reinvestment while connecting existing residents to the benefits of future revitalization.

A promising example of such transformation is the Healthy Neighborhoods Initiative (HNI) in Baltimore. The HNI recognizes the critical role that healthy, attractive neighborhoods play in making the city and region thrive. The initiative focuses on "in the middle" neighborhoods that usually do not have compelling enough problems to attract headlines yet also fail to attract investment dollars because of troubled properties. The Healthy Neighborhoods Initiative builds from neighborhood strength, harnessing assets and utilizing market forces to reinvigorate the targeted neighborhoods. Housing investments that increase home ownership and value are coupled with civic engagement activities that strengthen the social fabric of the neighborhood. In the Belair-Edison neighborhood, for instance, median sale prices for homes on target blocks increased over 9 percent from 2002 to 2003—and it is existing residents who are benefiting from this revitalization. Foundations such as the Goldseker Foundation and the Baltimore Community Foundation have made strategic investments in the Healthy Neighborhoods Initiative, recognizing the importance of this approach to building thriving neighborhoods that are connected to the broader region.

Another important arena for action is reclaiming vacant and abandoned properties. Many distressed communities are not capturing the opportunity to transform vacant or abandoned properties into valuable, revenue-generating sites that can help revitalize a neighborhood. A promising local effort is in Genesee County, Michigan, where the treasurer's office has launched an ambitious effort to take ownership of abandoned and vacant properties. As of March 2003, the county had taken ownership of over 2,100 properties in the city of Flint and has established a Land Reutilization Council to help return the roughly 1,800 sites it currently holds back to productive use.[21] On the national front, Smart Growth America (SGA) is spearheading the National Vacant Properties Campaign to make the issue of vacant properties a local and national policy priority and building a national network of leaders and experts working on these issues.

The challenge is not limited to weak market cities. Economically vibrant regions also have distressed neighborhoods that are not sharing in the benefits of

---

Grocery Stores: Ensuring Neighborhood Livability

Market Creek Plaza, San Diego. Located in the low-income, diverse Diamond Neighborhoods in San Diego, Market Creek Plaza extends over nine acres on a property that once housed a munitions factory. This commercial and cultural center—anchored by a Food 4 Less supermarket—includes ethnic restaurants, a fitness center, and an open-air community amphitheater. An outdoor public art collection—mosaics, totems, and murals—in combination with the design of the plaza's buildings reflects the artistic traditions of the diverse ethnic and cultural groups in the neighborhoods. A trolley stop located at Market Creek Plaza connects neighborhood residents to other locales across the region, and also helps make this cultural and commercial center in the heart of the Diamond Neighborhoods a regional destination. A project of the Jacobs Family Foundation, Market Creek Plaza is a wonderful example of revitalizing a neighborhood and improving opportunities for its residents, using a much needed grocery store to anchor these efforts.

State of Pennsylvania. The state of Pennsylvania recently adopted a supermarket development initiative using state economic development dollars for planning grants and low-interest loans to bring supermarkets into underserved urban and rural communities. This is critically important because Pennsylvania has the second-lowest number of supermarkets per capita of any state in the nation. The supermarket initiative is part of a larger economic stimulus package, recognizing that supermarkets can be economic development drivers in disinvested communities, while also helping to meet the food needs of the residents who live there.

---

growth. Strategies to rebuild such places and create vital, stable, and supportive neighborhoods that are regional destinations—such as the Diamond Neighborhood that is home to Market Creek Plaza in San Diego—are a critical arena for regional equity action.

Helping communities make comebacks and become attractive, connected places with amenities and services does not in itself necessarily mean that regional equity is increasing. Ironically, when a metropolitan region experiences a strong economy, it can threaten, rather than enhance, the stability of low-income communities and the livelihood of residents. When neighborhoods are transformed, tenured residents are often replaced, a process usually referred to as gentrification. It is important to guarantee that residents who stayed during difficult times can remain in neighborhoods experiencing revival if they choose. In-depth information on tools and strategies to prevent resident displacement through the process of revitalization can be found in the PolicyLink Equitable Development Toolkit.

THE WAY FORWARD

Regional equity will improve the overall well-being of all communities as opportunity in employment, education, transportation, and housing become more evenly available. As more people find paths to success, the entire region realizes benefits through increased stability, security, and prosperity.

There has been notable progress toward regional equity in the past several years. Examples cited in this chapter show the dynamic efforts underway around the country. The diversity of issue areas in which regional equity is being advanced, and the breadth of actors who are leading this work, is exciting and inspiring. While there is much progress to celebrate, the road to building more equitable and inclusive regions is long. Some important areas of investment that are needed to sustain and bring to scale the promising efforts discussed in this chapter include the following:

More Resources

The goal of regional equity cannot be achieved without more resources to support the types of policies and programs highlighted in this article. Redirected and new public, private, and philanthropic revenue sources are needed to support the innovative policies needed to realize the vision of regional equity. More funding is also needed to support organizations who are working on regional equity, as well as to bring new stakeholders to these efforts.

Community and social justice advocates understand the importance of regional analysis and action, but for the most part they are only positioned to work in low-income, inner-city communities. There is usually no funding support for work that reaches outside those boundaries.

Supporting regional equity approaches is a smart investment for the public, private, and philanthropic sectors. Investing in transit systems that connect to employment centers should help more people find good jobs; over time, this may reduce their dependence on public benefits and help them contribute to the tax base. Likewise, fostering greater educational equity will strengthen the economic vitality of the region by preparing more people to be productive workers; and improving the environmental factors that contribute to maintaining good health will reduce health care expenditures.

New Capacities

Working regionally requires different skills and knowledge than working at the neighborhood or city level. It is critical that individuals and organizations build the capacity in planning, land use, and fiscal issues necessary to be active in regional equity decisions. Some of the skills and techniques that need to be acquired and improved include the use of data, mapping, and information to support policy change and inform campaigns; communications skills and messages to make the case for regional equity; identifying and engaging diverse stakeholders; and organizing urban core/inner-ring alliances. Sometimes this requires action in more than one jurisdiction. Other times, action must move to the state level to reach the desired impact.

Training, technical assistance, and translating existing research on regionalism into "practical on-the-ground solutions" is an important area in need of continued and enhanced investment.

New Collaborations, New Venues for Conversation and Action

Collaborations across sectors, across neighborhoods, and across jurisdictions are essential for moving the regional equity agenda. Examples of collaborations between smart growth and social justice advocates highlighted in this article are promising. They need to be stronger, more inclusive, and more frequent.

There are a growing number of urban-suburban alliances and inner-ring suburban coalitions that need to be supported and strengthened. Additionally, there are new constituencies that, if more deeply engaged, could be powerful allies. For instance, there is a great need to better understand regional equity issues for rural communities and make connections to rural constituents. Regional equity requires analyzing and tackling deep-rooted issues of inequity in America—it cannot be accomplished without honest and frank conversations about race. Venues for having these kinds of tough conversations in a focused, productive way are crucial.

Leadership

Organizations mentioned in this chapter are home to a new cadre of leaders. Support and cultivation of new, bold regional equity leadership in the community, philanthropic, public sector, and private sector should be encouraged.

- *Social Justice and People of Color Leadership*. This chapter points to the way in which social justice advocates and people of color are increasingly engaging in regional action. Strategies to support their involvement and deepen their analysis are needed. One promising effort supported by the Ford Foundation is the African American Forum on Race and Regionalism. Convened by Angela Glover Blackwell, Robert Bullard, and John A. Powell—African American leaders with strong organizations seeking to promote regional equity—the purpose of the forum is to craft a multifaceted agenda designed to promote broad alliances for regional equity.[22]
- *Philanthropic Leadership*. This chapter highlighted foundations that are leading the way in terms of funding and convening regional equity efforts. The Funders' Network for Smart Growth and Livable Communities' Regional and Neighborhood Equity Project is an important venue for building foundation leadership and collaboration on these issues.
- *Elected Officials*. Local and state elected officials who are trained on regional equity issues and solutions, networked with each other, and connected to social justice advocates are critical to advancing this work. For example, a bipartisan and growing number of governors—including Jennifer Granholm (Michigan), Ed Rendell (Pennsylvania), Mitt Romney (Massachusetts), and Mark Sanford (South Carolina)—are putting forward a smart-growth agenda. These important state leaders need the regional equity framework to ensure that their efforts reflect the needs, voice, and per-

spective of low-income communities and people of color. On the local level, the National League of Cities and other membership associations can educate public officials on regional equity principles, approaches, and solutions.

- *Private Sector.* Efforts to engage the private sector—developers, corporate executives, bankers/investors—on issues of regional growth and development should offer specific ways that they can participate in advancing the goals of regional equity. The work of Richard Baron, president and chief executive of McCormack Baron Salazar, exemplifies how private developers can profit while also promoting the goals of regional equity. Baron works to revitalize neglected urban neighborhoods in ways that both physically revitalize an area and include needed services such as quality public schools and recreational areas. Chris Leinberger, another private developer, has developed an innovative "value latching" concept. This approach will capture revenue from improving property values stimulated by downtown revitalization to fund affordable housing initiatives in Albuquerque, New Mexico.

A Supportive Infrastructure

Given the new alliances, strategies, and analyses that are needed, it is very challenging for social justice advocates to engage in regional conversations. Anchor institutions that can serve as intermediaries for broadly engaging a range of stakeholders on regional equity action are critical for fostering relationships and supporting change.

CONCLUSION

In the United States, as much as one-third of our built environment will need to be renovated or replaced between the years 2002–2025. When combined with population growth, at least one-half the development needed by 2025 has yet to be built.[23] How government, the private sector, and philanthropy respond to these development needs and related investment decisions will shape the country's future.

Applying regional equity values and policies can chart an equitable course for future development and investment decisions, helping to build a nation of inclusion and broad opportunity. The opportunity to build stronger alliances between advocates for social and economic justice and proponents for smarter growth management represents a potent force for change.

REFERENCED ORGANIZATIONS AND INITIATIVES

ACORN, http://www.acorn.org/
Action for Regional Equity, http://www.policylink.org/BostonAction/
Atlanta Neighborhood Development Partnership (ANDP), http://www.andpi.org/
Baltimore Community Foundation, http://www.bcf.org/
Bethel New Life, http://www.bethelnewlife.org/
The Community Development Partnership Network, http://www.cdpn.org/
C. S. Mott Foundation, http://www.mott.org/
Equitable Development Toolkit, http://www.policylink.org/EDTK
Figueroa Corridor Coalition for Economic Justice, http://www.saje.net/programs/
    fccej.php

Ford Foundation, http://www.fordfound.org/

Funders' Network for Smart Growth and Livable Communities, http://www
.fundersnetwork.org/

Gamaliel Foundation, http://www.gamaliel.org/

Goldseker Foundation, http://www.goldsekerfoundation.org/

Good Jobs First, http://www.goodjobsfirst.org/

Healthy Neighborhoods Initiative, http://www.ci.baltimore.md.us/neighborhoods/
mhninitiative.html

Institute for Wisconsin's Future, http://www.wisconsinsfuture.org/

Jacobs Center for Neighborhood Innovation, http://www.jacobscenter.org/

The James Irvine Foundation, http://www.irvine.org/

Leadership Conference on Civil Rights, http://www.civilrights.org/about/lccr/

Market Creek Plaza, http://www.marketcreek.com/

McCormack Baron Salazar, http://www.mba-development.com/

Metropolitan Organizing Strategy Enabling Strength (MOSES), http://www
.mosesmi.org/

Mexican American Legal Defense and Educational Fund, http://www.maldef.org/

Millennial Housing Commission, http://www.mhc.gov/

National League of Cities, http://www.nlc.org/nlc_org/site/

National Vacant Properties Campaign, http://www.vacantproperties.org/

New Partners for Smart Growth, http://www.outreach.psu.edu/C&I/SmartGrowth/

Nonprofit Housing Association of Northern California, http://www.nonprofit
housing.org/

Ohio Coalition for Equity and Adequacy of School Funding, http://www.ohio
coalition.org/

PICO, http://www.piconetwork.org/

PolicyLink, http://www.policylink.org/

Smart Growth America, http://www.smartgrowthamerica.org

Spanish Speaking Unity Council, http://www.unitycouncil.org/

Strategic Concepts in Organizing and Policy Education (SCOPE), http://www
.scopela.org/

Sustainable Communities Working Group, http://www.citnet.org/wg/communities/

Transportation and Land Use Coalition (TALC), http://www.transcoalition.org/

Urban Land Institute, http://www.uli.org/

William Penn Foundation, http://www.wpennfdn.org/

Working Partnerships USA, http://www.wpusa.org/

NOTES

We would like to thank Regan Douglass at PolicyLink for her research assistance in developing this chapter. We also thank PolicyLink program staff for their review of a draft manuscript.

Special thanks to Carl Anthony at the Ford Foundation, Earl Johnson at the Rockefeller Foundation, and Ben Starrett and Jesse Leon at the Funders' Network for Smart Growth and Livable Communities for their review of draft manuscripts.

Finally, we also thank several of our colleagues in the field with whom we had conversations about the state of regional equity. They include Carl Anthony, Ford Foundation; Richard Baron, McCormack Baron Salazar, Inc.; Hooper Brooks, Surdna Foundation; Kim Burnett, Community Development Partnership Network (CDPN); Anne Canby, Surface Transportation Policy Project (STPP); Christine Doby, C. S. Mott Foundation; Francisco Estrada, Mexican American Legal Defense and Educational Fund (MALDEF); Michael Fix, The Urban Institute; Anika Goss-Foster, Detroit LISC; Wade Henderson, Leadership

Conference on Civil Rights; M. von Nkosi, Atlanta Neighborhood Development Partnership/Mixed Income Communities Initiative; Carey Shea, formerly with the Surdna Foundation; Ben Starrett, Funders' Network for Smart Growth and Livable Communities; and Debby Warren, Southern Rural Development Initiative.

Editor's Note: This chapter is reprinted with permission of The Funders' Network and Policy Link. It is part of a series sponsored by the Funders' Network for Smart Growth and Livable Communities to translate the impact of sprawling development patterns and urban disinvestment on our communities and environment and to highlight the opportunities that could be created by smarter growth policies and practices.

1. The use of residents, instead of citizens, is intentional. It seeks to connect the principles of the civil rights movement to the current struggle (most apparent in California) for the rights of all residents, regardless of nationality or immigration status.

2. Chungmei Lee, *Racial Segregation and Educational Outcomes in Metropolitan Boston* (Cambridge, MA: Harvard Civil Rights Project, 2004).

3. PolicyLink and the Mexican American Legal Defense and Educational Fund, *Building New Schools in California: How Are We Addressing Overcrowding?* (Oakland, CA: Author, 2004).

4. See, for example, the Federal Housing Administration, *Underwriting Manual: Underwriting and Valuation Procedure Under Title II of the National Housing Act* (1938). Some applicable excerpts: "[Section] 935 . . . Natural or artificially established barriers will prove effective in protecting a neighborhood and the locations within it from adverse influences . . . [including] prevention of the infiltration of business and industrial uses, lower class occupancy, and inharmonious racial groups. . . . [Section] 937. Quality of Neighboring Development . . . Areas surrounding a location are investigated to determine whether incompatible racial and social groups are present, for the purpose of making a prediction regarding the probability of the location being invaded by such groups. If a neighborhood is to retain stability, it is necessary that properties shall continue to be occupied by the same social and racial classes."

5. The Michigan Land Use Leadership Council, *Michigan's Land, Michigan's Future: Final Report of the Michigan Land Use Leadership Council*, August 15, 2003.

6. Paul Jargowsky, *Stunning Progress, Hidden Problems: The Dramatic Decline of Concentrated Poverty in the 1990s* (Washington, DC: Brookings Institution Center on Urban & Metropolitan Policy, 2003).

7. Edward Glaeser and Matthew Kahn, *Decentralized Employment and the Transformation of the American City* (Washington, DC: National Bureau of Economic Research, 2001).

8. Richard Perez-Pena, "Study Finds Asthma in 25% of Children in Central Harlem," *New York Times*, April 19, 2003.

9. Myron Orfield is the Director of the Institute on Race and Poverty at the University of Minnesota, John A. Powell is the Director of the Kirwan Institute for the Study of Race and Ethnicity at Ohio State University, and David Rusk is a consultant based in Washington, D.C.

10. Millennial Housing Commission, *Meeting Our Nation's Housing Challenge* (Washington, DC: Author, 2002).

11. Rolf Pendall, "Local Land-Use Regulation and the Chain of Exclusion," *Journal of the American Planning Association* 66(2) (2000): 125–42.

12. Lance Freeman, *Siting Affordable Housing: Location and Neighborhood Trends of Low Income Housing Tax Credit Development in the 1990s* (Washington, DC: Brookings Institution Center on Urban & Metropolitan Policy, 2004).

13. California Tax Credit Allocation Committee, *Qualified Allocation Plan* (2001).

14. Massachusetts Housing Finance Agency, *Qualified Allocation Plan* (2004).

15. Glaeser and Kahn, *Decentralized Employment*.

16. See PolicyLink Equitable Development Toolkit: Equity in Transit Oriented Development Tool for a more comprehensive discussion: http://www.policylink.org/EDTK.

17. The California Partnership for Working Families, *Lifting Cities Out of Poverty: Opportunities and Challenges for the Emerging Community Benefits Movement* (Oakland, CA: Author, 2004).

18. *Missing the Bus: How States Fail to Connect Economic Development with Public Transit* (Washington, DC: Good Jobs First, 2003).

19. Edward Glaeser and Jesse Shapiro, *City Growth and the 2000 Census: Which Places Grew, and Why* (Washington, DC: Brookings Institution Center on Urban & Metropolitan Policy, 2001).

20. Paul Brophy and Kim Burnett, *Building a New Framework for Community Development for Weak Market Cities* (Denver, CO: The Community Development Partnership Network, 2003).

21. National Vacant Properties Campaign: http://www.vacantproperties.org/.

22. See PolicyLink, *Leadership for Policy Change*, for a more comprehensive discussion: http://www.policylink.org/Research/Leadership/.

23. Funders' Network for Smart Growth and Livable Communities, *Two Steps Forward, One Step Back: Research on the Prospects for the Smart Growth and Livable Communities Movement* (Coral Gables, FL: Author, 2004).

Conclusion

Do current laws and regulations promote sprawl? Do tax policies provide incentives for the wrong behaviors? Assuming we could go back 50 years and undo the interstate highway system, the federal mortgage subsidies, and the local property tax incentives to grow, how could we create different outcomes? Would cities thrive at the expense of outlying areas? Would the countryside grow corn and livestock instead of auto dependent commercial and industrial parks? Would all people benefit equally from the success? Would air, water, and land be protected from the effects of congestion?

DYNAMIC FOR CHANGE

The lack of action on sprawl may be changing. There are currently many efforts to develop policy prescriptions that go beyond traditional urban/rural conflict models. (Fishman, 1987) The environmental community with their tradition of developing methodologies to account for the externalities of land and water use may lead to positive change. If the tax analysts are prepared to explore the innate conflict between tax valuation and social equity, then new incentives can be created to reverse the trends. If the equity issue is addressed straight on and proactively in metropolitan regions, then an ethical model of regional development which maximizes choice for all citizens can emerge.

However, there are disturbing trends. Economic cycles create countercyclical politics that mitigates against long-range solutions. When the economy is booming, political pressure builds to act against development interests. When things slow, as they always do, the "growth machine" engages and there is pressure to do anything to get the economy moving again. Further, states under pressure do move to make changes in their land-use management regimes. This is easier to accomplish politically in the governor's office through executive fiat rather than by moving ponderously through the legislature to make more permanent changes.

Efficiency doesn't always yield effectiveness in public policy. Once the governor leaves office new state executives have different policies and can quickly dismantle structures that do not have legislative support.

This volume, and other treatises on sprawl, help identify the deep and often intractable causes and consequences of land-use policies overseen by local governments with limited geographies and conflicting demands for social and physical infrastructure. For those who have an interest in the long-term cumulative effects of these activities, there is some comfort in the broad coalition of interests that appear to be engaging in this debate as the twenty-first century begins. However, as H. L. Mencken said "For every complex problem, there is a solution that is simple, neat and wrong." There is a tendency in advocacy to need to break a problem into pieces in order to get anything moving in the policy arena. While that is important for momentum, it is problematic for sustainable systemic change. Sprawl, as Harriet Tregoning at the Smart Growth Leadership Institute says, "is planned and is part of a sophisticated interaction among and between many elements in the development system, each of which must be addressed to accomplish truly 'smart' growth alternatives."[1]

This volume is a reference work for practitioners and advocates who wish to understand and respond to a truly enormous set of issues that, in many cases, underpin American life in the last half of the twentieth century. In the span of time, this is an important 50-year period, but the changes wrought on the landscape are not immutable and the capacity for sophisticated interventions is available. It is our collective hope that we have provided a comprehensive enough resource for a strategic set of responses to this challenge in the beginning of the twenty-first century.

NOTE

1. Speech to Metropolitan Area Planning Council, May 2005.

Appendix I
Database Resources

There is an increasingly rich variety of data available for the sprawl researcher. A number of government agencies maintain time series data at various geographic levels. Other research and advocacy organizations provide data that is processed in various ways. One important caveat to any researcher of time series data—it is important to make sure that the geographic area being measured is the same in each consecutive series. For example, census definitions of metropolitan areas change over time. A variety of "work-arounds" are possible to normalize the data for true comparisons and most published research accounts for these differences.

Brookings Institution, Metropolitan Policy Program

The Metropolitan Policy Program of the Brookings Institution (www.brookings .edu/metro), headed by Bruce Katz, is an incredibly rich resource for current academic research on the impact of sprawl across a number of social, economic, environmental, and political sectors. Links are offered to numerous resources and databases. A list-serve is available for free to receive notices of current offerings.

Bureau of Economic Analysis

The Bureau of Economic Analysis (BEA), division of the U.S. Department of Commerce, provides accurate and timely information on the performance of the U.S. economy. For our purposes, BEA has defined 172 economic regions of the country that represent a larger geography than the census metropolitan and micropolitan regions and, ostensibly, provide a more rigorous definition of the regional economies that are the building blocks of the state and national economies.

Bureau of Labor Statistics

The Bureau of Labor Statistics of the U.S. Department of Labor defines labor markets as an area which offers employment within a reasonable distance to residential locations. There are 2,383 areas with 337 market areas with 42 interstate areas, and 2046 small labor market areas, 13 of which are interstate. Employment and unemployment statistics are maintained on this geography.

The Institute for Strategy and Competitiveness at Harvard Business School

The Institute for Strategy and Competitiveness, led by Michael E. Porter, Bishop William Lawrence University Professor, maintains a Web site called the "cluster mapping project" (http://data.isc.hbs.edu/isc/index.jsp), which allows registered users (non-fee-cluster data and fee-based—greater depth) to perform cluster analysis at four geographic levels—state, economic area (BEA), metropolitan (Census), and inner city. This analysis provided invaluable insights into the performance of local and export industries in the area.

The Lewis Mumford Center for Comparative Urban and Regional Research

Established at the University of Albany in 1988 to carry out both comparative and historical urban research, the Lewis Mumford Center honors the tradition of interdisciplinary scholarship established by Lewis Mumford (1895–1990), a native New Yorker who was internationally recognized as one of the most distinguished urbanists of the twentieth century. By promoting broad-based collaboration among urban scholars from a variety of fields and geographic settings, the Center's mission is to further Mumford's ideal of local involvement with global vision. To this end, Center projects and activities range from international urban conferences (July 1999 in Shanghai) to local planning initiatives and national endeavors that examine urban change over time.

The Center maintains a Web-based resource center called "Metropolitan Racial and Ethnic Change—Census 2000" (http://www.albany.edu/mumford/census/data.html), in collaboration with the Initiative on Spatial Structures in the Social Sciences at Brown University. Researchers can access and download extensive social data on metropolitan regions.

Metropolitan Area Research Corporation

Myron Orfield, president of the Metropolitan Area Research Corporation, has worked with over 30 metropolitan regions in the United States to link social and fiscal stress with sprawl and new metropolitan politics. His Web site (http://www.metroresearch.org) has summaries of the major studies and a series of maps showing patterns of social separation in these regions.

Natural Resources Conservation Inventory

One of the most widely used data sets in recent sprawl studies is the Natural Resources Conservation Inventory of the U.S. Department of Agriculture. This study compares the amount of rural land available in two periods—1982 and 1997—and draws out a variety of compelling statistics on the rate of land consumption throughout the United States during that 15-year period. These data are used in many studies to "sound the alarm" about the impact of sprawl on the surrounding countryside.

Rutgers University, Center for Urban Policy Research

The Center for Urban Policy Research at Rutgers University developed the State of the Nation's Cities: A Comprehensive Database on American Cities and Suburbs, a "comprehensive database on 77 American cities and suburbs. As of January 19, 1998, Version 2.2a of the database brings together over 3,000 variables from a wide variety of sources, allowing easy comparability of indicators on employment and economic development, demographic measures, housing and land use, income and poverty, fiscal conditions, and a host of other health, social, and environmental indicators." The database is available for downloading at http://policy.rutgers.edu/cupr/sonc/sonc.htm.

State of the Cities Data Systems

State of the Cities Data Systems (SOCDS) is available through the HUD User section of the U.S. Department of Housing and Urban Development at the following Web site address: http://socds.huduser.org/index.html. This is a very sophisticated interactive Web site that has historical data on every city and metropolitan area back to 1970. Other data sets are linked including crime statistics, building permits and other important information. One of the most useful features for sprawl concerns is the comparison between the central city and the surrounding suburban areas.

U.S. Census

By far the richest set of data, both current an historical is the Census Bureau of the U.S. Department of Commerce. Raw and processed data are available for the 2000 census and, with a little digging, for historical periods. Census data on sprawl impacts is available on the Web site (www.sprawlcity.org) and in the metropolitan policy section of www.brookings.edu as well as other research and policy sites.

"Where We Stand"—East-West Gateway Coordinating Council, St. Louis, Missouri

One last resource of note is the publication "Where We Stand" of the Regional Council serving the St. Louis region. The latest version, published in 2002, compares 36 metropolitan regions in the country on nine major factors (density, urban form, education, economics, etc.) Although deliberately constructed to benchmark St. Louis's performance in each of these factors with their peer regions, the data sets provide a set of reasonable metrics for all 36 metropolitan regions.

Web Sites for Sprawl Research

A Google search on sprawl/smart growth/sustainable development or other key phrases will general thousands of potential site visits. However, to assist the sprawl researcher, we've annotated the ones that we think are the most helpful. In most cases, the text provided is taken from the self-description that appears on the Web site. See also Appendix I for a list of data resources available with online access and download capability.

Alliance for Regional Stewardship, www.regionalstewardship.org

The Alliance for Regional Stewardship (ARS) is a national network of individuals and organizations identifying themselves as regional stewards who benefit by sharing experiences and working collaboratively on innovative approaches to common regional challenges. ARS recognizes the interdependency of the economy, environment, and society in regions. These stewards can come from business, government, education, or community sectors, but they share a common commitment to collaborative action and regional stewardship. ARS helps leaders learn about best practices from other regions, communicate to state/federal leaders and the media about regional challenges and innovations, and develop new leaders for regional stewardship efforts.

American Farmland Trust, www.farmland.org

Since its founding in 1980, American Farmland Trust (AFT) has helped win permanent protection for over a million acres of American farmland. The organization's hard work and sound strategies unite farmers, environmentalists, and policy makers.

AFT has been instrumental in a number of "costs of sprawl" studies, highlighting the economic value and fiscal importance of agricultural land to local jurisdictions.

American Forests, www.americanforests.org

American Forests is the nation's oldest nonprofit citizens' conservation organization. Citizens concerned about the waste and abuse of the nation's forests founded American Forests in

1875. American Forests' Ecosystem Restoration and Maintenance Agenda presents the core values and seeks to build support for policy goals. These goals focus on assisting communities in planning and implementing tree and forest actions to restore and maintain healthy ecosystems and communities. The organization also works with community-based forestry partners in both urban and rural areas to help them participate in national forest policy discussions. American Forests seeks to broaden awareness of the interdependence of communities and forests through their policy and communication activities with local partners.

American Planning Association, www.planning.org

The American Planning Association is a nonprofit public interest and research organization committed to urban, suburban, regional, and rural planning. APA and its professional institute, the American Institute of Certified Planners, advance the art and science of planning to meet the needs of people and society.

This is the official Web site of the American Planning Association. It is *the* Web site to peruse for land use planning regulations and resource materials.

Citistates Group, www.citistates.com

The Citistates Group is a network of journalists, speakers, and civic leaders focused on building competitive, equitable, and sustainable twenty-first-century metropolitan regions. The Group's forte is communications—using its journalistic, speaking, and facilitation skills to stimulate active debate on the real-world choices facing twenty-first-century American regions.

The Citistates Web site has links to a number of "Citistates" reports that Neal Peirce and Curtis Johnson have prepared on regions throughout America. A number of other resource materials are also available as links and an extensive recommended reading list.

Environmental Protection Agency, www.epa.gov

The official Web site of the U.S. Environmental Protection Agency provides extensive information on environmental laws and regulations, and many reports are available. One report identified in this volume provides an exhaustive documentation of all of the currently available technology tools and computer models on sprawl (www.epa.gov/tools.pdf.). While the words "sprawl" and "smart growth" do not appear on the home page, if these key words are used in the search engine, over 30 reports and publications are available for reference and downloading.

Fannie Mae Foundation, www.fanniemaefoundation.org

The Fannie Mae Foundation creates affordable homeownership and housing opportunities through innovative partnerships and initiatives that build healthy, vibrant communities across the United States.

The Foundation's journal, *Housing Policy Debate*, has numerous scholarly articles on sprawl and smart growth, particularly in relation to housing policy. Other publications of the Foundation have similar insights. All are downloadable from the Web site.

Funders' Network for Smart Growth and Livable Communities, www.fundersnetwork.org

The Funders' Network for Smart Growth and Livable Communities seeks to inspire, strengthen, and expand philanthropic leadership and funders' abilities to support organizations working to improve communities through better development decisions and growth policies. It brings together foundations, nonprofit organizations, and other partners to address the range of environmental, social, and economic problems caused by development strategies that fail to consider the big picture.

The network has published 16 "Translation Papers" on the relationship between smart growth and a number of key strategic policy issues including equity, environment, energy, arts, health. They are all available for downloading at the Web site.

Growth Management Leadership Alliance, www.gmla.org

The Growth Management Leadership Alliance (GMLA) is a network of leaders from state, provincial, and regional organizations in the United States and Canada that carry out programs to directly shape and implement smart growth policies and actions.

The Web site maintains a link of all of the advocacy organizations (who are members of GMLA) around the country.

International City/County Management Association, www.icma.org

The International City/County Management Association (ICMA) is the professional and educational organization for chief appointed managers, administrators, and assistants in cities, towns, counties, and regional entities throughout the world. ICMA provides technical and management assistance, training, and information resources to the local government community.

ICMA's publications, including planning and smart growth, are among the most sophisticated and widely respected resources available to professionals, citizens, and scholars on the operations of local government.

Metropolitan Area Research Corporation, www.metroresearch.org

The Metropolitan Area Research Corporation (MARC) is a nonprofit research and geographic information systems (GIS) firm with a history of service to the public interest, government, philanthropy, academia, and private research institutions. MARC's expertise lies in presenting cutting-edge demographic research through the striking spatial display of data.

This is Myron Orfield's Web site, with resources on metropolitan studies around the country.

National Association of Regional Councils, www.narc.org

The National Association of Regional Councils (NARC) is the preeminent alliance for fostering regional cooperation and building regional communities. It advocates for regional approaches with federal and state governments; provides training and technical assistance on the latest regional developments; and conducts research on timely regional topics. For more than three decades, NARC has represented multipurpose regional councils of government that assist community leaders and citizens in developing common strategies for addressing cross-cutting transportation, economic development, air and water quality, social equity, growth, and other challenges. Today, NARC welcomes membership from other public, private, academic, nonprofit, and civic regional organizations and interests as it works to engage the regional community in achieving regional excellence.

NARC's Web site provides links to the over 500 public sector regional councils around the country.

National Governors Association, www.nga.org

The National Governors Association (NGA) is the Web site for the nation's governors. NGA provides governors and their senior staff members with services that range from representing states on Capitol Hill and before the Administration on key federal issues to developing policy reports on innovative state programs and hosting networking seminars for state government executive branch officials. The NGA Center for Best Practices focuses on state innovations and best practices on issues that range from education and health to technology, welfare reform, and the environment. NGA also provides management and technical assistance to both new and incumbent governors, and is an excellent resource for state policies on growth and development.

National League of Cities, www.nlc.org

The National League of Cities represents municipal governments throughout the United States. Working in partnership with the 49 state municipal leagues, the National League of Cities serves as a resource to and an advocate for the more than 18,000 cities, villages, and towns it represents.

Numerous articles have appeared in *Nation's Cities Weekly*, the NLC newsletter, on smart growth and sprawl, from a city perspective.

Natural Resources Defense Council, www.ndrc.org

The Natural Resources Defense Council (NRDC) works to restore the integrity of the elements that sustain life—air, land, and water—and to defend endangered natural places. It seeks to establish sustainability and good stewardship of the Earth as central ethical imperatives of human society. NRDC affirms the integral place of human beings in the environment, and strives to protect nature in ways that advance the long-term welfare of present and future generations.

The NRDC Web site maintains a section on smart growth/sprawl from the environmental advocacy perspective with in-depth reports and links to many resources.

PLANetizen, www.planetizen.com

PLANetizen is a public-interest information exchange provided by *Urban Insight* for the urban planning, design, and development community, providing a daily source for urban planning news, job opportunities, commentary, and events. The organization felt that there was a need for an information exchange where professionals and citizens could get up-to-date planning and development information. It uses PLANetizen to try out new technologies, and donate our time and skills to build, expand, and support PLANetizen.

This Web site offers an up-to-the-minute resource on sprawl, smart growth, and other planning and development issues from a citizen's point of view.

Planning Commissioners Journal, www.plannersweb.com

This is the Web site of the *Planning Commissioners Journal*, a series of resources available to officials serving on local planning boards, and other practitioners.

PolicyLink, www.policylink.org

PolicyLink collaborates with a broad range of partners to implement strategies to ensure that everyone—including those from low-income communities of color—can contribute to and benefit from economic growth and prosperity. Among the regional equity approaches is equitable development, a comprehensive local, regional, and state framework emphasizing equitable public investment, the fair distribution of affordable housing, and community strategies to improve health.

PolicyLink is the primary source for insights into the social equity issues linked to sprawl.

Sierra Club, www.sierraclub.org

The Sierra Club promotes the responsible use of the earth's ecosystems and resources. It seeks to educate and enlist humanity to protect and restore the quality of the natural and human environment. The Sierra Club has an extensive set of resources on sprawl and practical strategies for stopping it. Their series on the costs of sprawl is available for download.

Smart Growth America, www.smartgrowthamerica.com

Smart Growth America is a coalition of nearly 100 advocacy organizations including national, state, and local groups working on behalf of the environment, historic preservation, social equity, land conservation, neighborhood redevelopment, farmland protection, labor, and town planning.

This is a sophisticated network of advocates and researchers with excellent materials on all aspects of sprawl available for download.

Smart Growth Leadership Institute, www.sgli.org

The Smart Growth Leadership Institute, a project of Smart Growth America, was created by former Maryland Governor Parris N. Glendening to help state and local elected, civic, and business leaders design and implement effective smart growth strategies.

Dedicated to forging new coalitions in the smart growth movement, their recent publication *Smart Growth Is Smart Business* (available for download) is just one example of the new means of connecting smart-growth strategies to other critical policy areas.

Smart Growth Network, www.smartgrowth.org

This Web site is developed and maintained as part of the Smart Growth Network (SGN). In 1996, the U.S. Environmental Protection Agency joined with several nonprofit and government organizations to form the Smart Growth Network (SGN) in response to increasing community concerns about the need for new ways to grow that boost the economy, protect the environment, and enhance community vitality. The Network's partners include environmental groups, historic preservation organizations, professional organizations, developers, real estate interests, and local and state government entities. The SGN works to encourage development that serves the economy, community, and the environment. It is a forum for raising public awareness of how growth can improve community quality of life; promoting smart growth best practices; developing and sharing information, innovative policies, tools, and ideas; and cultivating strategies to address barriers to and advance opportunities for smart growth.

SGN is a nationwide effort coordinated by the U.S. Environmental Protection Agency's (EPA) Division of Development, Community and Environment. EPA is supporting the Smart Growth Network (SGN) through cooperative partnerships with organizations such as the International City/County Management Association (ICMA) and the Sustainable Communities Network (SCN). ICMA serves as the organizational "home" of the SGN and runs its membership program.

Sprawl City Web Site, www.sprawlcity.org

This Web site emerges from the work of environmental authors Leon Kolankiewicz and Roy Beck to help the public make more ready use of federal data on sprawl and rural land loss. This Web site features U.S. government data and analysis of that data that allow the visitor to see the roles of contributing factors in the sprawl of individual urban areas, states, bioregions and the nation as a whole. The site uses census data and the natural Resources Conservation Inventory to tell the sprawl story.

Appendix III

Contact Information for Smart-Growth Alliances

During the last decade or more a number of "smart-growth" alliances have formed in states around the country. In an effort to identify them and provide contact information, we used the Growth Management Leadership Alliance. Only those organizations that are members of the Alliance are listed here.

States

California

California Futures Network
1414 "K" Street
Suite 600
Sacramento, CA 95814
Phone: 916-325-2533
Fax: 916-448-8246
info@calfutures.org

Colorado

Environment Colorado
1536 Wynkoop Street
First Floor, Suite 100
Denver, CO 80202
Phone: 303-573-3871
Fax: 303-573-3780
info@environmentcolorado.org

Florida

1000 Friends of Florida
926 East Park Avenue

P.O. Box 5948
Tallahassee, FL 32314-5948
Phone: 850-222-6277
Fax: 850-222-1117
www.1000fof.org

Georgia

The Georgia Conservancy
817 West Peachtree Street
Suite 200
Atlanta, GA 30308
Phone: 404-876-2900
Fax: 404-872-9229
mail@gaconservancy.org

Hawaii

Hawaii's Thousand Friends
305 Hahani Street
PMB 282
Kailua, HI 96734
Phone and Fax: 808-262-0682
htf@lava.net

Idaho

Idaho Smart Growth
P.O. Box 374
Boise, ID 83701
Phone: 208-333-8066
Fax: 208-336-6056
isg@idahosmartgrowth.org

Iowa

1000 Friends of Iowa
3524 6th Avenue
Des Moines, IA 50313
Phone: 515-288-5364
Fax: 515-288-6362
www.kfoi.org

Maine

GrowSmart Maine
Sparhawk Mill
81 Bridge Street
Yarmouth, ME 04096
Phone: 207-847-9275
www.growsmartmaine.org

Maryland

1000 Friends of Maryland
1209 N. Calvert Street
Baltimore, MD 21202
Phone: 410-385-2910
Fax: 410-385-2913
www.friendsofmd.org

Massachusetts

Massachusetts Smart Growth Alliance
18 Tremont Street
Suite 401
Boston, MA 02108
Phone: 617-263-1257
Fax: 617-248-0807
www.ma-smartgrowth.org

Michigan

Michigan Environmental Council
119 Pere Marquette Drive
Suite 2A
Lansing, MI 48912

Phone: 517-487-9539
Fax: 517-487-9541
mec@voyager.net

Michigan Land Use Institute
205 S. Benzie Boulevard
P.O. Box 500
Beulah, MI 49617
Phone: 231-882-4723
Fax: 231-882-7350
webinfo@mlui.org

Minnesota

1000 Friends of Minnesota
26 E. Exchange Street
Suite 317
Saint Paul, MN 55101
Phone: 651-312-1000
Fax: 651-312-0012
www.1000fom.org

Montana

Montana Smart Growth Coalition
P.O. Box 543
Helena, MT 59624
Phone: 406-449-6086
smartgrowth@mcn.net

New Jersey

New Jersey Future
137 West Hanover Street
Trenton, NJ 08618
Phone: 609-393-0008
Fax: 609-393-1189
njfuture@njfuture.org

New Mexico

1000 Friends of New Mexico
400 Gold Avenue SW
Suite 910
Albuquerque, NM 87102
Mailing Address:
P.O. Box 26176
Albuquerque, NM 87125-6176
Phone: 505-848-8232
Fax: 505-248-1361
amigos@1000friends-nm.org

North Carolina

North Carolina Smart Growth Alliance
205 West Main Street
Suite 211
Carrboro, NC 27510
Phone: 919-928-8700
Fax: 919-928-8707
email@ncsmartgrowth.org

Oregon

1000 Friends of Oregon
534 SW Third Avenue
Suite 300
Portland, OR 97204
Phone: 503-497-1000
Fax: 503-223-0073
info@friends.org

Pennsylvania

10,000 Friends of Pennsylvania
1315 Walnut Street
Philadelphia, PA 19107-4725
Phone: 215-985-3201
Fax: 215-985-3207
info@10000friends.org

Pennsylvania Environmental Council
130 Locust Street
Suite 200
Harrisburg, PA 17101
Phone: 717-230-8044
Fax: 717-230-8045
Toll-free contact numbers:
800-322-9214/888-590-7844
http://www.pecpa.org

Rhode Island

Grow Smart Rhode Island
235 Promenade Street
Suite 550
Providence, RI 02908
Phone: 401-273-5711
Fax: 401-228-6594
www.growsmartri.com

South Carolina

South Carolina Coastal Conservation
  League

328 East Bay Street
P.O. Box 1765
Charleston, SC 29401
Phone: 843-723-8035
Fax: 843-723-8308
scccl@charleston.net

Vermont

Vermont Forum on Sprawl
110 Main Street
Burlington, VT 05401
Phone: 802-864-6310
Fax: 802-862-4487
info@vtsprawl.org

Vermont Natural Resources
  Council
9 Bailey Avenue
Montpelier, VT 05602
Phone: 802-223-2328
www.vnrc.org

Wisconsin

1000 Friends of Wisconsin & The Land
  Use Institute
16 North Carroll Street
Suite 810
Madison, WI 53703
Phone: 608-259-1000
Fax: 608-259-1621
friends@1kfriends.org

Regional Groups

British Columbia

Smart Growth BC
402 West Pender Street
#201
Vancouver, BC V6B1T6
Phone: 604-915-5234
Fax: 604-915-5236
info@smartgrowth.bc.ca

California (Bay Area)

Greenbelt Alliance
631 Howard Street
Suite 510
San Francisco, CA 94105

Phone: 415-543-6771
Fax: 415-543-6781
info@greenbelt.org

Chesapeake Bay

Chesapeake Bay Foundation
Philip Merrill Environmental Center
6 Herndon Avenue
Annapolis, MD 21403
Phone: 410-268-8816
Phone: 410-269-0481 (from Baltimore)
Phone: 301-261-2350 (from D.C. metro)
www.cbf.org

Chicago, Illinois

Metropolitan Planning Council
25 East Washington
Suite 1600
Chicago, IL 60602
Phone: 312-922-5616
Fax: 312-922-5619
info@metroplanning.org

Greater Yellowstone Region

Greater Yellowstone Coalition
13 S. Willson
Suite 2
P.O. Box 1874
Bozeman, MT 59771
Phone: 406-586-1593

Fax: 406-556-2839
gyc@greateryellowstone.org

Gulf Coast

Gulf Coast Institute
3015 Richmond
Suite 250
Houston, TX 77098
Phone: 713-523-5757
Fax: 713-523-3057
www.gulfcoastideas.org

New York Metropolitan

Regional Plan Association
4 Irving Place, 7th Floor
New York, NY 10003
Phone: 212-253-2727
Fax: 212-253-5666
www.rpa.org

Piedmont, Virginia

Piedmont Environmental Council
45 Horner Street
Warrenton, VA 20188
Mailing Address:
P.O. Box 460
Warrenton, VA 20188
Phone: 540-347-2334
Fax: 540-349-9003
pec@pecva.org

Ahwahnee Principles for Resource-Efficient Communities

The Ahwahnee Principles are the cornerstone of New Urbanism. They were so named because they were written at the Ahwahnee Lodge in Yosemite National Park in 1991. They are included here because they represent a succinct representation of the development alternatives to sprawl. They can be found online on the Local Government Commission Web site at www.lgc.org/ahwahnee/principles.html.

Ahwahnee Principles

Preamble:

Existing patterns of urban and suburban development seriously impair our quality of life. The symptoms are: more congestion and air pollution resulting from our increased dependence on automobiles, the loss of precious open space, the need for costly improvements to roads and public services, the inequitable distribution of economic resources, and the loss of a sense of community. By drawing upon the best from the past and the present, we can plan communities that will more successfully serve the needs of those who live and work within them. Such planning should adhere to certain fundamental principles.

Community Principles

1. All planning should be in the form of complete and integrated communities containing housing, shops, work places, schools, parks and civic facilities essential to the daily life of the residents.
2. Community size should be designed so that housing, jobs, daily needs and other activities are within easy walking distance of each other.
3. As many activities as possible should be located within easy walking distance of transit stops.
4. A community should contain a diversity of housing types to enable citizens from a wide range of economic levels and age groups to live within its boundaries.
5. Businesses within the community should provide a range of job types for the community's residents.

6. The location and character of the community should be consistent with a larger transit network.
7. The community should have a center focus that combines commercial, civic, cultural and recreational uses.
8. The community should contain an ample supply of specialized open space in the form of squares, greens and parks whose frequent use is encouraged through placement and design.
9. Public spaces should be designed to encourage the attention and presence of people at all hours of the day and night.
10. Each community or cluster of communities should have a well-defined edge, such as agricultural greenbelts or wildlife corridors, permanently protected from development.
11. Streets, pedestrian paths and bike paths should contribute to a system of fully-connected and interesting routes to all destinations. Their design should encourage pedestrian and bicycle use by being small and spatially defined by buildings, trees and lighting; and by discouraging high speed traffic.
12. Wherever possible, the natural terrain, drainage and vegetation of the community should be preserved with superior examples contained within parks or greenbelts.
13. The community design should help conserve resources and minimize waste.
14. Communities should provide for the efficient use of water through the use of natural drainage, drought tolerant landscaping and recycling.
15. The street orientation, the placement of buildings and the use of shading should contribute to the energy efficiency of the community.

Regional Principles

1. The regional land-use planning structure should be integrated within a larger transportation network built around transit rather than freeways.
2. Regions should be bounded by and provide a continuous system of greenbelt/ wildlife corridors to be determined by natural conditions.
3. Regional institutions and services (government, stadiums, museums, etc.) should be located in the urban core.
4. Materials and methods of construction should be specific to the region, exhibiting a continuity of history and culture and compatibility with the climate to encourage the development of local character and community identity.

Implementation Principles

1. The general plan should be updated to incorporate the above principles.
2. Rather than allowing developer-initiated, piecemeal development, local governments should take charge of the planning process. General plans should designate where new growth, infill or redevelopment will be allowed to occur.
3. Prior to any development, a specific plan should be prepared based on these planning principles.
4. Plans should be developed through an open process and participants in the process should be provided visual models of all planning proposals.

Authors: Peter Calthorpe, Michael Corbett, Andres Duany, Elizabeth Moule, Elizabeth Plater-Zyberk, and Stefanos Polyzoides.
Editors: Peter Katz, Judy Corbett, and Steve Weissman.

Glossary

The definitions contained herein are meant to be generally descriptive of the terms included and are not attributable for legal purposes. In all cases, persons are advised to consult with local authorities for specific application of any concept or regulation described in this volume.

Abandoned Property: Real or personal property for which the state or local authorities cannot find the owners of record or their legitimate heirs.

Abandoned Vehicles: Junk cars without claim of ownership by the holder of the title. Often a significant nuisance factor in blighted areas.

Abatement: The forgiveness of all or part of a local tax lien on a property usually granted under state enabling laws to clear the title for new ownership.

Abstract of Title: A listing of all current and previous owners of a particular property provided to establish clear chain of title.

Abutter: Owners of property adjacent to the property of interest, usually required to be notified and who have legal standing in consideration of use changes in the property of interest.

Access Road: A private (or occasionally public) road to provide vehicles to enter and exit the property from the frontage road.

Accessory Apartment: Often referred to as in-law apartments, a supplemental dwelling unit in a traditionally single-family residential zone often restricted to a blood relative of one of the owners of the primary residence. *See also* **Multifamily Residential**; **Single-Family Residential**.

Acquisition Cost: The purchase price of a property including land and buildings.

Ad Valorem Tax: Literally "to the value," meaning taxes generated from the value of property, also referred to as property taxes.

Adaptive Reuse: The creation of an alternate use for an existing structure to allow the building to be brought back to productive consumption, e.g., the conversion of an obsolete school to elderly housing.

Adjustable Rate Mortgage (ARM): A financial instrument, usually accessed at times when interest rates are high, to allow a rate to change during the life of the loan. The amount of variation is usually capped within certain high and low levels. *See also* **Mortgage**.

Administrative Law: Regulations derivative of legislative authority, enforceable by administrative agencies; if necessary, decisions by those agencies may be appealed to the court of jurisdiction.

Adverse Impact: A negative impact of development activity. *See also* **Spillover Effect**.

Aerial Photography: A technical process of taking images of a specific geography and converting them to use for interpretation of land use activities. Usually taken by public agencies at regular intervals (e.g., every 10 years). *See also* **Satellite Imagery**.

Aesthetics: Those characteristics of land development related to design, form, visual impact, etc. Because these do not relate directly to health, safety, and public welfare, they are usually justified on the basis of community character and, on occasion, historic conformity.

Affluent: Refers to income and wealth. Applied often as an adjective to suburban areas with concentrations of high-income families.

Affordable Housing: A general term referring to housing that can be accessed by families below the median family income in an area.

Agglomeration: The economic effect of firms choosing to co-locate in the same general vicinity to take advantages of specialized labor, suppliers, customers, and support services. *See also* **Central Place Theory; Cluster Theory**.

Agricultural Use: A zoning district that specifically permits farming as an allowed use and restricts other commercial and residential uses to those compatible with farming.

Ahwahnee Principles: Adopted in 1991, these are the foundational concepts of new urbanism. *See* Appendix IV.

Aid to Families with Dependent Children (AFDC): A federal program, also known as "welfare," that, until the late 1990s, provided funds to states for distribution to families with dependent children. The philosophy and legal framework changed to create "Transitional Assistance to Needy Families" (TANF), which limits the time that a family receives benefits creating a "transitional" rather than a "permanent" entitlement.

Air Rights: The property rights of land owners to the space above their parcel. Used also as a right for sale in creating buildings over highways, railyards, etc.

Airsheds: The zone of contribution to the atmospheric conditions, particularly air pollution, in an area.

Allodial: The legal regime that allows individuals to have clear title on property and real estate without paying tribute to the monarch or government in place. *See also* **Feudal System**.

Alternative Dispute Resolution: A mediation service available to parties in a dispute to avoid litigation and court battles.

Ambient Air Quality: The air in the immediate vicinity of a receptor, used to define the parameters for calculating air pollution concentrations.

Amenities: Those ancillary uses in close proximity that add value to properties; examples include restaurants, parks, arts and cultural facilities, etc.

American Association of State Highway and Transportation Officials (AASHTO): The public-interest group formed to develop policies and criteria for state transportation activities. One particular function of interest to sprawl actors is the role that AASHTO standards play in determining local road layouts (width, safety, shoulders, drainage, pedestrian and bicycle accommodation, etc).

American Institute of Certified Planners (AICP): The professional organization that creates an examination and certificate program for land-use planners.

American Planning Association (APA): The professional organization providing training, standards, research, and other resources for professional and lay planning officials.

Amortized Loan: A financial instrument which allows the recipient to pay the principal back over a specified period in incremental payments that include interest.

Annexation: The ability of one incorporated municipal jurisdiction to add adjacent land to its geography.

Appraisal: The valuation of a property resulting from a formal procedure, conducted by a certified professional appraiser. Such appraisals are usually required by banks and other mortgage lenders to determine the true loan to value ration as part of the loan approval process.

Appreciation: The increase in the value of an asset over time, an important historical characteristic of real property. *See also* **Depreciation**.

Arterial Street: A major thoroughfare in a community providing vehicles access to commercial centers, etc. *See also* **Collector Roads; Limited Access Highways**.

Assessments: Taxes and special service fees applied to real property to generate revenue for governmental expenditures.

Assumable Mortgage: A loan instrument that allows the purchaser of a property to take over the existing loan on that property.

Attachment: A legal action taken to use property as a security for debt that is in arrears.

Auto-Dependent Land Use: A fundamental characteristic of sprawl where land uses, by their location and regulation, are segregated and diffuse so as to require access by a motor vehicle rather than transit, bicycles, or pedestrians.

Average Daily Traffic: A traffic engineering metric that describes the volume of traffic expected to use a highway in a 24-hour period. *See also* **Peak-Hour Traffic**.

Baby Boom: Referring to the demographic shift that occurred when World War II veterans returned and started families, creating a significant increase in the number of births.

Balloon Payment: A large residual payment of the remaining principal on a short-term loan due at the end of the loan period.

Base Map: A map containing basic geographic features including political boundaries, natural features such as water bodies, and transportation facilities.

Beltway: A limited-access highway built around a major urban center to facilitate the movement of nonlocal vehicular traffic through an area.

Benchmarking: Establishing a set of measures which allow a comparison of one area to another with a particular emphasis on improving the performance of the area to a level meeting or exceeding the performance of other areas.

Betterment: A public improvement, usually financed by the abutting property owners, e.g., sidewalks, sewers, etc.

Bicycle Path: A designated transportation facility set aside for bicycle access which may be co-located on a transportation corridor accommodating other modes (a bicycle lane on a highway or along a rail corridor).

Big-Box Retail: A large, usually over 25,000 square feet, retail facility with one establishment, focusing on a specialty market (e.g., shopper's clubs, building materials, office supplies).

Biodiversity: A scientific term referring to the diversity of biological species in a particular area.

Blight: Refers to dilapidated structures, abandoned property, vacant or abandoned buildings, and other unsightly conditions of property and real estate.

Blockbusting: An illegal practice of purchasing one unit in a residential neighborhood and selling to a racial or ethnic minority with the explicit purpose of scaring other residents to flee, selling off their property at substantial losses.

Blue-Collar: Refers to traditional nonoffice/nonretail employment, usually manufacturing, construction, etc., that does not require business attire. *See also* **White-Collar**.

Boomtowns: Communities that sprang up quickly to respond to a surge in new residential demand, usually based upon new employment opportunities.

Broker: A real estate agent who has secured a higher-level license that allows the supervision of other agents and the ownership of a real estate business.

Brownfields: Land and buildings contaminated by chemicals and other toxic materials from previous, usually industrial activity.

Buffer: Land set aside on one building lot for landscaping, fencing, or other methods of protecting abutters from visual or auditory impacts from activity conducted in the facilities on the property.

Build Absolutely Nothing Anywhere Near Anything (BANANA): A colloquial term in the planning community referring to community opposition to changes in land use. *See also* **Locally Unwanted Land Uses (LULU); Not in My Back Yard (NIMBY)**.

Buildable Lot: A parcel that, under existing land-use regulations, can accept construction to accommodate a permitted use on the property.

Building Codes: Regulations that specify materials, construction techniques, and other aspects of safe construction. Many states have a uniform code based on national standards created by BOCA. Electrical, plumbing, fire safety, and general construction codes are administered by local inspectors.

Building Permit: A legal request for, and permission granting activity for, building activity under local enforced codes.

Build-Out Analysis: A technical procedure which allows a calculation of the maximum amount of development that can still take place in a community based on existing zoning. *See also* **Holding Capacity**.

Bundle of Property Rights: The legal rights that inhere to property and real estate including the right to use, to sell, to pass on to heirs, etc. Subject to governmental regulations that restrict certain types of activity.

Bureau of Labor Statistics (BLS): The federal department that monitors and reports out on employment activity in the economy.

Business Cycle: The ebbs and flows of business activity based on supply and demand and other economic conditions.

Business District: Under zoning, a district that allows certain business uses, usually commercial office rather than retail or manufacturing.

Business Incubator: A building used to create support services and small space for start-up companies to minimize costs.

Capital Budget: That portion of state and local budgeting dedicated to acquisition of land buildings and high-cost durable goods. Usually involves multiyears of financing through bonding and other strategies.

Capital Expenditures: High-cost municipal expenditures such as schools, libraries, fire engines, etc., which require major investments that must be scheduled and financed differently than operating expenditures.

Capital Improvements Program: A scheduled, usually five-year, program updated annually, which allows the community to anticipate capital expenditures and accommodate the demands for infrastructure required by growth.

Carpool: A formal or informal commuting strategy that allows multiple individuals to share their vehicle with other occupants. Different participants may rotate driving duties and use of vehicles. More formal arrangements, vanpools, have a dedicated vehicle and a single driver. Passengers pay a share of the cost and the driver receives certain tax benefits.

Carpool Lanes: Highway lanes that are set aside during peak commuting times for multioccupant vehicles.

Carrying Capacity: The ability of the land to support a particular intensity of development based, primarily, on water supply and waste water treatment systems.

Cartography: The making of maps. With increasingly sophisticated computers and satellite imagery, geographic information systems allow static maps to become highly integrated analytical tools.

Case Law: Law built around legal precedent in court interpretation of certain judicial principles and constructs.

Caveat Emptor: Literally "buyer beware" as a caution to any financial transaction for the buyer to be diligent in exercising oversight of the purchase, warranties, and other rights and constraints implied in the agreement to purchase. *See also* **Due Diligence**.

Cellular Towers: Structures required to carry and enhance signals to cellular communications. Local and state regulations may be in conflict over siting of towers to meet industry requirements.

Census Block: The smallest unit of census geography used in urban areas to differentiate demographic characteristics of neighborhoods.

Census Tract: A unit of census geography that, in urban densities, is assembled from census blocks. However, in less dense areas, the tract may be the smallest unit.

Central Business District (CBD):   That portion of the community, usually referring to cities, where large-scale commercial activities, including office towers, and financial institutions are concentrated. Such areas may have a direct delineation in zoning ordinances or may be more informal. Some cities link the benefits of development in the CBD to other residential neighborhoods to enhance community acceptance and distribution of benefits.

Central Place Theory: A planning construct that posits that economic activity concentrates in specific locations based on a hierarchical distribution into various "districts" (e.g., heavy industrial, warehousing, distribution, etc.). *See also* **Agglomeration**.

Certificate of Occupancy: Issued by the building inspector certifying that the building has met all of the codes, approval conditions, and other legal requirements to be occupied by the new owners or tenants for the prescribed use permitted.

Chain of Title: The various transfers of ownership of a specific piece of property based on land records, which, if historically accurate, lead back to the original acquisition of the property by land grant and forward through successive transactions to the current owner.

Chattel: Personal property as distinguished from real estate.

Citizen Participation: A process, popularized in the second half of the twentieth century and then included in regulations for governmental actions, that allows people affected by a governmental decision to participate through specific channels, including court action if necessary, in directly influencing that decision.

City Beautiful Movement: From 1902, a planning philosophy linked with Burnham, Olmsted, McKim, and Saint-Gaudens that saw planning as an essential function of cities.

City Manager: A professional chief executive of a local government appointed by the elected oversight body but with the powers to oversee personnel, contracts, and, in many cases, appointments boards and commissions. Spawned during the Progressive Era as a response to corruption and patronage.

City Water: Potable water provided to residences, commercial establishments, industry, and other facilities by the local government through a central supply, treatment capacity, and piping.

Civil Rights: Those rights enumerated in the Constitution of the United States and protected and enforced by the executive and judicial branches.

Closing Costs: Those costs and fees required to be supplied by the buyer, and in some cases the seller, at the time of property transfer. Under federal and state law, these costs and fees must be itemized and disclosed to all parties in the transaction.

Cloud on Title: A current or prior claim or lien to a particular property that is considered an impediment which must be satisfied for a new owner to have the entire bundle of rights associated with a clear title.

Cluster Development: A development design technique that concentrates buildings on a portion of the site to allow the remaining land to be used for open space, recreation, or preservation of environmentally sensitive land areas. *See also* **Density Bonus**; **Planned Unit Development**.

Cluster Theory: Developed by Professor Michael Porter at the Harvard Business School, clusters are concentrations of industrial types that tend to concentrate in specific locations (*see* **Agglomeration**) and attract other firms in similar or supporting industries to locate in the same general area. Specialized support including education, legal and accounting services, focused suppliers, and labor with appropriate skills fill out the model. Examples include the tulip industry in Holland, the shoe industry in Italy, the wine industry in California, etc.

Coastal Zone: Under federal law, the land area, within certain prescribed boundaries that abut an ocean, gulf, or tidal area, which is protected from encroachment and prohibited from certain land uses.

Codicil: An amendment or attachment to a will that provides additional directives without altering the basic provisions of the original will.

Co-generation: The mixing of combustible solid waste (trash) and sludge residue from wastewater treatment facilities with other fuel sources as necessary to burn for generation of steam and electricity. *See also* **Incinerator**; **Solid Waste**.

Cohort Projection: A demographic forecasting technique built on monitoring various age segments (cohorts) through the forecasting period which, when considered with births, deaths, and in/out migration, gives and estimate of the population in a particular future period.

Collateral: Property (usually real estate, but may include personal and financial assets), which is pledged as security for a loan.

Collector Roads: A traffic engineering term meaning lesser roadways in a community which feed local traffic onto roads that provide throughput and connection to other major centers of activity. *See also* **Arterial Streets**; **Limited Access Highways**.

Combined Sewer Overflow: The mixing of stormwater and sanitary sewer flows in older urban systems that, on heavy storm events, cause a surge in wastewater that overwhelms the treatment capacity of the system.

Commercial Bank: A financial institution focusing on short-term loans as an alternative to savings and loans (thrifts).

Commercial Center: A portion of the community set aside for retail trade.

Common Law: Law built on current practice and precedent built on community standards as interpreted by the courts rather than formal legislation.

Community Bank Reinvestment Act: Federal law, paralleled in some states, requiring financial institutions to invest in the communities where they have offices. *See also* **Redlining**.

Community Development: Referring to the variety of activities in a local government involved with planning and overseeing development, including planning, zoning, economic development, permitting, and often including inspections and enforcement.

Community Policing: A technique of law enforcement designed to provide an active and visible presence of uniformed personnel in a neighborhood with an emphasis on community involvement in monitoring and preventing criminal activity.

Community Property: Under the laws of some states, this legal concept defines all property as held in common by both spouses in a marriage, requiring an equitable distribution in the event of dissolution.

Commuter Rail: A system of mass transit in some metropolitan areas using the same gauge of rail and similar equipment as longer-distance passenger rail.

Compact Development: A loosely defined term suggesting an alternative to sprawl by increasing allowable densities for residential development and non-auto dependent access.

Company Town: Referring to communities that were built about a single industry or firm and are dependent on the success of that enterprise for its vitality and potential existence.

Compensatory Damages: Provided voluntarily, but usually under legal sanction, to offset the damages caused by an individual or firm to life and limb or to property.

Comprehensive Plan: *See* **Master Plan**.

Computer Aided Design (CAD): A design and drafting computer program used for technical drawings and blueprints.

Computer Simulation: The use of computer models to generate potential future conditions in land-use, transportation, and other infrastructure requirements. More recently, sophisticated visualization enhancements have been added to simulation models that allow alternative scenarios to be displayed on maps, in three-dimensional virtual landscapes, and quantitative impacts displayed.

Conditional Use Permit: Allowing a use that served a public need (e.g., a medical facility), which under the regulations would not be permitted.

Condominium: A form of property ownership that allows individual units in a multiunit complex to be sold to separate owners. Owners also own an interest in the overall property and shared areas. Usually overseen by an association that provides for the upkeep, maintenance, and improvements. Unit owners participate in the associations based on their share of the property and pay a fee to the association for shared services.

Congestion Pricing: A traffic management practice designed to manage demand for transportation facilities during peak use periods by placing a surcharge on the use of the facility during those periods.

Congregate Housing: A form of residential living in which multiple individuals share a building. There are private areas for each occupant and common areas for cooking, eating, and other shared activities.

Conservation Area: An area set aside, permanently or for a designated period, to protect the land from encroaching development. Often associated with the additional purpose of protecting flora and fauna habitat, the areas may be publicly or privately owned and managed.

Conservation Subdivision: A modification of cluster and planned unit development with a specific emphasis of allowing low-impact development to be accommodated in harmony with natural areas.

Consistency: The provision in law and regulation that requires one set of activities to be certified as consistent with other laws and regulations before the activities can proceed. For example, transportation plans and projects must be deemed consistent with the air quality plans for an area.

Consolidated Metropolitan Statistical Area (CMSA): If an area that qualifies as a metropolitan area (MA) has 1 million people or more, two or more primary metropolitan statistical areas (PMSAs) may be defined within it. Each PMSA consists of a large urbanized county or cluster of counties (or cities and towns in New England) that demonstrate very strong internal economic and social links, in addition to close ties to other portions of the larger area. When PMSAs are established, the larger MA of which they are component parts is designated a consolidated metropolitan statistical area (CMSA). CMSAs and PMSAs are established only where local governments favor such designations for a large MA. See the *City County Data Book 2003*.

Constitutional Rights: Those rights and personal responsibilities itemized in federal and state constitutions that cannot be infringed upon by public or private action.

Construction Loan: A financial transaction that allows a builder or developer to secure resources for creating improvements to land and buildings which will be discharged at the time that the land and buildings are sold to new owners.

Contract Zoning: Similar to spot zoning, this practice allows the local land-use authority to create an agreement with a property owner to revise the zoning for that particular parcel according to agreed upon specifications. Of questionable legality.

Conventional Loan: A traditional loan from a financial institution to purchase a piece of property based exclusively on the value of the property and the buyer's financial resources, as an alternative to a loan guaranteed or subsidized by the government or one of its agencies.

Conveyance Tax: *See* **Real Estate Transfer Tax**.

Cookie-Cutter Subdivision: A derogatory colloquial term referring to tract-housing subdivisions which limit the styles of construction available to individual owners.

Co-op Housing: A form of residential ownership in which occupants have a share in a corporation that owns the complex and operates it for the benefit of the residents.

Core-Based Areas: The general concept of a metropolitan or micropolitan statistical area is that of a core area containing a substantial population nucleus, together with adjacent communities having a high degree of economic and social integration with that core. *See* www.census.gov.

Corporate Farm: Agricultural-use property owned and managed by a corporation rather than an individual or family.

Corporation: A legal framework for creating and conducting a business enterprise. Corporations operate under state and federal regulations and have the same capacity to transact enterprise as an individual providing some protection for the personal assets of the incorporators and investor.

Cost Recovery: A tax-law term referring to depreciation.

Cost-Benefit Analysis: A technical procedure used to justify major public expenditures by testing the value of the potential use (benefit) against the amount of financial burden (cost) placed on the taxpayers. *See also* **Fiscal Impact**.

Country Life Movement: A populist and informal focus on the values and benefits of rural living usually focused on agricultural activity with the skills and respect for land and nature that grows out of this lifestyle. Spawned in the first half of the twentieth century as a reaction to increasing urbanization of the country, the antecedents of this value system are clearly visible in the sprawl debate.

County Government: In most areas of the country, counties are that unit of local government that oversees unincorporated land and public services including police, fire, schools, infrastructure, many court and criminal justice activities, and other social services. In New England, where the vast majority of the land is contained in municipal corporations performing these same functions, counties are a vestigial level of government and in some states exist only as a geographical description.

Covenant: A legal instrument creating an agreement among multiple parties limiting the use of the properties described in the agreement. Usually incorporated into the deeds of the respective properties. *See also* **Deed Restrictions; Easement**.

Covenant Running with the Land: An agreement which is attached to the right to use property rather that a limitation imposed only on the current owners.

Cross Acceptance: A provision in law or regulation that streamlines a permitting process by allowing various boards and commissions to allow one board's action to also be accepted for another board subject to certain restrictions and specifications.

Cul-de-sac: A road that has only one point of entrance and egress that ends in a circular turn around. Property owners, particularly in residential areas, consider such a layout beneficial to single-family homes as a traffic limiting strategy. Traffic engineers require that such layouts be large enough to accommodate fire engines and other essential access.

Curb-Cut: The provision in local and state regulation to permit access to a frontage road for abutting property owners. As retail, commercial, and other traffic-intensive land uses are permitted, some jurisdictions require a consolidation of access points to allow for signalization and other traffic management strategies.

Curtesy: Those rights of a surviving husband to property owned by a deceased wife. *See also* **Dower Right**.

Datum: A "benchmark" horizontal plane (e.g., sea level) that is used to calculate other heights and depths.

Day Care Facility: A state licensed facility to provide child care during parental working hours.

Debt Service: The amount of funds set aside each year by a public entity to pay interest on bonds and other outstanding debt.

Dedication: A specific reservation and transfer of private property for a public use (streets, schools).

Deed: A legal instrument that is registered with the public land records recording ownership of a property described in the document. *See also* **Property Description; Title**.

Deed Restrictions: Legal limitations described in the deed which limit the bundle of rights normally associated with property ownership. *See also* **Covenant; Easement**.

Default: A judgment that a loan is in sufficient arrears as to be deemed that the borrower will not make payment. May also apply to other pledges, promises, or obligations of a legal nature

Defeasance Clause: Legal language included in a deed which establishes the basis under which a right to the property is eliminated when a specified action is taken (e.g., mortgage is cancelled when the principal is paid in full).

Deforestation: The elimination of all trees in an area due to natural (e.g., forest fire) or human action (e.g., clear-cutting).

Demographics: The science of cataloguing characteristics of human populations (e.g., race, gender, age, etc.) currently and measuring change over time.

Demolition: The destruction of a building or structure on a property. A permit is often required to assure that materials are disposed of properly.

Density: A term generally used in many zoning codes to describe the number of dwelling units allowed on an area of land, but it can also refer to the square footage of nonresidential space on a lot.

Density Bonus: A provision in local regulations that allows additional units to be constructed in a smaller area, usually to allow lower density in a natural or conservation area. *See also* **Cluster Development**; **Planned Unit Development (PUD)**.

Department of Housing and Urban Development (HUD): The federal agency established in 1965 to oversee a variety of programs assisting cities, including rental and home ownership subsidies, urban renewal, and its antecedent block grants, etc.

Depreciation: The decline in residual value of an asset over time. *See also* **Appreciation**.

Design Guidelines: Specifications for building form, facade, size, bulk, etc., drawn from architectural standards.

Detention Basin: An area set aside to capture runoff from construction or other land-disturbing activities.

Developer: An individual or firm whose interest in real estate is transforming it from one use to a more intense use and then turning the property over to a new owner.

Development Agreement: A legal instrument which sets internal specifications for a specific site, beyond the minimum requirements under the laws and regulations.

Development of Regional Impact: Used in a number of growth-management laws and regulations, this refers to developments of a size and scale to have impacts far beyond the abutting owners (e.g., shopping mall, large residential complex, industrial plant).

Development Right: *See* **Highest and Best Use**.

Dillon's Rule: Refers to a 1868 court case presided over by a judge named John F. Dillon which confirmed that local governments are creatures of the state and can only perform functions that they are specifically authorized to perform. *See also* **Enabling Acts**; **Home Rule**; **Local Government**.

Discrimination: The intentional or unintentional restriction of access to residential units, employment, and public accommodations based on race, gender, age, or other condition.

Distressed Neighborhood: *See* **Blight**.

Dower: The legal right of a female spouse to her husband's property at time of his death. *See also* **Curtesy**.

Downtown: *See* **Central Business District**.

Downtown Improvement District: A legal district established under land-use regulations which allows the assessment of a "betterments fee" for public improvements including amenities.

Downzoning: A legal action taken to modify the use allowances in a zoning district to a lower threshold of density, floor area ratio, size, bulk, etc.

Drainage Basin: The topographical feature (natural or man-made) that allows surface runoff to collect for storage, aquifer recharge, or eventual migration to other surface water.

Due Diligence: The process of securing adequate information to protect a property owner from undisclosed impediments on the property. *See also* **Caveat Emptor**.

Due Process: The legal process that guarantees that the rights of citizens, including property owners, are protected under the constitution and laws of the governments exercising jurisdiction over them.

Duplex: A residential structure with two units one of which may be occupied by the owner and the other rented to a tenant. Both units may be rented. *See also* **Triple Decker**.

Dwelling Unit: A residential unit occupied by one or more individuals.

Earnest Money: Funds given as a pledge to honor a contract (e.g., a deposit).

Earth Removal: The physical process of removing sand, gravel, topsoil, and other materials from one location for use in another.

Easement: The legal granting of a right to use all or part of a piece of property for a limited access (pipeline, road, etc.). *See also* **Covenant**; **Deed Restrictions**.

Economic Base: Referring to firms in an area whose primary activity is exporting goods and services outside of the region.

Economic Development: The interface between governmental entities and private sector firms seeking to locate, expand, or, in some cases, be retained in an area.

Economic Life: The useful life of a building, structure, or other durable good.

Ecosystem: The universe of life and its supporting conditions in an area.

Edge City: A term coined by author Joel Garreau referring to significant communities on the periphery of traditional metropolitan areas.

Education: *See* **Public Education**.

Effluent: The residual wastewater and materials still contained or dissolved within it that leaves a wastewater treatment facility.

Elastic City: A term coined by author David Rusk referring to cities, essentially in the South and West, that have the ability to annex unincorporated land in adjacent counties.

Emblements: Agricultural products grown on the land.

Eminent Domain: Taking a piece of private property for public use. This legal procedure requires the public entity to provide just compensation to the private property owner.

Employer-Assisted Housing: A form of subsidy in high-cost housing markets where firms offset the cost of rents and home ownership to attract and retain workers.

Empty Nester: Families who continue to reside in their home after the children have departed.

Enabling Acts: Refers to the power vested in state legislatures to restrict or provide legal authorization to local governments. *See also* **Dillon's Rule**; **Home Rule**.

Encroachment: When land uses have a negative or external impact on abutting uses.

Encumbrance: Anything that decreases the value of the property or its use (lien, judgment, easement, etc.).

Endangered Species: A legal and scientific definition referring to flora or fauna that are threatened with extinction.

Energy Efficient: Referring to buildings, structures, appliances that consume energy without significant waste.

Enterprise Zone: An area of economic distress targeted for intensive revitalization by attracting firms with tax subsidies, indigenous workforce training, and other focused activities.

Environmental Impact: Under the NEPA, the identification of the impacts of human activity on the natural environment which must be mitigated to allow the development to proceed.

Environmental Justice: Environmental justice is based on the principle that all people have a right to be protected from environmental pollution and to live in and enjoy a clean and healthful environment. Environmental justice is the equal protection and meaningful involvement of all people with respect to the development, implementation, and enforcement of environmental laws, regulations, and policies and the equitable distribution of environmental benefits. (From the Environmental Justice Policy of the Executive Office of Environmental Affairs, p. 1.)

Equal Protection: A civil right guaranteed under the Fourteenth Amendment of the U.S. Constitution.

Equalization: The technical and financial process of standardizing the assessments on real property.

Equity: A social and economic principle measuring the differential impact of policies on different populations.

Erosion: The carrying away of topsoil and other earthen materials by moving water or, in severely drought ridden areas, by the wind.

Escheat: When property reverts to the local government due to the death of the owner without a will or established heirs.

Escrow: The legal and financial process of holding monies paid on deposit for property transfers or for future tax payments by real estate firms or lending institutions.

Estate: The assets of a deceased person including real and personal property that are disposed of under the laws of the state.

Estoppel: A legal term referring to a person relying on the statement, incorrectly, that someone is acting as someone else's agent.

Euclid, Ohio: A city in the Cleveland area that became memorialized in the U.S. Supreme Court case validating zoning.

Euclidean Zoning: A conventional nickname for traditional as-of-right or self-executing zoning in which district regulations are explicit; residential, commercial, and industrial uses are segregated; districts are cumulative; and bulk and height controls are imposed. The term is derived from the 1926 U.S. Supreme Court decision *Euclid (Ohio) v. Ambler Realty Co.*, which upheld comprehensive zoning. (From Michael Davidson and Fay Dolnick, *A Planners Dictionary* [Chicago: American Planning Association, 2004], p. 166.)

Eutrophication: The process of a lake or pond gradually being transformed into a swamp bog, wetland, or even land through the decay of organic material.

Eviction: The lawful expulsion of a tenant from the leased property due to a default in the tenant's compliance with the lease.

Evidence of Title: A legal instrument that provides a basis for claiming ownership to real property.

Exactions: The extraction of fees or other concessions from land owners wishing to develop property into a higher use. *See also* **Impact Fees**; **Rational Nexus**.

Exclusionary Zoning: The practice of creating social impediments to the ownership of land and real estate by restrictive land use regulations. *See also* **Inclusionary Zoning**; **Snob Zoning**.

Expiring Use: The removal of a rental property from the role of supplying low- and moderate-income families when the subsidies expire.

Externality: *See* **Spillover Effect**.

Exurban: Those lands on the periphery of a metropolitan area that are ripening for more intense development as the market creates a demand for lower cost lots.

Facade: The front part of a building which faces the street and presents an aesthetic presence as part of the visual streetscape.

Fair Housing Acts: Legislation, both federal and state, which requires landlords and sellers of real estate to make their properties available for lease or sale to individuals regardless of race, creed, color, physical disability, gender, or national origin. Some laws extend these protections to other individuals preventing discrimination based on having children, sexual orientation, and so on.

Fair Market Value: The appraised value of a property based on current market conditions and comparable properties in the area.

Faith-Based Organizations: Nonprofit service providers that have their principal operational values grounded in sectarian religion.

Fannie Mae: The agency established by the federal government to underwrite and guarantee mortgages.

Farm Belt: The Midwestern region of the country which has an agriculture-based economy.

Farmers Home Administration: The federal agency which provides a variety of services to agricultural-based businesses, including low interest loans.

Federal Deposit Insurance Corporation (FDIC): The agency established to underwrite the savings and loan industry providing protection to individual depositors in the event of bank failure.

Federal Home Loan Bank: The agency responsible for overseeing banks which primarily provide loans and mortgages for residential property.

Federal Reserve System: The organization which oversees the commercial banking system, monitoring the national economy and using its power to set interest rates as a means of controlling inflation.

Fee Simple Absolute: The purest form of real estate ownership in which the entire bundle of property rights is retained by the owner.

Feudal: A land ownership system that places all real estate in the hands of the monarch and his minions requiring others (subjects) to lease the land. *See also* **Allodial**.

FHA Loans: Originally, the Federal Housing Administration, which provided low interest, federally guaranteed loans to qualified home buyers. *See also* **Veterans Administration Loans**.

First-Tier Suburbs: The municipalities which sprang up around central cities and are now experiencing both the advantages and disadvantages of urban growth and decline.

Fiscal Disparity: An economic and social construct designed to measure the differential capacity of cities and towns to generate revenue to meet their demands for public services and improvements.

Fiscal Impact: An analytical discipline which allows planners to calculate the revenue that will be generated from a particular land use and then compare it to the demand for services that the land use will require. *See also* **Cost-Benefit Analysis**.

Fiscal Zoning: The practice of determining the optimal land uses to be permitted in zoning districts based on their net positive fiscal impact.

Flag Lots: Parcels of land created in a subdivision which have a very limited frontage providing access to a large buildable lot behind another parcel creating a "flaglike" picture with the short frontage and access as the "pole" and the larger back lot as the "flag."

Flood Control: Regulations which limit development and build flood management systems (dikes, storage areas, etc.) adjacent to rivers that experience significant seasonal variations in water flow.

Floor Area Ratio: The floor area of a building or buildings on a lot divided by the lot area. This is frequently used as a zoning tool that regulates the density of a development as it relates to the size of the lot. The higher the ratio, the more dense the development. *See also* **Land to Building Ratio**.

Forecasting: A technical procedure using current and historical data to predict future economic, social, or demographic conditions and their impacts on an area.

Foreclosure: The legal procedure for reclaiming property used to secure a loan/mortgage in the event of default.

Fraud: The deliberate and intentional misrepresentation of the facts in order to secure support, financial and otherwise, for a business venture or real estate transaction.

Frontage: The boundary of a property that abuts a road or highway. Most zoning regulations contain a minimum frontage requirement.

Garden Apartment: A small rental unit, usually in a large complex, which is enhanced by the capacity to grow plants in a small window box or shrubs on adjacent plots.

Gated Community: A residential area, usually under some form of homeowners' association, which provides security by a shared perimeter wall and access to the area through a secure common entrance.

Gentrification: Literally meaning that the "gentry" (re)occupy an area. The term applies to older residential areas which are discovered by bargain-hunting property owners who improve the units and the area, making it attractive and more valuable, but, as a consequence, price out the lower-income residents who can no longer afford to live in the area.

Geography: The study of human settlements on the land over time.

Geology: The study of the earth's surface and subsurface with a primary focus on the rocks and minerals and the historical dynamics that create observable and important differences in the make up of an area.

Geographical Information System (GIS): The ability to create and manipulate spatial data to make maps and analyze the interaction of special characteristics on particular areas and monitor changes over time. The advent of computers and now high-end desktop software allow computer-based mapping to become an essential part of community planning.

Grandfathering: A legal process which allows current uses to continue in a zone, after the ordinance changes and such uses would no longer be permitted. *See also* **Nonconforming Use**.

Greenbelt: The creation of a permanent open-space reservation around urban areas to help shape development and protect urban environments from losing their natural connections.

Greenfield Development: Using open vacant land for development rather than redeveloping or in-filling existing areas. *See also* **Leapfrog Development**.

Greenway: A dedicated open natural area through a developed area to allow active and passive recreation.

Grid Pattern: A development plan which lays out proposed residential, commercial, and other uses along a street network of parallel and perpendicular roads creating square blocks and linear development.

Gridlock: A traffic engineering term referring to a congestion situation which is so overloaded that no vehicles can move.

Ground Cover: A landscaping description of flowers, shrubs, plants, grass, and other natural vegetation as a way to reclaim a site after construction activity is finished.

Groundwater: Water naturally occurring below the earth's surface that is extracted by a well.

Group Homes: Residential facilities that are established to allow nonrelated individuals to live together for an extended period, usually based on physical or mental disability, or due to a temporary condition such as release from incarceration or protection from abuse or neglect.

Growing Smart: *See* **1000 Friends Movement**; **Smart Growth**.

Growth Boundary: A boundary located to mark the outer limit beyond which development is prohibited or discouraged in order to minimize sprawl by containing development within the boundary over a specific period of time.

Growth Management: A wide range of land-use planning techniques that determine the amount, type, and rate of development in a given community and attempt to steer such development where most appropriate based on infrastructure, development constraints, environmental factors, and the like.

Habendum Clause: A portion of a deed which specifies the type of interest/ownership being transferred (e.g., fee simple, **life estate**).

Habitat: Referring primarily to that geography and set of conditions necessary to sustain species of wildlife.

Habitat for Humanity: An organization which supplies volunteer labor to build residences for indigent families.

Hazardous Materials: Toxic substances created for or by industrial processes which require special handling, disposal, and management in the event of spills.

Height Limits: The specification in zoning ordinances of the maximum number of stories allowed based on fire codes and the availability of equipment to suppress fires in these buildings. Height restrictions are also enforced by the FAA in the flight paths near airports.

Heir: An individual entitled to inherit the assets of someone at the time of death. If a person dies intestate (without a will), the state determines the rightful heirs.

High Occupancy Vehicle (HOV) Lane: The designation of a specific lane of a highway during certain times of the day for vehicles occupied by two or more persons.

Highest and Best Use: The use of a property that would bring the owner the most income.

High-Rise Apartment: Residential units in dense urban areas characterized by many stories.

Historic District: A special zoning district requiring all building, renovations, and improvements to adhere to strict design guidelines (paint color, no aluminum siding, no modern windows, etc.).

Holding Capacity: The theoretical amount of capacity of the land to support development based on current infrastructure. *See also* **Build-Out Analysis**.

Home Equity Loan: Using a portion of the value of one's personal residence as security for obtaining a personal loan, not to finance the property itself.

Home Mortgage Disclosure Act (HMDA): Federal law governing the requirements of financial institutions to disclose their lending practices.

Home Occupation: Under zoning regulations, the allowed use, usually by special permit, to conduct a business in a private residence.

Home Ownership: The purchase of residential real estate for individual or family occupancy, rather than for rental.

Home Rule: The authority, granted under some state constitutions that allows local governments to petition the state legislature to expand their ability to provide services. *See also* **Dillon's Rule**; **Enabling Acts**; **Local Government**.

Homelessness: A social condition present in many communities, in which individuals or families do not live in a residence but, instead, reside in shelters or on the streets.

Homeowners Association: A legal organization, established in certain residential locations, of multiple property owners that oversees commonly held assets, usually infrastructure (common well, package treatment plant, private road) or amenities (swimming pool).

Homestead: Private homes usually held harmless in bankruptcy proceedings.

Housing Authority: A legal entity created by local jurisdictions to build, manage, and maintain public housing.

Housing Market: The supply and demand for residential units within a geographical area. Usually segmented between rental and owner occupied.

Housing Project: Referring to large-scale subsidized residential complexes built and managed by housing authorities for low-income families.

Housing Rehabilitation: Renovation of substandard residential units.

Human Services: Those social services provided by government to assist certain sectors of the population (e.g., youth, elderly, etc.).

Hydrology: The science of managing and using ground and surface water.

Hypothecation: Using real estate as collateral for borrowing money.

Impact Analysis: The technical process of quantifying the impacts of development on the environment and on existing infrastructure to determine the extent of mitigation required.

Impact Fees: The assessment of a charge by a local government on new development to offset the costs of providing additional infrastructure and other public services to the development. *See also* **Exactions**; **Rational Nexus**.

Impermeable Surface: The coverage of land by buildings, paved roads, and parking lots creating a barrier to water passing through the soil and recharging ground water.

Improvement: Those buildings and structures added to a property by the private owner which add value. Public improvements are investments made using tax dollars, which add value to abutting owners including streets, sewers, sidewalks, water supply, etc.

Incinerator: A solid-waste facility designed to burn refuse. Many incinerators have been shut down or significantly reconditioned to meet air pollution requirements. Some incinerators use the energy to generate electricity. *See also* **Co-generation**; **Solid Waste**.

Inclusionary Zoning: The specific requirements included in some state laws to provide a percentage of affordable housing in every development. Some local jurisdictions in other states make such a provision in their local ordinances. *See also* **Exclusionary Zoning**; **Snob Zoning**.

Incorporeal Right: Easements or rights of way which are the explicit rights of others to access private property for specific purposes.

Indicators: A set of data and/or metrics used to track the performance of various socioeconomic functions in a region over time. Indicators, used correctly, measure the effect of policies created to enhance the quality or quantity of the area. Using time series data, the indicator provides feedback on the actions taken to implement the policy and allows for an adjustment in the actions to improve the results.

Industrial Parks: A corporation (public, private, or nonprofit) that creates, develops, and manages a large tract of land for industrial development.

Infill Development: The process of building new residential units on vacant or abandoned lots as a way to revitalize a neighborhood.

Inflation: An increase in the cost of goods and property which also has the effect of increasing the purchasing price and subsequent reduction in the value of a specific amount of financial resources.

Infrastructure Sufficiency: A legal test used in some jurisdictions which assures that adequate water, sewer, and transportation capacity exist before permitting new development.

Inheritance Tax: Tax burden on the transfer of property at the time of death. Currently a state legal regime.

Inner City: That portion of a city composed of dense residential development, usually a negative connotation implying blight.

Inner-Ring Suburbs: Incorporated municipalities which surround a central city.

Institute of Traffic Engineers: The organization which, among other things, publishes standards for trip generation rates of various land uses which power traffic models.

Interchange: The access and egress of a major, limited-access highway. May provide ramps for traffic in all directions or partial access unidirectional on or off. Traditional configurations are cloverleaf and diamond.

Intercity: Describing various relationships of competition, cooperation, or connection between major cities.

Interest: A charge associated with the use of a financial institution's money. Alternatively, the return on funds invested in a bank.

Intergovernmental: Referring to relationships between layers of government (federal, state, county, municipal).

Intersection: The point of crossing between two (or more) thoroughfares.

Interstate Highway: Originally established in 1956 as part of the Federal Aid Highway Act, the goal was to provide coast-to-coast travel "without a traffic light." Major north/south routes have an odd number. East/west routes are even-numbered. Three-digit routes are spurs, bypasses, or connectors around the route number.

Interurban Transit: An alternate name for light rail and commuter rail transit service.

Intrinsic Value: Used in appraisals as a value accruing to a property based on the personal tastes of potential buyers.

Inverse Condemnation: A "taking" of private property without just or adequate compensation.

Joint and Severable Liability: A legal term referring to the burden on owners of assets to have those assets at risk in litigation (joint) and which can also be applied to one owner in the event that other owners are not associated with the case (severable).

Joint Tenancy: A form of ownership of property between several parties which allows the passage of all rights to the surviving owner(s) in the death of one of the parties.

Joint Venture: Two or more individuals acting together in a business enterprise for a specific project rather than a full partnership on all business activities.

Judgment: A court decision which settles a dispute between parties. Judgments against the real property of one of the parties must be recorded as a lien.

Just Compensation: A legal term describing the adequate provision of financial or other resources to an injured party or the owner whose property has been taken by eminent domain.

Labor Market: That geography from which workers can be drawn to firms based on reasonable commuting distances. Definitions of counties included in labor market areas are developed by the U.S. Department of Labor and do not cross state lines.

Land and Water Conservation Fund: A federal program administered by the U.S. Department of the Interior which provides monies to states to purchase land and, on occasion, water bodies, watersheds, and threatened coastal areas.

Land Classification: A system of identifying land areas by (un)suitability of use for certain activities, e.g., agriculture, wetlands, etc.

Land Grant: Under colonial settlement compacts, the king, through royal governors, would grant tracts of land to settlers willing to establish homesteads, harvest timber, plant crops, and begin to send products and raw materials back to the home country. Alternatively, a process of awarding original charters to certain colleges and universities based on the Morrill Acts of 1862 and 1890.

Land Owner: The individual(s) or firm(s) that holds title to a piece of property.

Land Parcels: Legal segments of land, subdivided according to the laws of the state and the community, that are deemed real property subject to the property laws of the state and local government in which they are located.

Land Records: The legal documents required to register all property transactions including transfers, subdivisions, liens, easements, covenants, etc. Each state designates the appropriate local locations where land records must be recorded, and here these documents may be reviewed by the public.

Land Rent: The financial consideration given to the owner of a property when the property is leased to a tenant.

Land Suitability Analysis: A technical procedure using soil surveys, aquifer locations, draining and runoff, flooding, depth to bedrock, and other land conditions to determine appropriate sustainable uses for the land.

Land Survey: A technical procedure performed by a licensed land surveyor defining the boundaries of a parcel. The location of buildings and structures, easements and covenants, rights of way, slope, wetlands, etc., may also be included.

Land to Building Ratio: A calculation of the relationship between the total land area (denominator) and the footprint of buildings and structures (nominator). *See also* **Floor Area Ratio**.

Land Trust: A public or private entity established to purchase land, usually for preservation or protection.

Land Use: The specification of various categories of buildings, structures, and enterprises that are permitted on land parcels within a jurisdiction. General categories include residential, commercial (retail and office), and industrial.

Landlord: A property owner who leases space in a building or on the land to a tenant.

Landscape Architecture: A professional discipline focused on enhancing the use of land areas to improve visual appeal, manage drainage, protect against erosion, buffer land uses from abutting properties through plantings and other barriers, etc.

Land-Use Regulation: The legal ordinances and derivative regulations that specify how land is subdivided and zoned, and what uses are permitted. Such regulations are enacted at the local level under state laws enabling such authority.

Large-Lot Zoning: A term used to describe the practice in some jurisdictions of requiring larger parcels in residential subdivisions than would be necessary to manage the safe operation of on-site water and septic systems. Often used pejoratively to highlight a practice that may have an exclusionary effect.

Leapfrog Development: A descriptive term referring to a tendency in sprawl for new development to bypass existing built-up areas into open rural environments. *See also* **Greenfield Development**.

Lease: A legal instrument created between a landlord and a tenant describing the conditions, financial and otherwise, that the owner requires to rent the space to the tenant.

Leasehold Estate: The right of a tenant to occupy or use a property during the period of the rental agreement.

Legal Description: The property description included in a deed specifying metes and bounds, locating benchmarks, and such other information as may be necessary to locate it by a land surveyor.

Leverage: The use of property to secure financing from sources other than the owner. This allows a small initial investment (equity position) for the owner to secure the property.

Levittown: Several communities developed in the Northeast by one developer in the second half of the twentieth century, purchasing a large tract of land and subdividing it into small lots, building starter houses based on uniform styles and models for young families. Recognized for both positive and negative impacts, these developments are often pointed to as early manifestations of sprawl.

Levy: The legal assessment of annual taxes on all properties in a jurisdiction.

Life Estate: A restriction in the rights to use the property to the lifetime of the designated person usually included in a will transferring the property to heirs.

Life-Cycle Costing: A full-cost allocation of capital investments over the expected useful life of the asset.

Light Industry: A descriptive term referring to industries which do not have heavy manufacturing processes (smokestack industries) associated with their research, development, and eventual manufacture.

Light Rail Transit: Trolleys and subways, operating on fixed rail guideways but not at the same gauge as regular rail facilities.

Limited Liability Corporation (LLC): A hybrid business arrangement, governed by state laws, that mixes various legal benefits and protections of corporations and partnerships.

Limited Partnership: A legal framework for property development and management where some partners (limited) are investors and others manage the enterprise. Limited partners are at risk only to the extent of their investment.

Limited-Access Highway: Major highways that restrict access by vehicles to designated interchange locations (e.g., Interstate Highways).

Linkage: A legal framework for allowing some of the revenues derived from intense commercial and industrial development to be used to benefit residential, particularly distressed areas, neighborhoods.

Liquidated Damages: In the case of a breach of an agreement by one party, the agreed-upon amount of compensation to the other party(ies).

Liquidity: The relative ease of turning a fixed asset (real or personal property) to cash without a significant loss.

Lis Pendens: A legal instrument notifying the owner (and lien holders, and, because it is a recorded transaction in the land records, the general public) that court action is pending affecting the property.

Littoral Rights: The alternative legal framework to riparian rights for land abutting water bodies designating the rights to use water and the boundary line of these properties at the high-water mark. *See also* **Riparian Right**.

Loan to Value Ratio: A calculation used in determining the amount of equity to be pledged by a financial institution for a mortgage based on the market value of the property established by an appraisal.

Local Government: Political subdivisions of the state including towns, townships, cities, and counties, organized to provide services within a designated geography. These governments are empowered to tax, expend, incur debts, and pass locally functional legislation. However, as "creatures of the state," unless a home-rule provision is included in the state constitution, they are only allowed to perform functions specifically enabled under state law. *See also* **Dillion's Rule**; **Home Rule**.

Local Legislative Body: Under the municipal charter, that body that is empowered to create and amend laws and regulations. Examples include city council, town meeting, etc. In counties, the Board of County Commissioners usually performs this function.

Locally Unwanted Land Uses (LULU):   Refers to land-use practices that bend to the will of a vocal citizenry to keep out whatever proposed uses have received negative attention. Examples include such different projects as hazardous waste facilities and group homes. *See also* **Build Absolutely Nothing Anywhere Near Anything (BANANA)**; **Not in My Back Yard (NIMBY)**.

Location Efficient Mortgage: A financial instrument that gives credit in the income calculations for residences near transit stations which reduce or eliminate the need for an automobile.

Loft Apartments: Inexpensive residential units located in industrial or warehouse districts. Often associated with artists who create live/work studios from high ceiling industrial buildings.

Low-Income Housing: Residential units built for families which meet threshold income levels. May include rental or ownership options with subsidies to the building or through a voucher to the tenant.

Mansionization: A recent phenomenon where small residential units are purchased and the majority of the unit is torn down to create a much larger unit on the same land.

Manufactured Housing: Prefabricated residential units that are created in a factory, then trucked to and assembled on a prepared site.

Manufacturing: Referring to industrial processes that create goods from raw materials or parts created in one location and assembled in a plant to make products.

Market Analysis: Similar to an appraisal but without the required certification, a comparison of a property to recent property transactions nearby to determine a listed selling price.

Market-Rate Housing: Residential units that are intended for sale or lease based on the current market without subsidies or income restrictions.

Mass Transit: *See* **Transit**.

Master Plan: A comprehensive long-range plan that is designed to guide growth, development, and resource protection in a given local or regional area. Typically, such a plan will analyze demographic and land-use data and will address issues in housing, transportation, economic development, environmental and open space, infrastructure, and historic and cultural resources. The plan will also contain an implementation element to ensure coordination and adoption of the plan's recommendations.

Megalopolis: Coined by geographer Jean Gottman in 1964 to refer to the merging together of urban areas (e.g., Boston to Washington) making discrete influences of each central city and region difficult to disaggregate.

Meridian: A geographical construct which establishes a system of lines running north and south over the earth's surface (longitude) that are used in surveys along with east/west lines (latitude) to locate properties and lay out plats.

Metes and Bounds: Using a designated point to begin the location and then using distances, direction of the boundary line, changes of direction (corners) back to the beginning point, a full description of the boundary of the parcel is created which is used for legal documents.

Metropolitan: A city and its surrounding area as defined by demographics, economics, and other criteria.

Metropolitan Government: A rare form of political subdivision in North America where a regional geography is under a single local government regime. Examples include city/county consolidation (Louisville, Kentucky) and true metropolitan government (Toronto, Canada).

Metropolitan Planning Organization (MPO): Under the 1973 Highway Act, states were required to designate MPOs to serve as a forum for cooperative decision making for local elected officials. Half of 1 percent of highway construction dollars were passed through to MPOs to create RTPs and, more significantly Transportation Improvement Progams giving "teeth" to regional planning by linking the programming of projects to plans for the first (and only) time. At least one MPO exists in every metropolitan area.

Metropolitics: Coined by Myron Orfield, this theory suggests that significant coalitions need to be created in regions between cities and fast-growing outlying areas to create a new politics to manage sprawl.

Micropolitan: A new census geography adopted in 2003 applying to smaller areas with an established core. Over 500 new areas have been identified with this definition.

Mill Building: Building constructed in many river-based cities in the late nineteenth century using water power to operate developing manufacturing processes.

Millage: A tax concept used to set the amount of property taxes due on real estate. A mill is equal to .001 cent. A millage rate of 25 mills would generate $.025 in taxes per dollar of assessed value.

Minimum Impact Development: A planning term applied to a series of strategies to integrate environmental sensitivity more closely to the application of community development standards.

Minimum Lot Requirements: Refers to the smallest land area allowed under local land use regulations to create a buildable lot in a zone.

Mitigation: Those required improvements to infrastructure (water, sewer, traffic) to accommodate the impacts of new development.

Mixed Use: Permitting multiple uses, normally segregated in traditional zoning (e.g., residential, industrial, commercial), in a designated zoning district to minimize auto dependency and enhance social interaction.

Mobility: The ability to move easily from place to place by various means including pedestrian, bicycle, transit, and auto.

Model Cities: A federal program adopted in 1966 as an alternative to urban renewal allowing a greater degree of participation of affected parties in the urban development process and integrating people-based strategies as an alternative to bricks and mortar.

Moderate-Income Housing: Residential units, owner occupied or rental, targeted to individuals and families of modest income based on a percentage of median family income in the area.

Moratorium: An action of questionable legality taken by a community to temporarily halt development.

Mortgage: Financial instruments used to assist prospective owners secure enough resources to purchase property. Loans are usually at a fixed percentage rate of interest (*see* **Adjustable Rate Mortgage [ARM]**) amortized over a long period of time. The mortgage is registered as a lien in the land records and the property is pledged as collateral for to secure the loan.

Mortgage Company: A non banking financial institution specializing in loaning funds to purchase property.

Mortgage Insurance: An insurance product sold to property owners to allow the financial institution to protect and recover its investment in the event of a default. In some cases such insurance is required to proceed with the closing and property transfer.

Multifamily Residential: A residential building with multiple units for leasing multiple tenants. *See also* **Accessory Apartments**; **Single-Family Residential**.

Multiple Listing: A real estate service that allows a property for sale to be available to many more potential buyers than a single agent or broker could achieve independently.

Multiplier: A mathematical calculation used to predict the local service employment that is generated from employment in regional export/basic industries.

Municipality: A legal public corporation set up under the laws of the state to create a political subdivision with the rights and responsibilities of local governments including taxation, public safety, education, land use regulation, and other services.

National Environmental Policy Act (NEPA):   The federal national environmental policy act passed in 1970 creating the council on environmental quality and the USEPA as well as the establishment of an Environmental Impact Statement for major public and private development actions.

National Flood Insurance: Established under federal law to underwrite the cost of insurance required on real estate transactions in flood-prone areas.

National Register: A listing of historical properties that requires significant protection of buildings and structures from demolition and significant alteration.

Natural Resources: Those naturally occurring renewable (forest, wildlife habitat, etc.) and nonrenewable (coal, oil, minerals) resources in an area. May also include water bodies and coastal areas.

Negative Equity: A condition occurring when the loan on a property exceeds the current market value. This may result in the financial institution calling the loan and requesting compensation by the owner for the loss of equity.

Neighborhood: A colloquial description of a unique or historically well-defined area of a city with residences and small-scale retail uses, elementary schools, places of worship, etc., based on current or prior settlements, ethnicity, or other factors.

Neotraditionalism: Referring to a movement in current community planning philosophy which harkens back to earlier days of city development where mixed uses were the norm.

New Urbanism: A school of city planning theory that advocates high density, mixed use development as an alternative to sprawl. *See also* **Ahwahnee Principles**.

Noise Control: Ordinances built on the **nuisance doctrine** that control the decibel level of ambient noise as a safety or health consideration.

Nonconforming Use: Uses permitted in a zoning district based on their continuous operation under previous regulations. Usually, the permit expires when the property is transferred.

Normative: A value judgment on the rightness or wrongness of a particular activity.

North American Industrial Classification System (NAICS): An alternative industrial classification system. *See also* **Standard Industrial Classification (SIC)**.

Not in My Back Yard (NIMBY): A populist reaction to development which would or could change the character of a local area. *See also* **Build Absolutely Nothing Anywhere Near Anything (BANANA); Locally Unwanted Land Uses (LULU)**.

Nuisance Doctrine: An underlying principle in land-use regulation that restricts permitted activity based on negative impacts on adjacent properties. *See also* **Spillover Effect**.

Occupancy Permit: *See* **Certificate of Occupancy**.

Occupational Classification: The official identification of various occupations into categories by the US Department of Labor for statistical and other official purposes (e.g., IRS codes for income tax forms).

Office of Management and Budget (OMB): The federal agency in charge of overseeing the uniform management and coordination of grants, contracts, programs, record keeping, etc.

Office Parks: Public or private developments which consolidate multiple commercial buildings in a single location. Often associated with suburban development near highway interchanges with significant auto dependency. Alternatively referred to as "campus style" office development with large greenspace buffering parcels and buildings.

Office Towers: Referring to high-density downtown commercial space featuring multistory, multitenant offices, usually with associated structured underground parking. Alternatively referred to as skyscrapers.

Official Map: A legal requirement in some state and local land-use regulations which creates a map of the community with the status of an ordinance, requiring legal actions by the associated board or commission to alter the map.

Off-Street Parking: Requirements under local ordinances for the availability of a specified number of parking spaces associated with particular land uses.

1000 Friends Movement: One of the original citizen-based public interest groups organized to call attention to consumptive land use practices. The first group bearing this title was organized by Henry Richmond in Oregon. A number of other states formed similar organizations. The phrase "smart growth" was coined by 1000 Friends of Massachusetts.

Open Space: Undeveloped land which may or may not be protected, temporarily or permanently, from changes in use.

Option: A legal term referring to an agreement for a fixed period of time, usually for a financial consideration, the ability of a single buyer to purchase the property for an agreed upon price.

Ordinance: An enforceable law or regulation created by a local legislative body.

Orthophoto: An aerial photograph. In some states and localities, these are available in digital form.

Overlay District: In a legally defined geographic area where existing zoning is in place, a smaller area is defined with alternate provisions that, under certain conditions, supersede the underlying regulations. Originally created to provide additional environmental provisions, this concept is now widely used to establish mixed-use areas in areas which permit only a single use (e.g., mill yards that are now converted to offices, artists' lofts, other residential use, charter schools, and restaurants and other amenities).

Owner Occupied Housing: Residential units that are lived in by the property owner rather than rented or leased out to a tenant.

Package Treatment Plant: An on-site septic system designed to serve multiple dwellings or commercial areas that do not have access to public waste water treatment. *See also* **Sewage Disposal**.

Parking Requirement: A provision in the zoning ordinance for a minimum number of spaces for temporary or longer term vehicles, usually associated with commercial and industrial uses but may also be a requirement for new residential construction.

Parks: Areas for active and passive recreation usually provided as a public good by the local or state governments.

Passive Recreation: Individual leisure activities (hiking, nature observation, etc.) as an alternative to organized collective activities (Little League, etc.).

Peak-Hour Traffic: Used by traffic engineers to define maximum-intensity use of a transportation facility (usually highways) and associated with "rush-hour" commuting. May be differentiated as morning and/or afternoon peak volumes. *See also* **Average Daily Traffic**.

Pedestrian: An individual engaged in walking as the current or primary means of personal mobility.

Pedestrian-Friendly Design: Buildings, neighborhoods, transportation facilities, cross-walks, safety regulations, and other architectural and engineering standards created to focus on foot traffic rather than automobiles or vehicular access.

Percolation Test: A technical procedure establishing the rate of diffusion of a measured volume of water from a test hole dug on the property. Used to determine whether an on-site septic system will leach properly.

Performance Bond: A monetary assurance required in local land use-regulations (usually subdivision requirements) to ensure that the approved plans for roads, drainage, and other improvements on the land will be built as approved and function as anticipated.

Performance Standards: Zoning regulations that govern uses based on specific standards of operation frequently relating to the potential impacts such uses may have on the environment, and nearby land, or development. Examples include regulations on noise, stormwater, light, odor, hazardous materials and waste, and traffic.

Permit Streamlining: An overhaul of local land use regulations designed to protect the rights of abutters and other interested parties but to limit the overlap, duplications, and sequential processing of local approvals to expedite the processing of applications. Usually targeted to industrial and commercial permitting, the goal may also include residential permits.

Permitted Use: In the zoning ordinance, those activities that are specifically allowed in the district.

Permitting Process: Describing the entire responsibilities of applicants for approval of a new or expanded use of a particular property.

Perpetuity: Legally, the inclusion of language in real estate and property transactions that allow the uses and ownership as currently established to continue indefinitely.

Phased Development: Voluntary or in some cases required development which is intentionally metered at a determined pace. Conditions for such consideration might be market absorption, financing, infrastructure availability, or community acceptance.

Physical Planning: Those activities associated with land development that include land clearing, construction activity, infrastructure development, etc. Other activities include "people-based" activities, including socioeconomic considerations, quality of life, etc.

Pine Barrens: Describing large, undeveloped tracts of land currently containing softwood trees and associated species, rather than hardwoods. Such areas may have been clear-cut or significantly harvested in earlier times. Many preservation efforts target these areas for protection because of their size, significance in the natural ecology, and relative ease of development.

Planned Community: A large land area under one ownership or management regime that can be developed with and integrated planning framework rather than parcel by parcel. Size varies from neighborhood scale development to entire "new towns" (e.g., Reston, Virginia; Columbia, Maryland).

Planned Unit Development (PUD): A large integrated development on a large tract of land that is planned and developed as a single project. It may contain both residential and nonresidential buildings, and is typically developed in conformance with specific zoning provisions allowing such a large development. Flexible guidelines as to how the development is sited on the parcel, as well as preservation of some open space are common under this scenario. *See also* **Cluster Development**; **Density Bonus**.

Planning Board/Commission: The local authority that oversees subdivision regulations and may interact on master plans, adoption or amendments to zoning regulation and various ancillary approvals including business use of a home, boundary disputes, road layout, drainage, performance bonds, etc.

Planning Process: Describing the entire local planning system including master plan, zoning, subdivision regulation, site-plan review, granting special permits, review and approvals of development applications, involvement of abutters and other interested parties, variances and exceptions by boards of appeals, and permitting. On occasion, the term applies colloquially to any discrete part of the system.

Plat: A map of a subdivision as approved by the planning board and filed as a legal land record. Also called "plot plan." Alternatively, "plat" may also apply to a map of the town or section of a town.

Points: One percent of the value of a loan, often charged by financial institutions to a mortgagee as a fee at the time of closing or refinancing.

Police Power: The ability to create and enforce laws and regulations for the protection of public health and safety. Land-use regulations are an example.

Pollution: The introduction of natural or man-made contamination into the land, water, or air.

Population: The number of persons in an enumerated district (census block, tract, civil division, county, state, etc.).

Potable Water: Water that is determined safe for human consumption.

Poverty: Individual or family income that is insufficient for subsistence living.

Poverty Rate: The numbers of individuals or families below a threshold of income established to determine the minimum amount of financial resources necessary to provide food, shelter, clothing, and other essentials.

Primary Metropolitan Statistical Area (PMSA): Primary Metropolitan Statistical Area used by the Census Bureau from 1980 to 2000 to define the major city and its area of significant influence. Replaced in 2003 by **Core-Based Areas**. *See also* **Consolidated Metropolitan Statistical Area (CMSA)**; **Standard Metropolitan Statistical Area (SMSA)**.

Prime Rate of Interest: The amount that financial institutions charge one another for the temporary use of funds, established by the Federal Reserve Bank.

Private Development: Land-use transformation created, developed, managed, and financed primarily by nongovernmental individuals and firms.

Property: Real or personal property of a significant enough value to be considered an asset for individuals or corporations. Includes land, buildings and structures, and air and mineral rights.

Property Description: The legal description of a parcel of land used in deeds and other property transactions, which includes metes and bounds, benchmarks from which a land surveyor could locate the property and its boundaries. *See also* **Deed**; **Title**.

Property Rights: Those bundle of rights that are legally attached to a property including the right to use, the right to sell, and the right to enjoy and exclude others from entering or occupying, etc.

Property Tax: The derivation of governmental revenues using the value of property as the basis. Also called "ad valorem" (to the value), this taxation regime is principally used to support local (municipal or county) governments including K–12 education.

Property Value: The determination of the relative value of one property based on local market conditions. The market value is what a willing buyer will pay to a willing seller. The assessed value is the legal value of the property, including the land buildings and structures, that is assigned by the local government for the purposes of calculating the taxes on the property.

Public Assistance: A general term applied to local and state welfare programs, usually for indigent families, but may encompass other transfer payments including food stamps, Medicaid, and even, in the broadest use, entitlements such as Social Security and Medicare.

Public Education: K–12 education provided to all eligible children through tax revenues provided to school districts.

Public Facilities: Various governmental buildings, structures, accouterments, parks, and other public spaces.

Public Health: A constitutional responsibility of the government along with safety and welfare. Refers as well to the activities of local government overseeing water supply, wastewater treatment, environmental protection, sanitary inspections of restaurants, food handlers, etc.

Public Hearing: A formal period of review and comment on pending actions by governmental agencies including land use decisions.

Public Housing: Residential units built, managed, and/or financed by governments or public agencies, usually for the benefit of low-income families.

Public Improvement: Any public good (road, water, sewer, recreational facility, building, etc.) built, financed, and/or managed by the government or one of its agencies.

Public Interest Group: An organized group of individuals, formed with the specific intent of influencing public policy, advocating changes in legislation and/or regulation, and monitoring the performance of governmental agencies to hold them accountable for implementing policies advocated by the group.

Public Notice: A legal announcement of a meeting by a governmental body to conduct business, take specific actions, solicit review, and comment on a proposed action, or adopt changes in laws and regulations.

Public Realm: A descriptive term meaning those things that are generally available to all citizens and individuals without the protections of private property rights, transaction fees, or other barriers to consumption or participation.

Public Schools: Generally referring to elementary and high school available by law to all residents of a community. Most states identify this as Kindergarten through 12th grade (K–12) although some states do not include kindergarten.

Public Services: Those governmental activities provided to the community and paid for by tax dollars including public safety, K–12 education, libraries, etc.

Public Transportation: Also referred to as mass transportation, these facilities include fixed-route bus service, light rail, commuter rail, sometimes water-based transit, and, though called paratransit, various forms of demand-actuated shared-ride services paid for or heavily subsidized by tax revenue.

Purchase and Sales Agreement: A legal instrument executed between a buyer and seller of real estate indicating that a firm offer has been made by the buyer subject to specified conditions (financing, inspections, etc.) and accepted by the seller.

Purchase of Development Rights: A legal transaction, enabled under state laws and regulations, which allows the government to acquire the value of the property that would inhere if sold for market value and, usually, converted to an alternate, more intense use. The owner of the property retains all other rights including operating any permitted business, agricultural operation, etc. Often used as a strategy to protect farmland.

Quality of Life: A ubiquitous planning term describing various positive (or negative) economic, social, environmental, and financial factors contributing to the general well-being of the community, a neighborhood, or some group of citizens who perceive threats to the existing conditions.

Quitclaim Deed: A legal instrument where a party surrenders any interest they have in a particular property.

Racism: A pernicious social construct built around the belief that one race is qualitatively better than another.

Rail Transit: Transit vehicles that use a fixed guideway for passage between two or more points. Categories include monorail, light rail (trolley/subway) and heavy rail (commuter trains using rails similar to intercity passenger and freight trains).

Rails to Trails: An organization advocating the reclamation of discontinued rail rights of way for recreational trails for hiking, bikeways, cross country skiing, etc.

Rapid Transit: Transit using a fixed guideway including trolleys, subways, and more recently rubber-tired vehicles on dedicated bus ways. Not traditionally applied to commuter rail service that is usually distinguished as "heavy rail transit."

Rational Nexus: The legal test applied to land use regulations, particularly the assessment of impact fees, which requires a reasonable relationship between the application of the regulation/fee and the impact of the use being regulated or assessed. *See also* **Exactions**; **Impact Fees**.

Real Estate: Land, buildings, structures, and other associated assets including air and mineral rights which under the laws of states are collectively defined as real property (distinguished from personal property) and which is owned, transferred from owner to owner, and considered an asset for the purposes of collateral for loans (mortgage), taxed by local authorities, and, at the time of death, passed on to heirs.

Real Estate Agent: A licensed individual who, for a fee or commission, acts on behalf of the seller of real property to list and advertise the property, solicit buyers, and oversee aspects of the transfer of the property to the new owner.

Real Estate Broker: Similar to a real estate agent, but usually the owner or manager in the sales organization overseeing other agents. Separate licensing requirements distinguish brokers from agents. Brokers must also be licensed as agents.

Real Estate Investment Trust (REIT): A legal instrument which allows multiple investors to purchase equity shares in real property and a mechanism to distribute profits from the income and asset appreciation value of the property.

Real Estate Transfer Tax: A legal assessment of a tax upon the transfer of real property based on the market value of the transaction. Laws vary on the application of the tax to the buyer, the seller, or a proportional assessment.

Reasonable Use Doctrine: A legal construct applied to the efficacy of regulations applied to the use of the property. Regulations should allow owners of property to use the property for the intents it was purchased without undue restrictions. Tests include "nuisance" and "hazard to health or safety."

Recharge Zone: A defined boundary around an aquifer or wellhead that is scientifically determined to be the area required to provide a sustainable flow of water from the well or system of wells drawing from the aquifer. Such zones have regulations restricting land use including storage of chemicals and petroleum products, application of fertilizer and pesticides, and amount of impermeable surface allowed.

Recreational Facilities: Buildings, structures, and defined land areas (ball fields, trails, boat ramps, etc.) set aside for passive and/or active use for sports, exercise, or other activities.

Recycling: A method of solid waste management (trash) that recovers materials such as glass, tin, aluminum, paper, plastics, etc. For reuse by industry rather than disposal in a landfill or other method. *See also* **Solid Waste**.

Redevelopment: The active removal of existing buildings and structures on a property to allow a new, higher and better use. *See also* **Urban Renewal**.

Redlining: The illegal practice by the financial services industry of defining certain parts of the community or neighborhoods as inappropriate for lending. *See also* **Community Bank Reinvestment Act**.

Regional Authority: A public agency or special district with powers and duties extending beyond the municipal or county jurisdictions but less than the entire state to manage various regional infrastructure systems (e.g., transit, ports, water, sewer). Such authorities rarely have general land use regulatory powers except over their own real estate including eminent domain.

Regional Economy: The reasonable geography of firms which helps establish distinctions between labor markets, commuting patterns, and export/service industry distinctions.

Regional Indicator: *See* **Indicator**.

Regional Planning: Broad-scale planning across municipal and county boundaries, but less than the entire state, that considers social, environmental, economic, and demographic policies designed to serve an entire region.

Regional Planning Agency: A public (or occasionally private or nonprofit) agency established to create plans and programs at a level between state and local governments. Most agencies are advisory in nature and draw their policy officials from constituent local governments.

Remedy: A legal sanction imposed on a firm or individual to rectify an illegal or unintended external harm to an abutting or neighboring property.

Rental Housing: Residential structures designed for lease to tenants rather than purchase and ownership by the occupants. The number of units available for rent varies substantially from one to large multifamily complexes.

Restrictive Covenant: A legal instrument which limits one or more of the bundle of rights that inhere to the property. Such covenants may be voluntary or derivative of laws or regulations. Illegal uses place restrictions on the right to use or sell in violation of federal, state, or local law (e.g., limiting sales to buyers based on race or ethnicity).

Retail: A category of land use, regulated by zoning that provides for shops and sales of merchandise to the general public.

Revenue: Income to the government generated by taxes an fees. Alternatively, income derived from the lease or sale of property.

Revitalization: Strategies focused on a particular community or neighborhood designed to enhance its attractiveness, functioning, and general socioeconomic performance.

Rezone: The legal change of the regulation of uses of property within an established zoning district.

Right of Way: A legal layout for a road, utility or other easement which allows a preemptive use of a portion of a property for certain defined activities.

Riparian Right: The rights of property owners abutting water bodies to access and use the water. *See also* **Littoral Rights**.

Riverfront: Referring to land adjacent to major nonstationary water bodies that gains an intrinsic value from its proximate location to the river. Many cities, originally built to use the rivers for transport, water supply, and wastewater effluent, are reclaiming these natural assets for enhancement, amenities, and other attractive uses.

Row Housing: A residential construction, usually in urban settings, that allows for zero lot-line units built side by side for an entire block, allowing for affordable rental and purchase of small units.

Rural: Describing land and uses of land primarily for agriculture, forestry, and other low-density human activity. Alternative distinctions are made for urban, suburban, and, more recently, exurban fringe areas.

Rust Belt: Essentially the Northeast and Midwest, characterized by heavy manufacturing, steel production, auto manufacturing, and "smokestack industries." *See also* **Sunbelt**.

Sand and Gravel Pit: A land use that allows the excavation of easily accessible subsurface materials (sand and gravel) for various uses. Most land use regulations that permit such operations require a restoration plan to be filed at the time of permit requiring the property owner to return the site to some level of natural condition.

Sanitary Landfill: A site used to dispose of human solid waste (trash and garbage) by burying it underground. In the late twentieth century, after numerous high publicity cases of contamination of ground and surface water through leachates from such facilities, many environmental agencies eliminated these as acceptable facilities and began aggressive strategies for sealing the areas to prevent migration of leachates off-site or into the groundwater below. *See also* **Solid Waste**.

Sanitary Sewers: Underground piping that carries human waste (sewage) away from residential, commercial, and industrial facilities to nearby treatment plants where the waste is processed for eventual discharge into a receiving river or stream.

Satellite Imagery: During the late twentieth century, technology originally deployed for space exploration became increasingly available for commercial use. Images taken by high-resolution cameras in satellites orbiting the earth are now used by planners to monitor significant changes in land use over time. *See also* **Aerial Photography**.

Savings and Loan: A portion of the financial services industry characterized by essentially local ownership providing loans and mortgages in local markets based primarily on savings of customers in the local area. After the Depression, the Federal Deposit Insurance Corporation (FDIC) insulated many of the small investors from loss by guaranteeing their funds up to $100,000. However, in the 1990s, many of these institutions suffered dramatically as regulations changed. The FDIC was forced to bail out investors at an unprecedented level.

Scenic Vistas: Those natural viewsheds that enhance the quality of the living environment and the value of the property. Some state and local regulations attempt to regulate development that would intrude on these "aesthetics."

Second Home: Residential dwellings built for the purpose of providing seasonal occupancy, primarily for recreational use.

Second Mortgage: A financial instrument designed to provide additional equity resources to the buyer of a property. The lender takes "second position" to the major mortgage provided in attempts to recover equity in any foreclosure proceedings in case of a default.

Section 8 Housing Voucher: Refers to a provision in the federal housing law that allows qualified renters to receive a "portable" subsidy (voucher) to take with them to use as scrip in securing a rental unit on the private market. The subsidy, in this case, is to the individual rather than to the housing unit.

Security Deposit: An additional sum (usually equivalent to one month's rent) that is paid by the renter to the landlord at the time of signing the lease, which is held in trust by the landlord as a pledge against damage to the unit and returned to the renter in full or in part, when the lease expires.

Sedimentation Control: In areas of high storm runoff particles of sand and loam (sediment) are carried into ponds, lakes, streams, and rivers, causing a build-up of deposits and eventual filling in or diversion of the water course. Local and state regulations require control measures to prevent such occurrences, particularly in construction areas where topsoil and other vegetation buffers have been removed.

Segregation: Legal or social separation of different racial, ethnic, and religious groups into different residential areas. Early legal regimes provided "de jure" segregation including public accommodations and K–12 education. Other socially enforced "de facto" segregation occurred as a mechanism for preserving economic and social homogeneity.

Sense of Place: A term of art used in current planning practice assisting citizens and political officials in defining what makes their particular locale, neighborhood, or community unique and articulating those measures that maintain or enhance this intuitive vision for the future.

Septic System: A method for treating human waste (sewage) on the property site. State and local regulations have increased over the last few decades to define the size, land area requirements, type of technology, and proximity to well water to protect the safety of current and prospective property owners. *See also* **Sewage Disposal**.

Service Sector: Originally, that portion of the local and regional economy that supplies the needs of the local area in contrast to the basic/export portion providing goods and services primarily to areas outside the local market. In modern economies, the service sector can often mean those firms providing a resource or support function (legal, accounting, financial) to other firms and which may serve a greater than local market.

Setback: In the local zoning ordinance, the distance that buildings and structures must be from the road. *See also* **Side Yard**.

Setback and Side Yard Requirements: A minimum distance by which a building must be separated from a lot line or street.

Settlement Pattern: Used by geographers as a way of describing how human interaction with the natural environment changes over time as population increases (or decreases).

Sewage Disposal: The method by which human waste (sewage) is removed from the buildings and structures and treated to eliminate pathogens and other materials. Rural and semirural disposal systems treat the wastes on-site (*see* **Septic System**) while more complex systems (**package treatment plants**) allow for multiple properties to be served by a single system. Urban densities require elaborate **sanitary sewers** and treatment plants to handle the volume.

Sheetrock Suburb: A descriptive term identifying postwar building technology that allowed rapid construction of large numbers of residences mimicking the assembly lines in factories producing other mass marketed products.

Shopping Center: Describing a variety of retail complexes on a single parcel of land, usually under a single ownership/property management company (*see* **Strip Commercial Development**). Most centers are designed primarily for automobile access.

Side Yard: That portion of the zoning ordinance that establishes the minimum distance a building or structure can be located near the property line of an adjacent property. *See also* **Setback**.

Sidewalk: A pedestrian access way across the road frontage of the property required by municipal ordinance and usually maintained by the abutting property owner.

Sight Distance: In the zoning ordinance, the requirement that access and egress to the property maintain a reasonable line of sight to provide safe entrance and exit onto adjacent roadways.

Sign Control: A provision in local land use regulation (usually zoning, site plan review, and occasionally historic district or architectural review) that specifies the type, size, illumination, and other requirements for signage on retail and commercial properties.

Single Occupant Vehicle: Used by traffic engineers and planners to describe the current mode of transportation of most cars and trucks on the road—one occupant, the driver, in one vehicle.

Single Room Occupancy Residence: A residential structure designed to provide long-term tenancy by individuals, living alone, and requiring only one room for their current circumstances.

Single-Family Residential: A specification in zoning districts that residential construction is limited to residences that allow occupancy for only one family unit. *See also* **Accessory Apartments**; **Multifamily Residential**.

Site-Plan Review: The review of a development plan for a particular site to ensure that all applicable zoning standards have been met. Many times these reviews are conducted to determine the impacts a project may have on the environment or infrastructure to ensure proper mitigation.

Slope: In topography, the level of incline of the land surface. Many local ordinances restrict construction on inclines greater than a certain percentage grade (steep slopes) to prevent accelerated runoff of stormwater and safety in accessing the property in inclement weather.

Sludge: The residual material from sewage treatment plants which must be disposed of under safe and sanitary conditions.

Slum: Residential areas that are characterized by overcrowding, unsafe and unsanitary structures, and other blighted conditions. *See also* **Tenement**; **Urban Renewal**.

Smart Growth: A term coined by 1000 Friends of Massachusetts that describes an alternative to sprawl, allowing growth in more sustainable and less land-consumptive ways. Picked up by many antisprawl activists, the term has become synonymous with the movement advocating change from our current land-use practices.

Smokestack Industries: A descriptive term referring to traditional manufacturing firms heavily dependent on processes that generated high volumes of air pollution (smokestacks). *See also* **Rust Belt**; **Stationary Sources**.

Snob Zoning: Refers to zoning which has the direct or indirect effect of creating economic barriers to participation in the residential market for persons of lower income than the current community standard. *See also* **Exclusionary Zoning**; **Inclusionary Zoning**.

Social Class: A determination of a person's or family's social standing based on occupational and wealth criteria.

Social Equity: The intentional inclusion of class and poverty concerns in the debate about land-use policies, with the explicit emphasis on increasing residential and economic opportunities and choice for citizens with limited choice due to race, class, and poverty.

Socioeconomic Analysis: The technical process for determining the social and economic stratification of a community, or a region based on such considerations as family income, housing tenure, occupational classification, and other indicators of wealth and social position.

Soil Survey: Prepared by the Soil Conservation Service of the U.S. Department of Agriculture, this procedure analyzes surface and subsurface soil conditions (e.g., sandy, clay, permeable and impermeable, rock and ledge). Such information is used by planners and engineers to determine arable soil for agriculture, layouts of septic systems, roads, and other infrastructure.

Solar Energy: A renewable energy source based on a variety of technologies designed to capture the sun's heat and light for human uses in residential and commercial design.

Solar Orientation: The location of buildings and structures based on the location of the sun during particular times of day and seasonal fluctuation. As a factor in urban design, buildings are arranged to allow adjacent properties to receive natural light without obstruction from other buildings.

Solid Waste: Refuse (trash and garbage) generated from human settlement requiring organized disposal efforts. *See also* **Co-generation**; **Incinerator**; **Recycling**; **Sanitary Landfill**; **Transfer Stations**.

Special Districts: A form of public entity created to manage a specific public system or function, usually with a dedicated revenue stream and independent bonding authority.

Special Exception: In a zoning ordinance, a provision that allows consideration of a specific use on a particular property that is not accepted under current district regulations. The exception requires action by the zoning authority or the zoning board of appeals.

Speculation: The purchase of real estate with the specific intent of holding it until the market allows disposition and a higher price rather than to use the property for the purposes intended.

Spillover Effect: The external, often unintended, consequences of a regulation or use of a property on adjacent properties or the community at large. Such consequences can be positive but are often negative. *See also* **Adverse Impact**; **Externality**.

Spot Zoning: Zoning which focuses exclusively on a particular piece of property. The practice is usually illegal.

Sprawl: Low-density, land-consumptive, auto-dependent development, primarily in areas peripheral to central cities, often associated with late twentieth-century suburban development.

Stakeholder Analysis: A technique of planning/visioning that begins with an exhaustive identification of all individuals and organizations that have an interest in the plan/vision who may affect the outcome, either positively or negatively. Once identified, these stakeholders are sought out and brought directly into the structure of the planning system to secure dialogue on issues, discussion of policies, consideration of concerns, formulation of compromises, and commitment to the outcomes.

Standard City Planning Enabling Act: Developed by the U.S. Department of Commerce in 1926, the act described the essential relationship between various structures essential to a land use planning system at the local level. This law became the basic framework that states adopted to enable planning.

Standard Industrial Classification (SIC): Established by the U.S. Department of Commerce, the industrial activities of firms have been classified for analytical purposes. Two-digit, three-digit, and four-digit classifications are used for gathering data on industrial performance for all industries in the U.S. *See also* **North American Industrial Classification System (NAICS).**

Standard Metropolitan Statistical Area (SMSA): A technical definition of the U.S. Census Bureau to determine the extended influence of central cities over their surrounding environs. This term was used through the 1980 Census when it was replaced by other definitions. *See also* **Consolidated Metropolitan Statistical Area (CMSA)**; **Core-Based Area**; **Micropolitan**; **Primary Metropolitan Statistical Area (PMSA).**

Standard State Zoning Enabling Act: Developed in 1926 by the U.S. Department of Commerce, this act provided the framework for states to enable local jurisdictions to segregate landed uses by districts (zones).

Stationary Sources: Under provisions of the Clean Air Act, these are sources of pollution located in a specific place, usually associated with manufacturing or electric utility generation. *See also* **Smokestack Industries.**

Storm Sewer: Piping laid to provide a rapid collection and dispersal of water distributed in urban areas by storm events. In some cases, particularly in older cities, these are combined with sanitary sewers (for the collection and dispersal of human waste) creating serious pollution from overflowing systems during major rainfall.

Stormwater: Water generated during periods of rainfall that is drained from human settlements by various natural and man-made systems, which, if not managed properly, can lead to flooding and pollution of waterways.

Stormwater Runoff: As stormwater moves over various land surfaces, it picks up a variety of contaminants including fertilizers, pesticides, and chemical and petroleum wastes that can generate concentrations of pollution large enough to affect human health. USEPA has established standards for various contaminants that are the basis for regulatory action.

Street Classification: Used by highway and traffic engineers to determine the nature of use of various parts of the road network. Examples of classifications include collector roads and arterial streets.

Street Layout: The requirement in local subdivision law to provide a street network for adequate traffic circulation within the subdivision and for access to collector and arterial streets abutting and adjacent to the subdivision.

Street Railway: Developed for urban areas in the late nineteenth and early twentieth centuries, the streetcar system used arterial city streets as the grid for laying out the routes for the horse-drawn cars to follow. Later the cars were electrified, becoming "trolleys" if the power came from overhead wires and "subways" if the power came through the "third" rail (unsafe above ground where other vehicles, pedestrians, etc., could come in contact).

Strip Commercial Development: Referring to small-scale shopping complexes that proliferated on major highways as communities zoned these areas for retail. Usually characterized by several stores in a small lot with access to the highway from a curb-cut.

These auto-dependent land uses are a particular characteristic of sprawl. *See also* **Shopping Center**.

Subdivision Regulations: Regulations governing the subdividing of lots into smaller lots in conformance with applicable zoning regulations. Requirements under these regulations include what is necessary for a complete plan application, procedures for review, design guidelines, enforcement, and appeals.

Sublease: A legal instrument allowing a tenant renting a property to allow a third party to occupy the property for a specified period of time for some financial consideration. Such subleases usually require permission of the landlord.

Subsidized Housing: Rental or, in some cases, owner-occupied residential property for which a portion of the lease or mortgage is underwritten by some financial assistance provided by a public entity at the federal, state or local level.

Suburb: Literally "under the influence of the city." In modern usage, places outside the limits of the major city's legal control which are integral to the metropolitan markets for housing, labor, retail products. In many cases, these places are incorporated with many of the same powers and duties of cities (taxation, land use control, K–12 education, etc.).

Sunbelt: Refers to Southern and Western states that emerged in the twentieth century as major business and residential locations, due primarily to their mild climate. *See also* **Rust Belt**.

Sustainable Development: Refers generally to economic activity that consumes fewer resources than it replaces. Often used as a description of the alternative to sprawling development.

Sweat Equity: That portion of labor and materials provided by a property owner that adds value to the property but does not require financial equity as well to create the value. In some cases, mortgage lenders consider this equity in calculating the loan to value relationship for a mortgage.

Takings: Referring to the Fifth Amendment of the Constitution which reads, in part, "nor shall private property be taken for public use without just compensation." Court cases have also been brought alleging that land-use regulations may be so restrictive that they are a "de facto" taking.

Tax Abatement: The relief of the payment of back taxes on a property by a new owner. Such abatements are granted by the community, usually under strict state guidelines.

Tax Base Sharing: A concept where the host community for a new development receives a portion of the new taxes and shares the balance with neighboring communities. The Twin Cities region is the only major metropolitan region that has enacted the framework for the entire area. Smaller experiments have followed in other areas.

Tax Increment Financing: Using the incremental increase in the value of property created by an infrastructure improvement to finance the cost of the improvement. Occasionally, tax revenues from the incremental increase in value for other community benefits.

Tax Lien: A legal sanction placed on a piece of property to allow the recovery of taxes due, which is usually satisfied at the time of sale but may be resolved at anytime.

Taxation: The collection of revenues for public purposes based on some legal framework for such collections. The traditional tax regimes are based on the value of real and personal property, sales transactions, and personal and corporate income. Numerous other regimes are also in municipal, state, and federal law.

Tax-Exempt: A provision in tax regimes to exempt certain activities, functions, properties, etc., from the burden of paying taxes that would otherwise be due. In property tax regimes, such exemptions are routinely granted for churches; nonprofit organizations including hospitals and private colleges and universities; and property owned by other governments and public agencies. On occasion provision is made for payments in lieu of taxes (PILOT) for city services.

Tax-Exempt Financing: Financing available for industrial and commercial development and some residential development using tax exempt bonds.

Telecommute: Providing employees with the opportunity to perform tasks from a remote location, including their residences, by using Internet and other telecommunication technology.

Tenancy in Common: A legal term meaning that multiple individuals are owners of a particular property with the same (i.e., undivided) interest in the property. The common alternative, particularly for married couples owning a residence, is "joint tenancy."

Tenant: An individual, business, or firm that rents or leases space from another owner of the property that is occupied for residential, commercial, industrial, or institutional use.

Tenement: A term of art applied to multifamily residences in dense urban settings. Often these buildings were substandard in construction and sanitary services, and subject to overcrowding. Often considered "slums" and "blight" as these facilities deteriorated over time. *See also* **Slum**; **Urban Renewal**.

Third Party: A legal term applying to persons or other interests in a transaction that are not direct participants in the transaction.

Title: The legal document which certifies ownership in real property or motor vehicles. *See also* **Deed**; **Property Description**.

Title Insurance: An insurance product designed to protect purchasers of property and their financial partners from errors in the certification of ownership from residual claims for other parties.

Title Search: A process of tracing the history of property ownership through the land records of the jurisdiction in which the property is located.

Topography: The measurement of the relative heights and depths of the land, usually relative to some scale, most often sea level. Cartographers delineate these features using isobars on a two-dimensional map or triangulated irregular network (TIN) which allows differences in height and depth to become more visible on a two-dimensional map by the density (tight or loose) of a series of connected triangles connecting various points.

Topsoil: A fertile layer of soil lying on the surface of the land made up primarily of decayed organic material (rather than clay or sand) capable of absorbing and holding moisture and therefore conducive to plant and crop support.

Town: A human settlement of reasonable size with multiple land uses but not complex enough to be considered a city. In New England, "towns" usually refer to incorporated municipalities with many powers similar to cities. In other states, incorporated towns are often called townships. On occasion, in other parts of the country, a town may refer to a location in the unincorporated portion of the county. In this case, the name is a general designation, like village, and no legal powers are exercised. *See also* **Township**.

Town Center: Often, the crossroads of the town where many public facilities are located (library, town hall, police, etc.). The settlement usually predates zoning and therefore, traditionally offers a mix of residential and small commercial activities in close proximity. *See also* **Village Center**.

Town Square: An open, common area, usually associated with the town center, where public ceremonies are held outdoors (parades, Fourth of July speeches and presentations, concerts, etc.). In colonial times, the town square was often the place to muster the militia or to graze livestock. Occasionally referred to as the "town common."

Townhouse: A form of multifamily residential construction featuring side-by-side units, rather than multistoried apartment buildings. Townhouses are often organized for sale under a condominium legal structure.

Township: A term of art, originally meaning a 6-mile-by-6-mile square laid out by government surveyors. However, in some states, the term also has a generalized meaning of an incorporated municipality other than a city. *See also* **Town**.

Tract House: A term applied to houses built in large subdivisions according to a very small number of immutable plans for original construction. Originally, many of these units were constructed as small "starter homes," but modern subdivisions often include larger units.

Traditional Neighborhood Development: The development of a small village center that includes a mix of uses and housing types, pedestrian- and bicycle-friendly environment, small-scale design, and generally higher densities to create a vibrant community where people can obtain goods and services within an easy walk from their home.

Traffic Analysis Zone (TAZ): A unit of geography, usually a combination of census tracks and blocks, but may include entire municipalities in low-density areas, that is used in traditional traffic models as an analysis unit for trip generation and trip distribution based on the land uses in the zone.

Traffic Calming: A concept generally concerned with reducing the impacts of traffic on a neighborhood through the installation of structures designed to slow the speed of motor vehicles.

Traffic Forecasting: A technical procedure, usually used for predicting the level of traffic that will be generated by a particular project and consequent mitigation requirements. Because of the potential for challenges, the "official forecasts" used in development reviews are certified by a qualified traffic engineer.

Traffic Models: A technical econometric modeling process which underpins all long-range projections of transportation demand and infrastructure supply and forms the basis for adding additional capacity to the system. The models usually accept the legal land-use framework (i.e., zoning) as inputs. Then, using traffic analysis zones (TAZ), the models generate the number of trips that will emerge from the zone. In a similar process, they determine the trips that will be attracted to the zone using a "gravity" model that bases its algorithm on the size of the activity in the TAZs and the distance between the TAZs (both characteristics of the intensity of gravitational forces—hence the term "gravity model"). From there, the models assign trips to the existing network and, if transit is available as a competing mode, will calculate the modal split.

Transfer of Development Rights: A legal framework that allow a "market" to develop around the rights of property owners to build to a certain level and density. These rights can be transferred from "sending" zones to "receiving" zones to allow greater density in the receiving zone and lower density in the sending zone.

Transfer Station: A solid waste–receiving location which assembles large quantities of refuse for hauling to alternate disposal facilities. Such facilities may or may not provide for recycling of recoverable materials (glass, tin, aluminum, etc.). *See also* **Solid Waste**.

Transit: Forms of multipassenger land-based transportation operating, usually, on fixed routes and charging a fare, serving local and metropolitan markets. In the past, such systems were run by private companies with franchises overseen as monopolies by state and local regulatory bodies. Currently, most transit is publicly owned and operated or service is contracted out to private carriers. Traditional distinctions are made in the transit systems between rubber-tired service (bus, express bus, vans, and shuttles), light rail (electrified trolleys or subways), and diesel- or electric-powered heavy/commuter rail. Some interstate bus and rail passenger services that provide a commuter function are described as transit in multistate regions.

Transit-Oriented Development: Land use strategies designed to take advantage of their proximate location to a transit station. A term of art now incorporated into "smart growth" and sustainable development programs.

Transportation Enhancement Program: A federal funding category included in the 1991 reauthorization of the highway bill, by then the Intermodal Surface Transportation Efficiency Act (ISTEA), which set aside 10 percent of one of the highway funding streams for "enhancements" to the system including bicycle, pedestrian, and historical and cultural uses.

Transportation Improvement Program (TIP): Part of the 1973 Highway Act introduced at the time of the creation of the Metropolitan Planning Organizations that required the creation of a five-year program of all federally funded surface transportation (highways and transit). Projects must be included state and local officials in the metropolitan program to receive certification for federal support. Linked directly to the Regional Transportation Plan, this regulation put the first real "teeth" into regional planning.

Trickle-Down Theory: A loosely developed economic "theory" that posits that benefits provided to the rich will eventually also benefit middle- and lower-income persons by "trickling down" through the economic transactions in a complex economy.

Trip Generation: A technical procedure for determining the number of person/vehicle trips that will generate from a particular land use. The Institute for Traffic Engineers sets the "industry standard" for all major site based land uses in a publication, periodically updated through empirical research.

Triple Decker: A form of residential construction, popularized in the early twentieth century in urban settings. The construction provided three floors in each building which were then leased as separate units. A family would buy the building, live on one floor and rent the other two units to pay for the financing and expenses. *See also* **Duplex.**

Underground Storage Tank: Tanks which are used to store chemicals, particularly petroleum products, which are buried in the ground. Under earlier regulatory systems, these tanks were allowed to be located without regard to leakage and potential contamination of soils and ground and surface water. After many well-publicized incidents, most states have adopted strict requirements for burial, containment systems, leak detection, and other requirements. Stiff fines are imposed on property owners, including residential home owners, whose tanks leak and contaminate surrounding areas.

Underground Utilities: The placement of gas, electrical, phone, cable TV, and other utilities, traditionally carried through residential areas on "telephone" poles. Many residential subdivision regulations now require this method to avoid weather-related service interruptions.

Undeveloped Land: Vacant land in a community that could convert to residential, commercial, industrial or other uses based on local land use regulations.

Unnecessary Hardship: A term of art that may take on a legal connotation leading to a cause of action in the courts if a regulation imposes an undue burden on property owners.

Urban: Referring to cities.

Urban Containment: The boundary, usually empirical rather than legal, that surrounds the extent of urban services (public water and/or sewer, and, on occasion, public transit) in a region that yields a series of policies to "contain urbanization" by restricting the extensions of these services into outlying areas.

Urban Design: An architectural concept describing the location and placement of dense urban development in a human scale by managing the visual form and impact as well as the streetscape, publicly accessible areas, ground floor/street level uses, sidewalks, plantings, and connections to other parts of the immediate area which might include amenities such as restaurants, retail, parks and open space, and, if available, waterfront and historical and cultural resources.

Urban Development Action Grant (UDAG): A now-defunct federal program managed by the U.S. Department of Housing and Urban Development that replaced the old urban renewal system and allowed cities to use public resources to intentionally stimulate economic development.

Urban Growth Boundary (UGB): A legal boundary around the urban area of a region designed to manage the sprawling of low-density development into the surrounding countryside. Used originally in Oregon, the UGB has also extended into other states and planning regimes as a way to contain urban development.

Urban Mass-Transit Act: Originally enacted in 1964, the act created a grant program to facilitate the takeover of private urban transit companies that were in financial distress. The act created a federal agency (now the Federal Transit Administration of the U.S. Department of Transportation) to administer grants for capital and operating expenses for transit systems now owned and operated by cities, states, and transit authorities.

Urban Renewal: Created in the 1950s as part of the Federal Housing Act, this program empowered cities to create redevelopment authorities with sweeping powers to acquire land, bulldoze slums, and return the land to private productive use, usually for commercial development. Widely criticized by urban activists in the 1960s for insensitive and cavalier attitudes towards the populations displaced by these activities, the program, which, in fact, was responsible for significant renewal of twentieth-century cities, was significantly transformed through the 1960s and 1970s and eventually abandoned as a method of reclaiming land for urban development. *See also* **Redevelopment**; **Tenement**.

Urban Service Area: Similar to the urban growth boundary, this concept, developed in the Twin Cities area, focused on policies that managed the extension of urban services (water, sewer, and transit, and urban highways used for commuting) through an intentional linkage to the impact of these services on changing land use patterns.

Urban Village: A term of art applied to concentrated mixed-use development in urban neighborhoods, made popular by new urbanists including, and especially Peter Calthorpe.

Urbanized Area (UA): An urbanized area (UA) consists of densely settled territory that contains 50,000 or more people. The U.S. Census Bureau delineates UAs to provide a better separation of urban and rural territory, population, and housing in the vicinity of large places. At least 35,000 people in a UA must live in an area that is not part of a military reservation (see www.census.gov).

U.S. Census Bureau: A division of the U.S. Department of Commerce that has the responsibility for conducting the decennial census required by the constitution. The modern Census Bureau maintains significant data on many demographic and socioeconomic aspects of American society. It has also worked with demographers and geographers to create a series of standardized definitions of various concentrations of human settlement (e.g., urban areas, metropolitan areas, etc.). Many of these definitions change over time as human settlements change in complexity and density.

Use Variance: A legal and technical decision to allow a variation of the interpretation of allowed uses in a zoning district. The decision to grant this change is made by the zoning authority, usually the zoning board of appeals. The criteria for making such decisions are different in different communities.

User Fees: Usually applied to the fees charged to individual property owners for consuming municipal services including water, sewer, trash pick-up, etc. The term is explicitly defined as an alternative to taxes and has been used in recent years as a policy decision to keep the tax rate as low as possible.

Utilities: Usually applied to private services provided to the community, including gas, electric, phone, and cable TV. Private water companies are defined in this way as well. In many cases, these services were operated as franchises, given a monopoly in the geographical area, and regulated by a public utility commission. Some public services including water and sewer are occasionally called utilities. In the late 1990s, much of the traditional operation of utilities was deregulated in a spirit of introducing competition into the utility environment.

Vacancy Rate: The amount of vacant leasable space in a segment of the real estate market. Applies differentially to office space and rental residential real estate.

Variance: Technical decision by a zoning authority (usually the zoning board of appeals) to allow a variation from the regulations applied to a specific piece of property for a particular use.

Vested Right: Those rights that are retained for certain properties within a zoning district for a specific period of time, even after the regulations for that district have changed. Designed to "grandfather" uses or regulatory conditions for current owners of property against changes that may impair the fair use of the property purchased under the previous regulatory framework.

Veterans Administration Loans: Loans enabling persons who have performed military service to purchase homes. This program fueled significant suburban development for servicemen and -women returning from World War II. Loans were offered at low interest and guaranteed by the government, making them desirable financial transactions for banks and real estate interests. *See also* **FHA Loans**.

Viewshed: An aesthetic term applied to the hillsides and scenic vistas in a particular area.

Village: A concentrated human settlement usually referring to a rural setting where residential, some commercial, and possibly government and religious functions are located in close proximity. This form of settlement usually is not constituted a municipality but represents part of the incorporated area.

Village Center: Similar to the definition of a village above but applied, now, to concentrated mixed-use centers in suburban and exurban locations under "smart growth" and "new urbanist" parameters for concentrating development and re-integrating uses as an alternative to traditional twentieth-century zoning districts. *See also* **Town Center**.

Waiver: A formal exemption from meeting a regulation or permit condition, usually granted by the authority overseeing the regulations.

Walkable Neighborhood: A term of art in the pedestrian advocacy community that means that the neighborhood or district is established with the explicit intent of maximizing pedestrian forms of transportation as an alternative to auto use.

Walking Distance: Used to define the optimal proximities of transit stops to residential concentration. The industry standard is one-fourth of a mile (i.e., pedestrians will not usually walk longer distances to access transit facilities).

Warranty: An explicit and legally binding statement that the producer will guarantee the performance of its products for a specific period of time. When applied in planning it indicates that a builder will "warrant" the building to perform as specified.

Warranty Deed: A deed which guarantees that the property has a clear title.

Wastewater Treatment: The process by which human waste and other sanitary and storm sewage is made safe for release into a receiving stream or other water body. On a smaller scale, individual properties may have an on-site septic or "package" treatment system that performs a similar function for sanitary wastes.

Water Rights: Water rights are defined differently in different parts of the country. Some states have right to use or withdrawal permits while Western states have a "riparian" rights doctrine, which gives rights to users based on their initial claims to the water.

Water Supply: The supply of potable water in a particular geography; may be ground or surface water and usually refers to public or multiuser private water systems.

Water Table: The location of groundwater in a particular area. May vary significantly even in small areas and fluctuates based on seasonal rainfall and withdrawals for use.

Waterfront: Land abutting water bodies, particularly coastal areas, harbors, riverbanks, and major lakes. Often considered an attractive location for intense development occasionally creating conflicts between marine and nonmarine uses.

Watershed: The land area surrounding a major water system (lakes, ponds, rivers, streams) that slopes toward the system and contributes surface runoff from rain and snow melt to the water. In recent years, watershed management has become the preferred method to protect water quality in many areas. Nonpoint source pollution from watershed run off may contribute significantly to the degradation of a major water body.

Well Water: Water drawn from the ground and supplied for drinking and other domestic uses. May be an on-site private system or a public/private multiuser system. A variety of land and soil conditions support groundwater supplies, recharge areas, and connections to surface water (lakes, ponds, rivers, and streams). Water-borne minerals may make the water "hard," requiring treatment. Pathogens and other chemicals entering the groundwater may make well water unsafe to drink. Public well systems are usually regulated for safety. Numerous, well-publicized incidents of contamination have brought additional attention and safeguards to groundwater use.

Wetlands: Technical soil conditions which support seasonal or year-round surface water necessary to support certain wildlife habitat.

White Flight: A term applied to racially motivated internal metropolitan migration of Caucasian families from cities to suburbs as cities became residential locations for racial minorities.

White-Collar: A term of art applied to office work, including sales, professional, managerial, and business services. In the twenty-first-century economy, the term is often applied to other occupations including retail. The term refers to the traditional business attire of male professionals: a "white shirt and collar" and usually a suit and tie. *See also* **Blue-Collar**.

Wilderness: Generally, lands not required for nor encroached upon by permanent human settlements.

Wildlife Habitat: Lands, wetlands, and water bodies required to sustain species of animals including reptiles, amphibians, and occasionally even freshwater aquatic species.

Wise-Use Movement: Referring to a public interest movement formed to protect the property rights of land owners and generally antagonistic to sprawl management, smart growth, and sustainable development interests.

Woodlots: Areas of forest and timber, usually in usually in urban and suburban settings and hence not considered traditional "forests" and usually managed by the local landowner for lumber or firewood.

Working Class: Loosely applied to families sustained by blue-collar wage earners.

Zero Lot Line: Used in a zoning ordinance to describe the side yard for attached units (i.e., no side yard required) for multifamily housing such as condominiums.

Zone of Contribution (ZoC): Used in environmental law related to water supplies, particularly groundwater, to define the area of greatest recharge to the water system. The ZoC is used to substantially restrict land uses that may lead to contamination of the supply (e.g., leaking underground tanks, chemical storage, hazardous materials, and applications of certain toxic pesticides and herbicides).

Zone of Emergence: A term used by Robert Woods and Albert Kennedy in 1969 to describe neighborhoods in transition based on race, income, and other characteristics.

Zoning: The legal framework for restricting uses of property to certain general types (residential, commercial, industrial) allowed by special permit, where buildings need to be located on the parcel (setback, side yard) and frontage and access requirements.

Zoning Authority: The board(s) of jurisdiction in creating and enforcing the zoning ordinance in the community. Under this rubric, the legislative body (e.g., city council, town meeting, county commission) creates the ordinance and amends it from time to time, usually with requirements for a super majority and usually upon the advice of the Planning Board. The local administration may reside in a special zoning enforcement officer or alternatively with the building inspector. Appeals of zoning decisions are heard first by a board of appeals and are also appealed to local and state courts.

Zoning Board of Appeals (ZBA): The legal board of jurisdiction which oversees variances or special exceptions to the uses allowed in a zoning district. The conditions under which a variance or special exception can be granted by the ZBA vary by community and by precedent. However, most communities have tightened these conditions in recent years to maintain the integrity of the zoning districts.

Zoning Envelope: The land area included in a zoning district or, alternatively, the allowable uses on a particular parcel based on the zoning regulations governing the district in which the parcel is located.

Zoning Variance: An application seeking permission to deviate from established zoning, generally on the basis of some form of hardship related to the property in question or the land on which it lies. Usually a demonstration must be made that the applicant, because of these circumstances, cannot enjoy the privileges of those in the vicinity in the same zoning district.

Comprehensive Bibliography

Abbott, Carl, and Sy Adler. 1989. "Historical Analysis as a Planning Tool." *Journal of the American Planning Association* 55(4): 467–73.

Aberley, Doug, ed. 1993. *Boundaries of Home: Mapping for Local Empowerment*. Philadelphia: New Society Publishers.

Abler, Ronald, ed. 1977. *A Comparative Atlas of America's Great Cities: Twenty Metropolitan Regions*. Minneapolis: University of Minnesota Press.

Abrams, Charles. 1965. *The City Is the Frontier*. New York: Harper and Row.

Acerrano, Anthony. 2002. "Wild Animal Attacks Appear on the Rise." *Sports Afield*, February 20.

Acquisition of Land for Future Highway Use: A Legal Analysis. 1957. National Research Council (U.S.) Highway Research Board. Special report 27. National Research Council. Publication, vol. 484. Washington, DC: National Research Council (U.S.). Highway Research Board. Committee on Highway Laws.

Adams, John, Mark D. Bjelland, Laura J. Hansen, Lena L. Laaken, and Barbara J. VanDrasek. 1998. *The Role of Housing Markets, Regulatory Frameworks, and Local Government Finance*. CTS 98-01. www.cts.umn.edu/trg/research/reports/TRG_01.html.

Adams, John S., Julie L. Cidell, Laura J. Hansen, Hyun-joo Jung, Yeon-taek Ryu, and Barbara J. VanDrasek. 1999. *Development Impact Fees for Minnesota? A Review of Principles and National Practices*. CTS 99-04. www.cts.umn.edu/trg/research/reports/TRG_03.html.

Adams, John S., Julie L. Cidell, Laura J. Hansen, and Barbara VanDrasek. 1999. *Synthesizing Highway Transportation, Land Development, Municipal and School Finance in the Greater Twin Cities Area, 1970–1997*. CTS 00-01. www.cts.umn.edu/trg/research/reports/TRG_04.html.

Adams, John S., Julie L. Cidell, Laura J. Hansen, and Barbara J. VanDrasek. 2002. *House Price Changes and Capital Shifts in Real Estate Values in Twin Cities–Area Housing Submarkets*. CTS 02-01. www.cts.umn.edu/trg/research/reports/TRG_07.html.

Adams, John S., Joel A. Koepp, and Barbara J. VanDrasek. 2003. *Urbanization of the Minnesota Countryside: Population Change and Low-Density Development Near Minnesota's Regional Centers, 1970–2000*. CTS 03-01. www.cts.umn.edu/trg/research/reports/TRG_10.html.

Adams, John S., and Barbara J. VanDrasek. In press. *Case Studies of Development in the Minneapolis–St. Paul Metropolitan Region*.

Adams, Russell B., Jr. 1977. *The Boston Money Tree*. New York: Crowell.

Addams, Jane. 1910. *Twenty Years at Hull-House: With Autobiographical Notes*. New York: Macmillan.

Adkins, John F., James R. McHugh, and Katherine Seay. 1975. *Desegregation: The Boston Orders and Their Origin*. Boston: Boston Bar Association Committee on Desegregation.

Ady, Robert M. 1990. *Locational Determinants for HighTech Firms*. New York: The Fantus Co.

AFT (American Farmland Trust). 1998. *Farming on the Edge*. Washington, DC: Author.

AFT (American Farmland Trust). 2002. *Farming on the Edge: Sprawling Development Threatens America's Best Farmland*. Washington, DC: Author.

Agrawal, A., and C. C. Gibson. 1999. "Enchantment and Disenchantment: The Role of Community in Natural Resource Conservation." *World Development* 27: 629–49.

Alden, J., and R. Morgan. 1974. *Regional Planning: A Comprehensive View*. New York: Halsted Press.

Alexander, Christopher W. 1964. *Notes on the Synthesis of Form*. Cambridge, MA: Harvard University Press.

Alexander, Ernest R. 1994. "The Non-Euclidian Mode of Planning: What Is It to Be?" *Journal of the American Planning Association* 60(3): 372–76.

Alexander, Ian. 1979. *Office Location and Public Policy*. New York: Longman.

Alinsky, Saul. 1971. *Rules for Radicals: A Practical Primer for Realistic Radicals*. New York: Random House.

Allaman, Peter M., Timothy J. Tardiff, and Frederick C. Dunbar. 1982. *New Approaches to Understanding Travel Behavior*. Washington, DC: Transportation Research Board, National Research Council.

Alland, Judith C. 1988. *Readings in Regional Development Impact Review: Process and Criteria*. Boston: Metropolitan Area Planning Council.

Alland, Judith C. 1995. *Metro Boston Brownfields Status Report, From Eyesore to Opportunity: Financing and Other Strategies to Recycle Contaminated Sites*. Boston: Metropolitan Area Planning Council.

Alonso, William. 1960. "A Theory of the Urban Land Market." *Papers of the Regional Science Association* 6: 149–58.

Alonso, William. 1964. *Location and Land Use: Toward a General Theory of Land Use*. Cambridge, MA: Harvard University Press.

Alterman, Rachelle, ed. 1988. *Private Supply of Public Services: Evaluation of Real Estate Exaction, Linkage, and Alternative Land Policies*. New York: New York University Press.

Alterman, Rachelle, and Duncan MacRae Jr. 1983. "Planning and Policy Analysis: Converging or Diverging Trends." *Journal of the American Planning Association* 49(2): 200–215.

Altshuler, Alan. 1969. *The City Planning Process*. Ithaca, NY: Cornell University Press.

Altshuler, Alan. 1977. "Review of *The Costs of Sprawl*." *Journal of the American Planning Association* 43(2): 207–9.

Altshuler, Alan. 1994. *The Governance of Urban Land: Critical Issues and Research Priorities*. Cambridge, MA: Lincoln Institute of Land Policy.

Altshuler, Alan, James P. Womack, and John R. Pucher. 1979. *The Urban Transportation System: Politics and Policy Innovation*. Cambridge, MA: MIT Press.

American Cities Corporation. 1970. *Hartford Process*. N.p.

American Law Institute. 1968. *A Model Land Development Code*. Philadelphia: Author.

American Planning Association. 1996. "Modernizing State Planning Statutes." *Planning Advisory Service*. Chicago: Author.

American Planning Association. 2002. *Growing Smart Legislative Guidebook*. Chicago: Author.

American/Canadian Metropolitan Intergovernmental Governance Perspectives. 1993. In Donald N. Rothblatt and Andrew Sancton, eds., *North American Federalism Project*, vol. 1. Berkeley, CA: Institute of Governmental Studies Press.

Amory, Cleveland. 1947. *The Proper Bostonians.* New York: E. P. Dutton.

Analysis of Zoning in the Greater Boston Area. 1980. Boston: Metropolitan Area Planning Council.

Anderson, David, and Gerard McCullough. 2000. *The Full Cost of Transportation in the Twin Cities Region.* CTS 00-04. www.cts.umn.edu/trg/research/reports/TRG_05.html.

Anderson, David, and Gerard McCullough. 2003. *The Distribution of Transportation Costs in the Twin Cities Region.* CTS 03-03. www.cts.umn.edu/trg/research/reports/TRG_15.html.

Anderson, Elijah. 1991. "Neighborhood Effects on Teenage Pregnancy." In Christopher Jencks and Paul E. Peterson, eds., *The Urban Underclass* (pp. 375–98). Washington, DC: The Brookings Institution.

Anderson, G., and H. Tregoning. 1998. "Smart Growth in Our Future?" In *Urban Land Institute on the Future of Smart Growth—Economy, Community, Environment.* Washington, DC: Urban Land Institute.

Anderson, Larz T. 1995. *Guidelines for Preparing Urban Plans.* Chicago: Planners Press of the American Planning Association.

Anglin, Roland. 1992. "Constructing a Planning Regime: Assessing the Beginning Phases of New Jersey's Plan for Development and Redevelopment." *Policy Studies Review* 11(3/4): 280–302.

Annotated Bibliography of Statistical Publications and Sources for Metropolitan Boston. 1985. Boston: Metropolitan Area Planning Council.

The Appraisal of Real Estate. 1992. 10th ed. Chicago: Appraisal Institute.

Arendt, Randall, Robert Yaro, Elizabeth A. Brabee, Harry L. Dodson, and Christine Reid. 1994. *Rural by Design: Maintaining Small Town Character.* Chicago: American Planning Association.

Argyris, Chris, Robert Putnam, and Diana McLain Smith. 1985. *Action Science.* San Francisco: Jossey-Bass.

Arnold, Chester L., Jr., and C. James Gibbons. 1996. "Impervious Surface Coverage: The Emergence of a Key Environmental Indicator." *Journal of the American Planning Association* 62(2): 243–58.

Arnold, Joseph L. 1971. *The New Deal in the Suburbs: A History of the Greenbelt Town Program, 1935–1954.* Columbus: Ohio State University Press.

Ascher, William. 1978. *Forecasting: An Appraisal for Policy-Makers and Planners.* Baltimore: The Johns Hopkins Press.

Ash, Maurice. 1969. *Regions of Tomorrow: Towards the Open City.* New York: Schocken Books.

Ashton, Adam. 2003. "Deer Related Accidents Cost $1.1 B." Associated Press, November 4.

Associated Press. 2003. "Officials Blame Air Pollution in Worsening Asthma Epidemic." December 17.

Associated Press. 2004. "Suspected in Death, Mountain Lion Is Shot in California Park." *Berkshire Eagle*, January 10, A3.

Association for the New Urbanism in Pennsylvania. 2004. *What Is the Transect?* Retrieved April 7, 2004, from htttp://www.anupa.org/transect.php.

Attoe, Wayne, ed. 1988. *Transit, Land Use, & Urban Form.* Austin, TX: Center for the Study of American Architecture.

Audirac, Ivonne, Anne H. Shermyen, and Marc T. Smith. 1990. "Ideal Urban Form and Visions of the Good Life: Florida's Growth Management Dilemma." *Journal of the American Planning Association* 56(4): 470–82.

Ausubel, Jesse H., and Robert Herman, eds. 1988. *Cities and Their Vital Systems: Infrastructure Past, Present, and Future.* Washington, DC: National Academy Press.

Automotive Safety Foundation. 1968. *Urban Transit Development in Twenty Major Cities.* Washington, DC: Author.

Axelrod, Dick, and Emily Axelrod. 2004. *You Don't Have to Do It Alone: How to Involve Others to Get Things Done*. San Francisco: Berrett-Koehler.

Baar, Kenneth. 1992. "The National Movement to Halt the Spread of Multifamily Housing, 1890–1926." *Journal of the American Planning Association* 58(1): 39–48.

Babcock, Richard. 1991. "Implementing Metropolitan Regional Planning." In Joseph Di-Mento and LeRoy Graymer, eds., *Confronting Regional Challenges* (pp. 79–88). Cambridge, MA: Lincoln Institute of Land Policy.

Babcock, Richard F. 1966. *The Zoning Game: Municipal Practices and Policies*. Madison: University of Wisconsin Press.

Babcock, Richard F., and Charles L. Siemon. 1985. *The Zoning Game Revisited*. Cambridge, MA: Lincoln Institute of Land Policy.

Backhaus, Gary, and John Murungi, eds. 2002. *Transformations of Urban and Suburban Landscapes: Perspectives from Philosophy, Geography, and Architecture*. Lanham, MD: Lexington Books.

Bagby, D. Gordon. 1980. "The Effects of Traffic Flow on Residential Property Values." *Journal of the American Planning Association* 46(1): 88–94.

Bahl, Roy W., and Robert E. Firestine. 1972. *Urban-Suburban Migration Patterns and Metropolitan Fiscal Structures*. Metropolitan Studies Program. Occasional Paper, vol. 8. Syracuse, NY: Syracuse University.

Balanced Growth Planning Manual. 1980. Boston: Metropolitan Area Planning Council.

Baldassare, Mark. 1986. *Trouble in Paradise: The Suburban Transformation in America*. New York: Columbia University Press.

Baldassare, Mark. 1989. "Citizen Support for Regional Government in the New Suburbia." *Urban Affairs Quarterly* 24: 460–69.

Baldassare, Mark. 1991a. "Attitudes on Regional Solutions and Structures." In Joseph Di-Mento and LeRoy Graymer, eds., *Confronting Regional Challenges* (pp. 105–20). Cambridge, MA: Lincoln Institute of Land Policy.

Baldassare, Mark. 1991b. "Is There Room for Regionalism in the Suburbs?" *Journal of Architectural and Urban Planning Research* 8: 222–34.

Baldassare, Mark. 1994a. "The Image Problem of Regional Government: Factors Contributing to Suburban Opposition." In Mark Baldassare, ed., *Suburban Communities: Change and Policy Responses* (pp. 195–208). Greenwich, CT: JAI Press.

Baldassare, Mark. 1994b. "Regional Variations in Support for Regional Governance." *Urban Affairs Quarterly* 30: 275–84.

Baldassare, Mark, ed. 1994. *Suburban Communities: Change and Policy Responses*. Greenwich, CT: JAI Press.

Baldassare, Mark, Joshua Hassol, William Hoffman, and Abby Kanarek. 1996. "Possible Planning Roles for Regional Government." *Journal of the American Planning Association* 62(1): 17–29.

Bamberger, Rita J., William A. Blazar, and George E. Peterson. 1985. *Infrastructure Support for Economic Development*. Chicago: American Planning Association.

Banerjee, Tridib, and Michael Southworth, eds. 1990. *City Sense and City Design: Writings and Projects of Kevin Lynch*. Cambridge, MA: MIT Press.

Banfield, Edward C. 1970. *The Unheavenly City*. Boston: Little, Brown and Company.

Banfield, Edward C. 1974. *The Unheavenly City Revisited*. Boston: Little, Brown and Company.

Bank of America, California Resources Agency, and Greenbelt Alliance. 1996. *Beyond Sprawl: New Patterns of Growth to Fit the New California*. San Francisco: Authors.

Barash, David P. 2004. *The Survival Game: How Game Theory Explains the Biology of Cooperation and Competition*. New York: Times Books.

Barber, B. R. 1984. *Strong Democracy: Participatory Politics for a New Age*. Berkeley: University of California Press.

Barker, Joel. 1985. *Discovering the Future: The Business of Paradigms*. St. Paul, MN: ILI Press.

Barker, Michael, ed. 1983. *Financing State and Local Economic Development*. Durham, NC: Duke University Press.

Barker, Theo, and Anthony Sutcliffe, eds. 1993. *Megalopolis: The Giant City in History*. New York: St. Martin's Press.

Barlow, I. M. 1991. *Metropolitan Government*. London: Routledge.

Barnebey, Mark P., Tom MacRostie, and Gary J. Schoenna. 1988. "Paying for Growth: Community Approaches to Development Impact Fees." *Journal of the American Planning Association* 54(1): 18–28.

Barnes, Gary, and Gary Davis. 1999. *Understanding Urban Travel Demand: Problems, Solutions, and the Role of Forecasting*. CTS 99–02. www.cts.umn.edu/trg/research/reports/TRG_02.html.

Barnes, Gary, and Gary Davis. 2001. *Land Use and Travel Choices in the Twin Cities, 1958–1990*. CTS 01-01. www.cts.umn.edu/trg/research/reports/TRG_06.html.

Barnes, William R. 1989. *The National System of City Regions*. Washington, DC: National League of Cities.

Barnes, William R., and Larry C. Ledebur. 1992. *City Distress, Metropolitan Disparities, and Economic Growth*. Washington, DC: National League of Cities.

Barnes, William R., and Larry C. Ledebur. 1998. *The New Regional Economies: The U.S. Common Market and the Global Economy*. Thousand Oaks, CA: Sage Publications.

Barnett, Jonathan. 1982. *An Introduction to Urban Design*. New York: Harper and Row.

Barnett, Jonathan. 1989. "Redesigning the Metropolis: The Case for a New Approach." *Journal of the American Planning Association* 55(2): 131–35.

Barnett, Jonathan. 1992. "Accidental Cities: The Deadly Grip of Outmoded Zoning." *Architectural Record* (February): 94, 98–101.

Barnett, Jonathan. 1995. *The Fractured Metropolis: Improving the New City, Restoring the Old City, Reshaping the Region*. New York: Icon Editions.

Barrett, Bernard. 1971. *The Inner Suburbs: The Evolution of an Industrial Area*. Carlton, Australia: Melbourne University Press.

Barrett, G. Vincent, and John P. Blair. 1982. *How to Conduct and Analyze Real Estate Market Feasibility Studies*. New York: Van Nostrand Reinhold Company.

Barrows, R. L. 1982. *The Roles of Federal, State, and Local Governments in Land-Use Planning*. Washington, DC: National Planning Association.

Bartholomew, Keith. 1999. "The Evolution of American Nongovernmental Land Use Planning Organizations." *Journal of the American Planning Association* 65(4): 357–63.

Bartik, Timothy J. 1991. *Who Benefits from State and Local Development Policies?* Kalamazoo, MI: W. E. Upjohn Institute for Employment Research.

Barton-Aschman Associates. 1970. *Commuter Parking at Highway Interchanges*. Washington, DC: U.S. Federal Highway Administration.

Bassett, Edward M. 1935. *Model Laws for Planning Cities, Counties, and States*. Cambridge, MA: Harvard University Press.

Battle for Land. 1974. NELI Outline, vol. 59. Boston: New England Law Institute.

Batty, Michael. 1994. "A Chronicle of Scientific Planning: The Anglo-American Modeling Experience." *Journal of the American Planning Association* 60(1).

Baxandall, Rosalyn, and Elizabeth Ewen. 2000. *Picture Windows: How the Suburbs Happened*. New York: Basic Books.

Beatley, Timothy. 2000. "Preserving Biodiversity: Challenges for Planners." *Journal of the American Planning Association* 66(1): 5–20.

Beaton, W. Patrick. 1980. "Regional Tax Base Sharing: A Conceptual Analysis." *Journal of the American Planning Association* 46(3): 315–22.

Beaton, W. Patrick. 1983. *Municipal Expenditures, Revenues, and Services: Economic Models and Their Use by Planners*. New Brunswick, NJ. Center for Urban Policy Research.

Beatty, Jack. 1992. *The Rascal King: The Life and Times of James Michael Curley, 1874–1958*. Reading, MA: Addison-Wesley.

Beauregard, Robert A. 1990. "Bringing the City Back In." *Journal of the American Planning Association* 56(2): 210–14.

Beauregard, Robert A. 1993. *Voices of Decline: The Postwar Fate of American Cities*. Cambridge, MA: Blackwell.

Beck, Roy, Leon Kolankiewicz, and Steven A. Camarota. 2003. *Outsmarting Smart Growth: Population Growth, Immigration, and the Problem of Sprawl*. Washington, DC: Center for Immigration Studies.

Bellah, Robert N, Richard Madsen, William M. Sullivan, Ann Swidler, and Steven M. Tipton. 1996. *Habits of the Heart: Individualism and Commitment in American Life*. Updated ed. London: University of California Press.

Bellevance, Russell C., ed. 1978. *Introduction to Real Estate Law*. St. Paul, MN: West Publishing Co.

Belzer, Dena, and Gerald Aulter. 2002. "Transit Oriented Development: Moving from Rhetoric to Reality." Washington, DC: The Brookings Institution Center on Urban and Metropolitan Policy and The Great American Station Foundation.

Bendavid-Val, Avrom. 1980. *Local Economic Development Planning: From Goals to Projects*. Chicago: American Planning Association.

Bendavid-Val, Avrom. 1991. *Regional and Local Economic Analysis for Practitioners*. 4th ed. New York: Praeger.

Benes, Peter, ed. 1980. *New England Meeting House and Church: 1630–1850*. Boston: Boston University.

Benevolo, Leonardo. 1967. *The Origins of Modern Town Planning*. Cambridge, MA: MIT Press.

Benfield, F. Kaid, Matthew D. Raimi, and Donald D.T. Chen. 1999. *Once There Were Greenfields: How Urban Sprawl Is Undermining America's Environment, Economy, and Social Fabric*. New York: Natural Resources Defense Council with the Surface Transportation Policy Project.

Benjamin, Gerald, and Richard P. Nathan. 2001. *Regionalism and Realism: A Study of Governments in the New York Metropolitan Area*. Washington, DC: Brookings Institution Press.

Ben-Joseph, Eran. 2002. "Smarter Standards and Regulations: Diversifying the Spatial Paradigm of Subdivisions." In Terry S. Szold and Armando Carbonell, eds., *Smart Growth: Form and Consequences*. Cambridge, MA: Lincoln Institute of Land Policy.

Bennett, Neil G., and David E. Bloom. 1990. "Plotting Our Destiny: Interpreting Our Demographic Trajectory." *Journal of the American Planning Association* 52(2): 135–39.

Benveniste, Guy. 1989. *Mastering the Politics of Planning: Crafting Credible Plans and Policies That Make a Difference*. San Francisco: Jossey-Bass.

Berger, Bennett M. 1971. *Looking for America: Essays on Youth, Suburbia, and Other American Obsessions*. Englewood Cliffs, NJ: Prentice-Hall.

Berger, Marilyn. 1989. *Urban Planning: A Guide to Reference Sources*. Chicago: Council of Planning Librarians.

Bergman, Edward M. 1974. *Eliminating Exclusionary Zoning: Reconciling Workplace and Residence in Suburban Areas*. Cambridge, MA: Ballinger Publishing Company.

Berke, Arnold. 1993/1994. "Seeking a Broader Vision for a Better American City: The Congress for the New Urbanism Launches Its Crusade." *Historic Preservation News* (December/January).

Berke, Phillip, and Maria Manta Conroy. 2000. "Are We Planning for Sustainable Development? An Evaluation of 30 Comprehensive Plans." *Journal of the American Planning Association* 66(1): 21–33.

Berkshire Eagle. 2004. "Unsafe at Any Speed." January 19, A6 [editorial].

Bernard, Richard, ed. 1990. *Snowbelt Cities: Metropolitan Politics in the Northeast and Midwest Since World War II*. Bloomington: Indiana University Press.

Bernhardt, Roger. 1991. *Property*. 2nd ed. St. Paul, MN: West Publishing Co.

Berry, Brian J. L., and Quentin Gillard. 1977. *The Changing Shape of Metropolitan America: Commuting Patterns, Urban Fields, and Decentralization Process 1960–1970*. Cambridge, MA: Ballinger.

Berry, Brian J. L., and Frank E. Horton. 1970. *Geographic Perspectives on Urban Systems*. Englewood Cliffs, NJ: Prentice-Hall.

Berry, Brian J. L., and Duane F. Marble. 1968. *Spatial Analysis: A Reader in Statistical Geography*. Englewood Cliffs, NJ: Prentice-Hall.

Berry, Brian J. L., and Lester Silverman, eds. 1980. *Population Redistribution and Public Policy*. Washington, DC: National Academy of Sciences.

Berry, Brian J. L., and Katherine B. Smith, eds. 1971. *City Classification Handbook: Methods and Applications*. New York: Wiley-Interscience.

Berube, Alan. 2003. *Census 2000: Key Trends & Implications for Cities*. Presentation to the Knight Center for Specialized Journalism "Cities, Suburbs, and Beyond," October 30. Washington, DC: The Brookings Institution, Center on Urban and Metropolitan Policy. PowerPoint presentation downloaded from brookings_metropolitan_policy_program@lyris.brookings.edu.

Binford, Henry C. 1985. *The First Suburbs: Residential Communities on the Boston Periphery 1815–60*. Chicago: University of Chicago Press.

Bingham, Richard D. et al. 1997. *Beyond Edge Cities*. New York: Garland.

Birch, David L. 1970. *The Economic Future of City and Suburb*. New York: Committee for Economic Development.

Birch, David L. 1979. *Using Dun and Bradstreet Data for Micro Analysis of Regional and Local Economics*. Cambridge, MA: MIT Program on Neighborhood and Regional Change.

Black, Harry. 1991. *Achieving Economic Development Success: Tools That Work*. Washington, DC: International City/County Management Association.

Blaesser, Brian W. 1998. *Discretionary Land Use Controls: Avoiding Invitations to Abuse of Discretion*. St. Paul, MN: West Group.

Blaesser, Brian W., and Alan C. Weinstein, eds. 1989. *Land Use and the Constitution: Principles for Planning Practice—An AICP Handbook*. Chicago: Planners Press of the American Planning Association.

Blaha, Katherine, and Peter Hamik. 2000. *Opportunities for Smarter Growth: Parks, Greenspace and Land Conservation*. Miami, FL: The Funders Network for Smart Growth and Livable Communities and The Trust for Public Land.

Blair, John P. 1995. *Local Economic Development: Analysis and Practice*. Thousand Oaks, CA: Sage Publications.

Blake, John B. 1959. *Public Health in the Town of Boston*. Cambridge, MA: Harvard University Press.

Blakely, Edward J. 1994. *Planning Local Economic Development: Theory and Practice*. 2nd ed. Thousand Oaks, CA: Sage Publications.

Blakely, Edward J. 2001. "Competitive Advantage for the 21st-Century City: Can a Place-Based Approach to Economic Development Survive in a Cyberspace Age?" *Journal of the American Planning Association* 67(2): 133–45.

Blanton, Kimberly. 2002. "The Haves and the Have Nots." *Boston Globe Magazine*.

Bledstein, Burton J., and Robert D. Johnston, eds. 2001. *The Middling Sorts: Explorations in the History of the American Middle Class*. New York: Routledge.

Blouin, Francis X., Jr. 1980. *The Boston Region 1810–1850: A Study of Urbanization*. Ann Arbor, MI: UMI Research Press.

Bluestone, Barry, and Bennett Harrison. 1982. *The Deindustrialization of America. Plant*

Closings, Community Abandonment, and the Dismantling of Basic Industry. New York: Basic Books.

Bluestone, Barry, and Bennett Harrison. 2000. *Growing Prosperity: The Battle for Growth with Equity in the Twenty-First Century*. Boston: Houghton Mifflin.

Bluestone, Barry, Bennett Harrison, and Lawrence Baker. 1981. *Corporate Flight: The Causes and Consequences of Economic Dislocation*. Washington, DC: Progressive Alliance: National Center for Policy Alternatives.

Bluestone, Barry, and Mary Huff Stevenson, eds. 2000. *The Boston Renaissance: Race, Space, and Economic Change in an American Metropolis*. With contributions from Michael Massaagli, Philip Moss, and Chris Tilly. New York: Russell Sage Foundation.

Bluestone, Barry, Gretchen Weismann, and Charles C. Euchner. 2001. *A New Paradigm for Housing in Greater Boston*. Boston: Center for Urban and Regional Policy.

Boarnet, Marlon, and Randall Crane. 1997. "L.A. Story: A Reality Check for Transit-Based Housing." *Journal of the American Planning Association* 63: 189–97.

Boarnet, Marlon G., and Nicholas S. Compin. 1999. "Transit-Oriented Development in San Diego County: The Incremental Implementation of a Planning Idea." *Journal of the American Planning Association* 65(1): 80–95.

Bobrowski, Mark. 1993. *Handbook of Massachusetts Land Use and Planning Law: Zoning, Subdivision Control, and Nonzoning Alternatives*. Boston: Little, Brown and Company.

Bogart, William T. 1998. *The Economics of Cities and Suburbs*. Upper Saddle River, NJ: Prentice Hall.

Bollens, John C., ed. 1964. *Exploring the Metropolitan Community*. Berkeley: University of California Press.

Bollens, John C., and Henry Schmandt. 1982. *The Metropolis*. New York: Harper and Row.

Bollens, Scott A. 1990. "Constituencies for Limitation and Regionalism: Approaches to Growth Management." *Urban Affairs Quarterly* 26: 46–67.

Bollens, Scott A. 1992. "State Growth Management: Intergovernmental Frameworks and Policy Objectives." *Journal of the American Planning Association* 60(4).

Bollens, Scott A. 1993. "Restructuring Land Use Governance." *Journal of Planning Literature* 7: 211–26.

Bollens, Scott A. 2002. "Urban Planning and Intergroup Conflict: Confronting a Fractured Public Interest." *Journal of the American Planning Association* 68(1): 22–42.

Bollens, Scott A., and David R. Godschalk. 1987. "Tracking Land Supply for Growth Management." *Journal of the American Planning Association* 53(3): 315–27.

Bond, C. Lawrence. 1989. *Houses and Buildings of Topsfield, Massachusetts*. Topsfield, MA: The Topsfield Historical Society.

Bonfanti, Leo. 1973. *The Massachusetts Bay Colony: Volume 1—Plymouth Colony to 1623*. Wakefield, MA: Pride Publications.

Borchert, John R. 1992. *Megalopolis: Washington, D.C., to Boston*. New Brunswick, NJ: Rutgers University Press.

Borgos, Michael F. 1979. "An Approach to Statistical Methods in Fiscal Impact Analysis." *Journal of the American Planning Association* 45(2): 127–33.

Borts, George H. 1960. *Regional Cycles of Manufacturing Employment in the United States*. New York: National Bureau of Economic Research.

Boskoff, Alvin. 1962. *The Sociology of Urban Regions*. New York: Appleton-Century-Crofts.

Bosselman, F. P., and D. L. Callies. 1971. *The Quiet Revolution in Land Use Control*. Washington, DC: U.S. Government Printing Office.

The Boston Conference: A City and Its Future. 1984. Boston: Massachusetts Institute of Technology.

Boston Facts & Figures. 1990. Boston: Boston Municipal Research Bureau.

Boston Facts & Figures. 1995. Boston: Boston Municipal Research Bureau.

The Boston Office Market: 1989–2000. 1990. Boston: Boston Redevelopment Authority.

"Boston's Charles River Basin: An Engineering Landmark." 1981. *Journal of the Boston Society of Civil Engineers Section, ASCE* 67(4): 200–387.

Boudeville, Jacques R. 1966. *Problems of Regional Economic Planning*. Edinburgh: Edinburgh University Press.

Bourne, Larry S. 1981. *The Geography of Housing*. New York: John Wiley & Sons—Halsted Press Division.

Bowen, Abel. 1829. *Bowen's Picture of Boston, or, The Citizen's and Stranger's Guide to the Metropolis of Massachusetts, and Its Environs*. Boston: A. Bowen.

Bowman, Ann. 1987. *Tools and Targets: The Mechanics of City Economic Development*. Washington, DC: National League of Cities.

Bowman, Ann O'M., and Richard C. Kearney. 2005. *State and Local Government*. 6th ed. Boston: Houghton Mifflin Company.

Boyer, Richard, and David Savageau. 1989. *Places Rated Almanac*. New York: Prentice-Hall.

Boyer, Richard, and David Savageau. 1993. *Places Rated Almanac*. New York: Prentice-Hall Travel.

Bradbury, Katharine L. 1988. "Shifting Property Tax Burdens in Massachusetts." *New England Economic Review, Federal Reserve Bank of Boston* (September/October): 36–48.

Bradbury, Katharine L. 1991. "Can Local Governments Give Citizens What They Want? Referendum Outcomes in Massachusetts." *New England Economic Review, Federal Reserve Bank of Boston* (May/June): 3–22.

Bradbury, Katharine L., and Lynn E. Browne. 1986. "Black Men in the Labor Market." *New England Economic Review, Federal Reserve Bank of Boston* (March/April): 32–42.

Bradbury, Katharine L., and Lynn E. Browne. 1988. "New England Approaches the 1990s." *New England Economic Review, Federal Reserve Bank of Boston* (January/February): 31–45.

Bradbury, Katharine L., Karl Case, and Constance R. Dunham. 1989. "Geographic Patterns of Mortgage Lending in Boston, 1982–1987." *New England Economic Review, Federal Reserve Bank of Boston* (September/October): 3–30.

Bradbury, Katharine L., and Helen F. Ladd. 1987. "City Property Taxes: The Effects of Economic Change and Competitive Pressures." *New England Economic Review, Federal Reserve Bank of Boston* (July/August): 22–36.

Bradlee, Francis Boardman Crowninshield. 1918. *The Boston and Lowell Railroad, the Nashua and Lowell Railroad, and the Salem and Lowell Railroad*. Salem, MA: The Essex Institute.

Bradley, James W. 1982a. *Historic and Archaeological Resources of Southeastern Massachusetts: A Framework for Preservation Decisions*. Boston: Secretary of State.

Bradley, James W. 1982b. *Historic and Archaeological Resources of the Boston Area: A Framework for Preservation Decisions*. Boston: Secretary of State.

Bradshaw, Michael. 1988. *Regions and Regionalism in the United States*. Jackson: University Press of Mississippi.

Bragado, Nancy, and Judy Corbett. 1995. *Building Livable Communities: A Policymaker's Guide to Infill Development*. San Diego, CA: Local Government Commission, funded by The Energy Foundation, U.S. Environmental Protection Agency.

Brameld, Theodore. 1957. *Cultural Foundations of Education: An Interdisciplinary Exploration*. New York: Harper & Brothers.

Branch, Melville C. 1978. "Critical Unresolved Problems of Urban Planning Analysis." *Journal of the American Institute of Planners* 44(1): 47–59.

Branch, Melville C. 1981. *Continuous City Planning: Integrating Municipal Management and City Planning*. New York: John Wiley & Sons.

Branch, Melville C. 1988. *Regional Planning: Introduction and Explanation*. New York: Praeger.

Breunig, Kevin. 2003. *Losing Ground: At What Cost? Changes in Land Use and Their Impact on Habitat, Biodiversity, and Ecosystem Services in Massachusetts*. Lincoln, MA: Mass Audubon.

Brevard, Joseph H. 1985. *Capital Facilities Planning*. Chicago: American Planning Association.

Brewer, Gene A. 2003. "Building Social Capital: Civic Attitudes and Behavior of Public Servants." *Journal of Public Administration Research and Theory* 13: 5–26.

Bridge to a Sustainable Future. 1995. Washington, DC: National Science and Technology Council.

Briffault, Richard. 1990. "Our Localism: Part I—The Structure of Local Government Law." *Columbia Law Review* 90: 1–115.

Brooks, David. 2000. *Bobos in Paradise: The New Upper Class and How They Got There*. New York: Simon & Schuster.

Brooks, Michael P. 1988. "Four Critical Junctures in the History of the Urban Planning Profession: An Exercise in Hindsight." *Journal of the American Planning Association* 52(2).

Brophy, Paul, and Kim Burnett. 2003. *Building a New Framework for Community Development for Weak Market Cities*. Denver, CO: The Community Development Partnership Network.

Brown, H. James, Robyn Swaim Phillips, and Neal A. Roberts. 1981. "Land Markets at the Urban Fringe: New Insights for Policy Makers." *Journal of the American Planning Association* 47(2): 131–44.

Browne, Lynn E. 1987. "Too Much of a Good Thing? Higher Wages in New England." *New England Economic Review, Federal Reserve Bank of Boston* (January/February): 39–53.

Browne, Lynn E. 1989. "Shifting Regional Forums: The Wheel Turns." *New England Economic Review, Federal Reserve Bank of Boston* (May/June): 27–40.

Browne, Lynn E. 1990. "Why Do New Englanders Work So Much?" *New England Economic Review, Federal Reserve Bank of Boston* (March/April): 33–46.

Browne, Lynn E. 1991. "The Role of Services in New England's Rise and Fall: Engine of Growth or Along for the Ride?" *New England Economic Review, Federal Reserve Bank of Boston* (July/August): 27–44.

Browne, Lynn E. 1992. "Why New England Went the Way of Texas Rather Than California." *New England Economic Review, Federal Reserve Bank of Boston* (January/February): 23–42.

Browning, Richard. 1998. "Impacts of Transportation on Household Energy Consumption." *World Transport Policy and Practice* 4(1).

Brueckner, Jan K., and Hyun-A Kim. 2000. *Urban Sprawl and the Property Tax*. http://www.igpa.uiuc.edu/publications/workingpapers/wp84-sprawltax.pdf (unpublished manuscript at 3).

Brunn, Stanley D., and James O. Wheeler, eds. 1980. *The American Metropolitan System: Present and Future*. New York: Wiley.

Bryce, Herrington J. 1979. *Planning Smaller Cities*. Lexington, MA: Lexington Books, D. C. Heath and Company.

Bryson, John M. 1995. *Strategic Planning for Public and Nonprofit Organizations: A Guide to Strengthening and Sustaining Organizational Achievement*. San Francisco: Jossey-Bass.

BTS (Bureau of Transportation Statistics). 1996. *U.S. Department of Transportation, Transportation Statistics Annual Report*. Washington, DC: Author.

Bucci, Robert S. 1999. *Metropolitan Area Planning Council Community Data Set: Fiscal Years 1976 to 1998*. Boston: John W. McCormack Institute, University of Massachusetts.

Buchsbaum, Peter A., and Larry J. Smith, eds. 1993. *State and Regional Comprehensive Planning: Implementing New Methods for Growth Management*. Chicago: American Bar Association.

Buder, Stanley. 1990. *Visionaries and Planners: The Garden City Movement and the Modern Community*. New York: Oxford University Press.

Builder Online. 1998. Washington, DC: Hanley-Wood, July.

Building Quality Communities: Making Local Land Use Decisions by Choice and Not by Chance. 2001. Washington, DC: National League of Cities.

Building Vibrant Communities: Linking Housing, Economic Development, Transportation, and the Environment. 2001. Implementing Massachusetts Executive Order 418. Boston: Commonwealth of Massachusetts.

Bullard, Robert D. et al. 1999. *Sprawl Atlanta: Social Equity Dimensions of Uneven Growth and Development*. Atlanta: Clark Atlanta University, The Environmental Justice Resource Center, January. Available at http://www.ejrc.cau.edu/sprlatlexcsum.html.

Bullard, Robert D., Glenn S. Johnson, and Angel O. Torres, eds. 2000. *Sprawl City: Race, Politics, and Planning in Atlanta*. Washington, DC: Island Press.

Buni, Andrew, and Alan Rogers. 1984. *Boston, City on a Hill: An Illustrated History*. Woodland Hills, CA: Windsor.

Bunker, Raymond. 1971. *Town and Country or City and Region?* Carlton, Australia: Melbourne University Press.

Bunting, William Henry. 1971. *Portrait of a Port: Boston, 1852–1914*. Cambridge, MA: Belknap Press.

Burchell, Robert W. et al. 1998. *The Costs of Sprawl—Revisited*. Washington, DC: National Academy Press.

Burchell, Robert W. et al. 2002. *Costs of Sprawl—2000*. Washington, DC: National Academy Press.

Burchell, Robert W., David Listokin, William R. Dolphin, and Lawrence Q. Newton. 1994. *Development Impact Assessment Handbook*. Washington, DC: Urban Land Institute.

Burnside, C. D. 1985. *Mapping from Aerial Photographs*. 2nd ed. New York: Wiley.

Burrows, Lawrence B. 1977. *Growth Management: Issues, Techniques, and Policy Implications*. New Brunswick, NJ: Center for Urban Policy Research.

Burtless, Gary, ed. 1996. *Does Money Matter? The Effect of School Resources on Student Achievement and Adult Success*. Washington, DC: Brookings Institution Press.

Business and Residential Growth in Metropolitan Boston. 1989. Boston: Metropolitan Area Planning Council.

Cairncross, Francis. 1991. *Costing the Earth: The Challenge for Governments, the Opportunities for Business*. Boston: Harvard Business School Press.

The California Partnership for Working Families. 2004. *Lifting Cities Out of Poverty: Opportunities and Challenges for the Emerging Community Benefits Movement*. Oakland, CA: Author.

Calthorpe, Peter. 1993. *The Next American Metropolis: Ecology, Community, and the American Dream*. New York: Princeton Architectural Press.

Calthorpe, Peter, and William Fulton. 2001. *The Regional City: Planning for the End of Sprawl*. Washington, DC: Island Press.

Calthorpe, Peter, and Henry Richmond. 1992. "Land Use & Transportation: Sustainable Growth." In Mark Green, ed., *Changing America: Blueprints for the New Administration*. New York: Newmarket Press.

Campbell, Scott. 1992. *Integrating Economic and Environmental Planning: The Regional Perspective*. New Brunswick, NJ: Center for Urban Policy Research.

Campoli, J., and A. S. MacLean. 2002. *Visualizing Density: Lower Density Catalog Images, 0.5–10.5 Units per Acre*. Cambridge, MA: Lincoln Institute of Land Policy.

Canada, Eric P. 1995. *Economic Development: Marketing for Results!* Wheaton, IL: Blaine, Canada Ltd.

Cannon, LeGrand. 1942. *Look to the Mountain*. New York: Bantam Books.

Canter, David. 1977. *The Psychology of Place*. New York: St. Martin's Press.

CARB (California Air Resources Board). 1994. *The Land Use–Air Quality Linkage*. Sacramento, CA: Author.

Carchedi, Guglielmo. 1977. *On the Economic Identification of Social Classes*. London: Routledge and Kegan Paul.

Carlson, Daniel, Lisa Wormser, and Cy Ulberg. 1995. *At Road's End: Transportation and Land Use Choices for Communities*. Washington, DC: Island Press.

Carlson, Stephen P., and Thomas W. Harding. 1990. *From Boston to the Berkshires: A Pictorial Review of Electric Transportation in Massachusetts*. Boston: Boston Street Railway Association.

Carpenter, Susan L., and W.J.D. Kennedy. 2001. *Managing Public Disputes: A Practical Guide for Professionals in Government, Business and Citizen's Groups*. 2nd ed. San Francisco: Jossey-Bass.

Carson, John Michael. 1973. *Community Growth and Water Resources Policy*. New York: Praeger.

Carson, Rachel. 1962. *Silent Spring*. Boston: Houghton Mifflin.

Case, Karl. 1986a. *Economics and Tax Policy*. Cambridge, MA: Lincoln Institute of Land Policy.

Case, Karl. 1986b. "The Market for Single-Family Homes in the Boston Area." *New England Economic Review, Federal Reserve Bank of Boston* (May/June): 38–48.

Case, Karl. 1991. "The Real Estate Cycle and the Economy: Consequences of the Massachusetts Boom of 1984–87." *New England Economic Review, Federal Reserve Bank of Boston* (September/October): 37–46.

Case, Karl, and Leah Cook. 1989. "The Distributional Effects of Housing Price Booms: Winners and Losers in Boston, 1980–88." *New England Economic Review, Federal Reserve Bank of Boston* (May/June): 3–12.

Case, Karl, and Robert J. Shiller. 1988. "The Behavior of Home Buyers in Boom and Post-Boom Markets." *New England Economic Review, Federal Reserve Bank of Boston* (November/December): 29–46.

Casella, Sam, John Kim Tschangho, Clyde W. Forrest, and Karen A. Przypyszny. 1984. *Tax Increment Financing*. Chicago: American Planning Association.

Catanese, Anthony J. 1972. *Scientific Methods of Urban Analysis*. Urbana: University of Illinois Press.

Census Data and Urban Transportation Planning. 1974. Washington, DC: Transportation Research Board, National Research Council.

Census Profiles of Boston Metropolitan Communities. 1991. Boston: Metropolitan Area Planning Council.

Center Revitalization Manual: A Guide to Improving Your Downtown. 1982. Boston: Metropolitan Area Planning Council.

The Central Mass. 1975. Reading, MA: The Boston & Maine Railroad Historical Society.

Cervero, Robert. 1986a. *Suburban Gridlock*. New Brunswick, NJ: Center for Urban Policy Research.

Cervero, Robert. 1986b. "Unlocking Suburban Gridlock." *Journal of the American Planning Association* 52(4): 389–406.

Cervero, Robert. 1987. "Forecasting on the PC: A Planner's Guide to Time Series Packages." *Journal of the American Planning Association* 53(4): 510–20.

Cervero, Robert. 1988. "Land-Use Mixing and Suburban Mobility." *Transportation Quarterly* 42: 429.

Cervero, Robert. 1989a. *America's Suburban Centers: The Land Use–Transportation Link*. Boston: Unwin Hyman.

Cervero, Robert. 1989b. "Jobs-Housing Balancing and Regional Mobility." *Journal of the American Planning Association* 55(2): 136–50.

Cervero, Robert. 1994. "Rail Transit and Joint Development: Land Market Impacts in Washington, D.C. and Atlanta." *Journal of the American Planning Association* 60(1).

Cervero, Robert, and Michael Duncan. 2002. "Transit's Value-Added Effects: Light and Commuter Rail Services and Commercial Land Values." *Transaction Research Record* 1805: 8, 15.

Cervero, Robert, and Michael Duncan. 2004. "Neighborhood Composition and Residential Land Prices: Does Exclusion Raise or Lower Values?" *Urban Studies* 41: 299, 307, 309.

Cervero, Robert, and Roger Gorham. 1995. "Commuting in Transit Versus Automobile Neighborhoods." *Journal of the American Planning Association* 61(2): 210–25.

Chadwick, George F. 1971. *A Systems View of Planning: Towards a Theory of the Urban and Regional Planning Process*. Oxford: Pergamon Press.

Chael, Marice. 2003. "The SmartCode: A Weapon to Fight the Sprawl War." *The Town Paper* 5(2). Retrieved April 9, 2004, from htttp://www.tndtownpaper.com/Volume5/smartcode.htm.

The Challenge of Prosperity: The Community Profile of the Boston Area in the Mid-1980's. 1989. Boston: The Social Policy Research Group.

Chandler, John. 1996. "Name and Boundary Changes of Cities and Towns of Massachusetts." Cape Cod, February 3. Located on the Mass Municipal Association Web site, http://www.mma.org/.

Chandler, Tertius. 1974. *3000 Years of Urban Growth*. New York: Academic Press.

The Changing Face of Boston Over 350 Years. 1980. Boston: Massachusetts Historical Society.

Chapin, F. Stuart, and Edward J. Kaiser. 1979. *Urban Land Use Planning*. 3rd ed. Urbana: University of Illinois Press.

Chapin, F. Stuart, and Shirley Weiss, eds. 1962. *Urban Growth Dynamics in a Regional Cluster of Cities*. New York: John Wiley & Sons.

Chapman, Jeffrey I. 1981. *Proposition Thirteen and Land Use: A Case Study of Fiscal Limits in California*. Lexington, MA: Lexington Books.

Chatburn, George Richard. 1923. *Highways and Highway Transportation*. New York: Thomas Y. Crowell Company.

Cheape, Charles W. 1980. *Moving the Masses: Urban Public Transit in New York, Boston, and Philadelphia, 1880–1912*. Cambridge, MA: Harvard University Press.

Chicoine, David L., and Norman Walzer, eds. 1986. *Financing Local Infrastructure in Nonmetropolitan Areas*. New York: Praeger.

Chinitz, Benjamin. 1989. "Growth Management from an Economist's Perspective." *Journal of the American Planning Association* 55(3): 338–39.

Chinitz, Benjamin. 1990. "Growth Management: Good for the Town, Bad for the Nation?" *Journal of the American Planning Association* 56(1): 3–8.

Chinitz, Benjamin, ed. 1964. *City and Suburb: The Economics of Metropolitan Growth*. Englewood Cliffs, NJ: Prentice-Hall.

Chiswick, Barry Raymond. 1974. *Income Inequality: Regional Analyses Within a Human Capital Framework*. New York: National Bureau of Economic Research, distributed by Columbia University Press.

Choosing to Compete: A Statewide Strategy for Job Creation and Economic Growth. 1993. Boston: Executive Office of Economic Affairs, Commonwealth of Massachusetts.

Christensen, Carol A. 1986. *The American Garden City and the New Towns Movement*. Ann Arbor, MI: UMI Research Press.

Cieslewicz, David J. 2002. "The Environmental Impacts of Sprawl." In Gregory D. Squires, ed., *Urban Sprawl: Causes, Consequences & Policy Responses* (pp. 23–38). Washington, DC: The Urban Institute Press.

Cisneros, Henry G. 1995. *Regionalism: The New Geography of Opportunity*. Washington, DC: U.S. Department of Housing and Urban Development.

Cisneros, Henry G., ed. 1993. *Interwoven Destinies: Cities and the Nation*. New York: W. W. Norton & Company.

Clapp, William Warland. 1969. *A Record of the Boston Stage*. New York: Greenwood Press.

Clarion Associates. 2000. *The Costs of Sprawl in Pennsylvania*. Philadelphia: 10,000 Friends of Pennsylvania.

Clark, Gordon L., Meric S. Gertler, and John Whiteman. 1986. *Regional Dynamics: Studies in Adjustment Theory*. Boston: Allen and Unwin.

Clark, Thomas A. 1979. *Blacks in Suburbs, a National Perspective*. New Brunswick, NJ: Center for Urban Policy Research.

Clark, William A. V., and Shila Patel. 2004. *Residential Choices of the Newly Arrived Foreign Born: Spatial Patterns and the Implications for Assimilation*. Los Angeles and Irvine: University of California, Los Angeles, and University of California, Irvine.

Clarke, Bradley H. 1981. *The Boston Rapid Transit Album*. Cambridge, MA: Boston Street Railway Association.

Clarke, Mary Stetson. 1974. *The Old Middlesex Canal*. Easton, PA: Center for Canal History and Technology.

Clawson, Marion. 1971. *Suburban Land Conversion in the United States: An Economic and Governmental Process*. Baltimore: Published for Resources for the Future by The Johns Hopkins Press.

Cobb, Nathan, and John N. Cole. 1980. *A Journey to Two Places: Cityside/Countryside*. Brattleboro, VT: The Stephen Greene Press.

Cohen, Abner, ed. 1974. *Urban Ethnicity*. London: Tavistock Publications.

Coleman, J. S. 1988. "Social Capital in the Creation of Human Capital." *American Journal of Sociology* 94 (supplement): 95–120.

Coleman, James S. 1966. *Equality of Educational Opportunity*. Washington, DC: Government Printing Office.

Coleman, Richard Patrick. 1971. *Social Status in the City*. San Francisco: Jossey-Bass.

Common Groundwork: A Practical Guide. 1993. Chagrin Falls, OH: Institute for Environmental Education.

Commonwealth Research Group and McGregor & Shea. 1995. "Cost of Community Services in Southern New England." Boston: Southern New England Forest Consortium.

Community Culture and the Environment: A Guide to Understanding a Sense of Place. 2002. U.S. EPA (EPA 842-B-01-003), Office of Water. Washington, DC: National Center for Environmental Publications and Information.

Community Profile Series. 1993. Boston: Executive Office of Communities and Development, Commonwealth of Massachusetts.

Community Values as Affected by Transportation; 7 Reports. 1963. Highway Research Board of the Division of Engineering and Industrial Research, National Academy of Sciences-National Research Council. Highway research record, no. 2. National Research Council. Publication, vol. 1065. Washington, DC: National Research Council (U.S.). Highway Research Board.

Commuting in a New Century: The New Program for Mass Transit. 1994. Boston: Executive Office of Transportation and Construction.

Comprehensive Land Use Inventory Report: Eastern Massachusetts Regional Planning Project. 1967. Cincinnati, OH: Vogt, Ivers and Associates.

Conant, James Bryant. 1961. *Slums and Suburbs: A Commentary on Schools in Metropolitan Areas*. New York: McGraw-Hill.

Connell, Katheleen M. 1972. *Regional New Towns and Intergovernmental Relations: Four Case Studies*. Detroit: Metropolitan Fund.

Connerly, Charles E., and Marc Smith. 1996. "Developing a Fair Share Housing Policy for Florida." *Journal of Land Use and Environmental Law* 12(1).

Connors, Donald L., and Michael E. High. 1987. "The Expanding Circle of Exactions: From Dedication to Linkage." *Law and Contemporary Problems* 50: 51–69.

Conroy, Michael E. 1975. *Regional Economic Diversification*. New York: Praeger.

Conservation Options: A Landowner's Guide. 1993. Washington, DC: Land Trust Alliance.

Conuel, Thomas. 1990. *Quabbin: The Accidental Wilderness*. Rev. ed. Amherst: University of Massachusetts Press.

Conzen, Michael P., and George K. Lewis. 1976. *Boston: A Geographical Portrait*. Cambridge, MA: Ballinger Publishing Company.

Cooper, M. 2001. An Evaluation of the Northeast Earth Institute's Effectiveness in Building Social Capital in New Hampshire Communities. Unpublished case study.

Cooperrider, David L., Peter F. Sorensen Jr., Diana Whitney, and Therese F. Yaeger, eds. 1999. *Appreciative Inquiry: Rethinking Human Organization Toward a Positive Theory of Change*. Champaign, IL: Stipes Publishing.

The Cost of Sprawl. 1997. Augusta: Maine State Planning Office.

"The Costs and Benefits of Alternative Growth Patterns: The Impact Assessment of the New Jersey State Plan." 2000. New Brunswick, NJ: Center for Urban Policy Research, Edward J. Bloustein School of Planning and Public Policy, September.

The Costs of Sprawl: Detailed Cost Analysis. 1974. Washington, DC: Real Estate Research Corporation and U.S. Government Printing Office.

The Costs of Sprawl in Delaware. 2000. Wilmington: The Delaware Chapter of the Sierra Club.

The Costs of Suburban Sprawl and Urban Decay in Rhode Island. 1999. Prepared by H. C. Planning Consultants and Planimetrics. Providence: Grow Smart Rhode Island.

Coughlin, Robert E., and James Fritz. 1971. *Land Values and Environmental Characteristics in the Rural-Urban Fringe*. Philadelphia: Regional Science Research Institute.

County Government in Massachusetts. 1945. Boston: The Massachusetts Association of Taxpayers' Associations.

Coyle, John Joseph. 1990. *Transportation*. 3rd ed. St. Paul, MN: West Publishing Company.

Crane, Jonathan. 1991a. "The Effects of Neighborhoods on Dropping Out of School and Teenage Childbearing." In Christopher Jencks and Paul E. Peterson, eds., *The Urban Underclass* (pp. 299–320). Washington, DC: The Brookings Institution.

Crane, Johnathan. 1991b. "How Much Does a School's Racial and Socioeconomic Mix Affect Graduation and Teenage Fertility Rates?" In Christopher Jencks and Paul E. Peterson, eds., *The Urban Underclass* (pp. 321–41). Washington, DC: The Brookings Institution.

Crane, Randall. 1996. "Cars and Drivers in the New Suburbs: Linking Access to Travel in Neotraditional Planning." *Journal of the American Planning Association* 62(1): 51–65.

Creese, Walter. 1966. *The Search for Environment*. New Haven, CT: Yale University Press.

Crocker, J. P., Jr., and W. R. Potapchuk. 1999. "Exploring the Elements of Civic Capital." *National Civic Review* 88(3): 175–96.

Cronin, Thomas E. 1970. "Metropolity Models and City Hall." *Journal of the American Institute of Planners* 36(3): 189–97.

Cudahy, Brian J. 1972. *Change at Park Street Under: The Story of Boston's Subways*. Brattleboro, VT: Stephen Greene Press.

Cuff, David J. 1982. *Thematic Maps: Their Design and Production*. New York: Methuen.

Cullingworth, J. B. 1993. *The Political Culture of Planning: American Land Use Planning in Comparative Perspective*. New York: Routledge.

Cullingworth, J. B., and S. C. Orr, eds. 1969. *Regional and Urban Studies: A Social Science Approach*. London: Allen & Unwin.

Dahl, Robert A. 1999. *On Democracy*. New Haven, CT: Yale University Press.

Dalton, Cornelius. 1984. *Leading the Way: A History of the Massachusetts General Court, 1620–1980*. Boston: General Court of Massachusetts.

Dalton, Linda C., and Raymond J. Burby. 1994. "Mandates, Plans, and Planners: Building Local Commitment to Development Management." *Journal of the American Planning Association* 60(4): 444–61.

Daly, Charles U., ed. 1968. *The Quality of Inequality: Urban and Suburban Public Schools*. Chicago: University of Chicago, Center for Policy Study.

Daniels, P. W., ed. 1979. *Spatial Patterns of Office Growth and Location*. Chichester: John Wiley.

Daniels, Thomas L. 1991. "The Purchase of Development Rights: Preserving Agricultural Land and Open Space." *Journal of the American Planning Association* 57(4): 421–31.

Daniels, Thomas L. 1999. *When City and Country Collide: Managing Growth in the Metropolitan Fringe*. Washington, DC: Island Press.

Daniels, Thomas L., John W. Keller, and Mark B. Lapping. 1988. *The Small Town Planning Handbook*. Chicago: Planners Press of the American Planning Association.

Daniels, Tom, and Katherine Daniels. 2003. *The Environmental Planning Handbook for Sustainable Communities and Regions*. Chicago: Planners Press of the American Planning Association.

Danielson, Michael N. 1976. *The Politics of Exclusion*. New York: Columbia University Press.

Davidoff, P., and L. Davidoff. 1971. "Opening the Suburbs: Toward Inclusionary Land Use Controls." *Syracuse Law Review* 22(2): 509–36.

Davidoff, Paul, and Thomas Reiner. 1962. "A Choice Theory of Planning." *AIP Journal*.

Davidson, Michael, and Fay Dolnick. 2004. *A Planners Dictionary*. Chicago: American Planning Association.

Davis, Judy, and Samuel Seskin. 1997. "Impacts of Urban Form on Travel Behavior." *Urban Lawyer* 29(2).

Davis, Judy S., Arthur C. Nelson, and Kenneth J. Dueker. 1994. "The New 'Burbs': The Exurbs and Their Implications for Planning Policy." *Journal of the American Planning Association* 60(1): 45–60.

Davis, Kingsley. 1959. *The World's Metropolitan Areas*. Berkeley: University of California Press.

De Chiara, Joseph, and Lee Koppelman. 1969. *Planning Design Criteria*. New York: Van Nostrand-Reinhold Company.

Deakin, Michelle Bates. 2002. "The Best High Schools." *Boston Magazine* (September): 98–105.

Dear, Michael. 1992. "Understanding and Overcoming the NIMBY Syndrome." *Journal of the American Planning Association* 58(3): 288–300.

A Decade of Change: Growth Trends in the Greater Boston Area—1990 to 2000. 2001. Boston: Metropolitan Area Planning Council.

A Decade of Change Community Profiles: Growth Trends in Greater Boston's 101 Communities—1990 to 2000. 2001. Boston: Metropolitan Area Planning Council.

DeGrove, John M. 1984. *Land, Growth and Politics*. Washington, DC: Planners Press of the American Planning Association.

DeGrove, John M., with Deborah A. Miness. 1992. *The New Frontier for Land Policy: Planning and Growth Management in the States*. Cambridge, MA: Lincoln Institute of Land Policy.

Delafons, John. 1962. *Land-Use Controls in the United States*. Cambridge, MA: MIT Press.

Denworth, Joanne R. 2001. "Growing Smarter Legislation—New Options for Multi-Municipal Planning and Implementation." Philadelphia: 10,000 Friends of Pennsylvania. Available at www.10000friends.org.

DeVillars, John. 2002. Foreword. In Terry Szold and Armando Carbonell, eds., *Smart Growth: Form and Consequence*. Cambridge, MA: Lincoln Institute of Land Policy.

Diamond, Douglas B., and George S. Tolley, eds. 1982. *The Economics of Urban Amenities*. New York: Academic Press.

Diamond, Henry L., and Patrick F. Noonan, eds. 1996. *Land Use in America*. Washington, DC: Island Press and Lincoln Institute of Land Policy.

Dickinson, Robert Eric. 1970. *Regional Ecology: The Study of Man's Environment*. New York: Wiley.

DiMento, Joseph, and LeRoy Graymer, eds. 1991. *Confronting Regional Challenges*. Cambridge, MA: Lincoln Institute of Land Policy.

Dionne, E. J. 2004. ". . . But First, an Earthly Idea." *Washington Post*, January 16, A19.

Dittmar, Hank. 1995a. "A Broader Context for Transportation Planning: Not Just an End in Itself." *Journal of the American Planning Association* 61(1): 7–13.

Dittmar, Hank. 1995b. "Putting a Stop to Sprawl." *Surface Transportation Policy Progress* (June).

Dobriner, William Mann. 1963. *Class in Suburbia*. Englewood Cliffs, NJ: Prentice-Hall.

Doeringer, Peter D., Philip I. Moss, and David G. Terkla. 1986. *The New England Fishing Economy: Jobs, Income, and Kinship*. Amherst: University of Massachusetts Press.

Dogan, Mattei, and John D. Kasarda, eds. 1988. *The Metropolis Era: A World of Giant Cities*. Newbury Park, CA: Sage Publications.

Doggett, Rosalyn P. 1969. "The Development Sector Approach to Regional Planning." *Journal of the American Institute of Planners* 35(3): 169–77.

Doggett, Tom. 2002. "Suburban Sprawl Blocks Water, Worsens U.S. Drought." Reuters News Service, August 29.

Dombeck, Mike. 2002. "Securing the Land Beneath Us." *Seattle Post Intelligencer*, March 31.

Donaldson, Scott. 1969. *The Suburban Myth*. New York: Columbia University Press.

Donovan, Shaun. 1994. *Moving to the Suburbs: Section 8 Mobility and Portability in Hartford*. Cambridge, MA: Joint Center for Housing Studies, Graduate School of Design, John F. Kennedy School of Government, Harvard University.

Doolittle, Fred C. et al. 1982. *Future Boston: Patterns and Perspectives*. Cambridge, MA: Joint Center for Urban Studies of MIT and Harvard University.

Dowall, David E. 1981. "Reducing the Cost Effects of Local Land Use Control." *Journal of the American Planning Association* 47(2): 145–53.

Dowall, David E. 1984. *The Suburban Squeeze: Land Conversion and Regulation in the San Francisco Bay Area*. Berkeley: University of California Press.

Downie, Leonard, Jr. 1974. *Mortgage on America: The Real Costs of Land Speculation*. New York: Praeger.

Downing, Paul B. 1973. "User Charges and the Development of Urban Land." *National Tax Journal* 26: 631–37.

Downs, Anthony. 1973. *Opening up the Suburbs: An Urban Strategy for America*. New Haven, CT: Yale University Press.

Downs, Anthony. 1979. "Key Relationships Between Urban Development and Neighborhood Change." *Journal of the American Planning Association* 45(4): 462–72.

Downs, Anthony. 1991. "Obstacles in the Future of U.S. Cities." *Journal of the American Planning Association* 57(1): 13–15.

Downs, Anthony. 1992. *Stuck in Traffic: Coping with Peak-Hour Traffic Congestion*. Washington, DC: The Brookings Institution.

Downs, Anthony. 1994. *New Visions for Metropolitan America*. Washington, DC: The Brookings Institution.

Doyle, Michael, and David Straus. 1976. *How to Make Meetings Work: The New Interaction Method*. New York: Wyden Books.

Doyle, Sir Arthur Conan. 1982. *Beyond the City: The Idyll of a Suburb*. Bloomington, IN: Gaslight Publications.

Dreier, Peter, Todd Swanstrom, and John Mollenkopf. 2001. *Place Matters: Metropolitics for the Twenty-First Century*. Lawrence: University Press of Kansas.

Drennan, Matthew P. 2002. *The Information Economy and American Cities*. Baltimore: Johns Hopkins University Press.

Drower, David J., David R. Godschalk, and Douglas R. Porter, eds. 1989. *Understanding Growth Management: Critical Issues and a Research Agenda*. Washington, DC: Urban Land Institute.

Drown, Merle. 2000. *The Suburbs of Heaven*. New York: Soho Press.

Drummond, William J. 1995. "Address Matching: GIS Technology for Mapping Human Activity Patterns." *Journal of the American Planning Association* 61(2): 240–51.

Duany, A., and E. Talen. 2002. "Transect Planning." *Journal of the American Planning Association* 68(3): 245–66.

Duany, Andres, Elizabeth Plater-Zyberk, and Jeff Speck. 2000. *Suburban Nation: The Rise of Sprawl and the Decline of the American Dream*. New York: North Point Press.

Dubbink, David. 1984. "I'll Have My Town Medium-Rural, Please." *Journal of the American Planning Association* 50(4): 406–18.

Dudek, Conrad L., and Gerald L. Ullman. 1992. *Freeway Corridor Management*. Washington, DC: Transportation Research Board, National Research Council.

Dueker, Kenneth J. 1987. "Geographic Information Systems and Computer Aided Mapping." *Journal of the American Planning Association* 53(3): 383–90.

Dueker, Kenneth J., and P. Barton DeLacy. 1990. "GIS in the Land Development Planning Process." *Journal of the American Planning Association* 56(4): 483–91.

Duensing, Edward E. 1994. *Information Sources in Urban and Regional Planning: A Directory and Guide to Reference Materials*. New Brunswick, NJ: Center for Urban Policy Research.

Duerksen, C. J. 1996. "Form, Character, and Context: New Directions in Land Use Regulations." Paper presented at the American Planning Association Annual Conference, April.

Duncan, Otis Dudley, Howard Schuman, and Beverly Duncan. 1973. *Social Change in a Metropolitan Community*. New York: Russell Sage Foundation.

Dunn, Edgar S., Jr. 1980. *The Development of the U.S. Urban System: Concepts, Structures, and Regional Shifts*. Baltimore: Published for Resources for the Future by the Johns Hopkins University Press.

Dunphy, Robert, and Kimberly Fisher. 1996. "Transportation, Congestion, and Density: New Insights." Transportation Research Record No. 1552. Washington, DC: Transportation Research Board.

Dunphy, Robert T. 1995. "Transportation Oriented Development: Making a Difference." *Urban Land* 10(1).

Easley, V. Gail. 1992. *Staying Inside the Lines: Urban Growth Boundaries*. Chicago: American Planning Association.

Easterling, Keller. 1993. *American Town Plans: A Comparative Time Line*. New York: Princeton Architectural Press.

Eck, Diana L. 2001. *A New Religious America: How a "Christian Country" Has Become the World's Most Religiously Diverse Nation*. New York: HarperSanFrancisco.

Eckardt, Wolf von. 1974. *A Place to Live: The Crisis of the Cities*. New York: Delacorte Press.

Economic Development Administration, U.S. Department of Commerce. 2003. "Defining Economic Development." Available at http://12.39.209.165/xp/EDAPublic/Research/EcoDev.xml#EDT.

Economic Impact Study of Massachusetts Route 128. 1958. Cambridge: Massachusetts Institute of Technology, Transportation Engineering Division.

Economic Impacts of Transportation Investment: The Road to Recovery in Massachusetts. 1992. Boston: Executive Office of Transportation and Construction, Commonwealth of Massachusetts.

Edel, Matthew, Elliott D. Sclar, and Daniel Luria. 1984. *Shaky Palaces: Homeownership and Social Mobility in Boston's Suburbanization*. New York: Columbia University Press.

Edmonston, Barry. 1975. *Population Distribution in American Cities*. Lexington, MA: Lexington Books.

Edwing, Reid, Rolf Pendall, and Don Chen. 2002. *Measuring Sprawl and Its Impact*. Washington, DC: Smart Growth America.

EIA (Energy Information Administration). 1996. *Annual Energy Outlook*. DOE/EIA-0383 (96). Washington, DC: U.S. Department of Energy, January.

Eisner, Robert. 1991. "Infrastructure and Regional Economic Performance: Comment."

New England Economic Review, Federal Reserve Bank of Boston (September/October): 47–57.

Eisner, Simon, Arthur Gallion, and Stanley Eisner. 1993. *The Urban Pattern*. 6th ed. New York: Van Nostrand Reinhold.

Eldredge, H. Wentworth, ed. 1967. *Taming Megalopolis*. Garden City, NY: Anchor Books.

Elias, C. E., Jr., James Gilles, and Svend Riemer. 1964. *Metropolis: Values in Conflict*. Belmont, CA: Wadsworth Publishing Company.

Ellickson, Robert C., and A. Dan Tarlock. 1981. *Land Use Controls: Cases and Materials*. Boston: Little, Brown and Company.

Emerson, M. Jarvin, and F. Charles Lamphear. 1975. *Urban and Regional Economics: Structure and Change*. Boston: Allyn and Bacon.

Employment and Income Forecasts. 1989. Boston: Metropolitan Area Planning Council.

Employment Location in Greater Boston: 1970–2010. 1983. Boston: Metropolitan Area Planning Council.

Employment Profile of the Massachusetts Economy 1988–91. 1992. Boston: Massachusetts Department of Employment & Training.

English, M., J. Peretz, and M. Manderschied. 1998. "Smart Growth for Tennessee Towns and Counties: A Process Guide (Draft)." Knoxville: University of Tennessee, Energy, Environment, and Resource Center.

Erasmus, Charles J. 1977. *In Search of the Common Good: Utopian Experiments Past and Future*. New York: Free Press.

Etzioni, A. 2000. "Back to We" (excerpts from *The Spirit of Community* [1993]). In *Discussion Course on Discovering a Sense of Place* (pp. 6-5–6-8). Available from the Northwest Earth Institute, 505 SW Sixth, Suite 1100, Portland, OR 97204.

Etzioni, Amitai. 1968. *The Active Society: A Theory of Societal and Political Processes*. New York: The Free Press.

Euchner, Charles C., ed. 2002. *Governing Greater Boston: The Politics and Policy of Place*. Cambridge, MA: Rappaport Institute for Greater Boston.

Evaluating the Role of the Automobile: A Municipal Strategy. 1991. Toronto: Healthy City Office, City of Toronto.

Evers, A. 2003. "Social Capital and Civic Commitment: On Putnam's Way of Understanding." *Social Policy and Society* 2: 13–21.

Everything You Always Wanted to Know About Levy Limits . . . But Were Afraid to Ask. 1988. Boston: Massachusetts Department of Revenue.

Ewing, Reid. 1997. "Is Los Angeles Style Sprawl Desirable?" *Journal of the American Planning Association* 63(1): 107–26.

Ewing, Reid, Rolf Pendall, and Don Chen. 2004. *Measuring Sprawl and Its Impact*. Washington, DC: Smart Growth America.

Ewing, Reid, Tom Schmid, Richard Killingsworth, Amy Zlot, and Stephen Raudenbush. 2003. "Relationship Between Urban Sprawl and Physical Activity, Obesity, and Morbidity." *American Journal of Health Promotion* (September).

Expanding Metropolitan Highways: Implications for Air Quality and Energy Use. 1995. Special Report, National Research Council (U.S.), Transportation Research Board, vol. 245. Washington, DC: National Academy Press.

Falbel, Stephen M. 1989. *The Demographics of Commuting in Greater Boston*. Boston: Central Transportation Planning Staff.

Falbel, Stephen M. 1998. *The Demographics of Commuting in Greater Boston*. 2nd ed. Revised, incorporating results of the 1990 Census. Boston: Central Transportation Planning Staff.

Falk, I., and S. Kilpatrick. 2000. "The Role of Social Capital in Rural Development: What Is Social Capital? A Study of Interaction in a Rural Community." *Sociologia Ruralis* 40: 87–110.

Faltermayer, Edmund K. 1968. *Redoing America: A Nationwide Report on How to Make Our Cities and Suburbs Livable*. New York: Harper and Row.

Faludi, Andreas, ed. 1973. *A Reader in Planning Theory*. Oxford: Pergamon Press.

Farr, Cheryl A. *Shaping the Local Economy: Current Perspectives on Economic Development*. Washington, DC: International City/County Management Association.

Feitelson, Eran. 1993. "The Spatial Effects of Land Use Regulations: A Missing Link in Growth Control Evaluations." *Journal of the American Planning Association* 59(4): 461–72.

Fernandez, Judith C., John Pincus, and Jane Peterson. 1982. *Troubled Suburbs: An Exploratory Study*. Santa Monica, CA: Rand Corporation.

Ferreira, Joseph, Jr. 1990. "Database Management Tools for Planning." *Journal of the American Planning Association* 56(1): 78–84.

Finch, Christopher. 1992. *Highways to Heaven: The AUTO Biography of America*. New York: HarperCollins.

Firey, Walter I. 1947. *Land Use in Central Boston*. Cambridge, MA: Harvard University Press.

The Fiscal Facts of Massachusetts Cities and Towns. 1987. Boston: Massachusetts Department of Revenue.

Fiscal Impact of Development. n.d. Boston: Metropolitan Area Planning Council.

Fischel, William A. 1985. *The Economics of Zoning Laws: A Property Rights Approach to American Land Use Controls*. Baltimore: The Johns Hopkins University Press.

Fischel, William A. 1990. *Do Growth Controls Matter? A Review of Empirical Evidence on the Effectiveness and Efficiency of Local Government Land Use Regulation*. Cambridge, MA: Lincoln Institute of Land Policy.

Fischel, William A. 2005. *The Homevoter Hypothesis: How Home Values Influence Local Government Taxation, School Finance, and Land-Use Policies*. Cambridge, MA: Harvard University Press.

Fischer, C. S. 1982. *To Dwell Among Friends: Personal Networks in Town and City*. Chicago: University of Chicago Press.

Fischer, David Hackett. 1994. *Paul Revere's Ride*. New York: Oxford University Press.

Fischler, Raphael. 1998. "The Metropolitan Dimension of Early Zoning: Revisiting the 1916 New York City Ordinance." *Journal of the American Planning Association* 64(2): 170–88.

Fiser, Webb S. 1962. *Mystery of the Metropolis*. Westport, CT: Greenwood Press.

Fisher, Andy. 1997. "What Is Community Food Security?" *Urban Ecology* (Spring).

Fisher, Irving D. 1986. *Frederick Law Olmsted and the City Planning Movement in the United States*. Ann Arbor, MI: UMI Research Press.

Fishman, Robert. 1987. *Bourgeois Utopias: The Rise and Fall of Suburbia*. New York: Basic Books.

Fishman, Robert, ed. 2000. *The American Planning Tradition: Culture and Policy*. Washington, DC: Woodrow Wilson Centre Press.

Fleissig, Will, and Vickie Jacobsen. 2002. *Smart Scorecard for Development Projects*. Washington, DC: Congress for New Urbanism and the U.S. Environmental Protection Agency.

Flint, Anthony. 2001. "Sprawl, Livability Called Voter Issues." *Boston Globe*, December 18.

Flint, Anthony. 2002. "Hello, Sprawl: Now That It's Past 495, the Need Rises to Manage It." *Boston Globe*.

Flora, C. B. 1997. "Innovations in Community Development." *Rural Development News* 21: 1–2. Available from the North Central Regional Center for Rural Development.

Flora, C. B., and J. L. Flora. n.d. *Measuring and Interpreting Social Capital on the Community Level: The Difference and Similarities between Social Capital and Entrepreneurial Social Infrastructure*. Retrieved August 9, 2002, from http://www.worldbank.org/poverty/scapital/library/flora2.htm.

Flora, J. L. n.d. *Social Capital and Communities of Place*. Retrieved August 9, 2002, from http://www.worldbank.org/poverty/scapital/library/flora1.htm.

Florida, Richard. 2003. *The Rise of the Creative Class: And How It's Transforming Work, Leisure, Community and Everyday Life*. New York: Basic Books.

Fodor, E. 1999. *Better Not Bigger: How to Take Control of Urban Growth and Improve Your Community*. Stony Creek, CT: New Society Publishers.

Foner, Eric. 1998. *The Story of American Freedom*. New York: W. W. Norton and Company.

For Our Common Good: Open Space and Outdoor Recreation in Massachusetts. 1988. Boston: Executive Office of Environmental Affairs, Commonwealth of Massachusetts.

Forbes, Allan. 1953. *Taverns and Stagecoaches of New England*. Boston: State Street Trust Company.

Forces in the New Economy: Implications for Local Economic Development. 1993. Washington, DC: National Council for Urban Economic Development.

Ford, L. R. 2000. *The Spaces Between Buildings*. Baltimore: Johns Hopkins University Press.

Forester, John F. 1999. *The Deliberative Practitioner: Encouraging Participatory Planning Processes*. Cambridge, MA: MIT Press.

Formisano, Ronald P. 1991. *Boston Against Busing: Race, Class, and Ethnicity in the 1960s and 1970s*. Chapel Hill: University of North Carolina Press.

Forrester, Jay Wright. 1969. *Urban Dynamics*. Cambridge, MA: MIT Press.

Fosler, R. Scott. 1991. *Local Economic Development*. Washington, DC: International City/County Management Association.

Foss, C., K. Hartnett, and M. Cooper. 2002. "A Three Infrastructures Approach to Land Use Planning in New Hampshire." *New Hampshire Audubon* 38 (August/September): 5–12.

Foster, Mark S. 1981. *From Streetcar to Superhighway: American City Planners and Urban Transportation, 1900–1940*. Philadelphia: Temple University Press.

Fowler, William M., Jr. 1985. *Boston Looks Seaward: The Story of the Port, 1630–1940*. Boston: Northeastern University Press.

Fowles, Jib. 1976. "An Overview of Social Forecasting Procedures." *Journal of the American Institute of Planners* 42(3): 253–63.

Fox, Maggie. 2003. "Urban Sprawl Makes Americans Fat." Reuters News Service, August 29.

Fox, Richard Gabriel. 1977. *Urban Anthropology: Cities in Their Cultural Settings*. Englewood Cliffs, NJ: Prentice-Hall.

Francis, J., and A. Leaby-Fucheck. 1998. "Smart Growth and Neighborhood Conservation." *Natural Resources & Environment* 13(1).

Francis, M. 1989. "Control as a Dimension of Public-Space Quality." In I. Altman and E. H. Zube, eds., *Human Behavior and Environment: Advances in Theory and Research* (pp. 147–72). New York: Plenum Press.

Frank, Jerome E. 1989. *The Costs of Alternative Development: A Review of the Literature*. Washington, DC: Urban Land Institute.

Franklin, Douglas E., Thaddeus J. Jankowski, and Raymond G. Torto. 1983. *Massachusetts Property Evaluation: Taxpayers' Rights and Legal Procedures*. Boston: Butterworth Legal Publishers.

Frankston, Janet. 2002. "Sprawl Linked Back to Lack of Affordable Housing." *The Atlanta Journal-Constitution*, September 30.

Fredland, Daniel R. 1974. *Residential Mobility and Home Purchase: A Longitudinal Perspective on the Family Life Cycle and the Housing Market*. Lexington, MA: Lexington Books.

Freeland, Richard M. 1992. *Academia's Golden Age: Universities in Massachusetts, 1945–1970*. New York: Oxford University Press.

Freeman, Lance. 2001. "The Effects of Sprawl on Neighborhood Social Ties." *Journal of the American Planning Association* 67(1): 69–77.

Freeman, Lance. 2004. *Siting Affordable Housing: Location and Neighborhood Trends of Low Income Housing Tax Credit Development in the 1990s*. Washington, DC: Brookings Institution Center on Urban and Metropolitan Policy.

Freilich, Robert. 2000. *From Sprawl to Smart Growth*. Chicago: Section of State and Local Government, American Bar Association.

Freilich, Robert H., and Michael M. Schultz. 1995. *Model Subdivision Regulation: Planning and Law*. 2nd ed. Chicago: Planners Press of the American Planning Association.

Frey, William H., and Alden Speare, Jr. 1988. *Regional and Metropolitan Growth and Decline in the United States*. National Committee for Research on the 1980 Census. The Population of the United States in the 1980s. New York: Russell Sage Foundation.

Frey, William H., Jill H. Wilson, Alan Berube, and Audrey Singer. 2004. *Tracking Metropolitan America into the 21st Century: A Field Guide to the New Metropolitan and Micropolitan Definitions*. Washington, DC: The Brookings Institution.

Fried, Lewis. 1990. *Makers of the City: Jacob Riis, Lewis Mumford, James T. Farell, and Paul Goodman*. Amherst: University of Massachusetts Press.

Frieden, Bernard J., and Lynne B. Sagalyn. 1989. *Downtown, Inc.: How America Rebuilds Cities*. Cambridge, MA: MIT Press.

Friedlaender, Ann Fetter. 1965. *The Interstate Highway System: A Study in Public Investment*. Amsterdam: North-Holland Publishing Company.

Friedman, Avi, with David Krawitz et al. 2002. *Planning The New Suburbia: Flexibility by Design*. Vancouver: UBC Press.

Friedman, J. 1987. *Planning in the Public Domain: From Knowledge to Action*. Princeton, NJ: Princeton University Press.

Friedmann, John. 1989. "Planning, Politics and the Environment." *Journal of the American Planning Association* 55(3): 334–38.

Friedmann, John. 1992. *Empowerment: The Politics of Alternative Development*. Cambridge, MA: Blackwell.

Friedmann, John. 1993. "Toward a Non-Euclidian Mode of Planning." *Journal of the American Planning Association* 59(4): 482–85.

Friedmann, John. 1994. "The Utility of Non-Euclidian Planning." *Journal of the American Planning Association* 60(3): 377–79.

Friedmann, John, and William Alonso, eds. 1975. *Regional Policy: Readings in Theory and Applications*. Cambridge, MA: MIT Press.

Frug, Gerald E. 1999. *City Making: Building Communities Without Building Walls*. Princeton, NJ: Princeton University Press.

Frye, Harry A. 1982. *Minuteman Steam: Boston & Maine Steam Locomotives, 1911–1958*. Littleton, MA: Boston and Maine Railroad Historical Society.

Fukuyama, Francis. 1992. *The End of History and the Last Man*. New York: Free Press.

Fullerton, Herbert H., and James R. Prescott. 1975. *An Economic Simulation Model for Regional Development Planning*. Ann Arbor, MI: Ann Arbor Science Publishers.

Fulton, William. 1993. "Sliced on the Cutting Edge: Growth Management and Growth Control in California." In Jay M. Stein, ed., *Growth Management and Growth Control in California* (pp. 113–28). Newbury Park, CA: Sage Publications.

Fulton, William, and Rolf Pendall. 2001. *Who Sprawls the Most? How Growth Patterns Differ Across the U.S.* Washington, DC: Center on Urban and Metropolitan Policy, The Brookings Institution.

Funders' Network for Smart Growth and Livable Communities. 2004. *Two Steps Forward, One Step Back: Research on the Prospects for the Smart Growth and Livable Communities Movement*. Coral Gables, FL: Author.

Furstenburg, Frank F., Jr., S. Philip Morgan, Kristen A. Moore, and James Peterson. 1987. "Race Differences in the Timing of Adolescent Intercourse." *American Sociological Review* 52: 511–18.

Future Development of Eastern Massachusetts Route 495 and Fringe Area, 1963 and 1975–1990. 1969. Boston: Massachusetts Department of Commerce and Development.

Future Directions for Boston and the Metro Region. 1989. A Roundtable Discussion of MetroPlan 2000 and a Blueprint for Boston. Boston: Boston Redevelopment Authority.

Gaffney, Mason. 1969. "Land Planning and the Property Tax." *Journal of the American Institute of Planners* 35(3): 178–83.

Gainsborough, Juliet F. 2001. *Fenced Off: The Suburbanization of American Politics.* Washington, DC: Georgetown University Press.

Gakenheimer, Ralph A. 1976. *Transportation Planning as a Response to Controversy: The Boston Case.* Cambridge, MA: MIT Press.

Gakenheimer, Ralph A. 1989. "Infrastructure Shortfall: The Institutional Problems." *Journal of the American Planning Association* 55(1): 14–23.

Gakenheimer, Ralph A., and Michael D. Meyer. 1979. "Urban Transportation Planning in Transition: The Sources and Prospects of TSM." *Journal of the American Planning Association* 45(1).

Galaty, Fillmore W., Wellington J. Allaway, and Robert C. Kyle. 1994. *Modern Real Estate Practice.* 13th ed. Chicago: Real Estate Education Company.

Gale, Dennis E. 1992. "Eight State-Sponsored Growth Management Programs: A Comparative Analysis." *Journal of the American Planning Association* 58(1).

Galloway, Thomas D., and Riad G. Mahayni. 1977. "Planning Theory in Retrospect: The Process of Paradigm Change." *Journal of the American Institute of Planners* 43(1): 62–69.

Galster, George, and Royce Hanson. 2001. "Wrestling Sprawl to the Ground: Defining and Measuring an Elusive Concept." *Housing Policy Debate* 12(4): 681–717.

Galster, George C., and Edward W. Hill, eds. 1992. *The Metropolis in Black and White: Place, Power, and Polarization.* New Brunswick, NJ: Center for Urban Policy Research.

Galster, George C., and Sean P. Killen. 1995. "The Geography of Metropolitan Opportunity: A Reconnaissance and Conceptual Framework." *Housing Policy Debate* 6(1): 7–43.

Galster, George C., and Ronald B. Mincy. 1993. "Understanding the Changing Fortunes of Metropolitan Neighborhoods: 1980–1990." *Housing Policy Debate* 4(3): 303–52.

Gans, Herbert J. 1962. *The Urban Villagers: Group and Class in the Life of Italian-Americans.* New York: The Free Press.

Gans, Herbert J. 1982. *The Levittowners: Ways of Life and Politics in a New Suburban Community.* New York: Columbia University Press.

Gans, Herbert J. 1990. "Deconstructing the Underclass: The Term's Dangers as a Planning Concept." *Journal of the American Planning Association* 56(3): 271–77.

GAO (General Accounting Office). 2002. *The Federal Government Could Help Communities Better Plan for Transportation That Protects Air Quality.* John B. Stephenson, Director, Natural Resources and Environment. Testimony before the Committee on Environmental and Pubic Works, U.S. Senate, U.S. General Accounting Office.

Gappert, Gary, ed. 1987. *The Future of Winter Cities.* Newbury Park, CA: Sage Publications.

Gardner, John W. 2002. *A New Spirit Stirring: Quotations from John Gardner.* Stanford, CA: Haas Center for the Public Service.

Gardner, Sarah S. 2004. "Review of *Urban Sprawl: Causes, Consequences & Policy Responses,* by Gregory D. Squires, ed." *Journal of Regional Science* 44(2).

Garland, Joseph E. 1981. *Boston's Gold Coast: The North Shore, 1890–1929.* Boston: Little, Brown and Company.

Garreau, Joel. 1991. *Edge City: Life on the New Frontier.* New York: Doubleday.

Garrett, Martin A., Jr. 1987. *Land Use Regulation: The Impacts of Alternative Land Use Rights.* New York: Praeger.

Garrison, William L., Richard L. Morrill, Brian J. L. Berry, Duane F. Marble, and John D. Nystuen. 1969. *Studies of Highway Development and Geographic Change.* New York: Greenwood Press.

Gehlbach, Frederick R. 2002. *Messages from the Wild: An Almanac of Suburban Natural and Unnatural History.* Austin: University of Texas Press.

Gelfand, Mark. 1975. *A Nation of Cities: The Federal Government and Urban America*. New York: Oxford University Press.

Geltner, David, and Norman G. Miller. 2001. *Commercial Real Estate Analysis and Investments*. Mason, OH: South-Western Publishing.

Gerston, Larry, and Peter Haas. 1993. "Political Support for Regional Government in the 1990s: Growing in the Suburbs?" *Urban Affairs Quarterly* 29: 154–63.

Getting to Smart Growth: 100 Policies for Implementation. 2002. Washington, DC: Smart Growth Network and International City/County Management Association.

Getzels, Judith, Martin Jaffe, Brian W. Blaesser, and Robert F. Brown. 1988. *Zoning Bonuses in Central Cities*. Chicago: American Planning Association.

Getzels, Judith, and Charles Thurow, eds. 1980. *Rural and Small Town Planning*. Chicago: American Planning Association.

Gibbs, Jack P. 1961. *Urban Research Methods*. Princeton, NJ: D. Van Nostrand Company.

Gihring, Thomas A. 1999. "Incentive Property Taxation: A Potential Tool for Urban Growth Management." *Journal of the American Planning Association* 65(1): 62–79.

Gilbert, Neil, and Harry Specht. 1977. *Dynamics of Community Planning*. Cambridge, MA: Ballinger Publishing Company.

Gildin, Hilail. 1983. *Rousseau's Social Contract: The Design of the Argument*. Chicago: University of Chicago Press.

Gillham, Oliver, with aerial photographs by Alex S. MacLean. 2002. *The Limitless City: A Primer on the Urban Sprawl Debate*. Washington, DC: Island Press.

Gindroz, Ray et al. 2003. *The Urban Design Handbook: Techniques and Working Methods*. New York: W. W. Norton.

Gindroz, Ray et al. 2004. *The Architectural Pattern Book: A Tool for Building Great Neighborhoods*. New York: W. W. Norton.

Glaab, Charles N., and Theodore Brown. 1967. *A History of Urban America*. London: Macmillan.

Gladwell, M. 2000. *The Tipping Point: How Little Things Can Make a Big Difference*. Boston: Little, Brown and Company.

Glaeser, E. L., D. Laibson, and B. Sacerdote. 2002. "Social Capital: An Economic Approach to Social Capital." *The Economic Journal* 112: 437–58.

Glaeser, Edward, and Matthew Kahn. 2001. *Decentralized Employment and the Transformation of the American City*. Washington, DC: National Bureau of Economic Research.

Glaeser, Edward, and Matthew Kahn. 2003. *Sprawl and Urban Growth*. Cambridge, MA: Harvard Institute of Economic Research.

Glaeser, Edward, and Jesse Shapiro. 2001. *City Growth and the 2000 Census: Which Places Grew, and Why*. Washington, DC: Brookings Institution Center on Urban and Metropolitan Policy.

Glasmeier, Amy K. 1991. *The High-Tech Potential: Economic Development in Rural America*. New Brunswick, NJ: Center for Urban Policy Research.

Glickfield, Madelyn, and Ned Levine. 1992. *Regional Growth, Local Reaction*. Cambridge, MA: Lincoln Institute of Land Policy.

Glickman, Norman J. 1977. *Econometric Analysis of Regional Systems: Explorations in Model Building and Policy Analysis*. New York: Academic Press.

Godschalk, David R. 1992. "In Defense of Growth Management." *Journal of the American Planning Association* 58(4): 422–24.

Godschalk, David R. 2000. "Smart Growth Efforts Around the Nation." *Popular Government* (Fall): 12–20.

Godschalk, David R., David J. Brower, Larry D. McBennett, and Barbara A. Vestal. 1977. *Constitutional Issues of Growth Management*. Chicago: American Society of Planning Officials.

Goldberg, Michael A. 1977. "Simulating Cities: Process, Product, and Prognosis." *Journal of the American Institute of Planners* 43(2): 148–57.

Golden Triangle Build-Out Analysis: An Extension of the Route 9 Corridor Planning Study, Fram-ingham/Natick. 1987. Boston: Metropolitan Area Planning Council.

Goldsmith, Stephen. 1997. *The Twenty-First Century City: Resurrecting Urban America.* Washington, DC: Regnery Publishing.

Goldston, Robert C. 1970. *Suburbia: Civic Denial; A Portrait in Urban Civilization.* New York: Macmillan.

Goldthorpe, John H., and Keith Hope. 1974. *The Social Grading of Occupations: A New Approach and Scale.* Oxford: Clarendon Press.

Gomez-Ibanez, Jose A. 1996. "Big-City Transit Ridership, Deficit, and Politics: Avoiding Reality in Boston." *Journal of the American Planning Association* 62(1): 30–50.

Goodman, John L., Jr. 1979. "Reasons for Moves Out of and Into Large Cities." *Journal of the American Planning Association* 45(4): 407–16.

Goodman, Paul, and Percival Goodman. 1960. *Communitas: Means of Livelihood and Ways of Life.* New York: Vintage Books.

Goodman, Robert. 1979. *The Last Entrepreneurs: America's Regional Wars for Jobs and Dollars.* New York: Simon and Schuster.

Gordon, Debra. 2003. "Sprawling Environments Contribute to Sprawling Waistlines." *Advances* (pamphlet series). Princeton, NJ: The Robert Wood Johnson Foundation.

Gordon, Peter, and Harry Ward Richardson. 1989. "Gasoline Consumption and Cities: A Reply." *Journal of the American Planning Association* 55(3): 342–46.

Gordon, Peter, Harry Ward Richardson, and Myung-Jin Jun. 1991. "The Commuting Paradox: Evidence from the Top Twenty." *Journal of the American Planning Association* 57(4): 416–20.

Gottlieb, R. 1993. *Forcing the Spring: The Transformation of the American Environmental Movement.* Washington, DC: Island Press.

Gottmann, Jean. 1964. *Megalopolis: The Urbanized Northern Seaboard of the United States.* Cambridge, MA: MIT Press.

Gottmann, Jean. 1990. *Since Megalopolis: The Urban Writings of Jean Gottman.* Baltimore: Johns Hopkins University Press.

Gottmann, Jean, and Robert A. Harper, eds. 1967. *Metropolis on the Move: Geographers Look at Urban Sprawl.* New York: Wiley.

Gowans, Alan. 1986. *The Comfortable House: North American Suburban Architecture, 1890–1930.* Cambridge, MA: MIT Press.

The Great Disruption: Human Nature and the Reconstitution of Social Order. 2000. New York: Simon and Schuster.

Greenberg, Donald. 1994. *The Politics Of Privilege: Governing the Affluent Suburb.* Lanham, MD: University Press of America.

Greenberg, Ilene. 1977. *The Massachusetts Growth Policy Development Act: Barriers to Public Learning.* Massachusetts Growth Policy Project. Cambridge, MA: Massachusetts Institute of Technology.

Grogan, Paul S., and Tony Proscio. 2000. *Comeback Cities: A Blueprint for Urban Neighborhood Revival.* Boulder, CO: Westview Press.

Grootaert, C. 1998. *Social Capital: The Missing Link?* Retrieved August 9, 2002, from http://www.worldbank.org/poverty/scapital/wkrppr/sciwp3.pdf.

Groves, Sanford M., and Maureen Godsey Valente. 1986. *Evaluating Financial Condition: A Handbook for Local Government.* Washington, DC: International City/County Management Association.

Growth Management Catalog: A Compendium of Growth Management Techniques. 1987. Boston: Metropolitan Area Planning Council.

Growth Management Techniques. 1978. Boston: Metropolitan Area Planning Council.

Gruen, Nina et al. 1995. *Housing in Suburban Employment Centers: Development Opportunities and Constraints.* Washington, DC: Urban Land Institute.

Gruen, Victor, and Larry Smith. 1960. *Shopping Town USA: The Planning of Shopping Centers*. New York: Van Nostrand Reinhold.

Guidelines for Enhancing Suburban Mobility Using Public Transportation. 1999. Washington, DC: National Academy Press.

Guldberg, Peter H., Frank H. Benesh, and Thomas McCurdy. 1977. "Secondary Impacts of Major Land Use Projects." *Journal of the American Institute of Planners* 43(3): 260–70.

Gustafson, Greg C., Thomas L. Daniels, and Rosalyn P. Shirack. 1982. "The Oregon Land Use Act: Implications for Farmland and Open Space Protection." *Journal of the American Planning Association* 48(3): 365–74.

Guttenberg, Albert Z. 1993. *The Language of Planning: Essays on the Origins and Ends of American Planning Thought*. Urbana: University of Illinois Press.

Haar, Charles M. 1954. "In Accordance with a Comprehensive Plan." *Harvard Law Review* 68: 1154.

Haar, Charles M. 1955. "The Master Plan: An Impermanent Constitution." *Law and Contemporary Problems* 20: 353.

Haar, Charles M. 1959. *Land-Use Planning*. Boston: Little, Brown and Company.

Haar, Charles M. 1996. *Suburbs under Siege: Race, Space, and Audacious Judges*. Princeton, NJ: Princeton University Press.

Haar, Charles M., ed. 1974. *President's Task Force on Suburban Problems: Final Report*. Cambridge, MA: Ballinger Publishing Company.

Haar, Charles M., and Jerold S. Kayden, eds. 1989. *Zoning and the American Dream: Promises Still to Keep*. Chicago: Planners Press of the American Planning Association.

Haar, Charles M., and Lance Liebman. 1985. *Property and Law*. 2nd ed. Boston: Little, Brown and Company.

Haar, Charles M., and Michael A. Wolf. 1989. *Land-Use Planning*. 4th ed. Boston: Little, Brown and Company.

Haar, Charles Monroe. 1973. *Housing the Poor in Suburbia: Public Policy at the Grass Roots*. Cambridge, MA: Ballinger Publishing Company.

Hack, Gary, Ralph A. Gakenheimer, Ruth Bonsignore, Amy Brown, and Lisa Cole. 1994. *The Future of Mobility in the Boston Suburbs: A Research Summary*. Cambridge, MA: MIT, Department of Urban Studies.

Hager, Louis P., ed. 1892. *History of the West End Street Railway*. Boston: Louis P. Hager.

Hale, Richard W. 1970. *Along the Coast of Essex County*. Boston: The Junior League of Boston.

Hall, E. T. 1951. *The Hidden Dimension*. Garden City, NY: Doubleday.

Hall, Kenneth B. 2001. *Community by Design: New Urbanism for Suburbs and Small Communities*. New York: McGraw-Hill.

Hall, Max. 1986. *The Charles: The People's River*. Boston: David R. Godine.

Hall, Peter. 1987. *Urban and Regional Planning*. 2nd ed. London: G. Allen and Unwin.

Hall, Peter. 1989. "The Turbulent Eighth Decade: Challenges to American City Planning." *Journal of the American Planning Association* 55(5): 275–82.

Hall, Richard H. 1969. *Occupations and the Social Structure*. Englewood Cliffs, NJ: Prentice-Hall.

Halprin, Lawrence. 1970. *The RSVP Cycles: Creative Processes in the Human Environment*. New York: G. Braziller.

Halprin, Lawrence, and Jim Burns. 1974. *Taking Part: A Workshop Approach to Collective Creativity*. Cambridge, MA: MIT Press.

Halsted, Ted. 2003. "The American Paradox." *The Atlantic Monthly* (January).

Hamer, Andrew Marshall. 1973. *Industrial Exodus from Central City: Public Policy and the Comparative Costs of Location*. Lexington, MA: Lexington Books.

Hamilton, David K. 1999. *Governing Metropolitan Areas: Response to Growth and Change*. New York: Garland.

Hamrin, Robert D. 1980. *Managing Growth in the 1980s: Toward a New Economics*. New York: Praeger.

Hanchett, Thomas W. 1994. "Federal Incentives and the Growth of Local Planning, 1941–1948." *Journal of the American Planning Association* 60(2): 197–208.

Handlin, Oscar. 1979. *Boston's Immigrants: 1790–1880, A Study in Acculturation*. Rev. and enl. ed. Cambridge, MA: The Belknap Press.

Hanna, Kevin S. 2000. "The Paradox of Participation and the Hidden Role of Information: A Case Study." *Journal of the American Planning Association* 66(4): 398–410.

Hanson, Mark E. 1992. "Automobile Subsidies and Land Use: Estimate and Policy Responses." *Journal of the American Planning Association* 58(1): 60–71.

Hanson, Susan, ed. 1986. *The Geography of Urban Transportation*. New York: Guilford Press.

Hanten, Edward W., Mark J. Kasoff, and F. Stevens Redburn, eds. 1980. *New Directions for the Mature Metropolis: Policies and Strategies for Change*. Cambridge, MA: Schenkman.

Hardin, Garrett. 1968. "The Tragedy of the Commons." *Science* 162: 1243–48.

Harlow, Alvin F. 1946. *Steelways of New England*. New York: Creative Age Press.

Harman, Harry H. 1976. *Modern Factor Analysis*. 3rd ed. Chicago: University of Chicago Press.

Harrigan, John J., and Ronald K. Vogel. 2003. *Political Change in the Metropolis*. 7th ed. New York: Longman.

Harrington, Michael. 1962. *The Other America: Poverty in the United States*. Baltimore: Penguin Books.

Harris, Charles Wesley. 1970. *A Research Brief on Councils of Governments and the Central City*. Detroit: Metropolitan Fund.

Harris, Curtis C. 1973. *The Urban Economies, 1985: A Multiregional, Multi-Industry Forecasting Model*. Lexington, MA: Lexington Books.

Harris, Curtis C., Jay O. Casey, Stanley J. Hille, and Charles E. Olson. 1974. *Regional Economic Effects of Alternative Highway Systems*. Cambridge, MA: Ballinger Publishing Company.

Harris, Richard, and Peter J. Larkham, eds. 1999. *Changing Suburbs: Foundation, Form, and Function*. New York: Routledge.

Harrison, Bennett. 1974. *Urban Economic Development: Suburbanization, Minority Opportunity, and the Condition of the Central City*. Washington, DC: The Urban Institute Press.

Hartzok, Alanna. "Pennsylvania's Success with Local Property Tax Reform: The Split Rate Tax." Available at www.earthrights.net/docs/success.html.

Harvey, Thomas N. 1996. *Assessing the Effects of Highway-Widening Improvements on Urban and Suburban Areas*. Washington, DC: National Academy Press.

Harwood, Douglas W. 1986. *Multilane Design Alternatives for Improving Suburban Highways*. Washington, DC: Transportation Research Board, National Research Council.

Hatry, Harry P., Mark Fall, Thomas O. Singer, and E. Blaine Liner. 1990. *Monitoring the Outcomes of Economic Development Programs: A Manual*. Washington, DC: The Urban Institute Press.

Hauser, Philip M., and Leo F. Schnore, eds. 1965. *The Study of Urbanization*. New York: John Wiley & Sons.

Hauser, Robert M., and David L. Featherman. 1977. *The Process of Stratification: Trends and Analyses*. New York: Academic Press.

Hauser, S. M. 2000. "Education, Ability, and Civic Engagement in the Contemporary United States." *Social Science Research* 29: 556–82.

Hawkins, Brett. 1968. "Fringe-City Life-Style Distance and Fringe Support of Political Integration." *American Journal of Sociology* 74: 248–55.

Hawley, Amos H., and Vincent P. Rock, eds. 1975. *Metropolitan America in Contemporary Perspective*. New York: John Wiley & Sons.

Hayward, J. 1989. "Urban Parks: Research, Planning, and Social Change." In I. Altman and

E. H. Zube, eds., *Human Behavior and Environment: Advances in Theory and Research* (pp. 193–216). New York: Plenum Press.

Healy, Robert G., and John S. Rosenberg. 1979. *Land Use and the States*. 2nd ed. Baltimore: Johns Hopkins University Press.

Heart, Bennet, Elizabeth Humstone, Thomas Irwin, Sandy Levine, and Dana Weisbord. 2002. *Community Rules: A New England Guide to Smart Growth Strategies*. Boston: Conservation Law Foundation and Vermont Forum on Sprawl.

Heddrick, Roger K. 1993. *Metropolitan Reorganization: A Response to Urban Fragmentation*. Chicago: Council of Planning Librarians.

Heikkila, Eric J. 2000. *The Economics of Planning*. New Brunswick, NJ: Center for Urban Policy Research.

Heimlich, Ralph E. 1989. "Metropolitan Agriculture: Farming in the City's Shadow." *Journal of the American Planning Association* 55(4): 457–66.

Henton, Douglas, John Melville, and Kim Walesh. 2003. *Civic Revolutionaries*. San Francisco: Jossey-Bass.

Henwood, K. 2002. *Issues in Health Development: Environment and Health: Is There a Role for Environmental and Countryside Agencies in Promoting Benefits to Health?* London: Health Development Agency.

Herbers, John. 1986. *The New Heartland: America's Flight Beyond the Suburbs and How It Is Changing Our Future*. New York: Times Books.

Herfindahl, Orris C. 1969. *Natural Resources Information for Economic Development: A Study*. Baltimore: Published for Resources for the Future by the Johns Hopkins University Press.

Higgins, Benjamin, and Donald J. Savoie. 1995. *Regional Development Theories and Their Application*. New Brunswick, NJ: Transaction Publishers.

Highways and Economic Development. 1959. Bulletin 227. National Research Council. Publication, vol. 687. Washington, DC: National Research Council (U.S.). Highway Research Board.

Hill, David. 1988. "Jane Jacobs's Ideas on Big, Diverse Cities: A Review and Commentary." *Journal of the American Planning Association* 54(3): 302–14.

Hirschhorn, Joel S. 2001. "Environment, Quality of Life, and Urban Growth in the New Economy." *Environmental Quality Management* 10(3): 1–8.

Hirschhorn, Joel S., and Paul Souza. 2001. *New Community Design to the Rescue: Fulfilling Another American Dream*. Washington, DC: National Governors Association.

Hiss, T. 1991. *The Experience of Place*. New York: Vintage Books.

Hobbes, Thomas. 1958 [1651]. *Leviathan, Parts One and Two*. Indianapolis, IN: The Liberal Arts Press.

Hogan, Dennis P., and Evelyn Kitagawa. 1985. "The Impact of Social Status, Family Structure, and Neighborhood on the Fertility of Black Adolescents." *American Journal of Sociology* 90(4): 825–55.

Holbrook, Stewart H. 1962. *The Old Post Road*. New York: McGraw-Hill.

Hollenbach, David. 1979. *Claims in Conflict: Retrieving and Renewing the Catholic Human Rights Tradition*. New York: Paulist Press.

Hollenbach, David. 2002. *The Common Good and Christian Ethics*. Cambridge: Cambridge University Press.

Hollinshead, Michael, and Ronald Thomas. n.d. *Electronic Town Meetings: Planning for the Information Age*. Videocassette. Chicago: Planning Commissioners Service.

Hollister, Robert M. 1987. *The Greening of Boston: An Action Agenda*. Boston: The Center for Public Service, Tufts University.

Holmes, Edward Henry. 1974. *Coordination of Urban Development and the Planning and Development of Transportation Facilities*. Washington, DC: Department of Transportation, Federal Highway Administration, Office of Planning.

Holmes, Richard. 1980. *Communities in Transition: Bedford and Lincoln Massachusetts, 1729–1850*. Ann Arbor, MI: UMI Research Press.

Holtzclaw, John. 1994. *Using Residential Patterns and Transit to Decrease Auto Dependence and Costs*. San Francisco: Natural Resources Defense Council; Costa Mesa, CA: California Home Energy Efficiency Rating Systems.

Homan, M. S. 1999. *Promoting Community Change: Making It Happen in the Real World*. Pacific Grove, CA: Brooks/Cole Publishing.

Homer-Dixon, Thomas. 2000. *The Ingenuity Gap: How Can We Solve the Problems of the Future?* New York: Alfred A. Knopf.

Hood, Clifton. 1993. *722 Miles: The Building of the Subways and How They Transformed New York*. New York: Simon & Shuster.

Hooper, Katherine S. 1995. *Innovative Suburb-to-Suburb Transit Practices*. Washington, DC: National Academy Press.

Hooper, Kevin G. 1989. *Travel Characteristics at Large-Scale Suburban Activity Centers*. National Cooperative Highway Research Program Report, 0077–5614; 323. Washington, DC: Transportation Research Board, National Research Council.

Hopkinton Build Out Analysis: Impacts of Privately Owned Sewage Treatment Facilities. 1988. Boston: Metropolitan Area Planning Council.

Hoppenfeld, Morton. 1967. "A Sketch of the Planning-Building Process for Columbia, Maryland." *Journal of the American Institute of Planners* 33.

"The Housing Gap." 2002. *Boston Globe*, May 30, Editorial Page.

Howard, Brett. 1976. *Boston, a Social History*. New York: Hawthorn Books.

Howard, Ebenezer. 1902. *Garden Cities of Tomorrow*. London: Swan Sonnenschein and Company.

Howe, Deborah A., and William A. Rabiega. 1992. "Beyond Strips and Centers: The Ideal Commercial Form." *Journal of the American Planning Association* 58(2): 213–19.

Howells, William Dean. 1881. *Suburban Sketches*. New and enl. ed. Boston: Houghton, Mifflin and Company.

Howes, Candace, and Ann R. Markusen. 1993. *Trading Industries, Trading Regions*. New Brunswick, NJ: Center for Urban Policy Research.

Howlett, Debbie. 2003. "Study Finds Traffic Congestion Bad and Getting Worse." *USA Today*, October 1.

Hoyle, Cynthia L. 1995. *Traffic Calming*. Chicago: American Planning Association.

Hoyt, William D. 1987. *Hanging On: The Gloucester Waterfront in Change, 1927–1948*. Gloucester, MA: Martin J. Horgan Jr.

Hu, Teh Wei. 1973. *Econometrics: An Introductory Analysis*. Baltimore: University Park Press.

Hufschmidt, Maynard, ed. 1969. *Regional Planning: Challenge and Prospects*. New York: Frederick A. Praeger.

Hughes, James W. 1972. *Urban Indicators: Metropolitan Evolution and Public Policy*. New Brunswick, NJ: Center for Urban Policy Research.

Hughes, Mark Alan. 1991. "Employment Decentralization and Accessibility: A Strategy for Stimulating Mobility." *Journal of the American Planning Association* 43(1): 288–98.

Humphrey, Thomas F. 1995. *Consideration of the 15 Factors in the Metropolitan Planning Process*. Washington, DC: National Academy Press.

Humphrey, Thomas J. 1985. *Boston's Commuter Rail: The First 150 Years*. Cambridge, MA: Boston Street Railway Association.

Humphrey, Thomas J., and Norton D. Clark. 1986. *Boston's Commuter Rail: Second Section*. Cambridge, MA: Boston Street Railway Association.

Hustedde, R. J. 1998. "On the Soul of Community Development." *Journal of the Community Development Society* 29(2): 153–65.

Huxtable, Ada Louise. 1989. *Will They Ever Finish Bruckner Boulevard?* Berkeley: University of California Press.

Hylton, Thomas. 1995. *Save Our Land, Save Our Towns: A Plan for Pennsylvania*. Harrisburg, PA: RB Books.

Infante, Rosemary, ed. 1994. *Economic Benefits of Land Protection*. Washington, DC: Land Trust Alliance.

Infrastructure and Economic Development: Literature Search. 1989. Boston: Metropolitan Area Planning Council.

Innes, Judith E., and David E. Booher. 1999. "Consensus Building and Complex Adaptive Systems: A Framework for Evaluating Collaborative Planning." *Journal of the American Planning Association* 65(4): 412–23.

Intergovernmental Cooperation in Highway Affairs: A Recommended Action Program for Effective Relationships. 1953. National Research Council (U.S.) Highway Research Board. Special report 9. National Research Council. Publication, vol. 267. Washington, DC: National Research Council (U.S.). Highway Research Board.

Intriligator, Michael. 1978. *Econometric Models, Techniques, and Applications*. Englewood Cliffs, NJ: Prentice-Hall.

IPCC (Intergovernmental Panel on Climate Change). 1995a. *Second Assessment Report, Summary for Policymakers*. New York: Author.

IPCC (Intergovernmental Panel on Climate Change). 1995b. *Summary for Policymakers of the Contribution of Working Group 1 to the IPCC Second Assessment Report*. New York: Author.

Irr, Caren. 1998. *The Suburb of Dissent: Cultural Politics in The United States and Canada during the 1930s*. Durham, NC: Duke University Press.

Isard, Walter. 1975. *Introduction to Regional Science*. Englewood Cliffs, NJ: Prentice-Hall.

Isard, Walter, and David F. Bramhall. 1960. *Methods of Regional Analysis: An Introduction to Regional Science*. Cambridge, MA, and New York: Published jointly by the Technology Press of the Massachusetts Institute of Technology and Wiley.

Isard, Walter, and Robert E. Coughlin. 1957. *Municipal Costs and Revenues Resulting from Growth*. Wellesley, MA: Chandler-Davis.

Isserman, Andrew M. 1977. "The Location Quotient Approach to Estimating Regional Economic Impacts." *Journal of the American Institute of Planners* 43(1): 33–41.

Jackson, John E., ed. 1975. *Public Needs and Private Behavior in Metropolitan Areas*. Cambridge, MA: Ballinger.

Jackson, Kenneth T. 1985. *Crabgrass Frontier: The Suburbanization of the United States*. New York: Oxford University Press.

Jackson, Richard, and Chris Kochtitzky. 2001. *Creating a Healthy Environment: The Impact of the Built Environment on Public Health*. Washington, DC: Sprawl Watch Clearinghouse, www.sprawlwatch.org.

Jackson, W. 1997. "Becoming Native to This Place." In H. Hannum, ed., *People, Land, and Community* (pp. 133–41). New Haven, CT: Yale University Press.

Jacobs, Allan B. 1978. *Making City Planning Work*. Chicago: American Society of Planning Officials.

Jacobs, Jane. 1961. *The Death and Life of Great American Cities*. New York: Random House.

Jacobs, Jane. 1969. *The Economy of Cities*. New York: Random House.

Jacobs, Jane. 1984. *Cities and the Wealth of Nations: Principles of Economic Life*. New York: Random House.

James, Franklin J., Jr., and Oliver Duane Windsor. 1976. "Fiscal Zoning, Fiscal Reform, and Exclusionary Land Use Controls." *Journal of the American Institute of Planners* 42(2): 130–41.

Janda, Kenneth, Jeffrey M. Berry, and Jerry Goldman. 2001. *The Challenge of Democracy: Government in America*. Boston: Houghton Mifflin.

Jargowsky, Paul. 2003. *Stunning Progress, Hidden Problems: The Dramatic Decline of Concentrated Poverty in the 1990s*. Washington, DC: Brookings Institution Center on Urban and Metropolitan Policy.

Jargowsky, Paul A., and Mary Jo Bane. 1991. "Ghetto Poverty in the United States, 1970 to 1980." In Christopher Jencks and Paul E. Peterson, eds., *The Urban Underclass* (pp. 235–73). Washington, DC: The Brookings Institution.

Jencks, Christopher, and Paul E. Peterson, eds. 1991. *The Urban Underclass*. Washington, DC: The Brookings Institution.

Jenkins, Stephen. 1913. *The Old Boston Post Road*. New York: G. P. Putnam's Sons.

Jennings, Michael D. 1989. "The Weak Link in Land Use Planning." *Journal of the American Planning Association* 55(2): 206–8.

John F. Kennedy School of Government, Harvard University, Saguaro Seminar. 2002. *Social Capital Community Benchmark Survey Short Form*. Cambridge, MA: Harvard University Press.

Johnson, Curtis. 2003. *Market Choices and Fair Prices: Research Suggests Surprising Answers to Regional Growth Dilemmas*. CTS 03-02. www.cts.umn.edu/trg/research/reports/TRG_17.html.

Johnson, Elmer W. 2001. *Chicago Metropolis 2020: The Chicago Plan for the Twenty-First Century*. Chicago: University of Chicago Press.

Johnson, Erin J., and Edward H. Ziegler, eds. 1993. *Development Agreements: Analysis, Colorado Case Studies Commentary*. Denver: The Rocky Mountain Land Use Institute.

Johnson, Roger. 1960. *The Economic Impact of Route 128*. Mimeographed. Boston: Associated Industries of Massachusetts.

Jones, Bernie. 1990. *Neighborhood Planning: A Guide for Citizens and Planners*. Washington, DC: Planners Press of the American Planning Association.

Jones, Douglas Lamar. 1981. *Village and Seaport: Migration and Society in Eighteenth Century Massachusetts*. Hanover, NH: University Press of New England.

Jones, Howard Mumford, and Bessie Zaban Jones. 1975. *The Many Voices of Boston: A Historical Anthology, 1630–1975*. Boston: Little, Brown and Company.

Joseph, Lawrence B., ed. 1993. *Affordable Housing and Public Policy: Strategies for Metropolitan Chicago*. Chicago: Center for Urban Policy Research.

Judd, Dennis R., and Paul Kantor, eds. 2002. *The Politics of Urban America: A Reader*. 3rd ed. New York: Longman.

Juergensmeyer, Julian C. 1996. *Property*. 2nd ed. St. Paul, MN: West Professional Training Programs.

Kahn, Herman. 1962. *Thinking about the Unthinkable*. New York: Horizon Press.

Kahn, Matthew E. 2001. "Does Sprawl Reduce the Black/White Housing Consumption Gap?" *Housing Policy Debate* 12(1): 77–86.

Kain, J. F. 1962. "The Journey to Work as a Determinant of Residential Location." *Papers of the Regional Science Association* 8: 137–60.

Kain, John F. 1970. "Rampant Schizophrenia: The Case of City and Regional Planning." *Journal of the American Institute of Planners* 36(4): 221–23.

Kaiser, Edward J., David R. Godschalk, and F. Stuart Chapin. 1995. *Urban Land Use Planning*. 4th ed. Chicago: University of Illinois Press.

Kane, Matt, and Peggy Sand. 1988. *Economic Development: What Works at the Local Level*. Washington, DC: National League of Cities.

Kane, Richard P. 1997. "The Ecological and Biological Benefits of Open Space." In *The Benefits of Open Space*. Morristown, NJ: The Great Swamp Watershed Association.

Kaplan, R., and S. Kaplan. 1989. *The Experience of Nature: A Psychological Perspective*. New York: Cambridge University Press.

Kaplan, Samuel. *The Dream Deferred: People, Politics, and Planning in Suburbia*. New York: Seabury Press.

Karr, Ronald Dale. 1996. *Lost Railroads of New England*. 2nd ed. Pepperell, MA: Branch Line Press.

Kasarda, John D. 1993. "Inner-City Concentrated Poverty and Neighborhood Distress: 1970 to 1990." *Housing Policy Debate* 4(3): 253–302.

Katz, Peter. 1994. *The New Urbanism: Toward an Architecture of Community*. New York: McGraw-Hill.

Kay, Jane Holtz. 1997. *Asphalt Nation—How the Automobile Took Over America and How We Can Take It Back*. New York: Crown Publishers.

Kay, Jane Holtz, and Pauline Chase-Harrell. 1986. *Preserving New England*. New York: Pantheon Books.

Keating, W. Dennis. 1994. *The Suburban Racial Dilemma: Housing and Neighborhoods*. Philadelphia: Temple University Press.

Kelbaugh, Doug, ed. 1989. *The Pedestrian Pocket Book: A New Suburban Design Strategy*. New York: Princeton Architectural Press in association with the University of Washington.

Kelley, Eugene J. 1956. *Shopping Centers: Locating Controlled Regional Centers*. Saugatuck, CT: Eno Foundation for Highway Traffic Control.

Kellogg, David H. 1960. "Areas for Regional Planning in Massachusetts, a Study." Boston: Massachusetts Department of Commerce, Division of Planning.

Kelly, Barbara, ed. 1989. *Suburbia Re-Examined*. Westport, CT: Greenwood Press.

Kelly, Barbara M. 1993. *Expanding the American Dream: Building and Rebuilding Levittown*. Albany: State University of New York Press.

Kelly, Eric Damian. 1993a. *Managing Community Growth: Policies, Techniques, and Impacts*. Westport, CT: Praeger.

Kelly, Eric Damian. 1993b. *Planning, Growth, and Public Facilities: A Primer for Local Officials*. Chicago: American Planning Association.

Kemmis, D. 1990. *Community and the Politics of Place*. Norman: University of Oklahoma Press.

Kendig, Hal. 1976. "Cluster Analysis to Classify Residential Areas: A Los Angeles Application." *Journal of the American Institute of Planners* 42(3): 286–94.

Kenessey, Zoltan. 1978. *The Process of Economic Planning*. New York: Columbia University Press.

Kennedy, Lawrence W. 1992. *Planning the City Upon a Hill: Boston Since 1630*. Amherst: University of Massachusetts Press.

Kettering Foundation. 1991. *Citizens and Politics: A View from Main Street America*. Dayton, OH: Author.

Kiefer, Matthew J. 2002. "From Sprawl to Smart Growth." *Boston Globe*, January 30.

Kihl, Mary, ed. 1990. *Intergovernmental Challenges for the 1990's*. Proceedings of the Intergovernmental Roundtable. Denver, CO: American Planning Association.

Kirlin, John. 1991. "Creating the Conditions for Devising Reasonable and Regional Solutions." In Joseph Dimento and LeRoy Grayme, eds., *Confronting Regional Challenges* (pp. 121–32). Cambridge, MA: Lincoln Institute of Land Policy.

Kitagawa, Evelyn Mae, and Donald J. Bogue. 1955. *Suburbanization of Manufacturing Activity Within Standard Metropolitan Areas*. Oxford, OH: Published jointly by Scripps Foundation for Research in Population Problems, Miami University, and Population Research and Training Center, University of Chicago.

Klain, Ambrose. 1971. *Zoning in Suburbia: Keep It, Reject It or Replace It?* Monticello, IL: Council of Planning Librarians.

Klaus, Susan L. 1991. "Efficiency, Economy, Beauty: The City Planning Reports of Frederick Law Olmsted, Jr. 1905–1915." *Journal of the American Planning Association* 57(4): 456–70.

Klein, Lawrence Robert. 1980. *An Introduction to Econometric Forecasting and Forecasting Models*. Lexington, MA: Lexington Books.

Klein, Richard D. 1990. *Everyone Wins! A Citizen's Guide to Development*. Washington, DC: Planners Press of the American Planning Association.

Klitgaard, Robert, and Gregory Treverton. 2003. "Assessing Partnerships: New Forms of Collaboration." Washington, DC: IBM Center for the Business of Government, March.

Klosterman, Richard E. 1978. "Foundations for Normative Planning." *Journal of the American Institute of Planners* 44(1): 37–46.

Klosterman, Richard E. 1990. *Community Analysis and Planning Techniques*. Savage, MD: Rowman & Littlefield.

Klosterman, Richard E., Richard K. Brail, and Earl G. Bossard. 1993. *Spreadsheet Models for Urban and Regional Analysis*. New Brunswick, NJ: Center for Urban Policy Research.

Knack, Ruth Eckdish. 2000. "Contrarians." *Planning Magazine*, American Planning Association 66(12).

Knapp, Gerrit J., and Lewis D. Hopkins. 2001. "The Inventory Approach to Urban Growth Boundaries." *Journal of the American Planning Association* 67(3): 314–26.

Knapp, Gerrit J., Lewis D. Hopkins, and Kieran Donaghy. 1995. *Do Plans Matter: A Framework for Examining the Logic and Effects of Land Use Planning*. Cambridge, MA: Lincoln Institute of Land Policy.

Knapp, Gerrit J., and Arthur C. Nelson. 1992. *The Regulated Landscape: Lessons on State Land Use Planning from Oregon*. Cambridge, MA: Lincoln Institute of Land Policy.

Koberg, Don, and Jim Bagnall. 1974. *The Universal Traveler: A Soft Systems Guide to Creativity, Problem-Solving, and the Process of Reaching Goals*. Los Altos, CA: Kaufmann.

Koch, Stella. 2000. *Taming the Sprawl Monster: The Costs of Suburban Sprawl*. Available at www.bewellnaturally.net/dcsprawl/costs.

Kolankiewicz, Leon, and Roy Beck. 2001. *Population, Immigration, and the Environment: Why Green Groups Abandoned the Goal of Population Stabilization*. Washington, DC: Center for Immigration Studies.

Kone, Linda D. 1994. *Land Development*. 8th ed. Washington, DC: Home Builder Press.

Kotkin, Joel. 1992. *Tribes: How Race, Religion, and Identity Determine the Success in the New Global Economy*. New York: Random House.

Kotkin, Joel. 2000. *The New Geography: How the Digital Revolution Is Reshaping the American Landscape*. New York: Random House.

Kotval, Zenia, and John Mullin. 1993. "A Balanced Approach to Industrial Planning: The Greenfield Versus Brownfield Debate." *Economic Development Commentary* 17(2): 18–23.

Kraft, Gerald, John R. Meyer, and Jean-Paul Valette. 1971. *The Role of Transportation in Regional Economic Development: A Charles River Associates Research Study*. Lexington, MA: Lexington Books.

Kraft, Michael E. 2001. *Environmental Policy and Politics*. 2nd ed. New York: Longman.

Kranz, Laura. 2003. "The Deadly Impacts of Sprawl." *Boston Globe*, January 21.

Kresge, David T. 1984. *Regions and Resources: Strategies for Development*. Cambridge, MA: MIT Press.

Kretzmann, John P., and John L. McKnight. 1997. *Building Communities from the Inside Out: A Path toward Finding and Mobilizing a Community's Assets*. Chicago: ACTA Publications.

Krieger, Alex, and David Cobb, eds., with Amy Turner. 2000. *Mapping Boston*. Cambridge, MA: MIT Press.

Krieger, Alex, and William Lennertz, eds. 1991. *Andres Duaney and Elizabeth Plater-Zyberk: Towns and Town-Making Principles*. New York: Rizzoli.

Krizek, Kevin, and Joe Power. 1996. *A Planner's Guide to Sustainable Development*. Chicago: American Planning Association, December.

Krueckeberg, Donald A. 1974. *Urban Planning Analysis: Methods and Models*. New York: Wiley.

Krueckeberg, Donald A. 1980. "From the Backyard Garden to the Whole U.S.A.: A Conversation with Charles W. Eliot, 2nd." *Journal of the American Planning Association* 46(4): 440–48.

Krueckeberg, Donald A., ed. 1983. *Introduction to Planning History in the United States*. New Brunswick, NJ: Center for Urban Policy Research.

Krueckeberg, Donald A., ed. 1994. *The American Planner: Biographies and Recollections*. 2nd ed. New Brunswick, NJ: Center for Urban Policy Research.

Krumholz, Norman, and John Forester. 1990. *Making Equity Planning Work: Leadership in the Public Sector*. Philadelphia: Temple University Press.

Kuhn, H. W., and A. W. Tucker, eds. 1950. *Contributions to the Theory of Games*, vol. 1. Princeton, NJ: Princeton University Press.

Kuklinski, Antoni, ed. 1974. *Regional Information and Regional Planning*. The Hague: Mouton.

Kunstler, James Howard. 1993. *The Geography of Nowhere: The Rise and Decline of America's Man-Made Landscape*. New York: Simon & Schuster.

Kunstler, James Howard. 1996. *Home from Nowhere: Remaking Our Everyday World for the Twenty-First Century*. New York: Simon & Schuster.

Kushner, J. A. 1994. *Subdivision Law and Growth Management*. Deerfield, IL: Clark Boardman.

Kutler, Stanley I. 1971. *Privilege and Creative Destruction: The Charles River Bridge Case*. Philadelphia: Lippincott.

Kuttner, Robert. 1984. *The Economic Illusion: False Choices Between Prosperity and Social Justice*. Boston: Houghton Mifflin.

Kwartler, Michael. 1989. "Legislating Aesthetics: The Role of Zoning in the Design of Cities." In Charles M. Haar and Jerold S. Kayden, eds., *Zoning and the American Dream: Promises Still to Keep*. Chicago: Planners Press of the American Planning Association.

Ladd, Helen F. 1993. *Land and Tax Policy*. Cambridge, MA: Lincoln Institute of Land Policy.

Laitos, Jan G. 1999. *Law of Property Rights: Limitations on Governmental Powers*. New York: Aspen Law and Business.

Lake, Robert W. 1981. *The New Suburbanites: Race and Housing in the Suburbs*. New Brunswick, NJ: Center for Urban Policy Research.

Lake, Robert W., ed. 1983. *Readings in Urban Analysis: Perspectives on Urban Form and Structure*. New Brunswick, NJ: Center for Urban Policy Research.

Land Use Impacts of Transportation: A Guidebook. 1999. Washington, DC: National Academy Press.

Landolt, P., and A. Portes. n.d. *Unsolved Mysteries: The Toqueville Files II: The Downside of Social Capital*. Retrieved August 9, 2002, from http://www.prespect.org/print/V7/26/26-cnt2.html.

Langdon, Philip. 1994. *A Better Place to Live: Reshaping the American Suburb*. Amherst: University of Massachusetts Press.

Langtry, Albert Perkins, ed. 1929. *Metropolitan Boston: A Modern History*. New York: Lewis Historical Publishing Company.

Lankevich, George J., ed. 1974. *Boston: A Chronological & Documentary History, 1602–1970*. Dobbs Ferry, NY: Oceana Publications.

Lawrence, Robert Means. 1922. *Old Park Street and Its Vicinity*. Boston: Houghton Mifflin.

Lazear, David G. 1991. *Seven Ways of Knowing: Teaching for Multiple Intelligences*. Palatine, IL: Skylight Publishing.

Leccese, Michael, and Kathleen McCormick, eds. 2000. *Charter of the New Urbanism*. Essays by Randall Arendt [et al.]. New York: McGraw-Hill.

Ledebur, Larry C., and William R. Barnes. 1993. *All in It Together: Cities, Suburbs and Local Economic Regions*. Washington, DC: National League of Cities.

Lee, Chungmei. 2004. *Racial Segregation and Educational Outcomes in Metropolitan Boston*. Cambridge, MA: Harvard Civil Rights Project.

Lee, Colin. 1973. *Models in Planning: An Introduction to the Use of Quantitative Models in Planning*. Oxford: Pergamon Press.

Leigh, Nancy Green. 1994. *Stemming Middle-Class Decline: The Challenges to Economic Development Planning*. New Brunswick, NJ: Center for Urban Policy Research.

Leinberger, Christopher. 1989. "Urban Villages." Albuquerque, NM: NARC Executive Directors.

Leinberger, Christopher B., and Christopher Lockwood. 1986. "How Business Is Reshaping America." *Atlantic Monthly* (October).

Leven, Charles L. 1978. *The Mature Metropolis*. Lexington, MA: Lexington Books.

Levin, Melvin. 1967. "Planners and Metropolitan Planning." *Journal of the American Institute of Planners* 33(2): 78–90.

Levin, Melvin R. 1963. *The Boston Regional Survey*. Boston: Massachusetts Mass Transportation Commission.

Levine, Hillel, and Lawrence Harmon. 1992. *The Death of an American Jewish Community: A Tragedy of Good Intentions*. New York: The Free Press.

Levine, Johnathan. 1998. "Rethinking Accessibility and Jobs-Housing Balance." *Journal of the American Planning Association* 64(2): 133–49.

Levinson, David M., and Ajay Kumar. 1994. "The Rational Locator: Why Travel Times Have Remained Stable." *Journal of the American Planning Association* 60(3): 319–32.

Levy, Brian C. 1996. *Massachusetts Zoning and Land Use Law*. Charlottesville, VA: Michie Law Publishers.

Levy, John M. 1981. *Economic Development Programs for Cities, Counties and Towns*. New York: Praeger.

Levy, Leonard Williams, ed. 1974. *Jim Crow in Boston: The Origin of the Separate but Equal Doctrine*. New York: Da Capo Press.

Lewin, Kurt. 1997. *Resolving Social Conflicts: And, Field Theory in Social Science*. Washington, DC: American Psychological Association.

Lewis, David Neville. 1971. *The Growth of Cities*. New York: Wiley-Interscience.

Lewis, Paul G. 1996. *Shaping Suburbia: How Political Institutions Organize Urban Development*. Pittsburgh, PA: University of Pittsburgh Press.

Lewis, Paul G., and Elissa Barbour. 1999. *California Cities and the Local Sales Tax*. Public Policy Institute of California. Available at http://www.ppic.org/content/pubs/r_799plr.pdf.

Lewis, Philip H., Jr. 1996. *Tomorrow by Design: A Regional Process for Sustainability*. New York: John Wiley and Sons.

Lewis, W. Cris. 1973. *Regional Growth and Water Resource Investment*. Lexington, MA: Lexington Books.

Leyy, John M. 1990. "What Local Economic Developers Actually Do: Location Quotients Versus Press Releases." *Journal of the American Planning Association* 56(2): 153–60.

Liberty, R. 1990. "Planned Growth: The Oregon Model." *Natural Resources & Environment* 13(1).

Liberty, Robert L. 1992. "Oregon's Comprehensive Growth Management Program: An Implementation Review and Lessons for Other States." *Environmental Law Reporter* 22: 10,367.

Lim, Gill C., ed. 1983. *Regional Planning: Evolution, Crisis, and Prospects*. Totowa, NJ: Allanheld, Osmun.

Lindeman, Bruce. 1976. "Anatomy of Land Speculation." *Journal of the American Institute of Planners* 42(2): 142–52.

Liner, E. Blaine, ed. 1986. *Compacts and Coalitions in Metropolitan Governance*. Cambridge, MA: Lincoln Institute of Land Policy.

Lingeman, Richard. 1980. *Small Town America, A Narrative History 1620 to the Present*. Boston: Houghton Mifflin.

Little, Charles E. 1990. *Greenways for America*. Baltimore: The Johns Hopkins University Press.

Little, Jane Sneddon. 1990. "New England's Links to the World Economy." *New England Economic Review, Federal Reserve Bank of Boston* (November/December): 33–50.

Liu, Ben Chieh. 1975. *Quality of Life Indicators in U.S. Metropolitan Areas, 1970*. Washington, DC: U.S. Environmental Protection Agency.

Livable Places, Inc. 2003. *Encouraging Transit Villages*. Retrieved April 20, 2004, from htttp://www.livableplaces.org/policy/todincentives.html.

Lochner, K., I. Kawachi, and B. P. Kennedy. 1999. "Social Capital: A Guide to Its Measurement." *Health & Place* 5: 259–70.

Logan, John R. 2002. "Choosing Segregation: Racial Imbalance in American Public Schools, 1990–2000." Albany, NY: Lewis Mumford Center for Comparative Urban and Regional Research at the University of Albany. Available at www.albany.edu/mumford/census/.

Logan, John R. 2003. *America's Newcomers*. Albany, NY: Lewis Mumford Center for Comparative Urban and Regional Research at the University of Albany.

Logan, John R., and Mark Schneider. 1981. "The Stratification of Metropolitan Suburbs: 1950–1970." *American Sociological Review* 46: 175–86.

Long, Larry. 1980. "Back to the Countryside and Back to the City in the Same Decade." In S. Laska and D. Spain, eds., *Back to the City*. New York: Pergamon Press.

Longstreth, Richard W. 1997. *City Center to Regional Mall: Architecture, the Automobile, and Retailing in Los Angeles, 1920–1950*. Cambridge, MA: MIT Press.

Lowry, Ira S. 1964. *A Model of Metropolis*. Memorandum RM-4035-RC. Santa Monica, CA: The Rand Corporation.

Lowy, Joan. 2001. "Predator Attacks Escalate as Americans Encroach on Wildlife Habitat." *National Geographic News*, news.nationalgeographic.com/news, August 27.

Luce, Thomas. 1998. "Regional Tax Base Sharing: The Twin Cities Experience." In Helen F. Ladd, *Local Government Tax and Land Use Policies in the United States*. Northhampton, MA: Edward Elgar.

Lucy, William H., and David L. Phillips. 2000. *Confronting Suburban Decline: Strategic Planning for Metropolitan Renewal*. Washington, DC: Island Press.

Lucy, William H., and David L. Phillips. 2001. *Suburbs and the Census: Patterns of Growth and Decline*. Washington, DC: Center on Urban and Metropolitan Policy, The Brookings Institution.

Lukas, J. Anthony. 1986. *Common Ground: A Turbulent Decade in the Lives of Three American Families*. New York: Alfred A. Knopf.

Lundberg, George A., Mirra Komarovsky, and Mary Alice McInerny. 1934. *Leisure: A Suburban Study*. New York: Columbia University Press.

Lupo, Alan. 1977. *Liberty's Chosen Home: The Politics of Violence in Boston*. Boston: Beacon Press.

Lupo, Alan, and Edmund P. Fowler. 1971. *Rites of Way: The Politics of Transportation in Boston and the U.S. City*. Boston: Little, Brown and Company.

Luria, Daniel D., and Joel Rogers Sr., eds. 1999. *Metro Futures: Economic Solutions for Cities and Their Suburbs*. Boston: Beacon Press.

Lynch, Kevin. 1960. *The Image of the City*. Cambridge, MA: MIT Press.

Lynch, Kevin. 1971. *Site Planning*. 2nd ed. Cambridge, MA: MIT Press.

Lynch, Kevin. 1976. *Managing the Sense of a Region*. Cambridge, MA: MIT Press.

Lynch, Kevin. 1981. *A Theory of Good City Form*. Cambridge, MA: MIT Press.

Mack, R. 1968. *Race, Class, and Power*. 2nd ed. New York: Van Nostrand Reinhold.

Mackun, Paul J., and Shawn R. Wilson. 2000. *Population Trends in Metropolitan Areas and Central Cities, 1990 to 1998*. Current Population Reports. P25-1133 [I.E. P20-1133], Population Characteristics. Washington, DC: U.S. Department of Commerce, Economics and Statistics Administration, U.S. Census Bureau.

Maclaren, Virginia. 1996. "Urban Sustainability Reporting." *Journal of the American Planning Association* 62(2): 184–202.

Madden, Janice Fanning. 2000. *Changes in Income Inequality Within U.S. Metropolitan Areas*. Kalamazoo, MI: W. E. Upjohn Institute for Employment Research.

Magdol, L., and D. R. Bessel. 2003. "Social Capital, Social Currency, and Portable Assets: The Impact of Residential Mobility on Exchanges of Social Support." *Personal Relationships* 10: 149–70.

Maguire, Charles A., and Associates, eds. 1948. *The Master Highway Plan for the Boston Metropolitan Area*. Boston: The Joint Board for the Metropolitan Master Highway Plan.

Major Employers in Boston Metropolitan Communities. 1992. Boston: Metropolitan Area Planning Council.

Maller, C., M. Townsend, P. Brown, and L. St. Leger. 2002. *Healthy Parks, Healthy People: The Health Benefits of Contact with Nature in a Park Context: An Annotated Bibliography*. Victoria, Australia: Deakin University and Parks.

Malme, Jane. 1993. *Preferential Property Tax Treatment of Land*. Cambridge, MA: Lincoln Institute of Land Policy.

Maltby, Edward. 1986. *Waterlogged Wealth: Why Waste the World's Wet Places*. Washington, DC: International Institutes for Environment and Health.

Mandelbaum, Seymour J., Jr., and Luigi Mazza, eds. 1996. *Explorations in Planning Theory*. New Brunswick, NJ: Center for Urban Policy Research.

Mandelker, Daniel. 2003. *Land Use Law*. 5th ed. Newark, NJ: LexisNexis.

Mandelker, Daniel R. 1993. *Land Use Law*. 3rd ed. Charlottesville, VA: Michie Company.

Mann, Richard A., and Mike Miles. 1979. "State Land Use Planning: The Current Status and Demographic Rationale." *Journal of the American Planning Association* 45(1): 48–61.

Mansfield, Howard. 1990. *Cosmopolis: Yesterday's City of the Future*. New Brunswick, NJ: Center for Urban Policy Research.

Mantell, Michael A., Stephen F. Harper, and Luther Propst, eds. 1990. *Creating Successful Communities: A Guidebook to Growth Management Strategies*. Washington, DC: Urban Land Institute.

MARC (Mid-America Regional Council). 2004. *The Facts About Lawn Chemicals*. www.marc.org.

Marcus, Norman. 1993. "Zoning from 1961 to 1991: Turning Back the Clock." In Todd W. Bressi, ed., *Planning and Zoning New York City* (pp. 61–102). New Brunswick, NJ: Center for Urban Policy Research.

Marks, Harold, and Salem Spitz. 1966. *A Review of Transportation Aspects of Land-Use Control*. Washington, DC: Highway Research Board, Division of Engineering, National Research Council, National Academy of Sciences.

Markusen, Ann R. 1985. *Profit Cycles, Oligopoly, and Regional Development*. Cambridge, MA: MIT Press.

Markusen, Ann R. 1987. *Regions: The Economics and Politics of Territory*. Totowa, NJ: Rowman and Littlefield.

Markusen, Ann R. 1989. *Regional Planning and Policy: An Essay on the American Exception*. New Brunswick, NJ: Center for Urban Policy Research.

Markusen, Ann R. 1990. *Trade, Industry, and Economic Development*. New Brunswick, NJ: Center for Urban Policy Research.

Markusen, Ann R. 1992. *Cities, Suburbs, and the Geography of Corporate Service Provision*. New Brunswick, NJ: Center for Urban Policy Research.

Markusen, Ann R., Yong-Sook Lee, and Sean DiGiovanna, eds. 1999. *Second Tier Cities: Rapid Growth Beyond the Metropolis*. Minneapolis: University of Minnesota Press.

Marlin, John T. 1986. *Book of World City Rankings*. New York: The Free Press.

Marsh, Margaret S. 1990. *Suburban Lives*. New Brunswick, NJ: Rutgers University Press.

Marshall, Alex. 2000. *How Cities Work: Suburbs, Sprawl, and the Roads Not Taken*. Austin: University of Texas Press.

Marston, S. A., and G. Towers. 1993. "Private Spaces and the Politics of Places: Spatioeconomic Restructuring and Community Organizing in Tuscon and El Paso." In R. Fisher and J. Kling, eds., *Mobilizing the Community: Local Politics in the Era of the Global City* (pp. 75–102). London: Sage Publications.

Martin, Roscoe Coleman. 1962. *Government and the Suburban School.* Syracuse, NY: Syracuse University Press.

Martin, Walter T. 1953. *The Rural-Urban Fringe: A Study of Adjustment to Residence Location.* Eugene: University of Oregon.

Martindale, Don, and R. G. Hanson. 1969. *Small Town and the Nation.* Westport, CT: Greenwood Press.

Masotti, Louis H. 1974. *Suburbia in Transition.* Edited with an introduction by Louis H. Masotti and Jeffrey K. Hadden. New York: New Viewpoints.

Masotti, Louis H., and Jeffrey K. Hadden, eds. 1973. *The Urbanization of the Suburbs.* Beverly Hills, CA: Sage Publications.

The Massachusetts Highway Story: 1949–1956. 1956. Boston: Massachusetts Department of Public Works.

Massachusetts Laws Relating to Municipal Finance and Taxation. 1988. Massachusetts Department of Revenue Municipal Bulletin. Vol. 29. St. Paul, MN: West Publishing Company.

Massam, Bryan H. 1980. *Spatial Search: Applications to Planning Problems in the Public Sector.* Oxford: Pergamon Press.

Massey, Douglass S., and Nancy A. Denton. 1993. *American Apartheid: Segregation and the Making of the Underclass.* Cambridge, MA: Harvard University Press.

Matthews, Richard K. 1986. *The Radical Politics of Thomas Jefferson: A Revisionist View.* Lawrence: University Press of Kansas.

The Mature Metropolis. 1978. Lexington, MA: Lexington Books.

Mayer, Susan E. 1991. "How Much Does a High School's Racial and Socioeconomic Mix Affect Graduation and Teenage Fertility Rates?" In Christopher Jencks and Paul E. Peterson, eds., *The Urban Underclass* (pp. 324–41). Washington, DC: The Brookings Institution.

McAdam, D., and R. Paulsen. 1993. "Specifying the Relationship between Social Ties and Activism." *American Journal of Sociology* 99 (November): 640–67.

McAdow, Ron. 1992. *The Charles River: Exploring Nature and History on Foot and by Canoe.* Marlborough, MA: Bliss Publishing Company.

McAndres, James, and Richard Voith. 1993. "Can Regionalization of Local Public Services Increase a Region's Wealth?" *Journal of Regional Science* 33(3): 279–302.

"The MCAS Results." 2002. *Boston Globe,* September 20, B5–B10.

McClaughry, J. 1997. "Bringing Power Back Home: Recreating Democracy on a Human Scale." In H. Hannum, ed., *People, Land, and Community* (pp. 133–41). New Haven, CT: Yale University Press.

McGuire, Therese J. 1987. "The Effect of New Firm Locations on Property Taxes." *Journal of Urban Economics* 22(2): 223–29.

McHarg, Ian. 1992 [1969]. *Design with Nature.* New York: John Wiley and Sons.

McKelvey, Blake. 1968. *The Emergence of Metropolitan America: 1915–1966.* New Brunswick, NJ: Rutgers University Press.

McKenzie, H. D. 1967. *The Metropolitan Community.* New York: Russell and Russell.

McKie, Madelyn, ed. 1988a. *The Planners Handbook.* Boston: Massachusetts Federation of Planning and Appeals Boards.

McKie, Madelyn, ed. 1988b. *The Zoning Guidebook.* Boston: Massachusetts Federation of Planning and Appeals Boards.

McLanahan, Sara, and Irwin Garfinkel. 1989. "Single Mothers, the Underclass, and Social Policy." *The Annals of the American Academy of Political and Social Science* 501: 92.

McLean, Mary L., Kenneth P. Voytek, Kevin P. Balfe, Thomas R. Hammer, and John F. McDonald. 1992. *Understanding Your Economy: Using Analysis to Guide Local Strategic Planning*. Developed by NCI Research, The Institute for Urban Economic Development. Chicago: Planners Press of the American Planning Association.

McMillen, Daniel P. 1989. "An Empirical Model of Urban Fringe Land Use." *Land Economics* 65: 138–45.

McNulty, Robert H., Dorothy R. Jacobson, and R. Leo Penne. 1985. *The Economics of Amenity: Community Futures and Quality of Life, A Policy Guide to Urban Economic Development*. Washington, DC: Partners for Livable Places.

McShane, Clay. 1994. *Down the Asphalt Path: The Automobile and the American City*. New York: Columbia University Press.

Medoff, Peter, and Holly Sklar. 1994. *Streets of Hope: The Fall and Rise of an Urban Neighborhood*. Boston: South End Press.

Mehrhoff, W. A. 1999. *Community Design: A Team Approach to Dynamic Community Systems*. London: Sage Publications.

Menand, Louis. 2001. *The Metaphysical Club*. New York: Farrar, Straus and Giroux.

Merrill, L. S. 1987. "The Road Not Taken: Two New England States Have Taken Widely Different Approaches to Planning and Development—With Surprisingly Similar Results." *Planning* 53(11): 22–24.

MetroPlan 2000. 1994. Boston: Metropolitan Area Planning Council.

MetroWest Growth Impacts Study. 1984. Boston: Metropolitan Area Planning Council.

Meurs, H., and R. Haaijer. 2001. "Spatial Structure and Mobility." *Transportation Research Part D: Transport and Environment* 6: 429.

Meyer, John R., and Jose A. Gomez-Ibanez. 1981. *Autos, Transit, and Cities*. Cambridge, MA: Harvard University Press.

The Michigan Land Use Leadership Council. 2003. *Michigan's Land, Michigan's Future: Final Report of the Michigan Land Use Leadership Council*. Lansing, MI: Author.

Middlesex Canal Heritage Park Feasibility Study. 1980. Boston: Metropolitan Area Planning Council.

Mier, R. 1995. "Economic Development and Infrastructure: Planning in the Context of Progressive Politics." In D. C. Perry, ed., *Building the Public City: The Politics, Governance, and Finance of Public Infrastructure* (pp. 71–102). London: Sage Publications.

Mier, Robert. 1993. *Social Justice and Local Development Policy*. Newbury Park, CA: Sage Publications.

Miernyk, William H. 1982. *Regional Analysis and Regional Policy*. Cambridge, MA: Oelgeschlager, Gunn, and Hain.

Millennial Housing Commission. 2002. *Meeting Our Nation's Housing Challenge*. Washington, DC: Author.

Miller, Donald. 1980. "Project Location Analysis Using the Goals Achievement Method." *Journal of the American Planning Association* 46(2): 195–212.

Miller, Donald L., ed. *The Lewis Mumford Reader*. New York: Pantheon Books.

Mills, C. Wright. 1959. *The Power Elite*. Cambridge: Oxford University Press.

Mills, Edwin S., and John F. McDonald, eds. 1992. *Sources of Metropolitan Growth*. New Brunswick, NJ: Center for Urban Policy Research.

Missing the Bus: How States Fail to Connect Economic Development with Public Transit. 2003. Washington, DC: Good Jobs First.

Mitchell, Robert Buchanan. 1954. *Urban Traffic, a Function of Land Use*. New York: Columbia University Press.

Model State and Regional Planning Law. 1955. Washington, DC: National Municipal League.

Moe, R. 1998. "Fed Up with Sprawl." *New York Times*, November 11.

Moe, Richard. 1994. "Communities at Risk: The Consequences of Sprawl." *Historic Preservation News* (December/January).

Moe, Richard, and Carter Wilkie. 1997. *Changing Places: Rebuilding Community in the Age of Sprawl*. New York: Henry Holt and Company.

Moltoch, Harvey. 1976. "The City as a Growth Machine: Toward a Political Economy of Place." *American Journal of Sociology* 82 (September): 309–32.

Monmonier, Mark. 1993. *Mapping It Out: Expository Cartography for the Humanities and Social Sciences*. Chicago: University of Chicago Press.

Montgomery, Jeff. 2003. "Sprawl May Make Flooding Worse." Available at www.delawareonline.com.

Montgomery, Lori. 2001. "Life in the 'Burbs: Lack of Good Walking Sites Can Weigh Heavily." *Washington Post*, January 30.

Moon, Daniel K. 1992. *The Green Book: Environmental Resource Directory of New England*. Wilmington, DE: The Green Book.

Moore, Terry, and Paul Thorsnes. 1994. *The Transportation/Land Use Connection: A Framework for Practical Policy*. Chicago: American Planning Association.

More, Sir Thomas. 1975. *Utopia*. New York: W. W. Norton and Company.

Morison, Samuel Eliot. 1979. *The Maritime History of Massachusetts: 1783–1860*. Boston: Northeastern University Press.

Morris, M. 2002. "Smart Communities: Zoning for Transit-Oriented Development." *Ideas at Work, Campaign for Smart Growth* 2(4).

Morrow, V. 2001. "Young People's Explanations and Experiences of Social Exclusion: Retrieving Bourdieu's Concept of Social Capital." *International Journal of Sociology and Social Policy* 21: 37–63.

Moskowitz, Harvey S. 1993. *The New Illustrated Book of Development Decisions*. New Brunswick, NJ: Center for Urban Policy Research.

Moving to Corn Fields: A Reader on Urban Sprawl and the Regional Future of Northeast Ohio. 1996. Cleveland, OH: Ecocity Cleveland.

Mowry, George. 1965. *The Urban Nation*. New York: Hill and Wang.

Moynihan, Cornelius. 1962. *Introduction to the Law of Real Property*. St. Paul, MN: West Publishing Company.

Moynihan, Daniel P. 1969. *Maximum Feasible Misunderstanding: Community Action in the War on Poverty*. New York: The Free Press.

Muller, Peter O. 1981. *Contemporary Suburban America*. Englewood Cliffs, NJ: Prentice-Hall.

Muller, Thomas. 1976. *Economic Impacts of Land Developments: Employment, Housing, and Property Values*. Washington, DC: The Urban Institute.

Mumford, Lewis. 1938. *The Culture of Cities*. New York: Harcourt, Brace and Company.

Mumford, Lewis. 1961. *The City in History: Its Origins, Its Transformations, and Its Prospects*. New York: Harcourt, Brace and World.

Municipal Planning and Subdivision Legislation. 1979. Massachusetts General Laws Chapter 41; Sections 81A-81J. Boston: Executive Office of Communities and Development; Secretary of State.

Munnell, Alicia H., and Leah Cook. 1990. "How Does Public Infrastructure Affect Regional Economic Performance?" *New England Economic Review, Federal Reserve Bank of Boston* (September/October): 11–33.

Munnell, Alicia H., and Leah Cook. 1991. "Financing Capital Expenditures in Massachusetts." *New England Economic Review, Federal Reserve Bank of Boston* (March/April): 52–79.

Munton, R.J.C. 1983. *London's Green Belt: Containment in Practice*. London: Allen and Unwin.

Muro, Mark, and Robert Puentes. 2004. *Investing in a Better Future: A Review of the Fiscal and Competitive Advantages of Smart Growth Development Patterns*. Washington, DC: The Brookings Institution Center on Metropolitan and Urban Development.

Murphy, Raymond E. 1974. *The American City: An Urban Geography*. 2nd ed. New York: McGraw-Hill.

Murphy, Thomas P., and Charles R. Warren, eds. 1974. *Organizing Public Services in Metropolitan America*. Lexington, MA: Lexington Books.

Murray, James A., and William Lamont Jr. 1978. *Action Handbook: Managing Growth in the Small Community*. The U.S. Environmental Protection Agency. Washington, DC: U.S. Government Printing Office.

Myers, Dowell. 1992. *Analysis with Local Census Data: Portraits of Change*. Boston: Academic Press.

Myers, Dowell. 1999. "Demographic Dynamism and Metropolitan Change: Comparing Los Angeles, New York, Chicago, and Washington, D.C." *Housing Policy Debate* 10(4): 919–54.

Myrdal, Gunnar. 1962. *An American Dilemma*. 20th anniversary ed. New York: Harper and Row.

National Air Quality: Status and Trends, Six Principal Pollutants-Particulate Matter. 1995. Washington, DC: Office of Air and Radiation, U.S. Environmental Protection Agency.

National Neighborhood Coalition. 2001. "Smart Growth for Neighborhoods: Affordable Housing and Regional Vision." Pamphlet.

Neckar, Lance M. 2003. *Urban Design and the Environment—Highway 61/Red Rock Corridor*. CTS 03-04. www.cts.umn.edu/trg/research/reports/TRG_13.html.

Needleman, L., ed. 1968. *Regional Analysis*. Baltimore: Penguin Books.

Neergaard, Lauran. 2003. "Sprawling Suburbs May Foster Obesity." Associated Press, August 29.

Nelson, Arthur C. 1988. "An Empirical Note on How Regional Urban Containment Policy Influences an Interaction Between Greenbelt and Exurban Land Markets." *Journal of the American Planning Association* 54(2): 178–84.

Nelson, Arthur C., James B. Duncan, Clancy J. Mullen, and Kirk R. Bishop. 1995. *Growth Management Principles and Practice*. Chicago: Planners Press of the American Planning Association.

Nelson, Kathryn P. 1980. "Recent Suburbanization of Blacks: How Much, Who and Where." *Journal of the American Planning Association* 46(3): 287–300.

Nelson, Kathryn P. 1992. "Housing Assistance Needs and the Housing Stock: Data for Comprehensive Housing Affordability Strategies." *Journal of the American Planning Association* 58(1).

Nesson, Fern L. 1983. *Great Waters: A History of Boston's Water Supply*. Hanover, NH: Published for Brandeis University by University Press of New England.

Netter, Edith M., and Ruth G. Price. 1983. "Zoning and the Nouveau Poor." *Journal of the American Planning Association* 49(2): 171–80.

Netzer, Dick, ed. 1998. *Land Value Taxation: Can It and Will It Work Today?* Cambridge, MA: Lincoln Institute of Land Policy.

Neuman, Michael. 1991. "Utopia, Dystopia, Diaspora." *Journal of the American Planning Association* 57(3): 344–45.

New England: An Economic Analysis: A Report Prepared for the New England Regional Commission. 1968. Cambridge, MA: Arthur D. Little.

New England Economic Almanac. 1982. Boston: Federal Reserve Bank of Boston.

New Hampshire Community Profiles: Canterbury. Retrieved March 8, 2003, from New Hampshire Employment Security Economic Labor and Information Bureau Web site, http://www.nhes.state.nh.us/elmi/htmlprofiles/pdfs/canterbury.pdf.

New Jersey Meadowlands Commission. "Tax Sharing in the Meadowlands District." Available at www.hmdc.state.nj.us/tax.html.

"The New Metropolitan Agenda." 1998. *Brookings Review* 16(4).

New Towns: A New Dimension of Urbanism. 1966. Chicago: International City Managers' Association.

Newman, Peter W. G., and Jeffrey Kenworthy. 1989a. *Cities and Automobile Dependence: A Sourcebook*. Aldershot, UK: Gower Publishing.

Newman, Peter W. G., and Jeffrey Kenworthy. 1989b. "Gasoline Consumption and Cities: A Comparison of U.S. Cities with a Global Survey." *Journal of the American Planning Association* 55(1): 24–37.

Nixon, Tom, and Tom Lisco. 1996. *Speed and Travel Times on Limited Access Highways in the Boston Metropolitan Region: 1994–1995*. Boston: Central Transportation Planning Staff.

N.J. DEP (New Jersey Department of Environmental Protection). 2003. *Final Report of the New Jersey Comparative Risk Project*. Trenton, NJ: Author, March.

No Land Is an Island: Individual Rights and Government Control of Land Use. 1975. San Francisco: Institute for Contemporary Studies.

Norley, David, Stuart Proudfoot, and Thomas Burns, eds. 1980. *Making Cities Work: The Dynamics of Urban Innovation*. Boulder, CO: Westview Press.

Norton, R. D. 1979. *City Life Cycles and American Urban Policy*. New York: Academic Press.

Nourse, Hugh O. 1968. *Regional Economics: A Study in the Economic Structure, Stability, and Growth of Regions*. New York: McGraw-Hill.

Now Is the Time: Places Left Behind in the New Economy. 1999. Washington, DC: U.S. Department of Housing and Urban Development.

Nyden, Philip W., and Wim Wiewel, eds. 1991. *Challenging Uneven Development: An Urban Agenda for the 1990's*. New Brunswick, NJ: Rutgers University Press.

Oakland, H. 1978. "Local Taxes and Interurban Industrial Location." In G. Break, ed., *Metropolitan Financing and Growth Management Policies*. Madison: University of Wisconsin Press.

Oakley, Raymond P. 1981. *High Technology Industry and Industrial Location*. Brookfield, VT: Gower Publishing.

Oates, Wallace E., and Robert M Schwab. "The Pittsburgh Experience with Land Value Taxation." In Helen F. Ladd, *Local Government Tax and Land Use Policies in the United States: Understanding the Links*. Northhampton, MA: Edward Elgar.

O'Connor, Thomas H. 1988. *South Boston: My Home Town*. Boston: Northeastern University Press.

O'Connor, Thomas H. 1991. *Bibles, Brahmins, and Bosses: A Short History of Boston*. 3rd ed. Boston: Trustees of the Boston Public Library.

O'Connor, Thomas H. 1993. *Building a New Boston: Politics and Urban Renewal 1950 to 1970*. Boston: Northeastern University Press.

O'Connor, Thomas H. 2001. *The Hub, Boston Past and Present*. Boston: Northeastern University Press.

ODLCD (Oregon Department of Land Conservation and Development). 1992. *Indicators of Urban Sprawl*. www.uoregon.edu/~pppm/landuse/sprawl.

Office of Technology Assessment. 1994. *Saving Energy in U.S. Transportation*. Washington, DC: Author.

Oge, Margo. 1995. *Automotive Emissions: Progress and Challenges*. Presentation to Automotive Management Briefing Session, Traverse City, MI, August 9.

Ohm, Brian, and Robert Sitkowski. 2002. "Enabling the New Urbanism." *Urban Lawyer* 34: 935–43.

Ohm, Brian, and Robert Sitkowski. 2003. "The Influence of New Urbanism on Local Ordinances: The Twilight of Zoning?" *Urban Lawyer* 35: 783–94.

Olanoff, Lynn. 2004. "Farms Grown Smaller, Poorer." (Newton) *New Jersey Herald*, February 5.

Oldenburg, Ray. 1999. *The Great Good Place: Cafés, Coffee Shops, Bookstores, Bars, Hair Salons, and Other Hangouts at the Heart of a Community*. New York: Marlowe and Company.

Olsen, Donald. 1986. *The City as a Work of Art*. New Haven, CT: Yale University Press.

Olson, M., Jr. 1965. *The Logic of Collective Action: Public Goods and the Theory of Groups*. Cambridge, MA: Harvard University Press.

OMS (Office of Mobile Sources, U.S. Environmental Protection Agency). 1993. *Automobiles and Ozone Fact Sheet*. Washington, DC: Author.

OMS (Office of Mobile Sources, U.S. Environmental Protection Agency). 1994. *Transportation Air Quality: Selected Facts and Figures*. Washington, DC: Author.

1000 Friends of Oregon. 1997. *Making the Connections: A Summary of the LUTRAQ Project*. Pamphlet.

Oosterbaan, John. 1980. *Population Dispersal: A National Imperative*. Lexington, MA: D. C. Heath and Company.

Open Space and Recreational Plan and Program for Metropolitan Boston. 1967. Boston: Metropolitan Area Planning Council.

Oppenheim, Norbert. 1980. *Applied Models in Urban and Regional Analysis*. Englewood Cliffs, NJ: Prentice-Hall.

Orfield, Gary, and John T. Yun. 1999. *Resegregation in American Schools*. Cambridge, MA: The Civil Rights Project, Harvard University.

Orfield, Myron. 1997. *Metropolitics: A Regional Agenda for Community and Stability*. Washington, DC: Brookings Institution Press.

Orfield, Myron. 2001. *Boston Metropatterns: A Regional Agenda for Community and Stability in Greater Boston*. Boston: Citizens' Housing and Planning Association.

Orfield, Myron. 2002. *American Metropolitics: The New Suburban Reality*. Washington, DC: Brookings Institution Press.

Organizing for Economic Development: Municipal and Regional Options. 1988. Boston: Mount Auburn Associates: Massachusetts Executive Office of Communities and Development.

Orton Family Foundation. 2004. *Making Community Connections: The Orton Community Mapping Program*. Steamboat Springs, CO: Author.

Osborne, David, and Ted Gaebler. 1992. *Reinventing Government: How the Entrepreneurial Spirit Is Transforming the Public Sector*. Reading, MA: Addison-Wesley.

Ostrom, Elinor. 1990. *Governing the Commons: The Evolution of Institutions for Collective Action, The Political Economy of Institutions and Decision*. New York: Cambridge University Press.

Ostrom, Elinor, and Roger B. Parks. 1973. *Suburban Police Departments: Too Many and Too Small?* Bloomington: Department of Political Science, Indiana University.

Owens, Bill. 1999. *Suburbia*. Edited by Robert Harshorn Shimshak. New York: Fotofolio.

Pack, Janet R. 1980. *Regional Growth: Historic Perspective*. Washington, DC: Advisory Commission on Intergovernmental Relations.

Pack, Janet Rothenberg. 2002. *Growth and Convergence in Metropolitan America*. Washington, DC: Brookings Institution Press.

Palen, John J. 1978. *The Urban World*. New York: McGraw-Hill.

Palen, John J. 1995. *The Suburbs*. New York: McGraw-Hill.

Palm, Risa. 1981. *The Geography of American Cities*. New York: Oxford University Press.

Paoli, Richard. 2003. "Survey Reveals What Women Really Want." *San Francisco Chronicle*, November 16.

Parkin, Frank, ed. 1974. *The Social Analysis of Class Structure*. London: Tavistock Publications.

Parsons, K. C. 1990. "Clarence Stein and the Greenbelt Towns: Settling for Less." *Journal of the American Planning Association* 56(2): 161–83.

Pastor, Manuel, Jr., and Peter Dreier. 2000. *Regions That Work: How Cities and Suburbs Can Grow Together*. Minneapolis: University of Minnesota Press.

Patton, Carl V., and David S. Sawicki. 1993. *Basic Methods of Policy Analysis and Planning*. 2nd ed. Englewood Cliffs, NJ: Prentice Hall.

Patton, Phil. 1986. *Open Road: A Celebration of the American Highway*. New York: Simon and Schuster.

Paving Our Way to Water Shortages: How Sprawl Aggravates the Effects of Drought. 2002. Washington, DC: Smart Growth America, Natural Resources Defense Council, America Rivers.

Pawlukiewicz, M. 1998. "What Is Smart Growth?" *Urban Land* 57(6).

Peet, Bill. 1970. *The Wump World*. Boston: Houghton Mifflin.

Peirce, Neal R., and Robert Guskind. 1993. *Breakthroughs: Re-Creating the American City*. New Brunswick, NJ: Center for Urban Policy Research.

Peirce, Neal R., Curtis W. Johnson, and John Stuart Hall. 1993. *Citistates: How Urban America Can Prosper in a Competitive World*. Washington, DC: Seven Locks Press.

Peiser, Richard B. 1989. "Density and Urban Sprawl." *Land Economics* 65(3): 193–204.

Peiser, Richard B. 1990. "Who Plans America? Planners or Developers?" *Journal of the American Planning Association* 56(4): 496–503.

Pelham, Thomas. 2003. "From the Ramapo Plan to Florida's Statewide Concurrency System." *Urban Lawyer* 35: 113.

Pendall, Rolf. 2000. "Local Land Use Regulation and the Chain of Exclusion." *Journal of the American Planning Association* 66(2): 125–42.

Perez-Pena, Richard. 2003. "Study Finds Asthma in 25% of Children in Central Harlem." *New York Times*, April 19.

Perloff, Harvey S. 1981. *Planning the Post-Industrial City*. Chicago: Planners Press of the American Planning Association.

Perloff, Harvey S., Jr., Edgar S. Dunn, Eric E. Lampard, and Richard F. Muth. 1960. *Regions, Resources, and Economic Growth*. Baltimore: Published for Resources for the Future by the Johns Hopkins Press.

Perry, Charles, and Lawrence E. Susskind. 1977. *The Massachusetts Growth Policy Development Act: Intent and Passage*. Cambridge, MA: Massachusetts Institute of Technology.

Perry, David C., ed. 1995. *Building the Public City: The Politics, Governance, and Finance of Public Infrastructure*. Thousand Oaks, CA: Sage Publications.

Persky, Joseph, and Wim Wiewel. 2000. *When Corporations Leave Town: The Costs and Benefits of Metropolitan Job Sprawl*. Detroit: Wayne State University Press.

Peterson, Paul E. 1981. *City Limits*. Chicago: University of Chicago Press.

Phillips, Bruce A. 1990. *Brookline: The Evolution of an American Jewish Suburb*. New York: Garland.

Phillips, Kenneth E., and Samuel L. Myers Jr. 1978. *Job Search, Spatial Separation of Jobs and Residences, and Discrimination in Suburban Labor Markets*. Santa Monica, CA: Rand Corporation.

Pickard, Jerome Percival. 1968. *Dimensions of Metropolitanism*. Washington, DC: Urban Land Institute.

Pickrell, Don H. 1992. "A Desire Named Streetcar: Fantasy and Fact in Rail Transit Planning." *Journal of the American Planning Association* 58(2): 158–76.

Piper, Robert R. 1977. "Transit Strategies for Suburban Communities." *Journal of the American Institute of Planners* 43(4): 381–85.

Pivo, Gary. 1990. "The Net of Mixed Beads: Suburban Office Development in Six Metropolitan Regions." *Journal of the American Planning Association* 56(4): 457–69.

A Plan for Tomorrow: A Comprehensive Long-Range Plan. 1989. (Available from the Town of Canterbury, NH.) Presented by the Canterbury Planning Board.

Planning and Community Equity: A Component of APA's Agenda for America's Communities Program. 1994. Chicago: Planners Press of the American Planning Association.

Planning for City, State, Region and Nation: Proceedings of the Joint Conference on Planning, May 4, 5, and 6, 1936. 1936. Chicago: American Society of Planning Officials.

Planning for Smart Growth: 2002 State of the States. 2002. Chicago: American Planning Association.

Platt, Harlan D. 1984. *A Boston Area Employment Model*. Boston: College of Business Administration, Northeastern University.

Platt, R. H. 1996. *Land Use and Society: Geography, Law, and Public Policy*. Washington, DC: Island Press.

Platt, R. H., and G. Macinko, eds. 1983. *Beyond the Urban Fringe: Land Use Issues of Nonmetropolitan America*. Minneapolis: University of Minnesota Press.

Platt, Rutherford H. 1991. *Land Use Control: Geography, Law, and Public Policy*. Englewood Cliffs, NJ: Prentice Hall.

Platt, Rutherford H. 1994. *The Ecological City: Preserving and Restoring Urban Biodiversity*. Amherst: University of Massachusetts Press.

Platt, Rutherford H. 1995. "The Water Supply Study for Metropolitan Boston: The Demise of Diversion." *Journal of the American Planning Association* 61(2): 185–99.

Platt, Rutherford H., Rowan A. Rowntree, and Pamela C. Muick, eds. 1994. *The Ecological City: Preserving and Restoring Urban Biodiversity*. Amherst: University of Massachusetts Press.

Pleck, Elizabeth Hafkin. 1979. *Black Migration and Poverty, Boston, 1865–1900*. New York: Academic Press.

Pleeter, Saul, ed. 1980. *Economic Impact Analysis: Methodology and Applications*. Boston: Martinus Nijhoff.

Plessas, Demetrius J., and Ricca Fein. 1972. "An Evaluation of Social Indicators." *Journal of the American Institute of Planners* 38(1): 43–51.

Policies for Land Use in Metropolitan Boston: PLUMB '78. 1978. Boston: Metropolitan Area Planning Council.

PolicyLink and the Mexican American Legal Defense and Educational Fund. 2004. *Building New Schools in California: How Are We Addressing Overcrowding?* Oakland, CA: Author.

Ponting, C. 1991. *A Green History of the World: The Environment and the Collapse of Great Civilizations*. New York: St. Martin's Press.

Poplin, D. E. 1979. *Communities: A Survey of Theory and Methods of Research*. New York: Macmillan.

Popper, Frank J. 1981. *The Politics of Land Use Reform*. Madison: University of Wisconsin Press.

Popper, Frank J. 1992. *Rethinking American Regional Planning*. New Brunswick, NJ: Center for Urban Policy Research.

Population Age Group Forecast. 1989. Boston: Metropolitan Area Planning Council.

Population and Employment Forecasts for the Boston Metropolitan Area. 1992. Boston: Metropolitan Area Planning Council.

Porta, S. 1999. "The Community and Public Spaces: Ecological Thinking, Mobility and Social Life in the Open Spaces of the City of the Future." *Futures* 31: 437–56.

Porter, Douglas. 2000. *The Practice of Sustainable Development*. Washington, DC: Urban Land Institute.

Porter, Douglas R. 1981. *Streamlining Your Local Development Process*. Washington, DC: National League of Cities.

Porter, Douglas R. 1997. *Managing Growth in America's Communities*. Washington, DC: Island Press.

Porter, Douglas R., ed. 2000. *The Practice of Sustainable Development*. Washington, DC: Urban Land Institute.

Porter, Douglas R., Ben C. Lin, Susan Jakubiak, and Richard B. Peiser. 1992. *Special Districts: A Useful Technique for Financing Infrastructure*. 2nd ed. Washington, DC: Urban Land Institute.

Porter, Michael. 1998. *Competitive Advantage: Creating and Sustaining Superior Performance*. New York: Free Press.

Porter, Michael E. 1980. *Competitive Strategy: Techniques for Analyzing Industries and Competitors*. New York: Free Press.

Porter, Michael E. 1991. *The Comparative Advantage of Massachusetts*. Cambridge, MA: The Monitor Company.

Porter, Michael E., Rebecca E. Wayland, and C. Jeffrey Grogan. 1992. *Toward a Shared Economic Vision for Massachusetts*. Boston: Challenge to Leadership.

Portes, A. 1998. "Social Capital: Its Origins and Applications in Modern Sociology." *Annual Review of Sociology* 24: 1–24.

Portney, Paul R., ed. 1976. *Economic Issues in Metropolitan Growth*. Baltimore: Published for Resources for the Future by the Johns Hopkins University Press.

Powell, John. 1999. "Race and Space." *Poverty and Race* (January/February). Available at http://www.prrac.org/topics/jan99/powell.htm.

Powell, John. 2002. *Racism and Metropolitan Dynamics: The Civil Rights Challenge of the 21st Century*. Minneapolis, MN: Institute on Race and Poverty. Available at http://www1.umn.edu/irp/publications/racismandmetrodynamics.pdf.

Powell, Lyman Pierson, ed. 1898. *Historic Towns of New England*. New York: G. P. Putnam's Sons.

Power, Thomas Michael. 1996. *Lost Landscapes and Failed Economies: The Search for a Value of Place*. Washington, DC: Island Press.

Powers, Mary G., ed. 1982. *Measures of Socioeconomic Status: Current Issues*. Boulder, CO: Westview Press.

Preliminary Report of the Joint Committee on Counties Relative to the Feasibility of State Takeover of All Essential and Necessary Functions and Services of County Government. 1991. Pursuant to Chapter 193 Section 10 of the Acts and Resolves of 1989. Boston: Commonwealth of Massachusetts, House of Representatives.

Pretty, J., M. Griffin, M. Sellens, and C. Pretty. 2003. *Green Exercise: Complementary Roles of Nature, Exercise and Diet in Physical and Emotional Well-Being and Implications for Public Health Policy*. Brighton: University of Sussex.

Primack, Mark L. 1983. *Greater Boston Park and Recreation Guide*. Chester, CT: The Globe Pequot Press.

Principles and Practice of Urban Planning. 1968. Washington, DC: International City Managers' Association.

Pringle, David. 2002. *Environmentalists Launch Anti-Sprawl Blitz*. Trenton, NJ: Garden State Clean Water Action.

Projecting Land-Use Change: A Summary of Models for Assessing the Effects of Community Growth and Change on Land-Use Patterns. 2000. Washington, DC: Office of Research and Development, United States Environmental Protection Agency.

Prop 2^1/$_2$ Turns 15. 1996. Boston: The Massachusetts Municipal Associations.

"Property Tax Exemptions to Promote Economic Development." 1994. *City and Town* 7(8): 1–2.

Pulsifer, David. 1868. *Guide to Boston and Vicinity: With Maps and Engravings*. Boston: A. Williams.

Pulsifer, David, and R. L. Midgley. 1857. *Sights in Boston and Suburbs, or, Guide to the Stranger*. Boston: James Munroe and Company.

Putnam, R. D. 2000. *Bowling Alone: The Collapse and Revival of American Community*. New York: Simon and Schuster.

Quantrill, Malcolm, and Bruce Webb, eds. 1993. *Urban Forms, Suburban Dreams*. College Station: Texas A&M University Press.

Radway, G. Frank. 1973. *Brahmins & Bullyboys: G. Frank Radway's Boston Album*. Boston: Houghton Mifflin.

Rasell, M. Edith, and Barry Bluestone, with charts by David Webster. 1997. *The Prosperity Gap: A Chartbook of American Living Standards*. Washington, DC: Economic Policy Institute.

Rasmussen, David W., and Charles Haworth. 1973. *The Modern City: Readings in Urban Economics*. New York: Harper and Row.

Rathkopf, Arden H., and Daren A. Rathkopf. 1993. *Rathkopf's The Law of Zoning and Planning*. 4th ed. & Supp. Edward H. Ziegler Jr., ed. New York: C. Boardman.

Rawls, John. 1972. *A Theory of Justice*. Cambridge, MA: Harvard University Press.

Rawls, John. 1993. *Political Liberalism*. New York: Columbia University Press.

Rees, John, Geoffrey Hewings, and Howard Stafford, eds. 1981. *Industrial Location and Regional Systems: Spatial Organization in the Economic Sector*. New York: J. F. Bergin Publishers.

Regional Community Population and Employment Outlook. 1989. Boston: Metropolitan Area Planning Council.

Regional Decline or Revival: An Interim Population Forecast for the Metropolitan Area 1980–2010. 1982. Boston: Metropolitan Area Planning Council.

Reidy, Chris. 1994. "Crusade of the 'Sprawl-Buster.'" *Boston Globe*, July 7.

"Reinventing the City." 2000. *Brookings Review* 18(3).

Reitze, Arnold W., Jr. 1974. *Environmental Planning: Law of Land & Resources*. Washington, DC: North American International.

A Report of Progress on the Massachusetts Highway Program and Other Department Activities. 1962. Boston: Massachusetts Department of Public Works.

Report on a Thoroughfare Plan for Boston. 1930. Prepared by the City Planning Board, Robert Whitten, Consultant. Boston: City of Boston.

Report on Regional Organization. 1980. Committee on Regional Organization. Boston: Metropolitan Area Planning Council.

A Report to Governor Foster Furcolo: Progress of the Massachusetts Highway Program and Other Department Activities. 1959. Boston: Massachusetts Department of Public Works.

A Report to Governor Foster Furcolo: Progress of the Massachusetts Highway Program and Other Department Activities. 1960. Boston: Massachusetts Department of Public Works.

A Report to Governor Foster Furcolo on the Progress of the 90/10 and 50/50 Highway Programs and Other Department Activities. 1958. Boston: Massachusetts Department of Public Works.

Reschovsky, Andrew, and Eugene Knaff. 1977. "Tax Base Sharing: An Assessment of the Minnesota Experience." *Journal of the American Planning Association* 43(4): 361–70.

Research on the Relationship Between Economic Development and Transportation Investment. 1998. Washington, DC: National Academy Press.

Retaining and Attracting Business and Industry in Metropolitan Boston. 1984. Digest of Presentations Given at Conference on 11/27/84. Boston: Metropolitan Area Planning Council.

Retsinas, Nicolas. 2002. "Declare a Truce on Sprawl." *Boston Globe*, January 1.

Rhodes, John, and Arnold Kan. 1971. *Office Dispersal and Regional Policy*. Cambridge: Cambridge University Press.

Richards, Lyn. 1990. *Nobody's Home: Dreams and Realities in a New Suburb*. New York: Oxford University Press.

Richardson, Harry Ward. 1969a. *Elements of Regional Economics*. Baltimore: Penguin Books.

Richardson, Harry Ward. 1969b. *Regional Economics: Location Theory, Urban Structure, and Regional Change*. New York: Praeger.

Richardson, J. 2000. *Partnerships in Communities: Reweaving the Fabric of Rural America*. Washington, DC: Island Press.

Richmond, Henry R. 1996. "Exploding the Myths of Sprawl." *Common Ground* 8(1).

Riis, Jacob. 1997 [1890]. *How the Other Half Lives: Studies Among the Tenements of New York*. New York: Penguin Books.

Ritzdorf, Marsha. 1990. "Whose American Dream? The Euclid Legacy and Cultural Change." *Journal of the American Planning Association* 56(3): 386–89.

Rivlin, Alice. 2000. "The Challenge of Affluence." Adam Smith Award Lecture, National Association of Business Economists, Brookings Institution, September 11. http://www.brook.edu/es/urban/speeches/challengesof.

Rivlin, L. G. 1987. "The Neighborhood, Personal Identity, and Group Affiliations." In I. Altman and A. Wandersman, eds., *Human Behavior and Environment: Advances in Theory and Research* (pp. 1–34). New York: Plenum Press.

Roakes, Susan L., and Harvey M. Jacobs. 1988. *Land Value Taxation and Urban Land Use Planning: An Annotated Bibliography*. Chicago: Council of Planning Librarians.

Robertson, Kent A. 1999. "Can Small-City Downtowns Remain Viable? A National Study of Development Issues and Strategies." *Journal of the American Planning Association* 65(3): 270–83.

Robinson, Carla Jean. 1989. "Municipal Approaches to Economic Development: Growth and Distribution Policy." *Journal of the American Planning Association* 55(5): 283–95.

Robinson, Susan G., ed. 1990. *Financing Growth*. Chicago: Government Finance Officers Association.

Robson, William Alexander, ed. 1972. *Great Cities of the World: Their Government, Politics, and Planning*. Beverly Hills, CA: Sage Publications.

Roddewig, Richard J., and Christopher J. Duerksen. 1989. *Responding to the Takings Challenge*. Chicago: American Planning Association.

Roddewig, Richard J., and Jared Shlaes. 1983. *Analyzing the Feasibility of a Development Project: A Guide for Planners*. Chicago: American Planning Association.

Rodriguez, Joseph A. 1999. *City Against Suburb: The Culture Wars in an American Metropolis*. Westport, CT: Praeger.

Rodriguez-Bachiller, Agustin. 1986. "Discontinuous Urban Growth and the New Urban Economics: A Review." *Urban Studies* 2: 79–104.

Rodwin, Lloyd. 1961. *Housing and Economic Progress: A Study of the Housing Experiences of Boston's Middle-Income Families*. Cambridge, MA: Harvard University Press and Technology Press.

Rodwin, Lloyd. 1970. *Nations and Cities: A Comparison of Strategies for Urban Growth*. Boston: Houghton Mifflin.

Roe, Kieran, ed. 1994. *Greenways: An Introduction*. Washington, DC: Land Trust Alliance.

The Role of Transit in Creating Livable Metropolitan Communities. 1997. Washington, DC: National Academy Press.

Rome, Adam Ward. 2001. *The Bulldozer in the Countryside: Suburban Sprawl and the Rise of American Environmentalism*. Cambridge: Cambridge University Press.

Romm, Joseph J., and Charles B. Curtis. 1996. "Mideast Oil Forever." *The Atlantic Monthly* (April): 57–74.

Rondinelli, Dennis A. 1975. *Urban and Regional Development Planning: Policy and Administration*. Ithaca, NY: Cornell University Press.

Rose, Jack Manley. 1941. *Northeast from Boston*. New York: G. P. Putnam's Sons.

Rose, Jerome G. 1974. *Legal Foundations of Land Use Planning: Cases and Materials on Planning Law*. New Brunswick, NJ: Center for Urban Policy Research.

Rose, Jerome G. 1979. *Legal Foundations of Land Use Planning: Textbook/Casebook and Materials on Planning Law*. New Brunswick, NJ: Center for Urban Policy Research.

Rose, Jerome G., and Robert E. Rothman, eds. 1977. *After Mount Laurel: The New Suburban Zoning*. New Brunswick, NJ: Center for Urban Policy Research.

Rose, Mark H. 1979. *Interstate: Express Highway Politics, 1941–1956*. Lawrence: Regents Press of Kansas.

Rosegrant, Susan, and David R. Lampe. 1992. *Route 128: Lessons from Boston's High-Tech Community*. New York: Basic Books.

Roseland, M. 1998. *Toward Sustainable Communities: Resources for Citizens and Their Governments*. Gabriola Island, BC, Canada: New Society Publishers.

Rosen, Jay, Davis Merritt Jr., and Lisa Austin. 1997. *Public Journalism Theory and Practice: Lessons from Experience*. Dayton, OH: Kettering Foundation.

Ross, Marjorie Drake. 1960. *The Book of Boston: The Colonial Period, 1630–1775*. New York: Hastings House Publishers.

Ross, Marjorie Drake. 1961. *The Book of Boston: The Federal Period, 1775–1837*. Boston: Hastings House Publishers.

Ross, Marjorie Drake. 1964. *The Book of Boston: The Victorian Period, 1837 to 1901*. New York: Hastings House Publishers.

Rossi, Robert J., and Kevin J. Gilmartin. 1980. *Handbook of Social Indicators*. New York: Garland STPM Press.

Rotberg, Richard I. 1977. *The Reorganization of the Government of Middlesex County: Analysis and Recommendations.* A Report Prepared at the Request of the Commissioners of Middlesex County. Boston: Massachusetts League of Cities and Towns.

Rothblatt, Donald N. 1994. "North American Metropolitan Planning: Canadian and U.S. Perspectives." *Journal of the American Planning Association* 60(4): 501–20.

Rothblatt, Donald N., ed. 1974. *National Policy for Urban and Regional Development.* Lexington, MA: Lexington Books.

Rubin, A. R., S. Hogye, and J. Hudson. 2000. "Development of EPA Guidelines for Management of Onsite/Decentralized Wastewater Systems." 2000 National Organization of Water Resources Administrators (NOWRA) Proceedings. Washington, DC: NOWRA.

Rubin, Barry M. 1981. "Econometric Models for Metropolitan Planning." *Journal of the American Planning Association* 47(4): 408–20.

Rudd, M. A. 2000. "Live Long and Prosper: Collective Action, Social Capital and Social Vision." *Ecological Economics* 34: 131–44.

Rusk, David. 1993. *Cities without Suburbs.* Washington, DC: The Woodrow Wilson Center Press.

Rusk, David. 1999. *Inside Game, Outside Game: Winning Strategies for Saving Urban America.* Washington, DC: Brookings Institution Press.

Rusk, David. 2002. "Trends in School Segregation." In Richard D. Kahlenberg, ed., *Divided We Fall: Coming Together through Public School Choice: The Report of the Century Foundation Task Force on the Common School.* New York: The Century Foundation Press.

Rusk, David. 2003. *Cities without Suburbs: A Census 2000 Update.* 3rd ed. Washington, DC, and Baltimore: Woodrow Wilson Center Press and Johns Hopkins University Press.

Rust, Edgar. 1975. *No Growth: Impacts on Metropolitan Areas.* Lexington, MA: D. C. Heath and Company.

Ryan, Barry, and Thomas F. Stinson. 2002. *Road Finance Alternatives: An Analysis of Metro-Area Road Taxes.* CTS 02-04. www.cts.umn.edu/trg/research/reports/TRG_09.html.

Rybczynski, Witold. 1999. *A Clearing in the Distance: Frederick Law Olmsted and America in the Nineteenth Century.* New York: Scribner.

Sabatier, Paul. 2003. *The Road to Assisi: The Essential Biography of Saint Francis.* Edited by Jon M. Sweeney. Brewster, MA: Paraclete Press.

Sacks, Seymour, Ralph Andrew, and David Ranney. 1972. *City Schools/Suburban Schools: A History of Fiscal Conflict.* Syracuse, NY: Syracuse University Press.

Sale, K. 2000. *Dwellers in the Land: The Bioregional Vision.* Athens: University of Georgia Press.

Salem: Maritime Salem in the Age of Sail. 1987. Washington, DC: U.S. Department of the Interior, National Park Service.

Salkin, Patricia. 1990. "Smart Growth at Century's End." *Urban Lawyer* 31: 601.

Sandel, Michael. 1982. *Liberalism and the Limits of Justice.* New York: Cambridge University Press.

Sanders, S. R. 2000a. "Homeplace." From *Orion* (Winter 1992). In *Discussion Course on Discovering a Sense of Place* (pp. 2-8–2-10). Available from the Northwest Earth Institute, 505 SW Sixth, Suite 1100, Portland, OR 97204.

Sanders, S. R. 2000b. "Web of Life." From *The Georgia Review* (1994). In *Discussion Course on Discovering a Sense of Place* (pp. 6-3–6-4). Available from the Northwest Earth Institute, 505 SW Sixth, Suite 1100, Portland, OR 97204.

Saunders, Tinah. 2002. "Atlanta Ranked as Fourth Most-Affordable Housing Market." *The Atlanta Journal-Constitution,* July 1.

Savitch, H. V. 1979. *Urban Policy and the Exterior City: Federal, State, and Corporate Impacts Upon Major Cities.* New York: Pergamon Press.

Sawicki, David S., and Patrice Flynn. 1996. "Neighborhood Indicators: A Review of the Literature and an Assessment of Conceptual and Methodological Issues." *Journal of the American Planning Association* 62(2): 165–83.

Saxenian, Analee. 1994. *Regional Advantage: Culture and Competition in Silicon Valley and Route 128*. Cambridge, MA: Harvard University Press.

SCCCL (South Carolina Coastal Conservation League). 1995. "Getting a Rein on Runoff: How Sprawl and the Traditional Town Compare." *South Carolina Coastal Conservation League Bulletin*, no. 7 (Fall).

Schaenman, Philip S., and Thomas Muller. 1975. *Measuring Impacts of Land Development: An Initial Approach*. Washington, DC: The Urban Institute.

Schaffer, Daniel, ed. 1988. *Two Centuries of American Planning*. Baltimore: Johns Hopkins University Press.

Schiffman, Irving. 1989. *Alternative Techniques for Managing Growth*. Berkeley: University of California Press.

Schmenner, Rodger W. 1982. *Making Business Location Decisions*. Englewood Cliffs, NJ: Prentice-Hall.

Schneekloth, Lynda H., and Robert G. Shibley. 1995. *Placemaking: A Collaborative Approach to Creating Community*. New York: Wiley.

Schneider, Mark. 1989. *The Competitive City: The Political Economy of Suburbia*. Pittsburgh, PA: University of Pittsburgh Press.

Schnore, Leo Francis. 1972. *Class and Race in Cities and Suburbs*. Chicago: Markham Publishing Company.

Schor, J. B. 1997. *Civic Engagement and Working Hours: Do Americans Really Have More Free Time than ever Before?* Paper presented at the Conference on Civic Engagement in American Democracy, Portland, ME, September.

Schorr, L. B. 1997. *Common Purpose: Strengthening Families and Neighborhoods to Rebuild America*. New York: Doubleday.

Schrank, David, and Tim Lomax. 2001. *2001 Urban Mobility Report*. College Station: Texas Transportation Institute, Texas A&M University.

Schwartz, Alex. 1992. *Cities, Suburbs, and the Geography of Corporate Service Provision*. New Brunswick, NJ: Center for Urban Policy Research.

Schwartz, Alex. 1993. "Subservient Suburbia: The Reliance of Large Suburban Companies on Central City Firms for Financial and Professional Services." *Journal of the American Planning Association* 59(3): 288–305.

Schwartz, Barry, ed. 1976. *The Changing Face of the Suburbs*. Chicago: University of Chicago Press.

Schwartz, Peter. 1996. *The Art of the Long View: Planning for the Future in an Uncertain World*. New York: Doubleday.

Schwarz, Loring LaB., ed. 1993. *Greenways: A Guideway to Planning, Design and Development*. Washington, DC: Island Press.

Schwarz, Roger. 2002. *The Skilled Facilitator: A Comprehensive Resource for Consultants, Facilitators, Managers, Trainers, and Coaches*. 2nd ed. San Francisco: Jossey-Bass.

Scott, Mel. 1969. *American City Planning Since 1890: A History Commemorating the Fiftieth Anniversary of the American Institute of Planners*. Berkeley: University of California Press.

Scott, Randall W., David J. Brower, and Dallas D. Miner, eds. 1975. *Management & Control of Growth: Issues, Techniques, Problems, Trends*. Washington, DC: Urban Land Institute.

Scott, Thomas M., and Barbara Lukermann. In press. *Public Policy, Transportation, and Regional Growth*.

Scully, Vincent. 1988. *American Architecture and Urbanism*. Rev. ed. New York: Holt.

Seely, Bruce Edsall. 1987. *Building the American Highway System: Engineers as Policy Makers*. Philadelphia: Temple University Press.

Sen, Amartya. 1999. *Development as Freedom*. New York: Random House.

Senge, Peter M. 1990. *The Fifth Discipline: The Art and Practice of the Learning Organization*. New York: Doubleday.

Senior, Derek, ed. 1966. *The Regional City: An Anglo-American Discussion of Metropolitan Planning*. Seminar on Metropolitan Planning, Ditchley Park, England, 1964; sponsored by the Ditchley Foundation in collaboration with the Town and Country Planning Association. Chicago: Aldine Publishing Company.

Seyfried, Warren R. 1991. "Measuring the Feasibility of a Zoning Bonus." *Journal of the American Planning Association* 57(3): 348–56.

Shand-Tucci, Douglass. 1988. *Built in Boston: City and Suburb, 1800–1950*. Amherst: University of Massachusetts Press.

Shand-Tucci, Douglass. 1999. *Built in Boston: City and Suburb, 1800–2000*. Rev. and exp. ed. Amherst: University of Massachusetts Press.

Sheer, Brenda Case, and Mintcho Petkov. 1998. "Edge City Morphology: A Comparison of Commercial Centers." *Journal of the American Planning Association* 64(3): 298–310.

Shefer, Daniel. 1970. "Comparable Living Costs and Urban Size: A Statistical Analysis." *Journal of the American Institute of Planners* 36(6): 417–21.

Shelton, Donn. 1972. *Regional Citizenship*. Detroit: Metropolitan Fund.

Shoup, Donald C. 1995. "An Opportunity to Reduce Minimum Parking Requirements." *Journal of the American Planning Association* 61(1): 14–28.

Shumsky, Neil Larry, ed. 1998. *Encyclopedia of Urban America: The Cities and Suburbs*. Santa Barbara, CA: ABC-CLIO.

Sierra Club. 1999. *Stopping Sprawl*. www.sierraclub.org/sprawl/report99/openspace.

Silver, Marc L., and Martin Melkonian, eds. 1995. *Contested Terrain: Power, Politics, and Participation in Suburbia*. Westport, CT: Greenwood Press.

Silverman, Robert A. 1981. *Law and Urban Growth: Civil Litigation in the Boston Trial Courts, 1880–1900*. Princeton, NJ: Princeton University Press.

Silverstone, Roger, ed. 1997. *Visions of Suburbia*. New York: Routledge.

Simmie, James M. 1983. "Beyond the Industrial City?" *Journal of the American Planning Association* 49(1): 59–76.

Sinclair, Upton. 1928. *Boston*. New York: A. and C. Boni.

Singer, Audrey. 2004. *The Rise of New Immigrant Gateways*. Washington, DC: The Brookings Institution.

Slone, Daniel K. 2003. "Overcoming Impediments to Implementation of New Urbanism." *New Urbanism: Comprehensive Report & Best Practices Guide, New Urban News*.

Small, Stephen J. 1992. *Preserving Family Lands: Essential Tax Strategies for the Landowner*. 2nd ed. Boston: Landowner Planning Center.

Smart Growth Network. 2001. "Affordable Housing and Smart Growth—Making the Connection." Washington, DC: Author.

Smith, Adam. 1976 [1776]. *An Inquiry into the Nature and Causes of the Wealth of Nations*. Edited by R. H. Cambell and A. S. Skinner. Oxford: Clarendon Press.

Smith, Alastair. 2002. *Mixed-Income Housing Developments: Promise and Reality*. Cambridge, MA: Joint Center for Housing Studies of Harvard University Neighborhood Reinvestment Corporation, October.

Smith, Carol A. 1976. *Regional Analysis*. New York: Academic Press.

Smith, David Alexander, ed. 1994. *Future Boston: The History of a City, 1990–2100*. New York: T. Doherty Associates.

Smith, Herbert H. 1993. *The Citizen's Guide to Planning*. 3rd ed. Chicago: Planners Press of the American Planning Association.

Smith, Kathryn J. 1988. *Massachusetts Outdoors: For Our Common Good*. Boston: Massachusetts Department of Environmental Management.

Smith, Laura J., John S. Adams, Julie L. Cidell, and Barbara J. VanDrasek. 2002. *Highway Improvements and Land Development Patterns in the Greater Twin Cities Area, 1970–1997: Measuring the Connections*. CTS 02-03. www.cts.umn.edu/trg/research/reports/TRG_08.html.

Smith, R. Marlin. 1987. "From Subdivision Improvement Requirements to Community Benefit Assessments and Linkage Payments: A Brief History of Land Development Exactions." *Law and Contemporary Problems* 50: 5–30.

Smith, Wallace. 1975. *Urban Development: The Process and the Problems*. Berkeley: University of California Press.

Smith, Zachary A. 2004. *The Environmental Policy Paradox*. 4th ed. Upper Saddle River, NJ: Prentice Hall.

Snyder, Ken, and Lori Bird. 1999. *Paying the Costs of Sprawl: Using Fair-Share Costing to Control Sprawl*. U.S. Department of Energy, www.sustainable.doe.gov.

So, Frank S., and Judith Getzels, eds. 1988. *The Practice of Local Government Planning*. 2nd ed. Washington, DC: International City/County Management Association.

So, Frank S., and Irving Hand, eds. 1985. *The Practice of State and Regional Planning*. Washington, DC: International City/County Management Association.

Sobin, Dennis P. 1971. *The Future of the American Suburbs: Survival or Extinction*. Port Washington, NY: Kennikat Press.

Solomon, Barbara Miller. 1989. *Ancestors and Immigrants: A Changing New England Tradition*. Boston: Northeastern University Press.

Sorenson, Ann A., Richard P. Green, and Karen Russ. 1997. *Farming on the Edge*. DeKalb, IL: American Farmland Trust.

Soule, David. 2003. "Defining and Managing Sprawl." Unpublished dissertation, Boston University.

Soule, David. 2004. "Confronting Housing, Transportation and Regional Growth." *Landlines* 16(2), available at http://lincolninst.edu/pubs/pub-detail.asp?id=889.

Soule, David, Joan Fitzgerald, and Barry Bluestone. 2004. *The Rebirth of Older Industrial Cities: Exciting Opportunities for Private Sector Investment*. Boston: The Center for Urban and Regional Policy at Northeastern University.

Soule, Michael E. 1991. "Land Use Planning and Wildlife Maintenance: Guidelines for Conserving Wildlife in an Urban Landscape." *Journal of the American Planning Association* 57(3): 313–23.

Southworth, Michael, and Eran Ben-Joseph. 1995. "Street Standards and the Shaping of Suburbia." *Journal of the American Planning Association* 61(1): 65–81.

Southworth, Michael, and Peter M. Owens. 1993. "The Evolving Metropolis: Studies of Community, Neighborhood and Street Form at the Urban Edge." *Journal of the American Planning Association* 59(3): 271–87.

Spain, Daphne. 1993. "Been-Heres Versus Come-Heres: Negotiating Conflicting Community Identities." *Journal of the American Planning Association* 59(2): 156–71.

Speare, Alden, Jr. 1993. *Changes in Urban Growth Patterns: 1980–90*. Cambridge, MA: Lincoln Institute of Land Policy.

Speare, Alden, Jr., Sidney Goldstein, and William H. Frey. 1975. *Residential Mobility, Migration, and Metropolitan Change*. Cambridge, MA: Ballinger Publishing Company.

Special Commission on Growth and Change: Final Report. 1990. Boston: Commonwealth of Massachusetts.

Speir, Cameron, and Kurt Stephenson. 2002. "Does Sprawl Cost Us All? Isolating the Effects of Housing Patterns on Public Water and Sewer Costs." *Journal of the American Planning Association* 68(1): 56–70.

Spigel, Lynn. 2001. *Welcome to the Dreamhouse: Popular Media and Postwar Suburbs*. Durham, NC: Duke University Press.

Sprawl: Beyond the Rhetoric. 2000. Cambridge, MA: Harvard Design School, Office of Executive Education.

"Sprawl: Not Just an Urban Issue." 1999. *Economic Development Digest* 10(7).

Sprawl Costs Us All. 2002. Washington, DC: Sierra Club.

Sprawl Costs Us All: A Guide to the Costs of Sprawl and How to Create Livable Communities in Maryland. 1997. Leonardtown, MD: Sierra Club.

Sprawl Hits the Wall: Confronting the Realities of Metropolitan Los Angeles. 2001. Los Angeles: Southern California Studies Center; Washington, DC: Brookings Institution Center on Urban and Regional Policy.

Squires, Gregory D. 2002. "Urban Sprawl and Uneven Development." In Gregory D. Squires, ed., *Urban Sprawl: Causes, Consequences and Policy Responses*. Washington, DC: Urban Institute Press.

Stacey, Benjamin, ed. 1947. *Source Book of New England Economic Statistics: A Publication of the Committee on Economic Research of the New England Council*. Boston Regional Office, U.S. Department of Commerce. Boston: New England Council. Committee on Economic Research; Federal Research Bank, Research and Statistics Department.

Stack, John F. 1979. *International Conflict in an American City: Boston's Irish, Italians, and Jews, 1935–1944*. Westport, CT: Greenwood Press.

Staley, Samuel R. 1999. *The Sprawling of America: In Defense of the Dynamic City*. Los Angeles: Reason Public Policy Institute.

Stanback, Thomas M. 1991. *The New Suburbanization: Challenge to the Central City*. Boulder, CO: Westview Press.

A Standard City Planning Enabling Act (SPCEA). 1928. Washington, DC: U.S. Department of Commerce.

Standard Industrial Classification Manual. 1987. Washington, DC: Office of Management and Budget.

A Standard State Zoning Enabling Act (SZEA). 1926. Washington, DC: U.S. Department of Commerce.

State of California. 2000. *California Transit Oriented Development Database (Caltrans)*. Sacramento: Author. Retrieved May 9, 2004, from http://transitorienteddevelopment.dot.ca.gov/.

State of North Carolina. 2000. *Traditional Neighborhood Development (TND) Guidelines*. Raleigh: North Carolina Department of Transportation, Division of Highways.

State of Oregon. 2000. *Neighborhood Street Design Guidelines: An Oregon Guide to Reducing Street Widths*. State of Oregon: Neighborhood Streets Project Stakeholders.

Statewide Growth Management: What's in It for the Cities. 1992. Lincoln, MA: 1000 Friends of Massachusetts.

Stegman, Michael A., and Margery Austin Turner. 1996. "The Future of Urban America in the Global Economy." *Journal of the American Planning Association* 62(2): 157–64.

Stegner, W. 2000. "The Sense of Place." From *Where the Bluebird Sings* (1992). In *Discussion Course on Discovering a Sense of Place* (pp. 1-3–1-6). Available from the Northwest Earth Institute, 505 SW Sixth, Suite 1100, Portland, OR 97204.

Stein, Clarence S. 1957. *Toward New Towns for America*. New York: Reinhold.

Stein, Jay M. 1995. *Classic Readings in Urban Planning: An Introduction*. New York: McGraw-Hill.

Stein, Jay M., ed. 1993. *Growth Management: The Planning Challenges for the 1990's*. Newbury Park, CA: Sage Publications.

Stein, Rob. 2004. "Car Use Drives Up Weight, Study Finds." *Washington Post*, May 31, A02.

Steiss, Alan Walter. 1975. *Models for the Analysis and Planning of Urban Systems*. Lexington, MA: Lexington Books.

Sternlieb, George. 1986. *Patterns of Development*. New Brunswick, NJ: Center for Urban Policy Research.

Sternlieb, George, and James W. Hughes. 1977. "New Regional and Metropolitan Realities of America." *Journal of the American Institute of Planners* 43(3): 227–41.

Sternlieb, George, and James W. Hughes, eds. 1975. *Post-Industrial America: Metropolitan Decline & Inter-Regional Job Shifts*. New Brunswick, NJ: Center for Urban Policy Research.

Sternlieb, George, and James W. Hughes, eds. 1981. *Shopping Centers USA*. Piscataway, NJ: Center for Urban Policy Research.

Stilgoe, John R. 1988. *Borderland: Origins of the American Suburb, 1820–1939*. New Haven, CT: Yale University Press.

Stockman, P. K. 1992. "Anti-Snob Zoning in Massachusetts: Assessing One Attempt at Opening the Suburbs to Affordable Planning." *Virginia Law Review* 78(7): 535–80.

Stone, Clarence N. 1989. *Regime Politics: Governing Atlanta, 1964–1988*. Lawrence: University of Kansas Press.

Stone, Dave. 2003. *Addressing Health Inequalities in Rural Communities Through Nature*. Paper to Rural Affairs Forum.

Stone, Donald N. 1974. *Industrial Location in Metropolitan Areas: A General Model Tested for Boston*. New York: Praeger.

Stone, P. A. 1973. *The Structure, Size, and Costs of Urban Settlements*. Cambridge: Cambridge University Press.

Strong, Ann L. 1979. *Land Banking*. Baltimore: The Johns Hopkins University Press.

Strong, Ann Louise, Daniel R. Mandelker, and Eric Damian Kelly. 1996. "Property Rights and Takings." *Journal of the American Planning Association* 62(1): 5–16.

Struyk, Raymond J. 1976. "Empirical Foundations for Modeling Urban Industrial Location." *Journal of the American Institute of Planners* 42(2): 165–73.

Suarez, Ray. 1999. *The Old Neighborhood: What We Lost in the Great Suburban Migration, 1966–1999*. New York: Free Press.

Successful Economic Development: Meeting Local and Global Needs. 1990. Baseline Data Report 22 (4). Washington, DC: International City/County Management Association.

Sucher, David. 1995. *City Comforts: How to Build an Urban Village*. Seattle: City Comforts Press.

Sum, Andrew M., Paul Harrington, Neeta P. Fogg, Ishwar Khatiwada, Mykhaylo Trub'skyy, and Sheila Palma. 2002. *The State of the American Dream in Massachusetts, 2002*. Boston: MassINC.

Susskind, Lawrence, and Jeffrey Cruikshank. 1989. *Breaking the Impasse: Consensual Approaches to Resolving Public Disputes*. New York: Basic Books.

Susskind, Lawrence E., and Michael Elliott. 1977. *A Survey of Local Growth Policy Committees and Their Impacts*. Cambridge, MA: Massachusetts Institute of Technology.

Susskind, Lawrence E., and Charles Perry. 1977. *The Impact of Local Participation on the Formulation of State Growth Policy in Massachusetts*. Cambridge, MA: Massachusetts Institute of Technology.

Susskind, Lawrence Elliott, ed. 1975. *The Land Use Controversy in Massachusetts: Case Studies and Policy Options*. Cambridge: Massachusetts Institute of Technology.

Sustainable America: A New Consensus for Prosperity, Opportunity, and a Healthy Environment for the Future. 1996. Washington, DC: The President's Council on Sustainable Development.

Sutcliffe, Anthony, ed. 1980. *The Rise of Modern Urban Planning: 1890–1914*. New York: St. Martin's Press.

Sutcliffe, Anthony, ed. 1984. *Metropolis: 1890–1940*. Chicago: University of Chicago Press.

Sutro, Suzanne. 1990. *Reinventing the Village*. Chicago: American Planning Association.

Suzuki, D., and A. McConnell. 1997. *The Sacred Balance: Rediscovering Our Place in Nature*. Vancouver: Greystone Books.

Swain, E. Susan, David Warm, Carl Kalish, Robert Grims, and David Anderson. 1992. *Regional Strategies for Local Government*. Washington, DC: International City/County Management Association.

Swanson, Carl V., and Raymond J. Waldman. 1970. "A Simulation Model of Economic Growth Dynamics." *Journal of the American Institute of Planners* 36(5): 314–22.

Sweetser, Frank Loel. 1962. *The Social Ecology of Metropolitan Boston: 1960*. Boston: Division of Mental Hygiene, Massachusetts Department of Mental Health.

Swenson, Carol, and Frederick Dock. 2003. *Urban Design, Transportation, Environment and Urban Growth: Transit-Supportive Urban Design Impacts on Suburban Land Use and*

Transportation Planning. CTS 03-06. www.cts.umn.edu/trg/research/reports/TRG _11.html.

Szold, Terry S. 2000. "Merging Place Making and Process in Local Practice." In Lloyd Rodwin and Biswaprina Sanyal, eds., *The Profession of City Planning: Changes, Images, and Challenges 1950–2000.* New Brunswick, NJ: Center for Urban Policy Research.

Szold, Terry S., and Armando Carbonell, eds. 2002. *Smart Growth: Form and Consequences.* Cambridge, MA: MIT, Lincoln Institute of Land Policy.

Takahashi, Lois M., and Gayla Smutny. 1998. "Development Inside Urban Growth Boundaries: Oregon's Empirical Evidence of Contingent Urban Form." *Journal of the American Planning Association* 64(4): 424–40.

Tannenwald, Robert. 1987. "Rating Massachusetts' Tax Competitiveness." *New England Economic Review, Federal Reserve Bank of Boston* (November/December): 33–45.

Tannenwald, Robert. 1989. "The Changing Level and Mix of Federal Aid to State and Local Governments." *New England Economic Review, Federal Reserve Bank of Boston* (May/June): 41–55.

Taylor, Andea Faber. 2003. "How Nature Heals Us: New Evidence that Natural Beauty, Even in Small Doses, Reduces Stress." *Utne Reader* (November/December).

Taylor, Frederick. 1911. *The Principles of Scientific Management.* New York: Harper & Brothers.

Taylor, Marcia Davis, and Miles Durfee. 1990. *Meeting Goals for Special Sector Economic Development: Tools That Work.* Washington, DC: International City/County Management Association.

Teaford, Jon C. 1979. *City and Suburb: The Political Fragmentation of Metropolitan America, 1850–1970.* Baltimore: Johns Hopkins University Press.

Thall, Bob. 1999. *The New American Village.* Baltimore: Johns Hopkins University Press.

Thernstrom, Stephan. 1973. *The Other Bostonians: Poverty and Progress in the American Metropolis, 1880–1970.* Cambridge, MA: Harvard University Press.

Thomas, G. Scott. 1998. *The United States of Suburbia: How the Suburbs Took Control of America and What They Plan to Do with It.* Amherst, NY: Prometheus.

Thomas, Ronald. 1978. "Designing with Communications." *Journal of Architectural Education* 7(3) (special issue).

Thomas, Ronald. 1981. *Cities by Design: A Guide for Public Officials.* Washington, DC: National League of Cities.

Thomas, Ronald, and Margaret Grieve. 1979. *Design for Low Income Neighborhoods.* Washington, DC: National League of Cities.

Thompson, Boyce. 1998. "Growing Smart: Whether You Call It Smart Growth or Sprawl, It's an Important Issue that We All Need to Address." *Builders*, National Association of Home Builders, July.

Thompson, Edward J. 2001. *Agricultural Sustainability and Smart Growth.* Miami, FL: The Funders Network for Smart Growth and Livable Communities and The American Farmland Trust.

TNC (The Nature Conservancy). 1998. *The 1997 Species Report Card: The State of U.S. Plants and Animals.* Arlington, VA: Author.

Tocqueville, Alexis de. 1945. *Democracy in America.* New York: Knopf.

Todisco, Paula J. 1976. *Boston's First Neighborhood: The North End.* Boston: Boston Public Library.

Toll, Seymour I. 1969. *Zoned America.* New York: Grossman Publishers.

Tolley, George S., Philip E. Graves, and John L. Gardner. 1979. *Urban Growth Policy in a Market Economy.* New York: Academic Press.

Toner, William, Efraim Gil, and Enid Lucchesi. 1994. *Planning Made Easy: A Manual for Planning Commissioners, Members of Zoning Boards of Appeal, and Trainers.* Chicago: Planners Press of the American Planning Association.

Tonnies, Ferdinand. 2001. *Community and Civil Society*. Edited by Jose Harris. Cambridge, MA: Cambridge University Press.

Toward a New Land Use Ethic. 1981. Warrenton, VA: Piedmont Environmental Council.

Toward a Sustainable Tax Policy: Tax Strategies to Promote Sustainable Development in Metro Boston. 2001. Prepared by the Metropolitan Area Planning Council in Conjunction with the McCormack Institute. Boston: U.S. Environmental Protection Agency.

Towards a Sustainable America. 1999. Washington, DC: The President's Council on Sustainable Development.

Traub, James. 2000. "What No School Can Do." *New York Times Magazine*, January 16.

Treyz, George I. 1993. *Regional Economic Modeling: A Systematic Approach to Economic Forecasting and Policy Analysis*. Boston: Kluwer Academic Publishers.

Tuckman, Bruce W., and Mary Ann C. Jensen. 1977. "Stages of Small Group Development Revisited." *Group and Organizational Studies* 2: 419–27.

Tyler, Poyntz, ed. 1957. *City and Suburban Housing*. New York: H. W. Wilson Co.

Ullmann, John E., ed. 1977. *The Suburban Economic Network: Economic Activity, Resource Use, and the Great Sprawl*. New York: Praeger.

Ulrich, Roger S. 1984. "Views Through a Window May Influence Recovery from Surgery." *Science* 224: 420–21.

Ulrich, Roger S., and Robert F. Simons et al. 1991. "Stress Recovery During Exposure to Natural and Urban Environments." *Journal of Environmental Psychology* 11: 201–30.

U.S. Bureau of the Census. 2000. *American Housing Survey, 1999*. http://www.census.gov/hhes/www/housing.

U.S. DOT (U.S. Department of Transportation). 1992. *National Personal Transportation Survey: Travel Behavior Issues in the 90s*. Washington, DC: Author.

U.S. DOT (U.S. Department of Transportation). 1996. *Transportation Air Quality: Selected Facts and Figures*. FHWA-PD-96–006. Washington, DC: Author.

U.S. DOT (U.S. Department of Transportation). 2001. *Fatality Analysis Reporting System*. National Center for Statistics & Analysis. Washington, DC: Author.

USDA (U.S. Department of Agriculture). 2000. *Summary Report: 1997 National Resources Inventory (revised December 2000)*. Washington, DC, and Ames, IA: Natural Resources Conservation Service and Statistical Laboratory, Iowa State University.

USDA (U.S. Department of Agriculture). 2002. *Urban Agriculture and Community Food Security in the United States: Farming from the City Center to the Urban Fringe*. Washington, DC: Author.

Utah Foundation. 2000. *Financing Government in Utah: A Historical Perspective*. Salt Lake City: Author.

Utt, Ronald D. 2002. "Will Sprawl Gobble Up America Lands? Federal Data Reveal Development's Trivial Impact." *The Heritage Foundation Backgrounder*. Washington, DC: The Heritage Foundation.

Van der Ryn, Sim, and Peter Calthorpe. 1986. *Sustainable Communities: A New Design Synthesis for Cities, Suburbs, and Towns*. San Francisco: Sierra Club Books.

Van Metre, P. C., B. J. Mahler, and E. T. Furlong. 2000. "Urban Sprawl Leaves Its PAH Signature." *Environmental Science & Technology* 34 (October 1): 4064.

Varady, David P. 1983. "Determinants of Residential Mobility Decisions." *Journal of the American Planning Association* 49(2): 184–99.

Varady, David P. 1990. "Influences on the City-Suburban Choice: A Study of Cincinati Homebuyers." *Journal of the American Planning Association* 49(2): 22–40.

Von Hoffman, Alexander. 1994. *Local Attachments: The Making of an American Urban Neighborhood, 1850 to 1920*. Baltimore: Johns Hopkins University Press.

Vranicar, John, Welford Sanders, and David Mosena. 1980. *Streamlining Land Use Regulation: A Guidebook for Local Government*. Washington, DC: U.S. Department of Housing and Urban Development, Office of Policy Development and Research.

Vtsprawl (Vermont Forum on Sprawl). 2004. "Exploring Sprawl." Retrieved January 23, 2004, at www.vtsprawl.org.

Wachs, Martin, Margaret Crawford, Susan Marie Wirka, and Taina Marjatta Rikala, eds. 1992. *The Car and the City: The Automobile, The Built Environment, and Daily Urban Life*. Ann Arbor: University of Michigan Press.

Wade, J. L. 1996. *Windows on the Future: The Two Worlds of Development*. Presidential address at the annual conference of the Community Development Society, Melbourne, Australia.

Wallace, David A., ed. 1970. *Metropolitan Open Space and Natural Processes*. Philadelphia: University of Pennsylvania.

Wallis, Allan. 1996. "Rebirth of City States and the Birth of the Global Economy." *National Civic Review* 85.

Wallis, Allan D. 1994a. "Evolving Structures and Challenges of Metropolitan Regions." *National Civic Review* (Winter–Spring).

Wallis, Allan D. 1994b. "Inventing Regionalism: A Two-Phase Approach." *National Civic Review* (Fall–Winter).

Wallis, Allan D. 1994c. "Inventing Regionalism: The First Two Waves." *National Civic Review* (Spring–Summer).

Wallis, Allan D. 1994d. "The Third Wave: Current Trends in Regional Governance." *National Civic Review* (Summer–Fall).

Walter, Bob, Lois Arkin, and Richard Crenshaw, eds. 1992. *Sustainable Cities: Concepts and Strategies for Eco-City Development*. Los Angeles: Eco-Home Media.

Walton, Mary. 1986. *The Deming Management Method*. New York: Dodd, Mead.

Walzer, Norman, and Glenn W. Fisher. 1981. *Cities, Suburbs, and Property Taxes*. Cambridge, MA: Oelgeschlager, Gunn & Hain.

Ward, M., K. Brown, and D. Lieb. 1998. "National Incentives for Smart Growth Communities." *Natural Resources & Environment* 13(1).

Warner, Sam Bass, Jr. 1977. *The Way We Really Live: Social Change in Metropolitan Boston Since 1920*. Boston: Trustees of the Public Library of the City of Boston.

Warner, Sam Bass, Jr. 1978. *Streetcar Suburbs: The Process of Growth in Boston (1870–1900)*. 2nd ed. Cambridge, MA: Harvard University Press.

Warner, Sam Bass, Jr. 2001. *Greater Boston: Adapting Regional Traditions to the Present*. Philadelphia: University of Pennsylvania Press.

Wassmer, Robert W. 2003. "The Influence of Local Fiscal Structure and Growth Control Choices on 'Big-Box' Urban Sprawl in the American West." In Dick Netzer, ed., *The Property Tax, Land Use and Land Use Regulation*. Northampton, MA: E. Elgar.

Weaver, Clifford L., and Richard F. Babcock. 1979. *City Zoning: The Once and Future Frontier*. Chicago: Planners Press of the American Planning Association.

Weber, Adna Ferrin. 1969. *The Growth of Cities in the Nineteenth Century: A Study in Statistics*. New York: Greenwood Press.

WED (Wisconsin's Environmental Decade). 2004. "Poison in the Grass." Pesticide Use Reporting and Reduction Project. Retrieved January 12, 2004, at http://www.clean wisconsin.org/.

Weiher, Gregory. 1991. *The Fractured Metropolis: Political Fragmentation and Metropolitan Segregation*. Albany, NY: State University of New York Press.

Weinberger, Rachel R. 2001. "Light Rail Proximity: Benefit or Detriment in the Case of Santa Clara County, California?" *Transportation Research Record* 1747: 104, 111.

Weisbord, Marvin. 1987. *Productive Workplaces: Organizing and Managing for Dignity, Meaning, and Community*. San Francisco: Jossey-Bass.

Weisbord, Marvin R. 1993. *Discovering Common Ground: How Future Search Conferences Bring People Together to Achieve Breakthrough Innovation, Empowerment, Shared Vision, and Collaborative Action*. San Francisco: Berrett-Koehler.

Weiss, Michael J. 1988. *The Clustering of America*. New York: Harper and Row.

Weitz, Jerry. 1999. *Sprawl Busting: State Programs to Guide Growth*. Chicago: Planners Press of the American Planning Association.

Wheatley, Margaret J. 2001. *Leadership and the New Science: Discovering Order in a Chaotic World*. Rev. ed. San Francisco: Berrett-Koehler.

Wheaton, William L. 1967. "Metro-Allocation Planning." *Journal of the American Institute of Planners* 33(2): 103–7.

Wheaton, William L., and Morton J. Schussheim. 1955. *The Cost of Municipal Services in Residential Areas*. Washington, DC: U.S. Department of Commerce.

White, L. 2002. "Connection Matters: Exploring the Implications of Social Capital and Social Networks for Social Policy." *Systems Research and Behavioral Science* 19: 25–269.

White, Louise G. 1979. "Approaches to Land Use Policy." *Journal of the American Planning Association* 45(1): 62–71.

White, Sammis B., Lisa S. Binkley, and Jeffrey D. Osterman. 1993. "The Sources of Suburban Employment Growth." *Journal of the American Planning Association* 59(2): 193–204.

White, William Foote. 1993. *Street Corner Society: The Social Structure of an Italian Slum*. Chicago: University of Chicago Press.

Whitehill, Walter Muir. 1966. *Boston in the Age of John Fitzgerald Kennedy*. Norman: University of Oklahoma Press.

Whitehill, Walter Muir. 1968. *Boston: A Topographical History*. 2nd ed. Cambridge, MA: The Belknap Press.

Whyte, William H. 1968. *The Last Landscape*. Garden City, NY: Doubleday.

Whyte, William H. 1988. *City: Rediscovering the Center*. New York: Doubleday.

Whyte, William H., Jr. 1958. "Are Cities Un-American?" In The Editors of Fortune, *The Exploding Metropolis* 23.

Wickersham, Jay. 1994. "The Quiet Revolution Continues: The Emerging New Model for State Growth Management Statutes." *Harvard Environmental Law Review* 18: 489.

Wickersham, Jay. 2001a. "Jane Jacobs's Critique of Zoning: From *Euclid* to Portland and Beyond." *Boston College Environmental Affairs Law Review* 28: 547–64.

Wickersham, Jay. 2001b. "Managing Growth without a Growth Management Statute: The Uses of MEPA." Boston, April 2.

Wickersham, Jay. 2003. "EIR and Smart Growth." *Urban Land* (May).

Wilkes, Brent. 1986. *Managing Small Towns: A Primer for Municipal Management for Towns with Populations under 20,000*. Boston: Massachusetts Municipal Association.

Wilkie, Richard W., and Jack Tage, eds. 1991. *Historical Atlas of Massachusetts*. Amherst: University of Massachusetts Press.

Wilkins, Charles S., Jr. n.d. "Concept Paper: Mixed-Income Rental Housing." Millennial Housing Commission Preservation and Production Task Forces, www.mhc.gov/papers/cpmirh.doc.

Will, George F. 1999. "Al Gore Has a New Worry: 'Smart Growth' to Cure 'Suburban Sprawl' Is the Newest Rationale for Government Growth." *Newsweek*, February 15, 76.

Willemain, Thomas R. 1980. *Statistical Methods for Planners*. Cambridge, MA: MIT Press.

Williams, Donald C. 2000. *Urban Sprawl: A Reference Handbook*. Santa Barbara, CA: ABC-CLIO.

Williams, Frank. 1922. *The Law of City Planning and Zoning*. New York: Macmillan.

Williams, Norman, and John M. Taylor. 1974. *American Planning Law: Land Use and the Police Power*. Wilmette, IL: Callaghan.

Williamson, Richard W. 2001. "Busting at the Seams: Gwinnett Schools Are Overcrowded and Getting Worse." *Creative Loafing*, January 27, http://atlanta.creativeloafing.com/2001-01-27/comment.html.

Willson, Richard W. 1995. "Suburban Parking Requirements: A Tacit Policy for Automobile Use and Sprawl." *Journal of the American Planning Association* 61(1): 29–42.

Windsor, Duane. 1979. "A Critique of *The Cost of Sprawl*." *Journal of the American Planning Association* 45(3): 279–92.

Wolch, Jennifer, and Michael Dear, eds. 1989. *The Power of Geography: How Territory Shapes Social Life*. Boston: Unwin Hyman.

Wolfe, Alan. 2000. *Moral Freedom: The Search for Virtue in a World of Choice*. New York: Oxford University Press.

Wolkoff, Michael J. 1985. "Chasing a Dream: The Use of Tax Abatements to Spur Urban Economic Development." *Urban Studies* 22(4): 305–15.

Wood, Denis. 1992. *The Power of Maps*. New York: Guilford Press.

Wood, Robert C. 1958. *Suburbia: Its People and Their Politics*. Boston: Houghton Mifflin.

Woodruff, Archibald M., ed. 1980. *The Farm and the City: Rivals or Allies?* Englewood Cliffs, NJ: Prentice-Hall.

Woods, Robert A., and Albert J. Kennedy. 1969. *The Zone of Emergence: Observations of Lower, Middle, and Upper Working Class Communities of Boston, 1905–1914*. Cambridge, MA: MIT Press.

Worster, Donald, ed. 1973. *American Environmentalism: The Formative Period, 1860–1915*. New York: Wiley.

Wright, Robert. 2000. *Nonzero: The Logic of Human Destiny*. New York: Pantheon Books.

Yaffee, Steven Lewis. 1977. *Municipal Involvement in the Formulation of State Growth Policy: The Implications of Traditional Local Planning Practice*. Massachusetts Growth Policy Project. Cambridge, MA: Massachusetts Institute of Technology.

Yankelovitch, Daniel. 1991. *Coming to Public Judgment: Making Democracy Work in a Complex World*. Syracuse, NY: Syracuse University Press.

Yankelovitch, Daniel. 1999. *The Magic of Dialogue: Transforming Conflict into Cooperation*. New York: Simon & Schuster.

Yaro, Robert, ed. 2002. *Promoting Smart Growth in Connecticut*. Cambridge, MA: Graduate School of Design, Harvard University.

Yaro, Robert, and Tony Hiss. 1996. *A Region at Risk: The Third Regional Plan for the New York–New Jersey–Connecticut Metropolitan Area*. New York: Regional Plan Association.

Yinger, John. 1998. "Testing for Discrimination in Housing and Related Markets." In Michael Fix and Margery Austin Turner, eds., *A National Report Card on Discrimination in America*. Washington, DC: The Urban Institute.

Zaitzevsky, Cynthia. 1982. *Frederick Law Olmstead and the Boston Park System*. Cambridge, MA: The Belknap Press.

The Zoning Act: Massachusetts General Laws 40-A. 1986. Current through 1986 Legislative Session. Boston: Executive Office of Communities and Development, Office of the Massachusetts Secretary of State.

Zoning Controversies in the Suburbs: Three Case Studies. 1968. Prepared for the Consideration of the National Commission on Urban Problems by Raymond & May Associates. National Commission on Urban Problems. Research Report No. 11. Washington, DC: Superintendent of Documents, U.S. Government Printing Office.

Zuckerman, Michael. 1970. *Peaceable Kingdoms: New England Towns of the Eighteenth Century*. New York: Vintage Books.

Index

About the Editor
and Contributors

DAVID C. SOULE is the associate director at the Center for Urban and Regional Policy at Northeastern University, where he conducts research on urban economic issues and tax policy and also teaches in the Political Science Department. He is the principal advisor to the Regional Futures Institute of the National Association of Regional Councils and a member of the board of directors and former officer of the Alliance for Regional Stewardship.

He recently stepped down as executive director of the Metropolitan Area Planning Council (MAPC) after more than 15 years of service. During his tenure, he oversaw the development of MetroPlan, a comprehensive plan for the future of the Boston metropolitan area. Prior to joining MAPC, Soule served as executive director of the Nashua Regional Planning Commission in Nashua, New Hampshire, for seven years. From 1971 to 1980, he served as deputy and planning director of the Capitol Region Council of Governments in Hartford, Connecticut.

In April 2003, Soule completed his Ph.D. in the Law, Policy, and Society program at Northeastern University, with a dissertation on managing sprawl; he has a bachelor's degree from Trinity College. Soule is also the primary staff for the New England Initiative, serving as a senior research associate for the Initiative at the Center for Industrial Competitiveness at the University of Massachusetts at Lowell and a lecturer in the College of Management at the University of Massachusetts in Boston.

ANGELA GLOVER BLACKWELL is the founder and chief executive officer of PolicyLink, a national nonprofit research, communications, capacity building, and advocacy organization working to advance policies to achieve economic and social equity. A renowned community-building activist and advocate, Blackwell served as senior vice president of the Rockefeller Foundation, where she oversaw the foundation's Domestic and Cultural divisions. Blackwell also developed Rockefeller's Building Democracy division, which focused on race and policy, and created the

Next Generation Leadership program. A lawyer by training, she gained national recognition as founder of the Oakland (California) Urban Strategies Council, where she pioneered new approaches to neighborhood revitalization. From 1977 to 1987, Blackwell was a partner at Public Advocates, a nationally known public interest law firm. She is a coauthor of *Searching for the Uncommon Common Ground: New Dimensions on Race in America* (2002).

ARI BRUENING is a land-use attorney in the Salt Lake City office of O'Melveny & Myers, LLP. Bruening graduated from Harvard Law School in 2005, where he was a *Harvard Law Review* editor and *Harvard Environmental Law Review* editor. He obtained a bachelor's degree with honors in philosophy from Brigham Young University, where he was the university graduation speaker and winner of the David H Yarn Philosophical Essay Contest. Bruening has also published a note on regionalism in volume 118 of the *Harvard Law Review*.

MEREDITH COOPER received a master's degree in environment and community from the Center for Creative Change at Antioch University Seattle and a bachelor's degree in humanities from the University of New Hampshire. Her graduate work was focused in the areas of land-use planning and social capital as an emerging principle in community development. Meredith has worked as a consultant with the NH Minimum Impact Development Partnership of the Jordan Institute on the "Three Infrastructures of NH Communities" land-use planning initiative and the NH Charitable Foundation's Social Capital Forum pilot initiative to develop a tool for Municipal Social Impact Assessment.

Cooper is currently a regional planner with the Southwest Region Planning Commission in Keene, New Hampshire, where her central duties include local land-use assistance such as consultation with municipal officials regarding land-use regulations and site-plan and subdivision review, Emergency Operations and Hazard Mitigation planning, and Brownfields Assessment Program management. Before joining the Planning Commission, Cooper worked as program coordinator for "Livable, Walkable Communities" with NH Celebrates Wellness; state coordinator for "Project Food, Land & People" with the NH Association of Conservation Districts; and conservation educator with the Merrimack County Conservation District in Concord, New Hampshire.

RADHIKA K. FOX is a senior program associate at PolicyLink, where she coordinates initiatives focused on promoting equitable development and regional equity. Fox works with community organizations and coalitions advancing policy campaigns; creates and conducts trainings on tools and strategies for advancing social and economic equity; and conducts research and writes about various issues related to affordable housing, economic development, and regional growth and development. She holds a bachelor's degree from Columbia University and a master's degree in city and regional planning from the University of California, Berkeley, where she was a HUD Community Development Fellow.

SARAH GARDNER teaches planning and is the associate director of the Center for Environmental Studies at Williams College in Williamstown, Massachusetts.

She serves on local and regional planning commissions in Berkshire County, Massachusetts. Her current research work is on land-use patterns and land-use politics in Massachusetts and comparative state environmental policy. Her recent article on brownfield politics in New Jersey is in *Recycling the City: The Use and Reuse of Urban Land* (2004).

DOUGLAS HENTON, the president and founder of Collaborative Economics, has more than 20 years' experience in economic development at the national, regional, state, and local levels. Henton is nationally recognized for his work in bringing industry, government, education, research, and community leaders together around specific collaborative projects to improve regional competitiveness. Henton founded Collaborative Economics in July 1993 after a decade as assistant director of SRI's International Center for Economic Competitiveness. At SRI, he directed major projects on the economic future of Hong Kong, the technopolis strategy in Japan, and regional development in China. Henton holds a bachelor's degree in political science and economics from Yale University and a master's degree in public policy from the University of California, Berkeley.

JAMES HLAWEK is in his final year at Harvard Law School, where he has worked as a research assistant for Professor Arthur Miller and currently is a primary editor for the *Harvard Law Review*. In addition, he was a research assistant at Northeastern University's Center for Urban and Regional Policy, focusing on a project that analyzed the impact of the Massachusetts property tax system on land-use planning. Prior to starting at Harvard, he obtained his MBA and worked as a consultant and an auditor for eight years.

CURTIS JOHNSON is president of The Citistates Group. Johnson's career is one of those rare combinations of activist and commentator. He has had leading roles in government, education, and civic organizations, and, since the mid-1980s, as an independent journalist on metropolitan issues. Living in the Twin Cities over the past three decades, Johnson also served as a community college president, the head of a large citizens organization, a policy adviser and chief of staff to a governor, and chairman of the Metropolitan Council. The Council is one of the earliest and premier regional organizations in the United States, responsible for growth management, establishing transportation and water priorities, and operating the transit and wastewater systems. As chairman, he successfully pushed for the region's first light rail line, for modernizing bus service, for reinvestments in the core of the region, and for better growth management policies. In recent years, Johnson has frequently played the role of moderator and sometimes mediator in the search for common ground among builders, local governments, regional policy makers, and environmentalists.

ZENIA KOTVAL is associate professor of urban and regional planning and director of Urban Planning Partnerships at Michigan State University. She has 15 years of planning experience. She holds a bachelor's degree in architecture and master's and Ph.D. degrees in regional planning. She is a member of the American Institute of Certified Planners. Her research interests focus on the link between theory and practice, with a special emphasis on local community and economic development and urban revitalization.

JOHN MELVILLE is principal and founder of Collaborative Economics. He has 13 years of experience in economic development and collaborative strategy development in the United States and internationally. Melville has served in numerous project leadership, task leadership, project support, and analytic roles in consulting engagements in North America, Asia, and Europe. He has specific expertise in human resource and education and training issues and strategies, especially their role in regional economic development.

As a senior policy analyst at SRI's Center for Economic Competitiveness, Melville authored or coauthored more than 20 economic strategy plans for communities and regions, authored a national guidebook on the role of education/training and economic development, and published articles on education. He helped launch state and local education, training, and economic development strategies in California, Pennsylvania, Oregon, Hawaii, Minnesota, Maryland, Hong Kong, and Spain. He holds a B.A. with honors in political science from Stanford University.

JOHN MOYNIHAN is the director of policy and resource development of the Planning Office for Urban Affairs (POUA) in the Roman Catholic Archdiocese of Boston. As the former director of the Harvard–Newton Tri School Program, The Metropolitan Education Center (MEC), and the Metropolitan Planning Project (MPP), he has decades of metropolitan experience. Since the Second Vatican Council, the Archdiocese of Boston, with his leadership and support, has built over 20 high-quality, mixed-income, residential developments in 14 communities throughout metropolitan Boston. The effort has paralleled the quest for human dignity and solidarity within both democratic societies and faith communities. Moynihan relates a progressive Catholic point of view about the urgency of this ethical quest in a forthcoming book entitled *Folded into Time*.

JOHN MULLIN is the dean of the Graduate School at the University of Massachusetts and director of the Center for Economic Development. He is also a professor of urban planning with a research focus on industrial planning. Dr. Mullin holds a bachelor's degree in government from the University of Massachusetts, a master's degree in city planning from the University of Rhode Island, a Master of Science degree in business administration from Boston University, and a Ph.D. in city planning from the University of Waterloo, Ontario, Canada. He is also a graduate of the U.S. Army War College. Dr. Mullin is a fellow of the American Institute of Certified Planners and a Senior Fulbright Scholar. He has written or edited over 100 book chapters, book reviews, technical reports, journal articles, and conference proceedings.

MYRON ORFIELD has become "the most influential social demographer in America's burgeoning regional movement," as Neal Peirce wrote in his nationally distributed column in Spring 2002. Both Peirce and David Broder of the *Washington Post* have featured Orfield's research on social and fiscal disparities in the United States and their political implications. As president of Minneapolis-based Ameregis Corporation, Orfield has produced more than 40 studies of major metropolitan areas, detailing patterns of regional disparity and inefficient, sprawling land use. The firm's studies are the backbone of Orfield's book, *American Metropolitics: The New Suburban Reality* (2002). Orfield served five terms in the Minnesota House of Representatives and one term in the State Senate, authoring a series of sweeping laws that brought about metropolitan reform that strengthened the nation's most substantial regional government and reformed land use and fiscal equity laws in the Twin Cities area. His legislative credentials serve him well as he works with local land use organizations across the nation, making the case for regional approaches to metropolitan governance. In 2001, he formed Ameregis, a company that grew out of his work with the Metropolitan Area Research Corporation (MARC), a nonprofit affiliate he founded.

Orfield has a bachelor's degree from the University of Minnesota, conducted graduate work at Princeton University, and earned a law degree from the University of Chicago, where he served as a member of the law review. After working as a law clerk for a federal appellate judge, Orfield was appointed assistant attorney general of Minnesota and appeared in significant cases before the U.S. Supreme Court and state and federal appellate courts. He also has practiced in the private sector and currently teaches as an adjunct professor at the University of Minnesota Law School.

JOHN PARR is a cofounder and principal of Denver-based Civic Results, a nonprofit organization that assists governments, businesses, and nonprofit institutions to collaboratively plan and implement initiatives that create measurable change in the physical, social, civic, and human infrastructure of communities and regions. He also serves as president/CEO of the Alliance for Regional Stewardship a national network of practitioners from the public, private, and nonprofit sectors that are using metropolitan or rural regional approaches for community problem solving. Parr is also an associate of the Citistates Group, working on issues of regional governance in the United States. He is a licensed attorney with extensive experience in public administration, strategic planning, mediation, public interest group management, and political campaign organization. From 1985 to 1995, Parr served as president of the National Civic League (NCL), an organization devoted to the improvement of political and governmental institutions and processes and community problem solving. He is a lecturer in the Graduate School of Public Affairs at the University of Colorado. He has taught in programs at Harvard University, Massachusetts Institute of Technology, the University of California at Los Angeles, and the University of Denver. Articles he has written have appeared in publications ranging from the University of Chicago *Policy Review* to *The Consensus Building Handbook*.

NEAL PEIRCE is Chairman of the Citistates Group. Peirce is a foremost writer, among American journalists, on metropolitan regions—their political and economic dynamics and their emerging national and global roles. With Curtis Johnson, he has coauthored the *Peirce Reports* (now called *Citistates Reports*) on compelling issues of metropolitan futures for leading media in more than 20 regions across the nation. *Boston Unbound*, released in May 2004, was the most recent of these. Other reports in recent years covered the San Diego–Tijuana citistate area for *San Diego Magazine*; South Florida for the Miami *Herald, El Nuevo Herald,* and the Fort

Lauderdale *Sun-Sentinel*; Kansas City for the Kansas City *Star*; and South Texas for the San Antonio *Express-News*.

In 1975, Peirce began—and today continues—the first national column focused on state and local government themes in the United States. Syndication is by the Washington Post Writers Group. His 10-book series on American states and regions culminated in *The Book of America: Inside 50 States Today* (1983). His more recent books were *Citistates: How Urban America Can Prosper in a Competitive World* and *Breakthroughs: Recreating the American City*.

Known widely as a lecturer on regional, urban, federal system, and community development issues, Peirce has been a familiar figure before civic, business, academic, and professional groups nationally. He has appeared on *Meet the Press*, the *Today*, *National Public Radio*, and local media across the country.

DAVID RUSK is an author, consultant, and a leading American regionalist who combines scholarship with practical political experience. He has been both a state legislator in New Mexico and mayor of Albuquerque, the nation's 36th largest city. In 1993, the American Planning Association called Rusk's first book, *Cities without Suburbs*, "must reading." His second book, *Baltimore Unbound*, was published in 1995. A third book has been commissioned by the Twentieth Century Fund.

Rusk's articles have been published in numerous papers including the *New York Times*, the *Washington Post*, and *Newsday*. His largest journalistic undertaking was "Renewing Our Community: The Rusk Report on the Future of Greater York," a 24-page supplement published by the York (Pennsylvania) *Daily Record* in November 1996. Rusk has not only traveled and lectured across the United States but also in such foreign cities as Berlin, Stuttgart, Frankfurt, Amsterdam, Delft, and Toronto. He has testified before legislative groups in Ohio, Michigan, Minnesota, Connecticut, and Virginia.

Rusk graduated Phi Beta Kappa in economics from the University of California at Berkeley. From 1963 to 1968, he was a civil rights and antipoverty worker with the Washington Urban League. He then was legislative and program development director for the U.S. Department of Labor's Manpower Administration. In 1971, he and his wife, Delcia Bence of Buenos Aires, Argentina, moved to Albuquerque, where they raised their three children. They now live and work out of Washington, D.C., where Mrs. Rusk serves as his research associate and business manager.

TERRY SZOLD is an adjunct associate professor of land-use planning. She has research interests in land-use planning and growth management and serves as her department's practitioner/educator in land use and growth management. Her recent work includes the preparation of cluster-housing regulations for the Town of Harvard and zoning and development guidelines for the Fenway Special Study Areas in Boston and the town of Guilford, Connecticut. She has been recently involved in the zoning update process in the Town of Brookline, Massachusetts; the alewife design and zoning project in Cambridge, Massachusetts; and preparation of zoning regulations and research addressing the "monster home" trend. She is co-editor of *Smart Growth: Form and Consequences* (2002) and is the 1996 recipient of the Faye Seigfriedt Award, American Planning Association, Massachusetts Chapter, and the 1994 Outstanding Community Leadership Award, North Suburban Chamber of Commerce.

RON THOMAS is executive director of the Northeastern Illinois Planning Commission (NIPC). Since joining the agency in 2000, he has focused the NIPC mission on providing more direct assistance to local communities based on their diverse planning, development, and environmental issues. He launched NIPC's award-winning Common Ground regional planning program and the innovative Full Circle community housing information center.

His career work includes a range of planning issues, such as land use, environment, housing, transportation (especially context-sensitive design), economic development, and many urban design and quality-of-life programs. He has pioneered extensive applied projects and published work on new planning approaches to visioning and strategic planning using innovative communication technology.

He is on the boards of Chicago Wilderness, Illinois Association of Regional Councils, the National Association of Regional Councils, the National Trust for Historic Preservation, and the Campaign for Sensible Growth, where he serves as co-chair. He holds graduate-level degrees in architecture and management and has conducted postgraduate work in communications. Thomas has a Master of Science in management from Antioch University. He is the author of numerous articles, including "Empowering Regions: Strategies and Tools for Community Decision Making," an Alliance for Regional Stewardship Monograph published in 2001, and "Taking Charge: How Communities Are Planning Their Futures," which he coauthored for the International City Management Association in 1988.

ALEXANDER VON HOFFMAN is a historian and specialist in housing and urban affairs. A senior research fellow at the Joint Center for Housing Studies since 1997, he currently directs a three-year project supported by, and in collaboration with, the United States Geological Survey, titled "Patterns and Process of Sprawl." The project explores metropolitan development from 1970 to the present. Among his other works on urban development are two coauthored Joint Center Working Papers titled "Forty Years of Fighting Sprawl: Montgomery County, Maryland, and Growth Control Planning in the Metropolitan Region of Washington, D.C." (2002); "The Historical Origins and Causes of Urban Decentralization in the United States" (2002); "All That Sprawl," *Boston Sunday Globe*, March 12, 2000; and "Housing Heats Up: Home Building Patterns in Metropolitan America," The Brookings Institution and Joint Center for Housing Studies, December, 1999.

JAY WICKERSHAM, a lawyer and architect, is a partner in the Cambridge, Massachusetts, law firm of Noble & Wickersham, LLP, and a lecturer in planning and environmental law at the Harvard Graduate School of Design and Kennedy School of Government. From 1998 to 2002, Wickersham was assistant secretary of environmental affairs for Massachusetts and director of the state's environmental impact review program. He is a contributing author to *Rathkopf's The Law of Zoning and Planning*, and he has written and lectured widely on smart growth, sprawl, and related subjects.

RALPH WILLMER, AICP, is the director of planning services at McGregor & Associates, a law firm in Boston specializing in environmental law. He has received a bachelor of science degree in resource management from the State University of New York College of Environmental Science and Forestry at Syracuse and a master's degree in urban and environmental policy from Tufts University. He has over 20 years of experience in the fields of environmental impact assessment, land-use planning, hazardous and solid waste management, citizen participation, policy formulation, environmental advocacy, and wetlands and water resource protection. Willmer has rewritten zoning codes, health rules, and subdivision regulations and has prepared master plans and open-space plans for many municipalities. He was recently a member of the American Planning Association (APA) National Board of Directors, is the chair of the Environmental Planning Division, and was a past president of the Massachusetts Chapter of APA. He is a member of the American Institute of Certified Planners.

ROBERT YARO is the president of the Regional Planning Association (RPA). Before assuming this role, Yaro served as RPA's executive director from 1990 to 2001. Headquartered in Manhattan, RPA is the oldest and most distinguished independent metropolitan research and advocacy group in the United States. At RPA, Yaro led the five-year effort to prepare RPA's Third Regional Plan, "A Region at Risk," which he coauthored in 1996. He chairs The Civic Alliance to Rebuild Downtown New York, a broad-based coalition of civic groups formed to guide redevelopment in Lower Manhattan in the aftermath of the September 11 attacks on the World Trade Center. Yaro is currently practice professor in city and regional planning at the University of Pennsylvania. He has also served on the faculties of Harvard and Columbia Universities. He holds a master's degree in city and regional planning from Harvard University and a bachelor's degree in urban studies from Wesleyan University. He is an honorary member of the Royal Town Planning Institute.

University of Nebraska Press